Lecture Notes in Information Systems and Organisation

Volume 79

Lecture Notes in Information Systems and Organization (LNISO) is a series of scientific books that explore the current state of information systems studies, in particular in the context of organizations, as well as behavioral and design aspects of information systems. The series offers an integrated publication platform for high-quality conferences, symposia and workshops proceedings. Books accepted for publication are selected based on a double-blind peer-review evaluation made by invited reviewers. The series is indexed in Scopus.

Aizhan Tursunbayeva • Francesco Virili
Alessio Maria Braccini
Editors

Technology-Driven Transformation

The Future of Work and Organizations

Springer

Editors
Aizhan Tursunbayeva
Department of Business and Economics
University of Naples "Parthenope"
Naples, Italy

Francesco Virili
Department of Economic and Social Sciences
Catholic University of the Sacred Heart
Piacenza, Italy

Alessio Maria Braccini
Department of Economics Engineering
Society and Business Organisation (DEIM)
University of Tuscia
Viterbo, Italy

ISSN 2195-4968 ISSN 2195-4976 (electronic)
Lecture Notes in Information Systems and Organisation
ISBN 978-3-032-01395-8 ISBN 978-3-032-01396-5 (eBook)
https://doi.org/10.1007/978-3-032-01396-5

This Springer imprint is published by the registered company Springer Nature Switzerland AG.
The registered company address is: Gewerbestrasse 11, 6330 Cham, Switzerland

Contents

Contributors

Giovanna Afeltra Department for the Promotion of Human Sciences and Quality of life, San Raffaele University, Rome, Italy

Rocco Agrifoglio Department of Business and Economics, University of Naples "Parthenope", Naples, Italy

Gilda Antonelli Economic Department, D'Annunzio University, Pescara, Italy

Aurora Ascatigno School of Advanced Studies, University of Chieti-Pescara, Chieti, Italy

Meseret Assefa Adamu Department of Information Systems, University of Agder (UiA), Kristiansand, Norway

Andrea Back University of St. Gallen, St. Gallen, Switzerland

Kira Bender Darmstadt University of Technology, Darmstadt, Germany

Alessia Berni Parthenope University of Naples, Naples, Italy

Filippo Bianchini Department of Computer, Control and Management Engineering Antonio Ruberti – DIAG,Sapienza University of Rome, Rome, Italy

Isabella Bonacci Universitas Mercatorum, Rome, Italy

Sara Bonesso Venice School of Management, Ca' Foscari, University of Venice, Venezia, Italy

Alessio Maria Braccini Department of Economics Engineering Society and Business Organisation (DEIM), University of Tuscia, Viterbo, Italy

Maximilian Breitruck University of St. Gallen, St. Gallen, Switzerland

Edgardo Bucciarelli University of Chieti-Pescara, Pescara, Italy

Franca Cantoni Università Cattolica del Sacro Cuore, Piacenza, Italy

Camilla Capogreco Università Cattolica del Sacro Cuore, Piacenza, Italy

Federica Ceci G. d'Annunzio University of Chieti, Pescara, Italy

Marco Cerri Università Cattolica del Sacro Cuore, Piacenza, Italy

Alfredo Colantonio International Telematic University Uninettuno, Roma, Italy

Laura Cortellazzo Venice School of Management, Ca' Foscari, University of Venice, Venezia, Italy

Markus Esswein Henkel KGaA, Düsseldorf, Germany

Alena Fedorova Ural Federal University, Yekaterinburg, Russia

Luiza Gaysina Parthenope University of Naples, Naples, Italy

Khaled Ghazy Ural Federal University, Yekaterinburg, Russia

Helwan University, Cairo, Egypt

Daria Höhener Institute of Information Systems and Digital Business, University of St. Gallen, St. Gallen, Switzerland

Ksenia Keplinger Max Planck Institute for Intelligent Systems, Stuttgart, Germany

Stefano Di Lauro Universitas Mercatorum, Rome, Italy

Domenica Lavorato "Parthenope" University of Naples, Naples, Italy

Benedict Lösser Institute of Information Systems and Digital Business, University of St. Gallen, St. Gallen, Switzerland

Francesca De Luzi Department of Computer, Control and Management Engineering Antonio Ruberti – DIAG,Sapienza University of Rome, Rome, Italy

Mattia Macrì Department of Computer, Control and Management Engineering Antonio Ruberti – DIAG,Sapienza University of Rome, Rome, Italy

Marcello Martinez University of Campania "Luigi Vanvitelli", Caserta, Italy

Antonio Mastrogiorgio University of Rome "UnitelmaSapienza", Rome, Italy

Jörg H. Mayer Darmstadt University of Technology, Darmstadt, Germany

Massimo Mecella Department of Computer, Control and Management Engineering Antonio Ruberti – DIAG,Sapienza University of Rome, Rome, Italy

Maria Menshikova Universitas Mercatorum, Rome, Italy

Maria Guariglia Migliore Sapienza University of Rome, Rome, Italy

Primiano Di Nauta University of Foggia, Foggia, Italy

Antonio De Nicola ENEA, CR Casaccia, Rome, Italy

Marko Ilmari Niemimaa Department of Information Systems, University of Agder (UiA), Kristiansand, Norway

Filomena Pagnozzi Economic Department, D'Annunzio University, Pescara, Italy

Dario Natale Palmucci Department of Management, University of Turin, Turin, Italy

Emanuele Patti Università Cattolica del Sacro Cuore, Piacenza, Italy

Lena-Marie Pätzmann University of St. Gallen, St. Gallen, Switzerland

Haiat Perozzo LIUC – Cattaneo University, Castellanza, Italy

Mauro Junior Dia Perozzo LIUC – Cattaneo University, Castellanza, Italy

Sabrina Pisano "Parthenope" University of Naples, Naples, Italy

Reiner Quick Darmstadt University of Technology, Darmstadt, Germany

Aurelio Ravarini LIUC – Cattaneo University, Castellanza, Italy

Alessia Regnicoli School of Advanced Studies, University of Chieti-Pescara, Chieti, Italy

Laura Roma Department of Business and Economics, University of Naples "Parthenope", Naples, Italy

Cesare Roncari LIUC – Cattaneo University, Castellanza, Italy

Rosa Anna Ruggiero Department of Modern Languages and Literatures, History, Philosophy and Law Studies – DISTU, University of Tuscia, Viterbo, Italy

Loris Santarelli G. d'Annunzio University of Chieti, Pescara, Italy

Alessandro Scaletti "Parthenope" University of Naples, Naples, Italy

Danila Scarozza Link Campus University, Rome, Italy

Vindhya Singh Max Planck Institute for Intelligent Systems, Stuttgart, Germany

Claudio Soregaroli Università Cattolica del Sacro Cuore, Piacenza, Italy

Paolo Spagnoletti Department of Information Systems, University of Agder (UiA), Kristiansand, Norway

Department of Business and Management, Luiss University, Rome, Italy

Emanuele Strada LIUC – Cattaneo University, Castellanza, Italy

Andrea Tomo University of Naples Federico II, Naples, Italy

Rebecca Trivelli University "G.d'Annunzio"of Chieti-Pescara, Pescara, Italy

Aizhan Tursunbayeva Department of Business and Economics, University of Naples "Parthenope", Naples, Italy

Francesco Virili Department of Business and Social Science, Catholic University of the Sacred Heart, Piacenza, Italy

Aleksandra Wagner Institute of Sociology, Jagiellonian University, Kraków, Poland

Pauline Weritz High Tech Business and Entrepreneurship Department, University of Twente, Enschede, The Netherlands

Stefano Za University "G.d'Annunzio" of Chieti-Pescara, Pescara, Italy

List of Figures

List of Tables

Work and Organisations of Tomorrow: Technology-Driven Change

Alessio Maria Braccini, Aizhan Tursunbayeva, and Francesco Virili

Abstract Technology-driven change continuously reshapes work environments, organisational structures, and managerial practices through digital transformation processes. This process, although technology-centric, fundamentally integrates social and organisational dynamics, creating unpredictable and emergent transformation paths influenced by human interactions, institutional contexts, and the technologies themselves. Consequently, traditional organisational structures are evolving into more fluid, agile, and platform-based arrangements. Effectively navigating the digital transformation process poses significant challenges, as the world of tomorrow will not just be the world of yesterday, but increasingly digitalised. This introductory chapter sets the framework for the content of this book, in which a set of research papers explores how digital technologies influence new work arrangements, organisational readiness, and human-technology interactions.

Keywords Digital transformation · Organisational innovation · New forms of work

---

A. M. Braccini (✉)
Department of Economics Engineering Society and Business Organisation (DEIM), University of Tuscia, Viterbo, Italy
e-mail: abraccini@unitus.it

A. Tursunbayeva
Department of Business and Economics, University of Naples "Parthenope", Naples, Italy
e-mail: a.tursunbayeva@uniparthenope.it

F. Virili
Department of Economic and Social Sciences, Catholic University of the Sacred Heart, Piacenza, Italy
e-mail: francesco.virili@unicatt.it

A. Tursunbayeva et al. (eds.), *Technology-Driven Transformation*, Lecture Notes in Information Systems and Organisation 79,
https://doi.org/10.1007/978-3-032-01396-5_1

1 Technology-Driven Change

The world of work and organisations is continuously reshaped by technology-driven change. Digital technologies – from ubiquitous connectivity and data analytics to advanced artificial intelligence – are significantly altering how work is conducted and how organisations are structured and managed [1]. Digital tools and platforms now mediate a vast portion of workplace activities, blurring traditional boundaries of time and space [2], enabling new modes of collaboration, and challenging long-established organisational practices. As a result, digital transformation has become a top strategic priority for contemporary managers [3] who try to interpret, anticipate, and steer the transformation process.

The effects produced by technology-driven transformation combine structures, practices, values, and beliefs, creating a changing force that frequently introduces tensions within existing institutions, organisations, ecosystems, industries, or fields [4]. These aspects make technology-driven change disruptive, continuously altering the status quo, designing actual or purported logics of interactions among organisational actors. Overall, two aspects characterise this technology-driven change process.

Firstly, even though technology is the driving force behind this type of change, the resulting digital transformation process is, in fact, a socio-technical process that extends beyond the mere adoption of technology and has the potential to reshape the internal work dynamics of organisations as well as their methods of interaction with their environment and stakeholders [1, 5].

Secondly, the digital transformation process aligns with the trends and dynamics of technological evolution, which typically does not exhibit a linear path and presents an emergent nature [6]. Human choices and institutional contexts influence this evolutionary process, but the emerging affordances and constraints of digital technologies themselves also propel it. In recent years, several key digital technologies – including the Internet, big data, and artificial intelligence – have generated significant interest and driven the evolution of digital transformation in unexpected and difficult-to-predict trajectories.

1.1 Digital Technology as the Driver of Change

Digital artefacts are central to changes driven by digital technology. Unlike traditional physical artefacts, digital artefacts lack physical properties; instead, they possess malleable characteristics that allow them to be shaped, adapted, and transformed for various contexts [7]. They are not constrained, as they can be reproduced limitlessly, often increasing in value upon replication. Furthermore, they can be distributed instantaneously around the globe with minimal transaction costs.

Digital artefacts emerge and are subsequently embedded in a broader context, whether personal or organisational, that is itself changing. This continual state of flux means that the status of digital artefacts is in constant transformation, rapidly reshaping or repurposing through updates, modifications, integrations with other systems, or the evolution of core technology [8]. Furthermore, digital artefacts are subject to interpretation, translation, and appropriation processes by goal-oriented actors, who endeavour to exploit the capabilities of digital artefacts for individual and organisational objectives [9–11]. As a result, digital artefacts are generative within the contexts in which they are embedded, promoting unplanned innovations beyond their original design.

1.2 Governing Technology-Driven Change

The emergent and unpredictable nature of the evolution of digital technology creates (ethical) challenges for individuals and organisations participating in the digital transformation process. The potential for negative outcomes have prompted a discussion on establishing principles for effective AI governance. Thus, many organizations have started putting forth proposals for guiding principles for Artificial intelligence, leading to an increasing interest in the concept of "Responsible AI" (RAI), which refers to a set of guidelines or normative statements regarding the governance of AI [12]. These guidelines encompass a range of topics, including digital artifacts, their development, implementation, use, and assessment guidelines.

Regarding the evolution of digital artefacts, both people and organisations are orthogonal and foundational. On one side, the evolution of core digital technology often seems distant from individuals and organisations. Digital technologies are explored, experimented with, developed, and diffused by a few key actors, such as large digital organisations, universities, and research centres. From this perspective, digital technology presents a challenge to individuals and organisations to adapt to emerging trends, adopt technological artefacts, and exploit their capabilities to reach their goals.

On the other hand, digital technology also evolves through the myriad interactions with other pieces of technology and existing institutional settings. This makes the evolution of digital technology influenced by a multitude of dispersed stakeholders, rendering its management a complex socio-technical undertaking [8]. Even if no single authority can influence, predict, or direct the trajectories of the evolution of digital artefacts, they are continuously influenced by multiple collective and decentralised interactions, as we are evidence by the phenomenon of the development. Even if it appears autopoietic, technology-driven evolution is only partially autonomous and evolves based on technical and socio-technical interactions [8, 13].

1.3 New Forms of Organisations and Institutional Arrangements

The cumulative effect of technology-driven change is visible in the transformations of how we organise for work, giving rise to new organisational forms and institutional arrangements. Traditional bureaucratic hierarchies and stable, long-term employment models are being supplemented (and sometimes supplanted) by more fluid [14], networked, and platform-based forms of organising [15]; however, this does not supplant the problem of organising [16]. Several new, digital technology-supported forms of organising and institutions are visible in reality.

For instance, digital platforms have established structures that differ significantly from traditional industrial firms. Platforms such as Uber, Airbnb, Amazon, and Upwork facilitate transactions and coordinate labour across organisational boundaries, forming ecosystems of users, workers, and providers. In this model, the platform owner supplies digital infrastructure and rules, while decentralised actors (drivers, hosts, developers, creators) generate much of the value [17, 18].

These developments also introduced new rules in the emerging economy, the gig economy, characterised by digital platforms that mediate work through algorithms, reshapes traditional employment relations by classifying many workers as independent contractors [17]. This evolution necessitates new considerations for labour rights, benefits, and responsibilities for worker training and safety, prompting legal adaptations like new laws for ridesharing.

Organisations are adopting agile team structures, cross-functional product squads, and decentralised authority. Digitally transformed companies emphasise flatter hierarchies and empowered teams responsive to data and customer feedback. Some firms take on a remote-first approach, collaborating mainly through digital tools, a trend accelerated by the pandemic. This requires strong digital communication infrastructures and a culture that supports cohesion without physical presence. Additionally, it necessitates re-evaluating leadership oversight, knowledge sharing, and maintaining organisational culture in a virtual environment.

At the institutional level, digital transformation acts as a change agent by blurring boundaries between sectors and stimulating regulatory evolution. For example, the boundary between the technology sector and other sectors is dissolving as many more companies running traditional businesses are increasingly digital. The digital transformation process per se can also be seen as an institutional change process, as it changes, threatens, and replaces existing institutional rules [4].

Finally, technology-driven change is ambivalent and contingent. Digital transformation can lead to greater efficiency, innovation, and even the democratisation of information, but it can also exacerbate inequalities, reproduce biases, and raise ethical dilemmas.

All these characteristics point to the fact that the work and organisations of tomorrow will not just be yesterdays, but more digital.

2 Exploring Technology-Driven Change

Understanding tomorrow's work and organisations requires an interdisciplinary lens, combining information systems research on the technological aspects with organisational studies on human and institutional factors. In this regard, this book builds on the historical collaborative tradition of information systems research within organisations studies [19]. The following chapters represent a selection of the best papers selected at the 2024 edition of the Italian Chapter of Association of Information Systems (AIS), Conference and collected in this topical book to provide an up-to-date overview of the research performed by scholars attending the Italian community of AIS in the domain of work and organisations of tomorrow.

Chapters included in this book focus on two specific sub-areas. A first area concerns specifically the future of work and work environment. Chapters within this group discuss, in Sect. 2.1, new forms of work and changes related to work consequent to digital technology evolution. A second area concerns instead the assessment of impacts, readiness, facilitating or hindering factors, as well as characteristics of people and technology when interacting. These chapters, in Sect. 2.2, discuss the results of research papers exploring these aspects.

2.1 Technology-Driven Change and New Work

Santarelli and Ceci, in their chapter "*Configuration of the Data Value Chain: Reflections on the Digital and Analogue Dimensions*," [20] investigate how organizations manage data value chains that operate across digital and physical spaces. Focusing on the National Park of Abruzzo, Lazio, and Molise, they highlight the complexities and organizational challenges of effectively transforming data into valuable assets.

In "*Employee Perception of Human-Robot Co-working: Evidence from the Hotel Sector in Russia, Egypt, and Italy*," Menshikova and colleagues [21] examine hotel employees' attitudes toward collaborative robots. Using mixed methods, they identify how social and psychological aspects influence robot acceptance and human-robot interaction across different cultural contexts.

Bonesso and colleagues, in "*The Strategic Role of HR in Hybrid Work Environments: An Application of the 'Harvard' Model*," [22] analyze how HR can lead and support hybrid work arrangements. Through a longitudinal case study and the Harvard model, they emphasize the importance of aligning HR practices with organizational goals in hybrid work environments and highlight the importance of continuous outcome monitoring.

In *"Gig Work in Organizations: Demystifying the Perspectives of Human Resource Management Professionals,"* Singh and colleagues [23] examine the evolving adoption of HRM practices for gig workers. Using natural language processing to analyze HR professionals' perspectives shared in YouTube videos, the study reveals that gig workers are increasingly integrated into standard organizational settings, reshaping traditional HRM practices.

Dario Natale Palmucci, in the chapter "*Technology Worsening Employees' Life: A Qualitative Study to Understand Determinants, Effects and Solutions*," [24] explores how constant connectivity enabled by technology can impact employee wellbeing. The findings stress the role of responsibility, offer practical implications for improving organizational safety conditions, and build the base for future researchers interested in exploring the determinants and effects of new work modalities.

Roma and Agrifoglio, in "*Exploring the Interpersonal Relationships in Virtual Reality: A Systematic Literature Review*," [25] examine how VR technologies transform interpersonal interactions. Their analysis identifies work, leisure, and learning as key domains, while highlighting research gaps concerning interpersonal interactions, the purpose of learning activities, the technology metaverse, and the context of virtual teams.

Mastrogiorgio and colleagues, in "*Algorithmic Transparency and Algorithmic Accountability in Organizations*," [26] examine how organizational actors may face legitimacy challenges when delegating decisions to opaque AI systems. They propose the conceptual roles of organizational actors as "Centaurs" or "Cyborgs" based on their interaction with AI in decision-making.

Finally, De Nicola and colleagues, in "*Gender-Aware Business Process Management*," [27] address the intersection of gender equity and business process management. They propose principles and methodologies for transitioning from gender-blind to gender-aware business process management, offering suggestions for enhancing modeling techniques, process mining, and gender-aware business process evaluation methods.

2.2 Readiness, Impact, and Assessment of Digital Technology

Breitruck and colleagues' paper, "*Towards Assessing Digital Maturity: Utilizing Real-Time Public Data for Organizational Benchmarking*," [28] introduces a novel Comparative Digital Maturity Model (CDMM), developed through focus groups and expert interviews with industry stakeholders. The CDMM aims to enable organizations to dynamically benchmark their digital maturity using real-time, publicly available news data, effectively overcoming the limitations of traditional static digital transformation models.

Höhener and Lösser, in their chapter "*Driving Factors in the Technology Acceptance of Generative Artificial Intelligence—Insights from an Exploratory Interview Study with Digital Leaders*," [29] developed a Generative AI Acceptance Model, which highlights trust, hedonic motivation, convenience, efficiency, and effectiveness as key antecedent factors. It further demonstrates that performance expectancy and perceived value creation, influenced by context factors, can serve as an appraisal that ultimately leads to behavioral intention and usage intensity.

In their chapter "*Fostering Organizational Cybersecurity Culture Amid Rapid Digital Transformation: A Case Study from Ethiopia*," Adamu, Spagnoletti, and Niemimaa [30] explore how organizations can cultivate cybersecurity culture during periods of rapid digital transformation. Drawing on a qualitative case study of a financial institution, they highlight critical strategies – including leadership initiatives, continuous training, and systematic updates to policies and guidelines – that enable organizations to reinforce cybersecurity practices and resilience in highly dynamic and evolving environments.

Pagnozzi, Weritz, and Antonelli, in "*The Metamorphosis Behind Digital Transformation: An Integrated Framework from Change Management*," [31] develop a conceptual framework linking societal change and digital transformation. Drawing on change management theory, they highlight the cultural and institutional shifts caused by digitalization and offer strategies to help organizations navigate these transformations effectively.

In their chapter "*Exploring Chatbot Adoption in the Italian Legal Domain: a Fuzzy-set Qualitative Comparative Analysis*," Bianchini and colleagues [32] examine the use of AI chatbots among legal knowledge workers. They identify two profiles of adopters – innovation-minded employees and critical thinkers – and reveal insights into chatbot usage behavior and perceived risks.

Trivelli and Za, in "*A Systematic Literature Review on Emerging Technology Adoption Across Time*," [33] provide a comprehensive analysis of organizational-level adoption of emerging technologies. Following Okoli's framework, and drawing on 48 published articles, they highlighted organizational, individual, environmental, and technological factors involved in the technology pre-adoption, adoption, and post-adoption stages.

In "*Determinants of Blockchain Adoption in Accounting: A Case Study Analysis*," Scaletti, Pisano, and Lavorato [34] apply the Technology-Organization-Environment framework to investigate blockchain adoption in accounting. Their qualitative case study suggests that technological benefits, such as enhanced transparency and operational efficiency, can serve as key drivers of adoption decisions, thereby providing empirical evidence on the antecedents of blockchain implementation.

Benedict Lösser, in the chapter "*State of the Art of Business Analytics for Enterprise Transformation Steering*," [35] examines the current state of business analytics in the context of enterprise transformations. Through a descriptive interview study, the chapter highlights the limited use of analytics in practice and advocates for their expanded adoption to bridge decision-making gaps in transformation projects.

In "*The Four 'E' Model – Evaluating Gen AI in a Balanced Way*," Mayer and colleagues [36] propose a comprehensive evaluation model for Generative AI adoption that incorporates efficiency, effectiveness, experience, and ESG considerations. Based on cross-industry survey data, they emphasize the need to assess sustainability impacts alongside technological benefits and suggest that their model can be used to identify best use cases.

Cantoni and colleagues, in "*Advances in Measuring Soft Skills in Project Management: A Technology-Mediated Approach to Capture Enacted Behavior*,"

[37] provide an overview of the most frequently used instruments for the assessment of soft skills, and suggest refinements in the measurement of soft skills in Project Management, advocating for a more flexible application of the measures outlined in the IMPA Key Competence Indicators. Their method emphasizes enacted behavior and reduces bias compared to traditional methods.

In *"Empowering SMEs: The Role of Generative AI in Knowledge Retention,"* Perozzo and colleagues [38] explore how Generative AI supports knowledge management and retention in SMEs. With the help of the socio-technical framework, they demonstrate the variables influencing knowledge sharing, emphasizing the interplay between individual motivation, organizational support and culture, and technological capability. They also stress that the employee perceptions must be carefully managed.

In their chapter, *"Digital Skills and Maturity in the Public Sector: A Review of EU Guidelines,"* Gaysina and colleagues [39] conduct a scoping review of grey literature on digitalization practices and digital skills in the public sector across the European Union. They propose a framework that links digital skills to various stages of digitalization maturity, emphasizing the need for continuous adaptation and advancement of digital skills in public sector training and development programs.

Finally, the chapter of Bucciarelli et al. *"What if the essential were invisible to decision-making? Designing an interactive eye-tracking study on the voluntary contribution mechanism"* [40] explores the use of eye-tracking as a way to predict eye movements during decision-making and its effects on economic outcomes. It proposes a novel experimental design using the public goods game framework to assess participants' understanding of the experimental instructions and the essential elements required to make real economic decisions.

References

1. Zammuto, R. F., Griffith, T. L., Majchrzak, A., Dougherty, D. J., Faraj, S., Dogherty, D. J., & Faraj, S. (2007). Information technology and the changing fabric of organization. *Organization Science, 18*, 749–762. https://doi.org/10.1287/orsc.1070.0307
2. Renkema, M., & Tursunbayeva, A. (2024). The future of work of academics in the age of Artificial Intelligence: State-of-the-art and a research roadmap. *Futures, 163*, 103453. https://doi.org/10.1016/j.futures.2024.103453.
3. Vial, G. (2019). Understanding digital transformation: A review and a research agenda. *Journal of Strategic Information Systems, 28*, 118–144. https://doi.org/10.1016/j.jsis.2019.01.003
4. Hinings, B., Gegenhuber, T., & Greenwood, R. (2018). Digital innovation and transformation: An institutional perspective. *Information and Organization, 28*, 52–61. https://doi.org/10.1016/J.INFOANDORG.2018.02.004
5. Fulk, J., & DeSanctis, G. (1995). Electronic communication and changing organizational form. *Organization Science, 6*, 337–349. https://doi.org/10.1287/orsc.6.4.337
6. Bailey, D. E., Faraj, S., Hinds, P. J., Leonardi, P. M., & von Krogh, G. (2022). We are all theorists of technology now: A relational perspective on emerging technology and organizing. *Organization Science, 33*, 1–18. https://doi.org/10.1287/ORSC.2021.1562
7. Piccoli, G. (2012). *Information systems for managers: Text and cases*. Wiley.

8. Kallinikos, J., Aaltonen, A., & Marton, A. (2013). The ambivalent ontology of digital artifacts. *MIS Quarterly, 37*, 357–370.
9. Orlikowski, W. J. (2007). Sociomaterial practices: Exploring technology at work. *Organization Studies, 28*, 1435–1448.
10. DeSanctis, G., & Poole, M. S. (1994). Capturing the complexity in advanced technology use: Adaptive structuration theory. *Organization Science, 5*, 121–147.
11. Sæbø, Ø., Federici, T., & Braccini, A. M. (2020). Combining social media affordances for organising collective action. *Information Systems Journal, 30*, 699–732. https://doi.org/10.1111/isj.12280
12. Mikalef, P., Conboy, K., Lundström, J. E., & Popovič, A. (2022). Thinking responsibly about responsible AI and 'the dark side' of AI. *European Journal of Information Systems, 31*, 257–268. https://doi.org/10.1080/0960085X.2022.2026621
13. Hanseth, O., & Lyytinen, K. (2010). Design theory for dynamic complexity in information infrastructures: The case of building Internet. *Journal of Information Technology, 25*, 1–19.
14. Samaan, D., & Tursunbayeva, A. (2024). Fluid workforce management in the health sector: Navigating the changing face of workforces and their management. *International Journal of Public Sector Management, 37*, 593–609. https://doi.org/10.1108/IJPSM-10-2023-0311.
15. Braccini, A. M., Sæbø, Ø., & Federici, T. (2019). From the blogosphere into the parliament: The role of digital technologies in organizing social movements. *Information and Organization, 29*, 100250. https://doi.org/10.1016/j.infoandorg.2019.04.002
16. Henfridsson, O., & Lind, M. (2014). Information systems strategizing, organizational subcommunities, and the emergence of a sustainability strategy. *Journal of Strategic Information Systems., 23*, 11–28. https://doi.org/10.1016/j.jsis.2013.11.001
17. Hamari, J., Sjöklint, M., & Ukkonen, A. (2016). The sharing economy: Why people participate in collaborative consumption. *Journal of the Association for Information Science and Technology, 67*, 2047–2059. https://doi.org/10.1002/asi.23552
18. Barnes, S. J., & Mattsson, J. (2017). Understanding collaborative consumption: Test of a theoretical model. *Technological Forecasting and Social Change, 118*, 281–292. https://doi.org/10.1016/j.techfore.2017.02.029
19. Orlikowski, W. J., & Barley, S. R. (2001). Technology and institutions: What can research on information technology and research on organizations learn from each other? *Management Information Systems Quarterly, 25*, 145–165. https://doi.org/10.2307/3250927
20. Santarelli, L., & Ceci, F. (2025). Configuration of the data value chain: Reflections on the digital and analogue dimensions. In A. Tursunbayeva, A. M. Braccini, & F. Virili (Eds.), *Technology-driven transformation: The future of work and organizations*. Springer Nature Switzerland AG.
21. Menshikova, M., Bonacci, I., Scarozza, D., Fedorova, A., & Ghazy, K. (2025). Employee perception of human-robot co-working: Evidence from the hotel sector in Russia, Egypt, and Italy. In A. Tursunbayeva, A. M. Braccini, & F. Virili (Eds.), *Technology-driven transformation: The future of work and organizations*. Springer Nature Switzerland AG.
22. Bonesso, S., Afeltra, G., & Cortellazzo, L. (2025). The strategic role of HR in hybrid work environments: An application of the 'Harvard' model. In A. Tursunbayeva, A. M. Braccini, & F. Virili (Eds.), *Technology-driven transformation: The future of work and organizations*. Springer Nature Switzerland AG.
23. Keplinger, K., Singh, V., Tursunbayeva, A., & Di Lauro, S. (2025). Gig work in organizations: Demystifying the perspectives of human resource management professionals. In A. Tursunbayeva, A. M. Braccini, & F. Virili (Eds.), *Technology-driven transformation: The future of work and organizations*. Springer Nature Switzerland AG.
24. Palmucci, D. N. (2025). Technology worsening employees' life: A qualitative study to understand determinants, effects and solutions. In A. Tursunbayeva, A. M. Braccini, & F. Virili (Eds.), *Technology-driven transformation: The future of work and organizations*. Springer Nature Switzerland AG.

25. Roma, L., & Agrifoglio, R. (2025). Exploring the interpersonal relationships in virtual reality: A systematic literature review. In A. Tursunbayeva, A. M. Braccini, & F. Virili (Eds.), *Technology-driven transformation: The future of work and organizations*. Springer Nature Switzerland AG.
26. Mastrogiorgio, A., Di Nauta, P., & Martinez, M. (2025). Algorithmic transparency and algorithmic accountability in organizations. In A. Tursunbayeva, A. M. Braccini, & F. Virili (Eds.), *Technology-driven transformation: The future of work and organizations*. Springer Nature Switzerland AG.
27. De Nicola, A., Guariglia Migliore, M., & Wagner, A. (2025). Gender-aware business process management. In A. Tursunbayeva, A. M. Braccini, & F. Virili (Eds.), *Technology-driven transformation: The future of work and organizations*. Springer Nature Switzerland AG.
28. Breitruck, M., Back, A., & Pätzmann, L.-M. (2025). Towards assessing digital maturity: Utilizing real-time public data for organizational benchmarking. In A. Tursunbayeva, A. M. Braccini, & F. Virili (Eds.), *Technology-driven transformation: The future of work and organizations*. Springer Nature Switzerland AG.
29. Höhener, D., & Lösser, B. (2025). Driving factors in the technology acceptance of generative artificial intelligence – Insights from an exploratory interview study with digital leaders. In A. Tursunbayeva, A. M. Braccini, & F. Virili (Eds.), *Technology-driven transformation: The future of work and organizations*. Springer Nature Switzerland AG.
30. Adamu, M. A., Spagnoletti, P., & Niemimaa, M. I. N. (2025). Fostering organizational cybersecurity culture amid rapid digital transformation: A case study from Ethiopia. In A. Tursunbayeva, A. M. Braccini, & F. Virili (Eds.), *Technology-driven transformation: The future of work and organizations*. Springer Nature Switzerland AG.
31. Pagnozzi, F., Weritz, P., & Antonelli, G. (2025). The metamorphosis behind digital transformation: An integrated framework from change management. In A. Tursunbayeva, A. M. Braccini, & F. Virili (Eds.), *Technology-driven transformation: The future of work and organizations*. Springer Nature Switzerland AG.
32. Bianchini, F., Braccini, A. M., De Luzi, F., Macrì, M., Mecella, M., & Ruggiero, R. A. (2025). Exploring Chatbot adoption in the Italian legal domain: A fuzzy-set qualitative comparative analysis. In A. Tursunbayeva, A. M. Braccini, & F. Virili (Eds.), *Technology-driven transformation: The future of work and organizations*. Springer Nature Switzerland AG.
33. Trivelli, R., & Za, S. (2025). A systematic literature review on emerging technology adoption across time. In A. Tursunbayeva, A. M. Braccini, & F. Virili (Eds.), *Technology-driven transformation: The future of work and organizations*. Springer Nature Switzerland AG.
34. Lavorato, D., Scaletti, A., & Pisano, S. (2025). Determinants of blockchain adoption in accounting: A case study analysis. In A. Tursunbayeva, A. M. Braccini, & F. Virili (Eds.), *Technology-driven transformation: The future of work and organizations*. Springer Nature Switzerland AG.
35. Lösser, B. (2025). State of the art of business analytics for enterprise Transformation steering. In A. Tursunbayeva, A. M. Braccini, & F. Virili (Eds.), *Technology-driven transformation: The future of work and organizations*. Springer Nature Switzerland AG.
36. Mayer, J. H., Bender, K., Esswein, M., & Quick, R. (2025). The Four "E" model – Evaluating Gen AI in a more balanced way. In A. Tursunbayeva, A. M. Braccini, & F. Virili (Eds.), *Technology-driven transformation: The future of work and organizations*. Springer Nature Switzerland AG.
37. Cantoni, F., Capogreco, C., Cerri, M., Patti, E., & Soregaroli, C. (2025). Advances in measuring soft skills in project management. A technology-mediated approach to capture the enacted behavior. In A. Tursunbayeva, A. M. Braccini, & F. Virili (Eds.), *Technology-driven transformation: The future of work and organizations*. Springer Nature Switzerland AG.
38. Perozzo, H., Ravarini, A., Dia Perozzo, M. J., Roncari, C., & Strada, E. (2025). Empowering SMEs: The role of generative AI in knowledge retention. In A. Tursunbayeva, A. M. Braccini, & F. Virili (Eds.), *Technology-driven transformation: The future of work and organizations*. Springer Nature Switzerland AG.

39. Tomo, A., Gaysina, L., Tursunbayeva, A., & Berni, A. (2025). Digital skills and maturity in the public sector: A review of EU guidelines. In A. Tursunbayeva, A. M. Braccini, & F. Virili (Eds.), *Technology-driven transformation: The future of work and organizations*. Springer Nature Switzerland AG.
40. Ascatigno, A., Bucciarelli, E., Colantonio, A., & Regnicoli, A. (2025). What if the essential were invisible to decision-making? Designing an interactive eye-tracking study on the voluntary contribution mechanism. In A. Tursunbayeva, A. M. Braccini, & F. Virili (Eds.), *Technology-driven transformation: The future of work and organizations*. Springer Nature Switzerland AG.

Configuration of the Data Value Chain: Reflections on the Digital and Analogue Dimensions

Loris Santarelli and Federica Ceci

Abstract The growing demand for improving data collection, use, and exploitation has prompted organisations to explore innovative tools and methodologies for effective data management. The data value chain (DVC) is a conceptual framework that encompasses the entire data lifecycle, from its aggregation to its strategic application, thereby facilitating the value extraction processes from data resources. However, the DVC comprises a series of processes and technologies that organizations must effectively configure to convert data into valuable assets. Consequently, its implementation poses considerable challenges. Furthermore, in various contexts, the activities that constitute the DVC occur not only in digital spaces but also in physical settings. This duality introduces an additional layer of complexity as the inherent differences between physical and digital operations require distinct approaches to coordination, integration, and management. Therefore, this paper aims to investigate a specific instance of the DVC that encompasses activities occurring across both digital and physical domains. Our research focuses on the National Park of Abruzzo, Lazio, and Molise (PNALM), where a combination of digital and analog technologies plays a critical role in supporting environmental and wildlife conservation efforts. Within this context, all organizational units involved in wildlife monitoring engage in data collection, sharing, and utilization, drawing on both traditional and digital data sources. Through this case, we contribute to the literature by deepening the understanding of the challenges organizations encounter in configuring and managing the Data Value Chain in complex environments.

Keywords Data value chain · Data ecosystems · Data management

L. Santarelli (✉) · F. Ceci
G. d'Annunzio University of Chieti, Pescara, Italy
e-mail: loris.santarelli@unich.it; f.ceci@unich.it

A. Tursunbayeva et al. (eds.), *Technology-Driven Transformation*, Lecture Notes in Information Systems and Organisation 79,
https://doi.org/10.1007/978-3-032-01396-5_2

1 Introduction

Ongoing advancements in data technologies are creating new opportunities for organizations to collaborate, share resources, and thrive in an increasingly interconnected business environment [1, 2]. Today, organisations consider data as a strategic asset, capable of driving changes in management strategies and decision-making processes [3–6]. In order to extract value from data, organizations focus on configuring their Data Value Chain (DVC). The DVC framework outlines five key steps through which data and technologies enable organizations to derive value from their data [7, 8]. Each step involves specific activities where data are not only owned, but also produced, shared, consumed, and reused across various domains, ultimately giving rise to data ecosystems [9, 10]. When referring to data, the term 'ecosystem' describes a network of actors who generate and share data while interacting with one another [7]. Such interactions require organizations to adapt and renew their relationships to align with new information flows and emerging opportunities. To fully leverage these opportunities, actors and technologies, which are the core elements of the ecosystem, must be well integrated. While technologies offer significant advances in data management, challenges remain, particularly in environments where traditional tools must be used alongside modern technologies. Indeed, in various contexts, the activities comprising a Digital Value Chain (DVC) are not confined solely to digital domains, such as online platforms, software systems, and virtual environments, but also extend into physical settings, including manufacturing facilities, retail spaces, and logistics operations. This dual domain introduces additional complexity, as digital and physical activities differ fundamentally in their characteristics, operational requirements, and technological infrastructure. As a result, distinct management strategies, resource allocations, and integration mechanisms are required to address the unique demands of each domain. The interplay between digital and physical environments further necessitates careful coordination to ensure operational continuity and to enhance the overall efficiency and effectiveness of the value chain.

The aim of this paper is to investigate the challenges in data management within such a specific configuration of the DVC, where various organizational areas use and share data through both digital and traditional technologies. This is particularly relevant in contexts characterized by fieldwork, where data are collected directly in the field for diverse purposes, across organizations from different sectors. In this study, we explore this configuration in the field of environmental safeguarding.

We developed a case study based on the National Park of Abruzzo, Lazio, and Molise (PNALM), dedicated to preserving wildlife and the natural landscape. In pursuit of its mission, PNALM employs strategies to promote the coexistence of humans and wildlife. Central to these strategies are numerous operations involving data, such as wildlife monitoring and censuses, which necessitate both digital and non-digital technologies. These technologies facilitate the collection, sharing, and usage of data across organizational domains, including technical, surveillance, or scientific areas. In these domains, information gathered by field operators are continuously collected and analyzed to support conservation efforts. Accordingly, this study is guided by the following research questions:

How does the integration of digital and traditional technologies impact the configuration of the data value chain within organizations? What challenges arise from this dual configuration?

To address these questions, we utilize qualitative data, including open-ended interviews and documents. Through this data, we unpack the DVC and explore the configuration and challenges within each phase. The remainder of the paper is structured as follows: first, we review the literature on the DVC to provide the study's foundational context. In the following section, we present the methodology, detailing the context, data collection process, and analysis techniques. Finally, we summarize our contributions and outline potential directions for future research.

2 Literature Review

2.1 Data Value Chain

Organizations that adopt data-driven technologies as strategic assets undergo transformations across multiple dimensions [3–5]. These transformations encompass the digitisation of traditional infrastructures [5], shifts in management strategies [4] and modification in decision-making processes [6]. However, these impacts are not immediate. To generate a shift in practices, data must acquire value through several steps, from acquisition to utilization [4, 11]. Understanding these steps is essential for identifying the process through which value can be derived from data. These stages are integral to the DVC model developed by Curry [12]. The DVC framework outlines how data flow through various steps: acquisition, analysis, curation, storage, and usage [4]. In particular, the DVC model describes the entire path of data from their initial acquisition to their final usage [3, 4] as follows. Data acquisition refers to the processes involved in collecting, validating, and organizing data prior to its storage in databases or other infrastructure. Data analysis involves preparing data for domain-specific applications, which include identifying relevant data, exploring patterns, and uncovering meaningful insights or hidden information. Data curation is the proactive management of data throughout its lifecycle, ensuring its quality, integrity, and reliability for effective usage. Data storage refers to the preservation and maintenance of data, ensuring its accessibility and scalability for future retrieval and reuse. Finally, data usage refers to the application of data-driven business activities that leverage data to gain performance advantages and support decision-making. Figure 1

Fig. 1 Data value chain from Curry [4]

illustrates the five steps of the data management process, from data acquisition to usage (Fig. 1).

The DVC represents a central framework for the future knowledge economy due to the opportunities it provides for the digital advancement of economic sectors [13]. It is designed to analyse activities related to data and technologies within organisational settings and forms a core component of the data ecosystem [4, 7]. The term ecosystem refers to '*a group of organizations related with varying degrees of multi-lateral, non-generic complementarities without hierarchical control*' [14]. Curry et al. [5] described a data ecosystem as '*a sociotechnical system enabling value to be extracted from data value chains supported by interacting organizations and individuals*.' Oliveira [10] adds that the data ecosystem is a complex network formed by actors collaborating to find, share, or use data to foster innovation, create value, and support new businesses. Data ecosystems are composed of actors linked through various relationships, sharing data to contribute to a common purpose [15]. Within data ecosystems, actors can be organizations or individuals assuming different roles. Key participants include data suppliers and consumers, data and technology providers, marketplaces, and end users [12].

Ecosystem literature typically identifies a framework composed of three levels: the core value chain, the extended value chain, and the big data ecosystem [4, 5, 15]. The DVC represents the central element of the data ecosystem as its core. This level illustrates the interconnections between direct data suppliers and the channels through which data value is distributed [7]. The extended value chain, the second level of the model, includes all actors who can influence market dynamics [7] and the macro level encompasses a community of interacting actors that surround organizations, technology platforms, and sectors [4].

Depending on its purpose, the core part of the ecosystem comprises a set of diverse configurations that organizations must manage to transform data into valuable assets. For example, the ecosystem may include technologies of varying natures or various actors linked by different purposes. Despite the significant challenges posed by this multiplicity, there is limited understanding of how to effectively organize the core value chain, particularly in terms of resources and technologies. Acknowledging these challenges is a crucial first step towards more effective data management. We identify and discuss these challenges by exploring the configuration of a DVC shaped by digital and traditional technologies and tools. We explore this particular configuration in a context where digital and non-digital technologies coexist, a feature that highlights unique organizational challenges. Our aim is to define and deepen our understanding of the core component of a data ecosystem, focusing specifically on the DVC. By unpacking the DVC, we aim to identify the interactions among actors participating in the DVC and how technologies and tools shape each step: data acquisition, data analysis, data curation, data storage, and data usage. This investigation helps us understand how actors within ecosystems behave and interact through both digital and traditional technologies, and it deepens our understanding of the challenges specific to this configuration, which is characteristic of many sectors where both types of technologies still coexist.

3 Methodology

3.1 Empirical Context

Our case study examines the organizational efforts of PNALM, dedicated to wildlife and nature safeguarding. To fulfil its mission, PNALM engages in a range of strategies that rely on both traditional and digital tools related to data management. These strategies encompass various data-related activities, such as monitoring activities, simultaneous counts, wildlife censuses, surveillance, and inspections. Within PNALM, multiple organizational areas share and manage data. These activities vary according to data sources and nature, depending on the actors involved and the objectives they are pursuing. These data-oriented tasks are carried out both in the field, where data are collected, and outside it.

Dedicated to environmental protection, PNALM has configured a DVC designed to facilitate data sharing both internally and externally. Internally, the DVC connects various organizational units, enabling coordinated efforts toward PNALM's shared mission. Externally, it functions as a point of engagement for stakeholders such as NGOs and academic institutions, who collaborate on common environmental objectives. This study focuses on the internal dimension of the DVC, where distinct organizational areas, such as technical, surveillance, and scientific domains, interact and cooperate to achieve shared goals. Within this context, effective data sharing across all organizational units is essential for the success of integrated conservation strategies.

Data collected from field operations are continuously gathered and analyzed, with both traditional and digital technologies playing vital roles throughout these processes. Technologies such as radio collars, mobile applications, and centralized databases, alongside both analog and digital communication tools, are employed to support data-related activities. A typical field scenario involves multiple teams, often working in dyads, tasked with monitoring specific wildlife populations. These teams collect data on variables such as animal location, group composition, and behavior within defined spatial and temporal boundaries. The process demands a high degree of organization and coordination, as teams physically navigate mountainous terrain to locate target species. Geolocation technologies, including radio collars and mobile apps, are utilized to trace animal movements, while traditional observation techniques complement the digital data collection efforts. Continuous communication among teams is essential; real-time updates are shared to report findings, avoid data duplication, and enhance operational efficiency. Ultimately, all collected data, regardless of format compared, stored, and utilized for multiple purposes, contributing to a holistic approach to wildlife monitoring and conservation within PNALM. Therefore, the context is characterized by the huge variety of complex activities and the necessity of using both traditional and digital technologies to collect and share information. These features make the DVC particularly complex, highlighting challenges at every step and motivating us to thoroughly explore this specific configuration.

3.2 *Case Study Design*

This study adopts a single-case study design to investigate how data sharing unfolds within an organizational context characterized by the simultaneous use of digital and traditional tools for data management. By unpacking the specific activities involved in data management, we examine each stage of the DVC and identify the challenges associated with them. The case study is based on three primary sources of data: archival documents, semi-structured interviews, and participatory observations.

Data Collection We collected data related to PNALM's initiatives, involved actors, activities, technologies, and projects. This phase involved gathering a wide range of secondary sources, including strategic reports, scientific publications, newspaper articles, social media posts, and datasets, to build a comprehensive understanding of the organizational context (see Appendix 1). The primary purpose of collecting secondary data was to inform the subsequent interview phase, allowing for a more targeted and context-aware approach.

In the second phase, we conducted 16 open-ended interviews with PNALM members holding diverse roles and backgrounds, including the Director, managers, rangers, auxiliaries, and external collaborators. Collectively, the interviews spanned 13 h and 19 min (see Table 1; additional details in Appendix 2). The interviews were guided by a protocol that covered themes such as professional roles, monitoring practices, technologies in use, inter-organizational relationships, data sharing

Table 1 Summary of the interview schedule

Interview steps	Actors	Durations
Step 1	Director, managers, rangers	5 interviews, 4 h 43 m
Step 2	Chief ranger, rangers, auxiliaries	4 interviews, 3 h 20 m
Step 3	Rangers, biologist	4 interviews, 2 h 55 m
Step 4	Tech. providers, ranger	3 interviews, 2 h 21 m
		16 interviews, 13 h 19 m

mechanisms, and collaborative efforts. All interviews were recorded, transcribed, and systematically coded to identify emerging themes and inform the development of the case study.

Finally, the Director granted us permission to participate in the activities as volunteers for a period of 8 days. During this time, we collected in-depth observational data, focusing on specific tasks and the use of both traditional and digital technologies. Observations were documented through detailed fieldnotes and subsequently expanded using an out-of-the-field dictionary [16, 17]. This approach enabled a richer understanding of PNALM's internal dynamics and data management practices. By triangulating insights from multiple sources, we enhanced the reliability and depth of our findings.

3.3 Coding Protocol

Our analytical protocol is grounded in inductive methods, beginning with an open coding approach. This initial phase was followed by iterative refinement and regrouping of codes to identify key organizational features related to data management. One primary coder conducted the initial coding, working in close collaboration with two researchers through multiple rounds of discussion to incorporate diverse perspectives and enhance the reliability of the coding process.

The coding was applied across all data sources, including archival documents, interviews, and field observations, and was firmly anchored in the conceptual framework of the DVC. As a first step, we developed a coding vocabulary by categorizing each data segment into specific dimensions of the DVC. This phase was essential in structuring our understanding of how data-related activities were distributed along the DVC. Subsequently, we grouped and analyzed activities corresponding to each step of the DVC, from data acquisition to data usage.

Table 2 presents definitions of each DVC stage, as drawn from the literature, alongside illustrative examples from our empirical data. This table serves to demonstrate the alignment between theoretical constructs and real-world practices observed within PNALM's operations.

During this phase, we aligned our empirical data with the DVC framework and proceeded to categorize and quantify the occurrences of both digital and traditional technologies used at each stage of the DVC. Using NVivo software, we conducted a detailed analysis of the frequency and co-occurrence of these technologies across the DVC steps (see Appendix 3).

In the subsequent phase, we performed a documentary and content analysis to identify the specific challenges associated with each stage of the DVC. This analysis allowed us to further classify the nature of these challenges, distinguishing between those that were technology-related and those stemming from other organizational or operational factors. This distinction was particularly important given the complexity inherent in PNALM's hybrid DVC configuration.

Table 2 Definitions and samples

Topics	Meaning	Samples from data
1. DVC phases		
Data acquisition	All the processes by which data are collected, checked, and organized.	*"I take care of all monitoring, management, and sometimes research of wildlife entities."*
Data analysis	All the processes making data ready for domain-specific usage, such as exploring and highlighting relevant information	*"Knowing how many animals are born in a year and knowing the year before how many were born, we know what the survival key is in the first year."*
Data curation	The active management of data over their lifecycle to ensure their quality and reliability for effective usage.	*"Spatial and temporal data are cross-referenced, and errors may often be made, but the aim is to minimise them, for storage and subsequent analysis."*
Data storage	The persistence of data as it need to be available for access and reuse in a scalable way.	*"Cards are collected, and, at the end of the sampling, we collect all the data, file it in the database, and start to think.*
Data usage	All the data-driven business activities requiring data as a tool to obtain advantages in performance.	*"Data used for management, territorial surveillance, to try to correct animal behaviours in some way, or to answer a number of research hypotheses."*
2. Technologies		
Traditional interaction	All interactions and exchanges with data among individuals or areas occurred directly in person, without the use of any digital tools.	*"We usually go together to the mountain, also with researchers from universities to share our knowledge."*
Digitally based interaction	All interactions and exchanges among individuals or areas occurred through communication tools based on information and communication technology.	*"We make a digital card that our system collects, and then, the technical office, based on the data we give them, processes the information."*

3.4 Content Analysis Protocol

Once the initial phase was completed, our data were systematically organized according to the steps of the DVC, from data acquisition to data usage (see Appendix 3). With this structure in place, we proceeded to the core coding process to identify and categorize the challenges emerging at each stage. Both primary and secondary data sources were incorporated into this analysis.

Documental Analysis We developed conceptual categories based on the characteristics of each document (see Appendix 1). Each document was reviewed to identify relevant segments related to data management and the use of technologies. These excerpts were subsequently integrated into the broader content analysis to ensure consistency across data types.

Content Analysis Following the guidelines proposed by [18], we conducted a content analysis that involved transcribing the thematic content and identifying key themes within the data. During the coding phase, relevant segments of text were selected and assigned to nodes within NVivo. These nodes were then grouped into thematic categories, which were further aggregated into higher-order dimensions. Each data source was systematically examined to extract recurring themes, which were then coded and structured accordingly.

To synthesize our findings, we developed a visual representation of the analysis process, depicting the progression from raw data to conceptual insights. The first stage involved identifying first-order concepts, labels used to describe specific activities, tools, structures, or artifacts mentioned in the data. In the second stage, these concepts were aggregated into second-order themes that are more abstract and grounded in existing literature.

The final structure of our analysis is presented in Fig. 2, illustrating the relationship between raw data, first-order concepts, and emergent themes.

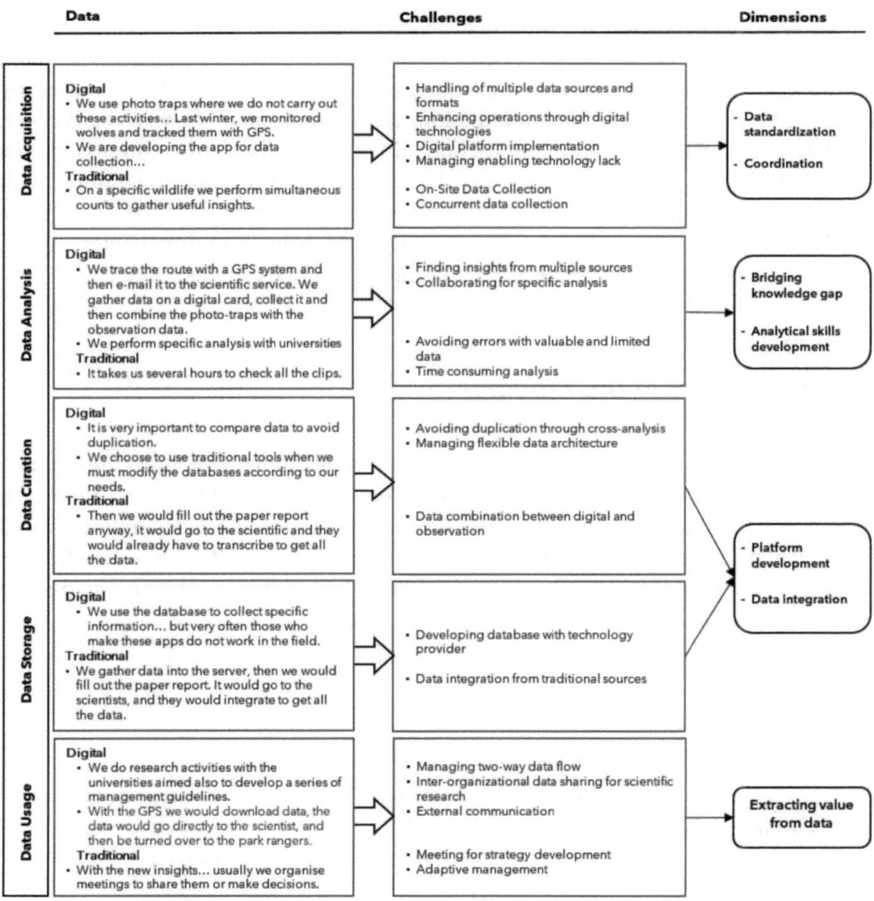

Fig. 2 Content analysis model

3.5 Data Analysis

Content analysis was employed to examine and explore the themes that emerged from the data. To deepen this analysis, we utilized the Matrix Coding Query feature in NVivo, which enabled us to identify intersections between coded items. This function allowed for a co-occurrence analysis of the data, facilitating the identification of patterns and relationships among nodes. Co-occurrences were determined by counting the number of words within sentences that referenced the concepts under investigation. This analytical approach revealed the nature of interactions occurring at each step of the DVC. By 'interaction,' we refer to the engagement of either traditional or digital technologies with data at each specific stage of the DVC. These interactions illustrate how various technologies contribute to the data value creation process.

Our results are framed and discussed in the corresponding findings section. Table 3 presents the relationships among the different sets of nodes and illustrates how specific interactions support value creation across the DVC.

Our results underscore the significance of both traditional and digital interactions, illustrating how data sharing occurs within the context of PNALM. We found that the data acquisition and data analysis phases are predominantly supported by traditional tools, with traditional interactions accounting for 77.16% of the activity, compared to 22.84% for digital interactions. In contrast, the data curation and data storage phases are characterized by a higher frequency of digital interactions, with digital tools accounting for 59.17% of activities, while traditional tools comprise 40.83%. Finally, data usage is predominantly driven by traditional interactions, highlighting the continued reliance on non-digital methods in this phase.

3.6 Discussion of the Findings

Our findings highlight an array of challenges organizations encounter in the data management process, particularly when the DVC is supported by both digital and traditional technologies. We identified the prevalence of these technologies and explored the challenges that emerge at each stage of the DVC. These challenges underscore the complexities organizations face in integrating and managing diverse technological tools throughout the data value chain.

Table 3 Interactions in the data value chain

DVC	Acquisition	Analysis	Curation	Storage	Usage
Traditional interactions	**77.16%**	**69.04%**	40.83%	35.44%	**62.72%**
Digital interactions	22.84%	30.96%	**59.17%**	**64.56%**	37.28%

Step I: Data acquisition We identified two complementary approaches to data collection. The first approach relies on technologies such as sensors and IoT devices, which are designed to capture large volumes of data from specific key points. The second approach, closely linked to the first, involves the collection of more targeted data directly from individuals engaged in the activities. Two prominent challenges emerged in this phase: data standardization and coordination. Data derived from multiple sources exhibit heterogeneity in various aspects, such as format and type. Addressing this heterogeneity is critical to avoiding standardization issues in subsequent steps of the DVC [19]. Coordination pertains to the need for synchronizing data collection activities to prevent duplication and other errors in data counting.

> We set specific days for simultaneous observation: rangers and the scientific service ascend to high altitudes with binoculars and spotting scopes to record and mark all the breeding units... There are evaluations that extend beyond simple counting, through permanent or artificial markings, we determine whether to collect that novel data or whether it has already been collected. (Extract from Interview I)

By employing both digital and traditional technologies, data acquisition encompasses a diverse range of data types. Digital technologies, such as IoT devices and GPS-based systems, facilitate automated data collection, while human intervention, supported by traditional methods and tools, completes this initial phase of the DVC.

Step II: Data Analysis Once relevant and supplementary data are collected, significant challenges arise during the analysis phase. In our case, we identified three primary objectives for data analysis: monitoring wildlife trends, understanding animal behaviour, and supporting scientific research. The integration of digital and traditional data sources presents challenges in synthesizing and triangulating insights from both types. These challenges include time-consuming analysis processes and the need for additional human resources. At this stage, the data ecosystem plays a critical role in facilitating data sharing beyond the organization. It supports the analysis process by attracting a range of stakeholders, including universities, NGOs, and other experts. A key challenge addressed by the data ecosystem is bridging knowledge, which fosters collaboration in working with unstructured and heterogeneous data [20].

> For instance, if we conduct a study on the characteristics of bear hibernation areas, this data can be transformed into models that, for instance, predict future patterns... (extract from Interview XIII)

> We collect data from photo-traps and spend hours watching all the videos one by one. We conduct the analysis internally, and we develop more skills with time. We monitor signs of presence by collecting genetic samples, which we then send to ISPRA for genetic analysis. Sometimes we ask universities for support with analyses. (extract from Interview I–IV)

Steps III and IV: Data Curation and Data Storage These steps are critical, as all data-driven activities depend heavily on the quality and accessibility of data. Given the dual nature of digital and traditional data sources, a key challenge is ensuring data quality and integrity while preventing duplication or loss. The challenges at these stages involve preparing data for seamless integration from various digital and traditional sources. Furthermore, to effectively manage data, the development of a centralized platform is essential, particularly to enhance the accessibility of all collected information. Multiple organizational areas must have easy access to the data in order to perform their activities and support ongoing research.

> We used to fill out paper reports anyway, which would then be transcribed into digital formats by the science department... We used to prefer to continue asking for paper reports, but this process often led to additional data and database modifications as required... (extract from Interview IV)
>
> In recent years, we have worked a lot on the digitisation of the app for data collection directly in the field, which significantly reduces errors and simplifies data-related activities and storage. (Extract from Interview I)

Given that data are collected from the field and sources of varying natures, it is essential that the platform be developed in close collaboration with those working on the ground. Furthermore, the platform must be flexible enough to accommodate all necessary data, ensuring that users do not have to rely on alternative tools to manage or access the information.

> The platform is helpful, but significant challenges remain. Creating a unified system requires effective communication between app developers and analysts. Without this collaboration, we risk encountering numerous issues related to data sources and types (extract from Interview X-XI-XII).

Step V: Data Usage In this final step, we examined the diverse uses of data, how it creates value, and how it attracts other stakeholders. First and foremost, to fully extract value from data, it is essential to ensure a two-way flow of information. Intra-organizational data sharing fosters collaboration and synergies across different organizational areas, facilitating more effective decision-making and coordinated efforts.

> We would download data; the data would go directly to the scientist and then be turned over to the park rangers. (extract from Interview VII)

We observed the use of data for various purposes, including research studies and continuous monitoring or data collection activities, which are built upon insights gained from previous data. Secondly, inter-organizational data sharing is frequently conducted for scientific research or analyses that require specialized knowledge beyond the organization's scope. This sharing is vital, as valuable data attract stakeholders who can leverage them for further analysis or decision-making. Finally, meetings focused on strategy development and adaptive management typically occur to reduce uncertainty and enhance decision-making through the use of data. Notably, we observed a predominance of face-to-face interactions during these meetings within the organization, highlighting the importance of personal collaboration in data-driven decision-making.

> Monitoring serves to assess both the state of the wildlife population, which then allows you to correlate this data with interventions you are doing in the area... We collect all the data, store them, and start to think about what to do. (extract from Interview XIII)

> So, there is dedicated time for 'lectures' in the office, through presentations or direct experience sharing... We simply need to meet, talk to each other, to assess what the goals and strategies are. (extract from Interview XIII)

Each step of the DVC plays a crucial role in enhancing organizational knowledge about the surrounding environment, attracting stakeholders through inter-organizational data sharing, fostering collaboration, and informing strategic decision-making. In summary, we have identified the challenges organizations face along the DVC from an ecosystem perspective. We demonstrate that effective data management necessitates coordinated human and technological efforts and highlight the challenges that arise during the integration of these configurations.

4 Conclusion

As organizations increasingly rely on data to gain deeper insights into their context and environment, effective data management becomes essential to unlocking its full value. To unlock greater value, data must be effectively collected, shared, and managed. The DVC framework provides an analysis of these processes, from data collection to the impact generated through its use within organizations. It is important to note that the DVC is not a standalone element; instead, it serves as the core of a broader ecosystem made up of various actors, roles, relationships, and resources [9].

By exploring this concept, we examine a network where different organizational areas contribute to the DVC by combining traditional and digital data sources. This integration presents various challenges in data management and value extraction. The coexistence of traditional and digital technologies remains widespread across multiple sectors, and numerous challenges persist, particularly in fields where data cannot be automatically collected or where traditional data systems are still in use.

We outlined the challenges faced by PNALM in managing the DVC for nature conservation and preservation. PNALM has implemented the DVC within a collaborative context, involving various organizations such as universities and research institutes, all working toward shared objectives. We illustrate how challenges arise when configuring a DVC composed of multiple data sources, both traditional and digital. Through an analysis of the data's journey across all steps of the DVC, from collection to usage, we observed the frequency and occurrence of each technology within the DVC phases. By examining its configuration, we identified the specific challenges linked to the simultaneous use of traditional and digital technologies within the DVC.

We demonstrate how the combined use of digital and traditional technologies presents challenges in four key dimensions: (1) data standardization and coordination during data collection, (2) bridging knowledge gaps and developing analytical skills for data analysis, (3) platform development and data integration for data storage, and (4) extracting value from data during its usage.

By addressing our research question, this paper contributes to the data management literature by exploring the roles and interplay between digital and traditional technologies in extracting value from the data. Specifically, it highlights how these technologies interact and the unique challenges organizations face. While previous literature has primarily focused on managing internal and external data exchanges and identifying potential challenges, our study offers deeper insights into these dynamics. We explored how interactions occur in a context where data are directly collected from the field, revealing how digital and traditional tools support data-related activities. Our study advances the understanding of challenges arising in the configuration of the DVC and contributes to the ongoing discourse in this stream of literature. Therefore, research in this field is extensive, and our findings contribute to prior discussions in the literature regarding DVC and ecosystems. In short, we assess the potential of the DVC for data value creation and highlight the major challenges arising from this process.

This research offers several practical implications for practitioners. First, the challenges identified throughout the DVC can assist in configuring data-related activities to ensure effective data management, implementation, and utilization. Second, our study provides valuable insights into the data management challenges faced by organizations operating within an ecosystem of multiple stakeholders. The integration of both digital and traditional data sources presents significant hurdles for ecosystem development, requiring careful attention to avoid errors and inflexibility. Enabling technologies are crucial, particularly when data is collected directly from the field. However, it is important to recognize that some challenges cannot be addressed solely by technological solutions. Effective organizational strategies are equally essential for managing data efficiently.

This study has several limitations that point to potential areas for future research. First, since it is based on a single case study, the generalizability of the findings may be constrained. Replicating this methodology in diverse contexts could strengthen the robustness of the results, uncover additional patterns, and enhance the overall reliability of the findings [21]. Second, while the DVC framework offers a solid conceptual foundation, the challenges identified are closely linked to its specific steps. Although this approach provides a structured perspective, it may overemphasize certain challenges while underrepresenting others, potentially impacting the results and limiting flexibility. Third, this paper consolidates challenges that may be relevant across various domains. Future research could examine or compare these challenges in other sectors, such as healthcare or finance, where both digital and traditional data systems continue to coexist. Additionally, this study focuses exclusively on the internal core of the ecosystem within a single organization, without considering all ecosystem partners. Future studies could extend the model to include an interorganizational DVC, thereby examining a broader and more decentralized ecosystem. As the data value chain and ecosystems literature underscore the importance of involving a diverse range of stakeholders at different levels, future research could explore the roles of these stakeholders or investigate alternative configurations of ecosystem components and resources. Finally, after identifying the challenges in structuring the core of the data ecosystem, further empirical investigations could offer detailed case studies on how these challenges are effectively addressed and managed in real-world scenarios.

Acknowledgments We acknowledge financial support under the National Recovery and Resilience Plan (NRRP), Mission 4, Component 2, Investment 1.1, Call for tender No. 1409 published on 14.9.2022 by the Italian Ministry of University and Research (MUR), funded by the European Union—NextGenerationEU—Project Title Data4Innovation—Data ecosystem governance toward enhancing data sharing for innovation: implications for organizations—CUP D53D23017780001—Grant Assignment Decree n. 1376 on 01/09/2023 by the Italian Ministry of University and Research (MUR).

Disclosure of Interests The authors have no competing interests to declare that are relevant to the content of this article.

Appendix 1 Overview of Archival Documents

Topics	Source of data	Volume (and description)
PNALM and organizations' collaboration and initiatives	Strategy report and articles from the website, organizations' webpage and newspapers	11 articles from webpages 8 PNALM reports 1 PNALM guide
Monitoring and technologies	Articles and posts published on the official website, social pages, newspaper	10 articles from webpages 9 PNALM annual reports 1 brochure 8 PNALM reports 1 INWIT reports
Projects for the preservation of nature	Articles and posts published on the official website, social pages, newspaper	3 articles from webpages 1 FLORANET report 1 GDE report Natura2000 data
Articles, scientific papers: history, economic efficiency, tourism, and areas management	Scholar and Scopus databases	8 papers (Geomantics for Green and Digital Transition, Wildlife research, Sustainable Development)
Sustainable tourism	Official website	1 PNALM report
Organizational structure	Official website and webpages	2 PNALM reports, plan, and organigram, 2 articles from webpages
Environmental information from Open Data	Public dataset	Natura2000 dataset OpenData Regione Abruzzo

Appendix 2 List of Interviews

Actor	Role	Length
Step 1		*PNALM site*
Wildlife Office Manager	Manager	1 h 43 m
Communication Office Manager	Manager	1 h 10 m
Volunteer Park Ranger	Newcomers	29 m
Pnalm Director	Director	49 m
Park Ranger	Experienced	32 m
Step 2		*Remote call*
Park Ranger	Chief	30 m
Auxiliary Park Ranger	Newcomers	1 h 15 m
Auxiliary Park Ranger	Newcomers	35 m
Park Ranger	Experienced	1 h
Step 3		*PNALM site*
Park Ranger	Chief	40 m
Park Ranger	Chief	40 m
Park Ranger	Experienced	40 m
Biologist	Experienced	55 m
Step 4		*Remote call*
Technology Provider	Sustainable Manager	45 m
Technology Provider	Sustainable Manager	45 m
Park Ranger	Newcomers	51 m
	Total time	13 h 19 m

Appendix 3 Configuration of Digital and Traditional Tools Within the Data Value Chain (Co-occurrences)

	Data Acquisition	Data Analysis	Data Curation	Data Storage	Data Usage
Technologies - Traditional - Digital	**77.16%** **22.84%**	**69.04%** **30.96%**	**40.83%** **59.17%**	**35.44%** **64.56%**	**62.72%** **37.28%**
Examples - Traditional	Paper sheets, telescope	Paper sheets	Paper sheets	Filed documents, physical samples	Database, platform
- Digital	IoTs (gps radio collar), drone, platform	Db (ArcGIS, ArcMap), Access	Access, Excel, R	Database, cloud, platform	Meetings
Activities	Monitoring, surveillance	Query, matrix	Data comparisons and cross-check	Data and paper sheets submission	Consultations, Research, Communication, and Decision making
From the interviews - Traditional aspects	*'We do simultaneous faunal counts twice a year using paper sheets... We are also now using a digital system.'*	*'Very often we prefer to continue asking for the paper, ... we then modify the databases as needed and have the opportunity on the paper to see some errors or duplications'*	*'We made an Excel spreadsheet in which we collected all the data we received during this last summer season and then passed it on to the scientific service'*	*'Paper sheets are collected, and, at the end of the sampling, we gather all the data, fileit in the database and start to think.'*	*'Monitoring basically is used to assess the state of the population and to correlate this data with the interventions you are doing in the area.'*
- Digital Aspects	*'In the case of wolf monitoring, we just trace the path taken by the wolf and collect it with a GPS system and then email it to the scientific service'*	*'We use Access and then everything is transformed into Excel to make matrices.'*	*'We use paper because it is possible for the same female to be spotted by two different units. It is then important compare data to avoid counting it twice.'*	*'We do digital surveys and so they are clearly all collected in a database.'*	*'Who deals with data has a role ofsuggesting management interventions. So, he has to suggest lines, routes, of course. It helps to make decisions.'*

References

1. Kapoor, R., Teece, D. J. (2021). *Three faces of technology's value creation: Emerging, enabling, embedding*.
2. Dosi, G. (1982). *Technological paradigms and technological trajectories a suggested interpretation of the determinants and directions of technical change*.
3. Watch, O. D. (2017). *The data value chain: Moving from production to impact*.
4. Curry, E. (2016). The big data value chain: Definitions, concepts, and theoretical approaches. In *New horizons for a data-driven economy: A roadmap for usage and exploitation of big data in Europe* (pp. 29–37). Springer International Publishing.
5. Curry, E., & Ojo, A. (2020). Enabling knowledge flows in an intelligent systems data ecosystem. In *Real-time linked dataspaces* (pp. 15–43). Springer International Publishing.
6. Brynjolfsson, E., & McElheran, K. (2016). The rapid adoption of data-driven decision-making. In *American economic review* (pp. 133–139). American Economic Association.
7. De Simone, C., Ceci, F., & Alaimo, C. (2023). *Data ecosystem and data value chain: An exploration of drones technology applications*. Presented at the.
8. Watch, O. (2017). *The data value chain: Moving from production to impact*.
9. Oliveira, M. I. S., & Lóscio, B. F. (2018). What is a data ecosystem? In *ACM international conference proceeding series*. Association for Computing Machinery.

10. Oliveira, M. I. S., de Barros Lima, G. F., & Farias Lóscio, B. (2019). Investigations into data ecosystems: A systematic mapping study. *Knowledge Information Systems, 61*, 589–630. https://doi.org/10.1007/s10115-018-1323-6
11. Rayport, J. F., & Sviokla, J. (1995). *Exploiting the virtual value chain*. Harvard Business Review.
12. Curry, E., Scerri, S., & Tuikka, T. (2022). *Data spaces design, deployment and future directions*. Springer International Publishing.
13. DG Connect. (2013). *A European strategy on the data value chain.*
14. Jacobides, M. G., Cennamo, C., & Gawer, A. (2018). *Towards a theory of ecosystems.*
15. Cavanillas, J. M., Curry, E., & Wahlster, W. (2016). *New horizons for a data-driven economy a roadmap for usage and exploitation of big data in Europe.*
16. Walford, G. (2009). The practice of writing ethnographic fieldnotes. *Ethnography and Education., 4*, 117–130. https://doi.org/10.1080/17457820902972713
17. Van Maanen, J. (1988). *Tales of the field on writing ethnography.*
18. Creswell, J. (2014) *Research design – Qualitative, quantitative, and mixed method.*
19. Wirén, M., Mäntymäki, M., & Najmul Islam, A. (2019). Big data value chain: Making sense of the challenges. *Digital Transformation for a Sustainable Society in the 21st Century* (pp. 125–137). https://doi.org/10.1007/978-3-030-29374-1_11.
20. Geisler, S., Vidal, M. E., Cappiello, C., Lóscio, B. F., Gal, A., Jarke, M., Lenzerini, M., Missier, P., Otto, B., Paja, E., Pernici, B., & Rehof, J. (2022). Knowledge-driven data ecosystems toward data transparency. *Journal of Data and Information Quality, 14*, 1–12. https://doi.org/10.1145/3467022
21. Yin, K. R. (2003). *Designing case studies research.*

Employee Perception of Human-Robot Co-working: Evidence from the Hotel Sector in Russia, Egypt, and Italy

Maria Menshikova, Isabella Bonacci, Danila Scarozza, Alena Fedorova, and Khaled Ghazy

Abstract Aligned with the evolution of Industry 5.0, which advocates for human-machine collaboration, the hotel sector has embraced new technologies and methods of work organisation referred to as Hospitality 5.0. Several studies contend that the concept of humans collaborating with advanced technologies is nascent and warrants thorough exploration through empirical analyses to mitigate negative impacts, enhance benefits, and ensure adequate conditions for collaboration. This study aims to analyse hotel employees' perceptions of cobots using a mixed-methods approach in order to explore their attitudes towards working alongside these collaborative robots. The attitudes of hotel employees were examined, focusing on some psychological and social aspects relevant to effective collaboration. Data was collected through employee questionnaires, the development of which was based on focus groups with experts. The research was conducted using a comparative analysis among respondents from Russia, Egypt, and Italy. It was discovered that social and psychological factors can significantly influence robot

M. Menshikova (✉) · I. Bonacci
Universitas Mercatorum, Rome, Italy
e-mail: maria.menshikova@unimercatorum.it; isabella.bonacci@unimercatorum.it

D. Scarozza
Link Campus University, Rome, Italy
e-mail: d.scarozza@unilink.it

A. Fedorova
Ural Federal University, Yekaterinburg, Russia
e-mail: A.E.Fedorova@urfu.ru

K. Ghazy
Ural Federal University, Yekaterinburg, Russia

Helwan University, Cairo, Egypt
e-mail: KEltabbakkh@at.urfu.ru

A. Tursunbayeva et al. (eds.), *Technology-Driven Transformation*, Lecture Notes in Information Systems and Organisation 79,
https://doi.org/10.1007/978-3-032-01396-5_3

acceptance and human-robot interaction in the workplace. Some similarities and differences in the perceptions of respondents from different countries were identified. The findings of the study can provide important insights for developing strategies and policies at the organisational level for the integration of collaborative robots in the hotel environment, as well as offer significant suggestions for HRM specialists to adequately prepare human resources for the organisational transformation related to Work 5.0.

Keywords Industry 5.0 · Hospitality 5.0 · Work 5.0 · Human-robot interaction · Social and psychological interaction factors · Employees' perception · Comparative analysis

1 Introduction

Aligned with the evolution of Industry 5.0, which advocates for human-machine collaboration, the hotel sector has embraced new technologies and methodologies referred to as Hospitality 5.0 by scholars [1, 2]. This paradigm shift gained prominence and development, particularly during the Covid-19 pandemic era [3, 4]. The synergistic effects of human and technological resources in the hotel sector not only hold promise for attracting more customers, enhancing their overall experience, and fostering competitive advantage, but also offer sustainability benefits through improved hygiene, cleanliness, and safety standards [5]. Numerous studies in recent years have analysed the impact of human-machine collaboration in hospitality, uncovering both positive and negative implications for companies and their stakeholders [5–7]. On the one hand, some authors [5] highlight how the incorporation of cobots into work processes leads to heightened productivity, efficiency, and staff growth due to stress reduction and task simplification. On the other hand, other scholars [8] identify challenges to future employability and career sustainability arising from the growing role of robots and artificial intelligence in service settings. Moreover, the importance of creating conducive work environments and investing in training and personnel development for successful human-robot collaboration within dynamic work environments is emphasised [5]. Concurrently, effective integration of cobots in hospitality is stressed, focusing on emotional intelligence training for frontline staff, ethical cobot management, and building trust with robotic counterparts [9]. Furthermore, some scholars assert that the success of human-robot collaboration hinges on employees' perceptions of robot partners, including perceived risk, playfulness, performance, and effort expectancy [10]. Additionally, working with service robots can evoke both positive and negative emotions, influencing individual intentions and behaviour at work [3].

Several studies contend that the concept of humans collaborating with advanced technologies is nascent and warrants thorough exploration, particularly through empirical analyses [6, 11]. To mitigate negative impacts, enhance benefits, and ensure adequate collaboration conditions, HR managers must focus on cultivating suitable work environments, fostering psychological climates, and developing supportive practices [12]. The workplace has been transformed by the advent of artificial intelligence, necessitating the collaboration and coordination of human employees with technological devices (robots) to achieve optimal work performance. It has become imperative for humans to collaborate and coordinate with robots to optimise performance and minimise errors [13]. Despite the importance of integrating robots into the work environment, there is currently no in-depth study of employees' perception of new types of collaboration, especially the social and psychological factors that can either facilitate or hinder the emergence of a new augmented environment in which human intelligence works alongside artificial intelligence to complete work tasks and provide better services to customers. In fact, some studies highlight the need for a deeper exploration of the human resources perspective on collaboration with robots, as the lack of worker involvement in designing robotic systems or applications deployed in workplaces may result in the omission of crucial information needed to enhance the human-centric nature of these technologies [14].

Moreover, some research further emphasises the need to better study the differences in adoption behaviour and acceptance of social robots between different adopter categories [15]. In this case, examining the differences among workers from various countries could provide an interesting contribution to understanding the phenomenon. This study aims to analyse hotel employees' perceptions of cobots using a mixed-methods approach [16] in order to explore their attitudes towards working alongside cobots. The data will be collected through employee questionnaires, the development of which was based on focus groups with experts. The pilot survey, refined through expert feedback, was preliminarily tested to validate the variables and items of the questionnaire. Thereafter, the questionnaire was launched in Russia, Egypt, and Italy for the final evaluation of workers' perceptions in the hospitality sector regarding collaboration with cobots. This research has been conducted as a comparative analysis to elucidate differences in cobot perception, considering social and psychological factors. By leveraging varied economic, social, and cultural contexts, this study aims to enhance understanding of the phenomenon and the generalisability of its findings. The research findings are important for identifying future research directions and guiding managers in implementing service robots in the hotel industry, facilitating human-robot collaboration through effective HRM practices.

2 Literature Review

2.1 Impact of Industry 5.0 on the Hospitality Sector

Industry 5.0 is considered a revolution in which humans and machines collaborate to enhance production methods and efficiency, with a primary emphasis on the human elements and technology involved in the production process. According to recent studies, Industry 5.0 supplements the industrial revolution with human-centric, resilient, and sustainable values [17, 18]. In fact, Industry 5.0 proposes a strategy for businesses that extends beyond the traditional views of productivity and efficiency as the primary goals, enriching the function and value of the industry in society. The Industry 5.0 concept places employee well-being at the core of the value creation process [19]. It employs innovative technology to provide prosperity beyond mere employment and development while respecting the principles of sustainability and Corporate Social Responsibility (CSR). Industry 5.0 is anticipated to combine high- speed, sophisticated machines with the cognitive, rational thinking, and emotional intelligence of people [20, 21]. In order to explore the evolution of Industry 5.0 concept within the scientific community and identify the future directions of the analysis some articles have been selected in the period from 2019 to 2024. To ensure a deeper understanding of the changes in the concept, scientific articles published in international peer-reviewed journals with the highest citation counts were selected. In Appendix 1 the definition of Industry 5.0 and its key elements are described better. The initial focus on improving production systems and increasing productivity and efficiency of processes gradually shifted to the need to find a balance in people-machine collaboration, underlying human centrality not only for better organisational results achievement, but also for the sustainability and resilience of the organisation. In this type of company operating within the modern Industry 5.0 framework, the key elements become well-being, health, and safety of workers, together with human resources development and prioritisation of human needs, not only inside (employees) but also outside the organisation (company's stakeholders: consumers, partners, society). The centrality of the human component is becoming increasingly significant in Industry 5.0 systems. These systems should be designed with the user in mind, prioritising comfortable work environments that enhance employee well-being and productivity. Along with this, flexibility and adaptability are essential, allowing innovative high-tech systems to respond effectively to changes in the external environment and workforce demands. By emphasising human centrality, companies can tap into the creative potential of their employees, fostering innovation and ensuring a quicker response to market shifts. By analysing the key elements of Industry 5.0 identified by the authors in recent studies, we can conclude that the focus on the centrality of human resources not only leads to more effective and resilient organisations but also cultivates a people-oriented culture crucial for success in today's business landscape. The application of Industry 5.0 in the hospitality sector has been studied through the literature review using the Prism Model (see Table 1). For the identification of documents for analysis, the following keywords were used: "Industry 5.0" AND "hospitality" OR "hotel."

The selected nine documents were examined in detail to understand the main directions of research concerning the relationship between the elements of Industry 5.0 and hospitality in recent years. The key findings of the studies, related to the relationship between the elements of Industry 5.0 and hospitality and presented in depth in Appendix 2, could be classified into the following five groups:

Table 1 The prism model

Phase	Description	Scopus	Google Scholar
Identification (n = 43)	Documents found	11	32
Screening (n = 32)	Abstract and keywords screening	7	25
Eligibility (n = 21)	Conference proceedings and articles in English in the period 2020–2024 with full version available	4	17
Inclusion (n = 9)	Full text screening	4	5

Source: Our elaboration

- *Operational efficiency.* Some studies [4, 22] highlight the scalability of Industry 5.0 design principles within the hospitality context, where the integration of emerging technologies (e.g. artificial intelligence, robotics, IoT and data analytics) improves service personalisation, operational efficiency, and data-driven decision-making processes.
- *Customer experience.* Other studies investigate the role of emerging technologies in ensuring hygiene and cleanliness during customer experience, underlining the importance of health, sanitation, and wellness, above all in the period of the COVID-19 pandemic [23]. Moreover, the interaction with robots creates emotional connection between customers and hotel brands, indicating that robot typology and traveller type can affect customer sentiment and overall satisfaction [24].
- *Human capital development.* Some research analysed knowledge, skills and attitudes that human resources working in the Hospitality 5.0 context must have. A significant gap was discovered between traditional hospitality knowledge and soft skills required in a technology-driven environment, emphasising the need for workforce development and alignment with strategic business objectives [25].
- *Social acceptance.* The social acceptance of robots and AI technologies in hospitality is a key determinant for their successful implementation, with studies suggesting that social listening and sentiment analysis could track the evolution of this acceptance [24, 26]. Perception of likeability, intelligence, and safety of the robots by the users could also have a significant effect on the social acceptance of new ways of interactions [27]. Moreover, the perception of risks and benefits of HRI could impact on the employees' agreement to interact with robots in the work environment [28].
- *Challenges of AI and robotics implementation.* Despite several benefits of emerging technologies implementation for organisations, some concerns over data privacy, cybersecurity issues, significant investments, and resistance to change are highlighted as barriers to integration and adoption by the organisations and their employees [22]. Some studies [29] have attempted to describe useful practices and initiatives to address these challenges and encourage the integration of technologies into organisational environments.

The main directions identified elucidates the multifaceted impact of Industry 5.0 elements on the hospitality sector, focusing on the interplay between technology customer experience, human capital, and social acceptance of the new methods of service providing based on robotics and artificial intelligence both by customers and by employees of the hotels and hospitality industry.

2.2 Work Transformation: Definition of Work 5.0 Concept

The transformations in the production process, service provision, and value creation in general have led to various changes in work approaches. In recent years, a new work philosophy has emerged, referred to by various scholars as Work 5.0 or Employment 5.0. This concept relates to the current iteration in the development of work and the workplace due to technological innovations, shifts in the global economy, and changing views regarding work-life balance. In the scientific literature, three main theoretical perspectives on the disruptive impact of digital transformation on work have been defined: socio-technical systems theory, skill-based technological change, and the political economy of digital transformation [30]. We can assert that Work 5.0 represents the most recent stage in the convergence of work and technology, aimed at developing productive and efficient work processes with the integration of a human-centric perspective. The philosophy of Work 5.0 aims to transform how work is performed. The term denotes an approach that places a premium on workplace innovations, including AI, robotics, and digital automation. Additionally, it emphasises the need to create a flexible workplace that can accommodate different needs of the company's stakeholders: employees, clients, partners, and society [31]. Another essential feature of Work 5.0 is the emphasis on building a more human-centred workplace. Creating a culture within the workplace that values and promotes employees' well-being and personal development, as well as ensuring that work is rewarding and meaningful, are both necessary steps in this process. Businesses invest in workforce engagement activities, such as health and wellness initiatives, professional development opportunities, and support for work-life balance. Additionally, organisations are putting considerable effort into fostering an inclusive and diverse workplace where employees from all backgrounds are acknowledged and respected [32, 33]. Work 5.0 is also characterised by a revolution in perspectives on the work environment. In this context, individuals need to identify and articulate their values while focusing on discovering meaning and purpose in their work. These values will influence their work-related choices and assist them in navigating the continuously evolving job market. As a result, organisations must make efforts to cultivate a supportive, collaborative, and motivating work environment to retain and develop talent. In fact, the human resources of any organisation must be prepared and ready for upcoming developments. In this context, it is becoming mandatory to retrain all employees to ensure they are qualified and suited to the changing needs of the external environment. It is evident that the soft skills required to work successfully in an environment where teams consist of both robots and humans will differ from those required a few years ago [34]. In conclusion, it is possible to argue that the concept of Work 5.0 is based on a radical transformation of traditional notions of labour and workplace. Advanced technologies, global economy, and changing values have all combined to produce: (1) more flexible work arrangements and behaviours, (2) a human-centred work organisation, (3) a purposeful and collaborative work environment, and (4) innovative technologies to support work processes and decision-making. Organisations that embrace these transitions and invest in their workforce will be well-positioned for success in the new business world.

2.3 Introduction of Cobots in the Work 5.0: Perception of the New Ways of Collaboration

As described previously, emerging technologies have a significant impact not only on the organisation of work and the redefinition of work environments, but also on the social aspects of work, such as relationships, cooperation, and collaboration. The framework of this paper (see Fig. 1) is based on the model of human-robot interaction [35]. In our case, the relationships between robots and employees in the hotel sector are perceived as interaction at the level of "human-robot collaboration," where work time and workspace are shared, and tasks are distributed in a collaborative interaction within a multi-agent robotic system. In this close collaboration between the actors of the new Work 5.0 system, multiple factors should be taken into consideration according to the sociological context of human-robot interaction [36]: physical interaction, social structures, psychological interaction (thoughts, feelings), and cultural context.

Cobots, or collaborative robots, are designed for direct human-robot interaction in a shared environment or when robots and people are in close proximity [37].

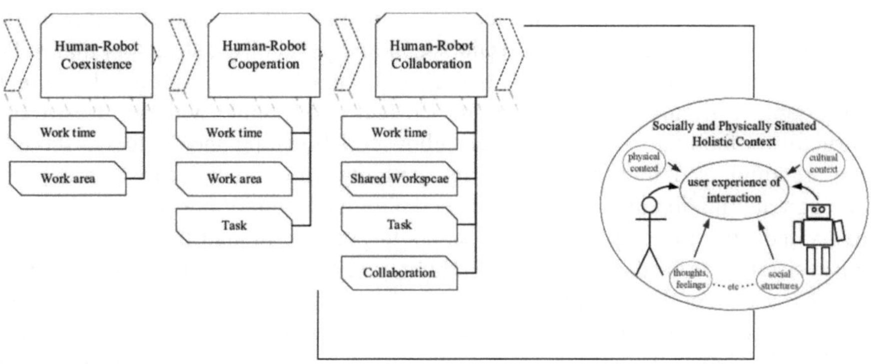

Fig. 1 The theoretical framework of human-robot interaction. Source: Our elaboration

Cobot applications promote human engagement with robots, unlike traditional industrial robotic uses that keep robots isolated. The safety of cobots may depend on features such as soft edges, lightweight materials, speed and force limitations, as well as software and sensors that ensure safe behaviour. Cobots are highly sensitive to unexpected impacts, allowing them to stop automatically when human employees identify any misplaced items in their path. In most cases, this makes them considerably more reliable than traditional industrial robots [38]. Cobots are designed to assist humans with functional tasks by interacting with them both physically and socially. Cobots are classified into two categories: (1) personal, used by individuals for non-commercial activities, such as domestic servant cobots, automated wheelchairs, pet exercise cobots, and personal mobility aid cobots; and (2) professional, used by businesses for commercial purposes, such as delivery cobots in offices, cleaning cobots for public areas, firefighting cobots, rehabilitation cobots, and surgical cobots [39]. Cobotic technologies and service automation have been incorporated into the tourism and hospitality industries, managing various areas and operations. Cobots currently being used in hotels perform several functions, such as greeting customers, preparing meals, providing room service, taking orders, managing check-in and check-out operations, offering information about the destination, and cleaning rooms, pools, and public areas. They can also cut grass, carry baggage, and deliver food and other goods. Cobots can operate 24/7, significantly exceeding the standard 40-hour workweek of human workers. Moreover, cobots can serve many clients simultaneously and perform these activities countless times without tiring or complaining [40]. The evolution of artificial intelligence cobots with social competencies allows for interactions between individuals and cobots that complement encounters in frontline service. As a result of these interactions, people tend to perceive cobots as social beings. Consequently, the potential issues arising from this unique social element are not solely related to the gadget's functionality or the basic logistics of integrating software, hardware, and other capabilities, but also to user behaviours and personal psychological factors [41]. This establishes the connection between humans and cobots as another significant challenge in the service environment [42]. In fact, some previous studies highlight that successful collaboration does not occur automatically. The creation of effective collaboration based on digital technologies may depend on certain social and psychological factors that individuals perceive when they: (1) recognise the value of the effort required; (2) feel comfortable with and trust the medium; (3) feel comfortable with and trust their instructor (or facilitator) as well as their fellow collaborators; and (4) feel as though they are immersed in a rich, engaging, and rewarding social experience [43]. Although automation and cobotics are becoming increasingly prevalent in the hospitality industry, the employment of cobots to perform human tasks may be met with resistance from the organisation's human resources. Recent studies indicate that the reasons for this resistance include the loss of human contact, as well as fears of an increase in unemployment and the dominance of machines in the labour market [44, 45]. Cobots that replace human employees might introduce a psychological issue to the traditional concept of service. For example, human interaction with a cobot may be avoided if it causes anxiety. In the context of the hotel industry, which relies primarily on personal contact, replacing human employees with cobots would alter the nature of the experience by introducing human-robot interactions and affecting users' attitudes and behaviours. Furthermore, technological anxiety is considered a significant socio-psychological factor influencing the adoption of new technologies [12, 46]. Even though there are many positive examples of robots supporting human partners, not everyone holds a positive attitude towards them. Cobots are less likely to be utilised if people have negative perceptions of them. Attitude is recognised as an individual's acquired judgement, reflecting a positive or negative emotion towards service robots, which influences the individual's intentions and behaviour. Attitudes develop due to complex psychological processes and act as motives for behavioural responses. They are crucial considerations in determining whether cobots are adopted [47–49]. Some scholars [39] surveyed consumers to discover how young people perceive the use of cobots in hotels. This research demonstrated that variations exist in how people evaluate innovative technology. Individuals will either accept or reject the adoption of such technology, and their acceptance or rejection will differ depending on individual characteristics and contextual features. Other authors [45] assessed the extent to which hotel guests are aware of the benefits and disadvantages of cobots, as well as how this awareness affects guests' intentions to use them. The results indicated that awareness of benefits and perceived value have a positive and significant impact on the willingness to engage with cobots. Conversely, awareness of disadvantages has a negative and significant impact on the intention to use cobots. Some findings highlighted the effect of automated service on customer experience. The authors claim that customers are proactively seeking opportunities to communicate and interact with cobots in order to establish a relationship with them [50]. Conversely, other scholars [51] found that potential consumers' attitudes towards human-like cobots are likely to be unfavourable. Based on the literature review, we can highlight that, on the one hand, several studies have focused on analysing the introduction of cobots from an organisational perspective, examining the benefits, obstacles, and certain application practices [13, 18, 20]. On the other hand, the perception of interaction with cobots from the customer's (or guest's) point of view has also been studied [2, 50, 51]. However, it appears that the analysis of employees' perceptions towards cobots is currently limited. The objective of this study is precisely to analyse the main psychological and social factors that influence the perception of cobots among workers in the hotel sector, in order to develop a model that can help overcome the obstacles linked to negative perceptions of cobots, thus enabling faster and more sustainable human- cobot integration. In particular, the research questions we wish to focus on in this study are as follows:

- What social and psychological interaction factors can hinder the introduction of cobots?
- What social and psychological interaction factors can facilitate the introduction of cobots in work processes?
- What are the differences and similarities in perception between workers from different countries, who therefore have diverse cultural contexts?

3 Research Methodology

The research methodology is based on the development and distribution of a questionnaire to employees of luxury hotels in three countries: Egypt, Italy, and Russia. The creation of the questionnaire was carried out systematically by following key steps: a literature review, expert evaluation through focus groups, and pre-testing. Since no validated tools for analysing employees' perceptions of human-robot collaboration were available at the start of the research, an analysis of the literature, expert evaluation, and pre-testing were conducted to verify whether the proposed model was coherent and to determine if the dimensions could be confirmed or modified. The pilot version of the toolkit was developed based on literature data and reviewed in focus groups that included experts from the hotel industry, employees working with robotics, and scientists in computer science and Human Resource Management (HRM). As a result of the expert discussions and the recommendations received, the toolkit (questionnaire) was finalised. The focus groups were conducted online with the participation of experts from three countries (Russia, Egypt, and Italy) to gather their input, critical appraisal, and content validation.

The final version of the questionnaire includes three sections: (1) Issues related to employees' perceptions of changes that have occurred in the workplace due to the introduction of robotic technologies into the working process; (2) Questions aimed at examining the Psychological Aspects (PA) and Social Aspects (SA) of employees' interactions with cobots; (3) Demographic characteristics of respondents (gender, age, and education level). The questionnaire contains 29 closed and open-ended questions, including dichotomous and scaled questions. The questions were written in Russian, English, and Italian to ensure they were easily understood by the participants. The pre-testing phase was conducted in each country, involving 10 participants to evaluate the developed tool. The final version of the survey involved Russian employees (167 respondents), Egyptian employees (159 respondents), and Italian employees (136 respondents). The set of respondents was formed using the non-probability purposive sampling method (staff from luxury hotels that are more advanced in terms of the use of digital technologies). The data collected were analysed using SPSS software. The data analysis was processed as follows. First, Cronbach's alpha coefficients were applied to test the internal reliability of the various Likert-type scales and questions. Second, descriptive data analysis was conducted to evaluate the socio-psychological aspects of hotel employees' attitudes towards human-cobot co-working. It is essential to determine the validity and reliability of all the constructs used in this research. Reliability assesses the degree to which measurements are error-free and provide consistent findings [52]. Cronbach's alpha coefficient is one of the most commonly used measures of reliability. According to Table 2, the respective Cronbach's alpha coefficients for the scales varied from 0.7 to 0.8. All coefficients are above the minimum value of 0.6, which is required for the acceptance of the questionnaire's reliability [53].

Table 2 Reliability of rating scales of the questionnaire

Scale	Egypt	Italy	Russia
	Cronbach's Alpha	Cronbach's Alpha	Cronbach's Alpha
Psychological aspects	0.721	0.713	0.752
Social aspects	0.801	0.772	0.781

Source: Our elaboration

Table 3 Participants' demographic characteristics

Demographic data		Egypt		Italy		Russia	
		Freq	%	Freq	%	Freq	%
Gender	Male	96	60.4	74	54.4	65	38.9
	Female	63	39.6	62	45.6	102	61.1
Age	25 years or younger	77	48.4	58	42.6	81	48.5
	From 26 up to 35	46	29.9	37	27.2	53	31.7
	From 36 up to 50	29	18.2	28	20.6	24	14.4
	over 50	7	4.4	13	9.6	9	5.4
Education	Secondary School or less	22	13.8	19	14.0	28	16.8
	University or Higher Institute Degree	129	81.1	107	78.7	135	80.8
	Postgraduate Degrees (Masters or PhD)	8	5.1	10	7.3	4	2.4
	Other	–	–	–	–	–	–

Source: Our elaboration

Table 3 shows the structure of responses from the surveyed employees of Russian, Egyptian, and Italian hotels regarding the changes that occurred at their workplaces due to the introduction of robotics.

As can be seen in Table 3, the majority of respondents in Russia were women (61.1%), while in Egypt, the majority of respondents were men (60.4%). In Italy, the gender distribution is quite balanced (54.4% are women and 45.6% are men). Regarding the age of the respondents, it is interesting to note that the majority in all countries are under 35 years old (78.4% in Egypt, 69.8% in Italy, and 80.2% in Russia). In all countries, the vast majority of respondents hold a university or higher institute degree (81.1% in Egypt, 78.7% in Italy, and 80.8% in Russia).

4 Results

The first question posed to the respondents aimed to understand which changes in the organisation are most perceived by workers due to the introduction of cobots in certain work activities. Table 4 shows employees' perceptions of the changes that have occurred in their workplaces due to cobotics. The responses from Russian and Egyptian respondents indicate that two-thirds of Russian employees report a partial reduction in the number of employees due to the introduction of cobots, whereas

Table 4 Changes occurred in the organisation due to the introduction of collaborative cobots

Answer alternatives	Egypt		Italy		Russia	
	Fred	%	Freq	%	Freq	%
The introduction of collaborative cobots involved the dismissal of employees	11	6.9	5	3.7	18	10.8
Partial reduction of the number of employees	77	48.4	15	11.0	116	69.4
Transferring some of the employees to distance work	66	41.5	78	57.4	47	28.1
The use of temporary or seasonal workers provided by other companies	58	36.5	11	8.0	39	23.3
Hiring new employees only on a short-term basis (from 1 to 6 months)	32	20.1	7	5.1	24	14.4
There were no changes	21	13.2	81	59.6	14	8.3
Other	–	–	14	10.3	28	16.7

Source: Our elaboration

this fact is noted by slightly fewer than half of Egyptian employees. In Italy, this aspect is almost imperceptible to the respondents (only 11%). At the same time, the distribution of responses regarding the transfer of some employees to remote work is perceived to a greater extent by Italians (57.4%), followed by Egyptian respondents (41.5%), while only 28.1% of Russian respondents noticed this type of change in work organisation. Regarding the involvement of temporary staff for similar activities, the responses were distributed as follows among Egypt, Russia, and Italy, respectively (36.5%, 23.3%, and 8.0%). It is noteworthy that one in ten Russian respondents perceives a greater possibility of layoffs due to the introduction of cobots, while only 6.9% of Egyptian respondents and 3.7% of Italian respondents chose this answer option. It is surprising that almost 60% of Italians have not noticed any changes due to the inclusion of cobots in their work environments (in contrast to a much smaller proportion of Egyptian respondents—13.2%—and Russian respondents—8.3%—who admitted not noticing any change in the work organisation). As another option, Russian workers note the constant adjustment of work tasks and responsibilities. 6.2% of Italian respondents stated that they had never interacted with a cobot and therefore did not perceive any changes directly in their work, whereas 4.1% of Italian respondents highlighted that they had to divide their work between office tasks and remote work (hybrid mode).

Based on the obtained set of answers to the scale questions in the questionnaire, a descriptive analysis was conducted to assess the socio-psychological aspects of the interaction between employees and cobots in the workplace (Table 5). The participants were asked to evaluate their degree of agreement with the statements, using a 5-point Likert scale, where 1 represents strong disagreement and 5 represents strong agreement.

Regarding the social aspects of human-robot interaction, some differences can be observed between respondents from different countries. The data shows that in Italy, compared to other countries (Russia and Egypt), organisations are currently less inclined to incorporate cobots into their work processes. The prestige

Table 5 Descriptive analysis of the employees' perception toward the "human-robot" working system

Scale Item	Italy		Russia		Egypt	
	M	SD	M	SD	M	SD
Social interaction factors						
In general, my organisation supports the use of cobots	3.01	1.102	3.83	0.736	3.27	0.926
People in my hotel who use cobots have more prestige than those who do not	2.62	0.602	3.86	0.491	4.38	0.849
The use of the cobot is appropriate to my various job-related tasks	2.83	1.046	3.92	0.396	3.97	0.973
The cobot's output is of excellent quality	2.66	0.911	3.90	0.428	3.40	0.791
I find using a cobot enjoyable	3.20	0.922	3.81	0.431	4.03	0.890
I fear that I will lose contact with my colleagues because of the cobot	3.41	0.860	3.93	0.655	4.21	0.811
I have no objection to sharing a workstation with a cobot	2.83	1.050	3.80	0.428	2.29	0.994
I have no objection if the cobot stores my personal information	2.62	1.353	2.87	0.447	2.15	0.880
I fear that I may lose my work due to the cobot	3.01	0.669	3.98	0.394	4.30	0.957
I feel safe while using the cobot	2.42	0.670	3.03	0.354	2.68	0.981
I can operate the cobot if someone teaches me how to use it first	3.81	0.971	3.76	0.379	3.01	0.808
Operating the cobot can enhance my job performance	3.44	0.498	3.89	0.431	3.41	0.915
Psychological interaction factors						
I feel uneasy if cobots really have emotions	3.27	1.050	2.23	0.588	3.41	0.821
Something terrible might happen if cobots developed into living beings	4.06	0.539	3.33	0.575	3.92	0.900
I feel relaxed dealing with cobots	3.22	1.163	3.77	0.744	2.70	1.092
If cobots had feelings, I would be able to make friends with them	2.27	1.686	3.88	0.631	2.62	0.956
I would feel comforted being with cobots that have emotions	2.43	1.204	3.66	0.578	2.31	1.006
I feel nervous operating a cobot in front of other people	2.60	0.665	2.00	0.329	2.27	0.948
I feel nervous just standing in front of a cobot	2.62	0.971	2.08	0.538	2.10	0.882
I think that if I depend on cobots too much, something terrible might happen	3.41	1.353	3.75	0.644	3.94	0.914
I feel paranoid talking with a cobots	2.20	0.741	2.09	0.605	2.46	0.907
I think that in the future, society will be dominated by cobots	3.41	1.138	3.92	0.634	4.01	0.894

Source: Our elaboration

associated with working with cobots in Italy is also perceived to a much lesser extent than in the other countries analysed. Furthermore, Italian respondents are the most hesitant regarding the excellent quality of the cobot's output. Most Egyptian respondents confirm that the use of cobots is appropriate for their job-related tasks, while Italian employees often believe that their work activities cannot be carried out by robot collaborators without task adaptations. Respondents in all three countries agreed on statements concerning concerns related to the processing of personal information by cobots and the lack of safety when using them. The primary concern among all workers relates to the loss of contact with "human" colleagues due to the introduction of cobots in managing certain tasks. In addition, Egyptian respondents are the most worried about losing their jobs due to the robotisation of some work processes, while the Italian participants appear to be less concerned about this issue. However, all workers interviewed expressed a willingness to collaborate with cobots. This statement is supported by an average score greater than 3.00 for the questions: "I can operate the cobot if someone teaches me how to use it first" and "Operating the cobot can enhance my job performance." In conclusion, it can be stated that despite some concerns related to the interaction with cobot colleagues, workers from Russia, Egypt, and Italy recognise their potential for improving their work performance (e.g. pleasantness of interaction, productivity). As regards the psychological aspects relating to the perception of cobots, there are some statements that align across the different countries, while others highlight differences that require attention and further analysis. All participants are convinced that society will be dominated by cobots in the future. This belief raises several psychological concerns among the respondents. The data appears to confirm a general trend of not wanting to become overly reliant on robot collaborators, as participants wish to maintain their decision-making autonomy and working freedom (all participants agree that depending too much on cobots could lead to negative consequences). Russian participants seem to have a greater psychological comfort when working with cobots; they feel more relaxed and less anxious in this new form of human-robot collaboration compared to their Italian and Egyptian colleagues, who, in any case, do not feel significantly worried from a psychological standpoint. Furthermore, a significantly larger proportion of Russian respondents would be willing to befriend cobots and would not be surprised if cobots had emotions (e.g. the average score obtained on the statement "If cobots had feelings, I would be able to make friends with them"). This could be a good starting point for fostering a positive working environment and greater trust towards cobot partners. Another interesting aspect to consider is the significantly higher standard deviation (on some statements) among Italian respondents compared to their colleagues from the other analysed countries (Russia and Egypt). The variation in responses from the Italians could be attributed to the fact that some of them claimed to have never interacted directly with cobots. The absence of direct experience may indeed influence their perceptions towards social aspects and heighten anxiety and insecurity regarding new forms of collaboration in work environments. In this case, preparing workers through HR management for future changes and promoting new ways of working, such as Industry 5.0, could be good practices to reduce resistance and prejudice towards advanced technologies, particularly in human-robot interactions, in the new work environments based on the principles of Industry 5.0 and Hospitality 5.0.

5 Discussion

This study has validated several findings from previous research [54]. Both enabling factors (social and psychological) and certain constraints for human-robot collaboration have been identified. In line with the research of several authors [13], the perceived benefits in terms of productivity, remote working, entertainment value, and the automation of repetitive tasks have been highlighted as factors that positively influence hotel employees' perceptions and increase their readiness to collaborate with cobots. Despite the majority of respondents expressing a willingness to cooperate with robot colleagues, several factors were identified that could negatively affect the work environment. One of the most significant concerns for all respondents was the potential loss of human contact with their colleagues within the organisation, with customers, and with partners in inter-organisational relationships. Furthermore, through the use of comparative analysis, some intriguing results have emerged regarding the perception of cobot introduction among employees of luxury hotels in the three analysed countries: Egypt, Russia, and Italy. It is noteworthy that there are both similarities and differences in the perception of collaboration with robots from a social and psychological perspective among respondents from different countries. Similar to previous studies, the implications of the findings for organisational management and HRM suggest that hotel staff should be prepared to collaborate with robots in the workplace [54]. This study confirms that the training and preparation of human resources for human-robot integration are imperative. Furthermore, in line with some previous evidence [9], our research highlights that trust in cobots' performance is essential for overcoming obstacles and embracing change. Additionally, the development of emotional intelligence towards robot colleagues can serve as a driver for optimising human-robot collaboration. In fact, respondents often currently experience negative emotions such as fear, confusion, and nervousness. However, it is worth noting that some participants feel relaxed and enjoy working with cobots. The implications of this study are significant for HRM, as it provides critical insights needed to develop effective measures for integrating robots into the hotel work environment. One of the primary challenges identified is the psychological and social barriers that exist in employees' perceptions of robotics in the workplace. Addressing these barriers is essential for fostering a collaborative atmosphere where humans and robots can function seamlessly together. Moreover, the study's results underscore the importance of considering national characteristics and the distinct features of the organisational environment in which this transformation is taking place. These contextual factors can greatly influence how employees react to new technologies and collaborative frameworks. By recognising these variations, HR professionals can better tailor their strategies to suit the specific needs and expectations of their workforce, thereby increasing acceptance and enhancing the overall effectiveness of cobot integration. This research can serve as a vital reference point for decision-makers at both the organisational and macro levels. Understanding the nuances of employee perceptions alongside the socio-cultural dynamics involved can facilitate a smoother transition to the new concept of Work 5.0. As workplaces increasingly adopt advanced technologies, it becomes imperative for organisations to not only implement these innovations but also to ensure that their employees are supported, informed, and engaged throughout the process. In conclusion, by leveraging the insights from this study, HRM can play a pivotal role in guiding organisations through the complex landscape of robotic integration, ultimately contributing to a more aligned and harmonious work environment that embraces the benefits of automation while addressing the human aspects of change.

6 Limitations and Further Research

The limitations of the study pertain to the absence, at this stage of the research, of an analysis based on personal characteristics (age, gender, educational qualifications) that may impact perceptions of working with cobot colleagues. These elements will be explored in further research to identify differences in perceptions of cobots among various groups of workers. Another limitation lies in the small sample size of respondents, which should be expanded in subsequent phases of the research to increase the generalisability of the results. Moreover, to gain a deeper understanding of the phenomenon, qualitative research methods could be incorporated. This would allow for broader insights into the dynamics of integration and interaction between hotel industry personnel and cobots. Considering the long-term perspective, the integration of cobots into Work 5.0 requires a thorough analysis and potential redefinition of HRM practices that can support the ongoing change. Consequently, further research on effective change management and HRM is needed.

Appendix 1 Analysis of the Industry 5.0 Evolution

Author	Definition of Industry 5.0	Key elements of Industry 5.0
Demir et al. (2019) [55]	Industry 5.0 may encompass both human-robot collaboration and the bioeconomy. Other themes, such as space life, space industries, and space mining, may represent the next revolution or be part of it. For efficient integration, it is necessary to consider potential issues related to human-robot collaboration from both an organisational and a human employee perspective.	Human-Robotic collaboration and Smart Society Bioeconomy and Sustainability Human-Robot Collaboration Issues: – Evolution in organisational behaviour, – Acceptance of robots, organisational structures and workflows, – Work ethics, – Discrimination against robots or people, – Privacy and trust, – Education and training, – Redesign of workplaces for robots.
Friedman and Hendry (2019) [56]	Industry 5.0 forces business professionals, information technology experts and philosophers to concentrate on taking human considerations into account while implementing new technologies in production systems	– Human consideration in the process of new technologies implementation – New technologies in the production system
Nahavandi (2019) [37]	In Industry 5.0, humans are reintroduced to the operation via collaborative workflows that include intelligent systems to maximise the benefits of both humans' and cobots' cognitive abilities in terms of improved process efficiency	– Collaborative workflows – Benefits of both humans' and cobots' cognitive abilities – Process efficiency
Adel (2022) [18]	Industry 5.0 is changing the paradigm and brings resolution, as it decreases the emphasis on technology and assumes that the potential for progress is based on collaboration among humans and machines	– Sustainability and environmental control – Efficiency and humans productivity – Creativity
Maddikunta et al. (2022) [57]	Industry 5.0 seems to be a human centred design in which the ideal human partner and cobots interact with human capital to enable customised autonomous production across corporate social networks.	– Human-centred design – Customised autonomous production across corporate social networks – People-machine collaboration – Task distribution (cobots: routine, labour-intensive activities; humans: personalisation and problem-solving)

(continued)

(continued)

Author	Definition of Industry 5.0	Key elements of Industry 5.0
Alves et al. (2023) [58]	Industry 5.0 is a strategy that puts the human factor at the centre of production, where the well-being of the worker is prioritised, along with more sustainable and resilient production systems. For human centricity, it is necessary to empower human beings to improve their individual skills and competencies in collaboration or cooperation with digital technologies.	– Human centricity – Sustainable and resilient – production systems – Worker well-being – Improvement of individual – skills and competencies – Collaboration and cooperation with digital technologies
Ivanov (2023) [59]	The major dimensions of Industry 5.0 are based on the technological- organisational framework. The major technological principles of Industry 5.0 are collaboration, coordination, communication, automation, data analytics processing, and identification. Industry 5.0 covers 4 areas: organisation, management, technology, and performance assessment. Industry 5.0 frames a new triple bottom line: resilient value creation, human well-being, and sustainable society	– Technological-organisational framework – Organization, management, technology, and performance assessment – New triple bottom line: (1) resilient value creation; (2) human well-being; (3) sustainable society
Wang et al. (2024) [60]	Human-centricity, a core value of Industry 5.0. It leads to the prioritisation of human needs, spanning from health and safety to self-actualization and personal growth.	– Human-centricity Prioritisation of Human needs Health and safety – Self-actualization Personal growth

Appendix 2 The Elements of Industry 5.0 in Hospitality

N.	Author(s)	Title	Main Findings
1	Pillai et al. (2021) [4]	COVID-19 and hospitality 5.0: Redefining hospitality operations	• The study examines the scalability of Industry 5.0 design principles into the hospitality context, leading to Hospitality 5.0 to improve operational efficiency. • The study delineates how Hospitality 5.0 technologies can ensure hygiene and cleanliness in various touchpoints in customer's journey. • The findings of the article serve as a foundation to understand how synergy between humans and machines can be achieved through Hospitality 5.0

(continued)

(continued)

N.	Author(s)	Title	Main Findings
2	Gaur et al. (2021) [23]	Role of artificial intelligence and robotics to foster the touchless travel during a pandemic: a review and research agenda	• The article sets out a research agenda that includes three dimensions: Artificial Intelligence & robotics, cleanliness & sanitation, and healthcare and wellness. • This study's findings suggest that AI and robotics may bring out definite research directions at the connection of health crisis and hospitality management, taking into account the COVID-19 crisis.
3	Ghazy and Fedorova (2022) [28]	Hotel Employees' Attitude and Acceptance Toward Human-Robot Co-Working Based on the Industry 5.0 Concept	• The findings revealed that, although the employees agreed to interact with robots and indicated that robots are helpful, enjoyable, and productive, they also pointed out that robots would control jobs.
4	Orea-Giner et al. (2022) [24]	Does the implementation of robots in hotels influence the overall tripadvisor rating? A text mining analysis from the Industry 5.0 approach	• The results of the study show a relationship between the categories of the functionality of robots/travellers and the rating given in a review. • The sentiment that increases review ratings the most is 'joy'. • In the case of the robot functionality, emotions and sentiments impact differently considering robot typology. • The results add new insights discussing the combination of robot typology and traveller type (solo, friends, couple, family, business). • The findings of the study confirm that incorporating robots into the guest experience benefits the relationship with the customer by creating an emotional link between customers and hotel brands.
5	Singh et al. (2023) [27]	Behavior of Delivery Robot in Human-Robot Collaborative Spaces During Navigation.	• The study is aimed towards evaluating human experience to explore the perceived social presence, role, and perception of a delivery robot exhibiting different behaviour conditions while navigating in a hotel corridor. • The experiment conducted in the study suggests that behaviour conditions have a significant effect on likeability, perceived intelligence, and perceived safety of the robot. • The participants' responses show that humans prefer an assistant role of a robot enabled with audio and visual aids exhibiting social behaviour

(continued)

(continued)

N.	Author(s)	Title	Main Findings
6	Callarisa-Fiol et al. (2023) [26]	Entrepreneurship innovation using social robots in tourism: a social listening study	• The results of the study are related to the acceptance of social robots in the tourism sector and specifically in hospitality. • Although service robots are being deployed at a rapid rate, the sentiment generated by this disruptive technology is still neutral. • The social acceptance of a technological innovation is a key aspect for its implementation. Social listening can be a useful methodology for monitoring the evolution of the social acceptance of a technology.
7	Dzia-Uddin et al. (2023) [61]	Systematic Literature Review of Employability Skills of Hospitality Graduates after Covid-19 Era.	• Three major themes emerged from the SLR: knowledge, skill, and attitudes of the human capital to be employed in Hospitality. • The results of this study provide information about the gap between traditional knowledge and additional soft and employability skills that are required in the current hospitality business environment, where technological tools transformed the service experiences in low-touch and high- tech.
8	Milton (2024) [22]	Exploring the Synergy of Artificial Intelligence and Financial Management in the Hotel Industry: A Critical Review of Innovations, Challenges, and Strategic Implications for Enhancing Operational Efficiency and Competitive Advantage.	• The findings underscore that AI technologies, encompassing predictive analytics, expenditure tracking systems, fraud detection algorithms, and personalised pricing strategies, are pivotal in revolutionising decision-making processes in hotels. • Despite the notable benefits of AI, impediments such as concerns over data privacy, biases within algorithms, and adherence to regulatory frameworks pose barriers to AI integration. • Factors such as organisational readiness, workforce development, and alignment with strategic business objectives emerge as critical determinants influencing the successful deployment of AI-driven solutions in hotels

(continued)

(continued)

N.	Author(s)	Title	Main Findings
9	Jabbar et al. (2024) [29]	Digital Transformation in Hotel Management: Optimizing Guest Experience in the Industry 4.0 Era.	• The findings indicate that integrating technologies such as property management systems, Internet of Things, artificial intelligence, and data analytics can enhance operational efficiency, service personalization, and data-driven decision- making in hotel management • The implementation of digital transformation faces challenges, such as significant investments, cybersecurity, and resistance to change. • Case studies of hotels that have successfully adopted digital technologies reveal best practices and valuable lessons, including the importance of top management support, strategic alignment, and stakeholder engagement.

Source: Our elaboration

References

1. Ashqar, R. I., Ramos, C., Sousa, C., & Matos, N. (2023). CRM and smart technologies in the hospitality. In *Marketing and smart technologies: Proceedings of ICMarkTech 2022* (Vol. 2, pp. 113–124). Springer Nature Singapore.
2. Gangwar, V. P., & Reddy, D. (2023). Hospitality industry 5.0: Emerging trends in guest perception and experiences. *Opportunities and Challenges of Business 5.0 in Emerging Markets*, 185–211.
3. Parvez, M. O., Öztüren, A., Cobanoglu, C., Arasli, H., & Eluwole, K. K. (2022). Employees' perception of robots and robot-induced unemployment in hospitality industry under COVID-19 pandemic. *International Journal of Hospitality Management, 107*, 103336.
4. Pillai, S. G., Haldorai, K., Seo, W. S., & Kim, W. G. (2021). COVID-19 and hospitality 5.0: Redefining hospitality operations. *International Journal of Hospitality Management, 94*, 102869.
5. Kumar, S., Yadav, M., & Kumar, D. (2024). Viability of man and machine as co-workers in the hotel industry. In *building smart and sustainable businesses with transformative technologies* (pp. 189–204). IGI Global.
6. Goel, P., Kaushik, N., Sivathanu, B., Pillai, R., & Vikas, J. (2022). Consumers' adoption of artificial intelligence and robotics in hospitality and tourism sector: Literature review and future research agenda. *Tourism Review, 77*(4), 1081–1096.
7. Verma, A., Grobbelaar, W., & Shukla, V. K. (2023). Smart innovation in the hospitality and tourism industry. In *Computational intelligence in urban infrastructure* (pp. 94–116). CRC Press.
8. Hussain, S., Singh, A. M., Mohanty, P., & Gavinolla, M. R. (2023). Next generation employability and career sustainability in the hospitality industry 5.0. *Worldwide Hospitality and Tourism Themes, 15*(3), 308–321.

9. Khoa, D. T., Gip, H. Q., Guchait, P., & Wang, C. Y. (2023). Competition or collaboration for human–robot relationship: A critical reflection on future cobotics in hospitality. *International Journal of Contemporary Hospitality Management, 35*(6), 2202–2215.
10. Song, Y., Zhang, M., Hu, J., & Cao, X. (2022). Dancing with service robots: The impacts of employee-robot collaboration on hotel employees' job crafting. *International Journal of Hospitality Management, 103*, 103220.
11. Singh, A. K., Tyagi, P. K., Jain, E., Tyagi, P., Singh, A. K., & Sharma, N. (2022). Robotics and artificial intelligence in hospitality sector: A descriptive bibliometric analysis and future research directions. In *2022 International Conference on Electronics and Renewable Systems (ICEARS)* (pp. 1484–1491). IEEE.
12. Li, J. J., Bonn, M. A., & Ye, B. H. (2019). Hotel employee's artificial intelligence and robotics awareness and its impact on turnover intention: The moderating roles of perceived organizational support and competitive psychological climate. *Tourism Management, 73*, 172–181.
13. Ghanghorkar, Y., & Pillai, R. (2024). Human–robot coordination and collaboration in industry 4.0. In *Digital transformation: Industry 4.0 to society 5.0* (pp. 195–219). Springer Nature Singapore.
14. Eurofound. (2024). *Human–robot interaction: What changes in the workplace?* Publications Office of the European Union.
15. Saari, U. A., Tossavainen, A., Kaipainen, K., & Mäkinen, S. J. (2022). Exploring factors influencing the acceptance of social robots among early adopters and mass market representatives. *Robotics and Autonomous Systems, 151*, 104033.
16. Gibson, C. B. (2017). Elaboration, generalization, triangulation, and interpretation: On enhancing the value of mixed method research. *Organizational Research Methods, 20*(2), 193–223. https://doi.org/10.1177/1094428116639133
17. Javaid, M., Haleem, A., Singh, R. P., Haq, M. I. U., Raina, A., & Suman, R. (2020). Industry 5.0: Potential applications in COVID-19. *Journal of Industrial Integration and Management, 5*(04), 507–530.
18. Adel, A. (2022). Future of industry 5.0 in society: Human-centric solutions, challenges and prospective research areas. *Journal of Cloud Computing, 11*(1), 1–15.
19. Alvarez-Aros, E. L., & Bernal-Torres, C. A. (2021). Technological competitiveness and emerging technologies in industry 4.0 and industry 5.0. *Anais da Academia Brasileira de Ciências, 93*.
20. Xu, X., Lu, Y., Vogel-Heuser, B., & Wang, L. (2021). Industry 4.0 and Industry 5.0—Inception, conception and perception. *Journal of Manufacturing Systems, 61*, 530–535.
21. Sindhwani, R., Afridi, S., Kumar, A., Banaitis, A., Luthra, S., & Singh, P. L. (2022). Can industry 5.0 revolutionize the wave of resilience and social value creation? A multi-criteria framework to analyze enablers. *Technology in Society, 68*, 101887.
22. Milton, T. (2024). Exploring the synergy of artificial intelligence and financial management in the hotel industry: A critical review of innovations, challenges, and strategic implications for enhancing operational efficiency and competitive advantage. *International Journal for Multidimensional Research Perspectives, 2*(2), 79–95.
23. Gaur, L., Afaq, A., Singh, G., & Dwivedi, Y. K. (2021). Role of artificial intelligence and robotics to foster the touchless travel during a pandemic: A review and research agenda. *International Journal of Contemporary Hospitality Management, 33*(11), 4079–4098.
24. Orea-Giner, A., Fuentes-Moraleda, L., Villacé-Molinero, T., Muñoz-Mazón, A., & Calero-Sanz, J. (2022). Does the implementation of robots in hotels influence the overall tripadvisor rating? A text mining analysis from the Industry 5.0 approach. *Tourism Management, 93*, 104586.
25. Dzia-Uddin, D. N., Minghat, A. D., & Zakaria, W. N. W. (2023). Systematic literature review of employability skills of hospitality graduates after covid-19 era. *International Journal of Academic Research in Business and Social Sciences., 13*(10).

26. Callarisa-Fiol, L. J., Moliner-Tena, M. Á., Rodríguez-Artola, R., & Sánchez-García, J. (2023). Entrepreneurship innovation using social robots in tourism: A social listening study. *Review of Managerial Science, 17*(8), 2945–2971.
27. Singh, K. J., Kapoor, D. S., Abouhawwash, M., Al-Amri, J. F., Mahajan, S., & Pandit, A. K. (2023). Behavior of delivery robot in human-robot collaborative spaces during navigation. *Intelligent Automation & Soft Computing, 35*(1).
28. Ghazy, K., & Fedorova, A. E. (2022). Hotel employees' attitude and acceptance toward human-robot co-working based on the industry 5.0 concept. *Changing Societies & Personalities, 6*(4), 906–926.
29. Jabbar, U. A., Prabowo, B. A., & Hanafi, R. A. (2024) Digital transformation in hotel management: Optimizing guest experience in the industry 4.0 era. *Proceeding of the International Global Tourism Science and Vocational Education, 1*(1), 177–190.
30. Kolade, O., & Owoseni, A. (2022). Employment 5.0: The work of the future and the future of work. *Technology in Society, 71*, 102086.
31. World Economic Forum. (2020). The future of jobs report 2020. World Economic Forum, Geneva, October. https://www3.weforum.org/docs/WEF_Future_of_Jobs_2020.pdf
32. Forbes. (2019). The future of work will be uniquely human. *Forbes*. Retrieved February 26, 2024, from https://www.forbes.com/sites/johnwinsor/2019/10/21/the-future-of-work-will-be-uniquelyhuman/?sh=1f34b40916b7
33. Gross-Gołacka, E., Kupczyk, T., Rzepka, A., Smolarek, M., & Szczepańska-Woszczyna, K. (2023). The concept of inclusion and diversity as an accelerator for building Society 5.0 and creating a managed organization in the 5.0 era. In *Innovation in the digital economy* (pp. 62–72). Routledge.
34. Grobbelaar, W., & Verma, A. (2024). Future employments in the hospitality industry. In artificial intelligence for smart technology in the hospitality and tourism industry (pp. 77–104). Apple Academic Press.
35. Galin, R., Meshcheryakov, R., & Kamesheva, S. (2020) Distributing tasks in multi-agent robotic system for human-robot interaction applications. In *International conference on interactive collaborative robotics* (pp. 99–106). Springer International Publishing.
36. Young, J. E., Sung, J., Voida, A., Sharlin, E., Igarashi, T., Christensen, H. I., & Grinter, R. E. (2011). Evaluating human-robot interaction: Focusing on the holistic interaction experience. *International Journal of Social Robotics, 3*, 53–67.
37. Nahavandi, S. (2019). Industry 5.0—A human-centric solution. *Sustainability, 11*(16), 4371.
38. Simões, A. C., Soares, A. L., & Barros, A. C. (2020). Factors influencing the intention of managers to adopt collaborative robots (cobots) in manufacturing organizations. *Journal of Engineering and Technology Management, 57*, 101574.
39. Ivanov, S. H., Webster, C., & Berezina, K. (2017). Adoption of robots and service automation by tourism and hospitality companies. *Revista Turismo & Desenvolvimento, 27*(28), 1501–1517.
40. Zhong, L., Zhang, X., Rong, J., Chan, H. K., Xiao, J., & Kong, H. (2020). Construction and empirical research on acceptance model of service robots applied in hotel industry. *Industrial Management and Data Systems, 121*(6), 1325–1352.
41. Kunz, W., Heinonen, K., Lemmink, J., & Lucas, B. (2018). Future service technologies: Business models, analytics, and experience. *Journal of Services Marketing, 33*(4), 479–487.
42. Chi, O. H., Denton, G., & Gursoy, D. (2020). Artificially intelligent device use in service delivery: A systematic review, synthesis, and research agenda. *Journal of Hospitality Marketing & Management, 29*(7), 757–786.
43. Hughes, S. C., Wickersham, L., Ryan-Jones, D. L., & Smith, S. A. (2002). Overcoming social and psychological barriers to effective on-line collaboration. *Journal of Educational Technology & Society, 5*(1), 86–92.
44. Hou, Y., Zhang, K., & Li, G. (2021). Service robots or human staff: How social crowding shapes tourist preferences. *Tourism Management, 83*, 104242.

45. Meidute-Kavaliauskiene, I., Cigdem, S., Yildiz, B., & Davidavicius, S. (2021). The effect of perceptions on service robot usage intention: A survey study in the service sector. *Sustainability, 13*(17), 9655.
46. Huang, H. L., Cheng, L. K., Sun, P. C., & Chou, S. J. (2021). The effects of perceived identity threat and realistic threat on the negative attitudes and usage intentions toward hotel service robots: The moderating effect of the robot's anthropomorphism. *International Journal of Social Robotics, 1599-1611.*
47. Cha, S. S. (2020). Customers' intention to use robot-serviced restaurants in Korea: Relationship of coolness and MCI factors. *International Journal of Contemporary Hospitality Management, 32*(9), 2947–2968.
48. Tussyadiah, I. P., Zach, F. J., & Wang, J. (2020). Do travelers trust intelligent service robots? *Annals of Tourism Research, 81*, 102886.
49. Pozharliev, R., De Angelis, M., Rossi, D., Romani, S., Verbeke, W., & Cherubino, P. (2021). Attachment styles moderate customer responses to frontline service robots: Evidence from affective, attitudinal, and behavioral measures. *Psychology and Marketing, 38*(5), 881–895.
50. Tung, V. W. S., & Au, N. (2018). Exploring customer experiences with robotics in hospitality. *International Journal of Contemporary Hospitality Management, 30*(7), 2680–2697.
51. Yu, C. (2020). Human-like robots as employees in the hotel industry: Thematic content analysis of online reviews. *Journal of Hospitality Marketing & Management, 29*(1), 22–38.
52. Tabachnick, B., & Fidell, L. (2007). *Using multivariate statistics* (5th ed., pp. 83–86). London.
53. Nunnally, J. C. (1978). *Psychometric theory*. McGraw-Hill.
54. Sadangharn, P. (2022). Acceptance of robots as co-workers: Hotel employees' perspective. *International Journal of Engineering Business Management, 14*, 18479790221113621.
55. Demir, K. A., Döven, G., & Sezen, B. (2019). *Industry 5.0 and human-robot co-working* (Vol. 158, pp. 688–695). Procedia Computer Science.
56. Friedman, B., & Hendry, D. G. (2019). *Value sensitive design: Shaping technology with moral imagination*. Mit Press.
57. Maddikunta, P. K. R., Pham, Q. V., Prabadevi, B., Deepa, N., Dev, K., Gadekallu, T. R., Ruby, R., & Liyanage, M. (2022). Industry 5.0: A survey on enabling technologies and potential applications. *Journal of Industrial Information Integration, 26*, 100257.
58. Alves, J., Lima, T. M., & Gaspar, P. D. (2023). Is industry 5.0 a human-centred approach? a systematic review. *Processes, 11*(1), 193.
59. Ivanov, D. (2023). The Industry 5.0 framework: viability-based integration of the resilience, sustainability, and human-centricity perspectives. *International Journal of Production Research, 61*(5), 1683–1695.
60. Wang, B., Zhou, H., Li, X., Yang, G., Zheng, P., Song, C., Wang, L., et al. (2024). Human digital twin in the context of industry 5.0. *Robotics and Computer-Integrated Manufacturing, 85*, 102626.
61. Dzia-Uddin, D. N., Minghat, A. D., & Zakaria, W. N. W. (2023). Systematic Literature Review of Employability Skills of Hospitality Graduates after Covid-19 (2023) Era. *International Journal Of Academic Research In Business And Social Sciences.*

The Strategic Role of HR in Hybrid Work Environments: An Application of the 'Harvard' Model

Sara Bonesso, Giovanna Afeltra, and Laura Cortellazzo

Abstract The shift to hybrid workplaces has accelerated following the COVID-19 pandemic, offering new opportunities for organizations to create value. While it is widely recognized that the HR function plays a crucial role in managing this transition, existing research has not sufficiently explored the strategic role of HR in effectively implementing hybrid work environments. This study addresses this gap by providing both theoretical and practical insights into how HR can lead and support hybrid work arrangements. Through the lens of the Harvard model, the research employs a longitudinal case study of an Italian company over 4 years, analyzing the HR department's interventions in collaboration with management and employees. The study examines how HR practices were co-designed to align with stakeholder interests and situational factors, ultimately creating a coherent strategy for hybrid work implementation. By integrating theory with practical application, this research contributes to the literature on HR management and hybrid work, offering a detailed exploration of the necessary alignment between HR practices and organizational goals in hybrid work environments, and highlighting the importance of continuous outcome monitoring.

Keywords HRM · Harvard model · Hybrid work environment · Strategic HRM practices

S. Bonesso (✉) · L. Cortellazzo
Venice School of Management, Ca' Foscari, University of Venice, Venezia, Italy

G. Afeltra
Department for the Promotion of Human Sciences and Quality of life, San Raffaele University, Rome, Italy
e-mail: giovanna.afeltra@uniroma5.it

A. Tursunbayeva et al. (eds.), *Technology-Driven Transformation*, Lecture Notes in Information Systems and Organisation 79,
https://doi.org/10.1007/978-3-032-01396-5_4

1 Introduction

The pandemic of Covid-19 has been a "great accelerator" for the digitalization of companies, changing work habits, lifestyles, and business strategies. Specifically, it has led to a significant increase in people working from home, accelerating the digital transformation of work [1] and giving rise to hybrid work arrangements, defined as a flexible arrangement where working hours are split between a company site and another location, often a home office [2].

The extant Hybrid work literature mainly focuses on the organizational benefits. Hybrid work is considered a way to achieve a competitive advantage [3] and it is also associated with a rise in employee motivation, commitment and job satisfaction [4], eliminating workplace distractions and improving the productivity of teleworkers [5]. HW also offers greater autonomy and flexibility to workers by blurring the lines between the traditional office and remote locations [6–8].

The most recent data from Gallup highlights that hybrid work arrangements are now the predominant model for remote-capable employees. In 2024, only 20% of these workers spent their entire week on-site, a significant drop from 60% in 2019 (Gallup 2024). This shift indicates that hybrid work arrangements are likely to remain a stable feature of the work environment [9]. To manage this phenomenon, some companies have invested in technology to support remote work, developed policies that promote work-life balance, and trained managers to handle distributed teams effectively [9]. An increasing number of companies are returning back to office, justifying their choice according to the need for direct collaboration, the nature of their work, and concerns about data security and productivity [10]. These companies may view the office environment as essential for fostering corporate culture, mentoring, and spontaneous collaboration that drives innovation [10].

The differences in the success of these work models underscore that it is not the tool or modality itself that guarantees success of hybrid work implementation, but how well it is integrated into the company's operations and culture [11]. The success of this implementation is often under the guidance of the HR departments. Labrador Fernández et al. (2023) have shown the crucial role of HR managers in facilitating the transformation of organizations into a more flexible business model with a culture of trust stressing the key role of HR departments in business decision-making during and after the pandemic. The external environment also influences internal HR configurations and it makes it necessary to differentiate the type of HR practices required in each hybridized work environment [2]. Therefore, various studies call for exploring a literature gap on how an organization may successfully operate in HW [6, 12]. In particular, Strategic Human Resource Management (SHRM) scholars have recently called for the need to expand both theory and practice to understand the strategic HR practices that support and champion a hybrid work environment [11, 13].

To answer this call, we draw on the Harvard model [14] to elucidate a contextualized and holistic view of the HRM role in implementing hybrid work systems and provide a broader perspective on stakeholders, and long-term organizational achievements [14, 15]. Thus, we address the following research question: "How do changes in stakeholder interests and situational factors influence HRM strategic practices and their impact on the successful implementation of hybrid work environments?". This research employs a qualitative methodological approach through the examination of a single case study. This case has been chosen for its potential to maximize insights into hybrid work HR strategies within a specific organizational context, allowing for an in-depth analysis in implementing hybrid work models after COVID-19.

2 Literature Background

2.1 SHRM and Hybrid Work

To delineate the configuration of SHRM within hybrid organizations, an initial exposition of the theoretical and conceptual underpinnings from both domains is provided. The discourse on hybrid organizations is commonly referred to within the specialized corpus as 'hybrid literature'. Hybrid work can be defined as a flexible equilibrium where working hours are split between a company location and another setting, typically a home office [2]. It is frequently associated with terms like "remote working" which refers to the ability of employees to work from any location, provided they have access to the organization's legacy systems, can collaborate with colleagues, and fulfil tasks ("flexibility in space"). This encompasses a variety of settings including homes, co-working spaces, parks, and other outdoor areas [16]. The term "agile working" is often used as a synonym to describe work optimization techniques that prioritize productivity, coordination, efficiency, and agility. Then a "flexible working system" that addresses efficiency and effectiveness through any combination of "autonomy, agility, coordination, and work tool optimization" is referred to as smart working [4].

The integration of HR practices into a hybrid cultural and economic system that balances regional and national values with global and local practices represents one of the greatest challenges for HRM in the post-COVID-19 era [17]. In light of this, a more contextualized understanding of the strategic role of HRM is needed, one that takes a longer, broader view of results and involves a thorough consideration of stakeholder requirements [15]. Jonsen and Jehn [18] suggest utilizing the Harvard model to explain hybrid work by incorporating its multi-stakeholder approach to analyze the diverse impacts and outcomes of hybrid work settings. The Harvard model, which emphasizes the integration of HRM policies with business strategy and the consideration of various stakeholders, is particularly suitable for understanding the complexities of hybrid work environments. According to these authors, by applying this model, organizations can better understand and manage the complexities of hybrid work, leading to more effective HR strategies and improved overall outcomes.

2.2 The Harvard Model

The application of an HRM business model is particularly useful to understand and integrate the role of HRM within the business strategy of the organization [19].

The Harvard model is considered an analytical and normative model [19, 20], and a very prominent model in SHRM as it allows the analysis of the HRM business process within three sub-processes: making HRM strategy; implementing HRM strategy; monitoring impact on the organization's achievements [19].

The Harvard model (see Fig. 1), due to its characteristics, remains a good representation of the reality of HRM in organizational life with significant reflections on organizational outcomes [14, 15]. This model is particularly applied in SHRM because it explains how employee interests (such as adaptability to new working conditions) combined with changes in situational factors (like cultural transitions) lead to HRM policy choices (particularly regarding job design, training, performance appraisal, etc.), which in turn affect long-term consequences (such as productivity, job satisfaction, etc.) [14].

The Harvard model has been applied in several different contexts. For instance, Brunetto et al. (2011) within the Australian context of a shortage of skilled professionals, relied on the model to conceptualize how changes in stakeholder interests, combined with situational factors, influence public sector HRM policy choices and subsequently impact HRM outcomes for various public sector employees. It has also been applied to shed light on the HRM practices in the Indian manufacturing

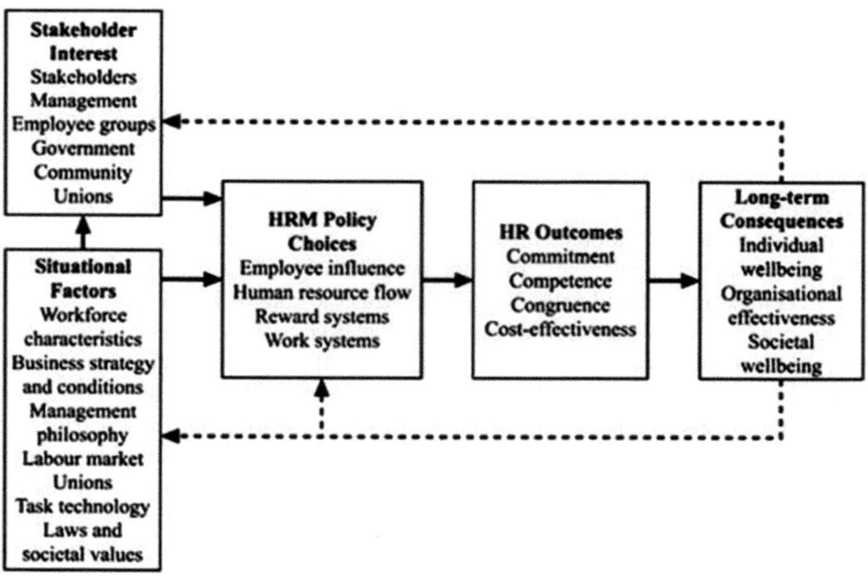

Fig. 1 The "Harvard Model" (Beer et al., 1985). Source: Beer et al. (1984), Fig. 2-1, p. 16, Map of the HRM Territory

sector and to understand the dynamic relationship between HRM practices and technological advancements [15, 21]. Its application is because the Harvard model provides a holistic perspective, integrating multiple stakeholders' interests—including employees, management, and society—into HR decision-making [14]. The model also stresses the importance of aligning HR policies with long-term organizational goals, which helps create a strategic, coherent approach when managing people. Additionally, it provides a framework for considering both internal factors, like organizational culture, and external influences, such as legal and economic conditions, making it adaptable to various contexts [22]. These strengths and broad scope make the Harvard Model a valuable tool for developing HR strategy in a way that balances diverse interests and promotes sustainable organizational success.

So far, its application in the context of a sustainable hybrid work environment still remains underexplored [18]. Therefore, we adopted this framework to provide a more contextualized view of the HRM role, and a broader perspective on stakeholders, with a wider, more long-term approach to organizational achievements [14, 15].

3 Methodology

3.1 Research Design

In this study, we employed a qualitative methodological approach using a single case study, specifically focusing on the organization "LARI" to explore the implementation of a hybrid work environment and the role of the HR department. This approach was selected due to its appropriateness in areas where empirical research is scant and crucial data for hypothesis development are lacking [23].

The method involves a deep dive into LARI's specific context, allowing for an intensive collection and analysis of data that reflects the unique experiences of workers and managers in developing new roles and services post-pandemic in Italy [24].

This single case study was chosen for its potential to provide detailed insights that could not be as readily extrapolated from a broader survey or multiple case studies [23]. Yin (2014) outlines that while single case studies provide deep insights, they are often criticized for their limited generalizability. However, when the case is well-chosen, it can offer rich, transferable knowledge that contributes to theory building. Furthermore, Eisenhardt, K. M. (1989) highlights the strength of a single case study in developing rich theoretical insights [25]. Despite some criticisms of this methodological approach, several authors have suggested the strengths of using a small sample for data collection if they provide compelling evidence that either supports or refines existing theories [26].

We selected the case study of "LARI" because of the following reasons. First, the company had not had the opportunity to experiment with hybrid working models before the pandemic. Before the pandemic, LARI was characterized by a culture heavily predicated on control. It operated with a traditional organizational structure, characterized by a clear hierarchy and a predominantly office-based work environment. Employees were primarily required to be physically present in the office, with designated workspaces and fixed working hours. Communication and collaboration were largely conducted face-to-face, with meetings and decision-making processes taking place in person. The structure was relatively rigid, with limited flexibility for remote work or alternative working arrangements. Departments functioned in silos, and the organization's emphasis was on maintaining standardized procedures and close supervision to ensure productivity and compliance with organizational policies.

The shift towards the new mode of work was significantly facilitated by the human resources department, and specifically by the new HR director hired during the pandemic. Thus, the case allows reconstruction of the interventions implemented by the HR Department from the onset of the pandemic up to 2024, deepening the understanding of how the role of the human resources department has illuminated strategic changes in its function. This investigation addresses the various facets of strategic human resource management, noting that both leadership and the organizational culture have undergone significant transformations within this 4-year temporal framework. Second, the company represents a case of successful implementation of a hybrid workplace, which obtained visibility at the local and national level, with the opportunity to monitor the impact of the HRM practice in the organizational context. In the case of "LARI", this Italian company operates under ATECO code 10.39, generated a 2022 revenue of 119 million euros, and employs around 150 individuals. The insights into this study were provided by the HR manager, four senior managers, and two collaborators.

By focusing on one exemplary case, the study aims to explore the complexity of implementing hybrid work models and the subsequent organizational transformations. This method is particularly valuable in capturing the lived experiences of individuals within the organization, thereby enriching the understanding of theoretical concepts in a real-world setting.

3.2 Data Collection and Research Protocol

The data collection for our case study of LARI adhered to foundational principles outlined by Yin (2014) including the use of multiple sources of evidence. We sought to ensure the reliability and completeness of the study through data triangulation, which allows for a more robust confirmation of research hypotheses. The sources included interviews with the HR manager, senior managers, and employees; company reports; websites; social media and relevant newspaper articles. We further triangulate data by looking at employee feedback about the company's work environment on different recruitment sites.

Following the methodologies recommended for case study research by Pagell (2004), and Yin (1999), our research framework included four main components: a semi-structured interview protocol, a targeted interview process, strategic respondent selection, and a detailed analysis strategy. The interviews were conducted via Zoom using a predefined set of questions to maintain uniformity while allowing flexibility to refine these questions after each session to deepen the relevance and insight into the topics discussed. A privacy notice was sent to participants in accordance with European regulations to ensure compliance and protect confidentiality. The interview protocol was structured following the components of the Harvard Model [14], to provide a comprehensive understanding of the strategic role of HR in implementing hybrid work environments.

We implemented a purposive sampling selecting individuals according to the following criteria: people who had been working in the company before the pandemic and were thus involved in a process of adaptation toward the hybrid work environment; respondents with different organizational perspectives in approaching the change (managers and collaborators); people with a different familiarity with and openness to remote working. We also selected people with careful consideration of gender, in order to identify possible differences in terms of expectations and benefits perceived by the HRM practices.

These approaches enabled the triangulation of data collected from interviews, a crucial process for ensuring the validity and reliability of our findings [27]. Regarding the data collection and coding: the data were collected through interviews of 90/120 min each and were initially transcribed with the aid of Panopto and subsequently reviewed by the authors. The data collection adhered to foundational principles outlined by Yin (2014) and it was distinguished into three phases [28, 29] (See Table 1).

The coding of the interviews was conducted by the authors following the framework of the Harvard model, identifying the items of each construct.

4 Findings

The findings that emerged from the analysis of the case are represented in Fig. 2.

The company we selected has a long-standing history of adhering to traditional working practices and had not previously experimented with hybrid work models before the pandemic. In recognizing the evolving nature of work environments, the company made substantial investments in its HR department to facilitate this transition by hiring a new HR manager in 2021. In implementing the new work model, the company extensively rely on its core values which are reported as follows: commitment to employee wellbeing; innovation and adaptability; community engagement; sustainability; and collaboration and inclusivity.

Table 1 Data sources

	Phase 1	Phase 2	Phase 3
Research task	Acculturation, identification of key parties, trust-building	Understanding of practices, development of analytical framework (theoretical focus emerges)	Empathetic understanding (inside view) and critical reflection on previous findings, more fine-grained perspective (critical view)
Internal document	Company hybrid work policy; Company training programmes	Company training programmes	Company documents on the redesign of the performance management system; Company training programmes
Media archive	Reports from the national observatory on smart working; articles published in the national and local press	Sustainability reports available on the company website; articles published in the company's social media platforms; articles published in national and local press and business magazines	Reports from national research institutes
Interviews	HR manager (200 min); Marketing Manager (120 min).	Accountant supervisor (100 min); Export manager (100 min); Customer service (90 min) Sustainability and CSR manager (120 min)	Food Regulatory Affairs Manager (120 min) HR manager (90 min)

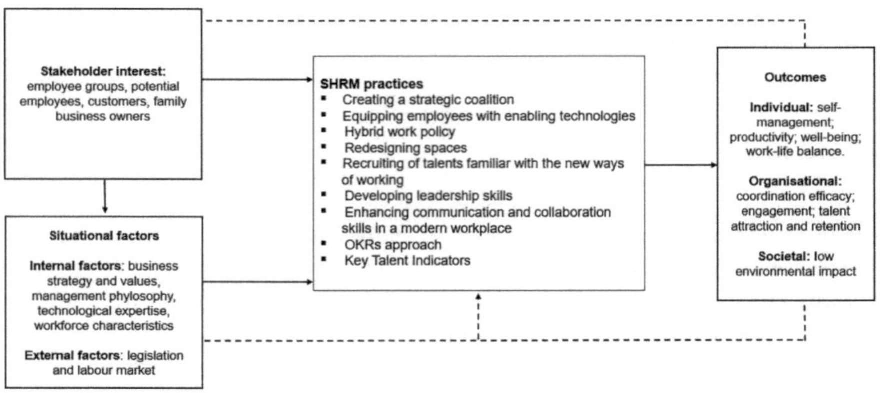

Fig. 2 LARI application of the Harvard model

4.1 Stakeholder Interest

In the context of the Harvard model, stakeholder interest refers to the importance of recognizing and integrating the various interests and expectations of all parties who are impacted by or have an influence on the organization.

In LARI, the primary stakeholder interests are the expectations of current and prospective employees. After a successful hybrid work trial, other departments, including customer service, marketing, and sales, requested similar arrangements. Feedback from a long-ignored suggestion box highlighted demands for more hybrid work and consistency across departments. Employees also expressed a desire for a better work-life balance, reflecting post-pandemic needs. Since 2001, their reputation has attracted candidates, but younger generations now prioritize hybrid work for better life balance.

> After an initial trial period of hybrid work of a shortened week involving a pilot group, the first requests also came from other company departments, including customer service in Italy and abroad, marketing, and sales in Italy; thus, all other employees who worked at the same location (HR manager).

> Upon entering the company, I came across a suggestion box that appeared untouched for quite some time, as indicated by the thick layer of dust covering it. Inside, I found numerous employee notes expressing a desire for increased opportunities for smart working, stronger discipline, and greater consistency across departments—concerns that had clearly surfaced in the aftermath of the pandemic (HR manager).

> No, I no longer want to live this life of being away from home for five days. So, I was the first person involved, but I must reiterate, fortunately, I also had many young people from my team (Marketing manager).

4.2 Situational Factors

Situational factors influence that impact the effectiveness of HR policies and practices within an organization. These factors provide the context in which HR strategies are formulated and implemented, and they can vary widely depending on a range of variables. The application of the LARI case allowed for the identification of internal and external situational factors. The former includes the management philosophy, the values of the organization, the level of digitalization in processes, the quality of remote facilities, and the characteristics of the workforce. Each of these factors plays a role in the design and effectiveness of HRM strategies, as explained by the HR manager:

> This is a company that, pre-pandemic, always operated in person. The company, both in terms of values and approach, has favored presence not out of a command-and-control logic, but because it is an entrepreneurial company that values connections, proximity to family, and the business (HR manager).

The external factors relevant to the case encompass the legislation that regulates the hybrid work arrangements and the characteristics of the labor market. Concerning the legal frameworks, in Italy Law No. 81/2017 established the basic rules for remote work, allowing employees to work outside the traditional office environment without a fixed location, as long as the tasks can be completed as per the employment contract. Starting in February 2020, following the spread of the COVID-19 pandemic, Italy implemented several measures to facilitate and maximize the adoption of smart working. Notably, Legislative Decree No. 6 of February 23, 2020, established smart working automatically in all employment relationships within areas deemed at risk during national or local emergencies, even without individual agreements typically required by law. Subsequent directives and regulations further emphasized flexible working arrangements to ensure the continuity of public services while protecting the health of citizens and workers. From January 1, 2024, smart working ended for public administration employees in Italy. However, it was extended until March 31, 2024, for private-sector parents with children under 14 years old and vulnerable workers, as per Article 18-bis of Law No. 191/2023.

As far as the characteristics of the labor market, the geographical location of LARI also significantly impacts its ability to recruit individuals with specialized skills. LARI was struggling to fill specific roles, therefore this scarcity required more innovative HR strategies, such as broader remote work policies that allow hiring beyond the local talent pool. The following quote exemplifies the aforementioned factors:

> The decision to adopt this approach was influenced, in my view, by the company's specific logistical requirements and the difficulty in finding staff willing to relocate. The pandemic has demonstrated the effectiveness of remote work, encouraging the company to offer greater flexibility (Sustainability e CSR manager).

> When the department expanded and I was looking for skills, people who already had a solid background, I recruited them from other companies, not from here in LARI. So, it's clear that I was the one who felt the impact of hybrid work more than my colleagues in other functions (HR manager).

4.3 SHRM Practices

The strategic application of SHRM practices in response to the identified stakeholder interests and situational factors include:

1. Creating a strategic coalition: forming alliances to align HR strategies with organizational goals for effective implementation.
2. Equipping employees with enabling technologies: Providing essential tools and technology for employees to work efficiently in hybrid environments.
3. Hybrid work policy: Implementing flexible work arrangements that combine remote and in-office work to enhance productivity.

4. Redesigning spaces: modifying physical workspaces to support both remote and on-site work environments seamlessly.
5. Recruiting talents familiar with new ways of working: hiring individuals adept in hybrid and flexible work setups for optimal team integration.
6. Developing leadership skills: training leaders to effectively manage, motivate, and support hybrid and remote teams.
7. Enhancing communication and collaboration skills: improving interpersonal skills for effective teamwork and communication in hybrid work settings.
8. OKRs approach: using Objectives and Key Results to align team efforts with company objectives and measure progress.
9. Key Talent Indicators: Identifying metrics to track talent acquisition, retention, and performance within the organization.

4.4 Outcomes

The implementation of these SHRM practices aims to achieve outcomes at three levels:

- Societal: such as reducing the organisation's environmental impact.
- Organisational: Enhancing coordination efficacy, improving engagement, and retaining top talent.
- Individual: Improving self-management, performance, productivity, well-being, and work-life balance.

The following quotes exemplify the perceived benefits derived from the new way of working.

> The working mode we have adopted not only does not take away time and energy but has proven to be more productive, improving both the company atmosphere and the efficiency and effectiveness of work (Sustainability and CSR manager).

> With the adoption of Teams as the primary communication platform, work-related exchanges have shifted away from WhatsApp. This transition has notably enhanced communication efficiency across the company, while also streamlining the management of phone contacts by reducing the need to route calls through the switchboard (Sustainability and CSR manager).

> We aim to concentrate office presence on specific days of smart working, partly for energy-saving reasons (Senior accountant).

> Office spaces have adapted to the new working mode, with more available workstations on smart working days and an office organization that promotes energy saving and sustainability (Senior accountant).

5 Managerial Implications and Future Research Directions

The study by tailoring the model in the context of hybrid work allowed the identification of the most salient HRM practices, providing a detailed description of their implementation. This means breaking down broader SHRM practices into more specific, targeted actions that can be more directly aligned with outcomes.

Our findings also show that to make the model more applicable and accepted by the management and the employees, a detailed framework for monitoring the outcomes attained is required. This allows for real-time tracking and analysis of the results of implemented SHRM practices, enabling an ongoing narrative about their effectiveness. By providing such a dashboard, organisations can better engage with the data, fostering a deeper understanding and responsiveness to the evolving needs of the workplace. However, in the context of hybrid work, the effectiveness of HRM policies should be evaluated based on their quality and impact rather than their quantity, providing a more nuanced understanding of their true effectiveness. Therefore, future research may investigate the real impact of each practice within organisations.

Further work is required to identify contextual factors that may differentiate the HR department approach in designing the SHRM practices, however, the preliminary evidence of the study offers new insights and a more nuanced application of the Harvard model, facilitating adaptations that better meet the specific needs and circumstances of different organisations that are in transition toward a hybrid work model. Future research should explore the trade-offs associated with the environmental impact of hybrid work, particularly the shift in energy costs from employers to employees. While hybrid work may reduce transportation-related carbon emissions, it could potentially increase overall energy consumption as employees incur higher energy costs at home, such as for heating, cooling, and powering devices. Additionally, future studies could investigate variations in employee responses to hybrid work based on factors such as gender, age, nationality, corporate area of affiliation, and tenure. These demographic variations could provide valuable insights into how different groups experience hybrid work.

6 Conclusion and Limitations

The study represents the first attempt to apply the Harvard model within the context of a sustainable work environment. The study advances the literature on SHRM and adds to the emerging field of study on hybrid working, providing an understanding of how the HR department may play a strategic role in supporting the organization and their leaders to navigate the complexity of the new way of working.

The model that emerged from the case emphasizes a systems approach where the various SHRM elements interact dynamically. This finding underlines the importance of aligning HRM practices with both internal and external environmental factors to enhance organizational performance and stakeholder satisfaction.

To be sustainable over time, the creation and implementation of a hybrid work environment require a continuous dialogue with stakeholders which translates into a process of co-design of HRM practice, which is progressively adjusted based on the adaptability demonstrated by the different parties.

This study is not free from limitations. In particular, we acknowledge that the Harvard model has several limitations as highlighted in the literature. One major critique is that it tends to be overly prescriptive and idealistic, assuming a level of alignment between stakeholders' interests and organisational goals that may not exist in practice [14]. Additionally, it often overlooks the practical challenges of implementation in diverse organisational contexts, making it less applicable in rapidly changing or less structured environments [22]. These limitations suggest that while the Harvard Model provides a valuable framework, it must be applied with caution, considering its potential gaps in addressing real-world organisational complexities.

References

1. Nagel, L. (2020). The influence of the COVID-19 pandemic on the digital transformation of work. *Int. J. Sociol. Soc. Policy., 40*, 861–875. https://doi.org/10.1108/IJSSP-07-2020-0323
2. Trevor, J., Holweg, M. (2022). Managing the New Tensions of Hybrid Work. *MIT Sloan Manag Rev.* 64
3. Aguiléra, A., Lethiais, V., Rallet, A., & Proulhac, L. (2016). Home-based telework in France: Characteristics, barriers and perspectives. *Transp. Res. Part Policy Pract., 92*, 1–11. https://doi.org/10.1016/j.tra.2016.06.021
4. Bailey, D., & Kurland, N. (2002). A review of telework research: Findings, new directions, and lessons for the study of modern work. *J. Organ. Behav., 23*, 383–400. https://doi.org/10.1002/job.144
5. Drumea, C. (2020). Work-related stress and subsequent productivity in a teleworking environment induced by pandemic-related confinement. Evidence from the public organizations. *Ovidius Univ. Ann. Econ. Sci. Ser., XX*, 337–341.
6. Bader, V., & Kaiser, S. (2017). Autonomy and control? how heterogeneous sociomaterial assemblages explain paradoxical rationalities in the digital workplace. *Manag. Rev., 28*, 338–358.
7. Bullini Orlandi, L., Veglianti, E., Zardini, A., & Rossignoli, C. (2024). Enhancing employees' remote work experience: Exploring the role of organizationaljob resources. *Technol. Forecast. Soc. Change., 199*(123), 075. https://doi.org/10.1016/j.techfore.2023.123075
8. Xie, J. L., Elangovan, A., & r., Hu, J., Hrabluik, C. (2019). Charting new terrain in work design: A study of hybrid work characteristics. *Appl. Psychol., 68*, 479–512. https://doi.org/10.1111/apps.12169
9. Pillai, S. V., & Prasad, J. (2022). Investigating the key success metrics for WFH/remote work models. *Ind. Commer. Train., 55*, 19–33. https://doi.org/10.1108/ICT-07-2021-0053
10. Lawler McHugh, T., Vinas, K. (2024). Trends - Boston College Center for Work & Family.
11. Otte, B. (2024). Recruiting for the hybrid generation. Tips for creating a successful business landscape through mentorship programs. *Strateg. HR Rev., 23*, 55–58. https://doi.org/10.1108/SHR-12-2023-0072

12. Gohoungodji, P., N'Dri, A. B., & Matos, A. L. B. (2023). What makes telework work? Evidence of success factors across two decades of empirical research: a systematic and critical review. *Int. J. Hum. Resour. Manag. 34*, 605–649 (2023). https://doi.org/10.1080/09585192.2022.2112259
13. Cascio, W. F. (2019). Training trends: Macro, micro, and policy issues. *Hum. Resour. Manag. Rev., 29*, 284–297. https://doi.org/10.1016/j.hrmr.2017.11.001
14. Beer, M., Spector, B., Lawrence, P., Mills, D., & Walton, R. (1985). Human resource management: A general manager's perspective. *Presented at the, 1985.*
15. Bondarouk, T., & Brewster, C. (2016). Conceptualising the future of HRM and technology research. *Int. J. Hum. Resour. Manag., 27*, 2652–2671. https://doi.org/10.1080/09585192.2016.1232296
16. Cuel, R., Cacciatore, E., Ravarini, A., & Varriale, L. (2022). Do organizations need a head of remote work? In R. Cuel, D. Ponte, & F. Virili (Eds.), *Exploring Digital Resilience* (pp. 274–286). Springer International Publishing. https://doi.org/10.1007/978-3-031-10,902-7_19
17. Elvira, M., & Davila, A. (2005). Emergent directions for human resource management: Research in Latin America. *Int. J. Hum. Resour. Manag., 16*. https://doi.org/10.1080/09585190500358703
18. Verma, A., Venkatesan, M., Kumar, M., & Verma, J. (2022). The future of work post Covid-19: Key perceived HR implications of hybrid workplaces in India. *J. Manag. Dev., 42*, 13–28. https://doi.org/10.1108/JMD-11-2021-0304
19. Cakar, F., Bititci, U. S., & MacBryde, J. (2003). A business process approach to human resource management. *Bus. Process Manag. J., 9*, 190–207. https://doi.org/10.1108/14637150310468
20. Torrington, D., & Hall, L. (1987). Personnel management: A new approach. *Prentice-Hall, 1987.*
21. Budhwar, P. S., & Khatri, N. (2001). HRM in context: Applicability of HRM models in India. *Int. J. Cross Cult. Manag., 1*, 333–356. https://doi.org/10.1177/147059580113005
22. Boxall, P., & Purcell, J. (2003). Strategy and human resource management. *Ind. Labor Relat. Rev., 57*. https://doi.org/10.1108/00251740310479368
23. Yin, R. K. (2014). *Case study research: design and methods*. SAGE.
24. Klaser, K., Cuel, R., & Casari, P. (2023). The future of hybrid work in Italy: A survey-based socio-technical-system analysis. *J. Innov. Knowl., 8*(100), 426. https://doi.org/10.1016/j.jik.2023.100426
25. Eisenhardt, K. M. (1989). Building theories from case study research. *Acad. Manage. Rev., 14*, 532–550. https://doi.org/10.2307/258557
26. Siggelkow, N. (2007). Persuasion with case studies. *Acad. Manage. J., 50*, 20–24. https://doi.org/10.5465/amj.2007.24160882
27. Jonsen, K., & Jehn, K. (2009). Using triangulation to validate themes in qualitative studies. *Qual. Res. Organ. Manag. Int. J., 4*, 123–150. https://doi.org/10.1108/17465640910978391
28. Cloutier, C., & Ravasi, D. (2021). Using tables to enhance trustworthiness in qualitative research. *Strateg. Organ., 19*, 113–133. https://doi.org/10.1177/1476127020979329
29. Farny, S., Kibler, E., & Down, S. (2019). Collective emotions in institutional creation work. *Acad. Manage. J., 62*, 765–799. https://doi.org/10.5465/amj.2016.0711

Gig Work in Organizations: Demystifying the Perspectives of Human Resource Management Professionals

Vindhya Singh, Aizhan Tursunbayeva, Ksenia Keplinger, and Stefano Di Lauro

Abstract The gig economy has expanded beyond platform-based work and is also transforming standard organizations that are accustomed to stable employment arrangements and long-term-oriented HRM practices. The shift towards gig workers and blended teams disrupts standard HR practices due to the short-term, transactional nature of gig work. This research investigates the implications of gig work on HRM practices in standard organizations. Specifically, we (1) examine the trends and perspectives of HR professionals on the use of gig work in standard organizations, (2) investigate whether HR professionals apply standard HRM practices for gig workers, and (3) conduct a longitudinal analysis of HRM perspectives applicable to gig workers before and post-COVID-19 pandemic. To achieve these research objectives, we employ natural language processing techniques to analyze more than 500 YouTube videos of HR professionals offering their opinions about gig work. The findings suggest that despite the widely conceived notion that gig workers are 'self-managed', various HRM practices are utilized in the context of gig work.

Keywords Gig work · HRM practices · Natural language processing

---

V. Singh · K. Keplinger (✉)
Max Planck Institute for Intelligent Systems, Stuttgart, Germany
e-mail: kkeplinger@is.mpg.de

A. Tursunbayeva
Department of Business and Economics, University of Naples "Parthenope", Naples, Italy

S. Di Lauro
Universitas Mercatorum, Rome, Italy

A. Tursunbayeva et al. (eds.), *Technology-Driven Transformation*, Lecture Notes in Information Systems and Organisation 79,
https://doi.org/10.1007/978-3-032-01396-5_5

1 Introduction

Gig work has emerged as a prominent labor phenomenon, recently attracting substantial attention from scholars and practitioners [1]. The term 'gig work' refers to a rapidly growing segment of the workforce [2], defined as "labor contracted and compensated on a short-term basis to organizations or individual clients through an external labor market" [3]. Gig workers are freelance contractors who hop between short-term work assignments, creating portfolios of jobs and often taking on multiple assignments with several organizations simultaneously [4]. They find their clients and customers through digital platforms and/or staffing agencies [5].

The gig workforce has a substantial impact on both individuals and organizations [6]. The standard employment arrangements are characterized by long-term commitments, open-ended structures, and emotional bonds [7]. These are often achieved through Human Resources Management (HRM) practices throughout the employee life cycle, including recruitment, training, and development, as well as career and succession planning. The increased use of gig workers and/or blended teams of standard and gig workers disrupts and transforms standard HRM practices due to the transactional, short-term nature of gig work. However, most scholarly efforts so far have focused on the experiences of gig workers and how individuals adapt to this new way of working, thus overlooking how organizations manage and integrate gig workers into workforce ecosystems. In their systematic literature review, Gautam and colleagues [8] found that studies on gig work "are not only a few in number but also widely scattered". However, there has been a rapid rise in the number of publications on gig work, emphasizing the need to evaluate HRM practices applicable to gig workers. Hence, this research focuses on investigating trends and perspectives of HR professionals on the adoption of gig work arrangements in standard organizations and the management of gig workers. Furthermore, by drawing on these perspectives, we investigate whether and how HR professionals apply standard HRM practices to the gig work context (gig workers are broadly acknowledged as 'self-managed' workers). In particular, we collected more than 500 YouTube videos featuring HR professionals discussing the ways of employing and managing gig workers in their organizations. We employed Natural Language Processing (NLP) techniques to analyze these videos, a methodology rapidly gaining traction in management research due to its ability to automatically model topics and generate theories from textual data [9, 10].

Our paper makes several significant contributions. First, it advances the literature on gig work by providing valuable insights into HRM perspectives on gig work in standard organizations and by demystifying how HRM practices are evolving with the rise of gig workers. Second, this research gives voice to a group of stakeholders often overlooked in the literature—HR professionals involved in hiring and managing gig workers to better accommodate their needs. Third, it develops a novel domain-specific dictionary for management researchers and utilizes state-of-the-art Artificial Intelligence (AI) models to extract insights from video data, showcasing the potential of human-machine collaboration in academic research. Fourth, it fosters interdisciplinary collaboration between management researchers and computer scientists by developing a fully functional automated pipeline that searches and fetches videos from YouTube, filters relevant content, converts it to audio, and transcribes it into text for NLP-based analysis.

2 Literature Review

The rise of the gig economy has resulted in multiple challenges for standard organizations, particularly in managing gig workers' performance [11]. Although a vast span of literature exists from the point of view of gig workers, several researchers suggested expanding the viewpoint to include the perspective of HR professionals [3, 12]. An interesting observation emerged from our literature research, indicating a divergence in perceptions towards gig work. On the one hand, some researchers fear that introducing HRM practices into gig work will hamper the flexibility and intrinsic nature of gig workers [13, 14]. On the other hand, other researchers have already examined the intersection of traditional HRM practices with the relatively newer work arrangements in the gig economy [15]. Furthermore, many call for a paradigm shift, urging HRM to include freelancers and independent workers, going beyond the standard organizational boundaries [16, 17].

This disparity in perspectives underscores the complexity and precarious nature of gig work. Previous research on the use of HRM in gig work highlights the collaborative value creation through diverse exchanges among gig workers, employers, and intermediary platform firms [18]. This discussion has been further advanced by examining the role of organizational needs and freelancers' psychological contracts in integrating HRM into gig workers' employment [3, 12]. Gig work fundamentally alters people management processes, as technology takes over some traditional HR tasks [19]. Roles, such as procurement and platform managers, become more pivotal. To sum up, recent studies detail the HRM responsibility shifts, outline new duties associated with gig work, and offer theoretical and practical recommendations for standard organizations adopting gig work. However, these studies miss the perspectives of HR professionals themselves, who are conceptualizing and implementing HR practices for gig workers.

The present research aims to fill this research gap, answering the following research question: "What are the HRM practices utilized by standard organizations for managing gig workers (initially perceived as self-managed workers)?

3 Research Methods

To analyze HR professionals' perspectives on gig workers in standard organizations, we selected keywords to access relevant YouTube videos. After applying filtering rules, we transcribed the videos using a Large Language Model (LLM).

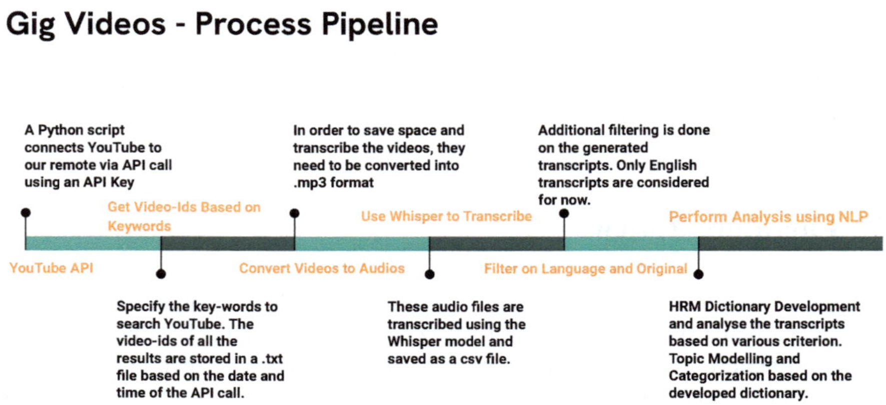

Fig. 1 Overview of data collection and data analysis processes

Using NLP techniques, we identified topics and prominent HRM practices discussed by professionals in the final dataset (see Fig. 1).

3.1 *Keyword Selection*

The first step was to create a dataset with suitable videos of HR professionals voicing their opinions about the role of gig work in organizations. We compiled a list of gig work-related keywords based on existing literature reviews. Additionally, we augmented these gig work-related keywords with two HRM-related terms, 'HRM practice' and 'human resource management,' as recommended by Bos-Nehles and colleagues [20]. We used the search string ('gig economy' OR 'gig work' OR 'HR interviews on gig economy') to scrape YouTube, the world's largest video website. The following Table 1 gives a summary of the keyword lists used and the final list of keywords that were used in our search. (*Keywords in bold are those shared between these two recent literature reviews on gig work.)

3.2 *Data Collection and Data Analysis*

Our initial search yielded approximately. 31,670 videos. We removed duplicates, videos unrelated to the gig workforce management, and videos simply explaining the terms and concepts in the gig economy. As we were specifically interested in the perspectives of HR professionals, we included videos of only those individuals who defined themselves as HR professionals and/or HR consultants in our dataset. We classified individuals as HR professionals and consultants if their titles included any of the HRM-related keywords, such as HR, Human Resources, People, Workforce, Employee, Human Capital, Manpower, Staff, Personnel, and Talent [21].

Table 1 Identifying relevant keywords

Research Paper	Keywords*
Kaine and Josserand, 2019	**'gig economy, work/**labour'; **'on-demand** economy, **work,** labour'; 'platform economy, work, labour'; 'digital work, worker'; 'micro-tasking'; 'crowd economy, work, labour'; 'uberization of economy, work, labour'; 'uber work, 'labour', 'collaborative economy, work', 'ride-sharing'; and 'amazon mechanical turk'
Cropanzano et al., 2023	'contract work,' **'gig economy,'** 'independent work,' **'gig work,' 'on-demand work,'** 'freelance,' 'digital nomad,' 'contingent work,' 'multiple jobholder,' and 'plural careerist.'
Additional Keywords	'gig economy,' 'gig work', 'HR interviews on gig economy'

Table 2 Details contained in the *snippet* object of the YouTube API

Properties	Description
snippet (object)	contains basic details such as the title and description of a search result
snippet.publishedAt (datetime)	date and time of creation for the video, downloaded based on the search criteria
snippet.liveBroadcastContent (string)	indicator of whether or not a video contains live broadcast content

Considering that scholars also have an important role in shaping the HR profession, we also included videos of HR scholars in our analysis. Further inclusion criteria were the language of the videos (English) [22], and their duration (longer than 2 min) [23]. These criteria were chosen to ensure sufficient informative content and quality of each video, as well as to ensure the videos were more likely to be the videos that other HR professionals would watch.

When an API call is made to YouTube to download videos based on keywords, one is provided with the option to download either *videos*, *channels*, or *playlists*. We downloaded the *videos* as we did not want to limit ourselves to specific *channels* or *playlists*. The YouTube API snippet (*snippet.liveBroadcastContent*), as shown in Table 2, indicated if videos were "live" or "upcoming." We excluded these videos because 'live' broadcasts were too long to analyze (the longest broadcast duration: 8 hours and 29 minutes), and 'upcoming' videos yielded no results.

Following the application of these filtering criteria, a total of 532 videos met the established standards. For a thorough analytical overview, we systematically retrieved metadata associated with all filtered videos, utilizing YouTube's API.

The next task of our process pipeline involved converting videos to audio. This step was required primarily for two reasons. First, to generate a high-quality transcription, we used Whisper, an automatic speech recognition system trained on 680,000 hours of supervised data collected from the web [24]. This model is limited to converting audio to text and lacks the functionality to convert videos to text. Second, to save memory space for further processing and analysis, we opted for audio files, making use of the Pytube Python library for the conversion of the video files to audio files in an MP3 format. The Pytube Python library was used for this purpose as it is a lightweight library with no third-party dependencies.

We downloaded 532 YouTube video IDs using the YouTube API. Of these, 481 video IDs remained after removing the duplicates. As we converted the videos to audio, 459 files remained. Some videos could not be downloaded as audio because they were 'Age Restricted' and required logging in. As we wished to scrape videos without restriction and the need to log in to YouTube, we were left with 459 audio files. Finally, the audios were transcribed, and we were left with 423 transcribed files. From the date of scraping to the date of transcription, there was a window of two weeks. During that time, some videos were removed, some changed their privacy settings, and some videos contained only music, so their transcription was impossible.

Next, we applied NLP quantitative techniques, such as topic modeling, on the transcripts generated from Whisper, to identify thematic groups based on probability distributions. This was done using the BERTopic model [25]. To get the best analytical insights from the text, we first cleaned the text and removed any mention of numerals, websites, or special characters. Next, we tokenized the text before feeding it to the BERTopic model and training it. Following the training of our BERTopic model, we iteratively examined various topics. The BERTopic model uses the c-TF-IDF score to generate features from textual documents based on the class they belong to. Essentially, c-TF-IDF is adopted for multiple classes by joining all documents per class from the TF-IDF formula. TF-IDF score is a product of Term Frequency (the frequency of any 'term' or word in a given 'document') and Inverse Document Frequency (IDF) accounts for the ratio of documents that include a specific 'term' or word. In our case, documents refer to the transcribed file of each YouTube video. However, unlike TF-IDF, which treats each document separately, c-TF-IDF groups all the documents belonging to the same class together. Therefore, each class comprises a single document, rather than a collection of documents. Additionally, we created a similarity matrix using cosine similarities for both c-TF-IDF and Transformers-based topic embeddings.

3.3 Dictionary Development and Categorisation

To identify HR practices utilized for managing gig workers in standard organizations, we adhered to the best practices in dictionary development [26]. In particular, we searched for the keyword "Human resource management" in article titles within the Scopus database in March 2024. This search brought 6506 returns. For all these records, we extracted the 20,164 "Author keywords". These were downloaded and analyzed in an Excel file. After removing 10,893 duplicate values, 9271 unique keywords remained. Separately, we conducted an additional search of scholarly articles relevant to HRM to identify a wide range of HRM practices.

Two authors independently coded the 9271 keywords into broad HRM practices categories. 59 percent of these were coded under the "Other" category because they were too broad to assign them to any specific HRM practice (e.g., 'Awareness', 'Analytic Hierarchy process', or 'Business strategy'). Subsequently, these independent codings were then reviewed by the remaining two authors. The inter-coder reliability was 97%, with coders disagreeing on only 253 keywords. These 253 keywords were discussed by the entire research team to identify the most suitable category. For instance, we discussed the keyword "Collaboration" assigned by one of the coders to the category "Motivation", and by another one to "Employee Relations", and agreed on the final assignment to the "Employee Relations" category. Next, we categorized transcripts into HRM practices (based on our developed dictionary) using string matching with a Python script.

4 Results

Although videos related to gig work have been present since 2015, a notable surge in discussions on gig work occurred particularly during and after the COVID-19 pandemic (2019–2021). Notably, more than half of the videos addressing gig work (281 out of 523) were published in 2023, indicating a rapidly growing contemporary interest and discourse on this subject (see Fig. 2).

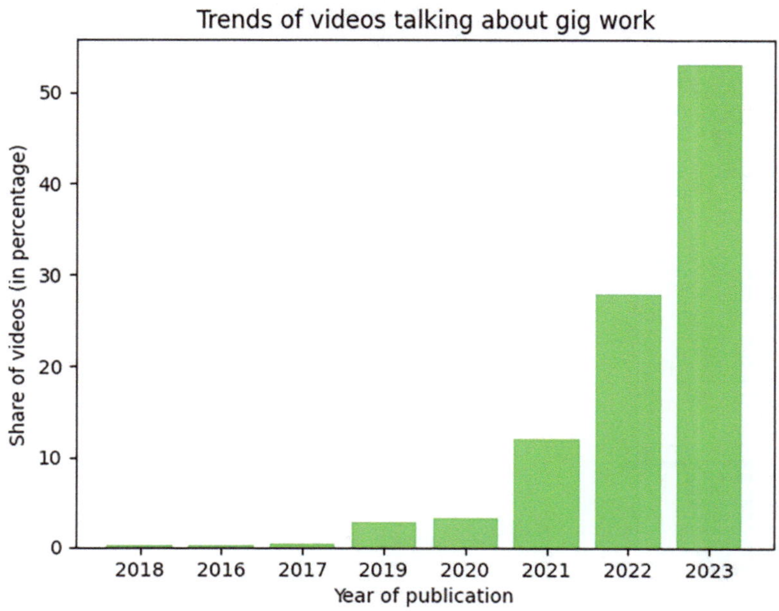

Fig. 2 YouTube videos featuring gig work in recent years

4.1 Topic Analysis: Overall and Post-COVID-19 Pandemic

Further, we explored the content of the videos, generating bar charts using c-TF-IDF scores to represent the prominence of topics. By selecting 10 descriptive words for each of the Top 20 automatically generated topics, we derived valuable insights from assessing the relative c-TF-IDF scores within and across topics. Through a manual review of the Top 20 topics, we identified and filtered the most coherent nine topics (see Fig. 3).

The analyzed video content encompasses various themes, including discussions on the gig economy and HRM practices. Some topics emphasize gig work as the future of employment, while others explore its transformative impact on standard working arrangements, notably the rise of work from home. A significant aspect is the examination of the growing freelancer population and its influence on standard working styles. Noteworthy discussions involve HR professionals addressing talent retention and the hiring of gig workers. In specific industries like technology and finance, there is a focus on gig workers as a contingent workforce, which is evident in top words, such as tech, companies, contingent workforce, and talent management from the Talent Management topic. Some videos attribute changes in the U.S. job landscape to the impact of the COVID-19 pandemic, while others highlight the role of AI in reshaping various industries. Upon in-depth examination of the video content, a notable upward trend is discerned in HR professionals' discussions about gig work, its impact, and the recent changes it has introduced (see Fig. 4).

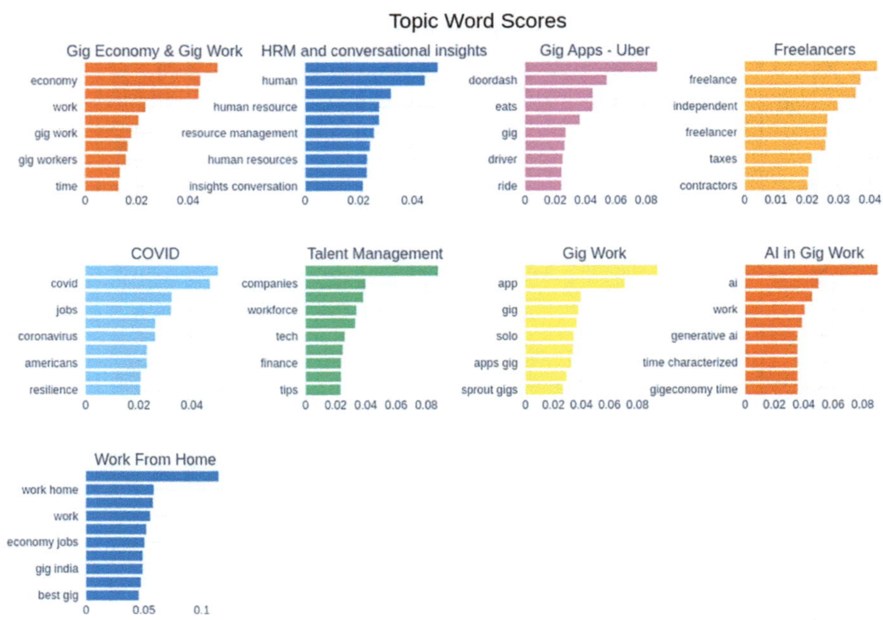

Fig. 3 Most discussed topics in our dataset. The bars represent the c-TF-IDF scores for each topic representation

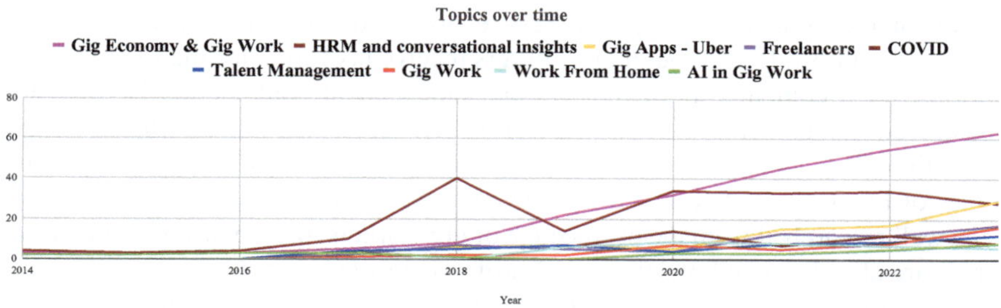

Fig. 4 Trends of topics as they emerged over a period of time

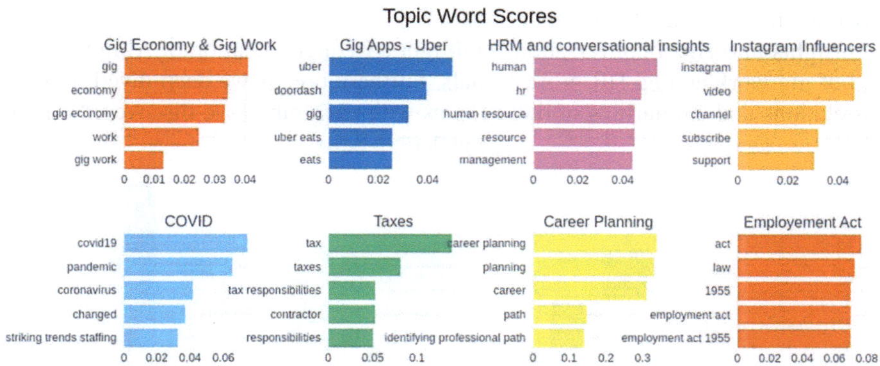

Fig. 5 Most frequently occurring topics post-COVID. The bars represent the c-TF-IDF scores for each topic representation

As COVID-19 appeared to be one of the most prominent topics, we delved deeper into this topic to understand the trends and evaluate the topics that emerged during and after the COVID-19 pandemic.

Our findings (see Fig. 5, Topic: Instagram Influencers) corroborate a recent study that analyzed and classified different platforms utilized by workers in the gig economy [27]. The study proposed five platform types, with one belonging to the subset of social media, encompassing workers categorized as content producers and influencers. These workers perform aspirational labor [28]. In our analysis, it appears to be a prominent topic during and after the COVID-19 pandemic, likely due to many individuals losing their regular jobs and turning to content production and influencer roles from their homes.

Additionally, within the topic of COVID-19, there were already discussions about the striking trends in hiring. Both in the overall and in-depth (post-COVID-19) topic analyses, HRM topics emerged prominently. This further draws attention to the fact that even though gig workers are usually perceived to be self-managed, with their rising presence in standard organizations, HRM practices are needed to manage them. These findings accentuate the fact that to integrate gig workers into workforce ecosystems, more often than not, discussing HRM practices is a need of the hour.

One theme for identifying gig workers revolves around their tax status and legal classification [29]. Even though gig workers receive tax forms for the services they perform for a company as freelancers and independent contractors, they are not considered standard employees and therefore often lack the same benefits and legal protection. This essence is very well captured by our topic modeling results. The topics of Freelancers, Taxes, and Employment Act capture this nuance, which has been well researched from the perspective of gig workers, but we discover that these topics are also discussed widely by HR professionals (see Fig. 5).

To gain further insights, we created a similarity matrix using cosine similarities for both c-TF-IDF and Transformers-based topic embeddings (see Fig. 6). This matrix visually represents the degree of similarity among specific topics. The topic 'Gig Economy' exhibits a high correlation with discussions involving apps like Uber and the COVID-19 pandemic.

Insights into HRM conversations highlight a frequent mention of AI in the context of gig work among HR professionals. Furthermore, as we deep-dived into the correlations and similarities of these topics with each other, we discovered a high

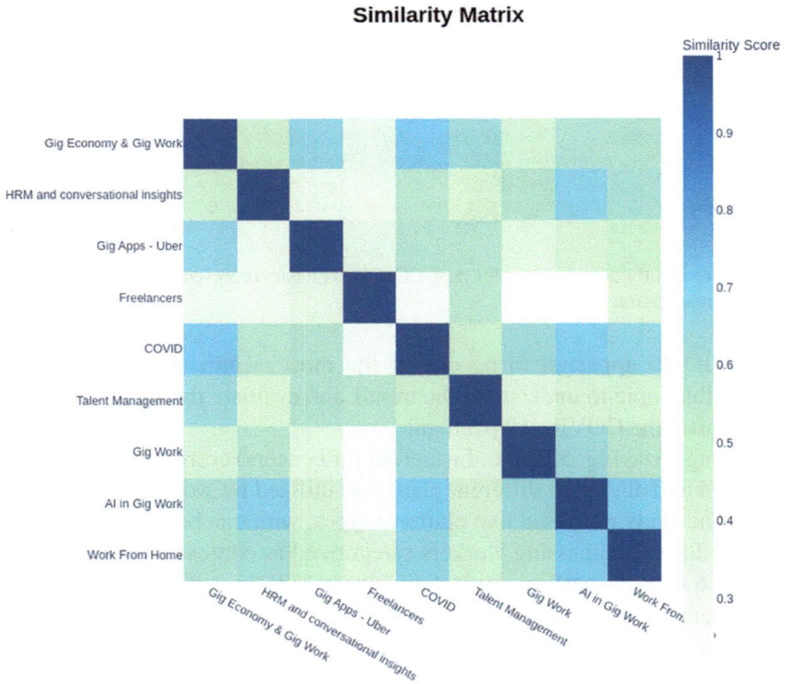

Fig. 6 Topic similarity matrix

degree of correlation between certain topics such as 'Gig Economy' and 'COVID'. Our findings align with studies done by researchers who analyzed the risks and possibilities for the special case of gig workers in the COVID-19 pandemic [30]. These topics exhibit a high co-occurrence because they have been studied together by both the researchers and practitioners of the domain, and HR professionals are no exception. There is also a high degree of correlation in topics such as 'Gig Economy' and 'Gig apps-Uber', as evidenced by prominent case studies about Uber or Doordash, such as the one conducted by Berger and colleagues [31].

In our dataset, the top three countries mentioned in the HRM conversations were India, the USA, and the UK (in descending order of the frequency of their mention).

4.2 *HRM Practices Applied to Gig Workers*

To explore the HRM practices specifically addressed by HR professionals in YouTube videos discussing gig work in standard organizations, we developed a novel, domain-specific dictionary and categorized the data accordingly.

Our findings (see Fig. 7) suggest that the category of Training and Development comprised the highest percentage of the discussions of HR professionals in our dataset (14.39%). Specifically, the HRM practices utilized in the gig work context included tailoring onboarding processes to gig workers to be short and easy to access, facilitating ongoing communication, and offering non-permanent staff training to enhance specific skills (as employers aim to attract talent for specific projects). Discussions revolved around but were not limited to companies being able to adopt a training platform or an app that enables gig workers to enroll, create profiles, and pre-qualify for gigs based on their work and training experience. This would synchronize work opportunities from job providers with the available gigs for qualified gig workers without requiring formal job interviews and commitments. Contrary to the assumption in the literature, which portrays gig workers as solely

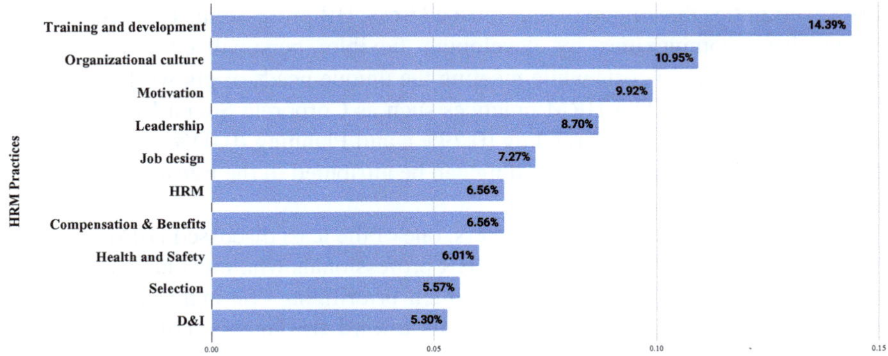

Fig. 7 Top 10 HRM practices discussed by HR professionals in the gig work context

responsible for their training and development [3], our results suggest that HR professionals seem to prioritize this topic. Furthermore, categories of Organizational Culture (10.95%), Motivation (9.92%), and Leadership (8.70%) were also among the most frequent HRM practices. In the category of Organizational Culture, the discourse focused on how HR professionals can provide gig workers with meaningful communication and a sense of belonging to their employer. In the category of Motivation, HR professionals suggested utilizing algorithms and monetary incentives to boost the motivation of gig workers.

Organizations incentivize gig workers with flexible rewards, such as monetary incentives tied to performance metrics (see also [3]). For example, food delivery gig workers earn rewards proportional to their activity level, encouraging increased motivation and productivity. HRM practices on Leadership in the gig work context included setting clear expectations and goals for gig workers to ensure they understand their responsibilities and align their efforts with organizational objectives; cultivating a supportive and inclusive work environment for gig workers, especially for women; and streamlining communication channels between gig workers and organizational stakeholders. These results point in the direction of the responsibilities and duties of HRM professionals, which should be the focal point of HRM associations and scholars as they envision the future. Furthermore, HRM practices such as Compensation and Benefits (6.56%), Health and Safety (6.01%), and Selection (5.57%) were among the frequently discussed HRM practices. The gig economy offers employers access to a broader talent pool, increased agility, reduced payroll costs, and enhanced innovation potential. Additionally, the discussions on these HRM practices also included how the gig work context poses challenges, including security issues and competitive risks to gig workers.

From the perspective of HR professionals, compensation and benefits for gig workers present significant challenges due to the lack of a clear regulatory framework and the diverse needs of this workforce. For example, in the Indian context, while some companies like Uber are actively designing systems to ensure fair compensation for gig workers, other multinational organizations continue to face challenges in optimizing pay and benefits across diverse worker categories. Contracts with gig workers are often open-ended and ambiguous, leading to legal and regulatory uncertainties that organizations must address. HR professionals discussed navigating these complexities by developing flexible, personalized compensation packages that balance costs while meeting the unique needs of gig workers.

It should be noted that HRM practices such as Corporate Social Responsibility (CSR) (0.87%), Employer Branding (0.79%), and Planning (0.04%) were the least discussed HRM practices. This finding can be attributed to the transactional, short-term nature of gig work (see Fig. 8).

The career progression of gig workers, one of the least discussed HRM practices (5.06%), is increasingly influenced by HR professionals who must navigate budget constraints and adapt hiring practices, often prioritizing contingent projects over long-term positions. As the leverage shifts toward freelancers, HR professionals discussed the need to recognize the growing autonomy and bargaining power of gig workers. Additionally, they also talked about how being tech savvy has become essential for all workers, including those in traditionally manual trades (such as

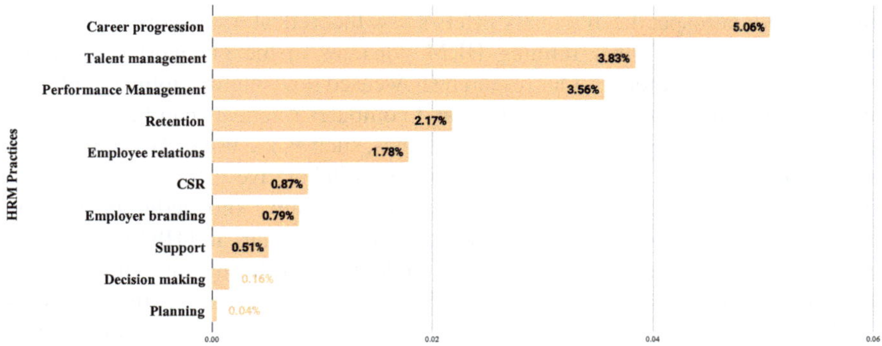

Fig. 8 10 Least discussed HRM practices by HR professionals in the gig work context

forklift operators, electricians, plumbers, etc.), as they must now adapt to digital tools and technologies (e.g., mobile and web technologies for job platforms and performance management) to stay competitive and meet client demands in an increasingly on-demand, digital world. Moreover, from the perspective of HR professionals, the sustainability of the gig economy (linked with CSR) is challenged by issues like inadequate healthcare and the reliance on low hourly rates, which lack sufficient support. There is uncertainty about whether the private or public sector will address these gaps, with questions about how to make gig work more viable in the long term. HR professionals discussed the need to advocate for systemic changes, such as universal healthcare or new legal frameworks, when talking about the USA, to support a sustainable gig economy that can provide essential benefits and protections for workers.

5 Discussion

Our paper carries several theoretical and practical implications. First, our findings provide valuable insights into HRM trends and HRM professionals' perspectives on managing gig workers in standard organizations. By challenging the notion of self-managed gig workers, we illustrate the relevance of HRM practices, such as training and development of gig workers, fitting them into organizational culture, and motivation and effective leadership in the gig work context, for modern standard organizations. Thus, the introduction of new dynamics by gig workers has the potential to reshape HRM's core principles, necessitating a reevaluation of conventional HRM theories and models [8]. Organizations should explore methods with which the most frequently mentioned HRM practices can be utilized for managing gig workers. An example can be studies that have already shown how organizations can carefully design their digital labor platforms and incorporate social media tools to support the self-motivation of gig workers [32]. With our research, we propose extending such studies to other HRM practices (such as Leadership, Training and Development, etc.) to support the smooth integration of gig workers in standard organizations. Second, our novel, domain-specific dictionary offers a new theoretical framework for examining, evaluating, and further refining HRM practices in the gig work context by researchers and practitioners. Our research showcased how interdisciplinary collaboration between management researchers and computer scientists can help us better understand the nuances of domain-specific topics, such as the use of HR practices in the gig work context. Similar interdisciplinary collaborative efforts can steer the course of future research studies by advancing our cumulative knowledge and thereby accelerating developments in the field of organizational studies and HRM. Third, our research offers a new interdisciplinary methodology for exploring emerging technologies-enabled forms of work, thus addressing the inadequacy of existing "conventional toolkits—theoretical and methodological, which are not well equipped to study the less obvious, indirect effects of digitalization" [33]. Lastly, insights from HR professionals on hiring, developing, and managing gig workers may inspire fresh perspectives on HRM that transcend the gig economy's boundaries and become applicable also for standard workers. Consequently, our findings may serve as a valuable resource for HR associations and scholars to envision the future of the HR profession and identify necessary interventions, such as redesigning HR professionals' responsibilities and duties, as well as updating HR educational programs.

Our findings also offer practical implications for organizations and HR professionals as they navigate the evolving landscape of work, characterized by the coexistence of standard and gig workers. Specifically, the results of topic modeling shed light on the growing role of AI in managing gig workers, particularly in areas such as recruitment, task allocation, performance management, and engagement. These findings support the results of previous studies [34, 35]. The emergence of 'AI in gig work' as a prominent topic among HR professionals underscores the need for organizations to integrate AI-driven practices into their HRM strategies proactively. By leveraging AI technologies effectively, organizations can enhance efficiency, streamline processes, and adapt to the changing demands of the modern workforce. The high importance of standard HR practices in the gig work context calls for organizations to reevaluate their HRM frameworks and tailor them to empower gig workers to thrive in their roles. Organizations can achieve this by investing in tailored training programs designed to meet the specific needs of gig workers, fostering a culture of motivation and recognition, and implementing performance management systems adapted to the short-term nature of gig work. Through these initiatives, organizations can maximize the potential of gig workers and ensure alignment with broader organizational objectives and values.

6 Future Work

Our results highlight a research area that warrants further investigation at the intersection of diversity dimensions and HRM practices in the gig work context. Specifically, investigating how gig workers of different ages, ethnicities, genders, etc., are managed in standard organizations could significantly enrich the domain of organizational research. It is essential to formulate targeted research questions and hypotheses to guide future research in this area to provide clearer direction for the scientific community. For instance, researchers could ask: "How do HRM practices differ when managing gig workers across various diversity dimensions such as age, ethnicity, and gender?" A potential hypothesis for empirical testing could be: "Gig workers from historically underrepresented groups are more likely to express dissatisfaction with HRM practices compared to their counterparts from majority groups." Expanding these discussions to include industry-specific variations would also be valuable.

One potential avenue for examining the influence of diversity dimensions on HR practices for managing gig workers would be conducting aspect-based sentiment analysis on the transcribed text of YouTube videos. A related research question could be: "What are the long-term trends in sentiment regarding HRM practices for gig workers, and how do these sentiments evolve concerning diversity dimensions over time?" Longitudinal tracking of sentiments would be particularly interesting from a research standpoint, as it allows for observing potential shifts and evolving perspectives over time within the HRM domain. By doing so, it would be possible to uncover more granular insights into the sentiments associated with each HRM practice category, further enriching our understanding of the specific HRM practices in the gig work context. Additionally, a hypothesis related to the sentiment analysis approach could be: "Sentiments expressed by HR professionals in YouTube videos about managing gig workers show significant variability based on the diversity dimensions of the workers being discussed, with more positive sentiments associated with discussions about younger or male gig workers."

Finally, future research should include the perspectives of gig workers, particularly at the intersection of diversity dimensions and HRM practices within the gig work context. Exploring these perspectives will provide deeper insights into the unique challenges faced by gig workers and inform more inclusive HRM strategies.

References

1. Kuhn, K. M. (2016). The rise of the 'gig economy' and implications for understanding work and workers. *Industrial and Organizational Psychology, 9*(1), 157–162.
2. Eurofound. *Eurofound Platform work.* Accessed 2023/10/25, from https://www.eurofound.europa.eu/it/topic/platform-work
3. Cropanzano, R., Keplinger, K., Lambert, B. K., Caza, B., & Ashford, S. J. (2023). The organizational psychology of gig work: An integrative conceptual review. *Journal of Applied Psychology, 108*(3), 492–519.
4. Sessions, H., Baer, M. D., Nahrgang, J. D., & Pychlau, S. (2023). From free pastures to penned in: The within-person effects of psychological reactance on side-hustlers' hostility and initiative in full-time work. *Journal of Applied Psychology, 108*, 1979–1997.
5. Schor, J. B., Attwood-Charles, W., & Cansoy, M. (2020). Dependence and precarity in the platform economy. *Theory and Society, 49*(5–6), 833–861.

6. Working Without Borders: The Promise and Peril of Online Gig Work. *Jobs group papers, notes, and guides*. The World Bank. Accessed 2025/03/11, from http://hdl.handle.net/10986/40066
7. Rahman, U. U., Rehman, C. A., Imran, M. K., & Aslam, U. (2017). Does team orientation matter? Linking work engagement and relational psychological contract with performance. *Journal of Management Development, 36*, 1–12.
8. Gautam, V., Mishra, A. A., & Maheshwari, M. (2024). Examining the relevance of Human Resource Management in gig work: A systematic literature review research agenda. *German Journal of Human Resource Management, 38*(4), 375–412.
9. Hannigan, T. R., Haans, R. F. J., Vakili, K., Tchalian, H., Glaser, V. L., Wang, M. S., Kaplan, S., & Jennings, P. D. (2019). Topic modeling in management research: Rendering new theory from textual data. *Academy of Management Annals, 13*(2), 586–632.
10. Egger, R. (2022). *Applied data science in tourism. Tourism on the Verge*. Springer.
11. Leicht-Deobald, U., Busch, T., & Schank, C. (2019). The challenges of algorithm-based HR decision-making for personal integrity. *Journal of Business Ethics, 160*(2), 377–392.
12. van den Groenendaal, S. M., Freese, C., Poell, R. F., & Kooij, D. (2022). Inclusive Human Resource Management in freelancers' employment relationships: The role of organizational needs and freelancers' psychological contracts. *Human Resource Management Journal, 33*(1), 224–240.
13. Dundon, T., & Rafferty, A. (2018). The (potential) demise of HRM? *Human Resource Management Journal, 28*(3), 377–391.
14. Rubery, J., & Johnson, M. (2018). *Human resource management: A critical approach*. Routledge.
15. Kuhn, K. M. (2021). Human resource management and the gig economy: Challenges and opportunities at the intersection between organizational HR decision-makers and digital labor platforms. In *Research in personnel and human resources management*. Emerald Publishing Limited.
16. Cross, D., & Swart, J. (2022). The (ir)relevance of human resource management in independent work: Challenging assumptions. *Human Resource Management Journal, 32*(1), 232–246.
17. Duggan, J., Sherman, U., Carbery, R., & McDonnell, A. (2020). Algorithmic management and app-work in the gig economy: A research agenda for employment relations and HRM. *Human Resource Management Journal, 30*(1), 114–132.
18. Meijerink, J., & Keegan, A. (2019). Conceptualizing human resource management in the gig economy: Toward a platform ecosystem perspective. *Journal of Managerial Psychology, 34*(4), 214–232.
19. Tillmann, A., & Koene, B. (2023). Gig work and its impacts on existing HR and organizational responsibilities and the role of HRM. *Academy of Management Journal, 1*.
20. Bos-Nehles, A., Renkema, M., & Janssen, M. (2017). HRM and innovative work behaviour: A systematic literature review. *Personnel Review, 46*, 1228–1253.
21. Tursunbayeva, A., Di Lauro, S., & Pagliari, C. (2018). People analytics—A scoping review of conceptual boundaries and value propositions. *International Journal of Information Management, 43*, 224–247.
22. Keelan, J., Pavri-Garcia, V., Tomlinson, G., & Wilson, K. (2007). YouTube as a source of information on immunization: A content analysis. *JAMA, 298*(21), 2482–2484.
23. Gaus, Q., Jolliff, A., & Moreno, M. A. (2021). A content analysis of YouTube depression personal account videos and their comments. *Computers in Human Behavior Reports, 3*, 100050.
24. Radford, A., Kim, J., Xu, T., Brockman, G., McLeavey, C., & Sutskever, I. (2022). Robust speech recognition via large-scale weak. *Supervision, arXiv*, 2212.04356.
25. Grootendorst, M. (2022). *B*ERTopic: Neural topic modeling with a class-based TF-IDF procedure. arXiv: 2203.05794
26. Pandey, S., & Pandey, S. K. (2019). Applying natural language processing capabilities in computerized textual analysis to measure organizational culture. *Organizational Research Methods, 22*(3), 765–797.
27. Vallas, S., & Schor, J. (2020). What do platforms do? Understanding the gig economy. *Annual Review of Sociology, 46*.

28. (Not) Getting paid to do what you love: Gender, social media, and aspirational work. *Yale Scholarship Online*. Accessed 2025/05/13, from https://doi.org/10.12987/yale/9780300218176.001.0001
29. Watson, G. P., Kistler, L. D., Graham, B. A., & Sinclair, R. R. (2021). Looking at the gig picture: Defining gig work and explaining profile differences in gig workers' job demands and resources. *Group & Organization Management, 46*(2), 327–361.
30. Spurk, D., & Straub, C. (2020). Flexible employment relationships and careers in times of the COVID-19 pandemic. *Journal of Vocational Behavior, 119*, 103435.
31. Berger, T., Frey, C. B., Levin, G., & Danda, S. R. (2020). Uber happy? Work and well-being in the 'Gig Economy'. *Economic Policy, 34*(99), 429–477.
32. Jabagi, N., Croteau, A.-M., Audebrand, L. K., & Marsan, J. (2019). Gig-workers' motivation: Thinking beyond carrots and sticks. *Journal of Managerial Psychology, 34*.
33. Orlikowski, W. J., & Scott, S. V. (2023). The digital undertow and institutional displacement: A sociomaterial approach. *Organization Theory, 4*(2).
34. Keegan, A., & Meijerink, J. (2023). Dynamism and realignment in the HR architecture: Online labor platform ecosystems and the key role of contractors. *Human Resource Management, 62*(1), 15–29.
35. Malik, R., Visvizi, A., & Skrzek-Lubasińska, M. (2021). The gig economy: Current issues, the debate, and the new avenues of research. *Sustainability, 13*(9), 5023.

Technology Worsening Employees' Life: A Qualitative Study to Understand Determinants, Effects and Solutions

Dario Natale Palmucci

Abstract In this study we analyze the effects of what we define "anytime & anywhere availability" (AAA), which is referred to the condition brought by technological advancement and in particular work activities carried out remotely, thanks to the actual technological devices and smartphones, away from dedicated workstations which often result on working beyond pre-established times and inability to break away and rest from work anywhere. The following qualitative study performed in various organizations explores the negative effects of this condition and reveals the crucial role played by sense of responsibility. Implications of the study are particularly relevant for both Human Resources departments to enhance efficiency in their organizational contexts and researchers who want to further understand determinants and effects of new work modalities. Also, the results of the study can be adopted by policy makers to design laws and guidelines that help organizations rethink their workplaces safety policies.

Keywords New work modalities · Technostress · Sense of responsibility

1 Introduction

Technological advancements, current advanced devices and smartphones availability, have given to employees the opportunity to perform work activities with greater flexibility [1] and better performance [2]. Not only, for workers further advantages of remote activities performed thanks technology advancements are related to: (a) for home workers the time saved for travel to commute in the office and the possibility of more easily reconciling personal needs, especially family needs, with work needs [3]. This aspect is particularly important for those who have to take care of

D. N. Palmucci (✉)
Department of Management, University of Turin, Turin, Italy
e-mail: darionatale.palmucci@unito.it

A. Tursunbayeva et al. (eds.), *Technology-Driven Transformation*, Lecture Notes in Information Systems and Organisation 79,
https://doi.org/10.1007/978-3-032-01396-5_6

children or non-self-sufficient elderly people, for whom the possibility of managing time and space independently represents a fundamental condition; (b) lower travel-related costs, including fuel, vehicle maintenance, public transport fares and parking [4]; (c) savings on the costs of meals outside the home, such as those incurred in canteens, bars and restaurants [5]; (d) acquisition of new skills in the field of smart working, since the focus is on weekly objectives managed individually with innovative digital tools [6]; (e) greater satisfaction linked to the autonomy acquired, as employees, being able to work in comfortable family environments and being able to manage their schedules based on personal needs, perceive greater trust from the organization [7].

However, both employees and managers are also dealing with some challenges. Indeed, although digitalization and new mixed working models have had a positive impact on the performance of people and companies, there is a risk that psychological safety is compromised, as workers often struggle to cope with stress and overwork because employees' inability to disconnect [8]. In other words, it is not clear when and how *the endless flexibility in terms of location and time* [9] *brought by mobile devices perpetually connected through the internet*, ends to be an opportunity and starts to be a risk. The one just mentioned is the gap that the present explorative study aims to cover since, although there are several studies focusing on remote working pros and cons in general, very little has been analyzed till now specifically to better explain determinants, effects and solutions for the "always connected" business reality.

Also, this piece of work contributes on the organizational wellbeing literature by suggesting a theoretical framework to explain the conditions that make AAA negative for employees' psychological safety.

2 Theoretical Framework

Smart working spread rapidly during the health emergency caused by Covid-19 and its use has become increasingly common, so much that it has become part of the "new normal" [10]. In the actual context in fact, many individuals spend the majority of their working days away from the offices, while still maintaining adequate performance levels, both on an individual and organizational level [11]. A recent published study carried out in UK for example [12], found that the increased frequency of working outside the office is positively associated with employees' self-reported hourly productivity, and, similar studies demonstrated that who spend a certain percentage of time working remotely often receive higher performance evaluation from their managers [11].

Moreover, by using mobile devices which are constantly connected through the internet, workers undoubtedly are more flexible in terms of location and time (e.g. through instant messenger, chat, etc.), re-defining the *"mobile working concept"* [13] and bringing undeniable advantages as granting a more efficient and streamlined communication and information flow and decreasing the need of static and costly workstations for the organizations [13].

Last but not least, according to what also reported in a recent important work that specifically analyzed *Working from Home* trends globally [14], it is important to mention one of the most recognized individual benefits: an average of about 1 h commuting time saved daily, ranging from 48 minutes in the United States to more than 90 min in eastern countries as India and China [14]. That said, *all that glitters is not gold* and new ways of working also mean to deal with some challenges. Indeed, although as seen digitalization and new mixed working models have had a positive impact on the performance of people and companies, there is a risk that psychological safety is compromised as workers often struggle to cope with stress, distractions and overwork [15]. More and more studies in fact reveal that levels of well-being are not optimal due to the excessive workload and related stress as well as the lack of time due to long working hours [8]. This clearly highlights how the growing demand for flexibility and the adoption of remote activities away from dedicated workplaces have increased pressure on workers, often negatively influencing their private sphere [16]. That's where this work comes into play and differs from other similar studies: we are not talking about remote working only, but on the condition of *anytime & anywhere availability* (AAA) brought by technological advancement and new flexible work modalities which often results on working beyond pre-established times and inability to break away and rest from work anywhere. In other words, the aim of this work is to spread light on the effects of the increasing opportunities (and above all, the risks) to instantly access work materials through the internet and to use mobile devices which enable constant connectivity [13], to manage the endless flexibility in terms of location and time [9] and, as a result, the uncontrolled Hyper-connection [17] which is redefining the way of doing business and social behavior at work.

To do so, it is necessary first of all provide a comprehensive analysis of the actual knowledge regarding remote work experience and understand the conditions of effectiveness of working from home, since this is the upstream topic as well as the closest one and most studied. Looking at this literature, we found that some studies focus on the relation between organizational culture and remote employees' satisfaction highlighting how an open and innovative organizational culture can impact motivation, communication, relationships, and teamwork, enhancing remote work satisfaction [18]. Not only, we found that also coherent organization policies and top management support are crucial in order to determine whether remote work and flexibility enhance performance. On this direction, Chatterjee and colleagues [19] reveals that remote work flexibility significantly boosts organizational performance, with company policies and top management support being crucial in the successful implementation of remote work strategies. In fact, the authors found that to enhance remote work flexibility, organizations should offer workplace and work time flexibility, along with support for infrastructural needs. In other words, adopting remote work systems positively affects employee satisfaction and productivity but top management support and organizational policies play crucial roles in moderating the effectiveness of remote work flexibility.

Then, if recent studies demonstrated that for organizations is crucial to shape a positive culture and develop flexible work policies endorsed by top management to better support remote employees and obtain positive outcomes from new working modalities, another fundamental aspect often reported by researchers is related to the relationship between the supervisor and the subordinate. On this, in a very much appreciated contribution exploring effective managerial practices for telecommuting, Lautsch and colleagues [20] by using data from surveys and interviews with 90 pairs of supervisors and subordinates (including both telecommuters and non-telecommuters), found that supervisors should maintain close contact with telecommuters, focusing on information sharing rather than strictly monitoring work schedules. In fact, according to the study, telecommuters who experienced this approach were more likely to report reduced work–family conflict, enhanced performance, and greater willingness to assist colleagues. In the same study the authors found also that supervisors should promote the separation of work and family boundaries among telecommuting employees, as this is linked to decreased work–family conflicts [20]. This confirms that supervisors' role is fundamental to ensure the efficiency of new work modalities as work– life balance and family supportive supervisor behavior impact teleworkers job performance [20].

Additional recognized theories that have tried to analyze the relation between homeworking and productivity are the Social Exchange Theory (SET) and the Affective Events Theory (AET).

Regarding the first one, the core idea of SET is that human relationships are shaped by a subjective cost-benefit analysis, where individuals are inclined to repeat actions that have been rewarded previously and the more frequently a specific behavior is rewarded, the more likely it is to occur again [21]. Applied to the work environments, individuals aim to maximize their utility in social interactions [22] and the nature of these exchanges varies based on the relationship with the other party (e.g., coworker, supervisor) and the benefits workers receive [23]. Therefore, SET can help understanding the link between homeworking and productivity by highlighting for example the reciprocal relationship between employers and employees. When employers offer flexibility, trust, and support, employees view these as rewards and reciprocate with higher commitment, loyalty, and productivity. This positive exchange fosters a supportive work environment, enhancing motivation and job satisfaction, which boosts productivity. However, this dynamic relies on the ongoing support from the organization and workers' perceived fairness, as any imbalance can negatively affect employee performance [24]. Thus, SET emphasizes the need for mutually beneficial relationships to maintain productivity in remote work settings and, above all, suggests that when technology replaces human interactions (with employees who may struggle to communicate effectively and address their needs, concerns, or aspirations), as a result the leader's role in enhancing employee performance and well-being is expected to grow in importance [25].

AET theory instead, focuses on how workplace events affect employees' emotions and how these emotions subsequently influence their job performance, attitudes, and behaviors [22]. In other words, it emphasizes the importance of emotions in the workplace, suggesting that emotional responses are a major factor driving work behavior, beyond logical or rational decision-making alone [23]. Thus, it first suggests that various work events influence employees' emotional states, which in turn affect their attitudes and behaviors, and then, unlike theories that focus on stable job characteristics, AET emphasizing the impact of everyday occurrences at work (as events that can range from minor—e.g., completing a small task, daily social interactions—to major—e.g., receiving a promotion). According to this theory, positive events are linked to positive moods, while negative events are associated with negative ones [38]. Applied to remote working, AET can explain how emotional experiences affect productivity. Positive aspects of working from home in fact, such as work-life balance, autonomy, and flexibility, can lead to satisfaction and increased motivation, boosted productivity [39]. Conversely, negative factors like isolation, poor communication or technical issues can cause frustration and disengagement, reducing productivity [40]. Consequently, effective emotional management by leaders—through regular support and feedback—can thus help address these negative emotions and improve productivity. Additionally, the ability to personalize one's workspace and reduced commuting stress contributes to a positive mood and enhanced work performance.

Beyond AET but in accordance with this last concept, also other studies indicate that individual differences cannot be ignored and for some employee telework can be a straightforward way to enhance well-being, while for others it can bring negative emotions [23]. For example, Anderson and colleagues [37] found that those who have low "openness" and opportunities for interactions could more easily experience negative consequences (e.g., social isolation) and thus organizations need to carefully assess whether teleworking is a beneficial arrangement for them or not.

In summary, there is plenty works and theories that tried to understand remote working effects on people and businesses. Some of them focus on positive outcomes (as performance and increased well-being satisfaction), others highlight the difficulties for workers of finding a balance between life and work. This has become a topic of growing concern for many workers in the post-Covid era and right here is placed the importance of this study: the negative effects of smart working and the work overload that often results involve both the mental and physical spheres [2], because, although regulations and procedures exist to guarantee the safety and health of workers, technology advancements and perpetual connectivity impact on psychological well-being has often been neglected. More in particular, as mentioned above, in this work we do not want to simply talk about remote working but to that *anytime & anywhere availability* (AAA) brought by technological advancement and new flexible work modalities which often results on working beyond pre-established times and inability to break away and rest from work anywhere. For these reasons we have started from the literature related to remote working and, with the subsequent qualitative research, we aim to first shed light on the still not clear relationships between AAA and both positive and negative outcomes of all these work activities carried out anytime and anywhere Second, since specifically for AAA little frameworks have been developed till now, we try to courageously sketch a rudimental first one to lay the foundations for future research. Consequently, research questions for our study are the following:

RQ1: What could be the key variables intervening between AAA and employees' performance, wellbeing and satisfaction, leading to optimal levels of these lasts?
RQ2: Is it possible to integrate these variables within a comprehensive framework?

3 Empirical Research

The extended analysis of the literature (mainly regarding remote working) analyzed in the previous paragraph represented a first preliminary activity for this empirical research. Thanks to that in fact, it has been possible to have an overview of all previous aspects addressed by researchers and thus lay the foundation for the subsequent qualitative study. As a result, to answer the two research questions and inspired by previous works aimed at exploring and providing insights similar to the subject of this study [27, 28], it has been decided to collect data by interviewing both managers and employees for a total of 31 different subjects from different organizational contexts. We would point out here that the decision to use qualitative data collected through interviews was primarily driven by prior research which has demonstrated that interviews are an effective method for assessing managerial behavior. This because this grants the possibility to discuss the problem directly with workers (in this case subordinates and managers), who are those who find themselves facing and therefore making decisions on various problems on a daily basis, including the workload caused by the increased flexibility. With regard to the sample, it has been chosen to adopt a heterogenous sample of participants working on different sectors and different companies in accordance with the explorative nature of the study and thus for a better understanding of the phenomenon and generalizability of the results [29]. In particular, it has been decided to collect data from both managers of different level and subordinates drawing inspiration from previous qualitative research who similarly explored the importance of this topic through interviews [20]. Furthermore, we chose to collect data from different managers and from different sectors and organizational contexts to ensure a greater exploratory impact and to overcome the limits of previous research [30]. Table 1 provides more details on the participants of our study.

Participants were preliminarily contacted to request their willingness in participate to the study and were grossly informed on its object (ensuring they had experience of flexible work modalities and use of advanced technological devices to access work materials). During this first approach, personal data were collected (e.g., age, level of seniority) among with information regarding the business context they worked. Then a meeting time/date for each participant was scheduled and subsequently singular virtual interviews lasting approximately 45 min were conducted. Before data collection, participants were assured that their interviews' content would remain anonymous and confidential. The interview protocol included

Table 1 Details of the sample adopted

N°	Age	Gender	Level of seniority	Industry/Sector	Size (N° of employees)
1	26–35	Male	Subordinate	Information Technology	Up to 250
2	26–35	Female	Subordinate	Public Sector	251–1000
3	26–35	Female	Manager	Energy	Over 5000
4	26–35	Male	Manager	Industrial	Over 5000
5	36–45	Male	Subordinate	Food industry	Over 5000
6	36–45	Female	Manager	Information Technology	Over 5000
7	36–45	Female	Manager	Pharmaceutical	1001–5000
8	36–45	Male	Manager	Automotive	1001–5000
9	36–45	Male	Manager	Information Technology	1001–5000
10	36–45	Female	Subordinate	Banking	1001–5000
11	36–45	Female	Manager	Banking	1001–5000
12	36–45	Male	Manager	Food industry	251–1000
13	36–45	Male	Manager	Business services	1001–5000
14	36–45	Female	Senior Manager	Business services	251–1000
15	46–55	Female	Senior Manager	Information Technology	1001–5000
16	46–55	Male	Senior Manager	Information Technology	Over 5000
17	46–55	Female	Subordinate	Business services	251–1000
18	46–55	Male	Manager	Public Sector	Over 5000
19	46–55	Female	Manager	Energy	251–1000
20	46–55	Male	Manager	Automotive	1001–5000
21	46–55	Female	Subordinate	Automotive	1001–5000
22	46–55	Male	Manager	Food industry	1001–5000
23	46–55	Male	Senior Manager	Information Technology	Up to 250
24	46–55	Female	Senior Manager	Consultancy	Over 5000
25	46–55	Female	Subordinate	Public Sector	1001–5000
26	46–55	Female	Manager	Public Sector	1001–5000
27	46–55	Male	Manager	Information Technology	Over 5000
28	46–55	Male	Subordinate	Information Technology	1001–5000
29	56–65	Male	Subordinate	Business services	1001–5000
30	56–65	Male	Senior Manager	Industrial	1001–5000
31	56–65	Male	Senior Manager	Information Technology	Over 5000

semi-structured questions in which participants were asked to share their experience with the flexibility brought by technology advancements in terms of time and space, to reveals problems in case they were experiencing and also advantages they were getting with new working modalities. They were also asked to share practical examples of issues they were struggle with, how they were managing the new remote business reality, the communicational issues and advantages they were experiencing and, in case of problems also to propose practical solutions both at a personal level and at organizational level.

Inspired by the literature review analyzed in the precedent paragraph, participants were also asked to express their feeling regarding the following aspects: (a) organizational policies, culture and openness regarding new working modalities in their contexts; (b) relation supervisor/subordinate they were experiencing when teleworking; (c) individual differences between colleagues they noticed regarding the interaction with technology and the adoption of new working modalities. The interviews ended asking participants their general feeling regarding the increasing general concern towards technostress and wellbeing at work. Subsequently the research team analyzed the interview data by transcribing the qualitative information, assigning preliminary codes, identifying recurring themes, considering differences and verifying the reliability and validity of the results following similar qualitative studies [15, 27].

4 Findings

4.1 Employees' Too Low Sense of Responsibility and AAA

In our fast-paced and interconnected world, technological devices have transformed the way we work, offering unparalleled flexibility and efficiency. With the rise of smartphones, laptops, and tablets, employees can now perform their tasks from virtually in any location, be it from home, a busy café, or even while on the go. This mobility seamlessly integrates work into daily life, dissolving the traditional boundaries of a fixed workplace [15].

Additionally, advanced communication tools and collaboration platforms keep employees connected with their teams and clients, no matter where they are. Video conferencing, instant messaging, and cloud-based file sharing enable easy meetings, project management, and task completion, overcoming geographical limitations: in other words, the capability to work at any time further boosts productivity and work-life balance, as employees can work during their peak hours, coordinate across time zones, and manage personal obligations more effectively [12].

However, if from one hand AAA enhances job satisfaction and cultivates a culture of trust and autonomy within the organization, from what analyzed in literature and according to the results of this qualitative study performed, with all this flexibility positive outcomes are not for granted and, although technological advancements allow work to be done from anywhere, this can also lead to negative performance in terms of both quantity and quality [31]. In fact, from the interviews analyzed have emerged several difficulties: one of the managers interviewed working as *head of digital innovation* for an important organization of the third sector said: "I am experiencing a lot of difficulties in managing the work of some resources who simply are not able to be responsible for their own activities when they are not present in the office. They often arrive late for online meetings (or simply they do not actively participate, or they do not make questions) and always seem to postpone activities until they are in the office, demonstrating that they do not have the right level of responsibility to manage their flexibility". On this direction, another interviewee who does not have supervisory responsibilities working for an IT company reported the following: "there are some colleagues with whom I find it extremely difficult to work when they are at home. For example, when I ask them updates on deliveries (on which my activities also depend) on an on-line call, the answer I get is often "yes, it's almost completed and next day that I will be in the office I will show you the work done". Needless to say that the work they later present is not completed and the deliveries of the whole team (including my activities) are slowed down by these behaviors. In summary, they are simply not responsible". Another participant working for an agency of the public sector reported: "since the pandemic it is difficult to reach certain colleagues who work remotely. When I call for an on-line meeting in one of those days they are working from home, they often decline the invitation answering "I can't that day because I work from home.." making for me difficult understanding when they are available for work or not. This behavior is also slowing down our responsiveness in providing answers and services to people and the community". Last but not least, most of the participants reported frustration in managing "an uncontrolled number of interruptions of any kind and from any source mail, wazzap, etc. I need to fight with that I am able to manage only thanks to my strong sense of responsibility that drives me to complete before the end of the day (and beyond the standard working hours) the work I have undertaken." as expressed from a 40 years old female manager working for a business services firm.

To recap what analyzed then, and in accordance with previous studies, new work modalities and AAA can have significant negative impacts. For example, this qualitative study aligns with previous studies that demonstrate the detrimental effects of interruptions on worker performance and their satisfaction. It is to say that continuous interruptions, whether stemming from technology in a remote work setting or from the home environment, can disrupt focus, reduce productivity, and lead to errors or unfinished tasks [31]. What also emerged and represents one of the key findings of this study, is, above all, the role of a lack of accountability leading often to a drop in employees' performance. In fact, following the interview analysis, we found that the freedom and the flexibility of AAA can sometimes cause distractions and a loss of focus if not properly managed and that performance is closely tied to an individual's sense of responsibility. Regarding this concept, there are numerous attempts from the scientific community to define it ethically, socially and psychologically. Not only, in the literature there are appropriate distinctions between the concept of responsibility in general and in relation to work and professional contexts [32]. Dose and Klimoski [33] in their work named "*Doing the right thing in the workplace: Responsibility in the face of accountability*" refer to responsibility as a controlled definition of expectations, enhanced personal control and an established importance of action. Gardner instead [32] emphasizes the concept of *going beyond*: "e.g., *to go beyond simply the consideration of interests*"; "*responsibility takes one beyond the safety of rules or codes, which tell you where you can stop*"; "*...that moral good provides the basis for independence and unconditionality that once more goes beyond contract*".

In this study, therefore, avoiding getting bogged down in a fruitless examination of various definitions but effectively drawing from those analyzed, we refer to a sense of responsibility as an inner commitment that encourages employees to fulfill their duties, obligations, or promises. It reflects to employees' understanding of their role and their readiness; to be accountable for their actions and decisions. This is the sense that often motivates people to complete tasks, meet expectations, and honor their commitments to both others and themselves. In other words, responsibility is key to ensuring that tasks are completed efficiently and deadlines are met and with too low sense of responsibility, in condition of AAA (and thus with a less structured setting), employees are less likely to stay motivated, organized, and committed to their work. From the analysis of the interviews, they seem not able to recognize the importance of maintaining high productivity levels and actively seek ways to address the challenges of AAA, such as interruptions and time management. In summary, without an adequate sense of responsibility, the lack of direct supervision and the informal nature of AAA can lead to procrastination, reduced productivity, and missed deadlines. This can result in a significant decline in work quality and overall performance, negatively affecting both the individual and the organization. In line with this reasoning, we may contend that:

Proposition 1 A too low level of workers' sense of responsibility leads to a decline in performance, difficulty in achieving objectives on time and a lowering of the level of service in general, particularly evident under AAA conditions.

4.2 Employees' Too High Sense of Responsibility and AAA

As seen in the previous section, new ways of working and the flexibility gained thanks to the actual technological devices and smartphones, away from dedicated workstations can negatively impact employees' performance and undermine the organizational efficiency in general when workers' sense of responsibility is absent or low.

On the other hand, from what analyzed in this work and according to the results of the qualitative study performed, with the huge flexibility typical of the AAA condition, having a too high level of sense of responsibility does not guarantee the absence of negative effects. In fact, not everyone is able to manage flexibility and AAA often risks a breakdown of the important boundaries between work life and personal life [17]. In fact, from some interview emerged a sort of inability to push-back requests that exceed in terms of workload, time and as well as the manner/modality in which they are made. Following is what reported from a manager interviewed: "When my supervisor writes me a request, no matter if it is already late in the afternoon or I am having lunch, I know a response is request in no more than two hours. There are no written rules, but this I think is the standard nowadays and to be honest I am not able to ignore my boss' request otherwise I feel guilty. This is why often I resume working extra-hours or during weekends". The content of the interview just mentioned is a concrete example of how much the increasing availability and access to information risk to cause overload and technostress [15] especially when workers feel a strong sense of responsibility toward their duties. Also, too high sense of responsibility in AAA conditions seem to lead to Hyper-connection which contributes itself in increasing stress and smart-working fatigue [17]. A young professional in fact, reported the following: "When I work from home, I worry that I won't be visible online and that I lose some chat or a call especially from my boss. As a result, I check continuously my phone, my email, our internal chat and even wazzap even if I know this causes more stress and I lose concentrion to complete practical tasks. I can't avoid doing it because I have always felt a strong sense of responsibility toward those who trust me".

To summarize, from our qualitative analysis seems evident how too high level of sense of responsibility in the actual AAA business reality can damage employees' wellbeing because of their "inability to stop and rest when needed instead of keep checking emails even when I wait in line at the supermarket (and I am not the only one in my team).." as reported from one interviewee who also reported an increasing of burnout cases in her organizational context as also indicated in recent studies [34]. Therefore, we propose that:

Proposition 2 A too high level of workers' sense of responsibility leads to a decline in wellbeing (in some cases even burnout), technostress, employees' inability to break away from devices, access work material and relax, particularly evident under AAA conditions.

4.3 Employees' Adequate and Balanced Sense of Responsibility and AAA

In the previous sections of our findings, we proposed that inadequate sense of responsibility brings both negative short-term and long-term consequences to employees and organization. In particular when sense of responsibility is too low, short term negative consequences are low performance and employees not able to guarantee deliverables on time. On the other hand, when sense of responsibility is too low, long term negative consequences as employees' burn out, stress, inability to break away from devices (and rest) will result on deterioration of health conditions, illnesses and at organizational level also turnover.

However, working remotely and using new available advanced devices from anywhere (and anytime) without commuting to work allows for a more adaptable schedule, enabling better balance between professional and personal responsibilities [3]. It also helps employees in doing cost saving as commuting costs, work attire expenses, and daily meal costs are significantly reduced [5]. In addition, the flexibility gained often result in higher productivity [11]. As also seen in the interviews performed, many find they can focus better and accomplish more without the typical office distractions, others feel very satisfied for having eliminated the daily time to commute to the office and for the opportunity to allocated this time to personal activities and better health (e.g., with reduced exposure to illnesses, less stress from commuting, and the ability to maintain a healthier lifestyle contribute to better overall health). Therefore, our qualitative study suggests that fostering a balanced sense of responsibility is crucial for safely and productively act in the actual AAA reality. Regarding safety, it is worth sharing the contents of an interview made to a senior manager working for an IT company: "I can't complain for the possibility brought by technology. I can access information from everywhere and if something is wrong and I need to quickly access to a report to make a decision and give instructions to my team on how to solve the problem, I can do it directly from my mobile before going out for dinner with no need to run back to the office. How can I complain? Sure, what's important is knowing when to stop working, and I realize that it's not easy for everyone to distinguish between what is an emergency and what isn't, what can be postponed and what can't, or when to decide to respond to a request later versus answering the phone immediately. In short, one needs to have a strong sense of responsibility and know when to stop, just like with a good glass of wine.".

The content of this interview confirms that sense of responsibility plays a crucial role in mediating the relation between AAA and positive/negative outcomes. In fact, in accordance with similar studies, the utility of technology advancement and information availability anytime and everywhere cannot be ignored and solely considered negative [15]. On the contrary, if properly adopted, technological devices empower employees to work more intelligently, providing the resources needed to excel in a dynamic and constantly evolving work environment. As we continue to embrace and adapt to these advancements, the future of work is set to become even more adaptable and inclusive.

In addition, what also emerged from the interviews and confirm what reviewed in the literature, supervisors (or relation between supervisors and supervisee) play a key role in making telework efficient by setting clear expectations, maintaining regular communication, fostering trust and autonomy, supporting work-life balance, providing necessary resources, encouraging collaboration, and monitoring performance [20]. These actions help ensure that teleworkers remain productive, safe, engaged, and satisfied with their work as also confirmed from one interviewee working for a consultancy firm who said: "I know that emails and chat anytime is causing stress, and I have few colleagues who are really suffering their supervisors' attitude to write them at any time. I heard of supervisors who often send to their supervisees email and work requests with tight deadlines on Friday evening and, right after, a wazzap message to ensure they have received the email. This is unhealthy and causes stress! I am lucky because my boss knows how to manage certain situations, she cares us, often she asks info on our work and health conditions and as a result we communicate better and we trust each other". To summarize, as AAA continues to play a major role in the modern work environment, both an adequate sense of responsibility and efficient supervisors are more important than ever. Therefore, we propose that:

Proposition 3 Sense of responsibility adequate and balanced is the essential condition to manage the flexibility brought by technology advancements, hyper connec-

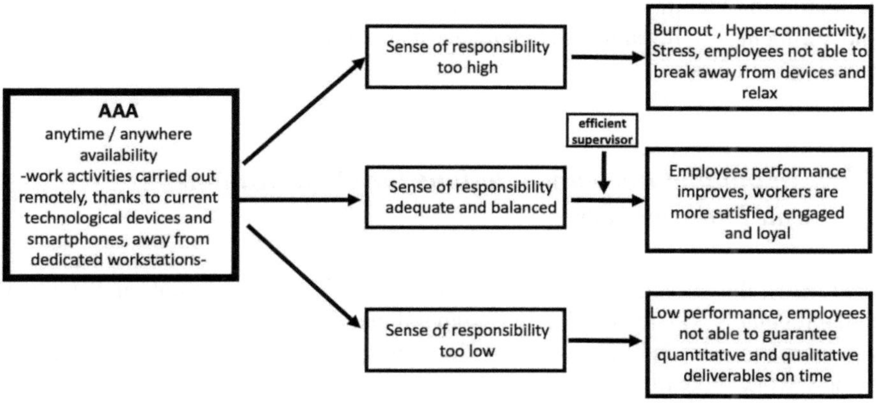

Fig. 1 The framework suggested

tivity and anytime/anywhere availability. In fact, if sense of responsibility is adequate, employees perform their work without jeopardizing their health, their performance improves, they are more satisfied, engaged and loyal. In addition, supervisors play a crucial role.

These are the key variables intervening between AAA and employees' performance, wellbeing and satisfaction, leading to optimal levels of these lasts and helped in answering RQ1. With regard to RQ2 that concerns the possibility to integrate these variables within a comprehensive framework, following is the frameworks we courageously try to suggest (Fig. 1):

5 Implications and Limits

5.1 Theoretical Implications

This study was mainly based on two components: (a) a solid base of scientific knowledge obtained thanks to the review of the literature that dealt with the topics under study; (b) an exploratory qualitative investigation that sought to better understand the objects of study. This made it possible to answer to the two research questions and thus:

- Understand the key variables intervening between AAA and employees' performance, wellbeing and satisfaction, leading to optimal levels of these lasts;
- Integrate these variables and suggest a comprehensive framework.

Thus theoretically, the main implication of the study is referred to this conceptual framework proposed that made it possible to understand the role of sense responsibility in mediating the relation between AAA and positive/negative outcomes, also adding to the literature on human resources management, organizational behavior and wellbeing by revealing the elements that can affect the effectiveness of new working modalities.

5.2 *Actionable Recommendations for Organizations and Policymakers*

Practically, the findings of this study may be relevant to governments and supranational regulatory bodies seeking to design policies and aiming to encourage organizations responsible behavior. As seen, the consequences of inadequate management of new work modalities in general and AAA in particular described in the study, represent opportunities to improve how information about workers safety is presented to individuals. Given the above, the following actionable recommendations are proposed to organizational leaders and policy makers:

- Build dedicated training paths: First of all, it is important to raise people's awareness of the issue of digital wellbeing and arouse a sense of urgency towards the problem, because only by acting promptly is possible to mitigate the consequences and slow down the dramatic advance of work-related stress [17]. Then, the results of this study can have significant application for the design of specific training programs aiming to, from one hand to achieve an adequate level of sense of responsibility within the workforce, from the other hand to build supervisory training programs aiming to develop, within the management communities, the right skills to manage the actual digital business reality. The study in fact confirmed that supervisor role is fundamental and this means they need to stay in regular contact with telecommuters, prioritizing information sharing over strict schedule monitoring [20] and, also, encourage clear boundaries between work and family life, which helps decrease work–family conflicts [35]. Once again, these findings highlight the importance of enhancing supervisors' tele-competences and train them in order to equip the organizations with the right skills to navigate the actual AAA reality.
- Re-define strategies for managing: organizational leaders should do as much as possible to strengthen an organizational culture that give greater prominence to the digital wellbeing and above all raise awareness among top managers on the situations employees are facing [17]. Also, the strategic HR Management function must to be aligned with new needs. For example, if it is true that people with adequate level of responsibility are those who are most likely to effectively and efficiently navigate AAA conditions, then these are aspects that the HR Talent acquisition in general (and the recruiters in particular) should carefully evaluate during selection processes.
- Re-think policies and rules: also, policy makers cannot fail to also take into consideration the psychological aspects in solving the problem since, as emerges from this study, it is essential to know the daily routine in which employees are

stuck, to be aware of the role of sense of responsibility and knowing that the most efficient way to mitigate the negative effects of remote working and no stopping use of technology devices is to balance the level of sense of responsibilities of workers. The above should therefore be taken into consideration in the creation and dissemination of any awareness campaigns and definition on new policies and rules. As today, there are only few countries in the world (e.g. Australia) where the law officially protects employees in case they refuse to monitor their devices outside the working hours (also without strictly prohibit employers from calling or messaging) and this can represent an essential preliminary first step to both give employees the 'right to disconnect' [17] and, at the same time, contribute to the development of an adequate (neither too low nor too high) sense of responsibility.

5.3 *Future Research*

Regarding the limits of the current work, the first consideration concerns the method used and the framework suggested. In this study, as already mentioned, we try to bravely propose a framework on the basis of the analysis of the relevant scientific literature and the qualitative analysis carried out. While this approach can be considered valid at this exploratory level, in order to provide the literature with a more robust contribution to explain the phenomenon, this investigation should be appropriately validated at a quantitative level in future studies. Consequently, the framework proposed as already mentioned, does not aim to be considered definitive, but rather as a preliminary attempt at understanding, in line with the exploratory nature of this study, determinants and effects of the actual AAA business condition.

Also, in this study the differences between different managers levels have not been considered and this could be proposed in future studies along with adding other categories of managers (e.g., low managers, middle managers) in order to increase the generalizability of the results. In fact, there could be differences between supervisors at the first managerial assignment and the ones who are more experienced. An additional element to investigate refers to the nature of the relation between junior subordinates and first line manager (which could be different to the one between already experienced professionals and their middle managers) All these peculiarities could help in better understanding the phenomenon.

Last but not least, the current study scarcely (in some cases not at all) considered the impact of other environmental and individual factors (e.g., organizational policies, social support, individual resilience, workaholism, technological preparedness or addiction) and these are elements that cannot be ignored in a future quantitative study aiming to valid the results obtained at this exploratory phase.

6 Conclusions

In summary, organizations must be aware of the advantages that new ways of working, the new digital reality and the AAA offer their collaborators and must not underestimate the important and positive influence of these on the digital transformation of the workplaces [15]. In fact, the opportunities arising from technological evolution are widely recognized and studied in both the academic and corporate fields. However, it is important to also recognize the risks and negative effects linked to inadequate management of these conditions [36], which must be carefully considered by management to ensure the long-term sustainable development of human capital. Today, the strategic role of companies goes beyond the simple management of work teams aimed solely at achieving objectives: it means instead paying attention to the psychological safety of workers and being aware of the conditions influencing their mental health (and thus the crucial role played by sense of responsibility according to the results of this study). Therefore, the effective management of remote employees becomes fundamental, ensuring their psychological safety on the one hand and maintaining a high level of motivation and performance on the other.

References

1. Gastaldi, L., Corso, M., Neirotti, P., & Paolucci, E. (2024). Smart working: Rethinking work practices to leverage employees' innovation potential. In *Proceedings of the 15th International CINet Conference*, Budapest.
2. Sekhar, C., & Patwardhan, M. (2023). Flexible working arrangement and job performance: The mediating role of supervisor support. *International Journal of Productivity and Performance Management, 72*(5), 1221–1238.
3. Darouei, M., & Pluut, H. (2021). Work from home today for a better tomorrow! How working from home influences work-family conflict and employees' start of the next workday. *Stress and Health, 37*(5), 986–999.
4. Kaya, M., & Arı, İ. (2023). The impact of remote working on Türkiye's energy consumption and greenhouse gas emissions: Learning from the experiences of Covid-19 era. *International Journal of Energy Studies, 8*(4), 701–729.
5. Battisti, E., Alfiero, S., & Leonidou, E. (2022). Remote working and digital transformation during the COVID-19 pandemic: Economic–financial impacts and psychological drivers for employees. *Journal of Business Research, 150*, 38–50.
6. Varma, A., Jaiswal, A., Pereira, V., & Kumar, Y. L. N. (2022). Leader-member exchange in the age of remote work. *Human Resource Development International, 25*(2), 219–230.
7. Khan, S., Rasheed, R., & Hyder, M. (2022). The impact of working remotely on employee job satisfaction: An SEM-PLS study of people working at universities. *Voyage Journal of Educational Studies, 2*(2), 84–102.
8. Risi, E., & Pronzato, R. (2021). Smart working is not so smart: Always-on lives and the dark side of platformisation. *Work Organisation, Labour & Globalisation, 15*(1), 107–125.
9. Bertschek, I., & Niebel, T. (2016). Mobile and more productive? Firm-level evidence on the productivity effects of mobile internet use. *Telecommunications Policy, 40*(9), 888–898.
10. Campbell, M., & Gavett, G. (2021). What covid-19 has done to our well-being, in 12 charts. *Harvard Business Review, 10.*

11. Choudhury, P., Khanna, T., Makridis, C. A., & Schirmann, K. (2024). Is hybrid work the best of both worlds? Evidence from a field experiment. *Review of Economics and Statistics*, 1–24.
12. Deole, S. S., Deter, M., & Huang, Y. (2023). Home sweet home: Working from home and employee performance during the COVID-19 pandemic in the UK. *Labour Economics, 80*, 102295.
13. Papagiannidis, S., & Marikyan, D. (2020). Smart offices: A productivity and well-being perspective. *International Journal of Information Management, 51*, 102027.
14. Aksoy, C. G., Davis, S. J., Barrero, J. M., Dolls, M., Bloom, N., & Zarate, P. (2022). Working from home around the world. *Brookings Papers on Economic Activity, 2*, 281–360.
15. Kokshagina, O., & Schneider, S. (2023). The digital workplace: Navigating in a jungle of paradoxical tensions. *California Management Review, 65*(2), 129–155.
16. Todisco, L., Tomo, A., Canonico, P., & Mangia, G. (2023). The bright and dark side of smart working in the public sector: Employees' experiences before and during COVID-19. *Management Decision, 61*(13), 85–102.
17. Palmucci, D. N., & Santoro, G. (2024). Managing employees' needs and well-being in the post-COVID-19 era. *Management Decision, 62*(12), 4138–4147.
18. Oleksa-Marewska, K., & Tokar, J. (2023). Organizational culture and job satisfaction of employees working remotely: A cross-cultural analysis. *Zeszyty Naukowe Politechniki Śląskiej. Organizacja i Zarządzanie, 182*.
19. Chatterjee, S., Chaudhuri, R., & Vrontis, D. (2022). Does remote work flexibility enhance organization performance? Moderating role of organization policy and top management support. *Journal of Business Research, 139*, 1501–1512.
20. Lautsch, B. A., Kossek, E. E., & Eaton, S. C. (2009). Supervisory approaches and paradoxes in managing telecommuting implementation. *Human Relations, 62*(6), 795–827.
21. Homans, G. C. (1958). Social behavior as exchange. *American Journal of Sociology, 63*(6), 597–606.
22. Cropanzano, R., & Mitchell, M. S. (2005). Social exchange theory: An interdisciplinary review. *Journal of Management, 31*(6), 874–900.
23. Mergener, A., & Trübner, M. (2022). Social relations and employees' rejection of working from home: A social exchange perspective. *New Technology, Work and Employment, 37*(3), 469–487.
24. Nemţeanu, S. M., Dabija, D. C., & Stanca, L. (2021). The influence of teleworking on performance and employee's counterproductive behaviour. *Amfiteatru Economic, 23*(58), 601–619.
25. Chernyak-Hai, L., & Rabenu, E. (2018). The new era workplace relationships: Is social exchange theory still relevant? *Industrial and Organizational Psychology, 11*(3), 456–481.
26. Weiss, H. M., & Cropanzano, R. (1996). Affective events theory. *Research in Organizational Behavior, 18*(1), 1–74.
27. Adisa, T., Ogbonnaya, C., & Adekoya, O. D. (2023). Remote working and employee engagement: A qualitative study of British workers during the pandemic. *Information Technology & People, 36*(5), 1835–1850.
28. Charalampous, M., Grant, C., & Tramontano, C. (2021). "It needs to be the right blend": A qualitative exploration of remote e-workers' experience and well-being at work. *Employee Relations: The International Journal, 44*(2), 335–355.
29. Palmucci, D. N. (2024). Decision making in human resources standard practices and change management innovation initiatives: The common destiny of being affected by biases. *EuroMed Journal of Business, 19*(4), 736–751.
30. J. Gustafsson, «Single case studies vs. multiple case studies: A comparative study,» 2017.
31. Barbieri, B. (2024). Enhancing productivity at home: The role of smart work and organizational support in the public sector. *Societies, 14*(4), 50.
32. Gardner, H. *Responsibility at work: How leading professionals act (or don't act) responsibly*. Wiley.
33. Dose, J. J., & Klimoski, R. J. (1995). Doing the right thing in the workplace: Responsibility in the face of accountability. *Employee Responsibilities and Rights Journal, 8*, 35–36.

34. Mariani, M. E. A. (2023). The rise and consolidation of digital platforms and technologies for remote working: Opportunities, challenges, drivers, processes, and consequences. *Journal of Business Research, 160*, 113617.
35. Campo, A. M. D. V., Avolio, B., & Carlier, S. I. (2021). The relationship between telework, job performance, work–life balance and family supportive supervisor behaviours in the context of COVID-19. *Global Business Review*, 09721509211049918.
36. Andrulli, R., & Gerards, R. (2023). How new ways of working during COVID-19 affect employee well-being via technostress, need for recovery, and work engagement. *Computers in Human Behavior, 139*, 107560.
37. Anderson, A. J., Kaplan, S. A., & Vega, R. P. (2015). He impact of telework on emotional experience: When, and for whom, does telework improve daily affective well-being? *European Journal of Work and Organizational Psychology, 24*(6), 882–897.
38. Miner, A. G., Glomb, T. M., & Hulin, C. (2005). Experience sampling mood and its correlates at work. *Journal of Occupational and Organizational Psychology, 78*(2), 171–193.
39. Silva, A. J., Neves, P., & Caetano, A. (2024). Procrastination is not only a "thief of time", but also a thief of happiness: It buffers the beneficial effects of telework on well-being via daily micro-events of IT workers. *International Journal of Manpower, 45*(1), 89–108.
40. Ugwu, F. O., Enwereuzor, I. K., & Mazei, J. (2023). Is working from home a blessing or a burden? Home demands as a mediator of the relationship between work engagement and work-life balance. *Applied Research in Quality of Life, 18*(1), 341–364.

Exploring the Interpersonal Relationships in Virtual Reality: A Systematic Literature Review

Laura Roma and Rocco Agrifoglio

Abstract The research aims to explore the evolution and impact of interpersonal interactions in virtual reality (VR) and the metaverse. Through a SLR it is possible to explore the multifaceted aspects of virtual interactions, including their purposes, technologies and contexts. Indeed, the analysis reveals that the main purposes are: (1) work-related activities, (2) leisure activities and (3) technology-mediated learning. Furthermore, the study explains the transition from conventional text-based communication to multi-sensory immersive experiences, emphasizing the influence of transforming virtual reality on interpersonal interactions using media richness theory. The primary technologies are text-based computer-mediated communication and the virtual community, which serve as the primary context for the development of interactors. The existing literary gap in the realm of managerial studies pertains to interpersonal interactions, to the purpose of learning activities, to the new metaverse technological issues and the contextual dimension of virtual teams. These are considerable as the starting points, the thematic pillars of the study, the motives on which create the formal structure and research design as well as significant for future research avenues.

Keywords Interpersonal interaction · Virtual reality · Metaverse · Media richness theory · SLR

L. Roma (✉) · R. Agrifoglio
Department of Business and Economics, University of Naples "Parthenope", Naples, Italy
e-mail: laura.roma001@studenti.uniparthenope.it; rocco.agrifoglio@uniparthenope.it

A. Tursunbayeva et al. (eds.), *Technology-Driven Transformation*, Lecture Notes in Information Systems and Organisation 79,
https://doi.org/10.1007/978-3-032-01396-5_7

1 Introduction

The COVID-19 pandemic has reshaped the way people interact, leading to a significant increase in the use of virtual communication channels like video calls for various purposes such as work, study and personal connections. However, prolonged engagement in video calls has been associated with reduced attention and concentration levels among participants, potentially contributing to feelings of isolation [1]. This shift towards virtual interactions has emphasized the importance of creating more immersive and engaging virtual experiences, leading to the exploration of the metaverse as a space for socializing, interacting and building relationships [2]. Early experiments with the metaverse in the gaming industry showed how individuals could connect and collaborate towards common goals. Today, metaverse offers opportunities for spontaneous interactions and shared experiences based on common interests. In this way, it plays a pivotal role in exemplification of transposed reality into virtual immersive dimensions. The virtual communities, operating web-mediated interaction, initially, revolved around shared interests like gaming, fashion, culinary arts, literature and technical hobbies, with participants offering their expertise to assist others in overcoming challenges [3]. At qualitative level, a prime illustration of collaborative knowledge creation is showcased in platforms like Wikipedia, where users are empowered to contribute information that is subsequently reviewed and modified by fellow users [4]. Subsequent to the popularity of blogs and forums, the emergence of social networks revolutionized interaction by enabling the dissemination of multimedia content related to personal experiences and interests among friends and like-minded individuals [5]. In light of the fact that the phenomenon of increasingly frequent online interactions represents a burgeoning area of scholarly inquiry, it was undertaken a systematic literature review aimed at examining and synthesizing previous research studies that have explored the interpersonal interaction within the realm of virtual reality, employing a thematic analysis of the findings in order to elucidate potential avenues for future research endeavors in this dynamic field of study [6]. The objective of the research is to establish the impact of the evolution of technology on social interaction in the virtual reality and metaverse. The authors determine the state of the art of managerial literature in relation to interpersonal interactions in virtual reality and metaverse. The systematic review of the literature has been conducted with the objective of answering the following research questions: (i) What are the purposes of social interaction in virtual reality and the metaverse? (ii) Which technologies facilitate social interactions in virtual reality and the metaverse? (iii) What kind of contexts facilitate the development of social interaction? The paper is structured as follows: (1) the introductive paragraph is useful for guiding the reader into the motives, objective and summarized pillars of the research; (2) the background context is an examination of the evolution of interpersonal interactions within organizational environments; (3) the methodology refers to the systematic literature review carried out on Scopus and 28 thematic journals by the PRISMA method used to select the final dataset, which consisted of 62 results; (4) the results address the research questions pertaining to the primary purposes of interaction in virtual reality, the technologies employed and the contexts in which the interactions occur; (5) the discussions highlighted the main results obtained in the systematic review of the literature relating to the purposes, technologies and contexts of social interaction. (6) the conclusion identifies the gaps in the literature, the research limits and proposed items for future research

2 Background: The Media Richness Theory, the Evolutionary Path of Communication Technologies and the Transformed Landscape of Interpersonal Interactions

Interpersonal relationships within organizations are crucial for achieving common goals and enhancing performance. The relationships involve the exchange of outputs between workers or collaboration among them to produce shared outcomes [7]. Communication is a key factor influencing relationships, promoting cooperation, increasing employee commitment, improving performance, increasing satisfaction and reducing turnover rates within the organization [8]. Effective communication aims to reduce uncertainty and ambiguity by providing precise information and processing complex data to ensure clarity and understanding among employees [9]. Interpersonal relationships within organizations are crucial for achieving common goals and enhancing performance. The Media Richness Theory (MRT), developed by Daft and Lengel in 1986 [10], posits that the effectiveness of communication within organizations depends on the appropriateness of the media used and the nature of the communicative task at hand. This theory is underpinned by four key criteria: immediate feedback (such as the speed at which messages are sent and received), language variety (the presence of symbols enabling the conveyance of a wide range of meanings in a message), personal focus (the capacity to tailor the message to suit the recipients' specific circumstances) and multiple cues (the variety of communication channels utilized to compose a message) [11]. The MRT is based on the idea that different communication media vary in their ability to convey complex and effectively ambiguous information [11]. Richer media, characterized by immediate feedback, multiple cues, language variety and personal focus, are better suited for tasks involving high levels of uncertainty and ambiguity [12]. In contrast, less rich media are more appropriate for tasks with lower levels of complexity and ambiguity, where immediate feedback and multiple cues are less critical [13]. The theory emphasizes the importance of aligning the richness of the communication medium with the informational requirements of the task at hand to optimize communication effectiveness [14]. Face-to-face interaction is considered the most enriched medium due to its ability to provide immediate feedback, convey multiple cues through non-verbal communication and allowing for natural linguistic expression [11]. In contrast, media with low communicative richness, such as emails and forums, lack immediate feedback and multiple cues, leading to asynchronous interactions primarily reliant on text-based communication [12]. The evolution of communication technologies has transformed the landscape of interpersonal interactions within organizations. Instant messaging platforms have mitigated the limitations of asynchronous communication by introducing real-time feedback mechanisms. These platforms have incorporated features like image, audio and video sharing, diversifying the modes of interaction available to users and enhancing the richness of communication. Audio messages, in particular, play a crucial role in clarifying ambiguities by providing cues through voice intonation, thereby enriching the communication experience. Furthermore, voice and video calls facilitated by mobile phones or Voice over Internet Protocol (VoIP) services have enhanced immediate feedback provision by integrating visual cues like facial expressions and non-verbal signals into interactions. In the post-COVID era, the dynamics of interpersonal relationships in the workplace have undergone significant transformations, especially with the emergence of the metaverse as a new frontier for work interactions. The shift towards remote work during the pandemic has accelerated the adoption of virtual environments, leading to the exploration of metaverse offices as potential future teleworking models [15]. Organizations have been compelled to rapidly digitalize their operations and fostering a transition to virtual workplaces, also highlighting the need to adapt to this new paradigm. The pandemic, by necessitating remote working, seems to emphasize the importance of exploring innovative ways to maintain and enhance social connections in virtual settings. As organizations grapple with these shifts, the implications for employee engagement, communication and teamwork come to the forefront. In this direction, the metaverse transposed presents a unique landscape for redefining how individuals interact and collaborate within organizations, becoming a valuable object of study, as the one proposed.

3 Methodology

The choice for conducting a systematic literature review (SLR) is due by the need for understanding the evolution of interpersonal interaction in the transposed virtual reality environments. The SLR is a methodology that allows scholars to select, analyze and synthesize the existing studies in order to draw clear conclusions about the current state of knowledge on a particular topic [16]. The value of such reviews in providing a holistic view of the existing literature was emphasized by Elsbach and van Knippenberg [17]. According to Snyder [18], SLRs are instrumental in addressing research questions that individual studies may not be able to address by integrating evidence from different empirical findings. In addition, Hulland and Houston [19] and Paul and Criado [20] emphasized that SLRs add value by providing readers with a state-of-the-art understanding of existing knowledge, identifying gaps and inconsistencies, suggesting directions for future research to advance knowledge in the area under review. It is noted that SLR is considered a scientific tool rather than a mere literary summarized exhibition [21], as it requires a defined and rigorous criterion to effectively address test hypotheses and theories, thus minimizing

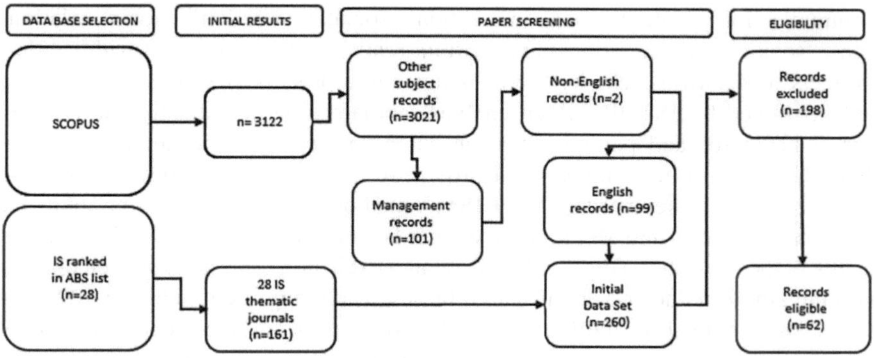

Fig. 1 Flow diagram for the selection of literature reviewed based on PRISMA

systematic error or bias [21–23]. The searching modes are based on the PRISMA (Preferred Reporting Items for Systematic Reviews and Meta-Analyses) model [24], which is represented by a flowchart outlining the stages of identification, screening and eligibility (Fig. 1). This model is essential for conducting a comprehensive way of understanding the status quo and through the literature search it ensures that all relevant studies are included in the analysis. The phases of the SLR implemented include two main stages: data collection and data analysis. In the data collection phase, the dataset consists of records selected from a single database and 28 thematic journals, whereas in the data analysis phase, the final dataset is examined descriptively [25]. This approach ensures a systematic approach adhering to the principles of the well-structured SLR methodology, as represented by its representative explications. In its lines and borders design, it contributes to the advancement of knowledge in the field of interpersonal interaction related to the transposed reality into virtual environments.

3.1 Data Collection

The first stage of data collection starts identifying an appropriate source of scientific journals, books and peer-reviewed conference proceedings useful for the SLR. To ensure a comprehensive data set, SCOPUS, a widely used search engine for academic literature, was selected. Although Scopus is one of the most comprehensive databases in the academic field, it does not include some scientific journals related to business information systems (IS). For this reason, a selection of ad hoc Journals in IS area has been implemented with the aim to extract papers referred to the study referring themes. The selection activity has been operated using the ABS ranking updated to the year 2021, evaluating by the keyword "information system", the scientific journals related to the ambit. The scientific journals related to business information systems identified to extend the results obtained from the Scopus database are 28 as reported in detail by the Appendix 1. The research query formulated refers to specific subject terms such as 'interpersonal relationship' (or 'interpersonal communication', 'interpersonal interaction', social interaction', 'social relationship', 'social communication') and 'virtual reality' (or 'metaverse') within titles, abstracts or keywords. The keywords underwent a process of validation through a tool facilitated by JSTOR, which enables scholars to systematically analyze and extract keywords and patterns from an extensive corpus of academic literature. Using bibliometric techniques, wildcards were used to include both singular and plural forms of the keywords. The PRISMA method (Preferred Reporting Items for Systematic Reviews and Meta-Analyses) has been implemented to identify relevant results in the flow chart (Fig. 1). Inclusion and exclusion criteria have been applied with the aim to reduce potential search biases. The string used yielded 3,122 relevant results published until May 2024, extracted from the Scopus database. Following the primary objective of the research, that is to explore the managerial aspects related to the relational dynamics of virtual reality, in filtering the main dataset for achieving a more specific and detailed result, a subset of 101 papers out of the total 3,122 results has been extracted. Two non-English results were then eliminated, leaving a dataset of 99 records. In addition, for a more comprehensive and holistic determination of the literary base, searching within the 28 thematic information system journals' web pages, 161 eligible results have been selected by the human sensitivity approach (Appendix 1). In this way, 161 results have been added to the previous 99 results, creating an initial dataset of 260 documents. The eligibility criteria in selecting literary contributions exclude 198 papers not aligned with the research objectives. After screening and eligibility assessment, the final dataset for the subsequent analysis accounts for 62 publications.

3.2 *Data Analysis*

The second step, Dataset Analysis, is a descriptive examination of the sample composed of the eligible 62 publications, taken into account in the way of obtaining information on related to the publication trends over the years (Fig. 2) and documents by type (Fig. 3).

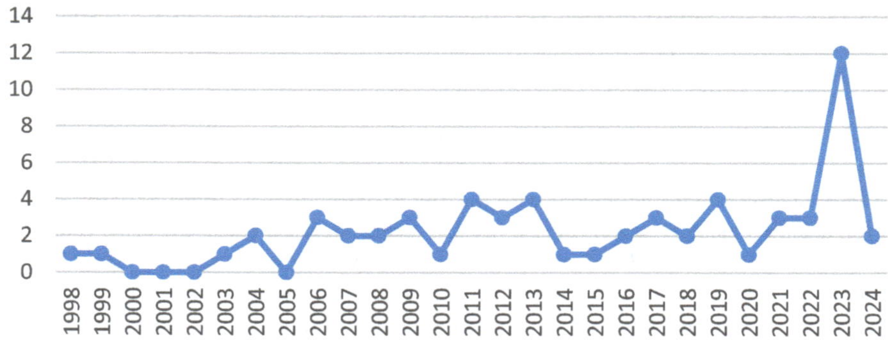

Fig. 2 Document by years

Fig. 3 Document by type

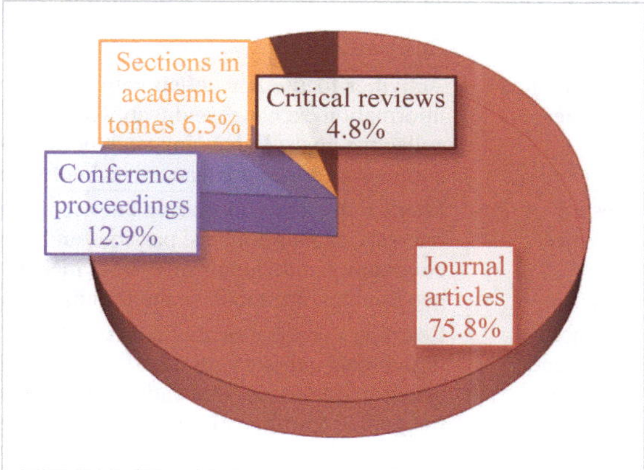

The research field of interpersonal interaction in virtual reality has its first publications in the early years of the twenty-first century (Fig. 2) because it correlates with the use of the Internet, the birth of virtual communities and the introduction of the first social networks. In this period, the interpersonal interaction seems to be mediated by text messages, consisting in formulating the base for the creation of a virtual community. However, the interest in this field of research has exponentially increased in recent years thanks to the emergence of the metaverse, immersive and interactive virtual reality.

Figure 3 shows the sources in the original dataset: mainly journal articles (75.8%), followed by conference proceedings (12.9%), sections in academic tomes (6.5%) and critical reviews (4.8%).

4 Results

The final dataset is an ad hoc structured with the aim to gain insights into (1) the main purposes for interpersonal interaction in virtual reality; (2) the main technologies used to interpersonal interact in virtual reality; (3) the main contexts of interpersonal interaction in virtual reality. The following sub-sections, resulting from the accurate thematic analysis behind the SLR, identify the aforementioned pillars in detail.

Table 1 The main purposes of interpersonal interaction in virtual reality

Purpose	Description	References
Work-related activities	Activities focused on collaborative project development, information exchange and teamwork aimed to achieve collective goals. Enhancing team performance through effective communication and advanced technological platforms	[26–59]
Leisure activities	Interactions focus on sharing knowledge about common interests such as hobbies, passions and games. In a virtual community, individuals interact to meet people in different geographical locations, make friends and support each other	[39, 40, 60–78]
Technology-mediated learning	Learning experiences are facilitated by technology, where individuals interact with others to acquire new knowledge and skills. Encompasses innovative teaching methods and integrative learning approaches in virtual environments	[79–83]

4.1 The Main Purposes for Interpersonal Interaction in Virtual Reality

Interpersonal interactions in the virtual environment serve a variety of purposes, such as (1) work-related activities, (2) leisure activities and (3) technology-mediated learning. Table 1 shows the main reason of interpersonal interaction in virtual reality.

4.1.1 Work-Related Activities

In terms of work, interactions within virtual reality revolve around establishing new methods of communication, collaboration and cooperation between geographically [26] dispersed individuals who share a common goal. The emergence of the Covid-19 pandemic has undeniably compelled individuals to remain within their homes, subsequently leading to a significant shift wherein professional interactions transitioned to the digital realm, thereby merging the previously distinct domains of home and workplace environments [44]. This encroachment into personal spaces, which are often shared with various members of the familial unit, has resulted in considerable challenges in maintaining a work-life balance, particularly for those individuals who are also fulfilling the role of caregivers or parents [44]. The pandemic period highlights that online interactions served to diminish the traditionally recognized hierarchical distance that existed between organizational leaders and their subordinates, thereby facilitating a mode of direct communication that transcended the limitations imposed by physical separation [44–46]. In the pre-pandemic landscape, individuals engaged in remote work frequently seem to encounter a sense of social and professional isolation, which in turn appears in restricting their access to career advancement opportunities [44]. Although the implementation of scheduled meetings has been shown to enhance team coordination and promote productivity it simultaneously results to move a noticeable decline in informal and spontaneous exchanges among colleagues, which are often crucial for fostering a collaborative work environment [44]. Consequently, the practice of remote seems to pauperize interactions, conducting to adverse effects on the fulfillment of essential relational needs and subsequently diminishing overall work engagement levels among employees [45]. The advent of Information and Communication Technology (ICT) has the potential to bolster work involvement by addressing the intrinsic needs for social and emotional connectivity, with the latter playing a pivotal role in cultivating an individual's sense of belonging both to toward the referring their workplace and the broader organizational context [45]. Nonetheless, it is pertinent to note that interactions conducted via video conferencing platforms are frequently perceived to be both mentally taxing and physically exhausting when compared to traditional face-to-face encounters. This is the result of evidence expressed by many individuals involved with high frequency in such virtual meetings [44, 46].

By contrast, using virtual teams offers the advantage of increasing working efficiency by interacting and sharing knowledge [27, 35], thus accelerating individual progress without having to repeat the mistakes of experienced colleagues. In this way, the capabilities afforded by Information Technology (IT) facilitate interaction among various organizations that may be situated at considerable geographical distances, thereby enabling the exchange of innovative knowledge that is specifically aimed at enhancing the effectiveness of products and improving the efficiency of processes [47]. The incorporation of social networks in professional settings enhances knowledge sharing and significantly boosts employee productivity while providing essential support during crises, highlighting the critical impact of social interactions [48, 49]; moreover, employees' positions within social media frameworks are influenced by various centrality measures, including degree, closeness, betweenness and eigenvector centrality, which collectively define their connectivity and influence within the network [50]. Link structures, in this context, pertain to the different types of relationships existing among members of a network. They play a crucial role in affecting both job performance and overall satisfaction among employees. These interpersonal ties can be categorized into two distinct types: (1) strong ties, characterized by the formation of close and frequent relationships that provide substantial emotional support and foster enhanced collaboration; and (2) weak ties, formed by individuals with infrequent and superficial interactions, act as essential links between diverse groups within an organization [50]. The efficacy and performance of work teams are heavily influenced by the nature of communication occurring among team members. The fundamental governor factor of the working teams is trust [51]. The concept of trust is derived from the perceptions that team members hold regarding each other's abilities and integrity in the short term, as well as from a sense of benevolence that is cultivated over the long term [54, 55]. Interestingly, teams' members of artificial intelligence (AI) systems are often regarded as possessing specific features: the AI members have superior capabilities and comprehensive knowledge; however, the non-humans are typically perceived as lacking the benevolence that is inherent to human interactions, which serves as a purely human factor that cannot be replicated by AI systems [55].

The establishment of clear and timely communication channels is absolutely critical to the overall success of virtual teams, as such communication fosters cohesion and alignment among team members [52]. Communication can be categorized as either socio-emotional or task-oriented in nature, with socio-emotional communication sometimes being deprioritized in favor of expediting work processes; however, it is crucial to recognize that task-oriented communication remains indispensable for maintaining quality control [53]. Notably, task-oriented communication tends to be more efficient when conducted through face-to-face interactions as opposed to mediated communication systems [53]. This dimension is functionally represented in trust-building actions [54, 55]. The building of trust is a fundamental aspect that is typically developed through face-to-face interaction; however, in the short term it can be replaced by a conceptual approach "swift trust" to the achievement of medium-term goals [28, 52, 56]. In the longer term, a lack of face-to-face contact may result in the virtual team disbanding [28, 36]. In work team, the establishment of trust acts as a catalyst for encouraging individuals to engage in proactive behaviors, which is accomplished through the mechanisms of frequent communication and the provision of feedback [54]. Trust serves as a moderating factor in the dynamics of team interactions, as it fosters the use of a positive tone characterized by expressions of empathy and mutual support among team members [54].

In addition to the pivotal role that trust plays, the phenomenon of team cohesion emerges as another significant factor that contributes to the enhancement of performance levels and the acceleration of consensus-building processes within the group [56]. The cohesive dynamics inherent within teams comprising virtual groups emerge and evolve through the establishment of a shared narrative that effectively addresses and elucidates the inherent challenges associated with comprehending the behaviors and actions of members who are not subjected to continuous visual and/or auditory interactions, which often complicates the process of mutual understanding and collaboration among participants [59]. However, it is essential to acknowledge that when cohesion reaches excessive levels, it may give rise to the detrimental phenomenon known as groupthink, wherein decisions are made hastily without the requisite consideration of alternative viewpoints or potential consequences [56]. Furthermore, relational conflicts often stem from inherent social differences among members, which can inhibit both cohesion and trust within the team dynamic [56]. Notably, individuals belonging to minority groups frequently exhibit a preference for engaging in virtual environments characterized by low social presence, as this preference serves to mitigate the risks associated with retaliation and punitive reactions from others [57]. In contrast, task-related conflicts tend to exert a positive influence on team performance, as they enhance the quality and depth of discussions, ultimately facilitating a greater likelihood of achieving group acceptance for proposed solutions [53, 56]. In the context of teams that include artificial intelligence (AI) members, it has been observed that the frequency and intensity of conflict tend to be lower compared to teams composed solely of human participants, especially when the AI members demonstrate high levels of performance [55].

In addition to what aforementioned and with the aim to create a holistic view on the emerging results, it is useful to deeply problematize the interpersonal relationships among team members, able to influence the ways and outcomes of relation. It is necessary to say that interpersonal relationships are significantly shaped by various factors, including individual personality traits (such as extroversion and introversion), interaction styles (which can range from constructive to aggressive or passive-defensive) and the cumulative experiences of the members [58]. Individuals who identify as extroverts typically display a propensity to engage more actively in team activities, which often leads to enhanced cohesion and a higher level of acceptance regarding the solutions proposed within the group [58]. Moreover, a constructive style of interaction is positively correlated with improved group performance, in stark contrast to aggressive or passive-defensive styles that tend to obstruct effective communication and collaboration within the team [58]. Additionally, the collective experience of team members translates into the production of higher quality proposals for solutions, thereby enriching the decision-making process [58].

Given this frame, in which inoculates the discourse on the possible transposition of the reality toward a virtual environment, it seems to be necessary to compare the dimensionality differences existing between virtualized contexts, from the past to the present evolutionary paths.

Initially, textual forms shaped how messages got interpreted, eliciting responses based on the emotional nuances conveyed. Currently, the immersive virtual environment facilitates worker interactions more effectively than 2D technologies [33] through the presence of avatars, which enhance non-verbal communication through improved facial expressions, more accurately reflecting the speaker's intentions [34]. In a professional environment, the immersive world facilitates seamless data sharing, offering 3D visualization of work-related materials and enables virtual manipulation [41], thereby enhancing interactions between individuals from different professions [30, 37, 41]. As a result, the virtual world serves as a platform for understanding organizational dynamics and supporting decision-making processes by validating solutions transposed into virtual environments [32]. Numerous studies [29, 31, 38, 40, 42] have highlighted the potential of using the metaverse in management contexts, focusing on interactions between employees and interactions between employees and consumers. The purpose of work-related interactions in virtual reality extends beyond teamwork to virtual communities that address industry-specific needs through the continuous dissemination of industry updates [43]. In addition, virtual communities are emerging between individuals within the same professional sphere outside of work hours, providing a platform for seeking support and sharing valuable professional insights [39].

4.1.2 Leisure Activities

Among the purposes of leisure activities, an important aspect of interpersonal interactions in virtual reality relates to the enjoyment of leisure. Facilitated by dedicated platforms [60, 63] or social network fan pages [61], this leisure activity involves individuals interacting on the base of common interests. Subsequently, there is a strong interest in sharing knowledge among community members and fostering interactions [39, 69–71]. Moreover, participation in crowdsourcing is encouraged or discouraged by the description of the task modulated by clarity and specificity and influenced by the emotional tone used [73]. Some individuals seek suggestions and advice on topics of interest, while others offer their expertise for reasons of community membership and social recognition. Participation within virtual communities is significantly moderated by the degree of cohesion present, which pertains to the closeness and connections that individuals establish with one another, as well as their attachment to the community itself, which reflects the emotional bonds that members forge with the community [77]. The most actively engaged members within these communities are often driven by intrinsic motivations, primarily derived from the satisfaction and pleasure associated with helping others through the sharing of knowledge and resources [76]. However, it is important to note that the introduction of extrinsic motivations, such as virtual rewards and the expectation of reciprocal assistance, tends to diminish the intrinsic motivation that drives highly active participants [76]. In contrast, those members who are less engaged or inactive may find themselves incentivized to share knowledge through the provision of virtual rewards [76]. The quality of discussions that unfold within online communities is directly influenced by the degree of internalization, which refers to the alignment of personal values and norms with those espoused by other community members and is indirectly affected by identification, which denotes the psychological involvement and emotional investment of the user in the virtual community [78]. In addition to the exchange of information, virtual interactions within communities are also aimed at meeting new people, making friends and receiving support [40, 64, 68, 72, 80]. Nonetheless, the concept of homophily prevalent within groups and social networks results in individuals often being exposed exclusively to opinions that mirror their own, a phenomenon that reinforces existing differences and constrains opportunities for mutual understanding and dialogue between diverse groups [74]. Conceivably, offline and online worlds merge through the organization of events advertised on social networks, where strangers get to know each other well enough to coordinate travel to the event [67]. During these events, content such as videos and photos is shared to update the virtual community and the relationships formed can continue through post-event online interactions [67]. Virtual communities originated in gaming environments that encouraged the new generation to engage and congregate in 3D spaces to communicate and collaborate on shared goals [62, 65]. Users typically enter the virtual realm through the utilization of avatars, which serve as digital representations that can function either as extensions or replacements of their real selves. The characteristics of these avatars, including their anthropomorphic features, vocal attributes, physical attractiveness and resemblance to the user, play a crucial role in shaping the attitudes and behaviors that individuals adopt within the virtual landscape, as well as the nature of their interactions with other users [75]. These factors collectively influence the confidence that users possess when it comes to collaborating with others in a digital context [75]. Furthermore, interactions within the early 3D virtual reality platforms such as Second Life have evolved into the diverse immersive worlds of the metaverse [66].

4.1.3 Technology-Mediated Learning

The ultimate purpose of virtual reality interactions extends to the educational environment, such as students learning in immersive classrooms through experiential learning [80, 82] and continued engagement in virtual communities after school [79]. The advent of Web 2.0 e-learning platforms has empowered employees to effectively access, create and evaluate a wide array of learning resources through the utilization of key performance indicators (KPIs), all while engaging in active discussions within dedicated forums that facilitate knowledge sharing and collaborative learning [83]. Furthermore, the integration of immersive technologies with museum culture demonstrates how digital heritage is transformed into an interactive educational tool, fostering enjoyable interactions between students and docents [81].

4.2 The Main Technologies of Interpersonal Interaction in Virtual Reality

Interpersonal interactions in the virtual world used a variety of technologies, such as (1) text-based computer-mediated communication, (2) immersive technology communication. Table 2 shows the main technologies of interpersonal interaction in virtual reality as derived by the thematic analysis made on the SLR.

4.2.1 Text-Based Computer-Mediated Communication (TBCMC)

Text-based computer-mediated communication has evolved into a wide range of tools and platforms for both asynchronous and synchronous information exchange. Although it has largely been replaced by more sophisticated technologies, the fax [27] was once an important means of sending scanned documents over phone lines. Email [26–28, 69, 71] has emerged as a fundamental pillar of digital communication, enabling the seamless exchange of text messages and attachments, revolutionizing both personal and professional correspondence. In addition, document sharing platforms [28, 50, 84] have become invaluable tools that allow multiple users to access, edit and collaborate on documents in real time or asynchronously, ultimately increasing productivity and improving teamwork. In addition, bulletin board systems (BBS) [26, 60, 71, 73, 85, 86] were early forms of online communities where users could post messages and engage in discussions, predating the modern Internet forums we are familiar with today.

Table 2 The main technologies of interpersonal interact in virtual reality

Modes	Technology	References
Text-Based Computer-Mediated Communication (TBCMC)	Fax	[27]
	E-mail	[26–28, 69, 71]
	Document Sharing	[28, 50, 84]
	Bulletin Board System	[26, 60, 71, 73, 85, 86]
	Forums	[36, 39, 43, 69, 76, 78, 79, 83–85, 87]
	Blogs	[39, 50, 70, 71, 84, 86]
	Chat Tools	[27, 50, 69, 79, 84]
	Mobile Phones	[28, 84]
	Instant Messaging (e.g., ICQ, MSN, Yahoo Messenger)	[26–28, 36, 39, 41, 71, 86]
	Voice over IP	[28, 41]
	Online Meetings	[27, 39, 44–47, 51–54, 56–59, 77]
	Video Calls	[28, 36, 44–46, 84]
	Social media (e.g., Facebook, Twitter, Instagram)	[36, 48, 49, 61, 67–69, 74, 84]
	Enterprise Social Media	[87]
Immersive Communications	Real-time Multisensory Social Interaction	[33, 41, 62, 65, 66]
	Virtual Reality	[30, 32, 42, 68, 75, 80, 82]
	Augmented Reality	[18, 20, 40, 43]
	Extended Reality	[43]
	Mixed Reality	[81]
	Artificial Intelligence	[55, 80]
	Machine Learning	[64]
	Blendshape (facial expression reproduction)	[62]
	Metaverse	[29, 31, 38, 40, 42, 66]

Forums [36, 39, 43, 69, 76, 78, 79, 83–85, 87] are online platforms that allow users to initiate posts and threads, fostering community discussions on a variety of topics. Blogs [39, 70, 71, 84, 86], on the other hand, are websites or web pages that are regularly updated by individuals or groups and serve as effective platforms for sharing opinions, news and various other forms of content. Blogs serve as a valuable tool for corporations, enabling them to disseminate pertinent information regarding current developments and advancements within their respective industries, thereby keeping both employees and stakeholders informed about significant professional news and trends that may impact their operations [50]. Chat tools [27, 50, 69, 79, 84] are real-time text-based communication utilities that facilitate instant messaging between users, contributing to fast and efficient interactions. In addition, mobile phones [28, 84] have become ubiquitous portable communication devices that support voice calls, text messaging and Internet access, significantly changing the way people communicate. Instant messaging services [26–28, 36, 39, 41, 71, 86] such as ICQ, MSN and Yahoo Messenger have gained popularity for enabling real-time text-based communication between users, further enhancing connectivity. Voice over IP (VoIP) [28, 41] technology has emerged as a breakthrough innovation, enabling voice communication over Internet protocols.

Online meetings [27, 39] are platforms that streamline the virtual meeting experience by integrating video, audio and text capabilities to support remote collaboration. The necessity for conducting remote meetings has become increasingly prevalent, particularly during times when physical proximity among team members is not feasible due to various circumstances, as evidenced by numerous studies [47, 51–54, 56, 58, 59, 77]. The global outbreak of the Covid-19 pandemic has fundamentally transformed the landscape of interpersonal interactions, making it imperative to utilize advanced technology platforms for communication, as in-person meetings pose considerable health risks associated with the transmission of infectious diseases [44–46]. Video calls [28, 36, 84] have become increasingly popular as a means of real-time video communication, bridging geographical distances and allowing users to see and hear each other during interactions. An augmented sense of social presence within virtual interactions can yield substantial relational advantages; however, it can simultaneously impose unique challenges, particularly for individuals belonging to underrepresent or minority groups within the workplace [57]. In contrast, virtual environments characterized by diminished social presence have the potential to alleviate disparities and reduce the likelihood of adverse reactions directed toward individuals from minority backgrounds, thereby fostering a more inclusive atmosphere [57]. In conclusion, social media platforms [36, 61, 67–69, 74, 84] such as Facebook, Twitter and Instagram have revolutionized online interactions by providing digital spaces where users can create, share and engage with content and each other, ultimately creating vibrant online communities. Moreover, the role of social networks within organizational contexts serves to amalgamate the collective knowledge and expertise of employees, acting as a rich reservoir of information while also providing crucial emotional support to address various challenges and obstacles that may arise in professional settings [48, 49]. Enterprise social media platforms function as internal communication channels within organizations, designed to facilitate the transmission of messages to either specific individuals or large groups, as well as to publish posts concerning professional updates, maintain wikis, manage company blogs and establish a cohesive network among the members of the organization [87].

4.2.2 Immersive Technology Communication

Immersive communication technology is designed to facilitate more compelling and lifelike virtual interactions through the integration of advanced sensory modalities. The objective is to enhance the realism and immersion of virtual interactions through the integration of various sensory inputs, thereby improving the overall experience. Three-dimensional virtual environments [32, 41, 62, 65], such as Second Life [66], have emerged as a means of creating a virtual world where users can interact with each other and the digital environment using avatars, which effectively creates a profound sense of presence in the virtual world.

Virtual reality (VR) [30, 32, 42, 68, 80, 82] is a technology that creates a simulated physical presence in a virtual environment by utilizing headsets. The objective is to provide users with immersive experience that enhances communication using visual and auditory stimuli. The utilization of VR technology has been demonstrated to markedly enhance the manner in which individuals interact within virtual environments, primarily through the utilization of avatars, which serve as digital representations of the users engaged in these immersive experiences [75]. In contrast, augmented reality (AR) [42, 68, 81, 82] superimposes digital information on the real world, thereby enhancing the user's perception. This technology enables the creation of interactive experiences that seamlessly blend the physical and digital realms. Extended reality (XR) [42] is a term that encompasses virtual reality (VR), augmented reality (AR) and mixed reality (MR). It represents a spectrum of environments where real and virtual elements are combined to create unique user experiences.

The term 'mixed reality' (MR) [81] encompasses a range of technologies that merge the real and virtual worlds, creating new interactive environments where physical and digital objects coexist and interact in real-time. The integration of these two distinct realms provides users with a high level of interactivity and immersion. Furthermore, the integration of artificial intelligence (AI) into virtual environments serves to enhance interactivity and customization to such an extent that it can facilitate the formation of virtual teams composed of AI entities, thereby revolutionizing the traditional paradigms of team collaboration and interaction [55]. The integration of AI [80] technologies into virtual settings enables the communication experiences to be more dynamic and responsive to user needs. Machine learning [64], a subset of AI, enables systems to learn and adapt from user interactions, thereby improving the level of personalization in virtual environments.

The degree of immersion experienced in the metaverse is contingent upon the utilization of virtual reality (VR) headsets [72], which comprise a 'helmet' and frequently two controllers. These controllers can either be connected to a personal computer (PC) or operate independently. Although prolonged use of such devices may induce fatigue, research indicates that users may be able to adapt to them over time. Additional devices, such as haptic gloves and garments [72], provide tactile feedback that resembles interacting with physical objects, thereby enhancing the immersive experience.

It is evident that the role played by the headsets' built-in sensors is of significant importance. These sensors monitor user movements (head tracking) to view real-world positions in the virtual realm, track eye movements (eye tracking) to convey user expressions and incorporate an audio system to heighten the sense of immersion. Blendshape technology [62] represents an advanced facial animation technology that captures and reproduces facial expressions. It plays a pivotal role in the enhancement of non-verbal communication in virtual settings, accurately depicting emotions and gestures.

The metaverse [29, 31, 38, 40, 42], a concept first proposed by Neal Stephenson in his 1992 novel Snow Crash, describes a hypothetical future iteration of the internet as a single, universal and immersive virtual world. The interconnected world would facilitate social interaction with avatars, virtual reality (VR) and augmented reality (AR) technologies for an enhanced and realistic experience.

4.3 The Main Contexts of Interpersonal Interaction in Virtual Reality

Interpersonal interactions in the virtual world developed a variety of contexts, such as (1) virtual teams, (2) virtual communities. Table 3 shows the main context of interpersonal interaction in virtual reality.

4.3.1 Virtual Team

The study of SLR indicates that the typical composition of virtual teams is within professional environments. The objective of such teams is the facilitation of collaboration between individuals who are dispersed geographically [47]. Research pertaining to virtual teams predominantly concentrate on the essential elements that

Table 3 The main contexts of interpersonal interact in virtual reality

Context		Description	References
Virtual Teams	Textual	Interactions within virtual teams facilitated by textual technologies such as email, instant message, shared documents and online meetings	[26–28, 35, 36, 44–47, 51–57, 59]
	Immersive	Interactions within virtual teams through immersive technologies like virtual reality and metaverse, fostering collaboration and communication through advanced virtual environments	[29, 30, 41]
Virtual Communities	Textual	Interactions within virtual communities using textual technologies such as blog, forum, social networks and instant messaging to share interests and information and to make friends	[39, 43, 48–50, 60, 61, 63, 67, 69–71, 73, 74, 76–79, 83–87]
	Immersive	Interactions within virtual communities through immersive technologies like virtual reality and metaverse, allowing users to engage in advanced social and learning experiences	[31–34, 38, 40, 42, 62, 64–66, 68, 72, 75, 80, 82]

contribute to their effectiveness, including but not limited to the development of trust, the fostering of cohesion among team members and the optimization of communication practices [47, 51–54, 56–59], extending to the examination of teams that incorporate artificial intelligence members as a part of their composition [55]. However, this scholarly perspective underwent a significant transformation as a direct result of the onset of the Covid-19 pandemic, necessitating the formation of virtual teams, due by the fact that traditional face-to-face meetings were rendered impossible accordingly to public health mandates aimed at mitigating the virus spread [44–46]. Evidence on virtual teams demonstrate that they interact primarily through text-based communication [26–28, 35, 36], including email, instant messaging, online meetings and more recently, immersive virtual environments [29, 30, 41] such as metaverse devices.

4.3.2 Virtual Community

The outcome of SLR regarding the context in which there are more interpersonal interactions is the virtual community, particularly due to the fact that these interactions predominantly take place in less formal activities where individuals come together based on shared interests such as hobbies, passions and gaming, or to exchange information [60, 61, 63, 69–71, 76, 83]. The motivation behind individuals joining virtual communities is different, encompassing a range of factors, including the desire to connect with individuals who share similar interests and values, the aim to form new friendships despite geographical distance, the objective to strengthen existing relationships and to seek and offer support to someone [67]. In addition to the realm of leisure activities, there exist virtual communities that are specifically tailored to address the professional landscapes, which are fundamentally designed to facilitate the solicitation of advice, the provision of support and the encouragement of collaboration among users who operate within the same occupational domain [48, 49, 84]. The collective sharing of experiences and expertise within a similar work environment, not only fosters a sense of cohesion among individuals but also lets users to actively engage in the integration of their diverse knowledge structure and background through meaningful interactions. In this way they generate exchanges within the virtual community framework [73, 79, 83]. Such dynamic interactions ultimately contribute to the enrichment of professional understanding and the enhancement of collaborative efforts, thereby significantly advancing the collective capacity of the community members involved [39, 43, 50]. The initial research efforts in the area concentrate on the identification of the influencing factors on the richness in engagement levels within these communities [60, 61, 77, 84, 87]. The emerging results demonstrate that the objective is to encourage members to actively participate by following posts and engaging in discussions through comments or new postings [76, 78, 85, 86]. With the evolutionary scenario of ICTs and the increasing needs imposed by globalized contexts the potential of virtual communities is enhanced itself through social networking platforms, which has further enhanced the virtual communities' experience by offering convenient access from any time and any location through mobile devices. This frame facilitates direct, private interactions via instant messaging and introducing additional features such as voice and video calls.

The evolution of virtual communities is further advanced with the advent of 3D gaming, imposing users to generate avatars for engaging within gaming communities [75]. Among these, as aforementioned adolescents predominantly utilized virtual environments like Second Life [66] to construct their identities, to seek refuge from daily pressures and partake in social interactions within a secure and regulated setting. Metaverse-based communities represent the most recent phase in this evolution, offering users the opportunity to engage without a specific goal, freely exchange interests and foster friendships with individuals residing in different places [31–34, 38, 40, 42, 62, 64–66, 68, 72, 80–82].

5 Discussion

The results emerging from the literature review demonstrate how the primary purpose of interpersonal interactions in virtual reality is to work collectively towards a common goal, regardless of the context. This is evident in the fact that, in both work and leisure contexts, collaboration among individuals is encouraged by the pursuit of winning a game. In this way, interactions facilitate the sharing of interests and the creation of shared knowledge. In addition to the pursuit of leisure, the sharing of common interests is also a key aspect of these activities. This leads to interactions that facilitate the construction of shared knowledge. The leisure activities purpose also encourages interactions between individuals who are unknown to each other, with the aim of facilitating the making of friendships. Furthermore, it becomes evident that the primary reason for adolescents entering three-dimensional virtual reality is to establish an environment in which they can define their identity, distance themselves from the stress of everyday reality and experience their own reality within a controlled environment [33]. In contrast, developments in the metaverse have been driven by the expansion of boundaries of reality into different virtual worlds, facilitating interaction with distant individuals, the consolidation of relationships and the creation of new ones. In professional environments, collaborations among individuals who are geographically separated or unable to meet in person, as a result of the Covid-19 pandemic, are established with the objective of disseminating knowledge to enhance a process or product. Consequently, virtual teams necessitate explicit and prompt communication channels, which are underpinned by trust and cohesion. The nature of the relationships among team members is influenced by the individual personality traits, communication styles and experiences of the members. Existing literature emphasizes the importance of in-person meetings for fostering trust among members; however, in urgent situations, this requirement may be circumvented to address immediate task demands. This occurrence is referred to as 'swift trust,' which tends to diminish over the medium to long term if interactions remain exclusively virtual. The dissemination of knowledge transpires not solely via virtual work teams, but also through digital communities within social networks or/and enterprise social media platforms where professionals from a particular domain interchange information, guidance and assistance in an informal manner. Another purpose noted in interactions in the virtual world is learning. However, this has received less attention than other purposes, as the use of interpersonal interaction as a teaching tool in virtual realities is less explored.

With regard to the results pertaining to the technologies employed for interaction in virtual reality, the majority of studies focus on computer-mediated communication, such as emails in the workplace, forums, blogs and bulletin board systems in the leisure activities, which involve asynchronous interaction among participants. The real-time feedback communication was introduced by the advent of instant messaging, concern also exchange of image, audio and video which clarify any ambiguities that may arise during interactions. Mobile phones or Voice over Internet Protocol (VoIP) services, which subsequently evolved to include video calls, let an increase of immediate feedback in interpersonal interaction and the integration of voice and visual cues, such as facial expressions and non-verbal signals. Social communication is mediated by avatar thought text, images, gestures or even voice in the three-dimensional virtual. The communications have immediate feedback among participants, but limited interaction channel such as text, image and voice. According to the media richness theory, modes of communication such as chat platforms, telephonic conversations, Voice over Internet Protocol (VoIP, and virtual meetings utilizing video conferencing enhance the effectiveness of communication by facilitating immediate feedback, offering a diverse linguistic experience through audiovisual elements and providing multiple cues through various available communication channels. Nonetheless, amplifying social presence is not invariably the optimal approach for interpersonal engagement; in fact, within groups comprising minorities, the strategy of minimizing the visibility of differences often serves as a mechanism to alleviate potential conflicts. An evolution in three-dimensional realities is the metaverse, where immediate interaction among avatars included body language and facial expressions. Furthermore, technological advances have facilitated an increase in corporeality in interactions within these virtual environments, enabling tactile interactions such as a pat on the back for encouragement or reassurance, which can be achieved using specialized gloves [72].

The results of the review indicate that the contexts in which relationships develop are predominantly virtual communities, which are primarily created for the purpose of sharing knowledge on common interests. The use of forums, blogs and bulletin boards are technologies that facilitate asynchronous interaction between a generalized group of subjects, with the majority of communication being textual. However, the addition of images and videos has become increasingly common. Virtual communities are also created with the aim of encouraging learning among participants, with the sharing of materials, information and advice. Additionally, they are used to support workers in the same sector or in the same working reality. With the advent of social networks, virtual communities can interact via instant messaging, which allows for prompt interaction with each other. Furthermore, the sharing of multimedia messages such as photos, audio and videos is also possible. Another context that emerges from the literature review concerns the formation of virtual teams in professional environments, which rely upon text-based tools such as emails and instant messaging. Furthermore, regular virtual meetings are held with the objective of enhancing communication and collaboration. The paucity of research in this field has led scholars to posit that face-to-face interactions are crucial for the establishment of trust among team members. The proposed contribution is based precisely on the need to find a complementary solution to face-to-face interactions in order to create the necessary trust for the improvement of the collaborative work teams in the medium and long term. Moreover, the metaverse can be a valid solution to meet the needs of creating remote interactions, managing to generate trust directly in the immersion of virtual reality, necessary to strengthen the cohesion of the virtual work team.

6 Conclusion

The Covid-19 pandemic has highlighted the need for social interactions and the inability of current technologies to communicate proximity, due to limited communication channels that do not take into account corporeality and thus body language or facial expressions, signals of greater communication. The aim of the paper is to highlight the evolutionary impact of technology in social interactions through a systematic review of the literature, focusing on the main purposes, such as those related to work, leisure and learning; to map the technologies used in virtual interactions, analyzing them from the point of view of media richness; and finally to identify the main contexts of evolution, such as virtual communities and virtual work teams. The use of MRT allows to highlight the inadequacy of communication through the current panorama of technologies and the possibility of satisfying these needs through the development of technologies linked to the metaverse.

The results underline a limited number of studies [30, 41] that have investigated the potential of the metaverse to facilitate knowledge sharing among individuals, enrich collaboration through virtual experimentation and provide a shared meeting space for team collaborators. In addition, the managerial literary production and the subsequent review provided reveal a dearth of contribution about interaction for learning activities purposes in virtual reality and a paucity of research concerning virtual work teams within the metaverse. On this outcome it is possible to structure the future avenues of the research. Despite the incorporation of journals that has aided in enhancing and establishing a more comprehensive literary coverage, the limitations of the research are related to the analysis of a single database such as Scopus, which only refers to the management literature to obtain the papers to be analyzed. Another limitation is the lack of an empirical study on how social interactions take place in virtual reality today and how the metaverse can become a means to replace face-to-face interactions. Consequently, future research should address the question of whether the potential of engagements in the metaverse as a supplement or even a substitute for face-to-face interactions could strengthen existing relationships and facilitate the formation of new connections. The managerial literature review reveals a dearth of contribution about interaction for learning activities purposes in virtual reality and a paucity of research concerning virtual work teams within the metaverse. Future research should investigate the evolution of virtual reality and its impact on social interactions, with a particular focus on learning activities and work teams. Experimental approaches could be implemented in effectively demonstrate, by direct observation, the effects, the preferences, potential and risks of the evolutionary trends in transposing real environments and paths into virtual ones.

Appendix 1

N°	Thematic journal in Information System ranked by the ABS list	Initial results	Final results
1	International Journal of Accounting Information Systems	2	–
2	Journal of Accounting and Management Information Systems	–	–
3	Journal of Information Systems	–	–
4	Information Systems Research	2	1
5	Journal of the Association for Information Systems	1	–
6	MIS Quarterly: Management Information Systems	–	–
7	European Journal of Information Systems	18	2
8	Information Systems Journal	15	1
9	Journal of Information Technology	11	1
10	Journal of Management Information Systems	25	8
11	Journal of Strategic Information Systems	3	–
12	Information Systems Frontiers	20	4
13	AIS Transactions on Human-Computer Interaction	–	–
14	Business & Information Systems Engineering	4	1
15	Communications of the Association for Information Systems	–	–
16	Enterprise Information Systems	8	–
17	Information Systems and e-Business Management	–	–
18	Information Systems Management	3	1
19	Journal of Computer Information Systems	21	–
20	Pacific Asia Journal of the Association for Information Systems	–	–
21	Scandinavian Journal of Information Systems	–	–
22	The Data Base for Advances in Information Systems	14	3
23	Australian Journal of Information Systems	5	2
24	International Journal of Business Information Systems	7	–
25	International Journal of Information Systems and Change Management	1	–
26	International Journal of Information Systems in the Service Sector	–	–
27	International Journal of Web Information Systems	–	–
28	International Journal of Information Systems and Supply Chain Management	1	–
	Total Results	161	24

Appendix 2

1. Baralou, E., & McInnes, P. (2013). Emotions and the spatialisation of social relations in text-based computer-mediated communication. *New Technology, Work and Employment*, *28*(2), 160-175.
2. Baruch, Y., & Lin, C. P. (2012). All for one, one for all: Coopetition and virtual team performance. *Technological Forecasting and Social Change*, *79*(6), 1155-1168.
3. Baskerville, R., & Nandhakumar, J. (2007). Activating and perpetuating virtual teams: Now that we're mobile, where do we go?. *IEEE transactions on professional communication*, *50*(1), 17-34.
4. Bruni, R., Piccarozzi, M., & Caboni, F. (2023). Defining the Metaverse with challenges and opportunities in the business environment. *Journal of Marketing Theory and Practice*, 1-18.
5. Du, J., Shi, Y., Zou, Z., & Zhao, D. (2018). CoVR: Cloud-based multiuser virtual reality headset system for project communication of remote users. *Journal of Construction Engineering and Management*, *144*(2), 04017109.
6. Flores-Albornoz, J., Asis, E. H., Asnate-Salazar, E. A. S., Espinoza-Rodríguez, H., Ramirez-Asis, N., Pandey, D., & Dadheech, P. (2023). Metaverse: the development of human culture in the future and cyberspace. In *Applications of Neuromarketing in the Metaverse* (pp. 52-61). IGI Global.
7. Goel, L., Junglas, I., Ives, B., & Johnson, N. (2012). Decision-making in-socio and in-situ: Facilitation in virtual worlds. *Decision Support Systems*, *52*(2), 342-352.
8. Hennig-Thurau, T., Aliman, D. N., Herting, A. M., Cziehso, G. P., Linder, M., & Kübler, R. V. (2023). Social interactions in the metaverse: Framework, initial evidence, and research roadmap. *Journal of the Academy of Marketing Science*, *51*(4), 889-913.
9. Huang, D., Yao, Y., Tang, W., & Ding, Y. (2018, December). Facial tracking and animation for digital social system. In *Proceedings of the 16th ACM SIGGRAPH International Conference on Virtual-Reality Continuum and its Applications in Industry* (pp. 1-8).
10. Saksilapachai, W., Mayakul, T., Wattanasirichaigoon, S., & Kiattisin, S. (2019, December). Communication process management within virtual work for startup entrepreneur. In *2019 fourth Technology Innovation Management and Engineering Science International Conference (TIMES-iCON)* (pp. 1-4). IEEE.
11. Stoller, J. K. (2021). On the power of spontaneous collisions: preserving culture and effectiveness in the pandemic. *BMJ Leader*, *5*(3).
12. Yao, X., Turoff, M., & Chumer, M. J. (2010). Designing a group support system to review and practice emergency plans in virtual teams. *International Journal of Emergency Management*, *7*(2), 137-150.
13. Dwivedi, Y. K., Hughes, L., Baabdullah, A. M., Ribeiro-Navarrete, S., Giannakis, M., Al-Debei, M. M., ... & Wamba, S. F. (2022). Metaverse beyond the hype: Multidisciplinary perspectives on emerging challenges, opportuni-

ties, and agenda for research, practice and policy. *International journal of information management*, *66*, 102,542.

14. Chen, Z. Z., & Liu, M. T. (2006, October). Computer mediated communication, social network and service industry. In *2006 International Conference on Service Systems and Service Management* (Vol. 2, pp. 1346-1349). IEEE.
15. Uludag, K. (2024). Use of Virtual Academic Environments During the Coronavirus Pandemic. In *Exploring the Use of Metaverse in Business and Education* (pp. 275-285). IGI Global.
16. Owens, D., Mitchell, A., Khazanchi, D., & Zigurs, I. (2011). An empirical investigation of virtual world projects and metaverse technology capabilities. *ACM SIGMIS Database: the DATABASE for Advances in Information Systems*, *42*(1), 74-101.
17. Schöbel, S. M., & Leimeister, J. M. (2023). Metaverse platform ecosystems. *Electronic Markets*, *33*(1), 12.
18. Shih, H. P., & Huang, E. (2015). Influence mechanisms that leverage participation quality in a professional virtual community: the social-relationship perspective. *Journal of Global Information Management (JGIM)*, *23*(4), 77-100.
19. Waizenegger, L., McKenna, B., Cai, W., & Bendz, T. (2020). An affordance perspective of team collaboration and enforced working from home during COVID-19. *European Journal of Information Systems*, *29*(4), 429-442.
20. Singh, H., & Dev, V. (2023). ICT-Driven Work Engagement Interventions in Work-From-Home: The Mediating Role of the Need for Relatedness. *Australasian Journal of Information Systems*, *27*.
21. Lal, B., Dwivedi, Y. K., & Haag, M. (2023). Working from home during Covid-19: doing and managing technology-enabled social interaction with colleagues at a distance. *Information Systems Frontiers*, *25*(4), 1333-1350.
22. Cui, T., Tong, Y., Teo, H. H., & Li, J. (2020). Managing knowledge distance: IT-enabled inter-firm knowledge capabilities in collaborative innovation. *Journal of Management Information Systems*, *37*(1), 217-250.
23. Wu, L. (2013). Social network effects on productivity and job security: Evidence from the adoption of a social networking tool. *Information systems research*, *24*(1), 30-51.
24. Cao, X., Guo, X., Liu, H., & Gu, J. (2015). The role of social media in supporting knowledge integration: A social capital analysis. *Information Systems Frontiers*, *17*, 351-362.
25. Schötteler, S., Laumer, S., & Schuhbauer, H. (2023). Consequences of Enterprise Social Media Network Positions for Employees: A Literature Review and Research Agenda. *Business & Information Systems Engineering*, *65*(4), 425-440.
26. Sarker, S., Ahuja, M., Sarker, S., & Kirkeby, S. (2011). The role of communication and trust in global virtual teams: A social network perspective. *Journal of management information systems*, *28*(1), 273-310.
27. Powell, A., Piccoli, G., & Ives, B. (2004). Virtual teams: a review of current literature and directions for future research. *ACM SIGMIS Database: the DATABASE for Advances in Information Systems*, *35*(1), 6-36.

28. Kahai, S. S., & Cooper, R. B. (1999). The effect of computer-mediated communication on agreement and acceptance. *Journal of Management Information Systems*, *16*(1), 165-188.
29. Jarvenpaa, S. L., Knoll, K., & Leidner, D. E. (1998). Is anybody out there? Antecedents of trust in global virtual teams. *Journal of management information systems*, *14*(4), 29-64.
30. Dennis, A. R., Lakhiwal, A., & Sachdeva, A. (2023). AI agents as team members: Effects on satisfaction, conflict, trustworthiness, and willingness to work with. *Journal of Management Information Systems*, *40*(2), 307-337.
31. Curşeu, P. L. (2006). Emergent states in virtual teams: a complex adaptive systems perspective. *Journal of Information Technology*, *21*(4), 249-261.
32. Windeler, J., Harrison, A., & Sundrup, R. (2024). Under the Radar or Into the Spotlight: How Does Social Presence Affect Minorities in Virtual Groups?. *ACM SIGMIS Database: the DATABASE for Advances in Information Systems*, *55*(2), 98-119.
33. Balthazard, P., Potter, R. E., & Warren, J. (2004). Expertise, extraversion and group interaction styles as performance indicators in virtual teams: how do perceptions of IT's performance get formed?. *ACM SIGMIS Database: The Database for Advances in Information Systems*, *35*(1), 41-64.
34. Fiore, S. M., McDaniel, R., & Jentsch, F. (2009). Narrative-based collaboration systems for distributed teams: Nine research questions for information managers. *Information Systems Management*, *26*(1), 28-38.
35. Bock, G. W., Ng, W. L., & Shin, Y. (2008). The effect of a perceived leader's influence on the motivation of the members of nonwork-related virtual communities. *IEEE Transactions on Engineering Management*, *55*(2), 292-303.
36. Chih, W. H., Hsu, L. C., & Liou, D. K. (2017). Understanding virtual community members' relationships from individual, group, and social influence perspectives. *Industrial Management & Data Systems*, *117*(6), 990-1010.
37. Eynard, R., Pallot, M., Christmann, O., & Richir, S. (2015, June). Impact of verbal communication on user experience in 3D immersive virtual environments. In *2015 IEEE International Conference on Engineering, Technology and Innovation/International Technology Management Conference (ICE/ITMC)* (pp. 1-8). IEEE.
38. Lawrence, L. (2003). 'These are the voyages…': interaction in real and virtual space environments in leisure. *Leisure studies*, *22*(4), 301-315.
39. López Vargas, K., Runge, J., & Zhang, R. (2022). Algorithmic assortative matching on a digital social medium. *Information Systems Research*, *33*(4), 1138-1156.
40. Mäntymäki, M., & Riemer, K. (2014). Digital natives in social virtual worlds: A multi-method study of gratifications and social influences in Habbo Hotel. *International journal of information management*, *34*(2), 210-220.
41. Richter, S., & Richter, A. (2023). What is novel about the Metaverse?. *International Journal of Information Management*, *73*, 102,684.
42. Simons, I. (2019). Events and online interaction: The construction of hybrid event communities. *Leisure Studies*, *38*(2), 145-159.

43. Chakraborty, D., Polisetty, A., Khorana, S., & Buhalis, D. (2023). Use of metaverse in socializing: Application of the big five personality traits framework. *Psychology & Marketing*.
44. Wang, K., & Tai, C. F. (2011, May). The influence of social presence on continual participation in online communities: The relational view based on social identity theory. In *2011 International Joint Conference on Service Sciences* (pp. 110-115). IEEE.
45. Pallot, M., Ruland, R., Traykov, S., & Kristensen, K. (2006, June). Integrating shared workspace, wiki and blog technologies to support interpersonal knowledge connection. In *2006 IEEE International Technology Management Conference (ICE)* (pp. 1-8). IEEE.
46. Zheng, Y., Zhao, K., & Stylianou, A. (2013). The impacts of information quality and system quality on users' continuance intention in information-exchange virtual communities: An empirical investigation. *Decision support systems*, *56*, 513-524.
47. Liang, Y., & Wang, Y. (2021, November). Investigation on the Influence of Virtual Reality Displays on People's Interaction. In *2021 International Conference on Culture-oriented Science & Technology (ICCST)* (pp. 6-10). IEEE.
48. Wu, S., Liu, Q., Zhao, X., Sun, B., & Liao, X. (2024). Attracting solvers' participation in crowdsourcing contests: The role of linguistic signals in task descriptions. *Information Systems Journal*, *34*(1), 6-38.
49. Kwon, H. E., Oh, W., & Kim, T. (2017). Platform structures, homing preferences, and homophilous propensities in online social networks. *Journal of Management Information Systems*, *34*(3), 768-802.
50. Aljaroodi, H. M., Adam, M. T., Chiong, R., & Teubner, T. (2019). Avatars and embodied agents in experimental information systems research: A systematic review and conceptual framework. *Australasian Journal of Information Systems*, *23*.
51. Kim, D. J., Salvacion, M., Salehan, M., & Kim, D. W. (2023). An empirical study of community cohesiveness, community attachment, and their roles in virtual community participation. *European Journal of Information Systems*, *32*(3), 573-600.
52. Zhao, L., Detlor, B., & Connelly, C. E. (2016). Sharing knowledge in social Q&A sites: The unintended consequences of extrinsic motivation. *Journal of Management Information Systems*, *33*(1), 70-100.
53. Shih, H. P., & Huang, E. (2014). Influences of Web interactivity and social identity and bonds on the quality of online discussion in a virtual community. *Information Systems Frontiers*, *16*, 627-641.
54. Monahan, T., McArdle, G., & Bertolotto, M. (2008). Virtual reality for collaborative e-learning. *Computers & Education*, *50*(4), 1339-1353.
55. Cole, R. N., & DeVine, L. (2023). Identifying the impact of innovative teaching approaches and integrative learning on the performance of students enrolled in biotechnology programs. *Journal of Commercial Biotechnology*, *28*(4).

56. Economou, M., & Tost, L. P. (2007). Educational tool or expensive toy? Evaluating VR evaluation and its relevance for virtual heritage. In *New Heritage* (pp. 258-276). Routledge.
57. Farooqui, N. A., Pandey, M., Mirza, R., Ali, S., & Khan, A. N. (2023). 8 Exploratory study of the parental perception of social learning among school-aged children based on augmented and virtual reality. *Augmented and Virtual Reality in Social Learning: Technological Impacts and Challenges*, *3*, 117.
58. Wang, M. (2011). Integrating organizational, social, and individual perspectives in Web 2.0-based workplace e-learning. *Information Systems Frontiers*, *13*, 191-205.
59. Wang, W. T., & Hung, H. H. (2019). A symbolic convergence perspective for examining employee knowledge sharing behaviors in company-hosted virtual communities. *Information Resources Management Journal (IRMJ)*, *32*(2), 1-27.
60. Chang, H. H., & Chuang, S. S. (2011). Social capital and individual motivations on knowledge sharing: Participant involvement as a moderator. *Information & management*, *48*(1), 9-18.
61. Chiu, C. M., Hsu, M. H., & Wang, E. T. (2006). Understanding knowledge sharing in virtual communities: An integration of social capital and social cognitive theories. *Decision support systems*, *42*(3), 1872-1888.
62. Lowry, P. B., Romano, N. C., Jenkins, J. L., & Guthrie, R. W. (2009). The CMC interactivity model: How interactivity enhances communication quality and process satisfaction in lean-media groups. *Journal of Management Information Systems*, *26*(1), 155-196.

References

1. Barankevich, R., & Loebach, J. (2022). Self-care and mental health among college students during the COVID-19 pandemic: Social and physical environment features of interactions which impact meaningfulness and mitigate loneliness. *Frontiers in Psychology, 13*, 879408.
2. Liang, Z., da Costa Junior, M. G., & Piumarta, I. (2020). Opportunities for improving the learning/teaching experience in a virtual online environment. In *2020 IEEE international conference on teaching, assessment, and learning for engineering (tale)* (pp. 243–250). IEEE.
3. Spencer, B. L., Doran, K. S., & Burcham, L. R. (2021). The virtual streptococcal seminar series and trainee symposium: Adaptations of a research community during the COVID-19 pandemic. *Journal of Microbiology & Biology Education, 22*(1), 10–1128.
4. Lochhead, I., & Hedley, N. (2021). Designing virtual spaces for immersive visual analytics. *KN-Journal of Cartography and Geographic Information, 71*(4), 223–240.
5. Bradbury, A., Schertz, S., & Wiebe, E. (2022). How does virtual reality compare? The effects of avatar appearance and medium on self-disclosure. In *Proceedings of the Human Factors and Ergonomics Society Annual Meeting* (Vol. 66, No. 1, pp. 2036–2040). Sage.
6. Webster, J., & Watson, R. T. (2002). Analyzing the past to prepare for the future: Writing a literature review. *MIS Quarterly*, xiii–xxiii.
7. Kleinbaum, A. M., Stuart, T. E., & Tushman, M. L. (2013). Discretion within constraint: Homophily and structure in a formal organization. *Organization Science, 24*(5), 1316–1336.

8. Tuzun, I. K. (2013). Organizational levels of analysis of communication satisfaction and identification in relation to job satisfaction. *Journal of Economics, Business and Management, 1*(1), 1–5.
9. Schäfer, M. S., & Fähnrich, B. (2020). Communicating science in organizational contexts: toward an "organizational turn" in science communication research. *Journal of Communication Management, 24*(3), 137–154.
10. Daft, R. L., & Lengel, R. H. (1986). Organizational information requirements, media richness and structural design. *Management Science, 32*(5), 554–571.
11. Bergener, K., & Hofmann, S. (2012). Collaborative media choice processes in virtual teams. In *8th International Conference on Collaborative Computing: Networking, Applications and Worksharing (CollaborateCom)* (pp. 372–380). IEEE.
12. Badger, M., Kaminsky, E., & Behrend, S. (2014). Media richness and information acquisition in internet recruitment. *Journal of Managerial Psychology, 29*(7), 866–883.
13. Liu, C. L. (2014). The impact of social cues and effectiveness in check-in advertising. *Kybernetes, 43*(7), 984–1002.
14. Tang, J., Zhao, Y., & Zhang, P. (2012). Moderating effects of perceived affordances on users' adaptive media use. In *Proceedings of the 2012 iConference* (pp. 576–578).
15. Šímová, T., Zychová, K., & Fejfarová, M. (2024). Metaverse in the virtual workplace. *Vision, 28*(1), 19–34.
16. Denyer, D., & Tranfield, D. (2009). Producing a systematic review.
17. Elsbach, K. D., & van Knippenberg, D. (2020). Creating high-impact literature reviews: An argument for 'integrative reviews'. *Journal of Management Studies, 57*(6), 1277–1289.
18. Snyder, H. (2019). Literature review as a research methodology: An overview and guidelines. *Journal of Business Research, 104*, 333–339.
19. Hulland, J., & Houston, M. B. (2020). Why systematic review papers and meta-analyses matter: An introduction to the special issue on generalizations in marketing. *Journal of the Academy of Marketing Science, 48*, 351–359.
20. Paul, J., & Criado, A. R. (2020). The art of writing literature review: What do we know and what do we need to know? *International Business Review, 29*(4), 101717.
21. Petticrew, M., & Roberts, H. (2008). *Systematic reviews in the social sciences: A practical guide*. Wiley.
22. Cronin, P., Ryan, F., & Coughlan, M. (2008). Undertaking a literature review: a step-by-step approach. *British Journal of Nursing, 17*(1), 38–43.
23. Campbell Collaboration. (2017). Campbell systematic reviews: Policies and guidelines.
24. Moher, D., Liberati, A., Tetzlaff, J., Altman, D. G., Antes, G., Atkins, D., Tugwell, P., et al. (2014). Preferred reporting items for systematic reviews and meta-analyses: The PRISMA statement. *Revista Espanola de Nutricion Humana y Dietetica, 18*(3), 172–181.
25. Gundolf, K., & Filser, M. (2013). Management research and religion: A citation analysis. *Journal of Business Ethics, 112*, 177–185.
26. Baralou, E., & McInnes, P. (2013). Emotions and the spatialisation of social relations in text-based computer-mediated communication. *New Technology, Work and Employment, 28*(2), 160–175.
27. Baruch, Y., & Lin, C. P. (2012). All for one, one for all: Coopetition and virtual team performance. *Technological Forecasting and Social Change, 79*(6), 1155–1168.
28. Baskerville, R., & Nandhakumar, J. (2007). Activating and perpetuating virtual teams: Now that we're mobile, where do we go? *IEEE Transactions on Professional Communication, 50*(1), 17–34.
29. Bruni, R., Piccarozzi, M., & Caboni, F. (2023). Defining the Metaverse with challenges and opportunities in the business environment. *Journal of Marketing Theory and Practice*, 1–18.
30. Du, J., Shi, Y., Zou, Z., & Zhao, D. (2018). CoVR: Cloud-based multiuser virtual reality headset system for project communication of remote users. *Journal of Construction Engineering and Management, 144*(2), 04017109.

31. Flores-Albornoz, J., Asis, E. H., Asnate-Salazar, E. A. S., Espinoza-Rodríguez, H., Ramirez-Asis, N., Pandey, D., & Dadheech, P. (2023). Metaverse: The development of human culture in the future and cyberspace. In *Applications of neuromarketing in the Metaverse* (pp. 52–61). IGI Global.
32. Goel, L., Junglas, I., Ives, B., & Johnson, N. (2012). Decision-making in-socio and in-situ: Facilitation in virtual worlds. *Decision Support Systems, 52*(2), 342–352.
33. Hennig-Thurau, T., Aliman, D. N., Herting, A. M., Cziehso, G. P., Linder, M., & Kübler, R. V. (2023). Social interactions in the metaverse: Framework, initial evidence, and research roadmap. *Journal of the Academy of Marketing Science, 51*(4), 889–913.
34. Huang, D., Yao, Y., Tang, W., & Ding, Y. (2018). Facial tracking and animation for digital social system. In *Proceedings of the 16th ACM SIGGRAPH International Conference on Virtual-Reality Continuum and its Applications in Industry* (pp. 1–8).
35. Saksilapachai, W., Mayakul, T., Wattanasirichaigoon, S., & Kiattisin, S. (2019). Communication process management within virtual work for startup entrepreneur. In *2019 4th Technology Innovation Management and Engineering Science International Conference (TIMES-iCON)* (pp. 1–4). IEEE.
36. Stoller, J. K. (2021). On the power of spontaneous collisions: Preserving culture and effectiveness in the pandemic. *BMJ Leader, 5*(3).
37. Yao, X., Turoff, M., & Chumer, M. J. (2010). Designing a group support system to review and practice emergency plans in virtual teams. *International Journal of Emergency Management, 7*(2), 137–150.
38. Dwivedi, Y. K., Hughes, L., Baabdullah, A. M., Ribeiro-Navarrete, S., Giannakis, M., Al-Debei, M. M., Wamba, S. F., et al. (2022). Metaverse beyond the hype: Multidisciplinary perspectives on emerging challenges, opportunities, and agenda for research, practice and policy. *International Journal of Information Management, 66*, 102542.
39. Chen, Z. Z., & Liu, M. T. (2006). Computer mediated communication, social network and service industry. In *2006 International Conference on Service Systems and Service Management* (Vol. 2, pp. 1346–1349). IEEE.
40. Uludag, K. (2024). Use of virtual academic environments during the coronavirus pandemic. In *Exploring the use of metaverse in business and education* (pp. 275–285). IGI Global.
41. Owens, D., Mitchell, A., Khazanchi, D., & Zigurs, I. (2011). An empirical investigation of virtual world projects and metaverse technology capabilities. *ACM SIGMIS Database: The DATABASE for Advances in Information Systems, 42*(1), 74–101.
42. Schöbel, S. M., & Leimeister, J. M. (2023). Metaverse platform ecosystems. *Electronic Markets, 33*(1), 12.
43. Shih, H.-P., & Huang, E. (2015). Influence mechanisms that leverage participation quality in a professional virtual community: The social-relationship perspective. *Journal of Global Information Management, 23*, 77–100. https://doi.org/10.4018/JGIM.2015100104
44. Waizenegger, L., McKenna, B., Cai, W., & Bendz, T. (2020). An affordance perspective of team collaboration and enforced working from home during COVID-19. *European Journal of Information Systems, 29*(4), 429–442.
45. Singh, H., & Dev, V. (2023). ICT-driven work engagement interventions in work-from-home: The mediating role of the need for relatedness. *Australasian Journal of Information Systems, 27*.
46. Lal, B., Dwivedi, Y. K., & Haag, M. (2023). Working from home during Covid-19: Doing and managing technology-enabled social interaction with colleagues at a distance. *Information Systems Frontiers, 25*(4), 1333–1350.
47. Cui, T., Tong, Y., Teo, H. H., & Li, J. (2020). Managing knowledge distance: IT-enabled inter-firm knowledge capabilities in collaborative innovation. *Journal of Management Information Systems, 37*(1), 217–250.
48. Wu, L. (2013). Social network effects on productivity and job security: Evidence from the adoption of a social networking tool. *Information Systems Research, 24*(1), 30–51.

49. Cao, X., Guo, X., Liu, H., & Gu, J. (2015). The role of social media in supporting knowledge integration: A social capital analysis. *Information Systems Frontiers, 17*, 351–362.
50. Schötteler, S., Laumer, S., & Schuhbauer, H. (2023). Consequences of enterprise social media network positions for employees: A literature review and research agenda. *Business & Information Systems Engineering, 65*(4), 425–440.
51. Sarker, S., Ahuja, M., Sarker, S., & Kirkeby, S. (2011). The role of communication and trust in global virtual teams: A social network perspective. *Journal of Management Information Systems, 28*(1), 273–310.
52. Powell, A., Piccoli, G., & Ives, B. (2004). Virtual teams: A review of current literature and directions for future research. *ACM SIGMIS Database: The DATABASE for Advances in Information Systems, 35*(1), 6–36.
53. Kahai, S. S., & Cooper, R. B. (1999). The effect of computer-mediated communication on agreement and acceptance. *Journal of Management Information Systems, 16*(1), 165–188.
54. Jarvenpaa, S. L., Knoll, K., & Leidner, D. E. (1998). Is anybody out there? Antecedents of trust in global virtual teams. *Journal of Management Information Systems, 14*(4), 29–64.
55. Dennis, A. R., Lakhiwal, A., & Sachdeva, A. (2023). AI agents as team members: Effects on satisfaction, conflict, trustworthiness, and willingness to work with. *Journal of Management Information Systems, 40*(2), 307–337.
56. Curşeu, P. L. (2006). Emergent states in virtual teams: a complex adaptive systems perspective. *Journal of Information Technology, 21*(4), 249–261.
57. Windeler, J., Harrison, A., & Sundrup, R. (2024). Under the radar or into the spotlight: How does social presence affect minorities in virtual groups? *ACM SIGMIS Database: The DATABASE for Advances in Information Systems, 55*(2), 98–119.
58. Balthazard, P., Potter, R. E., & Warren, J. (2004). Expertise, extraversion and group interaction styles as performance indicators in virtual teams: How do perceptions of IT's performance get formed? *ACM SIGMIS Database: The Database for Advances in Information Systems, 35*(1), 41–64.
59. Fiore, S. M., McDaniel, R., & Jentsch, F. (2009). Narrative-based collaboration systems for distributed teams: Nine research questions for information managers. *Information Systems Management, 26*(1), 28–38.
60. Bock, G. W., Ng, W. L., & Shin, Y. (2008). The effect of a perceived leader's influence on the motivation of the members of nonwork-related virtual communities. *IEEE Transactions on Engineering Management, 55*(2), 292–303.
61. Chih, W. H., Hsu, L. C., & Liou, D. K. (2017). Understanding virtual community members' relationships from individual, group, and social influence perspectives. *Industrial Management & Data Systems, 117*(6), 990–1010.
62. Eynard, R., Pallot, M., Christmann, O., & Richir, S. (2015). Impact of verbal communication on user experience in 3D immersive virtual environments. In *2015 IEEE International Conference on Engineering, Technology and Innovation/International Technology Management Conference (ICE/ITMC)* (pp. 1–8). IEEE.
63. Lawrence, L. (2003). 'These are the voyages…': Interaction in real and virtual space environments in leisure. *Leisure Studies, 22*(4), 301–315.
64. López Vargas, K., Runge, J., & Zhang, R. (2022). Algorithmic assortative matching on a digital social medium. *Information Systems Research, 33*(4), 1138–1156.
65. Mäntymäki, M., & Riemer, K. (2014). Digital natives in social virtual worlds: A multi-method study of gratifications and social influences in Habbo Hotel. *International Journal of Information Management, 34*, 210–220. https://doi.org/10.1016/j.ijinfomgt.2013.12.010
66. Richter, S., & Richter, A. (2023). What is novel about the Metaverse? *International Journal of Information Management, 73*, 102684.
67. Simons, I. (2019). Events and online interaction: The construction of hybrid event communities. *Leisure Studies, 38*(2), 145–159.

68. Chakraborty, D., Polisetty, A., Khorana, S., & Buhalis, D. (2023). Use of metaverse in socializing: Application of the big five personality traits framework. *Psychology & Marketing*.
69. Wang, K., & Tai, C. F. (2011). The influence of social presence on continual participation in online communities: The relational view based on social identity theory. In *2011 International Joint Conference on Service Sciences* (pp. 110–115). IEEE.
70. Pallot, M., Ruland, R., Traykov, S., & Kristensen, K. (2006). Integrating shared workspace, wiki and blog technologies to support interpersonal knowledge connection. In *2006 IEEE International Technology Management Conference (ICE)* (pp. 1–8). IEEE.
71. Zheng, Y., Zhao, K., & Stylianou, A. (2013). The impacts of information quality and system quality on users' continuance intention in information-exchange virtual communities: An empirical investigation. *Decision Support Systems, 56*, 513–524.
72. Liang, Y., & Wang, Y. (2021). Investigation on the influence of virtual reality displays on people's interaction. In *2021 International Conference on Culture-oriented Science & Technology (ICCST)* (pp. 6–10). IEEE.
73. Wu, S., Liu, Q., Zhao, X., Sun, B., & Liao, X. (2024). Attracting solvers' participation in crowdsourcing contests: The role of linguistic signals in task descriptions. *Information Systems Journal, 34*(1), 6–38.
74. Kwon, H. E., Oh, W., & Kim, T. (2017). Platform structures, homing preferences, and homophilous propensities in online social networks. *Journal of Management Information Systems, 34*(3), 768–802.
75. Aljaroodi, H. M., Adam, M. T., Chiong, R., & Teubner, T. (2019). Avatars and embodied agents in experimental information systems research: A systematic review and conceptual framework. *Australasian Journal of Information Systems, 23*.
76. Zhao, L., Detlor, B., & Connelly, C. E. (2016). Sharing knowledge in social Q&A sites: The unintended consequences of extrinsic motivation. *Journal of Management Information Systems, 33*(1), 70–100.
77. Kim, D. J., Salvacion, M., Salehan, M., & Kim, D. W. (2023). An empirical study of community cohesiveness, community attachment, and their roles in virtual community participation. *European Journal of Information Systems, 32*(3), 573–600.
78. Shih, H. P., & Huang, E. (2014). Influences of Web interactivity and social identity and bonds on the quality of online discussion in a virtual community. *Information Systems Frontiers, 16*, 627–641.
79. Monahan, T., McArdle, G., & Bertolotto, M. (2008). Virtual reality for collaborative e-learning. *Computers & Education, 50*(4), 1339–1353.
80. Cole, R. N., & DeVine, L. (2023). Identifying the impact of innovative teaching approaches and integrative learning on the performance of students enrolled in biotechnology programs. *Journal of Commercial Biotechnology, 28*(4).
81. Economou, M., & Tost, L. P. (2007). Educational tool or expensive toy? Evaluating VR evaluation and its relevance for virtual heritage. In *New heritage* (pp. 258–276). Routledge.
82. Farooqui, N. A., Pandey, M., Mirza, R., Ali, S., & Khan, A. N. (2023). 8 Exploratory study of the parental perception of social learning among school-aged children based on augmented and virtual reality. *Augmented and Virtual Reality in Social Learning: Technological Impacts and Challenges, 3*, 117.
83. Wang, M. (2011). Integrating organizational, social, and individual perspectives in Web 2.0-based workplace e-learning. *Information Systems Frontiers, 13*, 191–205.
84. Wang, W. T., & Hung, H. H. (2019). A symbolic convergence perspective for examining employee knowledge sharing behaviors in company-hosted virtual communities. *Information Resources Management Journal (IRMJ), 32*(2), 1–27.
85. Chang, H. H., & Chuang, S. S. (2011). Social capital and individual motivations on knowledge sharing: Participant involvement as a moderator. *Information & Management, 48*(1), 9–18.

86. Chiu, C. M., Hsu, M. H., & Wang, E. T. (2006). Understanding knowledge sharing in virtual communities: An integration of social capital and social cognitive theories. *Decision Support Systems, 42*(3), 1872–1888.
87. Lowry, P. B., Romano, N. C., Jenkins, J. L., & Guthrie, R. W. (2009). The CMC interactivity model: How interactivity enhances communication quality and process satisfaction in lean-media groups. *Journal of Management Information Systems, 26*(1), 155–196.

Algorithmic Transparency and Algorithmic Accountability in Organizations

Antonio Mastrogiorgio, Primiano Di Nauta, and Marcello Martinez

Abstract In this contribution, we explore the effects of algorithmic transparency and algorithmic accountability on organizations. Algorithmic transparency refers to the idea that algorithms should be transparent to the people who use, regulate, and are affected by those algorithms. This means that the input, processes, and their use should be known, even though the algorithms do not necessarily need to be fair. Algorithmic accountability refers to the idea that organizations should be held responsible for decisions made by the algorithms they use, even if they are unable to explain how the algorithms produce their results.

Considering that algorithms are increasingly substituting many human activities—making decisions in place of humans—organizational actors may not always agree with algorithmic decisions, yet they remain legally accountable for their choices. We posit that organizational actors may face an internal legitimacy challenge regarding rationalization and consensus when their preferences do not align with the opaque decisions made by the algorithm. We discuss the role played by organizational actors, as Centaurs or Cyborgs, depending on whether they totally delegate specific tasks to AI or deeply interact with AI to enhance their own decisions. We maintain that the contemporary emphasis on AI does not include an accurate and comprehensive reflection on the long-term effects on organizational systems.

A. Mastrogiorgio (✉)
University of Rome "UnitelmaSapienza", Rome, Italy
e-mail: antonio.mastrogiorgio@unitelmasapienza.it

P. Di Nauta
University of Foggia, Foggia, Italy
e-mail: primiano.dinauta@unifg.it

M. Martinez
University of Campania "Luigi Vanvitelli", Caserta, Italy
e-mail: marcello.martinez@unicampania.it

A. Tursunbayeva et al. (eds.), *Technology-Driven Transformation*, Lecture Notes in Information Systems and Organisation 79,
https://doi.org/10.1007/978-3-032-01396-5_8

Keywords Algorithmic transparency · Algorithmic accountability · Explainability · Centaurs · Cyborgs · AI act

1 Introduction

Isaac Asimov, the famous science fiction American writer of the twentieth century, describes in a chapter of his renowned work, the *Foundation* series, a dystopian future in which nuclear power plants were managed by priests who were ignorant of their functioning. These priests were solely involved in the replication of cryptic rituals and ceremonies necessary for the plants' operations. Far from being fictional science, contemporary society is gradually moving toward a similar scenario. A fundamental concern in the current debate on AI revolves around the idea that decisions made by algorithms lack transparency and are consequently not easily understood by humans. Despite this lack of transparency, humans are legally accountable for their decisions. To some extent, individuals are increasingly required to endorse algorithmic decisions based solely on their effectiveness, without fully comprehending how those decisions were made [1, 2].

Algorithmic transparency and algorithmic accountability are two notions gaining importance in contemporary debates. *Algorithmic transparency* refers to the idea that algorithms should be transparent to the people who use, regulate, and are affected by them. This means that the inputs, processes, and their uses should be known, even though the algorithms do not necessarily need to be fair. *Algorithmic accountability*, on the other hand, emphasizes that organizations should be held responsible for the decisions made by the algorithms they use, even if they cannot fully explain how the algorithms produce their results.

In our paper, we explore the effects of algorithmic transparency and accountability on organizations. As AI increasingly replaces many human activities, including decision-making, organizational actors face a potential misalignment between human and AI decisions. This misalignment extends beyond the performance of the decisions and affects the overall organizational dynamics. Organizational actors may not always agree with AI decisions, yet they remain legally accountable for them. Consequently, they grapple with internal challenges related to both the difficulty of rationalizing algorithmic decisions and the loss of consensus when algorithms replace human decision-makers.

Our paper must be also conceptualized within the general problem of a common regulatory and legal framework for AI (considering that in the EU, the AI Act came into force on 1 August 2024).

The rest of the paper is organized as follows. In Sect. 2, we review the current debate on the transparency and accountability of AI. In Sect. 3, we explore the impact of transparency and accountability in organizations. In Sect. 4, we discuss the organizational implications through the notion of Centaurs and Cyborgs. The last Sect. 5 offers a conclusion.

2 Theoretical Background

The relevance of algorithmic transparency and algorithmic accountability is mirrored by the regulatory debate taking place at the institutional level in several advanced countries. In April 2023, the European Commission launched the European Centre for Algorithmic Transparency [3] with the explicit aim of contributing with scientific and technical expertise to the Digital Services Act [4]. The European Audiovisual Observatory, which is a public service organization part of the Council of Europe in Strasbourg [5] recently published a new, in-depth report, about the regulation of algorithms [6]. This report is useful for understanding the state of the debate and anticipating its evolution.

The general debate can be framed through the *black box* problem. In the words of Cappello (2023, p. 80), "A "black box" is generally understood as a system which can be viewed in terms of its inputs and outputs, but not in terms of its internal workings. In the context of algorithmic decision-making, this black box refers to the lack of transparency in how algorithmic or AI systems operate and make decisions, meaning that there is no way of explaining how an automated system achieved a particular decision" [6]. It's important to note that black-box models may not be understood even by domain experts, unlike the so-called white-box models that are understandable to experts in the domain.

The black box problem is strictly related to the *explainability* of AI algorithms, particularly Machine Learning (ML) algorithms. The High-Level Expert Group on AI, created by the European Commission, proposes an articulated definition of the problems linked to explainability. According to their guidelines, "Explainability concerns the ability to explain both the technical processes of an AI system and the related human decisions (e.g. application areas of a system)" (p. 18). Or rather, "Explainability concerns the ability to explain both the technical processes of an AI system and the related human decisions (e.g., application areas of a system)" [7].

They further emphasize that "explanations of the degree to which an AI system influences and shapes the organisational decision-making process, design choices of the system, and the rationale for deploying it, should be available (hence ensuring business model transparency)" [7].

de Streel A., et al. (2020)—following the UK Data Protection Authority, The Information Commissioner's Office (ICO)—articulate explainability in the following points [8]:

- Rationale explanation: the reasons that led to a decision, delivered in an accessible and non-technical way;

- Responsibility explanation: who is involved in the development, management and implementation of an AI system, and who to contact for a human review of a decision;
- Data explanation: what data has been used in a particular decision and how;
- Fairness explanation: steps taken across the design and implementation of an AI system to ensure that the decisions it supports are generally unbiased and fair, and whether or not an individual has been treated equitably;
- Safety and performance explanation: steps taken across the design and implementation of an AI system to maximize the accuracy, reliability, security and robustness of its decisions and behaviours;
- Impact explanation: the impact that the use of an AI system and its decisions has or may have on an individual, and on wider society;

It is important to note that the notion of explainability is traditionally distinct from the one of *interpretability*, where "Model Explainability aims to communicate the reasoning of AI/ML/DL [Artificial Intelligence/Machine Learning/Deep Learning] technology to end users, while model interpretability focuses on in-powering model transparency so that users will understand precisely why and how a model generates its results" (p. 197) [9].

2.1 Algorithmic Transparency and Algorithmic Accountability

Within the general debate about explainability, we encounter the common distinction between algorithmic transparency and algorithmic accountability. The European Audiovisual Observatory [5] provides articulate and useful definitions for both algorithmic transparency and algorithmic accountability.

With reference to *algorithmic accountability* "The concept of "accountability" refers to the idea that someone is responsible for their actions, meaning that a person has to explain and justify their decisions or acts, and then to make amends for any fault or error. In law, accountability refers to legal responsibility for actions, decisions and their consequences, which is not necessarily linked to natural persons if understood broadly" (p. 77) [6]. With reference to *algorithmic transparency* Capello (2023) provides an articulate definition declaring that "Transparency enables those affected by a decision or action to know the reasons for that action or decision, and to enable the affected party to evaluate the quality of these reasons" (p. 86) [6]. The author adds: "where algorithmic systems are implemented, appropriate levels of transparency are recommended with regard to inter alia the use, design and basic processing criteria and methods of these systems. For instance, in the EU, the Proposal for an AI Act requires that so-called high-risk AI systems be designed and developed in such a way to ensure that their operation is sufficiently transparent to enable users to interpret the system's output and use it appropriately" [6]. Such definitions and articulations were based on the Proposal for an AI Act [10].

Hence, algorithmic transparency refers to the idea that algorithms should be transparent to the people who use, regulate, and are affected by those algorithms. This means that the input, processes, and their use should be known, even though the algorithms do not necessarily need to be fair. Algorithmic accountability refers to the idea that organizations should be held responsible for decisions made by the algorithms they use, even if they are unable to explain how the algorithms produce their results.

It is important to note that explainability is not an absolute category; rather, we observe different degrees of explainability. There exists a general trade-off between explainability and performance: typically, the more a model is explainable, the less performative it is for a given task. For instance, while a linear regression model is easily understood compared to a neural network, the latter is more performative for specific tasks [9]. Generally speaking, performance comes at the expense of transparency. However, it is also essential to recognize that performance and transparency should not be viewed in Manichean terms. An algorithm can exhibit varying levels of transparency and performance. In other words, we can compare several classes of models for a specific task [11], each characterized by a specific trade-off between transparency and performance.

Interestingly, in EU the AI Act came into force on 1 August 2024 after being approved by the European Parliament (on 13 March 2024) and by the Council (on 21 May 2024) [10].

Our emphasis on the European scenario is not casual: the regulatory framework in the EU is considered one of the most advanced by international observers. We can reasonably expect that many democratic countries will align with the EU framework in the coming years, considering that historically, EU regulations have often served as a precursor for addressing many social concerns and ethical dilemmas. Given that the notions of algorithmic transparency and algorithmic accountability have been formulated as legal constructs, we expect they will permeate organizations through the regulatory system.

3 Theoretical Development

The use of AI in organizational settings is a well-established area of research, particularly in the context of information systems applied to HR [12, 13], with applications in specific domains such as healthcare [14, 15].

While many scholars highlight the promises of AI in organizational settings [16, 17] about its potential risks and misunderstandings [18, 19]. Recent research places particular emphasis on the ethics of people analytics and related biases, including racial and gender bias [20–23]. In HR applications, algorithmic decisions are perceived as less fair than identical decisions by humans [24].

The kind of problem we are discussing here differs from that of unfair decisions made by an algorithm. Here, we assume a sharp distinction between the quality of a decision and its value implications, or rather, we highlight the distinction between factual judgments and value judgments. In more detail, the quality of decision-making is entirely independent of its fairness: we could make a fair decision that is completely opaque, and we could make an unfair decision that is completely transparent. This independence is encapsulated in the very definition of transparency (provided in the previous sections), which has been deliberately formulated prescinding from fairness. Nevertheless, the independence between facts and values, far from being neutral, does not eliminate but rather exacerbates ethical concerns as it introduces a new class of problems: an organizational actor is accountable not only for the opaque decision made by an algorithm but, precisely because of this opacity, we believe that the actor will increasingly be held accountable for its long-range ethical consequences.

3.1 When Humans Do Not Align with Machine Decisions

The issue of explainability of AI in organizational settings remains an under-investigated domain, probably because the technology and the regulatory framework, far from being stable, are still evolving. To understand the relevance of this matter, let's consider this mental experiment based on the prototypical case of an HR department in a public institution involved in the hiring process for a new public manager. This standard process typically involves several steps, where the candidates admitted to the shortlist for a final interview are normally ranked. Let us suppose that, within the first stage of the selection process, a hiring committee divides the pool of evaluated candidates into three groups: (a) a set of fit candidates likely to be included in the shortlist for an interview; (b) a "grey zone" composed of candidates whose fit is lower but who possess important features; (c) a set of inadequate candidates who should not be included in the shortlist for the final interview.

Now, let's imagine a different situation in which the hiring committee decides to fully delegate the selection process to AI. This prototypical situation—where an HR department relies on an algorithm—is plausible, considering that using AI to support human decision-making is a natural trend in contemporary organizational practices. There is evidence that job applicants react negatively toward AI-based selection practices [25]. In our mental experiment, the selection process is delegated to a powerful algorithm that has been trained for the same task and successfully used in other similar organizations, particularly within HR departments. The algorithm generates its own ranking of the candidates. Notice that common machine learning (ML) algorithms are intrinsically non-transparent, making it challenging to understand their underlying logic. The hiring committee can use the algorithm's results without comprehending how the results were generated, given that the underlying model relies on intricate relationships among many variables and operates nonlinearly.

The eventual alignment or misalignment between human and machine decisions is crucial. If human and machine decisions align (i.e., the ranking of candidates is the same), there are good reasons to hypothesize that AI will be considered an "endorser" of the human decisions. In this scenario, the decisions made by the algorithm corroborate and strengthen those made by humans.

However, the situation changes dramatically in cases of misalignment—when human decisions substantially differ from those made by the algorithm. Let's imagine that the algorithm produces a ranking where the candidates at the top belong to the "grey zone" of the ranking created by humans. In other words, AI selects some individuals as the best candidates, even though the hiring committee initially considered them implausible. This misalignment is not unlikely and represents a probable scenario. Indeed, we can expect that the decisions made by algorithms should not merely replicate human decisions but rather improve the quality of human decision-making precisely because they select different (and potentially better) alternatives.

Should the hiring committee member endorse the decision made by the AI, or should they discard it? The plausible misalignment between human and AI decisions creates several consequences. More precisely, the problem is not merely about the different performance in decision-making between humans and machines; it is about the organizational consequences of the eventual misalignment. Indeed, if the hiring committee members decide to discard the human decision and adopt the ranking created by the machine, they should also account for the decision made by the machine—potentially hiring the "wrong" person (i.e., a manager who will be unsuccessful). On the contrary, if the hiring committee members choose to discard the decision made by the algorithm, they must take full responsibility for a decision not endorsed by AI.

The organizational implications of discarding human decisions in favor of machines can be analyzed in terms of rationalization and consensus.

Rationalization In the "realm" of decision-making, individuals often construct meaningful, consistent, and plausible narratives about how choices were made. Non-understandable decisions create discomfort, regardless of their quality. This phenomenon is so pronounced that humans often fall prey to "hindsight" stories, where they retroactively create explanations for decisions after the fact [26, 27]. People naturally gravitate toward coherent and straightforward accounts of decision processes, rather than embracing the inherent opacity of decision-making [28].

Translating this human tendency to the domain of algorithms introduces a new layer of complexity. When an algorithm makes a good but non-transparent decision, it can lead to discomfort for the human decision-maker. The feeling of being replaced by a machine, coupled with the inability to understand (or learn from) the algorithm, creates frustration and dissonance. In such scenarios, the actors responsible for the machine's decision may find themselves at odds with the algorithm's choice.

A decision-maker who legally endorses an opaque decision made by AI may also be psychologically vulnerable. For instance, consider an individual legally accountable for an airplane that transports people, yet is entirely maneuvered by AI. The impossibility of rationalizing how decisions were made, coupled with the necessity of being accountable for those decisions, creates a significant organizational challenge related to the (im)possibility of understanding both the decision process and its outcomes.

This (im)possibility could lead to internal dissonance. In some cases, humans are held accountable for an unsuccessful decision they never made and do not understand. Interestingly, in other cases, humans are accountable for a successful decision they never made and cannot comprehend. Rationalizing unearned success poses a problem that organizations may face in the future.

Consensus If an individual actor cannot rationalize a decision made by a machine, it is likely that the actor will struggle to communicate and explain this decision to other organizational individual actors. When a machine's decision diverges from the one proposed by humans, the decision maker, accountable for the machine decision, is subject to a decrease of consensus among its subordinates and peers. Justifying a decision made solely by a machine, without human agreement, is problematic. If a human decision maker lacks trust in AI but legally endorses its decision, her/his legitimacy may be compromised.

We cannot expect an increase of commitment if the individual, legally accountable for a decision, does not endorse the decision, because of its opacity. A good but non-transparent decision, made by the machine but not endorsed by the humans that account for this decision, is also a decision that reduces the legitimacy of the humans.

It is important to note that the decrease in consensus, far from being the end of the story, leads to additional detrimental consequences. For instance, consider our example where an AI-hired manager (who was an implausible candidate for the human hiring committee) joins the organization. In the best-case scenario, the organizational response is cold. The new manager may not be welcomed by the boss (whose interest was expressed by the hiring committee), resulting in challenges regarding acceptance by peers.

Hence, machine intelligence, due to its opacity, likely amplifies opacity in organizational dynamics. This arises from the ambiguity created by machine decisions. The problem of consensus also persists because it is impossible to predict ex ante whether specific organizational actors will agree or disagree with an artificial decision. In other words, the mere presence of machine decisions introduces opacity, as actors cannot form reasonable expectations about the "black box" of machines decisions.

Consider our example: when a new manager is hired by a human committee, organizational actors have reasonable expectations based on the preferences and attitudes of the hiring committee (which is somewhat predictable). However, the same cannot be said for machines: their decisions are unpredictable not only due to opacity but also because they lack human trait and will, that would make their future choices discernible. Consequently, the very presence of machine decision-making alters the "rules of the game" regarding consensus. It is important to note that artificial decisions are preferred only when they entail losses, but reducing opacity through explanations does not increase delegation to AI [29].

Speculatively, the (mis)alignment between humans and machines redefines Barnard's classical view of efficiency: while humans and machines may share aligned intents and goals, humans may struggle to anticipate how artificial systems will orient the decision-making process.

4 Organizational Implications

Bankins et al. (2024) present a systematic review of empirical research that illuminates the implications of AI use in the workplace [30]. The study focuses on several key themes, including (1) human–AI collaboration, (2) perceptions of algorithmic and human capabilities, (3) worker attitudes towards AI, (4) AI as a control mechanism in algorithmic management of platform-based work, and (5) labor market implications of AI. The acceleration of AI in the last 5 years has opened new issues that render traditional research programs on Information Systems somewhat obsolete. We are gradually transitioning from an era in which artificial systems merely served as tools to one where they function as autonomous agents, competing with humans.

In our previous example, we explored an extreme scenario where the entire decision-making process is entirely delegated to a machine, effectively replacing human decision-making. However, a more prudent approach involves not directly comparing humans and machines in absolute terms. Instead, we should consider which tasks algorithms excel at compared to humans, identify situations where human-made decisions are preferable, and explore ways to integrate the strengths of both.

4.1 A Nuanced Approach: Centaurs and Cyborgs

With reference to the attitudes of organizational actors towards AI, Dell'Acqua et al. (2023) propose an effective distinction between *Centaurs* (like the mythical half-horse/half-human creature) and *Cyborgs* [31]. Centaurs represent such individuals delegating their solution-creation activities to the AI or to themselves. In their own words (p. 16) the approach of Centaurs "involves a similar strategic division of labor between humans and machines closely fused together. Users with this strategy switch between AI and human tasks, allocating responsibilities based on the strengths and capabilities of each entity. They discern which tasks are best suited for human intervention and which can be efficiently managed by AI" [31]. Cyborgs represent such individuals that tend to integrate the task with the technology through a continuous interaction. In their own words (p. 16) the approach of Cyborgs "is about intricate integration. Cyborg users don't just delegate tasks; they intertwine their efforts with AI at the very frontier of capabilities. This strategy might manifest as alternating responsibilities at the subtask level, such as initiating a sentence for the AI to complete or working in tandem with the AI" [31].

In the previous example, we explored the extreme situation where the entire decision-making process was entirely delegated to a machine. However, the categories of Centaurs and Cyborgs introduce a nuanced approach.

Let's consider a situation in which the hiring committee adopts the attitude of a Centaur. Imagine breaking down the decision process into subprocesses, each with a fine-grained articulation of necessary operations. Here, AI intelligence supports only sub-tasks. For instance, AI could extract relevant information from candidates' CVs or compare competences against external benchmarks. In this specific case, an individual's knowledge of the strengths of AI is used to switch between human and AI, with reference to specific sub-tasks. Transparency becomes less stringent because algorithms operate where they excel, and their opacity is confined to those specific sub-tasks. The overall decision process remains, to some degree, under human control even if the details are somewhat opaque.

Let's consider another situation in which the hiring committee adopts the attitude of a Cyborg. In this case, the hiring committee relies on AI for each of the sub-tasks throughout the entire workflow. The committee actively engages with AI to elicit useful outputs and continually questions the system to experiment and refine its output. This approach is more intricate, requiring a deeper understanding of the potential of generative AI. It involves ongoing interaction with AI, where actions include providing examples of correct answers before posing questions, asking AI to explain specific decisions, directing AI's focus to particular data, adding data after an initial output, and even expressing disagreement with AI decisions [31]. As a result, the hiring committee integrates and revises the entire decision-making process based on the results generated by the algorithms. Essentially, the human decision maker becomes "augmented" through the use of AI. However, transparency in this specific case becomes a "noisy" construct. Establishing a clear boundary between human and machine decision-making becomes nearly impossible due to their deep integration, which doesn't follow a linear or temporal pattern. Opacity arises from the continuous interaction between humans and machines.

Fully delegating decisions to AI is an extreme scenario. Typically, organizational actors assume the roles of Centaurs or Cyborgs, depending on whether they delegate specific tasks to AI or engage in deep interaction to enhance their decision-making. We believe that distinguishing between Centaurs (who selectively delegate to AI) and Cyborgs (who actively collaborate with AI) provides a valuable analytical framework for exploring how transparency and accountability will impact organizations in the short- and mid-term.

5 Conclusions

While there is significant debate about the risks of AI intelligence for society [32], the effects of AI in organizational settings remain an under-investigated topic [30]. Among organizational scholars, the promise of AI seems to surpass its perils.

We believe that this situation in the organizational debate deserves balance through considering that AI may be non-neutral in preserving organizational practices. To increase overall trust in AI, human organizational actors can actively work to reduce opacity through dedicated organizational standards and access to knowledge [33]. However, such expedients can only mitigate the problem as they do not eliminate the organizational consequences of artificial decisions. Once a decision is delegated to a machine, the role of human decision-makers takes on a different meaning. In the best case, organizational actors become mere endorsers of decisions made by AI—a faith-like endorsement, given that common ML algorithms are typically opaque and not easily explained. Humans remain accountable for AI-driven decisions, even though they cannot fully understand the intricacies of AI processes.

The good news is that fully delegating decisions to AI is an extreme case. Normally, individual actors play the roles of Centaurs or Cyborgs, depending on whether they delegate specific tasks to AI or engage in deep interaction to improve their own decision-making.

5.1 Last Remarks

During the 1960s, Herbert A. Simon famously predicted that "machines will be capable, within twenty years, of doing any work a man can do". This prediction, shared by many other notable scientists of that era, turned out to be surprisingly inaccurate. In the 1980s, several AI research projects were abandoned due to their lack of success. Until recently, a significant number of prominent scholars remained skeptical (and many still do) about the possibility of replicating human intelligence through artificial systems. However, the disillusionment has unexpectedly waned in the last 5 years, thanks to the acceleration of AI—particularly through the development of large language models (LLMs). These models offer new possibilities that were unimaginable until recently. Rather than a mere acceleration, this development resembles a singularity, making precise predictions challenging.

While the distinction between Centaurs and Cyborgs provides a viable framework for analyzing the short- and mid-term effects of AI on organizations, the long-term impact of AI—along with algorithmic transparency and accountability—on organizational culture, employee roles, public trust, and other aspects remains an open question. We believe that considering the long-term impact of AI is inherently challenging, and maintaining an agnostic stance is opportune. Given our inability to predict AI's evolution over the past 5 years, forecasting its future developments and effects for the next decades becomes even more complex. Rather than asking how AI will specifically affect organizations in the long term, we should question whether the prevailing concept of "what an organization is" will remain unchanged. Hence, providing long-term practical guidelines—such as best practices and policy recommendations—poses difficulties. Not only such guidelines could be ineffective, but the very notions of best practices and policy recommendations could be at stake.

Organizational scholarship faces a similar dilemma. Organizational scholars find themselves in an uncomfortable position where AI might offer superior solutions about organizational matters compared to their own insights. Paying close attention to the disruptive effects of AI on economic systems becomes crucial for navigating the intricate landscape of AI adoption within organizations.

Disclosure of Interests The authors have no competing interests to declare that are relevant to the content of this article.

References

1. Ghassemi, M., Oakden-Rayner, L., & Beam, A. L. (2021). The false hope of current approaches to explainable artificial intelligence in health care. *The Lancet Digital Health, 3*(11), e745–e750.
2. McCoy, L. G., Brenna, C. T., Chen, S. S., Vold, K., & Das, S. (2022). Believing in black boxes: Machine learning for healthcare does not need explainability to be evidence-based. *Journal of Clinical Epidemiology, 142*, 252–257.
3. European Centre for Algorithmic Transparency (ECAT). https://algorithmic-transparency.ec.europa.eu/index_en
4. Digital Services Act (DSA). https://digital-strategy.ec.europa.eu/en/policies/digital-services-act-package
5. European Audiovisual Observatory. https://www.obs.coe.int/en/web/observatoire/
6. Cappello, M. (Ed.). (2023). *Algorithmic transparency and accountability of digital services*. IRIS Special, European Audiovisual Observatory, Strasbourg. https://rm.coe.int/iris-special-2023-02en/1680aeda48
7. High-Level Expert Group on AI, Guidelines. https://ec.europa.eu/newsroom/dae/document.cfm?doc_id=60419
8. de Streel, A., Bibal, A., Frenay, B., & Lognoul, M. (2020). *Explaining the black box: When lax controls AI*. Centre on Regulation in Europe. www.cerre.eu
9. Vermesan, O., Piuri, V., Scotti, F., Genovese, A., Labati, R. D., & Coscia, P. (2023). Explainability and interpretability concepts for edge AI systems. In O. Vermesan & D. Marples (Eds.), *Advancing edge artificial intelligence* (pp. 197–227). River Publishers.
10. Council of the EU, Press release, 21 May 2024 10:17. https://www.consilium.europa.eu/en/press/press-releases/2024/05/21/artificial-intelligence-ai-act-council-gives-final-green-light-to-the-first-worldwide-rules-on-ai/
11. Bossi, F., Di Gruttola, F., Mastrogiorgio, A., D'Arcangelo, S., Lattanzi, N., Malizia, A. P., & Ricciardi, E. (2022). Estimating successful internal mobility: A comparison between structural equation models and machine learning algorithms. *Frontiers in Artificial Intelligence, 5*, 848015.
12. Berni, A., Moschera, L., & Tursunbayeva, A. (2023). Artificial intelligence in human resource management: Objectives and implications. In D. La Torre, F. P. Appio, H. Masri, F. Lazzeri, & F. Schiavone (Eds.), *Impact of artificial intelligence in business and society* (pp. 85–104). Routledge.
13. Di Lauro, S., Tursunbayeva, A., Antonelli, G., & Moschera, L. (2023). La diffusione dei People Analytics: tendenze nella gestione HR in Italia. *Sviluppo & Organizzazione, 309*, 18–29.
14. Tursunbayeva, A. (2019). Human resource technology disruptions and their implications for human resources management in healthcare organizations. *BMC Health Services Research, 19*(1), 268.

15. Tursunbayeva, A., & Renkema, M. (2023). Artificial intelligence in health-care: Implications for the job design of healthcare professionals. *Asia Pacific Journal of Human Resources, 61*(4), 845–887.
16. Chalutz-Ben Gal, H., & Tursunbayeva, A. (2023). Artificial intelligence, human talent, and trust: A management tool for assessing and supporting AI adoption in HRM. In *European Academy of Management 2023 Conference proceedings*.
17. Za, S., & Braccini, A. M. (2017). Tracing the roots of the organizational benefits of IT services. *Lecture Notes in Business Information Processing, 279*, 3–11.
18. Martinez, M. (2024). L'era delle Cyber-organizzazioni. *MIT Sloan Management Review Italia* 2 Marzo/Aprile.
19. Smacchia, M., & Za, S. (2023). Intelligenza Artificiale: cosa emerge nel dibattito Organizzativo e Manageriale? *Prospettive in Organizzazione*, 8 Novembre 2023.
20. Gupta, M., Parra, C. M., & Dennehy, D. (2022). Questioning racial and gender bias in AI-based recommendations: Do espoused national cultural values matter?. *Information Systems Frontiers, 24*(5), 1465–1481.
21. Smacchia, M., & Za, S. (2023). *Exploring artificial intelligence bias, fairness and ethics in organisation and managerial studies*. ECIS 2023 Research Papers, 362.
22. Tursunbayeva, A., Di Lauro S., & Berni A. (2024). L'impatto dell'intelligenza artificiale sulla diversità e sull'inclusione nel processo di reclutamento. *Prospettive in Organizzazione* 6 Marzo 2024.
23. Tursunbayeva, A., Pagliari, C., Di Lauro, S., & Antonelli, G. (2021). The ethics of people analytics: Risks, opportunities and recommendations. *Personnel Review, 51*(3), 900–921.
24. Newman, D. T., Fast, N. J., & Harmon, D. J. (2020). When eliminating bias isn't fair: Algorithmic reductionism and procedural justice in human resource decisions. *Organizational Behavior and Human Decision Processes, 160*, 149–167.
25. Gonzalez, M. F., Liu, W., Shirase, L., Tomczak, D. L., Lobbe, C. E., Justenhoven, R., & Martin, N. R. (2022). Allying with AI? Reactions toward human-based, AI/ML-based, and augmented hiring processes. *Computers in Human Behavior, 130*, 107179.
26. Fischhoff, B. (2007). An early history of hindsight research. *Social Cognition, 25*, 10–13.
27. Fischhoff, B. (1975). Hindsight ≠ foresight: The effect of outcome knowledge on judgment under uncertainty. *Journal of Experimental Psychology: Human Perception and Performance, 1*(3), 288–299.
28. Mastrogiorgio, A., & Lattanzi, N. (2023). Opaque decision-making in organizations. *International Journal of Organizational Analysis, 31*(5), 1243–1256.
29. Candrian, C., & Scherer, A. (2022). Rise of the machines: Delegating decisions to autonomous AI. *Computers in Human Behavior, 134*, 107308. (2022).
30. Bankins, S., Ocampo, A. C., Marrone, M., Restubog, S. L. D., & Woo, S. E. (2024). A multilevel review of artificial intelligence in organizations: Implications for organizational behavior research and practice. *Journal of Organizational Behavior, 45*(2), 159–182.
31. Dell'Acqua, F., McFowland, E., Mollick, E. R., Lifshitz-Assaf, H., Kellogg, K., Rajendran, S., Krayer L., Candelon, F., & Lakhani, K. R. (2023). *Navigating the jagged technological frontier: Field experimental evidence of the effects of AI on knowledge worker productivity and quality*. Harvard Business School, Working Paper 24-013.
32. Bostrom, N. (2014). *Superintelligence: Paths, dangers, strategies*. Oxford University Press.
33. Bedué, P., & Fritzsche, A. (2022). Can we trust AI? An empirical investigation of trust requirements and guide to successful AI adoption. *Journal of Enterprise Information Management, 35*(2), 530–549.

Gender-Aware Business Process Management

Antonio De Nicola, Maria Guariglia Migliore, and Aleksandra Wagner

Abstract Business processes have been widely addressed by the research community in the last 25 years. Researchers and practitioners have developed methods and software for facilitating modelling, their analysis, and reengineering. However, the intersection of business process management with gender equity has received limited attention. This paper addresses this gap by first posing key research questions about these interwoven themes for future research activities. We then outline foundational principles for gender-aware business process management. Next, we discuss how existing methodologies and technologies can be used to transition from gender-blind to gender-aware business process management. In detail, we discuss possible enhancement of modelling techniques, process mining, and video-surveillance. Finally, we propose a methodology for evaluating whether a business process within an enterprise is gender-aware. If it is not, our methodology provides a structured approach for rethinking and reengineering the process to incorporate gender-aware principles.

Keywords Business process · Business process management · Gender

A. De Nicola (✉)
ENEA, CR Casaccia, Rome, Italy
e-mail: antonio.denicola@enea.it

M. Guariglia Migliore
ENEA, CR Casaccia, Rome, Italy

Sapienza University of Rome, Rome, Italy
e-mail: maria.guarigliamigliore@uniroma1.it

A. Wagner
Institute of Sociology, Jagiellonian University, Kraków, Poland
e-mail: aleksandra.wagner@uj.edu.pl

A. Tursunbayeva et al. (eds.), *Technology-Driven Transformation*, Lecture Notes in Information Systems and Organisation 79,
https://doi.org/10.1007/978-3-032-01396-5_9

1 Introduction

During the past 25 years researchers and practitioners have created methods and software to aid in the modelling, design, analysis, and reengineering of Business Processes (BP)s [1]. Indeed, these have been extensively studied by the research community from the business, behavioural, and technological perspectives. According to Dumas et al. [1], "*Business Process Management (BPM) is the art and science of overseeing how work is performed in an organization to ensure consistent outcomes and to take advantage of improvement opportunities*". Hence, it is a set of practices dedicated to managing business processes throughout their entire lifecycle. However, despite the abundance of existing studies, there are only a few that intersect this topic with the issue of gender equity [2].

Traditional business process management has primarily focused on optimizing process performance to reduce costs, execution times, error rates, and to increase production levels. While Industry 4.0 [3] is dedicated to using advanced technologies to enhance efficiency and effectiveness, Industry 5.0 [4] aims to create value by also considering social and environmental dimensions. Since business processes are crucial for the transition to Industry 4.0 and the upcoming Industry 5.0, and gender equity is essential for achieving social sustainability in industries, we believe there is an urgent need to integrate a gendered assessment approach into business process management studies.

The general aim of this paper is to spark a reflection on business processes to determine whether the scarcity of studies addressing gender equity is leaving certain research areas unexplored and hindering the full participation of women in the production system. Hence, we pose the following research questions about these interwoven themes. **(RQ1) What are the principles that should be followed to make business process management gender-aware? (RQ2) What are the phases of the business process management lifecycle that could be analysed through the lens of gendered assessment? (RQ3) Can digital transition facilitate the shift from traditional business process management to gender-aware business process management? (RQ4) How to decide if a business process is gender aware or needs to be reengineered?**

We define a gender-aware business process as one that incorporates the principles of gender equity and justice while ensuring its own efficiency. Inspired by the Gender Innovation Approach [5, 6, 7] [25], gender-aware business process harness the creative power of sex, gender, and intersectional analysis for improving management. Conversely, we define a gender-blind business process as one that, to ensure process efficiency disregard the mentioned principles.

To the purpose of answering to the research questions, we outline some principles for gender-aware business process management inspired by the recommendations of the European Institute for Gender Equality (EIGE) [8]. Next, we discuss how existing methodologies and technologies can be used to transition from gender-blind to gender-aware business process management. In detail, we propose possible enhancement of modelling techniques, process mining, and video-surveillance.

Finally, we describe a framework to assess whether business process management in an enterprise is gender-aware or needs to be rethought to consider the gender awareness principles. This article is therefore conceptual. It aims to outline a possible path for transforming business processes to meet the requirements of Industry 5.0 in terms of accessibility, sustainability and efficiency. At the same time, it is an invitation for discussion and further research in an area that we have identified as a gap in existing knowledge.

The rest of the paper is structured as it follows. Section 2 presents the related work. Section 3 outlines the principles for gender-aware business process management. Section 4 describes the framework for gender-aware business process management. Section 5 describes how existing technological solutions can be used to achieve gender-aware business process management. Section 6 presents a methodology for gender-aware business process reengineering. Section 7 concludes the work with some possible payoffs of gender-aware BPM.

2 Related Work

All the phases of business process management have been deeply investigated by the research community. Among these works, we cite the book of Dumas et al. [1] that outlines process identification, process modelling, process discovery, process analysis, process redesign, process implementation, and process monitoring as the principal activities of the BPM lifecycle.

The assessment of gender gap in STEM subjects has recently attracted researchers' interest, leading them to employ more advanced methods that go beyond the mere calculation of conference attendance rates or school and university enrollments [9]. Indeed, these new approaches encompass techniques based on complex network analysis, and semantic analysis.

The need to include gender data in the big data revolution was recognised by the Cape Town Global Action Plan for Sustainable Development Data, launched on 15 January 2017 at the first United Nations World Data Forum. The Action Plan directly called for the mobilisation of resources and the coordination of efforts for capacity building, which must be achieved "*not only through the integration of big data and analytics into planning and decision-making, but also by working with governments, policy makers and the wider international community to address the gaps in women's access to ICTs and other tools and activities that generate new sources of data*" [10]. The need for gender awareness in business processes is even more urgent when we consider the increasing role of algorithms in corporate governance. Gender bias in the operation of algorithms was next to racial bias, which was diagnosed early on by academics analysing the problem [11].

Hence, despite a large literature on business process management as well as on gender and inclusion only a few works address the interweaving of these two topics. Among them, Gorbacheva et al. [2] analysed 10,405 BPM-related LinkedIn profiles using a text mining technique called latent semantic analysis to the aim of checking if there is the issue of female underrepresentation also in this STEM (Science Technology Engineering Math) sector. The study revealed that women are underrepresented among BPM professionals and suggested potential existence of gender stereotypes [12]. Then, Memon et al. [13] did a study in India to investigate organizational commitment of female employees in the information technology business process management sector. One example of an initiative that proposes using a gender lens in the human rights due diligence process is Gender-Responsive Due Diligence platform (see https://www.genderduediligence.org), which intends to support companies to actively manage any adverse human rights and labour impacts in their supply chains. Screening and due diligence gender-related data is recommended by British International Investment to identify business performance gender opportunities and risks in value chain (see https://gendertoolkit.bii.co.uk/due-diligence/) [14]. Despite these first practical tools and the growing body of literature on the risk of discrimination against women in the digital revolution [15] and the risk of detrimental impact on them in global supply chains [16, 17], the potential of gender-responsive business processes to improve management in organisations remains untapped. While several studies have demonstrated the positive impact of gender diversity on corporate social responsibility [18–20], there is still a lack of a systematic basis for understanding gender-responsive business processes and their key principles.

Compared to existing papers, our work is the only that critically analyses business process management and the lack of a gender perspective. At the same time, it suggests the next step after research and design in implementing gender innovation in management practice.

3 Principles for Gender-Aware Business Process Management

Sara is a process engineer working in a semiconductor company. Her job takes her to a clean room where she works on production machines. The clean room is a safe environment but can always be prone to gas leaks or possible fires. She has been pregnant for three months and wants to minimize any risk to the unborn child. Unfortunately, enterprise policies do not allow any exemptions for Sara, who is therefore forced to work in the clean room. During her shift, a fire occurs and Sara is transported to the hospital for a fetal health check.

This is just one realistic example of an industrial process that does not take into account the peculiarities of being a woman. According to the Industry 5.0 paradigm, enterprises should balance efficiency, effectiveness, and environmental and social sustainability. Since gender inclusiveness is one of the aspects of social sustainability, gender aware business process management should incorporate some principles to guarantee gender fairness. Hence, a first objective of this paper is to identify these principles. To this end, we started from the analysis of gender equality plans [8] to see if these could be used for gendered assessment. The list of the principles is as it follows:

1. Work-life balance;
2. Gender-balance in leadership and decision making;
3. Gender equality in recruitment and career progression;
4. Integrating the gender dimension into BP research and teaching content;
5. Measures against gender-based violence, including sexual harassment.

For example, in alignment with the work-life balance principle, gender-aware business process management should account for workers' specific needs, such as those involving care responsibilities for parents or children, which could cause higher levels of stress. Societal expectations often dictate that women should provide more care for family members at the end of life [21]. One solution is to design activity schedules that accommodate these responsibilities. Similarly, in line with the principle of gender balance in leadership and decision-making, women should be actively involved in decision-making activities and in determining which processes need reengineering. Moreover, according to the principle of gender equality in recruitment and career progression, women should have the same opportunities as men, especially in STEM fields. Additionally, integrating the gender dimension into BPM research and teaching content is crucial. It is well-known that fewer women than men are involved in business process management [12]. Therefore, it is urgent to increase this number through promotional initiatives at schools and universities. Finally, following the principle of implementing measures against gender-based violence, it is advisable to adopt monitoring measures, such as video-surveillance, to enhance safety in isolated or high-risk environments.

4 Framework for Gender-Aware Business Process Management

4.1 BPM Lifecycle

Business process management encompasses tools, techniques, methods, and methodologies aiming at supporting all stages of the BP lifecycle [1]. It consists of several phases, each varying in relevance depending on the perspective of the BPM analyst, whether more business-oriented or more technological. For instance, in the process monitoring phase, a business analyst would focus on process performance indicators such as costs, and production levels, while a technician would be concerned with the technical setup needed to collect data during the process execution or the methods to analyse data. The BPM lifecycle typically includes the following phases [1]: *BP identification*, *BP discovery* (or *as-is BP modelling)*, *BP analysis*, *BP redesign*, *BP implementation*, and *BP monitoring*.

BP identification is the phase focused on identifying the processes relevant to the business problem at hand. *BP discovery* is the phase when the current version of the as-is process is represented as a model. *Process analysis* is the phase when the issues of the as-is process are identified, documented, and quantified using performance indicators. *Process redesign* is the phase when the issues identified during analysis are addressed, and changes are identified to improve the performance measures. *Process implementation* is the phase when the changes planned during process redesign are put into action and executed. *Process monitoring* is the phase when relevant data related to the redesigned process are collected and analyzed to assess performance measures.

4.2 Incorporating Gender-Aware Principles in BPM Phases

We have reviewed the phases of business process management (BPM) in relation to gender-aware BPM principles to identify potential modifications. The result is a matrix, with columns representing the BPM phases, rows representing the principles, and cells containing the gender-aware initiatives that can be implemented to enhance BPM with a gender perspective. We refer to this matrix as the framework for gender-aware business process management. This is shown in Fig. 1 and a possible application of it is described in the following. It is important to note that the matrix in Fig. 1 is not intended to be exhaustive; rather, it represents one possible application of the Gender-Aware BPM framework.

The *BP identification phase* is crucial for pinpointing processes that are pertinent to the business problem at hand. To implement the work-life principle in the identification process, one can consider the potential differences that can be caused by sex and gender that influence the patterns of work-life balance definitions without treating groups of men, women, or gender-diverse people as homogenous. To adhere to the principle of gender balance in leadership and decision-making, it is essential to actively involve women in this phase. This approach ensures diverse perspectives,

	BP identification	BP discovery	BP analysis	BP redesign	BP implementation	BP monitoring
Work-life balance	Consider the potential differences that can be caused by sex and gender that influence the patterns of work-life balance definitions	Define modelling constructs to capture work-life balance	Check whether activities ensure work-life balance	Ensure work-life balance	Adopt technologies (e.g., video meeting) and practices (e.g., smart working) to ensure work-life balance	Measure the degree of implementation of work-life practices
Gender-balance in leadership and decision making	Involve women in BP identification	Assign decisional roles to women	Check rates of women with decisional roles	Ensure equal participation in decisional roles	Implement techniques for data mining of process traces for gender gap detection	Record traces for gender gap detection
Gender equality in recruitment and career progression			Check rates of women partecipating to BPs	Ensure involvement of women	Implement techniques for data mining of process traces for gender gap detection	Record traces for gender gap detection
Measures against gender-based violence, including sexual harassment		Add modelling constructs to address gender-based violence	Check whether activities can lead to gender-based violence	Adopt countermeasures for activities that can lead to gender-based violence	Implement video surveillance for detection of gender-based violence	Video surveillance

Fig. 1 Framework for gender-aware business process management

leading to more comprehensive and inclusive decision-making. Engaging women at this stage not only enhances the quality of process identification but also promotes equitable leadership, driving better outcomes and fostering an environment of equality and representation within the organization.

To integrate the work-life balance principle in the *BP discovery phase*, it is beneficial to define modelling constructs that capture aspects of work-life balance, such as flexible work arrangements or support for caregiving responsibilities. These constructs ensure that the model reflects considerations important to employee well-being. Furthermore, to implement the principle of gender balance in leadership and decision-making, it is essential to assign decisional roles to women within the modelling process. Involving women in these roles not only enriches the decision-making with diverse insights but also promotes equity in leadership. This dual approach enhances the accuracy and inclusiveness of the process model, aligning it with contemporary values of gender equity and balanced work environments. Then, to implement the principle concerning the measures against gender-based violence, including sexual harassment, new modelling constructs addressing gender-based violence, such as monitoring activities, could be beneficial.

In the *BP analysis phase*, issues within the as-is process are identified, documented, and quantified using performance indicators. To implement the work-life balance principle, it is critical to evaluate whether activities support or hinder work-life balance for employees. This can include assessing factors like flexible scheduling and workload distribution. To address gender balance in leadership and decision-making, it is important to monitor the rates of women in decisional roles. This analysis helps ensure equitable representation and influence in leadership positions. For advancing gender equality in recruitment and career progression, it is essential to track the participation rates of women in various business processes. This ensures that recruitment practices are inclusive and that women have equal opportunities for career advancement. Additionally, to comply with measures against gender-based violence, including sexual harassment, activities within the process should be scrutinized to identify any potential risks of gender-based violence. This involves ensuring that the workplace environment and processes do not perpetuate or tolerate any form of violence or harassment.

To implement the work-life balance principle effectively in the *BP redesign phase*, it is crucial to ensure that both formal policies and informal practices support work-life balance. This includes recognizing and rewarding additional time devoted to work, while also promoting a culture that values and respects personal time and commitments outside of work. For the principle of gender balance in leadership and decision-making, it is essential to ensure equal participation in decisional roles. This can be achieved by actively encouraging and empowering women to take on leadership positions and ensuring their voices are heard and considered in decision-making processes. Regarding gender equality in recruitment and career progression, efforts should focus on actively involving women in recruitment processes and creating pathways for their advancement within the organization. This includes implementing policies and practices that mitigate bias and promote equal opportunities for career development. To address measures against gender-based violence, including sexual harassment, it is critical to adopt proactive measures to prevent activities that can lead to such violence. This involves creating a safe and respectful workplace environment where all employees feel protected and empowered to report any incidents of harassment or violence.

To uphold the work-life balance principle in *BP implementation*, adopting technologies like video meetings and practices such as smart working can play a crucial role. These tools facilitate flexible working arrangements that accommodate employees' personal responsibilities and promote a healthier balance between work and life. For achieving gender balance in leadership and decision-making, implementing techniques for data mining of process traces is essential. This approach helps identify and address gender gaps in leadership roles and decision-making processes, ensuring equitable opportunities for participation and advancement. Similarly, for promoting gender equality in recruitment and career progression, utilizing data mining techniques of process traces is pivotal. By analyzing these traces, organizations can identify any biases or barriers that hinder women's progress and take proactive measures to eliminate them, fostering a more inclusive and fair recruitment and career advancement process. To combat gender-based violence, including sexual harassment, implementing video-surveillance can aid in detecting and preventing such incidents within the workplace. This measure enhances safety and creates a secure environment where all employees feel protected and respected.

To support the work-life balance principle effectively in *BP monitoring*, it is important to measure the degree of implementation of work-life practices. This includes evaluating how well policies and initiatives aimed at promoting work-life balance are being implemented and utilized within the organization. For promoting gender balance in leadership and decision-making, recording traces for gender gap detection is crucial. By systematically capturing and analyzing data related to leadership roles and decision-making processes, organizations can identify disparities and take corrective actions to ensure equitable representation and participation. Similarly, for advancing gender equality in recruitment and career progression, recording traces for gender gap detection is essential. This involves monitoring recruitment practices, career progression opportunities, and identifying any biases or barriers that may impede women's advancement within the organization. To address measures against gender-based violence, including sexual harassment, implementing video-surveillance can aid in monitoring and preventing such incidents in the workplace. Video-surveillance [22] serves as a proactive measure to enhance security and create a safe environment where all employees feel protected and respected.

5 Enhancing Gender-Aware BPM via Digital Transition

Digital transition is the shift from traditional, often manual, processes and systems to ones that are enhanced by digital technologies [23]. It is a key factor enabling Industry 4.0 and the upcoming Industry 5.0. To achieve a successful digital transition, an enterprise must operate across multiple levels: at business strategy level, at process level, and at operations level. The layered perspective of digital transition is shown in Fig. 2.

At the business strategy level, enterprises need to innovate their existing business models to explore new revenue channels enabled by digital technologies. This includes leveraging data analysis and recommender systems to support decision-making processes and enhance strategic planning.

At the process level, implementing digital twins is essential for simulating systems and making real-time adjustments to parameters, thereby optimizing operations. Automation through digital technologies can significantly increase efficiency and productivity. Additionally, mining process logs can provide valuable insights for continuous process improvement and refinement.

At the operational level, a range of technologies is available, including cloud computing, prompt engineering, Large Language Models (LLMs), Artificial Intelligence (AI), virtual reality, data analytics, the Internet of Things (IoT), and video-surveillance. These technologies facilitate workforce digitalization, support business process automation, and enable the implementation of digital twins.

In the following, we discuss potential enhancements to digital technologies that could facilitate the achievement of gender-aware business process management.

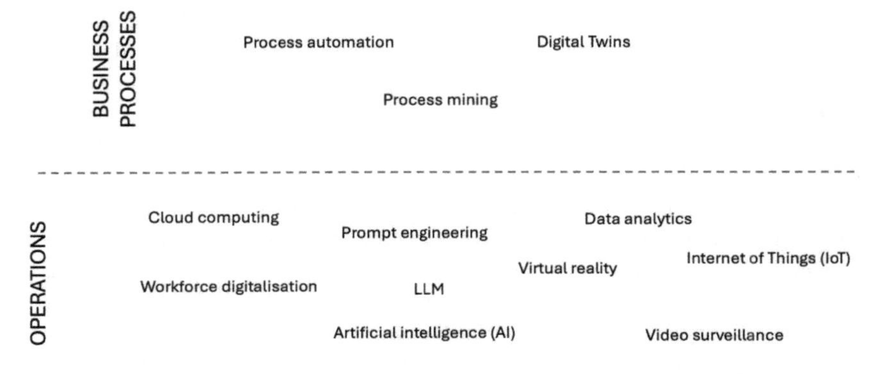

Fig. 2 Digital transition from a layered perspective

5.1 Gender-Aware Business Process Modelling

Business process modelling necessitates the use of constructs and rules to create models that are both clear and concise in representing how operations evolve over time. Practitioners commonly employ various notations and languages, such as Business Process Model and Notation (BPMN), Functional Resonance Analysis Method (FRAM), and Event-driven Process Chains (EPC), to achieve this goal. These modelling techniques provide robust frameworks for depicting the sequence of activities, decision points, and dependencies within business processes, thereby enabling organizations to analyze and optimize their workflows. However, while these notations capture essential aspects related to process efficiency and effectiveness, they often overlook critical gender and sex-specific considerations. This gap can lead to models that fail to address the diverse needs of a gender-diverse workforce, potentially perpetuating inequalities and limiting the inclusiveness of the designed processes.

Incorporating constructs that explicitly model work-life balance is one way to address this gap. Work-life balance is a significant factor affecting employee well-being and productivity, and its needs can vary significantly across different gender groups. For instance, including elements that capture flexible working arrangements, access to childcare, and varying personal responsibilities can provide a more accurate representation of how these factors influence employee participation and performance. By integrating these constructs, process models can reflect the realities of modern work environments, where balancing professional and personal life is crucial for all employees. This approach not only supports better employee engagement but also helps organizations design processes that accommodate diverse needs, leading to a more inclusive workplace.

Additionally, addressing gender dynamics within decision-making activities is essential for promoting equity and inclusiveness in business process modelling. Traditional models may not sufficiently represent how decision-making power is distributed among different gender groups, which can obscure potential biases and inequalities. Constructs that specifically highlight the gender distribution in decision-making roles can provide valuable insights into who holds influence and how decisions are made. This level of detail allows organizations to identify and rectify imbalances, ensuring that decision-making opportunities are equitably available to all employees. Furthermore, such constructs can facilitate the monitoring and analysis of gender representation over time, helping organizations implement and track progress towards gender equality goals.

Lastly, monitoring activities and the representation of gender within process models can significantly enhance the understanding and management of gender equity in business processes. By including constructs that measure the participation rates and engagement of different gender groups in various activities, organizations can gather data on how inclusive their processes are in practice. This information is crucial for identifying barriers that may prevent certain groups from fully participating and for developing targeted interventions to promote inclusivity. Additionally, visualizing the gender distribution within process roles can highlight areas where specific gender groups are underrepresented or face challenges, allowing for more informed and effective policy-making. Integrating these gender-aware elements into business process modelling not only improves the accuracy and relevance of the models but also supports the creation of more equitable and supportive work environments for all employees.

5.2 *Process Mining for Gender Gap Detection*

As previously mentioned, mining process logs is a crucial technique in the digitalization of industries and the realization of Industry 4.0. This technique involves analyzing the data recorded in event logs to gain insights into the actual functioning of business processes. One significant application of process mining is in the detection of gender gaps within an organization. This analysis can uncover a variety of issues, such as the tendency for decision-making activities to be predominantly performed by men, or the excessive amount of operational time that encroaches on family time, disproportionately affecting certain groups.

Furthermore, process mining can play a pivotal role in ensuring that business processes comply with gender equality principles and policies. By providing a data-driven view of how processes are executed, it allows organizations to identify and address gender disparities effectively. For example, it can reveal whether men or women are disproportionately represented in specific roles or activities, how work is distributed across genders, and whether there are patterns of behaviour that disadvantage one group over another.

The insights gained from process mining can be used to design interventions that promote more equitable work environments. This might include adjusting the allocation of decision-making roles to ensure a balanced representation, implementing measures to better support work-life balance for all employees, or revising process workflows to eliminate biases. Moreover, process mining can support continuous monitoring and improvement, helping organizations to track progress over time and make data-driven adjustments as necessary.

Overall, process mining not only enhances operational efficiency but also serves as a valuable tool for fostering gender equality within the workplace. By uncovering hidden disparities and providing actionable insights, it supports the creation of a more inclusive and fair working environment, aligning with broader organizational goals of diversity and inclusion.

5.3 AI-Powered Video-Surveillance for Preventing Gender-Based Violence

Activities conducted in isolated locations, such as the engine room of a cruise ship, can pose significant safety risks for women due to the potential for sexual harassment and other forms of gender-based violence. In these environments, traditional video-surveillance, monitored by human operators, may prove ineffective, especially if the surveilled area is extensive and challenging to oversee continuously.

To address these limitations, advancements in artificial intelligence (AI) and automatic image recognition techniques offer new opportunities for enhancing safety through unmanned video-surveillance systems. AI-powered video-surveillance can automatically detect unusual or suspicious behaviour without the need for constant human monitoring, thereby providing a more reliable and efficient solution for large and complex areas.

These AI systems can be trained to recognize patterns and indicators of potential harassment or violence, such as unauthorized access to restricted zones, prolonged loitering, or physical altercations. Upon detecting such incidents, the system can trigger real-time alerts, allowing for immediate intervention by security personnel. This automated approach not only improves the responsiveness of surveillance but also reduces the likelihood of incidents going unnoticed due to human oversight or fatigue.

Implementing AI-driven video-surveillance can significantly enhance the safety of isolated work environments, making it more feasible for women to undertake roles that have traditionally been dominated by men. By mitigating the risks associated with gender-based violence, these technologies contribute to creating a more inclusive and equitable workplace, where women can participate fully and safely in all types of activities.

Moreover, the use of unmanned video-surveillance aligns with broader efforts to leverage digital technologies for improving workplace safety and operational efficiency. It underscores the potential of AI to transform traditional practices, providing robust solutions that enhance security while promoting gender equality. As organizations continue to embrace such innovations, they can expect to foster safer, more diverse, and more inclusive working environments.

In summary, the integration of AI-based image recognition in video-surveillance represents a significant advancement in preventing sexual harassment and other forms of violence in isolated work settings. This technology not only addresses the limitations of human-operated systems but also empowers women to engage in a wider range of professional activities, contributing to a more balanced and inclusive workforce.

6 Gender-Aware Business Process Reengineering

Business Process Reengineering (BPR) was originally defined by Hammer & Champy in the nineties as "*the fundamental rethinking and radical redesign of the business processes to achieve dramatic improvements in critical, contemporary measures of performance, such as cost, quality, service and speed*" [24]. The work of Hammer & Champy has influenced the research on BPR for decades. However, we note that the definition still focuses on productivity goals and leaves out the social implications of change including those related to gender.

We revisited the business process management lifecycle to show how the different constituent phases should be modified to meet gender-aware principles. The resulting methodology is sketchily depicted in Fig. 3.

To effectively reengineer a business process, it is crucial to start by identifying the process through the collaborative efforts of both women and men. The participation of all genders in this initial phase ensures a comprehensive understanding of the process, taking into account diverse perspectives and experiences. This inclusive approach helps to identify key areas that may benefit from reengineering and lays the foundation for a more balanced and equitable redesign.

In the subsequent BP discovery (modelling) phase, it is essential to apply gender-aware constructs to the modelling process. This involves utilizing innovative constructs that reflect critical aspects such as work-life balance, decision-making activities, and the gender of actors involved in the process (as detailed in subsection 5.1). By integrating these constructs into the modelling phase, the resulting process models will better represent the diverse needs and roles of all participants, providing

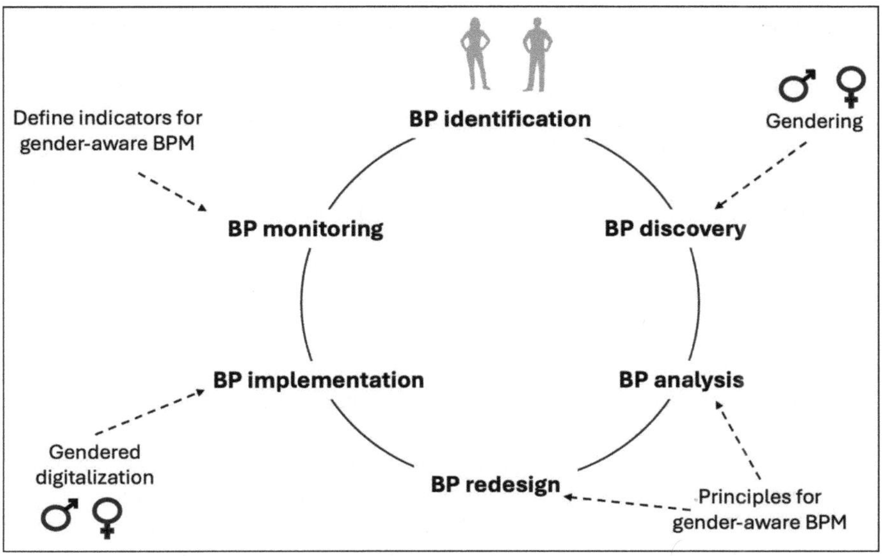

Fig. 3 Gender-aware business process lifecycle

a more accurate and inclusive depiction of how operations evolve over time. This gendered modelling approach ensures that the specific impacts on different genders are considered from the outset, facilitating the development of processes that are equitable and supportive for everyone involved.

Following the discovery phase, the BP analysis and BP redesign phases should explicitly incorporate the principles for gender-aware BPM, as outlined in subsection 4.2. During analysis, it is critical to identify and document gender-related issues, such as potential biases in decision-making roles or disparities in work-life balance. The redesign phase should then focus on addressing these issues by implementing changes that promote gender equity. This might involve altering workflows to provide equal opportunities for leadership and participation, or modifying policies to support work-life balance across all genders.

In the BP implementation phase, the adoption of appropriate digital technologies is key to ensuring the integration of gender-aware principles. Technologies such as process mining tools, AI-driven analytics, and automated monitoring systems can be utilized to enforce compliance with gender equity standards and to provide real-time feedback on the process's performance from a gender perspective. These technologies facilitate the practical application of gender-aware designs, helping to embed inclusivity into the day-to-day operations of the business.

Finally, it is imperative to establish and monitor gender-aware indicators to evaluate the effectiveness of the BP redesign. These indicators should measure the extent to which the reengineered process has transformed from a gender-blind to a gender-aware process. Metrics might include the representation of different genders in decision-making roles, the balance of work-life integration, and the participation rates of all genders in various process activities. Regular monitoring and analysis of these indicators will help to identify areas for further improvement, ensuring that the process remains aligned with gender equity goals and continues to support an inclusive organizational culture.

Overall, a gender-aware approach to business process reengineering not only enhances the inclusivity and fairness of business processes but also contributes to a more engaged and diverse workforce. By systematically incorporating gender considerations at each stage of the BPM lifecycle, organizations can foster a more equitable environment that recognizes and addresses the needs of all employees.

7 Conclusion

The payoffs of gender-aware business process management can be considered from both external and internal perspectives.

The former can be assessed in terms of image and reputation benefits. An organisation that is perceived as ensuring equal working conditions and career development for men, women and gender-diverse people can attract more potential employees, which secures human resources, and diverse expertise can support innovation potential. Addressing equality standards makes the organisation more resilient for the future. Equality expectations are more visible, so addressing them helps to legitimise decisions. An inclusive approach helps to attract a wide range of stakeholders: investors, influencers, customers.

Internally, gender awareness helps to improve operational and commercial models. Systematically integrating a gender perspective into business processes optimises the use of resources and reduces the risks associated with misperceptions based on stereotypes, prejudice or ignorance. It can lead to innovation in management processes [7].

In this paper, we have identified the key principles essential for making Business Process Management (BPM) gender-aware (refer to **RQ1**). We then analyzed the phases of the BPM lifecycle, examining them through the lens of gendered assessment by cross-referencing with the identified principles (refer to **RQ2**). We also explored how digital transformation can facilitate the transition from traditional BPM to gender-aware BPM (refer to **RQ3**). Additionally, we revised the BPM lifecycle to provide guidelines on evaluating whether a business process is gender-aware (refer to **RQ4**) or, if necessary, how to reengineer it for inclusivity.

Looking forward, our future work will focus on experimenting with the framework for gender-aware BPM within an industrial context to validate and refine its effectiveness.

Acknowledgments We gratefully acknowledge the partial support of the gEneSys (Transforming Gendered Interrelations of Power and Inequalities in Transition Pathways to Sustainable Energy Systems) project, which has received funding from the European Union's Horizon Europe—Culture, creativity and inclusive society—under grant agreement no. 101094326.

Disclosure of Interests The authors have no competing interests to declare that are relevant to the content of this article.

References

1. Dumas, M., La Rosa, M., Mendling, J., & Reijers, H. A. (2018). *Fundamentals of business process management*. Springer.
2. Gorbacheva, E., Stein, A., Schmiedel, T., & Müller, O. (2015). A gender perspective on business process management competences offered on professional online social networks. In *Proceedings of the 23rd European conference on information systems, ECIS 2015*.
3. Lu, Y. (2017). Industry 4.0: A survey on technologies, applications and open research issues. *Journal of Industrial Information Integration, 6*, 1–10.
4. Maddikunta, P. K. R., Pham, Q.-V., Prabadevi, B., Deepa, N., Dev, K., Gadekallu, T. R., Ruby, R., & Liyanage, M. (2022). Industry 5.0: A survey on enabling technologies and potential applications, Journal of Industrial Information. *Integration, 26*.
5. Gender-responsive due diligence platform. Retrieved August 13, 2024, from https://www.genderduediligence.org
6. Schiebinger, L., & Klinge, I. (Eds.). (2020). *Gendered innovations 2: How inclusive analysis contributes to research and innovation (Luxembourg: Publications Office of the European Union, 2020)*. Foreword by EC Commissioner for Innovation, Research, Culture, Education and Youth, Mariya Gabriel.

7. Tannenbaum, C., Ellis, R. P., Eyssel, F., Zou, J., & Schiebinger, L. (2019). Sex and gender analysis improves science and engineering. *Nature, 575*(7781), 137–146.
8. European Institute for Gender Equality: Gender Equality in Academia and Research - GEAR tool. (2022). https://eige.europa.eu/gender-mainstreaming/toolkits/gear/what-gender-equality-plan-gep?language_content_entity=en
9. De Nicola, A., & D'Agostino, G. (2021). Assessment of gender divide in scientific communities. *Scientometrics, 126*, 3807–3840. https://doi.org/10.1007/s11192-021-03885-3
10. Abreu Lopes, C. & Bailur, S. (2018, January). UN women, gender equality and big data. *Making gender data visible.*
11. Saka, E. (2021). Big data and gender-biased algorithms. In K. Ross (Ed.), *The international encyclopedia of gender, media, and communication*. John Wiley & Sons, Inc.
12. Gorbacheva, E., Stein, A., Schmiedel, T., et al. (2016). The role of gender in business process management competence supply. *Business and Information Systems Engineering, 58*, 213–231. https://doi.org/10.1007/s12599-016-0428-2
13. Memon, N. Z., & Satpathy, B. (2017). Antecedents and consequences of organizational commitment: A gender study in the IT-BPM sector of India. *Management and Labour Studies, 42*(4), 306–315.
14. British International Investment. (2024). Investment process. Screening and due diligence. Retrieved August 13, 2024, from https://gendertoolkit.bii.co.uk/due-diligence/
15. Wajcman Young, E., & Fitzmaurice, A. (2020). *The digital revolution: Implications for gender equality and women's rights 25 years after Beijing, discussion paper nr 36*. UN Women.
16. Barrientos, S., Bianchi, L., & Berman, C. (2017). Women workers in global supply chains: Rights and remedy.
17. Tobalagba, A. (2020). Corporate human rights due diligence and assessing risks of sexual violence in large-scale mining operations. *Australian Journal of Human Rights, 26*(2), 347–365. https://doi.org/10.1080/1323238X.2020.1813377
18. Ruel, S., & Fritz, M. M. C. (2021). Gender diversity in supply chains: towards more sustainable decisions? Evidence from interviews. *Supply Chain Forum: An International Journal, 22*(3), 205–222. https://doi.org/10.1080/16258312.2021.1948307
19. Yarram, S. R., & Adapa, S. (2021). Board gender diversity and corporate social responsibility: Is there a case for critical mass? *Journal of Cleaner Production, 278*, 123319. https://doi.org/10.1016/j.jclepro.2020.123319
20. Zaid, M. A., Wang, M., Adib, M., Sahyouni, A., & Abuhijleh, S. T. (2020). Boardroom nationality and gender diversity: Implications for corporate sustainability performance. *Journal of Cleaner Production, 251*, 119652. https://doi.org/10.1016/j.jclepro.2019.119652
21. Morgan, T., Williams, L., Trussardi, G., & Gott, M. (2016). Gender and family caregiving at the end-of-life in the context of old age: A systematic review. *Palliative Medicine, 30*, 616. https://doi.org/10.1177/0269216315625857
22. Bouma, H., Villani, M. L., van Rooijen, A., Räsänen, P., Peltola, J., Toivonen, S., De Nicola, A., Guarneri, M., Stifini, C., & De Dominicis, L. (2023). An integrated fusion engine for early threat detection demonstrated in public-space trials. *Sensors, 23*(1), 440. https://doi.org/10.3390/s23010440
23. Westerman, G., Bonnet, D., & McAfee, A. (2014). *Leading digital: Turning technology into business transformation*. Harvard Business Review Press.
24. Hammer, M., & Champy, J. (1993). Reengineering the corporation: A manifesto for business revolution. *Business Horizons, 36*(5), 90–91.
25. GIA. (2023). What is gendered innovations? http://genderedinnovations.stanford.edu/what-is-gendered-innovations.html

Towards Assessing Digital Maturity: Utilizing Real-Time Public Data for Organizational Benchmarking

Maximilian Breitruck, Andrea Back, and Lena-Marie Pätzmann

Abstract This paper details the creation of a novel Comparative Digital Maturity Model (CDMM), enabling organizations to dynamically benchmark their digital maturity against peers by utilizing real-time, publicly available news data sources. Traditional Digital Transformation (DT) models typically rely on static data such as annual reports, interviews, and questionnaires. Addressing this gap, our model adopts a Practice-Based View (PBV) within a Design Science Research (DSR) methodology, ensuring a robust, iterative development process through focus group discussions and expert interviews in collaboration with industry stakeholders. The results demonstrate that the CDMM effectively captures the evolving nature of DT across sectors, providing continuous, up-to-date assessments that overcome the limitations of static evaluations.

Keywords Digital maturity model · Practice based view · Organizational benchmarking

1 Introduction

Today, digital transformation is present in all organizations in one way or another. Consequently, organizations no longer differ in whether they have started their digital transformation but rather in how far they have progressed in this endeavor [1]. In relation to this progress, the literature primarily discusses an organization's maturity level concerning digital transformation [2].

M. Breitruck (✉) · A. Back · L.-M. Pätzmann
University of St. Gallen, St. Gallen, Switzerland
e-mail: maximilian.breitruck2@unisg.ch

A. Tursunbayeva et al. (eds.), *Technology-Driven Transformation*, Lecture Notes in Information Systems and Organisation 79,
https://doi.org/10.1007/978-3-032-01396-5_10

Accordingly, companies exhibit varying degrees of maturity depending on their progress. This maturity level often serves as an internal indicator for companies to plan their further course of action concerning the transformation [3]. Like other strategic initiatives within an organization [4], benchmarking with competitors in the same sector is crucial for adjusting one's strategy [5]. Particularly for determining their digital maturity (DM) level, a multitude of frameworks already exist that enable organizations to assess their own stage of maturity in this regard (e.g [6, 7].). However, these, too, are snapshots, providing a depiction of an organization's maturity at a specific point in time. Currently, the literature does not yet provide approaches for dynamically assessing the maturity levels of competing firms over time [8, 9]. This lack in trajectorial research is particularly due to the fact that the majority of existing frameworks rely on qualitative data from interviews with corporate representatives or questionnaires that must be completed by such [7–9]. Continuous evaluation of the maturity level is challenging, and the approach of some papers to analyze the annual reports of respective companies is only of limited use since these reports are published only once a year and often contain limited information on Digital Transformation DT [10]. Parallels can indeed be drawn to the Environment, Social, and Governance research area, where public data is also utilized to develop approximation scores for Environmental, Social, and Governance (ESG) performance. This approach has significantly reduced the resource intensity associated with such assessments [11, 12].

In general, the concept of maturity models in the field of Information Systems (IS) is no longer a novelty. There are maturity models for various facets of IT components within organizations, primarily aimed at helping to identify the current developmental status of an organization and systematically support its improvement. This also applies to the domain of Digital Maturity Models (DMMs), as a multitude of these already exist in the literature [13–15]. However, the development of DMMs that can express maturity over time while simultaneously evaluating and comparing multiple organizations has been scarcely pursued despite being frequently mentioned as a research gap [8, 13]. Nevertheless, the literature emphasizes that exploring this area could significantly advance maturity model research. This could provide a valuable opportunity to compare developments between organizations, potentially leading to new insights into best practices, avoidable mistakes, and other relevant factors [8, 13].

Based on the trends within e.g. ESG research a novel approach could be beneficial here that leverages the wealth of publicly available data, which is updated more frequently and can, therefore, offer more current insights, facilitating the development of a tool for continuous monitoring and benchmarking of digital maturity. This could fill the gap in longitudinal digital maturity research and enable practitioners to continuously monitor their own organization's status in relation to competitors, securing and expanding their position in the market environment and learning from potential digital leaders within the industry.

Based on this gap, the following research question can be derived: *How can a practitioner-oriented model be developed to map the evolutionary patterns of digital maturity in organizations, utilizing public data to enable benchmarking against competitors?* This question will be systematically addressed by iteratively applying the Design Science Research method according to Hevner et al. [16] enriched with DMM design-specific elements of Becker et al. [17] DSR methodology. The central components used for the design of the DMM are a literature review, focus group discussions, and expert interviews. Consequently, the following study is structured into a theoretical foundation in Sect. 2, a detailed description of the research methodology and its application in Sect. 3, and the finalized DMM and its application in Sect. 4. Finally, Sect. 5 reflects on the research project, its results, and limitations.

2 Theoretical Foundation

2.1 Digital Transformation Maturity

The term "Digital Transformation" is pivotal within contemporary Information Systems (IS) research, leading to a plethora of heterogeneous definitions and constructs attempting to capture the concept in a holistic manner [9]. Many of these approaches (e.g. [12, 13]) consider DT as an array of capabilities that an organization must develop to undergo a fundamental change [6].

The primary objective of this transformation process is to adapt to the changing environment (e.g., technological innovations, change in consumer expectations, etc.), thereby ensuring the organization remains compatible with the alterations at its interfaces, whether they be with partner companies, customers, or other [18]. The term "Digital Maturity" has emerged as a proven indicator for assessing the level of transformation in this context, as a transformation can never truly be complete but can only grow from one stage of maturity to the next [8]. An organization can thus never be fully transformed but can only be "more mature" at a given moment than, for example, its competitor firms. As long as there are new technologies and opportunities to further develop organizational dimensions, such as, e.g. the business model, underlying business processes, etc., there will also be additional levels of maturity that an organization can achieve [3].

Pöppelbuß and Röglinger [8] have noted that at the core of every DMM lies the description of maturity levels, which are the groundwork for assisting organizations in their transformation processes. However, they also noticed that DMMs differ in their goal in terms of what they want to enable their users. To ensure that DMMs fulfill their purpose as effectively as possible, they have established design principles for the creation of DMMs. As they discovered that they had slightly diverging goals within DMM creation, they additionally differentiated their efforts between three types of DMMs. In addition to the descriptive and prescriptive types, they also derive the comparative type of DMMs. The descriptive type addresses the design of DMMs that aim to describe the maturity degree of an organization, whilst prescriptive DMMs want to enable organizations to reach a higher maturity degree. The comparative type is characterized by its utility in internal and external benchmarking; therefore, every model has its own focus whilst maintaining the core of describing the digital maturity degree [8].

2.2 Practice-Based View

According to Bromiley and Rau [19], a company's competitive advantage does not solely originate from its resource endowment, as posited by the Resource-Based View, but rather is attributed to organizational practices that distinguish it from its competitors. These practices can be defined as "a defined activity or set of activities," where the correct combination of these practices and deep knowledge of them can lead to superior performance [19].

This theory can also be applied to the construct of DT by recognizing that existing DMMs primarily focus on organizational capabilities, which ultimately manifest as a set of practices. These practices must be implemented to eventually build the organizational ability to become more digitally mature. Correspondingly, applying and knowing specific practices can lead to a competitive advantage. Therefore, the implementation of such practices is desirable for organizations, which in turn motivates the targeted assessment or measurement of the presence of these practices.

2.3 News Data Text Mining

The construct of text mining has evolved significantly over the years but can still be seen, as in its original form by Feldman and Dagan [20], as a construct aimed at extracting relationships or previously unrecognized information from large volumes of textual data. This foundational goal underscores the method's capacity to uncover valuable insights by analyzing text at scale. Since its widespread adoption, this methodology has increasingly been applied to publicly accessible data sources such as social media and news data. By leveraging these continuously expanding datasets, text mining has been used to obtain quantitative insights regarding various fields of interest [21]. However, this approach also comes with critical challenges, such as the potential for biases in the news data, the variability in data quality, and the complexity of accurately interpreting context within textual information. These factors can impact the reliability of the insights derived, necessitating careful consideration and validation in any analysis. However, this approach also entails critical aspects, such as the potential for biases in the news data, the variability in data quality of the news sources, and the complexity of accurately interpreting context within textual information [22].

In the existing literature, such data is commonly used to approximate otherwise not retrievable types of information [23]. For example, in the finance sector, news data is often utilized to forecast stock price developments or approximate organizations' Environmental, Social, and Governance (ESG) values [24]. This approach is particularly useful for obtaining estimates of values that would otherwise require direct, organization-internal information, which can be both time-consuming and resource-intensive. This makes the assessment of DM very appealing, which typically relies on the evaluation of internal documents and interviews with company representatives. In previous DMM research, the text-mining approach was primarily limited to analyzing annual company reports [25].

3 Research Methodology

3.1 Research Design

As the central research methodology, Design Science Research will be employed as this approach has been specifically developed for the creation of innovative artifacts solving real world organizational problems [26]. Based on the fundamental construct of DSR according to Hevner et al. [16], a combined approach between the six-step process of Peffers et al. [27] and the nine-step process of Becker et al. [17] will be utilized to design the artifact, as outlined in Fig. 1. As the process of Peffers et al. [27] is constructed for the general design of artifacts within the IS domain, maturity-model-specific steps of Becker et al.'s [17] process will be added to ensure an even more rigorous design and evaluation process. This research design is in line with previous publications that focus on the creation of DMMs and can, therefore, be seen as suitable [9, 13]. Even though the focus here should primarily be on the model's design, researchers have called several times to assess the concept of digital maturity in a longitudinal study [9], making the research entry point problem-centered, according to Peffers et al. [27]. Therefore, the problem definition and motivation should also be within the scope of this research as the fundamental step for the latter design of the artifact addressing the specific problem.

Following the previous four steps, the model will be developed iteratively over four cycles, within steps 5 and 6, during which the existing model will be alternately validated or revised with the assistance of corporate representatives, experts, and researchers from the domain along four central evaluation cycles as per Sonnenberg and vom Brocke [28]. A multi-methodological approach is employed here, involving empirical and conceptual approaches in the respective iterations. This method allows for the integration of information from existing literature and the prior experiences of the researchers (*conceptual*), as well as insights from practitioners (*empirical*), into the development and evaluation of the model [29].

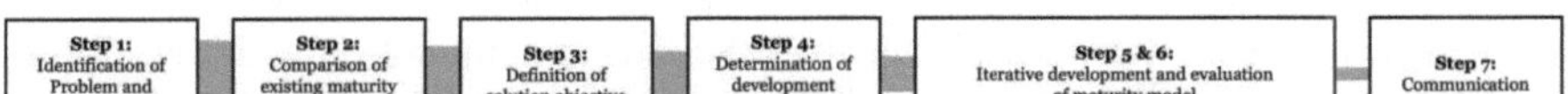

Fig. 1 Design process (adapted from Peffers et al. [27] and Becker et al. [17])

3.2 Model Development

Beginning with the initial step of *identifying the problem and motivation (1)*, it can be established that, as initially described, there is a significant gap in the literature concerning comparative DMMs. This is mostly due to the lack of a data basis for such benchmarking-oriented models. However, to gain an initial assessment of the current status of competitors, a very detailed DMM analysis of the companies is optional; instead, an approximation can already be helpful for comparing an organization with its peers [30].

When *comparing currently existing maturity models (2)* as we did within step two of our research process, it has been noted that there is a wide range of DMMs for accurately determining the maturity level of individual companies, therefore descriptive DMMs. However, there is a lack of an approach to compare multiple companies at once on a larger scale to identify potential differences between them and the associated varying maturity levels.

Based on these findings and the primary motivation, the requirements for the artifact to be developed, our DMM, were derived in the third step, resulting in the *definition of a clear solution objective (3)*. The central starting point for this step was the design principles developed by Pöppelbuß and Röglinger [8], which were explicitly crafted for various types of DMMs. The central goal of this model is to use publicly available data to determine the development of digital maturity across an entire sector, including all its market participants, in real time. This enables benchmarking between companies, making it clear what the digital leaders in the respective sector are doing differently or better.

This also influenced the *design strategy used for model development (4)*. Becker et al. [17] distinguish between three approaches: the complete development of a new model, the improvement of an existing model, and the combination of structures and contents from existing models. We opted for the third approach, extracting and recombining existing content and structures from current DMMs. In addition to utilizing existing DMMs, we also incorporated additional literature from the field of digital transformation to ensure that our model includes a sufficient amount of relevant practices in this area. We also added new components specifically regarding the data foundation and calculation logic, as no existing approaches could incorporate such large datasets into DMMs.

As outlined in the methodology description, a four-cycle approach was adopted for the penultimate phase of *model development and evaluation (5&6)*, following the guidelines set by Becker et al. [17] for the development as well as Sonnenberger and vom Brocke [28] for the evaluation, as depicted in Fig. 2.

The development process began accordingly by extracting organizational capabilities and subordinate practices from existing DMMs as well as thematically similar literature within the *first iteration*. For this purpose, a structured literature review was performed using the scientific database Scopus in conjunction with the following search string: *TITLE (((digital AND transformation) OR (digital AND maturity)) AND (framework OR model))*. Due to the already extensive range of literature

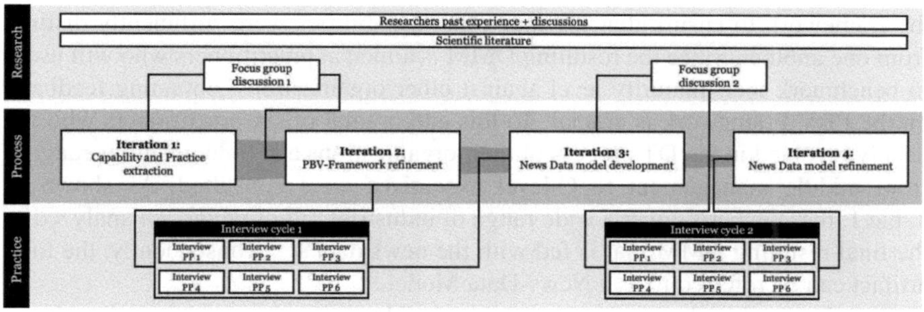

Fig. 2 Artifact design process

available, we decided to limit our initial search to "titles only" rather than including abstracts and keywords as is usual because the resulting literature often deviated significantly from the core area. The best matches were found through title searches accordingly, partly due to the high specificity of the topic. From there, we screened the abstracts of all papers and excluded those that were either inaccessible or not suitable for further proceedings based on their quality, which was mainly determined through the use of the AJG as well as VHB rankings. Building on this, organizational practices of digital transformation were identified and aligned with the structure of a previous publication by one of the authors [31]. The framework utilized in this previous publication distinguishes between eight pillars of digital transformation (Technology & Infrastructure, Process Automation & Optimization, Cybersecurity & Governance, Data & Analytics, Digital Skills & Training, Cybersecurity & Governance, Business Model Innovation, Customer Experience, Digital Leadership & Culture) and subdivides these into further organizational capabilities, with practices then being assigned to these capabilities.

For this publication, a total of 313 papers were screened, consisting of initially identified papers (289) and additional papers found through a forward-backward search process (24). After extracting the practices, the assignment of these to the respective capabilities was iteratively repeated until all co-authors were satisfied with the allocations. The cumulative number of identified practices was 167. The outcome of the first iteration was then validated and expanded through a focus group discussion. The focus group was carefully selected to include one professor and four research associates, all with significant backgrounds in IS. These participants were chosen based on their familiarity with the topic of DT, especially DMMs. The focus group was conducted using a semi-structured format, where participants were asked questions about the alignment of the initially retrieved practices with already existing capabilities. The aim here was to make sure that the alignment of practice to capability was not solely based on the author's opinion but rather also reached a consensus with a broader set of researchers.

The *second iteration* involved refining the revised version of the PBV Framework, which was already challenged once more within the last iteration by the focus group discussion. This included expanding or, in certain aspects, reducing components of the framework to ensure that the individual capabilities were sufficiently distinct from one another. Since the resulting DMM is aimed at practitioners who will use it to benchmark their maturity level against other organizations, obtaining feedback on the PBV Framework is crucial. To this end, a total of six practitioners who are deeply involved in the DT process of their organizations and hold positions ranging from middle management to C-level executives were consulted. As shown in Table 1, these experts cover a wide range of industries, all of which are analyzed in the final resulting DMM that is fed with the news data set. Consequently, the final artifact can be referred to as a News-Data Model.

Building on this, the actual News-Data Model was constructed in the *third iteration*. Based on the PBV Framework, the model is designed to measure the maturity level using news data input. The News Data Model, therefore, uses the structure of the PBV and applies it to a news data set. For this purpose, specific keywords were assigned to each practice, which then served to identify the news volume per practice. The selection of these keywords involved using the descriptions of the practices from the identified papers, as well as utilizing the Python library NLTK to find synonyms based on these initial keywords that could represent the practice in potential news articles. Additionally, alongside the keywords, the calculation logic for the score was developed. This model component identified the previously established practices in the news data set, which contains data from STOXX 600 companies and will be used as the test sample for this publication. This specific dataset was retrieved from YukkaLab, a news data provider that has accumulated over a billion articles over the course of the last 3 years. Based on these data points, a score could then be assigned to each company for each practice, derived from the company's relative size-adjusted news volume compared to industry peers, formed on a monthly basis to provide more detail compared to yearly scores. This score is then aggregated across two levels, resulting in a final maturity score for each company per month, as well as scores per pillar and capability. To validate this part of the DMM, a second focus group discussion was conducted with two experts from the partner company YukkaLab, from whom the data basis, namely the news articles, was sourced. Here, the keyword architecture and the conception of the calculation logic were further developed, as YukkaLab already has a variety of models that measure other factors of organizations using news data.

In the *fourth iteration*, we once again engaged the same experts as in the prior expert interviews to validate the model one final time. We did this by showing them

Table 1 Expert interview partner overview

IPP	Position	Industry	Revenue
1	Ex-Chief Innovation Officer & Senior Advisor	Insurance	83.63 bn
2	VP / Group IT Manager	Manufacturing	32.2 bn
3	Head of Data & AI Consulting	Telecommunications	11.07 bn
4	Chief Technology Officer	Insurance	5.4 bn
5	Executive Director Strategy and Enterprise Architecture	Healthcare	4.5 bn
6	Chief Data Officer	Banks	3.24 bn

the outputs of the model concerning their respective organizations and discussing the trends over a 3-year period. This allowed us to compare the external perspective provided by the News Data Model with the internal assessment of the maturity level from the experts' viewpoint. During this process, the applicability of our model was primarily assessed by enabling practitioners to validate their maturity levels and discuss benchmarking results with competitors from their industry. This allowed for a validation of their standing relative to the competition. As described by Sonnenberg and vom Brocke [28], in this final validation, it is essential to identify the usefulness and actual applicability of the artifact, which was ensured through the conducted expert interviews. As a concluding task, the feedback received, albeit marginal, regarding the News DMM was incorporated, ensuring that the adjustments were meaningful for the organizations surveyed and the model in general. The aim was to refine the scoring process to make it more accurate without developing a bias towards the surveyed companies.

4 News DMM

As described in the research methodology, the final DMM consists of two components that were iteratively designed by practitioners and researchers. The first is the PBV Framework, which serves as the foundation for the News Data Model. The PBV Framework comprises eight pillars, which are further divided into 29 capabilities, ultimately resulting in 167 practices. To provide an overview of this foundational model and its contents, the following section will explain the individual pillars, related capabilities, and exemplary practices. This aims to facilitate understanding the subsequent News Data Model built upon this framework, which is visualized in Fig. 3.

4.1 PBV Framework

Starting with the pillar of *Technology and Infrastructure*, six capabilities are essential for implementing this part of digital transformation through the underlying practices. These capabilities are subdivided into a further 38 practices, primarily focusing on developing and designing artificial intelligence algorithms [32], their integration within the organization, and the application of technologies such as IoT or blockchain [33]. They also address the use of external infrastructure and its security [34]. The forefront consideration is that these technologies should be applied and integrated in a purposeful and beneficial manner, enabling the organization to gain a competitive advantage. Therefore, practices related to the systematic collection of these data are included in this segment as well [35].

The second pillar, *Process Automation & Optimization*, also includes supporting practices that are crucial for defining and iteratively improving organizational

DMM-PBV-Framework		
Pillar	Capability	Practice
Technology & Infrastructure	AI Deployment	Systematic AI Integration, Strategic AI Planning, ML Algorithm Development & Implementation, Deep Learning Application, Neural Network Design & Application, AI Operational Management
	IoT Utilization	IoT Network Deployment, IoT Systems Integration, Smart Device Management, IoT Security Enhancement, IoT Data Analytics, IoT Ecosystem Development
	Blockchain Based Security Enhancement	Blockchain Infrastructure Implementation, Smart Contract Development, Decentralized Security Solutions, Cryptographic Data Protection, Blockchain Network Management, Decentralization Strategy
	External Infrastructure Utilization	Cloud Computing Integration, SaaS Solutions Adoption, PaaS Systems Utilization, IaaS Management, Third-Party Cloud Services Utilization, External Infrastructure, Hybrid Cloud Strategies
	Infrastructure Securitization	Cybersecurity Framework Implementation, Network Security Enhancement, Data Protection, Information Security Management, Data Encryption, Security Protocol Development
	Structured Data Harvesting	Data Mining, Big Data Analysis, Data Analytics, Data Storage Optimization, Automated Data Collection, Data Processing
Process Automation & Optimization	Process Definition & Improvement	Process Mapping, Process & Workflow Optimization, Lean Process Management, Business Process Redesign, Continuous Process Improvement, Process Automation Integration, Process Performance Monitoring
	Process Standardization Establishment	Standardization Protocol Development, Uniformity Enforcement, Operational Efficiency, Process Documentation, Quality Control, Best Practices Implementation, Compliance and Regulatory Adherence
Cybersecurity & Governance	Data Management	Robust Data Governance, Lifecycle Data Management, Secure Data Protocols, Comprehensive Data Auditing, Information Architecture Optimization, Access Control Systems, Data Backup and Recovery
	Compliance Assurance	Regulatory Compliance Alignment, Compliance Training Programs, Policy and Legal Compliance Review, Effective Policy Implementation, Compliance Auditing and Monitoring, Risk Assessment and Management, Standardized Compliance Reporting
	Efficiency Auditing	Performance Efficiency Analysis, Process and Workflow Evaluation, Resource Utilization Review, Technology and Auditing Tools, Cost-Benefit and ROI Analysis, Operational Review and Inspection, Benchmarking and Best Practices
	Data Integrity	Data Integrity Assurance, Error Detection and Correction, Consistency and Standardization, Data Quality Metrics and Indicators, Data Integrity Policy and Standards, Comprehensive Data Cleansing
	Reputation Safeguarding	Brand and Reputation Monitoring, Crisis Management and Response, Public Relations and Image Management, Customer Feedback and Insights, Digital Presence and Online Reputation, Strategic Reputation Planning, Media Communication and Relations
Data & Analytics	Decision Support	Advanced Decision Analytics, Predictive Modelling Techniques, BI Solutions, Strategic Planning Analytics, Analytics Reporting, Decision Algorithms, Insight Visualization
	Process Transparency	Transparency Enhancement, Visibility Analysis, Open Processes, Process Documentation, Transparent Reporting, Stakeholder Engagement, Accountability Measures in Process Management
	Analytics Solutions	Comprehensive Data Analytics, Innovative Analytics Implementation, Integrated Data Systems, Analytics Solution Development, Automated Analytics Tools
Digital Skills & Training	Skills Acquisition Trainings	Digital Skill Development, Training Programs, Learning and Development, Professional Growth Enhancement
	Device Proficiency	Device Usage Training, Technology Proficiency, User Training, Equipment Handling, Operational Training
	Technology Interaction	Technology Interaction, Technology Interaction Optimization
Business Model Innovation	Core competency focus	Core Development, Focus Strategy, Strength Identification, Capability Focus
	Outsourcing efficiency	Outsourcing Implementation, Partnership Management, Service Delegation, Operational Delegation, Strategic Delegation
	Revenue stream innovation	Model Innovation, Revenue Development, Diversification Strategies, New Revenue Streams, Monetization Strategies
	Ecosystem creation	Ecosystem Building, Network Partnerships, Collaboration Cultivation, Ecosystem Growth, Strategic Collaboration, Integration Strategies
Customer Experience	Customer need alignment	Customer Need Identification, Market Demand Analysis, Customer Preference Assessment, Market Adaptation
	Service innovation	Service Design Innovation, Service Delivery Optimization, Customer-Centric Solutions, Service Model Redefinition, Service Value Addition
Digital Leadership Culture	Strategy/Culture Alignment	Strategic Alignment, Culture Modification, Strategy Development, Integration of Culture, Implementing Strategies, Transforming Culture
	Leadership-Driven Change	Leadership Development, Managing Change, Strategic Guidance, Role Definition, Initiative Leadership, Change Leadership, Transformational Guidance
	Change Management Excellence	Initiative Implementation, Managing Transformation, Change Strategy Execution, Organizational Redesign, Adopting Changes, Leading Change
	Adaptability and Resilience	Adaptability Enhancement, Organizational Resilience Development, Flexibility Cultivation, Strategy Adaptation Readiness, Agility Implementation, Responsive Strategy Planning

Fig. 3 PBV Foundation Framework

processes. Practitioners also mention key aspects such as lean process management, process redesign, continuous development, and techniques such as Robotic Process Automation (RPA) [36–38]. These practices constitute a significant part of their efforts in this area, helping to enhance efficiency and effectiveness across organizational operations.

The third pillar, *Cybersecurity & Governance*, encompasses essential practices required for the security of organizational IT infrastructure, driven by the need to protect data collected through various technologies. This includes, e.g., implementing robust data governance and adjusting compliance regulations to meet legal standards [34, 39, 40]. In the validation phase, practitioners highlighted this as a critical area that is often under-addressed in digital transformation strategies, emphasizing the necessity of incorporating these practices to ensure the integrity and security of organizational data and operations.

The fourth pillar, *Data & Analytics*, builds on the previous pillars and includes practices that enable organizations to transform the data they collect into structured knowledge and value creation. This is achieved by systematizing the data in Business Intelligence (BI) systems and other tools to make it actionable [41]. For this purpose, these systems, including data pipelines, must be conceptualized and integrated, ultimately providing a more transparent overview of the organization and its processes [42, 43].

The deployment of these and other digital technologies within organizations necessitates that all employees who interact with them are trained and empowered to use them effectively [44]. To address this, the pillar of *Digital Skills & training* includes practices, e.g., aimed at embedding training programs within the company or fostering the cultivation of learning communities. These practices are oriented towards systematically enhancing digital proficiency across the organization, ensuring that employees are not only familiar with but proficient in the use of new technologies [45, 46].

Indeed, the adoption of new technologies alone is not sufficient for the digital maturity of an organization. The service offering and the business model itself must also evolve in the digital age [47, 48]. To facilitate this, the pillar of *Business Model Innovation* includes practices that enable the enhancement or redefinition of core areas, support the creation of new distribution and revenue channels, and ease the development of ecosystems [43, 48, 49]. This pillar focuses on ensuring that businesses adapt to digital changes and proactively innovate and transform their business models to seize new opportunities and maintain competitiveness in a rapidly changing market.

A central related aspect of this prior pillar is the *customer's experience*. Alongside business model innovation, this touchpoint must also be further developed as part of DT [50, 51]. In this context, practices that precede business model design, such as identifying changing customer needs or market shifts, are crucial. Additionally, subsequent practices, such as improving service design and delivery, play a significant role [51–54]. These practices ensure that organizations anticipate and react to customer expectations and market dynamics changes and enhance the overall customer experience.

To effectively leverage all technological changes in the form of new methods or tools at the organizational level, it is crucial to have strong digital leadership and change management embedded within the organization [55–57]. The pillar of *Digital Leadership Culture* includes practices that contribute to aligning the digital strategy with the organizational culture, facilitating leadership-driven change. This alignment is essential for organizations to evolve through digital transformation (DT) projects deliberately, thereby enhancing their adaptability to external factors and simultaneously increasing their resilience against such challenges [34, 55–58].

4.2 News Data Model

As mentioned in the research methodology, the first step after creating the PBV Framework was to define keywords for each practice, which are used to search for these practices in news data. Each keyword was ensured to consist of at least two words to avoid recognizing overly generic content that matches only one word as a practice. Additionally, the keyword catalog was iteratively developed in collaboration with both the focus group and researchers until a consensus was reached.

For instance, Table 2 lists all the practices and corresponding keywords for the capability "Leadership-Driven Change", which belongs to the pillar of Digital Leadership Culture. These keywords were then set up in the YukkaLab interface, which is necessary to extract the associated news volume data as a CSV dataset. The actual text mining process involved applying the pre-established set of keywords to the news dataset. This approach allowed for identifying and quantifying how often each keyword, representing the respective practice, appeared per company per month across all relevant articles. The CSV dataset containing these numbers, which is available for each practice per company, includes this respective news

Table 2 Keyword examples for the capability "Leadership-Driven Change"

Practice	Keywords
Leadership Development	["leadership training", "leadership skills", "executive development", "leadership growth", "management training"]
Managing Change	["change management", "transition management", "organizational change", "change initiatives", "change strategies"]
Strategic Guidance	["strategic leadership", "leadership direction", "visionary leadership", "strategic vision", "leadership influence"]
Role Definition	["leadership roles", "role clarification", "role responsibilities", "executive roles", "management roles"]
Initiative Leadership	["change initiatives", "project leadership", "initiative management", "program leadership", "project direction"]
Change Leadership	["leadership in change", "change champions", "leading transformation", "change facilitation", "transformation leadership"]
Transformational Guidance	["transformation leadership", "guiding change", "transformation strategy guidance", "change guidance", "leading innovation"]

volume—i.e., the number of articles available for each practice and the company per day. For the calculation of the first score, namely the score at the practice level, this daily volume was aggregated monthly.

A distribution for each month was then created for every STOXX Supersector, which represents a normed industry and already defines a fixed set of companies, using 10 percentiles. Based on this distribution, each practice was assigned a monthly score ranging from 1 to 10, which depends on the percentile in which the specific volume of the practice is located. A score of 0 was assigned if no volume was present, i.e., the firm does not have any relevant articles containing keywords for the specific practice this month. To ensure that this distribution does not favor larger companies due to their higher news volume, a weighting based on the total news volume of each company was applied before creating the distribution. This adjustment ensures that companies with lower total news volumes are not disadvantaged. It is important to note that the total news volume was used, not just the volume focused on digital transformation (DT), to avoid distorting the measured variable (DT maturity).

Based on this initial score, the scores for the respective capabilities were created by summing up the practice scores for all practices belonging to a capability, thus creating a capability score. This score was then used to derive a pillar score, which represents the overall estimated maturity of each organization per pillar on a scale from 0 to 1. This was done by dividing the aggregated score of all capabilities per pillar by the number of capabilities and normalizing it to a scale from 0 to 1. The same procedure was applied using the pillar scores for the final DT Maturity Score. This resulted in the final Maturity Score, which approximates an organization's overall maturity within the digital transformation context. As a result, the entire formula for determining the overall maturity level is composed, which is illustrated in eq. 1, and whose constituent components are detailed in Table 3.

$$Overall\,Maturity\,Score = \frac{1}{K}\sum_{K}^{k=1}\left(\frac{\sum_{i \in Pillark} \max_t \left(\sum_{j=1}^{n_i} S_{ij,t}\right)}{\sum_{i \in Pillark} 10 \times n_i}\right) \tag{1}$$

Based on this calculation logic, the maturity level of 590 companies was determined. Building on this data, two central analysis options were developed, which were used in the second round of practitioner expert interviews to validate the model and allow for a prototypical use of the model. The first option is the visualization of maturity levels at both the overall and pillar levels, allowing practitioners to compare their organization and its approximated maturity with those in the same industry within the STOXX 600. This provides them with an initial insight into how their organization performs in comparison to industry peers. Based on this initial assessment, a targeted benchmarking can be performed with particularly strong competitors or industry leaders. The direct benchmarking functionality at the pillar, capability, and practice levels offers the opportunity to specifically see in which aspects their organization is performing worse or better than others over time.

Table 3 Overall Maturity Score formula variable-overview

Variable	Description
$S_{ij,t}$	Score of the *j*-th practice within the *i*-th capability at time *t*, ranging from 0 to 10 based on percentile ranking in volume
n_i	Number of practices within the *i*-th capability
$\sum_{n_i}^{j=1} S_{ij,t}$	Sum of scores of all practices within capability *i* at time *t*, representing the total score for capability *i* at that time
$max_t()$	The maximum score for capability *i* across all time periods, indicating the highest level of development achieved by the capability
$10 \times n_i$	Maximum possible score for capability *i*, calculated by the number of practices times the maximum score per practice
$\sum_{i \in Pillar\ k}()$	Sum over all capabilities contributing to pillar *k*
P_k	The score for pillar *k*, computed as the ratio of the sum of adjusted maturity scores for all capabilities contributing to it over the sum of their maximum potential scores
K	Total number of pillars evaluated, used to average the pillar scores to ensure equal contribution to the overall maturity score
$\frac{1}{K}\sum_{K}^{k=1}(\ )$	Averaging the scores across all pillars to compute the overall maturity score

4.3 Model Application Interface

As described in the research methodology, a prototype interface of the model was used for validation with practitioners. This encompasses multiple visual representations regarding the maturity scores of various companies and initial benchmarking functionality. A key view initially shown to practitioners within the validation interview provides an overview of an entire supersector and each company's overall maturity score, as illustrated in Fig. 4 for the supersector banks.

Next, practitioners could delve deeper into the details of their organization with a visualization of the individual pillars. This allows them to separately assess and interpret the model's approximation of their organization's performance across different thematic areas, i.e., the pillars, providing a more granular view of where strengths and potential areas for improvement lie, as visualized in Fig. 5. Following this, practitioners can focus specifically on individual pillars, or the capabilities associated with those pillars and benchmark these against other organizations. Figure 6 shows a benchmarking example for four companies from the banking supersector and the Capability *AI-Deployment* within the pillar *Technology & Infrastructure*.

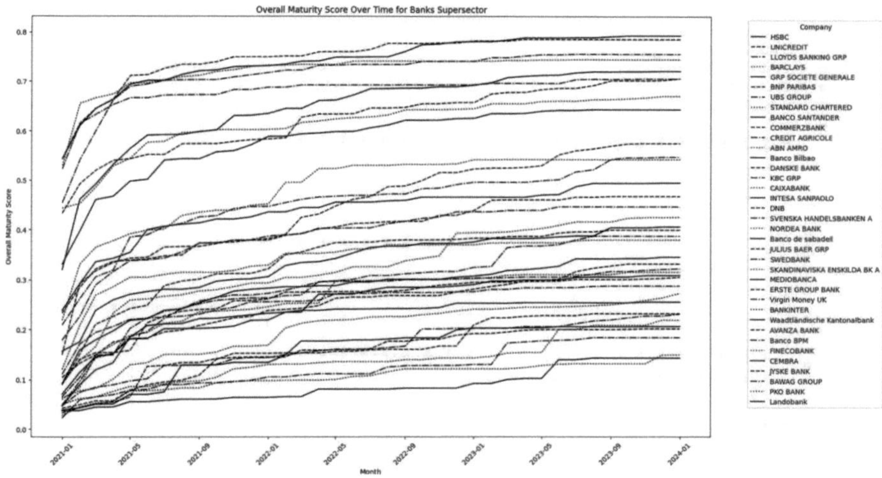

Fig. 4 Supersector overview banks

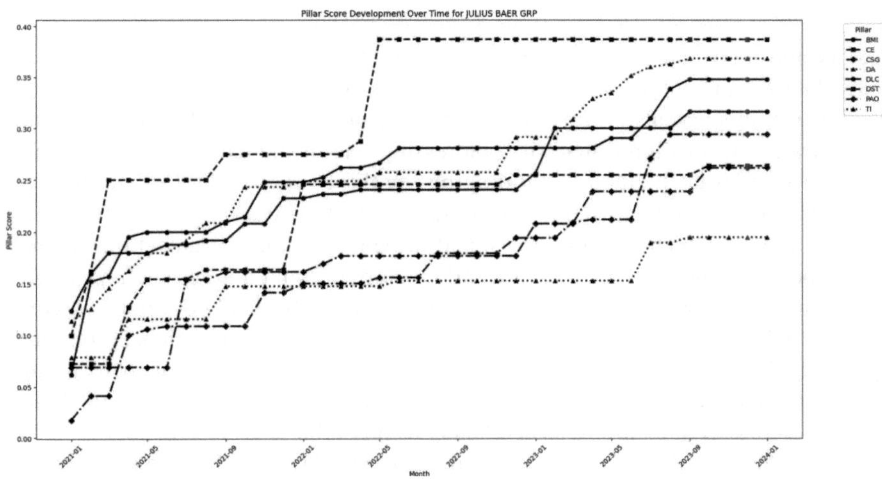

Fig. 5 Pillar maturity overview

5 Discussion

The initial goal of this study, which also served as the primary motivation, was to find a way to use accessible, large-scale data sets to approximate the digital maturity of organizations. From the outset, it was anticipated that the level of detail and the informative value would not match the depth provided by qualitative assessments conducted through surveys of multiple company members. This approach's crucial advantage was the ability to measure digital maturity in real-time across entire

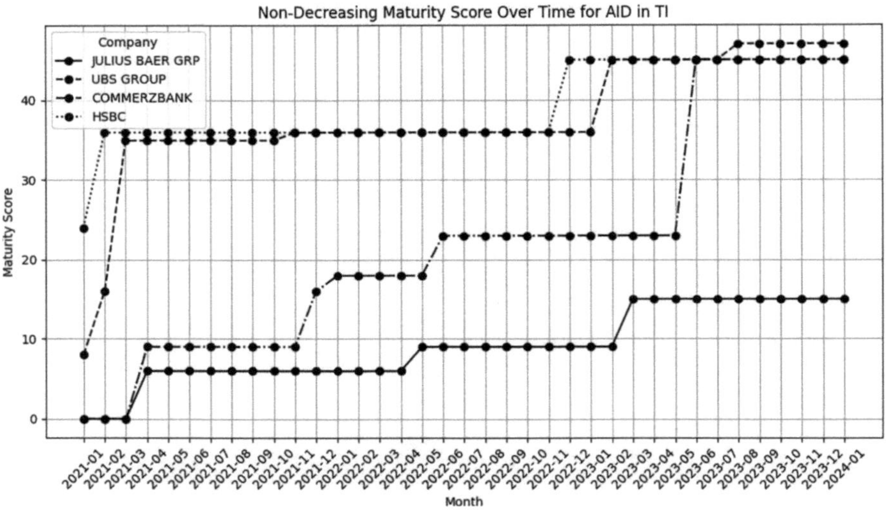

Fig. 6 Pillar benchmarking example

sectors and their constituent companies, unlike the more isolated assessments of individual organizations commonly found in existing literature. From a research perspective, this was also fitting because the use of such data enables the depiction of the trajectory of digital maturity, addressing one of the central calls for future research in relevant literature. Building on the three types of DMMs outlined by Pöppelbuß and Röglinger [8], the appropriate model type was identified as the comparative model, which is primarily aimed at benchmarking organizations against each other. This model type is significantly underrepresented in research, primarily due to the lack of suitable data sources. Subsequently, this study developed a comparative DMM based on news data inputs, using a Design Science Research approach. The model was iteratively refined through the inclusion of focus groups and qualitative expert interviews, ensuring that it reflects the dynamics of digital maturity across organizations, as accurately as possible.

The underlying theory of the PBV, alongside the methodology, was central to this research design. Although scarcely used in DT research to date, the PBV provides a foundation for understanding that organizations can distinguish themselves and gain a competitive advantage not only through different resource allocations but also, or especially, through the presence of certain organizational capabilities constituted through practices. In discussions of DT, there is often a focus on the implementation of new technologies and infrastructure, while the organizational component, which is crucial for successful implementation, is frequently overlooked. The PBV addresses this gap effectively, as it allows for a comprehensive exploration of practices identified in the literature, distributed across all DT areas.

Closely linked to this research design and the underlying PBV framework are also the limitations of this model and the associated study. Firstly, starting with the nature of a static practice framework, especially for rapidly evolving concepts like DT, new practices continually emerge that could be implemented to achieve even higher maturity. While the framework in use is sufficiently comprehensive, research is historically often temporally ahead of practice in implementing developed content, albeit with a certain lead time. However, for a long-term comparative assessment, there must be a mechanism for dynamic expansion of the PBV framework to accommodate ongoing changes and additions in DT practices. Secondly, the data base used, namely news data, is highly susceptible to biases related to several factors, such as the hype around certain topics or the publication activity of organizations, which complicates keeping the scores comparable. Therefore, additional model factors are needed in the future to systematically reduce such biases. Thirdly, the model's calculation logic has been kept very general so far, with the same importance assigned to all factors of the PBV framework. However, certain sectors may have particularly critical components in the DT process which should be weighted differently. This leads to three opportunities that future research should address to make the approximated results of such comparative DMMs even more accurate.

Interests The authors have no competing interests to declare that are relevant to the content of this article.

References

1. Vial, G. (2021). Understanding digital transformation. *Managing Digital Transformation*, 13–66. https://doi.org/10.4324/9781003008637-4/UNDERSTANDING-DIGITAL-TRANSFORMATION-GREGORY-VIAL
2. Haryanti, T., Rakhmawati, N. A., & Subriadi, A. P. (2023). The extended digital maturity model. *Big Data and Cognitive Computing, 7*, 17. https://doi.org/10.3390/BDCC7010017
3. Gökalp, E., & Martinez, V. (2021). Digital transformation capability maturity model enabling the assessment of industrial manufacturers. *Computers in Industry, 132*, 103522. https://doi.org/10.1016/J.COMPIND.2021.103522
4. Prašnikar, J., Debeljak, Ž., Ahčan, A., Praš, J., Debeljak, Ã. Ã., & Ahč An, A. (2005). Benchmarking as a tool of strategic management. *Total Quality Management and Business Excellence, 16*, 257–275. https://doi.org/10.1080/14783360500054400
5. Gurbaxani, V., & Dunkle, D. (2018). Gearing up for successful digital transformation center for digital transformation. *MIS Quarterly Executive, 18*(3), 6.
6. Hortovanyi, L., Morgan, R. E., Herceg, I. V., Djuricin, D., Hanak, R., Horvath, D., Mocan, M. L., Romanova, A., & Szabo, R. Z. (2023). Assessment of digital maturity: the role of resources and capabilities in digital transformation in B2B firms. *International Journal of Production Research, 61*, 8043–8061. https://doi.org/10.1080/00207543.2022.2164087
7. Berghaus, S., & Back, A. (2016). Gestaltungsbereiche der digitalen transformation von unternehmen: entwicklung eines reifegradmodells. *Die Unternehmung, 70*, 98–123.
8. Pöppelbuß, J., & Röglinger, M. (2011). *What makes a useful maturity model? A framework of general design principles for maturity models and its demonstration in business process management* (p. 28). Universität Augsburg.
9. Thordsen, T., Murawski, M., & Bick, M. (2020). How to measure digitalization? A critical evaluation of digital maturity models. In *Lecture Notes in Computer Science (including subseries Lecture Notes in Artificial Intelligence and Lecture Notes in Bioinformatics). 12066 LNCS* (pp. 358–369). https://doi.org/10.1007/978-3-030-44999-5_30

10. Eremina, Y., Lace, N., & Bistrova, J. (2019). Digital maturity and corporate performance: The case of the Baltic states. *Journal of Open Innovation: Technology, Market, and Complexity, 5*, 54. https://doi.org/10.3390/JOITMC5030054
11. Lee, H., Lee, H., Park, H., Kim, J. H., & Jung, H. S. (2024). ESG2PreEM: Automated ESG grade assessment framework using pre-trained ensemble models. *Heliyon, 10*, e26404. https://doi.org/10.1016/j.heliyon.2024.e26404
12. Fischbach, J., Adam, M., Dzhagatspanyan, V., Mendez, D., Frattini, J., Kosenkov, O., & Elahidoost, P. (2023). Automatic ESG assessment of companies by mining and evaluating media coverage data: NLP approach and tool. In *Proceedings - 2023 IEEE international conference on big data, BigData 2023* (pp. 2823–2830). https://doi.org/10.1109/BIGDATA59044.2023.10386488
13. Thordsen, T., & Bick, M. (2023). A decade of digital maturity models: Much ado about nothing? *Information Systems and e-Business Management, 21*, 947–976. https://doi.org/10.1007/s10257-023-00656-w
14. Berghaus, S., Back, A.: Disentangling the fuzzy front end of digital transformation: Activities and approaches. (2017).
15. Becker, J., Niehaves, B., Poeppelbuss, J., & Simons, A. (2010). Maturity models in IS research.
16. Hevner, A. R., March, S. T., Park, J., & Ram, S. (2004). Design science in information systems research. *MIS Quarterly, 28*, 75–105. https://doi.org/10.2307/25148625
17. Becker, J., Knackstedt, R., & Pöppelbuß, J. (2009). Developing maturity models for IT management. *Business & Information Systems Engineering, 1*, 213–222. https://doi.org/10.1007/S12599-009-0044-5
18. Hanelt, A., Bohnsack, R., Marz, D., & Marante, C. A. (2020). A systematic review of the literature on digital transformation: Insights and implications for strategy and organizational change. *Journal of Management Studies, 58*, 1159–1197. https://doi.org/10.1111/joms.12639
19. Bromiley, P., & Journal, D. R.-S. M. (2014). Undefined: Towards a practice-based view of strategy. *Strategic Management Journal, 35*, 1249–1256. https://doi.org/10.1002/smj.2238
20. Feldman, R., Dagan, I., & Hirsh, H. (1998). Mining text using keyword distributions. *Journal of Intelligent Information System, 10*, 281–300. https://doi.org/10.1023/A:1008623632443
21. Hotho, A., Nürnberger, A., & Paaß, G. (2005). A brief survey of text mining. *Journal for Language Technology and Computational Linguistics, 20*, 19–62.
22. Aras, H., Hackl-Sommer, R., Schwantner, M., & Sofean, M. (2014). *Applications and challenges of text mining with patents*. IPaMin@ KONVENS.
23. Ashtiani, M., & Raahemi, B. (2023). News-based intelligent prediction of financial markets using text mining and machine learning: A systematic literature review. In *Expert Systems with Applications*. Elsevier.
24. Borms, S., Boudt, K., Holle, F. V., & Willems, J. (2021). Semi-supervised text mining for monitoring the news about the ESG performance of companies. In *Data science for economics and finance: Methodologies and applications*. https://doi.org/10.1007/978-3-030-66891-4
25. Wen, H., Zhong, Q., & Lee, C. (2022). *Digitalization, competition strategy and corporate innovation: Evidence from Chinese manufacturing listed companies*. Elsevier.
26. Vom Brocke, J., Hevner, A., & Maedche, A. (2020). Introduction to design science research. In *Design science research. Cases* (pp. 1–13). Springer. https://doi.org/10.1007/978-3-030-46781-4_1
27. Peffers, K., Tuunanen, T., Rothenberger, M. A., & Chatterjee, S. (2007). A design science research methodology for information systems research. *Journal of Management Information Systems, 24*, 45–77. https://doi.org/10.2753/MIS0742-1222240302
28. Sonnenberg, C., & Vom Brocke, J. (2012). Evaluations in the science of the artificial - Reconsidering the build-evaluate pattern in design science research. In *Lecture Notes in Computer Science (including subseries Lecture Notes in Artificial Intelligence and Lecture Notes in Bioinformatics). 7286 LNCS* (pp. 381–397). https://doi.org/10.1007/978-3-642-29863-9_28
29. Nickerson, R. C., Varshney, U., & Muntermann, J. (2013). A method for taxonomy development and its application in information systems. *European Journal of Information Systems., 22*, 336–359. https://doi.org/10.1057/EJIS.2012.26

30. Zaino, N. A., & D'Errico, J. (1989). Optimal discrete approximations for continuous outcomes with applications in decision and risk analysis. *Journal of the Operational Research Society, 40*, 379–388. https://doi.org/10.1057/JORS.1989.56
31. Breitruck, M. (2024). *Decomposing the construct of digital transformation: An in-depth exploration of its integral pillars using the viable system models perspective*. University of St. Gallen. https://www.alexandria.unisg.ch/handle/20.500.14171/122674
32. Marcel Ramadhan, A., Trisetyarso, A., Abdurachman, E., & Zarlis, M. (2023). Digital transformation adoption: An extended step-by-step framework. *Journal of System and Management Sciences., 13*, 45–63. https://doi.org/10.33168/JSMS.2023.0204
33. Ma, C., Mao, J. Y., & An, X. P. (2022). The driving forces behind the phenomenal rise of the digital economy in China. *Management and Organization Review, 18*, 803–815. https://doi.org/10.1017/mor.2022.34
34. Lacombe, I., & Jarboui, A. (2023). Governance and management of digital transformation projects: an exploratory approach in the financial sector. *International Journal of Innovation Science., 15*, 611–635. https://doi.org/10.1108/IJIS-02-2022-0034
35. Shan, R., & Shan, T. (2022). Digital transformation method for healthcare data. In *Lecture notes in computer science (including subseries Lecture notes in artificial intelligence and lecture notes in bioinformatics)* (pp. 48–63). Springer. https://doi.org/10.1007/978-3-030-96282-1_4
36. Nowak, A., Pawlowski, J., & Schellenbach, M. (2022). The competency-based business process management-employee-centered process improvement for digital transformation. In *Communications in computer and information science* (pp. 103–117). Springer. https://doi.org/10.1007/978-3-031-07920-7_9
37. Shinde, S., & Cormican, K. (2023). From pain points to scale points: Exploring barriers to lean digital transformation. In *IFIP advances in information and communication technology* (pp. 108–121). Springer. https://doi.org/10.1007/978-3-031-25741-4_11
38. Josyula, S. S., Suresh, M., & Raghu Raman, R. (2023). How to make intelligent automation projects agile? Identification of success factors and an assessment approach. *International Journal of Organizational Analysis., 31*, 1461–1491. https://doi.org/10.1108/IJOA-05-2021-2749
39. Surani, A., Bawaked, A., Wheeler, M., Kelsey, B., Roberts, N., Vincent, D., & Das, S. (2023). Security and privacy of digital mental health: An analysis of web services and mobile applications. In *Lecture notes in computer science (including subseries Lecture notes in artificial intelligence and lecture notes in bioinformatics)* (pp. 319–338). Springer. https://doi.org/10.1007/978-3-031-37586-6_19
40. Gökalp, E., Şener, U., & Eren, P. E. (2017). Development of an assessment model for industry 4.0: Industry 4.0-MM. In *Communications in computer and information science* (pp. 128–142). Springer Verlag. https://doi.org/10.1007/978-3-319-67383-7_10
41. Mucha, T., Ma, S., & Abhari, K. (2023). Riding a bicycle while building its wheels: The process of machine learning-based capability development and IT-business alignment practices. *Internet Research, 33*, 168–205. https://doi.org/10.1108/INTR-10-2022-0769
42. Eichholz, J., Knauer, T., & Winkelmann, S. (2023). Digital maturity of forecasting and its impact in times of crisis. *Schmalenbach Journal of Business Research, 75*, 443–481. https://doi.org/10.1007/s41471-023-00171-1
43. Florek-Paszkowska, A., Ujwary-Gil, A., & Godlewska-Dzioboń, B. (2021). Business innovation and critical success factors in the era of digital transformation and turbulent times. *Journal of Entrepreneurship, Management and Innovation, 17*, 7–28. https://doi.org/10.7341/20211741
44. Crupi, A., Del Sarto, N., Di Minin, A., Gregori, G. L., Lepore, D., Marinelli, L., & Spigarelli, F. (2020). The digital transformation of SMEs – A new knowledge broker called the digital innovation hub. *Journal of Knowledge Management, 24*, 1263–1288. https://doi.org/10.1108/JKM-11-2019-0623
45. Cetindamar Kozanoglu, D., & Abedin, B. (2021). Understanding the role of employees in digital transformation: Conceptualization of digital literacy of employees as a multi-dimensional organizational affordance. *Journal of Enterprise Information Management, 34*, 1649–1672. https://doi.org/10.1108/JEIM-01-2020-0010

46. Fu, F., Zha, W., & Zhou, Q. (2023). The impact of enterprise digital capability on employee sustainable performance: From the perspective of employee learning. *Sustainability (Switzerland), 15*. https://doi.org/10.3390/su151712897
47. Troisi, O., Visvizi, A., & Grimaldi, M. (2023). Digitalizing business models in hospitality ecosystems: Toward data-driven innovation. *European Journal of Innovation Management, 26*, 242–277. https://doi.org/10.1108/EJIM-09-2022-0540
48. Ulrich, P., & Fibitz, A. (2020). Blessing or curse: does digitalization foster business model innovation? Evidence from a quantitative empirical study. *Corporate and Business Strategy Review., 1*, 44–65. https://doi.org/10.22495/cbsrv1i2art4
49. Jin, J., Ma, L., & Ye, X. (2020). Digital transformation strategies for existed firms: From the perspectives of data ownership and key value propositions. *Asian Journal of Technology Innovation, 28*, 77–93. https://doi.org/10.1080/19761597.2019.1700384
50. Martínez-Peláez, R., Ochoa-Brust, A., Rivera, S., Félix, V. G., Ostos, R., Brito, H., Félix, R. A., & Mena, L. J. (2023). Role of digital transformation for achieving sustainability: Mediated role of stakeholders, key capabilities, and technology. *Sustainability (Switzerland), 15*, 11221. https://doi.org/10.3390/su151411221
51. Hafsi, M., & Assar, S. (2020). Does enterprise architecture support customer experience improvement? Towards a conceptualization in digital transformation context. In *Lecture notes in business information processing* (pp. 411–427). Springer. https://doi.org/10.1007/978-3-030-49418-6_28
52. Hu, L., & Basiglio, A. (2023). A multiple-case study on the adoption of customer relationship management and big data analytics in the automotive industry. *TQM Journal, 36*, 1–21. https://doi.org/10.1108/TQM-05-2023-0137
53. Prokopenko, O., Zholamanova, M., Mazurenko, V., Kozlianchenko, O., & Muravskyi, O. (2022). Improving customer relations in the banking sector of Ukraine through the development of priority digital banking products and services: Evidence from Poland. *Banks and Bank Systems, 17*, 12–26. https://doi.org/10.21511/bbs.17(3).2022.02
54. Mahanta, P., & Mohamed, A. G. (2020). Digital transformation – A call for business user experience driven development. In *Lecture notes in computer science (including subseries Lecture notes in artificial intelligence and lecture notes in bioinformatics)* (pp. 161–166). Springer. https://doi.org/10.1007/978-3-030-40907-4_16
55. Niu, S. J., Park, B. I., & Jung, J. S. (2022). The effects of digital leadership and ESG management on organizational innovation and sustainability. *Sustainability (Switzerland), 14*, 15639. https://doi.org/10.3390/su142315639
56. Gledson, B., Zulu, S. L., Saad, A. M., & Ponton, H. (2024). Digital leadership framework to support firm-level digital transformations for Construction 4.0. *Construction Innovation, 24*, 341–364. https://doi.org/10.1108/CI-12-2022-0328
57. Ramadan, M., Bou Zakhem, N., Baydoun, H., Daouk, A., Youssef, S., El Fawal, A., Elia, J., & Ashaal, A. (2023). Toward digital transformation and business model innovation: The nexus between leadership, organizational agility, and knowledge transfer. *Administrative Sciences, 13*, 185. https://doi.org/10.3390/admsci13080185
58. Business School, H. *Boards in challenging times: Extraordinary disruptions leading through complex and discontinuous challenges*. Joint Research Programme on Board Leadership.

Driving Factors in the Technology Acceptance of Generative Artificial Intelligence: Insights from an Exploratory Interview Study with Digital Leaders

Daria Höhener and Benedict Lösser

Abstract The adoption pace of Generative Artificial Intelligence (GAI) is swift, yet the factors specifically affecting GAI acceptance remain underexplored. Building on the long-standing tradition within information systems to elucidate technology acceptance, this paper adopts an exploratory approach given the novelty of GAI. An interview study involving thirteen experienced digital leaders from established companies has been conducted to understand GAI acceptance among human agents. The inquiry has led to developing the GAI Acceptance Model (GAIAM), which highlights trust, hedonic motivation, convenience, efficiency, and effectiveness as antecedent factors. The proposed model demonstrates that performance expectancy and perceived value creation, influenced by context factors, serve as appraisals that ultimately lead to behavioral intention and usage intensity. GAIAM may serve as an initial model for grounding the acceptance of GAI at an individual level of analysis and encourages further research in this area. Additionally, the hypothesized model provides practitioners with guidance on which levers they can proactively manage to increase the intensity of GAI usage among human agents.

Keywords Generative artificial intelligence · Technology acceptance · Interview study

D. Höhener (✉) · B. Lösser
Institute of Information Systems and Digital Business, University of St. Gallen, St. Gallen, Switzerland
e-mail: daria.hoehener@unisg.ch; benedict.loesser@unisg.ch

A. Tursunbayeva et al. (eds.), *Technology-Driven Transformation*, Lecture Notes in Information Systems and Organisation 79,
https://doi.org/10.1007/978-3-032-01396-5_11

1 Introduction

Generative Artificial Intelligence (GAI) significantly transforms the socio-technical landscape, influencing significant macroeconomic outcomes [1]. This rapid evolution challenges society to keep pace. Within the given context, the discourse surrounding GAI technology, as a subset of Artificial Intelligence (AI), is particularly vivid, encapsulating both "utopian visions of unprecedented productivity and dystopian fears of humanity's demise" [2]. Agrawal [3] notes the immense potential of GAI yet acknowledges that factors influencing its acceptance, and thus the adoption of GAI technology, remain underexplored. This observation is somewhat surprising, especially since examining user acceptance of technologies is a well-established area of inquiry within Information Systems (IS) research [4, 5].

Various researchers have addressed the changing factors influencing the acceptance of AI in general, including Jöhnk et al. [6] and Agrawal [3]. However, these investigations have been somewhat fragmented, leaving the critical factors that are decisively influential still unclear [7]. To address this gap, Gursoy et al. [8] proposed a model tailored explicitly to general AI device acceptance, suggesting that traditional, universally applied acceptance models may not be suitable for AI [8]. This perspective aligns with Wu [5], who argues for extending existing models to accommodate evolving technologies.

To that end, transitioning from traditional AI to GAI marks a significant shift, mainly due to advancements such as generative pre-trained transformers (GPT) that enable the creation of content in conversational styles across various output formats such as text, code, or music [5]. The output capabilities of GAI that are nearly indistinguishable from human-generated output fundamentally alter usage dynamics [1], rendering the GAI phenomenon uniquely distinct. This shift significantly transforms the role of human agency in the use of IS artifacts, as GAI tools are no longer consistently subordinate. Consequently, users implicitly become human agents of the IS artifacts, who "can now delegate more complex tasks and even outcome preferences" [9]. Therefore, changes in the acceptance of GAI are anticipated.

Current research and explanatory models fail to capture GAI's acceptance adequately, including the well-established Unified Theory of Acceptance and Use of Technology (UTAUT) model [4, 10]. The inadequacy stems from their focus on technologies that have not previously exhibited such a degree of personalization and adaptability in interactions. Indeed, existing studies have addressed AI device use acceptance; however, these do not broadly focus on technology acceptance by employees within organizations but rather explore the acceptance of AI devices in specific activities [8]. Therefore, these models are incomplete in addressing the context of GAI, leading to the research question pursued by this study: What elements conceptualize individual GAI technology acceptance from a human agent perspective, and what measure is used to assess this acceptance?

Consequently, we explore the antecedents, appraisals, and novel outcomes of GAI-technology acceptance, as explicitly called for by Ooi et al. [1]. This investigation is conducted from the perspective of thirteen highly experienced digital leaders, such as Chief Digital Officers (CDOs) from enterprises across various industries. These C-level executives were selected for the study because their leadership roles are characterized, in part, by an understanding of how technological changes impact people and how organizations must align with them [11]. Thus, a qualitative, practitioner-focused approach is deemed suitable for illuminating the "key influences on acceptance" within a "real-world environment" [12]. Following the proposal by Mogaji et al. [13], interviews are a suitable and effective method to delve into the factors influencing GAI acceptance. Based on recommendations by Wu [5], we adopt a grounded theory approach articulated by Strauss & Corbin [14], recognized leaders in qualitative research methodology. Following the guidance provided by Gioia et al. [15] to ensure rigor, we derive inductive insights through structured qualitative analysis. This study presents an exploratory, hypothesized GAI acceptance model (GAIAM) comprising five main antecedents for GAI acceptance: trust, hedonic motivation, convenience, effectiveness, and efficiency. These elements collectively contribute to behavioral intention and ultimately affect the usage intensity of GAI from the human agent's perspective.

With these insights, a) the research community can understand how existing technology acceptance models might be adapted to incorporate GAI from a practical perspective, and (b) digital leaders can derive strategies to enhance acceptance of GAI within their organizations.

2 Research Context

2.1 Generative Artificial Intelligence Through a Socio-Technical Lens

As a research discipline, IS is optimally positioned to explore both the technical and human components of digital technologies [16, 17]. Such an exploration is, therefore, often rooted in the widely recognized and accepted lens of socio-technical systems (STS), which are instrumental in understanding "how they jointly influence the ability of people to act together" [18]. As noted by other authors, GAI should be regarded "as an integral component of larger" STS [19]. STS are ideal for examining technical and social systems within a specific context, providing a comprehensive framework that acknowledges their intertwined impact [20]. Viewing through the lens of STS facilitates understanding how interactions can be optimized for the best possible output. Consequently, technology acceptance theories are considered "core IS-frames" and are coherent with the "socio-technical tradition" [21], serving as a key explanatory factor. The reciprocal relationship between technological advancements and societal implications concerning GAI is elucidated through three contingencies developed by Sabherwal and Grover [2]: "the balance between automation and augmentation, the congruence of physical and digital realities, and the retention of human bounded rationality."

Regarding the technology, GAI encompasses deep learning models that generate new content based on existing training data [22, 23]. This machine learning architecture, such as GPT-4, falls under what is known as the model level. Furthermore, the system level encompasses the infrastructure—from the model to the user interface. Examples include ChatGPT for text generation, Midjourney for image generation, ElevenLabs for synthesized speech generation, and GitHub Copilot for code generation. The third layer constitutes the application level, which refers to the actual use cases being executed, such as producing an SEO-optimized text [24]. This application level represents the primary focus of this research. All three layers are set against societal implications such as ethical responsibility in usage to uphold privacy, transparency, accountability, and regulatory compliance, to name a few [1, 2].

2.2 Technology Adoption Through Individual Acceptance

Given the intense discourse surrounding GAI, which oscillates between fears due to ethical concerns, hallucinations, misapplications, and hopes for productivity enhancements [25], understanding GAI's acceptance remains challenging [26]. The complexity persists despite the long tradition of technology acceptance research within IS [5]. Still, understanding what constitutes acceptance is fundamental. Kelly [7] defines it as a "predictive measure that encapsulates a personal choice".

Two historically significant acceptance models stand out: the Technology Acceptance Model (TAM) and the UTAUT. TAM, introduced in 1989 by Davis, initially differentiated between two determinants of technology acceptance: perceived usefulness and perceived ease of use [27]. Two years later, TAM was expanded to include additional constructs—subjective norm, image, job relevance, output quality, result demonstrability, experience, and voluntariness, culminating in TAM2 [28]. In 2008, TAM3 further extended the model by adding influencing factors on perceived ease of use, specifically four anchors and two additional factors [29]. Overall, TAM is regarded as a "key tool in understanding technology adoption" [13] and is known for its theoretical simplicity [5]. Nevertheless, there have been numerous other attempts to explain technology acceptance, none of which have achieved the same level of recognition. However, the increasing fragmentation led Venkatesh et al. [4] to design the UTAUT, which synthesized eight theoretical acceptance models, including TAM [7, 22, 30]. UTAUT aims to achieve more excellent predictive capability and increased comprehensiveness. It includes the dependent variable of behavioral intention and the independent variables of performance expectancy, effort expectancy, social influence, and facilitating conditions, which are influenced by gender, age, experience, and voluntariness of use [4]. UTAUT was further refined to include additional determinants such as hedonic motivation, price value, and habit in UTAUT2 [10], which is considered "one of the most complete models explaining technology acceptance and use" with high predictive power [22, 31].

Regarding the applicability of the two models for understanding GAI acceptance, they offer only limited explanatory potential. TAM, with its three primary modifications [4, 10, 27–29] and the two versions of the UTAUT [4, 10], fall short of adequately understanding the specific acceptance of GAI despite their reliance on various factors [30]. Such limitation primarily stems from the interplay between technological progress and societal impacts concerning GAI, which inherently influence technology acceptance and cannot be adequately addressed by the two models: TAM is losing relevance as it does not account for the dynamic context as well as "emotional and social drivers" [13]. According to Mogaji et al. [13], the predictability of TAM in assessing GAI acceptance is correspondingly challenging. Furthermore, TAM is particularly suited for existing, not novel, emerging technologies [23]. UTAUT is considered inadequate for explaining the acceptance of GAI, among others, due to its lack of trust components central to accepting AI frontiers [7, 16]. Furthermore, the human-like capabilities of GAI intensify collaboration between humans and machines, a dynamic not reflected in the UTAUT model [10, 19]. This is also noted by Kelly et al. [7], who argue that traditional technology acceptance models, such as TAM or UTAUT, should only be used in the context of "non-intelligent" technology as "their predictors were irrelevant for AI usage".

Gursoy et al. [8] reinforce this observation by attempting to develop an AI-device use acceptance model (AIDUA). However, its comprehensiveness remains unclear [7] and has not yet been widely applied in extensive studies [23]. Moreover, AIDUA is unsuitable for understanding GAI acceptance in businesses as it primarily targets AI devices in customer service roles [8], which is insufficient for the broader GAI application scope.

Beyond the AIDUA model, initial attempts have been made to elucidate GAI technology acceptance. Nonetheless, such studies have predominantly examined the use of ChatGPT by students within educational settings [31, 32], offering explanations that are insufficient for the business context and limited to a single GAI application.

3 Research Method

3.1 Qualitative Interview Study Design

To understand the antecedents, appraisals, and measuring units of GAI technology acceptance, it is necessary to identify these factors first. Thus, we apply exploratory qualitative research [33]. Quantitatively verifying the weight of potential technology acceptance factors, as typical in acceptance research [4, 10, 27–29], is only feasible once the influencing factors have been identified and GAI has reached a higher level of usage maturity. Given the recent accelerations in GAI technology developments [30], this level of maturity has not yet been achieved. Currently, most organizations are still in an exploratory phase regarding the distinct capabilities of the technology [1], particularly concerning the profound integration into existing processes and structures [34]. In alignment with our research question, we have chosen a qualitative interview study for our research design. Our theory development is guided by the methodologies of Strauss & Corbin [33], where the consolidated understanding is "grounded" in data sourced from experienced experts. In our research, digital leaders serve as knowledge carriers and are viewed through a neo-positivist lens, specifically as "competent truth tellers", as conceptualized by Schultze & Avital [35]. The interviewees are distinguished by their focus on innovation at the intersection of technological advancements [11], including GAI. As human agents of GAI, they can be considered at the forefront of investigations into what influences individual acceptance of GAI technology. This positioning provides them with unique insights that can be gathered to consolidate a contemporary perspective from various industries on the influencing factors of individual GAI acceptance.

Consistent with comparable research, our objective is to analyze the real-world phenomenon within its socio-organizational context [36]. We have selected the acceptance of GAI from the perspective of the human agent, meaning the individual level, as our unit of analysis [37]. While an investigation into GAI tool sourcing by organizations might involve research streams from the procurement field, this is not the objective of our current study. Instead, we focus on understanding which factors influence the human agent and affect acceptance. The selection is particularly suitable for our context, as even the TAM originated from inductive qualitative research [38], facilitating synergy between data collection and analysis [33].

3.2 Data Collection

Interviews, as a data collection method, serve as an ideal instrument to obtain "nuanced and authentic accounts of participants" through conversations [35]. To achieve rigor in examining contemporary phenomena within IS research, we ensure reporting of the development progress as suggested by Levina [38].

In total, 13 interviews were conducted with highly experienced digital leaders, predominantly Chief Digital Officers, between February and May 2024. Participants were approached directly and were informed of our research intentions, aiming to recruit interviewees from various industries and different company sizes for theoretical sampling, as shown in Table 1 [33, 39].

In qualitative research, utilizing interviews as a data source is well-established [40]. We adhered to data saturation to ensure an adequate sample size [33], where statements in the final interviews became repetitive, and no new insights emerged. This repetition indicates saturation had been achieved, implying a comprehensive capture of the phenomena under investigation within the collected data.

The in-depth interviews were conducted one-on-one in a semi-structured interview format, as suggested by Myers & Newman [41]. The initial third of the discussions focused on the participants' experiences with GAI acceptance and the extent

Table 1 Interview Partners

Interview Partner (IP)	Job Title Interviewee	Industry of Company Interviewee is Working	Number of Employees
1	Chief Digital Officer	Security	> 16′000
2	Vice President & Head of Center of Excellence Artificial Intelligence	Technology	> 56′000
3	Chief Digital Officer	Energy	< 1′000
4	Chief Digital Officer	Pharma	> 20′000
5	Group Chief Digital Officer	Retail	> 95′000
6	Chief Digital Officer	Construction	> 6′000
7	Director Data & Insights	Energy	> 1′000
8	Head of Advanced Analytics & Robotics	Insurance	> 11′000
9	Chief Digital Officer	Fashion	< 1′000
10	Chief Digital Officer	Automotive	> 7′000
11	Director Digital Business	Banking	> 10′000
12	Chief Digital Officer	Banking	> 1′000
13	Chief Commercial & Digital Officer	Technology	> 8′000

of GAI application in their organizations, facilitating direct engagement in conversation, as suggested by Schultze & Avital [35]. Subsequently, the discussion explored factors prevalent in existing acceptance models and their applicability in the GAI context. Finally, discussions sought to identify potential vital constructs and antecedents for GAI technology acceptance and their implications for the individual in an organizational context.

3.3 Data Analysis

The interviews were recorded and transcribed in agreement with the interviewees, as Sarker et al. recommended, emphasizing explicit coding for analysis [39]. A qualitative data analysis software was employed for structured coding. Following an open coding process, according to Strauss & Corbin [33], 465 in-vivo codes were documented. Similarities and differences were consolidated, akin to axial coding [33], resulting in 189 first-order concepts [15]. During the second-order analysis, continuous reevaluation was performed to ensure that the combined concepts adequately described the phenomenon [15]. The data analysis process formed 35 second-order themes, which were then clustered into ten aggregated dimensions (see Table 1) and are summarized in the following sections. As the interviews were primarily conducted in German, we translated relevant quotes into English to enhance the manuscript's accessibility and comprehension.

4 Findings

4.1 People-Centered Approach

When integrating new technologies, it is often not the technology that acts as the bottleneck, but instead the human element (IP12), as several interview participants (IP2, IP12) noted. Such an understanding underscores the necessity of adopting a people-centered approach. This is also affirmed in the literature, which notes that the collaboration of GAI with humans is at the core of the challenge [19]. Consequently, it becomes evident that human factors play a critical role in the individual acceptance of technology and must be effectively influenced and managed. Based on these findings, aggregated dimensions as antecedents—trust, hedonic motivation, convenience, efficiency, and effectiveness—were identified. Such implications suggest that these five components, representing individual levers, influence the multi-step process of determining the willingness to utilize, in the form of appraisal, akin to the AIDUA model [8]. Performance expectancy and perceived value creation act as appraisals for the outcome of GAI technology acceptance and are influenced by context factors. In this case, these are deliberately considered as external factors, as they affect the individual level but simultaneously represent external influences. The two elements, behavioral intention and usage intensity, ultimately belong to the outcome of individual technology acceptance, as everyone's usage intensity indicates the acceptance level.

To assign the following findings to statements by the interview partners (IP), we use the format of IPX, while X is a number between 1 and 13, to ensure transparent traceability (Table 2).

4.2 Antecedents of GAI Technology Acceptance

Trust is essential to accept GAI technology, as confirmed through interviews. Several factors contribute to it: maintaining a human-in-the-loop enhances trust (IP2, IP6, IP8, IP12), as does personal solid resilience (IP7), which can address technical challenges such as data security (IP2, IP5, IP10, IP13), GAI-generated hallucinations (IP3, IP9, IP10, IP13), and fears of personal redundancy (IP4, IP5, IP8, IP10), all of which ultimately influence acceptance. Concerning technical issues, volatility, such as the inconsistency in coherent outputs manifested as hallucinations (IP3, IP9, IP10, IP13), is a barrier to building trust in the technology (IP8). General data security concerns (IP5, IP13) must be taken seriously, and fears related to data breaches (IP2, IP10) and ensuing data leaks (IP2, IP9) need addressing. Regarding personal concerns, the fear of diminishing personal significance, fear of job loss, and subsequent rationalization negatively impact trust in human agents (IP4, IP5, IP8, IP10). These issues highlight the complexity of factors that must be managed to foster trust and acceptance of GAI technology. Thus,

Table 2 Findings

Dimensions	Second-Order Themes	Exemplary Interview Excerpts
Trust	Human in the Loop	*"[...] and therefore, it is necessary to try to instill trust, establish clear rules [...]"* (IP13)
	Resilience	
	Data Security	
	Hallucination	
	Redundancy	
Hedonic Motivation	Curiosity	*"[...] then we have the top third who are always informed and for whom everything is always too slow, and who intrinsically would have liked all new things yesterday."* (IP1)
	Inspiration	
	Mindset	
	Training	
	Trend	
Convenience	Habit	*"The more regular and routine the use of these systems becomes, the stronger the habituation effect."* (IP2)
	Usability	
	Seamless Integration	
	Simplicity	
Effectiveness	Perception	*"[...] does the tool significantly enhance their capabilities?* (IP4)
	Quality	
Efficiency	Scalability	*"I also believe that performance must be adequate."* (IP10)
	Parallelization	
Performance Expectancy	Demonstrability	*"[...] customer is better informed [...] quickly get up to speed and have the necessary information."* (IP5)
	Relevance	
Perceived Value Creation	Meaningfulness	*"[...] the most crucial factor for acceptance is when the technology is applied in genuinely meaningful use cases."* (IP11)
	Recurring Benefit	
Contextual Factors	Adaptability	*"Since the fundamentals are either not yet in place or only partially so, we are currently launching a data governance initiative, beginning with documentation as a sub-project and advancing metadata and master data management in collaboration with IT."* (IP7)
	Digital Maturity	
	Experience	
	Financial Flexibility	
	GAI Readiness	
	Governance	
	Lock-In Effect	
	Regulatory	
	Reputation	
Behavioral Intention	Attitude	*"[...] people will seriously try it out and subsequently use it."* (IP10)
	Beliefs	
Usage Intensity	Usage Duration	*"[...] the proof is in the living."* (IP4)
	Usage Frequency	

trust—shaped by ethical concerns and personal fears—depends on consistently including human oversight.

UTAUT [4, 10] and researchers such as Huy et al. [22] noted that *hedonic motivation* is critical to technology acceptance. This concept refers to "the fun and pleasure derived from using a technology" [10], also evident in the current explorative interview study. Fostering curiosity is a critical motivator that enhances intrinsic motivation to use GAI (IP2, IP4, IP7, IP11, IP13). An explorative mentality is associated with an increased capability for experimentation (IP10, IP13), and this affinity for innovation can be fostered through easily accessible opportunities for experimentation (IP1), which in turn inspire ideas on how GAI can be profitably utilized in daily operations, thereby enhancing acceptance (IP6). Ultimately, "mindset is key" (IP10). A mindset open to change is a crucial lever for hedonic motivation, which impacts GAI acceptance (IP10, IP11–13). This can be encouraged through training (IP10), whereby such events can minimize doubts about GAI (IP4, IP10, IP12). Furthermore, the current media presence is well-suited to enhance technology acceptance by showcasing the fun and pleasure associated with GAI, with attractiveness bolstered by hype (IP7). Accordingly, *hedonic motivation* is a crucial driver of the appraisal for GAI technology acceptance, fueled by fun and curiosity combined with an open mindset.

The *convenience* of GAI applications significantly influences their acceptance, as voiced by many interview participants (IP2–3, IP5–10, IP12–13). Specifically, usability is a substantial factor aimed at increasing acceptance. Therefore, ease of use and intuitive understandability are positive drivers (IP3, IP8–9, IP10, IP12). Convenience is mainly an accelerator when an organization's "simplicity over complexity" approach is pursued (IP5). The more accessible the technology and the less effort it requires from human agents, the more positively it impacts usage intensity (IP6). Moreover, convenience includes the seamless integration into existing core business systems (IP5, IP7). In other words, the more advantageously GAI can be embedded into existing organizational setups (IP13) and process landscapes (IP12), and the better it can address interface issues (IP8), the more beneficial it becomes. Finally, since humans are creatures of habit, convenience develops over time (IP12–13). To summarize, GAI, with its impact growing as it becomes more accessible, must be convenient for human agents to increase positive appraisal.

Enhancements in *effectiveness* positively impact GAI acceptance. The surveyed digital leaders observed this mainly in two dimensions: On one hand, an increase in the quality of outputs enhances perceived effectiveness (IP4–5, IP8, IP10, IP12–13); on the other hand, perception also influences effectiveness (IP4). In this context, an increase in quality refers to producing adequate outputs that match the desired outcomes, thereby enhancing effectiveness by minimizing the inputs required from human agents (IP5, IP10). Perception refers to the ability to recognize or showcase the functions of GAI, meaning that human agents can directly see the benefits they gain from using it. If it is immediately apparent how GAI supports problem-solving, content generation, and so on, then the likelihood of its utilization increases (IP4). To summarize, effectiveness increases adoption if improved output quality and visibility are enhanced.

Efficiency emerges as the final antecedent for GAI technology acceptance. Scalability, defined as the capacity to process large volumes of data in this case, results in a perceived boost in efficiency from the human agent's perspective, which positively influences acceptance (IP3, IP5, IP9, IP10). The parallelization of activities, handling multiple requests or tasks simultaneously enabled by GAI, results in time savings (IP9), which also signifies an efficiency boost from the perspective of the human agent. Hence, enhancing perceived time savings and overall productivity manifests as efficiency, ultimately influencing a positively correlated appraisal.

4.3 Appraisals of GAI Technology Acceptance

The current study proposes that performance expectancy and perceived value creation are central elements that directly contribute positively to the acceptance of GAI technology.

Performance expectancy is the extent to which human agents expect a GAI application to assist them in achieving their goals. It is addressed in UTAUT [4, 10] and also referred to as appraisal in AIDUA [8], and encompasses demonstrability and relevance according to the interview participants of this study. Demonstrability refers to the ability of human agents to see or understand the potential of GAI (IP5, IP9). For example, when the human agent observes GAI performing tasks better and faster, such as generating content or accelerating code testing, their tendency to adopt the technology increases. The visibility of successful use cases enhances the willingness to use GAI (IP4, IP10). Relevance implies that the technology closely correlates with the needs or inputs of the human agents and that information is readily accessible (IP7), forming an expectation regarding the utility provided. Caution is advised if outputs are unsatisfactory, as these are considered acceptance killers (IP7). In UTAUT, performance expectancy is regarded as the primary driver of technology acceptance for use intention [10], while in AIDUA, performance expectancy, along with effort expectancy, determines the "emotions toward AI device use" [8].

In the context of GAI, digital leaders regard *perceived value creation* as fundamental. The concept encompasses the degree to which human agents recognize the value of a GAI application through utility assessment. It relies on meaningfulness and recurring benefits. Meaningfulness refers to the creation of added value (IP2, IP4, IP7, IP12–13), the provision of purposeful solutions (IP2, IP9, IP11, IP13), and genuine value creation (IP5, IP7). The added value is evident in problem-solving acceptance (IP12) and utility provision (IP7, IP13). The concept of meaningfulness is articulated through the "so what" factor (IP13), and value creation is made transparent through the visibility of added value (IP7). Recurring benefits ensure genuine value creation through consistent advantages (IP5), while repeatability secures a standardized value generation (IP2).

Context factors influence performance expectancy and perceived value creation. Still, they are not direct influencers of human agents' technology acceptance since they address the organizational rather than the individual level of analysis. However, these factors cannot be ignored as they exert considerable external influence. Among the components identified by interviewees are organizational adaptability, which is understood as the ability to recognize and adapt to changes (IP5, IP7, IP12), and digital maturity, hypothesizing that a higher maturity level correlates positively with perceived value creation and performance expectancy at the individual level (IP4, IP6, IP8, IP13). In other words, digital maturity can indicate acceptance of new technologies, including GAI, at the human agent level (IP4, IP6). In addition, experience in dealing with the adoption processes of new technologies is influential, as learning curves can be increased (IP2). A stable financial situation with resources available for innovation also facilitates adoption (IP6, IP9), as does a general readiness for GAI, which is enhanced through inter-organizational exchanges (IP13) and an understanding of the relationship between input and output factors (IP1, IP7, IP9). Furthermore, stable yet flexible governance frameworks accelerate acceptance (IP7, IP13). The dominance of a few large tech players often casts a shadow over smaller GAI technology providers, creating a perceived lock-in effect, particularly within ecosystems like the Microsoft Suite as a standard office solution (IP5). Regulatory concerns, including uncertainties about copyright (IP5, IP8) and upcoming legislation (IP11), also negatively influence GAI technology acceptance. Finally, particularly for reputable brands, concerns about potential reputational damage from careless handling of GAI are a significant barrier to acceptance (IP7, IP8).

4.4 Behavioral Intention Leads to Usage Intensity

Behavioral intention is identified as the initial outcome of the influence of antecedents and the intensity of appraisals in the interviews. The intention concretely manifests actual usage and the associated attitude toward one's behavior (IP10). Furthermore, personal beliefs, whether behavioral or normative, justify the usage behavior (IP4). These findings underscore the direct implications of antecedent factors and appraisal processes on the decision to engage with GAI technologies.

The behavioral intention in the context of GAI ultimately leads to use behavior that manifests in *usage intensity*. With this, factors such as frequency of usage (IP4; IP5) and duration length (IP4) are implied. Some digital leaders surveyed have deeply integrated GAI applications into their operations (IP4, IP8). In contrast, others note that the intensity of use varies by application area, with GAI being extensively used in software development (IP5) but less so in other places (IP10). It can be observed that usage intensity measures the GAI technology acceptance of a human agent. The more frequently the use is made, the higher the implicit acceptance is. The question is no longer if GAI is used but rather the intensity of its use (IP5). This distinction sets our findings apart concerning the outcome of behavioral intention from those of TAM [4, 10, 27–29] and UTAUT [4, 10]. Rather than merely assessing use behavior, our approach evaluates the intensity of use, which serves as a more meaningful unit for measuring acceptance.

5 Discussion

5.1 Theoretical Contribution and Practical Implications

From the insights gathered, we developed GAIAM, as shown in Fig. 1. In this model, antecedents are depicted as influencing factors that affect appraisals, which in turn influence outcomes. The hypothesized model is derived from insights obtained through interviews and subsequent coding processes leading to aggregated dimensions, detailed in the previous chapter. Additionally, perceived value creation not only influences behavioral intention but also affects performance expectancy, as indicated by various interview participants. This influence occurs as expectations of performance increase when a technology generates significant value (IP1, IP7–8, IP10, IP13).

GAIAM builds upon existing acceptance models in IS research, outlined in Chap. 2.2, and refines the conceptualizations of prevailing AI acceptance studies specifically for GAI as follows: When it comes to the identified antecedents, *trust* is a driving factor in accepting AI technologies, as highlighted by other authors, including Kelly [7]. Resilience positively correlates with trust, whereas other second-order themes, such as data security concerns, exert a negative effect. *Hedonic motivation*, featured in both UTAUT2 [10] and AIDUA [8], reflects the fun mentality, which gains further relevance due to the human-like qualities of GAI outputs. *Convenience*, a current megatrend, also plays a significant role in the antecedents of GAI technology acceptance, emphasizing the ease of use of applications. *Efficiency*, mentioned in the literature as one of the considerable attributes of GAI [23], along with effectiveness [1], is relevant to the human agent. Findings from McKinsey support this, suggesting that using GAI can lead to an annual increase in work productivity of between 0.1 and 0.6%, thus enhancing *efficiency* [42]. *Perceived value*

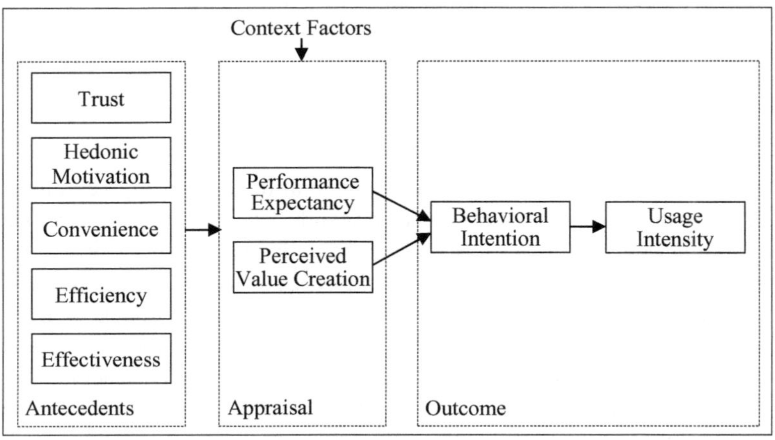

Fig. 1 GAIAM

creation measures the value anticipated from a GAI application. It influences *performance expectancy*, a construct also present in both UTAUT [4, 10] and AIDUA [8] frameworks, which assesses the expectation of GAI applications in supporting goal achievement. *Context factors* include social factors, as identified by Lee et al. [26]. Ultimately, as a measure of GAI acceptance by human agents, these constructs lead to a *behavioral intention*. This is in line with UTAUT1 and UTAUT2, which recognize the prediction of behavioral intention to use a technology as a measure of technology acceptance [4, 10]. They note that behavioral intention is "the key predictor of technology use" [10] and is even considered the "strongest predictor." These models build on many preceding individual acceptance research studies, identifying behavioral intention as a suitable measure [4]. In our context, intention is understood not as the intention to adopt but rather as the intention to continue use [43]. Further, in terms of continued use, behavioral intention culminates in a manifestation of *usage intensity*.

In terms of theoretical contribution, we have conceptualized with GAIAM how GAI technology acceptance is shaped at the level of the human agent. By doing so, we build upon the tradition of IS acceptance research and thus expand existing models such as UTAUT, TAM, or AIDUA, as illustrated in the comparison above. We argue that exogenous constructs, similar to the findings of Dwivedi et al. [30], also influence acceptance, as indicated by the *context factors*. It remains unclear whether the identified antecedents and appraisals will remain applicable in the medium to long term for GAI; as Vial [44] noted, while there may be a positive impact in the short to medium term, the long-term implications remain uncertain, particularly in how ethical debates may diminish acceptance.

Regarding practical implications, GAIAM indicates which levers should be used by human agents to increase the intensity of GAI usage. It highlights the importance of added value, which plays a significant role in the usage intensity of GAI. Considering the generated added value is crucial when prioritizing proof of concepts, as it can enhance intensity. Aligning such an approach with organizational goals is essential for achieving a sustainable advantage using GAI technology.

5.2 Limitations

To interpret the outcomes accurately, it is essential to acknowledge certain limitations that can be explored in subsequent research. Accordingly, we point out two relevant limitations. First, this study is fundamentally qualitative. Efforts were made to include a variety of company sizes and industries to facilitate generalization in a "natural setting" [37]; however, the insights gained represent a snapshot at the time of the interviews and reflect the perspectives of the limited number of interviewees. Although the participants are recognized as experienced digital leaders, this does not equate to a "variety of voices" [41]. Cultural differences were not considered, as the study was primarily conducted in Switzerland and Germany, despite some interviewed digital leaders working in globally operating companies. Second, we recognize that our findings cannot be transferred to specific application areas of GAI as the subject of the study was intentionally quite broad, allowing for generalization. Third, derived from GAIAM, no best practices have been specified for how companies can address and positively influence the identified antecedents.

6 Concluding Remarks and Future Research

The paper's objective was to develop a hypothesized model that explains the acceptance of GAI technology from a human agent perspective. To accurately represent human-technology interaction, thirteen experienced digital leaders were involved as interview participants in a qualitative interview study using the STS lens. The study is relevant as the impact of GAI "gradually unfolds" [2] in light of its remarkable characteristics [19]. GAIAM includes the antecedents of trust, hedonic motivation, convenience, efficiency, and effectiveness, which influence perceived value creation and performance expectancy appraisals. These, in turn, determine behavioral intention and, ultimately, usage intensity as the measuring unit for GAI technology acceptance.

Further research based on this exploratory approach can be conducted in various ways. For instance, the study could be repeated once GAI is no longer predominantly in the experimentation phase to illustrate changes over time. Additionally, other interview participants, such as developers or legislators, could be included to provide a broader foundation for the results. An industry-specific study would also offer intriguing insights into the specific determinants affecting GAI acceptance with a more focused scope. Beyond that, ethical implications—increasingly emerging in the GAI discourse—represent an intriguing area for further investigation regarding their impact on acceptance levels. Finally, and most straightforwardly, it is essential to statistically analyze the model hypothesized in this research to determine the significance of each antecedent and appraisal. That approach is similar to other research, such as that by Gursoy et al. [8]. Examining the weighting of individual constructs, which is customary in acceptance models [4, 10, 28, 29], allows for further analysis. The additional quantitative research can support validating and refining the proposed model's components and their interrelations.

Disclosure of Interests The authors have no competing interests to declare that are relevant to the content of this article.

References

1. Ooi, G., et al. (2023). The potential of generative artificial intelligence across disciplines: Perspectives and future directions. *Journal of Computer Information Systems*, 1–32.
2. Sabherwal, R., & Grover, V. (2024). The societal impacts of generative artificial intelligence: A balanced perspective. *Journal of the Association for Information Systems, 25*(1), 13–22.

3. Agrawal, K. P. (2023). Towards adoption of generative AI in organizational settings. *Journal of Computer Information Systems, 37–191*.
4. Venkatesh, V., Morris, M. G., Davis, G. B., & Davis, F. D. (2003). User acceptance of information technology: Toward a unified view. *MIS Quarterly, 27*(3), 425–478.
5. Wu, P. F. (2012). A mixed methods approach to technology acceptance research. *Journal of the Association for Information Systems, 13*(3), 172–187.
6. Jöhnk, J., Weissert, M., & Wyrtki, K. (2021). Ready or not, AI comes – An interview study of organizational AI readiness factors. *Business & Information Systems Engineering, 63*(1), 5–20.
7. Kelly, S., Kaye, S., & Oviedo-Trespalacios, O. (2023). What factors contribute to the acceptance of artificial intelligence? A systematic review. *Telematics and Informatics, 77*(1).
8. Gursoy, D., Chi, O. H., Lu, L., & Nunkoo, R. (2019). Consumers acceptance of artificially intelligent (AI) device use in service delivery. *International Journal of Information Management, 49*(1), 157–169.
9. Baird, A., & Maruping, L. M. (2021). The next generation of research on is use: A theoretical framework of delegation to and from agentic IS artifacts. *MIS Quarterly, 45*(1), 315–341.
10. Venkatesh, V., Thong, J. Y. L., & Xu, X. (2012). Consumer acceptance and use of information technology: Extending the unified theory of acceptance and use of technology. *MIS Quarterly, 36*(1), 157–178.
11. Oberer, B., & Erkollar, A. (2018). Leadership 4.0: Digital leaders in the age of industry 4.0. *International Journal of Organizational Leadership, 7*(4), 404–412.
12. Williams, M. D., Rana, N. P., & Dwivedi, Y. K. (2015). The unified theory of acceptance and use of technology (UTAUT): A literature review. *Journal of Enterprise Information Management, 28*(3), 443–488.
13. Mogaji, E., Viglia, G., Srivastava, P., & Dwivedi, Y. K. (2024). Is it the end of the technology acceptance model in the era of generative artificial intelligence? *International Journal of Contemporary Hospitality Management, 120*(1).
14. Strauss, A. L., & Corbin, J. M. (1990). *Basics of qualitative research: Grounded theory procedures and techniques* (2nd ed.). SAGE Publications.
15. Gioia, D. A., Corley, K. G., & Hamilton, A. L. (2012). Seeking qualitative rigor in inductive research: Notes on the Gioia methodology. *Organizational Research Methods, 16*(1), 15–31.
16. Berente, N., Gu, B., Recker, J., & Santhanam, R. (2021). Managing artificial intelligence. *MIS Quarterly, 45*(3), 1433–1450.
17. Sarker, S., Chatterjee, S., Xiao, X., & Elbanna, A. (2019). The sociotechnical axis of cohesion for the is discipline: Its historical legacy and its continued relevance. *MIS Quarterly, 43*(3), 695–719.
18. Resnick, P. (2000). Beyond bowling together: Sociotechnical capital. In *Human-computer interaction in the new millennium* (pp. 247–272). ACM Press.
19. Nah, F., Cai, J., Zheng, R., & Pang, N. (2023). An activity system-based perspective of generative AI: Challenges and research directions. *AIS Transactions on Human-Computer Interaction, 15*(3), 247–267.
20. Bostrom, R. P., & Heinen, J. S. (1977). MIS problems and failures: A socio-technical perspective. Part I: The causes. *MIS Quarterly, 1*(3), 17–32.
21. Ravarani, A., Margherita, E. G., & Islind, A. S. (2024). Human-centric digital technology: Socio-technical lenses for a new era of artificial intelligence. In *Call for papers itAIS 2024. itAIS, Piacenza.*
22. Van Huy, L., Nguyen, H. T. T., Vo-Thanh, T., Thinh, N. H. T., & Dung, T. T. T. (2023). Generative AI, why, how, and outcomes: A user perspective. *Transactions on Human-Computer Interaction, 15*(1), 1–31.
23. Gupta, R., Nair, K., Mishra, M., Ibrahim, B., & Bhardwaj, S. (2024). Adoption and impacts of generative artificial intelligence: Theoretical underpinnings and research agenda. *International Journal of Information Management Data Insights, 4*(1).
24. Feuerriegel, S., Hartmann, J., Janiesch, C., & Zschech, P. (2024). Generative AI. *Business & Information Systems Engineering, 66*(1), 111–126.

25. Alavi, M., Leidner, D. E., & Mousavi, R. (2024). A knowledge management perspective of generative artificial intelligence. *Journal of the Association for Information Systems, 25*(1), 1–12.
26. Lee, S., Jones-Lang, M., Chung, M., Kim, N., & Choi, J. (2024). Who is using ChatGPT and why? Extending the unified theory of acceptance and use of technology (UTAUT) model. *Information Research, 29*(1), 54–72.
27. Davis, F. D. (1989). Perceived usefulness, perceived ease of use, and user acceptance of information technology. *MIS Quarterly, 13*(3), 319–340.
28. Venkatesh, V., & Davis, F. D. (2000). A theoretical extension of the technology acceptance model: Four longitudinal field studies. *Manage Science, 46*(2), 186–204.
29. Venkatesh, V., & Bala, H. (2008). Technology acceptance model 3 and a research agenda on interventions. *Decision Sciences, 39*(2), 273–315.
30. Dwivedi, Y. K., Rana, N. P., Jeyaraj, A., Clement, M., & Williams, M. D. (2019). Re-examining the unified theory of acceptance and use of technology (UTAUT): Towards a revised theoretical model. *Information Systems Frontiers, 21*(3), 719–734.
31. Budhathoki, T., Zirar, A., Njoya, E. T., & Timsina, A. (2024). ChatGPT adoption and anxiety: A cross-country analysis utilising the unified theory of acceptance and use of technology (UTAUT). *Studies in Higher Education, 49*, 831.
32. Yilmaz, F. G. K., Yilmaz, R., & Ceylan, M. (2023). Generative artificial intelligence acceptance scale: A validity and reliability study. *International Journal of Human–Computer Interaction, 40*, 8703.
33. Strauss, A. L., & Corbin, J. M. (1998). *Basics of qualitative research techniques and procedures for developing grounded theory* (2nd ed.). SAGE Publications.
34. Dwivedi, Y. K., Rana, N. P., Jeyaraj, A., Clement, M., & Williams, M. D. (2019). Re-examining the Unified Theory of Acceptance and Use of Technology (UTAUT): Towards a revised theoretical model. *Information Systems Frontiers, 21*(3), 719–734.
35. Schultze, U., & Avital, M. (2011). Designing interviews to generate rich data for information systems research. *Information and Organization, 21*(1), 1–16.
36. Yin, R. K. (2016). *Qualitative research from start to finish* (2nd ed.). The Guilford Press.
37. Khan, S. (2014). Qualitative research method: Grounded theory. *International Journal of Business and Management, 9*(11), 224–233.
38. Levina, N. (2021). All information systems theory is grounded theory. *MIS Quarterly, 45*(1), 489–494.
39. Sarker, S., Xiao, X., & Beaulieu, T. (2013). Qualitative studies in information systems: A critical review and some guiding principles. *MIS Quarterly, 37*(4).
40. Marshall, B., Cardon, P., Poddar, A., & Fontenot, R. (2013). Does sample size matter in qualitative research?: A review of qualitative interviews in is research. *The Journal of Computer Information Systems, 54*(1), 11–22.
41. Myers, M. D., & Newman, M. (2007). The qualitative interview in IS research: Examining the craft. *Information and Organization, 17*, 2–26.
42. McKinsey & Company. (2023). *The economic potential of generative AI.*
43. Jeyaraj, A., Dwivedi, Y. K., & Venkatesh, V. (2023). Intention in information systems adoption and use: Current state and research directions. *International Journal of Information Management, 73.*
44. Vial, G. (2019). Understanding digital transformation: A review and a research agenda. *Journal of Strategic Information Systems, 28*(2), 118–144.

Fostering Organizational Cybersecurity Culture Amid Rapid Digital Transformation: A Case Study from Ethiopia

Meseret Assefa Adamu, Paolo Spagnoletti, and Marko Ilmari Niemimaa

Abstract Digital transformation introduces significant cybersecurity challenges for organizations, with its rapid pace further complicating the development of a robust cybersecurity culture (CSC). While previous studies have focused on building, developing, and conceptualizing CSC under relatively stable conditions, they often overlook the challenges posed by rapid digital transformation (RDT) and lack detailed insights into the initiatives and key factors that promote a desirable CSC amid RDT. This study employs a qualitative research methodology, collecting data from a financial institution undergoing RDT through semi-structured interviews and archival documents. The findings provide empirical insights into the cybersecurity challenges RDT presents and identify critical factors that contribute to cultivating a desired CSC in such a dynamic context. Theoretically, this research demonstrates that organizations can develop a desired CSC through deliberate actions, such as regular training, leadership initiatives, and updating policies and guidelines, even amid rapid organizational changes. Practically, it deepens the understanding of CSC in dynamic settings and provides strategies to enhance security and address cybersecurity challenges in times of rapid transformation.

Keywords Cybersecurity culture · Rapid digital transformation · Cybersecurity challenges · Cybersecurity initiatives · Factors of cybersecurity culture

M. A. Adamu (✉) · M. I. Niemimaa
Department of Information Systems, University of Agder (UiA), Kristiansand, Norway
e-mail: meseret.a.adamu@uia.no; marko.niemimaa@uia.no

P. Spagnoletti
Department of Information Systems, University of Agder (UiA), Kristiansand, Norway

Department of Business and Management, Luiss University, Rome, Italy
e-mail: paolo.spagnoletti@uia.no; pspagnoletti@luiss.it

A. Tursunbayeva et al. (eds.), *Technology-Driven Transformation*, Lecture Notes in Information Systems and Organisation 79,
https://doi.org/10.1007/978-3-032-01396-5_12

1 Introduction

Many organizations are rushing to invest in large-scale implementation and integration of emerging digital technologies [1, 2], causing significant organizational disruption [1]. The implementation and integration trigger changes and challenges [2, 3] that significantly impact organizations in many ways, such as culture and operations [4]. CSC is a subculture of organizational culture [5] potentially affected by the implementation and integration of digital technologies (digital transformation) [2, 6]. Digital transformation increases the exposure of organizational operations to cyberattacks [3, 7], and the rapidity of the transformation exacerbates the problem. RDT is the rapid implementation of emerging digital technologies and strategies to enhance business operations, automation, and workflows [8]. However, this rapid integration can lead to significant challenges and consequences [1, 9], particularly concerning organizational cybersecurity. For example, in March 2024, an Ethiopian commercial bank experienced significant system disruptions following the rapid implementation and integration of digital technologies. This led to unauthorized transactions and exposed several cyber vulnerabilities. This resulted in a prolonged interruption in banking services and a loss of multi-billion Ethiopian currency or 40 million U.S. dollars due to the incident [10].

In response to the challenges, organizations primarily invest in technical cybersecurity initiatives. These include increasing cybersecurity budgets, adopting new technologies, and enhancing process security through preventative, detective, and corrective controls [1, 11, 12]. However, according to recent reports, more than 83% of security incidents are due to human-related issues [13]. The increased cyberattacks targeting human elements as vulnerable links require comprehensive security measures [14–16]. Researchers argued that in addition to the technological solutions [17, 18], initiatives not primarily focused on technology or the implementation of technical solutions also play a critical role in organizational cybersecurity [19–22]. These initiatives contribute to fostering a desired CSC [5, 23], which involves creating an environment that enhances an organization's cybersecurity posture by promoting security values, supporting employee behaviors, and shaping a cybersecurity mindset. As RDT exacerbates these challenges [24], it becomes imperative for organizations to cultivate the desired CSC to mitigate significant risks [9, 25]. Failure to do so exposes organizations to heightened risks [12, 26].

Numerous previous studies have broadly addressed CSC within organizations, focusing on its conceptualization [27, 28], proposing frameworks [29–32], and identifying factors influencing CSC development [30, 31, 33, 34] in a relatively stable organizational state. However, the dynamic nature of RDT introduces significant challenges to CSC development, requiring swift organizational adaptation and deliberate efforts to shape employees' mindsets and foster a desired CSC during rapid changes. This study employs a qualitative research methodology, collecting data from Ethiopian financial institutions undergoing RDT through semi-structured interviews and document analysis. It aims to overcome the inherent resistance to cultural change and effectively cultivate a desired CSC within the context of rapid organizational change, thereby mitigating diverse cyber risks posed by RDT. This research is guided by the following question: How can organizations foster a desired CSC amid RDT?

The following sections of this paper will present a review of related literature, research methodology, data analysis, and a discussion of the findings. The paper will conclude with insights drawn from the discussion.

2 Literature Review

CSC is the perception of how people view cybersecurity and how these perceptions translate into behavior that leads to successfully safeguarding data, systems, and people within an organization [4, 27]. CSC, a subset of organizational culture, focuses on how employees interact with information assets in the cyber domain and exhibit security-related behaviors [5, 23]. It guides interactions with cyberspace to ensure the security of digital assets [14, 30]. In this study, we refer to this concept as a desired CSC, described in the literature as a positive [30], strong [5] CSC that involves nurturing security values, shaping employee behaviors, fostering a shared cybersecurity vision [35, 36], prioritizing cybersecurity through organizational measures and integrating it into everyday practices [37].

There is a consensus in the literature on the need for organizations to develop CSC [23]. The importance of CSC becomes even more pronounced during digital transformation [23]. Previous studies recommended that CSC helps to mitigate these risks [38], encouraging employees to be cautious and responsive to potential breaches [19, 39]. Furthermore, a CSC promotes a sense of collective responsibility [30, 31], where everyone in the organization is invested in maintaining the security of the digital environment [12]. It creates an environment where every employee at all levels understands his/her role in protecting the organization from cyber threats [4, 40], guiding the activities of the organization and its employees toward safe cybersecurity practices [19], shaping the behavior [5], and making them the first line of defense [28], with a strategic and systematic approach [23]. Hence, fostering CSC means creating an environment that boosts organizational cybersecurity posture by promoting security values, supporting employee behaviors, and shaping a cybersecurity mindset [41].

As organizations increasingly rely on emerging digital technologies to modernize and integrate their operations, the potential for cyber threats also rises [5]. The RDT presents a series of challenges, especially in the cybersecurity domain, that often outpace the ability of organizations to adequately protect themselves from cyber threats [1, 25]. Furthermore, the rapid adoption of digital technologies has enabled cybercriminals to become more sophisticated [25, 42], making it more difficult for organizations to comprehend and manage cybersecurity risks effectively [40].

Despite its significance, the concept of RDT lacks a clear definition in the academic literature. It is often mentioned in various papers to describe the urgency of transformation driven by factors such as COVID-19 [1, 25]. These pressures lead organizations to implement digital transformation initiatives in a "rapid" manner [9], significantly impacting the organization's core structure [8], including its CSC. RDT thus represents the forced, swift, and time-constrained implementation of digital technologies within an organization, differing from the typical linear or incremental digital transformation initiatives.

During RDT, organizations rapidly change their operations, which affects the deep structure of an organization and the development of a desired culture to adapt to new digital realities. Scholars specializing in organizational culture argue that changing organizational culture is generally a slow and challenging process that resists quick implementation [43]. Organizations undergoing RDT must therefore deal with the resistant nature of cultural change and foster a desired CSC through targeted organizational initiatives to mitigate the cyber risk associated with RDT. In this context, "initiatives" refer to non-technical organizational cybersecurity measures, actions, or strategies that complement technological or technical solutions [5].

3 Research Methodology

3.1 Approach

This study adheres to the approach recommended by Walsham [43] to obtain in-depth insights on the cybersecurity challenges of RDT, initiatives to tackle these challenges, and factors nurturing CSC within organizations. It applies an interpretative case study methodology to investigate one of Ethiopia's largest banks undergoing RDT. A case study method was employed to gain an in-depth understanding of CSC in a context characterized by RDT.

3.2 Case Description

Since 2020, Ethiopia has enthusiastically initiated an extensive nationwide RDT, marked by the adoption of "Digital Ethiopia 2025", which is geared towards establishing a digital economy in 2025 and is anticipated to yield significant benefits for the country [44]. According to Digital Ethiopia 2025 [54], a pivotal avenue for this transformation involves creating IT-enabled services across organizational levels. The objective is to achieve comprehensive digital transactions by leveraging and enhancing the connectivity of the banking system and the interoperability of digital platforms and services on a national scale [44, 45]. Consequently, financial institutions are rapidly adapting their digital banking infrastructure to facilitate faster and more seamless data (and money) transfers, compelled by the need to implement a robust and accountable digital finance and payments system as per the National Bank of Ethiopia's (NBE's) directives [44, 45].

The Ethiopian banking sector comprises the NBE, a state-owned development bank, a government-owned commercial bank, and twenty-eight private banks. This study empirically investigates how the Ethiopian banking sector perceives and adopts CSC during RDT, focusing on a case study of one of the largest banks. We purposely select a bank for our study due to its pivotal role in shaping the country's digital future. The bank has over 37.9 million account holders across 1900 branches, 6.6 million mobile and internet banking users, 8.3 million active ATM cardholders, and 17 million mobile banking users. According to the latest data, the bank employs more than 50,000 people and controls over 67 percent of the nation's total banking services, deposits, loans, and foreign exchange, with the remaining 33 percent spread among twenty-eight other banks. The bank leads the market in terms of assets, deposits, branches, and workforce, cementing its dominant position in the Ethiopian financial sector and ranking among the largest banks in East Africa [46]. The bank's cybersecurity division and departments are centralized, with designated cyber-responsible offices or personnel at each branch nationwide.

3.3 Data Collection and Analysis

Primary data was collected through semi-structured interviews and document analysis, engaging experts in various managerial and professional roles within the bank. Eight Participants (IS security Directors (D01), Managers (M01, M02, M03, M04, M05), and Experts (EX01, EX02)) were selected based on their current roles and experiences. They represented different levels and roles, both management and non-management. Additionally, a total of seven digital banking experts and system users (Bankers) (B01, B02, B03, B04, B05, B06, B07) were interviewed to gain insights into how these initiatives affect employees.

The interview guide was customized according to the background of each informant. Initial interviews were conducted with the Director of Information System Security Management, department managers, and experts to explore cybersecurity challenges and the bank's response. The interviews were conducted online, totaling more than nine hours, and were transcribed in full. Furthermore, data from strategic and policy documents, including the Ethiopian Digital Transformation Strategy, NBE Directive, INSA National Cyber Security Policy, bank cybersecurity awareness framework, security policy, the bank magazine, and cybersecurity reports, were utilized to gain additional insights through triangulation.

The interviews, conducted in Amharic, Ethiopia's official working language, were audio-recorded and later translated and transcribed into English. The transcripts were coded using NVivo 20 and thematically analyzed following Braun and Clarke's guidelines [47]. The process of identifying common ideas and connections in the interviews involved several steps. First, the transcripts were carefully read and analyzed to become familiar with the data. Then, a coding process was used to label and categorize relevant portions of the transcripts, assigning descriptive codes to capture key concepts or themes related to the research objective. This resulted in the formation of two main themes: "Cybersecurity Challenges" and "Initiatives." The first theme addresses the major challenges of cybersecurity associated with RDT, while the second theme pertains to the initiatives applied by the bank to tackle these challenges. Further, to achieve a comprehensive understanding of the context, insights from employees working on digital banking systems and document analysis were integrated. Finally, findings were analyzed by examining the relationship between concepts, linking each initiative to factors described in previous literature on CSC, and identifying relationships or conceptual connections.

4 Findings

In the last few years, driven by the government's digital transformation agenda and accelerated by COVID-19, Ethiopian digital banking has rapidly transformed. According to the informant, before 2018, over 90% of banking services were not digital. The current digital transformation strategy aims to be completed within five years and necessitates the banking sector's involvement as a key enabler of this transformation. These changes have been forced by external pressure and are notably rapid, resulting in significant implementation of emerging technologies to transform services and operations in the bank. An informant described the situation: *"A few years back, the banking sector was described as manual, only 10% of the service was electronic, but not integrated. Forced by the present national digital transformation strategy, the digital landscape in the banking industry has leapfrogged very fast." [D01].*

As outlined in the Digital Ethiopia 2025 strategy, National Digital Payment plays a pivotal role in the country's digital transformation journey, with the banking sector serving as a crucial facilitator. Implementing and integrating digital banking platforms such as card banking, internet banking, mobile banking, and other digital payment platforms has fueled the growing adoption of digital payments nationwide. *"The digital landscape in the banking industry has undergone rapid advancements, leading to surprising transformations in technological advancements within banking services [...]." [M01].*

As the bank implements RDT and increasingly relies on digital technologies for daily operations, the need to prioritize cybersecurity becomes more evident. Rapid integration of emerging technologies affects current cybersecurity measures and exposes systems to vulnerabilities. An informant described the scenario as: *"Digital transformation without a proper security strategy can be best described as a process that takes one step forward and two steps backward." [E02].* Our empirical data shows that organizations must be constantly vigilant in the face of the ever-evolving cyber threat landscape. An informant described the situation as: *"The current digital transformation projects fail to focus on the risk of cybersecurity and compliance." [M04].*

Therefore, it is important to identify challenges, apply organizational measures to address the challenges, and foster a desired CSC amid RDT.

4.1 Challenges of RDT

Digital transformation without fostering a desired CSC is a recipe for cyber disaster [48]. Organizations must implement initiatives and take appropriate action to address challenges, protect sensitive information, prevent data breaches, and maintain customer trust [6, 48]. RDT in the Ethiopian banking sector brings several challenges. Below, we look at the cybersecurity challenges arising due to RDT based on our empirical data.

Disruption of Cybersecurity Operations One significant challenge posed by RDT is the disruption it causes to an organization's cybersecurity operations. The rapid implementation of new tools and systems outpaces existing cybersecurity operations and workflows, disrupting established processes and practices. This disruption affects cybersecurity tasks, processes, and systems, altering employee actions and departmental operations. *"One of the challenges of the transformation we have identified is the interruption of the existing operations that can cause a new and massive cyberattack/incident [...]." [M03].* Such disruption creates significant cybersecurity challenges that require a proactive approach to address technological, human, and procedural aspects. One proactive measure is to adjust workflows and the overall organizational cybersecurity framework. The complexity of cyber threats demands an in-depth understanding of various technologies and processes, making it difficult for organizations to keep up.

Increased Attack Surface Another major challenge from our data is the increased attack surface and vulnerability to cyber threats due to RDT. The expanded attack surface allows threat actors to target poorly managed cybersecurity operations, exploit vulnerabilities, and create opportunities for unauthorized access and potential exploitation. An informant exemplifies the problem: *"The ongoing transformation at our bank has made cyber incidents more complex, leading to longer breach detection and resolution times. This has caused financial losses and harmed customer relationships. In September 2023, we suspended banking operations for two days after an employee clicked a phishing email." [M01].*

This challenge also carries financial implications, as cyberattacks can have devastating consequences. RDT poses a trust erosion challenge, raising concerns among customers, partners, and stakeholders about banks' data protection capabilities, potentially resulting in business loss and legal repercussions. *"The data breach harms the organization's brand image and ability to attract and retain customers. This reputational damage can have long-term effects, hindering the organization's growth and success." [D01].* Additionally, the expanded attack surface from RDT exposes integrated banking systems to external community members, making them vulnerable targets for attackers. An informant discussed the situation: *"Another major challenge is the low cybersecurity awareness among users of digital banking services like mobile banking, internet banking, POS cards, and ATMs, with many incidents traced back to customers." [M05].*

4.2 Initiatives to Address Challenges

Our data highlights key cybersecurity initiatives the bank applied to address challenges from RDT. The bank used various strategies, targeting non-technical initiatives and organizational processes, to foster a cybersecurity culture. The most significant initiatives are explained below.

Restructuring and Reorganizing Departments To address the challenges, the bank restructured its cybersecurity division and appointed new leadership. This fosters a CSC by ensuring effective leadership. Our data highlights the role of this restructuring and leadership commitment in shaping CSC during RDT. The informants described the situation as *"To address cybersecurity challenges, the bank reinstated its cybersecurity division, restructured departments, appointed new leaders, and redesigned workflows with a focus on human factors." [D01].*

Furthermore, as can be seen from our empirical data, the restructured department and leadership facilitate collaboration between different departments, as cybersecurity is a cross-functional issue that requires input from various stakeholders. A clear hierarchy and defined roles and responsibilities help to ensure that cybersecurity measures are implemented effectively. *"[...] with the recent structural changes in the bank's security division, several distinct yet interconnected departments have been established." [D01].* All the departments are interconnected and play an important role in empowering and shaping human behavior toward cybersecurity. *"One of the important departments established recently following the transformation is the Cybersecurity Transformation Department." [M01].* An informant exemplified how the department established and explained the role and responsibilities of the department: *"As part of the restructuring initiative, our bank established the Cybersecurity Transformation Department tasked with assessing and addressing cybersecurity challenges arising from rapid digital transformation, collaborating with other departments for proactive solutions." [M01].*

Open and Clear Communication and Collaboration As can be seen from the empirical data, the bank undergoing RDT must better address the evolving cyber threats, and require open and effective communication and collaboration across all departments and individuals. This fosters a sense of collective responsibility and ensures everyone is working towards the same goal of protecting the organization. Our empirical data show that leaders in the bank establish a culture of openness and clear communication with employees at all levels, where employees feel comfortable reporting potential security threats and any malicious activities without fear of retribution. This also facilitates departmental collaborations in the bank. *"Very recently, we have started a hierarchical security briefing (reporting) session daily among staff and an immediate manager, weekly among managers in parallel departments, every two weeks among managers with directors, and once a month with vice presidents." [M03].*

Timely incident reports via the correct channels are crucial to prevent damage. The bank urges employees to report confidentially, drawing on its practical experience in this area. One of the informants described the situation with a piece of evidence: *"Recently, an employee reported a timely fraudulent activity through our established channel. After evaluation, it was confirmed as a serious phishing attack with potential harm to the bank. This incident caught the attention of top management, leading to recognition and a reward for the reporting employee." [M02].*

Collaboration and communication with employees at all levels are essential for reporting threats and incidents, ensuring they understand policies and procedures, providing necessary awareness training, and keeping them informed about new updates they need to follow in their daily practices. *"[...] new cybersecurity-related updates, policies, and standards are consistently communicated to employees at every level." [M02].*

Financial and Resource Allocation for Rapid Response Initiatives Many top managers in the bank did not recognize the importance of the non-technical aspects of cybersecurity. Some saw these initiatives as luxuries or mere meeting topics, focusing primarily on maximizing profits and minimizing expenses, especially the CEO. Additionally, board members were heavily focused on political aspects. *"Years ago, cybersecurity initiatives were considered a luxury in our bank. However, with the transformation strategy and NBE's 2020 directive, top managers now support cybersecurity initiatives. Yet, there's still a gap in this area." [D01].* Proper awareness and a positive tone from top management help shift employees' attitudes towards cybersecurity, making it a valued priority throughout the organization. When cybersecurity becomes a concern for top managers, it can influence every employee, shaping the organization's core values toward cybersecurity, and achieving a desired CSC becomes more attainable. *"NBE Directive 2020 garnered top management support, mandating a cybersecurity department, 3% budget allocation for training, and regular reporting to NBE and INSA." [D01].*

Budget and resource limitations are critical considerations in the planning and execution of cybersecurity initiatives and implementation programs, especially during the RDT phase. An informant described as: *"Most cybersecurity initiatives require budget and timely decisions, which greatly affect the quality and effectiveness of initiatives." [M03].* Hence, top managers must meticulously plan their budgets and resources to ensure effective support for the success of cybersecurity initiatives.

Update/Upgrade Cybersecurity Policy Another important initiative that this study can derive from the empirical data is to update or improve the bank's cybersecurity policy and guidelines. *"The cybersecurity policy, procedure, and guidelines* *are reshaped or tuned to fit with the existing digital landscape of the bank [...].” [D01].* The National Bank of Ethiopia, a national regulatory body of financial institutions, set a directive in 2020 that provides binding guidelines for the banking sector to redesign cybersecurity policy in line with the RDT. Based on the directive, cybersecurity policy, standards, guidelines, and procedures are reshuffled, updated, and upgraded in line with the underlying organization’s objectives. *“[...] the initiatives our bank took were cybersecurity policy revision and cybersecurity awareness training, both aimed at influencing employee behavior towards cybersecurity (making employees cyber-disciplined and alert).” [M01].*

The document analysis also shows that the bank has tuned strategies, guidelines, policies, and procedures towards the present that promote secure behaviors and practices. Regularly reviewing and updating these policies ensures that they remain effective against the latest threats. This process involves assessing the organization’s current cybersecurity posture, identifying potential vulnerabilities, and implementing the necessary changes. Additionally, training staff on the latest cybersecurity practices and fostering a culture of security can significantly enhance an organization’s overall cybersecurity posture.

Current, Continuous, and Regular Awareness Training As our data shows, employee awareness training is another critical initiative used to address cybersecurity-related challenges posed due to RDT. Therefore, risk-based, continuous, and regular training programs are conducted in the bank to educate employees on the latest cyber threats posed by RDT and the best practices to avoid them. These programs are tailored to the bank’s specific needs and the employee roles. This initiative’s objective is thus to enhance cybersecurity competency among employees. *“The bank has a dedicated awareness and training department focused on improving employee competency [...]. It utilizes various methods such as online and classroom training, simulations, campaigns, TV/social media programs, and daily security updates for awareness.” [M03].*

Continuous and up-to-date training is critical to keeping up with the rapidly evolving cybersecurity landscape. As new threats and vulnerabilities emerge regularly, it is essential to keep employees informed of these developments. Including risk-based, regular, refresher, and updated courses in the training program helps to ensure that employees’ knowledge and skills remain up-to-date. The bank’s Cybersecurity Awareness Program Framework 2023 highlights that ongoing training is considered an integral part of the company’s comprehensive cybersecurity strategy. An informant justified this fact: *“In our bank, awareness training focuses on daily practices, security policies, guidelines, and cyber risk incidence. We update programs and content based on the situation, delivering training as frequently as needed.” [M03].*

According to the bank’s Cybersecurity Awareness Program Framework 2023, regular assessments evaluate training and awareness effectiveness, pinpointing areas for improvement. Tailoring awareness training to individual capacities and preferences by recognizing the level of competence, understanding, and awareness among employees is more effective. Ongoing efforts aim to influence employee behavior in response to increasing cyber risks. An informant described it as: *"The awareness training starts from the top manager and goes down to the lower level [...] training aligned with personal preferences and pace, and performance should be regularly assessed per the goal of the awareness training...." [M03].*

As part of the employee awareness approach, in times of emergency and urgent security communication, the bank utilizes users' working computer screensavers to convey news and critical security tips. "[...] *operational computers are managed via Active Directory. New incident alerts are broadcast to all employees within 2 minutes. Active users receive notifications on their screensavers, while inactive users get notified upon computer login, allowing prompt action." [E02].*

According to the NBE directive, financial institutions are required to constantly review and update their cybersecurity measures to counter the latest threats. This involves regularly updating security protocols, learning from breaches, and using these lessons to enhance future responses. The directive also encourages banks to adopt a proactive approach to anticipate and mitigate risks before they escalate into costly incidents, empowering employees and integrating them into the bank's cybersecurity strategy.

Promote Employee Mindfulness Our empirical data demonstrates that the bank actively promotes and encourages employees to maintain presence and alertness at work. This initiative entails promoting full engagement, focus, and awareness in the workplace. An informant described this issue as *"...the bank reduced employee workload and stress [...], fostering a positive work environment, [...]. " [M03].* The bank promotes employees' mindfulness to encourage safe practices and establish a nuanced, continuous operation that supports organizational and personal well-being in their daily work.

Conduct Community Awareness Campaigns Another important initiative derived from the empirical data is community awareness campaigns that aim to promote online safety among customers and the external community. *"We recognize that cybersecurity protection isn't solely one institution's responsibility. Promoting the human aspect isn't enough; it requires collective effort. Alongside stakeholders like INSA, we conduct campaigns to raise awareness within customers and the external community." [M04].* According to the Cyber Security Readiness report by INSA for Digital Strategy, the bank aimed to bridge the awareness gap in the external community by employing various methods. These included sending security alerts and tips via SMS, distributing pamphlets, posting tips on the bank's website, and featuring them on a bank TV program broadcast by a national television station (Fig. 1).

This study also gathered insight from bankers working within the bank's digital banking systems to understand how the initiatives impact employees' daily operations and long-term security behavior. Their responses confirm that the initiatives influence their behavior positively. *"Before the transformation that began in 2020, our awareness and concern for cybersecurity, risk management, hygiene practices,*

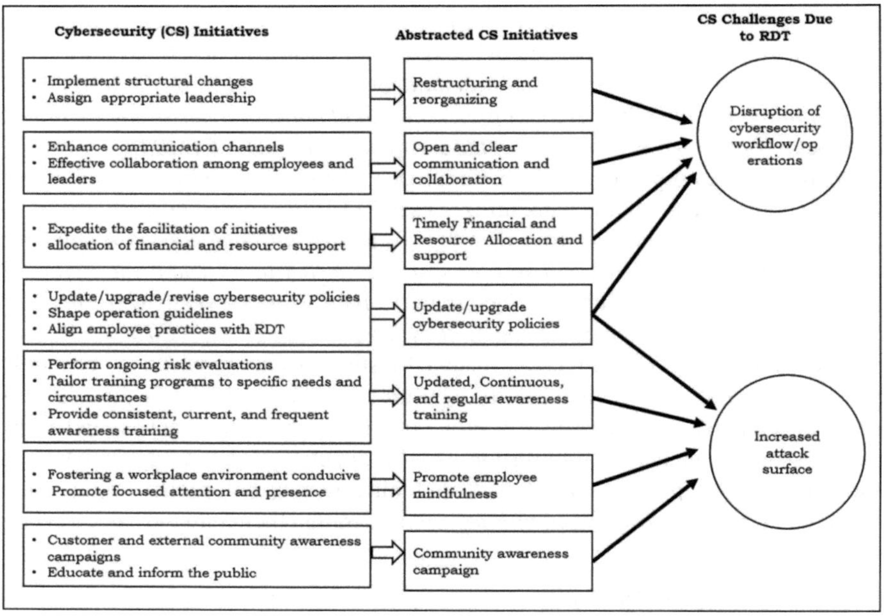

Fig. 1 Cybersecurity initiatives in response to the challenges posed by RDT

and overall security awareness were relatively low." [B03]. "I believed cybersecurity was solely the responsibility of the IT department. But now I understand it's my responsibility too." [B01]. "Recently, the bank implemented several initiatives focusing on cybersecurity that significantly enhanced my understanding and awareness of cybersecurity." [B06]. "The initiatives help me a lot. I am now more aware of the risks and understand my responsibilities in maintaining cybersecurity than before." [B05].

In summary, our empirical analysis shows that fostering a desired organizational CSC to address cybersecurity challenges brought by RDT necessitates several key initiatives. Each of the initiatives is vital for daily operations and shaping a cybersecurity mindset among employees in the long term.

5 Discussion

The empirical findings of this study addressed the top two cybersecurity challenges and several key initiatives applied by the bank to address the challenges. As discussed below, after identifying the major challenges and initiatives, the initiatives were abstracted by analyzing components, characteristics, and key elements or concepts. Each initiative was then linked to the CSC factors described in previous literature [33, 34] by looking for relationships or conceptual connections to support broader generalizations from our specific case study. While existing literature identifies numerous factors influencing CSC in stable organizational contexts, our refined conceptualization, linked to existing literature, has narrowed the list to seven salient contributing factors, as shown in Table 1. These factors are essential for effectively fostering CSC amidst the challenges posed by RDT.

In this section, we discuss the two major cybersecurity challenges identified, the corresponding key initiatives applied by the bank to overcome the challenges, and the associated contributing factors to foster CSC in line with the RDT and aimed at influencing the values, beliefs, behavior, and mindset of employees in the long run.

The first major CSC challenge posed by RDT was the disruption of cybersecurity workflows and operations. Cybersecurity workflow and operations encompass a series of coordinated and interconnected activities designed to protect an organization from potential cyber threats and attacks. Disruption of CS workflow refers to an interruption in the normal and effective functioning of cybersecurity processes and practices within an organization [6]. Our findings show that this issue can arise due to RDT, leading to an awareness gap among employees. To address this challenge, the bank implemented several initiatives. One initiative involved restructuring and reorganizing departments and assigning the right leader to operate more smoothly, remain competitive, and achieve cybersecurity objectives amid RDT. Another initiative focused on fostering open and clear communication between employees, leaders, and departments, promoting hierarchical collaboration. Additionally, the bank allocated financial and other resources for rapid response efforts. These initiatives have significantly contributed to addressing the challenge. Further, based on the concepts of the initiatives the associated factors identified from the previous literature that contribute to fostering CSC amid RDT are organizational structure and leadership [24, 34, 49], collaboration and communication [12, 33, 39, 40, 50] and top management support [34, 50–52] respectively.

Table 1 Salient factors that contribute to fostering a desired CSC amid RDT

CS initiatives	Derived Salient Factors	Expected outcomes
Restructuring and reorganizing departments	Organizational structure and leadership	Clear roles and responsibilities, integrated processes, and top-down commitment.
Open and clear communication and collaboration	Collaboration and communication	Seamless, transparent, and open communication
Financial and resource allocation and support	Top management support	Prioritize cybersecurity
Updated, continuous, and regular training	CS awareness and training	Improve Competency
Updating cybersecurity policy	Cybersecurity policy	Improve Compliance
Promote employees mindfulness	Employee mindfulness	Vigilant and proactive
Community awareness campaign	Awareness campaign	Awareness enhancement

The second major challenge identified in this study was that RDT has expanded the attack surface for cybercriminals. This challenge refers to the increased scope and vulnerability of an organization's potential cyber-attack points due to the rapid implementation of emerging digital technologies and transformation initiatives, extending even to the outside community. To address this, the bank implemented several cybersecurity initiatives. These include continuous risk assessments, regular security audits, training needs assessments, designing tailored training programs, and providing continuous, up-to-date awareness training to enhance employee competency and foster a security-first mindset. Another initiative was updating cybersecurity policy to shape workplace practices. Additionally, it was crucial to promote employee awareness, encouraging careful attention to their actions, active engagement, and proactive adjustment to prevent incidents. A community awareness campaign was also conducted to address the attack effectively due to the RDT [38, 53]. The corresponding contributing factors identified associated with the initiatives that contribute to fostering CSC amid RDT are therefore, cybersecurity awareness and training [23, 33, 34, 38], cybersecurity policy [12, 24, 33, 34], employee mindfulness [24] and awareness campaign [6, 34, 53, 54] respectively.

Hence, as summarized in Table 1 below, based on our empirical data, this study identifies several initiatives, derives salient factors from prior research, and anticipates their expected impact on fostering a desired CSC within an organization, demonstrating the basis for initiatives to support broader generalizations of the phenomena.

Our finding shows that fostering a CSC amidst RDT necessitates at least seven fundamental factors. Previous literature [33, 34] extensively outlined many factors contributing to fostering CSC in organizations operating within stable states. In a stable organizational state, factors contributing to fostering CSC revolve around established norms, practices, and structures that have evolved to mitigate cyber risks effectively. These factors often emphasize consistency, adherence to established protocols, and a shared understanding of cybersecurity responsibilities among employees. However, during RDT, organizations rapidly change technology and operations that disrupt deep structure or organizational culture to adapt to new digital realities, making it crucial to address the challenges that arise in fostering CSC during this rapid organizational transformation.

The identified factors comprise the need for rapid implementation of emerging technologies and threats, agility in responding to emerging risks, and the ability to embed cybersecurity principles into employees' day-to-day practices and mindsets. These factors focus on organizational initiatives applied to address cybersecurity challenges posed by RDT. This reveals significant contextual variations between organizations undergoing RDT and stable state organizations, the temporal disparity between the rapid pace of organizational change and the gradual process of developing CSC, the dynamic nature of cybersecurity challenges, and the shifting attack surface due to rapid changes.

6 Conclusion

This study examines the major cybersecurity challenges and corresponding initiatives, based on qualitative data collected from financial institutions undergoing RDT. Further, these initiatives were aligned with existing literature, leading to the identification of seven salient factors that contribute to fostering a CSC amid RDT.

This research contributes to the existing literature by offering practical and theoretical insights. Theoretically, it highlights the challenges of fostering organizational CSC amid rapid organizational changes, particularly during RDT. It presents that organizations can foster a desired CSC through deliberate actions, such as regular training, leadership initiatives, and refining policies and guidelines, even in the face of swift organizational change. Practically, it deepens the understanding of CSC in dynamic environments and provides insights to foster organizational CSC against cybersecurity challenges amid RDT.

The generalizability of insights from a single case study may be questioned beyond its specific context. While our research focuses on fostering CSC amidst RDT in the highly regulated banking sector, we argue that the concepts discussed could apply more broadly. Future research could explore how identified factors influence cybersecurity behaviors and propose models or frameworks for fostering CSC amid RDT. Furthermore, integrating the organizational culture framework with the multilayer temporality concept can help address the temporal disparities in fostering CSC and RDT. Exploring the impact of national or community culture on organizational security culture and investigating the impact of CS initiatives on cultural groups within organizations can be other intriguing areas of investigation. Additionally, while our research utilized an interpretative qualitative approach, integrating quantitative data through a mixed-methods approach could yield further insights and facilitate the triangulation of information from various sources and perspectives.

References

1. Nurhas, I., Aditya, B. R., Jacob, D. W., & Pawlowski, J. M. (2022). Understanding the challenges of rapid digital transformation: The case of COVID-19 pandemic in higher education. *Behaviour & Information Technology, 41*, 2924–2940.
2. Vial, G. (2021). Understanding digital transformation: A review and a research agenda. *Managing Digital Transformation*, 13–66.
3. Baskerville, R., Rowe, F., & Wolff, F.-C. (2018). Integration of information systems and cybersecurity countermeasures: An exposure to risk perspective. *ACM SIGMIS Database: The Database for Advances in Information Systems, 49*, 33–52.
4. Dhillon, G., Syed, R., & Pedron, C. (2016). Interpreting information security culture: An organizational transformation case study. *Computers & Security, 56*, 63–69.
5. Corradini, I. (2020). *Building a cybersecurity culture in organizations: How to bridge the gap between people and digital technology*. Springer Nature.

6. Saeed, S., Altamimi, S. A., Alkayyal, N. A., Alshehri, E., & Alabbad, D. A. (2023). Digital transformation and cybersecurity challenges for businesses resilience: Issues and recommendations. *Sensors, 23*, 6666.
7. Möller, D. (2020). *Cybersecurity in digital transformation: Scope and applications*. Springer.
8. Hansen, A. M., Kraemmergaard, P., & Mathiassen, L. (2011). Rapid adaptation in digital transformation: A participatory process for engaging IS and business leaders. *MIS Quarterly Executive, 10*.
9. Baz, M., Alhakami, H., Agrawal, A., Baz, A., & Khan, R. A. (2021). Impact of COVID-19 pandemic: A cybersecurity perspective. *Intelligent Automation & Soft Computing, 27*.
10. BBC. (2024). *Commercial Bank of Ethiopia glitch lets customers withdraw millions*. BBC. https://www.bbc.com/news/world-68599027.amp
11. Dornheim, P., & Zarnekow, R. (2023). *Determining cybersecurity culture maturity and deriving verifiable improvement measures*. Information & Computer Security.
12. Pavlova, E. (2020). Enhancing the organisational culture related to cyber security during the university digital transformation. *Information & Security, 46*, 239–249.
13. Verizon.com: Data breach investigations report 2022. Verizon.com. https://www.verizon.com/business/resources/reports/
14. Ubowska, A., & Królikowski, T. (2022). Building a cybersecurity culture of public administration system in Poland. *Procedia Computer Science, 207*, 1242–1250.
15. Glaspie, H. W., & Karwowski, W. (2018). Human factors in information security culture: A literature review. In *International Conference on Human Factors in Cybersecurity*. Springer.
16. Martins, A., & Elofe, J. (2002). *Information security culture*. Springer.
17. Baskerville, R., Spagnoletti, P., & Kim, J. (2014). Incident-centered information security: Managing a strategic balance between prevention and response. *Information & Management, 51*, 138–151.
18. Huang, K., & Pearlson, K. (2019). For what technology can't fix: Building a model of organizational cybersecurity culture. In *Proceedings of the 52nd Hawaii International Conference on System Sciences*.
19. Zimmermann, V., & Renaud, K. (2019). Moving from a "human-as-problem" to a "human-as-solution" cybersecurity mindset. *International Journal of Human-Computer Studies, 131*, 169–187.
20. Bulgurcu, B., Cavusoglu, H., & Benbasat, I. (2010). Information security policy compliance: an empirical study of rationality-based beliefs and information security awareness. *MIS Quarterly*, 523–548.
21. Nasir, A., Arshah, R. A., & Ab Hamid, M. R. (2017). Information security policy compliance behavior based on comprehensive dimensions of information security culture: A conceptual framework. In *Proceedings of the 2017 international conference on information systems and data mining*.
22. Da Veiga, A. (2019). Achieving a security culture. In *Anthology on business aspects of cybersecurity* (pp. 72–100). IGI Global.
23. Alshaikh, M. (2020). Developing cybersecurity culture to influence employee behavior: A practice perspective. *Computers & Security, 98*, 102003.
24. Hassandoust, F., & Johnston, A. C. (2023). Peering through the lens of high-reliability theory: A competencies driven security culture model of high-reliability organisations. *Information Systems Journal*.
25. Thangam, D., Arumugam, T., Velusamy, K., Subramanian, M., Ganesan, S. K., & Suryakumar, M. (2022). COVID-19 pandemic and its brunt on digital transformation and cybersecurity. In *Cybersecurity crisis management and lessons learned from the COVID-19 pandemic* (pp. 15–42). IGI Global.
26. Da Veiga, A. (2016). A cybersecurity culture research philosophy and approach to develop a valid and reliable measuring instrument. In *2016 SAI computing conference (SAI)*. IEEE. https://doi.org/10.1109/SAI.2016.7556102

27. Da Veiga, A., Astakhova, L. V., Botha, A., & Herselman, M. (2020). Defining organisational information security culture—Perspectives from academia and industry. *Computers & Security, 92*, 101713.
28. Thomson, K.-L., Von Solms, R., & Louw, L. (2006). Cultivating an organizational information security culture. *Computer Fraud & Security, 2006*, 7–11.
29. Alhogail, A., & Mirza, A. (2014). A framework of information security culture change. *Journal of Theoretical & Applied Information Technology, 64.*
30. Da Veiga, A. (2018). An approach to information security culture change combining ADKAR and the ISCA questionnaire to aid transition to the desired culture. *Information & Computer Security, 26*, 584–612.
31. Schlienger, T., & Teufel, S. (2003). Information security culture-from analysis to change. *South African Computer Journal, 2003*, 46–52.
32. Da Veiga, A., & Eloff, J. H. (2010). A framework and assessment instrument for information security culture. *Computers & Security, 29*, 196–207.
33. Mwim, E. N., & Mtsweni, J. (2022). *Systematic review of factors that influence the cybersecurity culture*. Springer.
34. Uchendu, B., Nurse, J. R., Bada, M., & Furnell, S. (2021). Developing a cyber security culture: Current practices and future needs. *Computers & Security, 109*, 102387.
35. Daugherty, J. L., & Dark, M. J. (2021). The cybersecurity mindset: A critical literacy for adult learners. In *Global citizenship for adult education* (pp. 334–343). Routledge.
36. Karyda M. (2017). Fostering information security culture in organizations: A research agenda.
37. Schoenmakers, K., Greene, D., Stutterheim, S., Lin, H., & Palmer, M. J. (2023). The security mindset: characteristics, development, and consequences. *Journal of Cybersecurity, 9.*
38. Reid, R., & Van Niekerk, J. (2014). Towards an education campaign for fostering a societal. In *Cyber security culture*. HAISA.
39. Ioannou, M., Stavrou, E., & Bada, M. (2019). Cybersecurity culture in computer security incident response teams: Investigating difficulties in communication and coordination. In *2019 international conference on cyber security and protection of digital services (cyber security)*. IEEE.
40. Van Niekerk, J., & Von Solms, R. (2010). Information security culture: A management perspective. *Computers & Security, 29*, 476–486.
41. Adamu, M. A., Niemimaa, M. I., & Spagnoletti, P. (2024). Towards a three-tiered framework for fostering organizational cybersecurity culture. EMCIS 2024. *Lecture Notes in Business Information Processing, 536*. Springer. https://link.springer.com/chapter/10.1007/978-3-031-81325-2_22
42. Shahi, C., & Sinha, M. (2021). Digital transformation: Challenges faced by organizations and their potential solutions. *International Journal of Innovation Science, 13*, 17–33.
43. Alvesson, M., & Sveningsson, S. (2015). *Changing organizational culture: Cultural change work in progress*. Routledge. https://doi.org/10.4324/9781315688404
44. FDRE. (2020). *Digital Ethiopia 2025: A strategy for Ethiopia's inclusive prosperity.* Addis Ababa.
45. National Digital Payments Strategy 2021. National Bank of Ethiopia, Addis Ababa. (2021).
46. Minney, T. (2023). East Africa's top banks in 2023. *African Business.* https://african.business/2023/09/finance-services/east-africas-top-banks-in-2023
47. Braun, V., & Clarke, V. (2006). Using thematic analysis in psychology. *Qualitative Research in Psychology, 3*, 77–101.
48. Stewart, H. (2023). Digital transformation security challenges. *Journal of Computer Information Systems, 63*, 919–936.
49. Hasib, M. (2022). Cybersecurity leadership: Powering the modern organization. *Tomorrow's Strategy Today.*
50. Reegård, K., Blackett, C., & Katta, V. (2019). The concept of cybersecurity culture. In *29th European safety and reliability conference.*

51. Tsoeu, M. A., & da Veiga, A. (2022). A Cyber4Dev security culture model. In *International conference on advanced research in technologies, information, innovation and sustainability*. Springer.
52. Hu, Q., Dinev, T., Hart, P., & Cooke, D. (2012). Managing employee compliance with information security policies: The critical role of top management and organizational culture. *Decision Sciences, 43*, 615–660.
53. Tolah, A., Furnell, S. M., & Papadaki, M. (2021). An empirical analysis of the information security culture key factors framework. *Computers & Security, 108*, 102354.
54. Bada, M., Sasse, A. M., & Nurse, J. R. (2019). Cyber security awareness campaigns: Why do they fail to change behaviour? *arXiv preprint arXiv:190102672*.

The Metamorphosis Behind Digital Transformation: A Framework from Change Management

Filomena Pagnozzi, Pauline Weritz, and Gilda Antonelli

Abstract Digital transformation has significantly reshaped human interactions and business operations, leading to changes in social structures, norms, values, and behaviors within institutions. This paper examines the intersection of societal change and digital transformation through the lens of change management, focusing on three key issues: utilizing established theories to guide digital transformation, modifying institutional arrangements, and exploring the complex relationship between technology and societal change. The study employs a conceptual framework to analyze the impact of institutional logic and culture on digital transformation. It provides both theoretical and practical insights, enhancing the understanding of the interplay between technological and institutional changes. The paper also offers strategies for effective change management, equipping organizations to navigate the challenges and seize the opportunities of digital transformation.

Keywords Digital transformation · Change management · Institutional logic

1 Introduction

The digital transformation, a key driver of societal change, has fundamentally altered the way individuals interact, businesses operate, and governments function [1]. Societal change refers to transformative shifts that occur at the broader societal level, encompassing changes in social structures, norms, values, behaviors, and

---

F. Pagnozzi (✉) · G. Antonelli
Economic Department, University of G. d' Annunzio, Pescara, Italy
e-mail: filomena.pagnozzi@unich.it; gilda.antonelli@unich.it

P. Weritz
High Tech Business and Entrepreneurship Department, University of Twente, Enschede, The Netherlands
e-mail: p.weritz@utwente.nl

A. Tursunbayeva et al. (eds.), *Technology-Driven Transformation*, Lecture Notes in Information Systems and Organisation 79,
https://doi.org/10.1007/978-3-032-01396-5_13

institutions [2]. These changes impact society and can be influenced by various factors such as technological advancements, cultural shifts, economic developments, political movements, and environmental challenges. With the widespread adoption of digital technologies such as the Internet, social media, and data analytics, the dynamics of communication, commerce, and governance have been redefined [3]. More precisely, the rapid pace of technological innovation has transformed traditional industries, created new job opportunities, and posed regulatory and ethical challenges [4]. To navigate these shifts effectively, robust change management strategies are essential for organizations to adapt to evolving technological landscapes and mitigate potential disruptions. As such, understanding the intersection of societal change and digital transformation is essential for navigating the complexities of the modern world. Because of the complexity of the phenomenon and the remaining challenges for research to advance the field, we aim to address the various facets of this intersection and its implications for individuals, organizations, and societies at large. We identified three main issues which can be addressed by conceptually understanding digital transformation from a change management perspective.

First, although digital transformation has been studied for years from a process perspective, the field aims for new theories rather than looking back on what already exists and which established theories can offer a framework for transformation. Challenges and opportunities for change management in the face of digital transformation include resistance to change, navigating the complexities of multiple institutional logics, building digital capabilities, and fostering a culture of innovation. Effective change management strategies are essential for successful digital transformation, enabling organizations to adapt and thrive in this dynamic environment.

Second, digital technology is altering established institutional arrangements and changing the multiplicity of institutional logic in different domains of society. These logics encompass the deeply rooted beliefs, practices, and rules that guide institutional behavior. Digital transformation has implications for institutional arrangements and affordances, redefining roles and responsibilities within institutions and disrupting traditional hierarchies and power dynamics [5]. This disruption is explained by how digital technology impacts organizational structures and processes, necessitating new ways of thinking and operating within institutions [6].

Third, the relationship between technology and societal change is multifaceted, with digital transformation being conceptualized as constitutive of societal change [7]. Culture plays a crucial role in this transformation, influencing how societies adopt and integrate digital technologies [1]. For example, the manufacturing sector is embracing Industry 4.0 and smart factories, showcasing how digital technologies are revolutionizing production processes without considering the role of the employees. Similarly, the implementation of new ways of working, such as remote working, which requires an essential shift in technology modalities, is strongly influenced by the culture of the organizations that adopt it (i.e. public organizations or family businesses) as the employees [8]. Hence, the role of the organizational culture in this sociotechnical system of digital transformation is underdeveloped.

Based on these three key issues, this paper aims to delve deeper into the complexities of societal change and digital transformation, providing a comprehensive understanding of how these phenomena shape change. By providing a more in-depth exploration of this intersection, we try to uncover valuable insights that can inform strategic decision-making, policy formulation, and personal choices in an increasingly interconnected and digitized world. This article aims to enrich the theoretical repertoire by explaining the implications of technological change at the societal level.

The research question guiding this exploration is: *How does digital transformation unfold from a change management perspective in an institutional logic?*

We adopt a conceptual and theoretical approach to analyze this issue, using existing theories and literature to provide a solid framework for understanding the effects of digital technology on institutions and large-scale institutional change at the societal level. Similarly, we believe that organizational culture plays a crucial role in these changes. New ways of working, which generate transformations in practices, processes, decisions, and implemented technologies, are strongly influenced by organizational culture, which, in turn, reconsiders values, norms, and behaviors within organizations [9]. Indeed, cultural factors are essential in determining how digital transformation is perceived and implemented within organizations [8]. The prevailing norms, values, and beliefs in an organization can facilitate or hinder the adoption of new technologies and practices. Therefore, understanding the interplay between digital technology and organizational culture is critical to promoting effective and sustainable institutional change, highlighting that the role of organizational culture in this sociotechnical system of digital transformation is still underdeveloped. We consider the multiplicity of institutional logic, suggesting that different stakeholders and agents may benefit from and become active participants in the process of digital transformation. Technological change increases the compatibility of certain institutional logics while heightening contradictions and tensions, among others [10]. This duality serves as both a source for positive transformation and complex challenges [7], necessitating significant advances in theorizing the relationship between technological and institutional change [11–13].

This study makes significant contributions to both the theoretical and practical understanding of digital transformation within the context of societal and institutional change. Theoretically, it advances the discourse by examining the complex interplay between technological change and institutional logic, highlighting the multiplicity of institutional perspectives and the pivotal role of organizational culture. The research delves into how prevailing norms, values, and beliefs within organizations influence the adoption and implementation of new technologies, thereby shaping the trajectory of digital transformation. By focusing on the cultural dimensions, the study provides a nuanced view of how organizational culture can either facilitate or hinder the integration of digital technologies, contributing to a more comprehensive understanding of the socio-technical dynamics involved.

Practically, the study provides key insights into effective change management during digital transformation, emphasizing the need to cultivate a digital culture that aligns with organizational goals and societal expectations. It offers actionable guidance for leaders and policymakers to manage the complexities and contradictions of digital change by understanding institutional logics and cultural factors. This framework supports strategic, sustainable change and lays the groundwork for future qualitative research on the diverse impacts of digital transformation in different contexts.

The relevance of this study is underscored by the accelerating pace of technological change and its profound impact on institutions and societies. In an increasingly interconnected and digitized world, the findings offer a vital resource for stakeholders—including organizational leaders, policymakers, and researchers—looking to navigate the challenges and leverage the opportunities presented by digital transformation. By providing a deeper theoretical and practical understanding, the study equips these stakeholders with the knowledge to make informed strategic decisions, formulate relevant policies, and adapt to evolving societal norms and technological advancements.

2 Related Literature

2.1 Digital Transformation Literature

Digital transformation (DT) is a complex and widely discussed concept in current research, emphasizing its essential role in transforming modern organizations. First, DT and digitalization are usually used interchangeably as concepts related to politics, business, and social issues [14–16]. There is no single, universally accepted definition of DT in the literature, and several literature reviews have explored the topic [17–19].

As Kokkinakos et al. (2016) noted, advanced technologies such as social software and data analytics play a crucial role in reshaping everyday operations at all organizational levels [20]. This underscores the need for a clear definition of DT, a term frequently mentioned but often vaguely understood. According to a systematic literature review conducted by Reis et al. (2018), existing literature divides DT into three main elements: technological, organizational, and social [17].

From a technological perspective, DT involves using new digital tools like social media, mobile platforms, analytics, and embedded devices to achieve significant business improvements [21–23]. In this regard, Hanelt et al. (2020) defined DT as "organizational change that is triggered and shaped by the widespread diffusion of digital technologies" (p. 2), [24]. McDonald and Rowsell-Jones (2012) further assert that DT goes beyond merely digitizing resources, creating value and revenues from digital assets [23].

Organizationally, DT requires changes in existing processes or the development of new business models to enhance customer engagement and operational efficiency [25]. Socially, DT impacts all aspects of human life, improving customer experiences and fundamentally altering business and social interactions [26]. Furthermore, DT is a process that affects organizational values and identity [27].

Despite the various definitions (Table 1), there is general agreement that DT involves the strategic use of digital technologies to drive substantial business

Table 1 Digital transformation definitions

Author(s)	Definition
Fitzgerald et al. [21]	Use of new digital technologies, such as social media, mobile, analytics or embedded devices, in order to enable major business improvements like enhancing customer experience, streamlining operations or creating new business models
McDonald and Rowsell-Jones [23]	As such, the Digital Transformation goes beyond merely digitizing resources and results in value and revenues being created from digital asset
Solis et al. [24]	The realignment of, or new investment in, technology and business models to more effectively engage digital customers at every touch point in the customer experience lifecycle
Collin et al. [14]; Gimpel and Röglinger [15]; Kane et al. [16]	While digitization commonly describes the mere conversion of analogue into digital information, the terms Digital Transformation and digitalization are used interchangeably and refer to a broad concept affecting politics, business, and social issues
Martin [28]	Digital Transformation is now commonly interpreted as such usage of Information and Communication Technology, when not trivial automation is performed, but fundamentally new capabilities are created in business, public government, and in people's and society life
Westerman et al. [31]	Digital Transformation is defined as the use of technology to radically improve performance or reach of enterprises
Schallmo et al. [29, 30]	The DT framework includes the networking of actors such as businesses and customers across all value-added chain segments, and the application of new technologies. As such, DT requires skills that involve the extraction and exchange of data and the analysis and conversion of that data into actionable information. This information should be used to calculate and evaluate options to enable decisions and/or initiate activities. In order to increase the performance and reach of a company, DT involves companies, business models, processes, relationships, products, etc.
Stolterman and Fors [26]	Digital Transformation is the changes that digital technology causes or influences in all aspects of human life
Vial [18]	Digital Transformation is a process that encompasses significant changes through the introduction of information and communications technologies (ICTs)
Hanelt et al. [24]	Digital Transformation is organizational change that is triggered and shaped by the widespread diffusion of digital technologies
Wessel et al. [27]	Digital transformation activities leverage digital technology in (re)defining an organization's value proposition and involve the emergence of a new organizational identity
Kokkinakos et al. [20]	Advanced technologies such as social software and data analytics play a crucial role in reshaping everyday operations at all organizational levels
Reis et al. [17]	Digital Transformation encompasses three main elements: technological, organizational, and social aspects
Matt et al. [32]; Singh and Hess [33]	Digital Transformation primarily focuses on organizations, with significant differences in the types of technologies and the nature of transformations described.
Bharadwaj et al. [34]	Digital Transformation involves combinations of information, computing, communication, and connectivity technologies to trigger significant changes in an entity's properties

improvements and influence customer experiences, creating value and new capabilities across industries and society [28–31]. This comprehensive understanding highlights the transformative power of digital technologies and their critical role in modern organizational strategies.

In our paper, we consider the definition by Vial et al. (2019), which describes digital transformation as a process that encompasses significant changes through the introduction of information and communications technologies (ICTs) [18]. Vial et al. (2019), [18] made three main observations: first, DT definitions primarily focus on organizations; second, significant differences exist in the types of technologies and the nature of transformations described; and third, common terms such as "digital technologies" are used across definitions [32, 33]. For example, some definitions emphasize the radical improvement of enterprise performance [31], while others focus on integrating new technologies like social media and analytics to enhance customer experience and streamline operations [21].

Despite these variations, all definitions agree that DT involves leveraging digital technologies to achieve significant business improvements. Vial et al.'s (2019) semantic analysis revealed four essential properties of DT: the target entity, scope, means, and expected outcome [18]. They thus proposed a definition of DT as "a process that aims to improve an entity by triggering significant changes to its properties through combinations of information, computing, communication, and connectivity technologies." This definition is not organization-centric and acknowledges improvement as a potential but not a guaranteed outcome. By avoiding the term "digital technologies" and using Bharadwaj et al.'s (2013) definition, they ensure the conceptual clarity and adaptability of their definition over time [34].

Sources: Adapted from Reis et al. [17]; Vial [18]; Hanelt et al. [24]; Wessel et al. [27].

2.2 *Change Management Perspective*

Change management plays a vital role in addressing the complexities of digital technologies within organizations. As these advancements introduce a range of choices that affect various structures, processes, and strategies [35, 36], adept change management is necessary to ensure these changes support organizational objectives. This process helps firms utilize digital technologies to reshape their value propositions and develop new organizational identities [27]. Change management involves a structured approach to transitioning individuals, teams, and entire organizations from a current state to a desired future state. Effective change management is crucial as it minimizes resistance, maximizes engagement, and ensures that changes are implemented smoothly and sustainably [37]. With a strategic approach to managing change, organizations can avoid disruption, inefficiency, and failure to achieve their goals.

In the present paper, we follow Kotter's "8 Steps to Change" framework (2012), [38]. The 8 Steps are: (1) create a sense of urgency; (2) building a coalition; (3)

develop a vision; (4) communicate the vision; (5) empower others to act; (6) generate short-term wins; (7) sustain acceleration; (8) institute the change.

First, *developing a sense of urgency* is essential. This involves creating a compelling reason for why change is necessary by highlighting market trends, competitive pressures, or internal challenges that necessitate immediate action. The goal is to instill a sense of urgency among stakeholders to rally support for the change initiative. Next, *forming a powerful guiding coalition* is crucial. This step requires assembling a group of people at different organizational levels with enough power and influence to lead the change effort, including key leaders and influencers within the organization who are committed to driving the change and can work together as a team. Following this, *creating a vision for change* becomes vital. A clear vision and strategy are needed to direct the change effort, outlining the desired future state of the organization and the steps required to achieve it. A well-articulated vision helps align and motivate employees toward the common goal. Once the vision is established, the next step is *to communicate* it effectively by embedding it within all aspects of the organization's operations. Consistent and transparent communication ensures that all employees understand and buy into the vision. Identifying and *removing obstacles* is another critical step. This involves pinpointing and eliminating barriers to change, which might include restructuring organizational processes, updating outdated systems, or addressing employee concerns and resistance. Recognizing and rewarding those who support the change can reinforce positive behaviors. Moreover, *generating short-term wins* helps build momentum and validate the effort. Achieving quick, visible successes early in the change process shows the benefits of the change, encouraging ongoing support and effort. To sustain momentum, *consolidating gains and producing more change* is necessary. This step requires building on the momentum gained from early wins, continuously analyzing the change process, making necessary adjustments, and ensuring that improvements are sustained and expanded. This stage helps prevent backsliding and ensures that the change becomes entrenched. Finally, *anchoring new approaches in the culture* ensures lasting change. For change to be enduring, it must become part of the organization's core culture, with new behaviors and practices solidified as the norm. Leaders must integrate these changes into every aspect of the organization, including policies, procedures, and employee development programs.

By following Kotter's 8 Steps to Change, organizations can effectively manage transitions, ensuring that changes are implemented, embraced, and sustained [38]. This approach helps organizations improve efficiency, adapt proactively to market demands, and achieve long-term strategic objectives.

2.3 Institutional Logic

The institutional logic perspective, introduced by Friedland and Alford (1991), emphasizes the importance of societal contexts in understanding organizational phenomena, portraying society as an interinstitutional system composed of various institutional orders, each characterized by its logic [39]. These logics, such as the market, state, democracy, family, and religion, differentiate areas of social life through distinct symbolic systems and ways of ordering reality. Thornton (2004) expanded this typology to include additional logic like corporate, profession, and community [40]. Institutional logics are ideal types—conceptual models that simplify complex realities to facilitate comparative analysis and understanding of societal dynamics and institutional change. This perspective is particularly useful for analyzing how different logics interact and influence organizational practices.

While there has been extensive research on the relationship between Information Technology (IT) and organizational change limited research has theorized the relationship between IT and societal change [27, 41]. Some scholars address this gap by utilizing institutional theory, particularly institutional logic, to develop a model of IT and societal change [7]. This model is crucial in an era of large-scale digital transformation, considering society as an interinstitutional system reflecting the multiplicity of logics at the societal level. They conceptualize societal change as shifts in the levels of centrality and compatibility of multiple logics, linking these changes to the materiality of technology through the concept of IT affordances.

We propose to enrich this framework by integrating into it the concept of IT affordances, which are the potential actions perceived in technological artifacts based on users' goals and contexts. IT affordances are not inherent properties of the technology itself but arise from the relationship between the technology, its users, and their environment [42–46]. As users engage with IT, their focus on specific affordances can highlight and activate corresponding institutional logic. For instance, users influenced by a community logic may prioritize affordances that enhance community building, while those guided by a market logic may focus on affordances that facilitate marketing activities.

This interaction between IT affordances and institutional logic reveals how technology can both shape and be shaped by societal structures.

By examining how these affordances align with or challenge existing institutional logic, including elements of authority, legitimacy, and norms, researchers can gain deeper insights into the mechanisms of institutional change [7]. For example, IT affordances that support hierarchical control can reinforce authority structures, while those promoting transparency can legitimize practices that enhance openness and accountability. Similarly, affordances that foster collaboration can shift norms towards more inclusive and collective behaviors.

Thus, the affordance-based institutional logic perspective offers an understanding of the interplay between technology and society, illustrating how technological engagements can drive new organizational practices and broader societal transformations. Furthermore, it can help to explain how digital technologies shape social and economic activities, revealing both positive and negative impacts. On the positive side, such activities have alleviated poverty [47, 48] by creating new economic opportunities and improving access to resources. They also increase social inclusion [49] by connecting marginalized groups to broader social networks and fostering political participation [50] by enabling more widespread and diverse public discourse. Conversely, the same technologies can increase systemic risks [51], potentially destabilizing economic systems and reducing employment standards [52] by automating jobs and creating precarious work conditions. Additionally, they can undermine democratic processes [53] by facilitating misinformation and manipulating public opinion. This duality underscores the need for a nuanced understanding of digital affordances within institutional logic to balance benefits and mitigate risks.

3 Toward a Societal Change Forming Digital Transformation

Institutional logic provides a framework for understanding how companies function, legitimize their actions, and maintain stability and continuity [54]. These logics shape individuals' and organizations' expectations, behaviors, and interactions within a given social system. Understanding institutional logic is crucial in the context of digital transformation because it highlights the fundamental principles that drive organizational change [7]. Institutional logic can group the specific patterns of beliefs, values, practices, and rules that guide behavior [55]. They reflect the dominant ways of thinking and acting within a social system and provide a framework for understanding how institutions operate, in this case, specifically for DT.

In this regard, we propose a framework considering Kotter's 8 steps [38] and sense of authority, sense of legitimacy and norms from affordance-based institutional logics [7, 54, 56].

Kotter's "8 Steps to Change" framework is selected for its comprehensive, structured approach that emphasizes cultural and behavioral dynamics, providing a holistic view essential for understanding digital transformation within institutional contexts. It is particularly valuable due to its focus on leadership and cultural embedding, making it an effective tool for analyzing and managing long-term organizational changes. By selecting Kotter's "8 Steps to Change" framework, the study leverages a well-established, comprehensive, and culturally sensitive model that aligns closely with its research objectives. The framework's focus on human factors, structured process, and proven applicability in complex change scenarios provides a strong foundation for analyzing how institutional logic and cultural dynamics influence digital transformation efforts. This selection not only enhances the study's methodological rigor but also ensures the relevance and practical applicability of the findings.

Initially, starting with a sense of authority, it is first necessary to establish a sense of urgency, creating awareness about the need for DT to remain competitive. Next, forming a powerful coalition of influential leaders supporting the transformation helps solidify the new authority structure. Creating a clear vision of what digital transformation wants to achieve provides authoritative guidance and inspires the organization, while effectively communicating this vision at all levels strengthens the authority of the coalition of leaders and promotes the adoption of the vision.

In particular, these first four steps (sense of urgency, powerful coalition, digital vision, and communication) are essential to redefine the sense of authority. A sense of authority based on these four elements is critical to legitimizing the transformation process by creating short-term successes and implementing pilot projects that demonstrate the benefits of digital transformation and reinforce the legitimacy of change. Using these initial successes to undertake larger, more complex projects further consolidates the legitimacy of the transformation process. Moving from merely having authority to being seen as legitimate is tied to individuals gaining new skills and capabilities. For this transition to be successful, the organization must foster empowerment and remove barriers, ensuring that all members are autonomous and responsible for tasks and actions.

These individual factors play a crucial role in cementing a sense of legitimacy within the organization, as they directly influence organizational culture and corporate identity. When members of the organization perceive that actions taken are legitimate and consistent with shared values, a solid foundation for acceptance of new norms and behaviors is created. This process is critical to the growth and development of organizational culture, as the new norms and behaviors adopted represent a tangible form of evolution and adaptation to the surrounding environment. The evolving organizational culture not only reflects external changes, such as those resulting from digital transformation, but can also guide and shape these changes, serving as a reference point for the organization's identity and cohesion [54]. Therefore, understanding and influencing the sense of legitimacy within the organization is critical to promoting positive and sustainable cultural change that sustains the organization's long-term success and resilience.

Furthermore, it is important to emphasize that this process is not static but dynamic: through continuous feedback and constant adaptation, norms evolve, and the organization grows in its digital capabilities. In this context, a sense of authority and legitimation plays a key role in maintaining a close alignment with the overall vision of the company. This ensures that the transformation is supported and deeply embedded in the organizational culture. This approach aims to promote a cultural change that not only reflects the new digital reality but also serves as a vehicle to strengthen the company's identity and foster a sense of unity among all members of the organization. Our paper proposes a new theoretical framework based on established theories and convincingly highlights the crucial role of institutional logic in understanding and guiding digital transformation within organizations. Through this model, we emphasize how institutional logic provides a conceptual framework for understanding the functioning of companies, legitimizing actions, and ensuring organizational stability. This conceptual framework, integrated with elements such as Kotter's model and concepts of authority, legitimacy, and norms, offers a structured guide for organizations engaged in digital transformation [7, 38]. Additionally, we underscore the importance of creating a digital culture within the organization, as it plays a fundamental role in shaping corporate identity and fostering the acceptance and adoption of digital changes [1, 54, 56]. This digital culture not only reflects external transformations but can actively influence such changes, providing a solid foundation for long-term success and resilience.

4 Discussion and Conclusion

This paper has sought to shed light on the intricate relationship between digital transformation and social change, recognizing their substantial influence on individuals, institutions and broader communities. By analyzing the complex interplay between technological advances, institutional structures and cultural dynamics, we have highlighted both the possibilities for transformative progress and the underlying challenges inherent in the digital transformation journey. As technology continues to reshape various aspects of our society, it is essential to understand how to skillfully navigate change in this digitally driven era. Our research has underscored the importance of implementing resilient strategies to combat resistance, stimulate innovation, and cultivate digital capabilities within organizations. We advance theoretical insights by elucidating the evolving interplay between technology and institutional norms, showing the range of institutional beliefs and practices, and recognizing the influential role of culture in shaping digital progress. In doing so, we also highlight the necessity of bridging organizational culture and technical transformations to promote a coherent change. By providing a theoretical framework built on existing literature and theories, we set the stage for further exploration of the ramifications of technological change on society.

Our research shows that while technology offers potential for improvement, it also brings with it several difficulties that need to be resolved through strategic leadership and cultural alignment. In addressing the problems raised in the motivation of the study, our framework effectively responds to each of them. Firstly, our approach demonstrates that it is not always necessary to reinvent the wheel. Using a solid theoretical foundation, we can avoid the risk of stagnating digital transformation research without significant advancements. This approach allows us to build on validated foundations and focus on developing new cutting-edge concepts and practices. Moreover, leveraging established theories enables us to refine existing models and propose nuanced adaptations that better align with contemporary digital realities.

Secondly, our framework provides a solid avenue for future research, encouraging scholars to explore various elements and influencing factors such as empowerment and leadership. Conducting qualitative research using case studies to confirm the conceptual domain of our model could be particularly useful as a next step. Longitudinal research techniques may potentially be used in future studies to analyze the long-term effects of digital transformation on organizational performance and culture. This approach deepens understanding of digital transformation in organizations and could identify new areas for investigation and intervention. For example, additional investigations could explore how specific organizations implement digital technologies and manage the changes accompanying them. This could reveal the practical challenges organizations face, such as overcoming resistance to change, integrating new digital tools with existing systems, and fostering a digital culture. This research could also explore how different industries adapt to digital transformation, identifying sector-specific strategies and challenges. In addition, future research could highlight successful strategies and best practices for coping with digital transformation, providing valuable insights for other organizations. In this way, it is also possible to try to create standard policies and practices that could probably differ by the sector in which the organization operates, as well as the size of the organization, the type of employees involved, etc. By examining the role of organizational culture and identity in digital transformation, future work could uncover how cultural values and identities influence the adoption and integration of digital technologies. Additionally, investigating how organizational identity evolves in response to digital transformation could provide valuable insights into preserving cultural consistency during major change initiatives.

Lastly, our work highlights the importance of digital culture in a sociotechnical system. By showing how organizational culture, which often concerns only social aspects (people and organizational structure), influences and is influenced by digital transformation, we demonstrate the close link between the technological and social dimensions of the organization [9]. This further underscores the importance of developing a robust and adaptable digital culture capable of effectively guiding and supporting organizational change in the long term.

In conclusion, we recommend that organizations invest in continuous cultural assessments to align their digital strategies with evolving cultural norms and values. Our paper proposes practical contributions by guiding organizations through the complex process of digital transformation effectively and systematically. Firstly, in creating a sense of urgency, emphasis is placed on conducting a thorough analysis of the market and competitive challenges. This enables the identification of emerging opportunities and threats resulting from digital transformation, highlighting the immediate need for change across the organization. Subsequently, in forming a guiding coalition, the focus is on identifying and involving key leaders and influencers within the organization. This step is crucial to ensure strong support and effective guidance during the transformation process, as these individuals can significantly shape the direction and approach to digital transformation. Finally, in developing a vision, the active involvement of organization members in this process is recommended. This ensures that the vision is not imposed from the top down but is instead co-created and shared by all members. This sense of ownership and widespread engagement is essential to ensure an effective response to institutional and cultural changes while maintaining strong organizational cohesion and identity. By creating a framework that integrates both technological and cultural dimensions, organizations can better navigate the complexities of digital transformation. Future research should explore the impact of emerging technologies on organizational culture, as well as the effectiveness of various change management strategies in different organizational contexts. Specifically, studies should examine how digital tools and platforms influence employee engagement, organizational cohesion, and cultural adaptation. By addressing these areas, we can provide actionable insights that will help organizations and scholars better manage the intersection of technology and culture, ultimately contributing to more successful and sustainable digital transformations.

Disclosure of Interests The authors have no competing interests to declare that are relevant to the content of this article.

References

1. Weritz, P., Braojos, J., & Matute, J. (2020). Exploring the antecedents of digital transformation: Dynamic capabilities and digital culture aspects to achieve digital maturity.
2. Rotatori, D., Lee, E. J., & Sleeva, S. (2021). The evolution of the workforce during the fourth industrial revolution. *Human Resource Development International, 24*(1), 92–103.
3. Feliciano-Cestero, M. M., Ameen, N., Kotabe, M., Paul, J., & Signoret, M. (2023). Is digital transformation threatened? A systematic literature review of the factors influencing firms' digital transformation and internationalization. *Journal of Business Research, 157*, 113546.
4. Markus, M. L., & Rowe, F. (2023). The digital transformation conundrum: Labels, definitions, phenomena, and theories. *Journal of the Association for Information Systems, 24*(2), 328–335.
5. Gegenhuber, T., Logue, D., Hinings, C. B., & Barrett, M. (2022). Institutional perspectives on digital transformation. In *Digital transformation and institutional theory* (Vol. 83, pp. 1–32). Emerald Publishing Limited.
6. Carroll, N., Hassan, N. R., Junglas, I., Hess, T., & Morgan, L. (2023). Transform or be transformed: the importance of research on managing and sustaining digital transformations. *European Journal of Information Systems, 32*(3), 347–353.
7. Faik, I., Barrett, M., & Oborn, E. (2020). How information technology matters in societal change: An affordance-based institutional logics perspective. *MIS Quarterly, 44*(3).
8. Pagnozzi, F., Pescatore, I., Cartone, A., & Antonelli, G. (2023). Organisational culture and hybrid work in the Italian public sector. In *ItAIS 2023 – 20th conference of the Italian Chapter of AIS*. University of Turin.
9. Pescatore, I., Pagnozzi, F., & Antonelli, G. (2024). Analysing the bottom-up approach to develop organisational culture in virtualised organisations. In A. Lazazzara, R. Reina, & S. Za (Eds.), *Towards digital and sustainable organisations. ItAIS 2022* (Lecture notes in information systems and organisation) (Vol. 65). Springer.
10. Berente, N., & Yoo, Y. (2012). Institutional contradictions and loose coupling: Post implementation of NASA's enterprise information system. *Information System Research, 23*(2), 376–396.
11. Orlikowski, W. J., & Barley, S. R. (2001). Technology and institutions: What can research on information technology and research on organizations learn from each other? *MIS Quarterly*, 145–165.
12. Scott, W. R. (2013). *Institutions and organizations: Ideas, interests, and identities*. Sage Publications.
13. Berente, N., & Seidel, S. (2022). Digital technologies: Carrier or trigger for institutional change in digital transformation? In *Digital transformation and institutional theory* (pp. 197–209). Emerald Publishing Limited.
14. Collin, J., Hiekkanen, K., Korhonen, J., Halén, M., Itälä, T., & Helenius, M. (2015). It leadership in transition-the impact of digitalization on Finnish organizations.
15. Gimpel, H., & Röglinger, M. (2015). Digital transformation: Changes and chances–insights based on an empirical study.
16. Kane, G., Palmer, D., Phillips, A., Kiron, D., & Buckley, N. (2015). *Strategy, not technology, drives digital transformation* (Vol. 14). MIT Sloan Management Review and Deloitte University Press.
17. Reis, J., Amorim, M., Melão, N., & Matos, P. (2018). Digital transformation: A literature review and guidelines for future research. *Trends and Advances in Information Systems and Technologies, 1*(6), 411–421.
18. Vial, G. (2019). Understanding digital transformation: A review and a research agenda. *The Journal of Strategic Information Systems*. https://doi.org/10.1016/j.jsis.2019.01.003
19. Mikalef, P., & Parmiggiani, E. (2022). An introduction to digital transformation. *Digital Transformation in Norwegian Enterprises, 1*.

20. Kokkinakos, P., Markaki, O., Koussouris, S., & Psarras, J. (2016). Digital transformation: Is public sector following the enterprise 2.0 paradigm? In *Digital transformation and global society* (pp. 96–105). Springer.
21. Fitzgerald, M., Kruschwitz, N., Bonnet, D., & Welch, M. (2013). *Embracing digital technology: A new strategic imperative*. MIT Sloan Management Review, Research Report.
22. Fitzgerald, M., Kruschwitz, N., Bonnet, D., & Welch, M. (2014). Embracing digital technology: A new strategic imperative. *MIT Sloan Management Review, 55*(2), 1.
23. McDonald, M., & Rowsell-Jones, A. (2012). *The digital edge: Exploiting information & technology for business advantage*. Gartner Inc.
24. Hanelt, A., Bohnsack, R., Marz, D., & Antunes Marante, C. (2020). A systematic review of the literature on digital transformation: Insights and implications for strategy and organizational change. *Journal of Management Studies, 58*(5), 1159–1197.
25. Solis, B., Lieb, R., & Szymanski, J. (2014). *The 2014 state of digital transformation*. Altimeter Group.
26. Stolterman, E., & Fors, A. (2004). Information technology and the good life. In *Information systems research* (pp. 687–692).
27. Wessel, L., Baiyere, A., Ologeanu-Taddei, R., Cha, J., & Blegind-Jensen, T. (2021). Unpacking the difference between digital transformation and IT-enabled organizational transformation. *Journal of the Association for Information Systems, 22*(1), 102–129.
28. Martin, A. (2008). Digital literacy and the "digital society". *Digital Literacies Concepts Policies Practices, 30*, 151–176.
29. Schallmo, D., Williams, C. A., & Lohse, J. (2019a). Digital strategy—Integrated approach and generic options. *International Journal of Innovation Management, 23*(08), 1940005.
30. Schallmo, D., Williams, C. A., & Boardman, L. (2019b). Digital transformation of business models – Best practice, enablers and roadmap. *Digital Disruptive Innovation, 36*, 119–138.
31. Westerman, G., Calméjane, C., Bonnet, D., Ferraris, P., & McAfee, A. (2011). *Digital transformation: A roadmap for billion-dollar organizations* (pp. 1–68). MIT Sloan Management, MIT Center for Digital Business and Capgemini Consulting.
32. Matt, C., Hess, T., & Benlian, A. (2015). Digital transformation strategies. *Business & Information Systems Engineering, 57*, 339–343.
33. Singh, A., & Hess, T. (2020). How chief digital officers promote the digital transformation of their companies. In *Strategic information management* (pp. 202–220). Routledge.
34. Bharadwaj, A., El Sawy, O. A., Pavlou, P. A., & Venkatraman, N. V. (2013). Digital business strategy: Toward a next generation of insights. *MIS Quarterly*, 471–482.
35. Baiyere, A., Grover, V., Lyytinen, K. J., Woerner, S., & Gupta, A. (2023). Digital "x"—Charting a path for digital-themed research. *Information Systems Research, 34*(2), 463–486.
36. Kaganer, E., Gregory, R. W., & Sarker, S. (2023). A process for managing digital transformation: An organizational inertia perspective. *Journal of the Association for Information Systems, 24*(4), 1005–1030.
37. Braojos, J., Weritz, P., & Matute, J. (2024). Empowering organisational commitment through digital transformation capabilities: The role of digital leadership and a continuous learning environment. *Information Systems Journal*.
38. Kotter, J. P. (2012). *Leading change*. Harvard Business Press.
39. Friedland, R., & Alford, R. R. (1991). Bringing society back. In W. W. Powell & P. J. DiMaggio (Eds.), *Symbols, practices and institutional contradictions. In the new institutionalism in organizational analysis* (pp. 232–263). The University of Chicago Press.
40. Thornton, P. H. (2004). *Markets from culture: Institutional logics and organizational decisions in higher education publishing*. Stanford University Press.
41. Leonardi, P. M. (2007). Activating the informational capabilities of information technology for organizational change. *Organization Science, 18*(5), 813–831.
42. Hutchby, I. (2001). Technologies, texts and affordances. *Sociology, 35*(2), 441–456.
43. Leonardi, P. M. (2011). When flexible routines meet flexible technologies: Affordance, constraint, and the imbrication of human and material agencies. *MIS Quarterly, 35*(1), 147–168.

44. Markus, M. L., & Silver, M. S. (2008). A foundation for the study of IT effects: A new look at DeSanctis and poole's concepts of structural features and spirit. *Journal of the Association for Information Systems, 9*(10/11), 609–632.
45. Seidel, S., Recker, J., & Vom Brocke, J. (2013). Sensemaking and sustainable practicing: Functional affordances of information systems in green transformations. *MIS Quarterly, 37*(4), 1275–1299.
46. Zammuto, R. F., Griffith, T. L., Majchrzak, A., Dougherty, D. J., & Faraj, S. (2007). Information technology and the changing fabric of organization. *Organization Science, 18*(5), 749–762.
47. Jha, S. K., Pinsonneault, A., & Dubé, L. (2016). The Evolution of an ICT platform-enabled ecosystem for poverty alleviation: The case of eKutir. *MIS Quarterly, 40*(2), 431–445.
48. Oborn, E., Barrett, M., Orlikowski, W., & Kim, A. (2019). Trajectory dynamics in innovation: Developing and transforming a mobile money service across time and place. *Organization Science, 23*(5), 1448–1461.
49. Andrade, A. D., & Doolin, B. (2016). Information and communication technology and the social inclusion of refugees. *MIS Quarterly, 40*(2), 405–416.
50. Selander, L., & Jarvenpaa, S. L. (2016). Digital action repertoires and transforming a social movement organization. *MIS Quarterly, 40*(2), 331–352.
51. Tarafdar, M., Gupta, A., & Turel, O. (2013). The dark side of information technology use. *Information Systems Journal, 23*(3), 269–275.
52. Brynjolfsson, E., & McAfee, A. (2012). *Race against the machine: How the digital revolution is accelerating innovation, driving productivity, and irreversibly transforming employment and the economy*. Digital Frontier Press.
53. Allcott, H., & Gentzkow, M. (2017). Social media and fake news in the 2016 election. *Journal of Economic Perspectives, 31*(2), 211–236.
54. Thornton, P. H., Ocasio, W., & Lounsbury, M. (2012). *The institutional logics perspective: A new approach to culture, structure and process*. OUP.
55. Haveman, H. A., & Gualtieri, G. (2017). Institutional logics. In *Oxford research encyclopedia of business and management*.
56. Thornton, P. H., & Ocasio, W. (2008). Institutional logics. In R. Greenwood, C. Oliver, T. B. Lawrence, & R. E. Meyer (Eds.), *The Sage handbook of organizational institutionalism* (pp. 99–129). SAGE Publications.

Exploring Chatbot Adoption in the Italian Legal Domain: A Fuzzy-Set Qualitative Comparative Analysis

Filippo Bianchini, Alessio Maria Braccini, Francesca De Luzi, Mattia Macrì, Massimo Mecella, and Rosa Anna Ruggiero

Abstract This paper explores the adoption and use of AI chatbots by knowledge workers in the Italian legal sector. Distancing from existing literature, which mainly explores chatbots as interactive agents and focuses on implications for human agency, in this research, we focus on chatbots as text manipulation tools that knowledge workers have to work with. We collected data from a sample of 39 respondents exploring causal factors influencing the usage behaviour of knowledge workers. The results of a fuzzy set Qualitative Comparative Analysis show two causal configurations of knowledge workers profiles willing to use AI chatbots: innovative-minded employees with a positive attitude towards innovation and workers who approach chatbot usage with critical thinking and in a teamwork setting. Our research has implications for research and practice, on the need to progress investigation of the lack of perceived risk of AI chatbots, and on the role of intensity of usage on the perception of chatbots.

Keywords AI chatbots adoption · Working with AI · fsQCA

F. Bianchini (✉) · F. De Luzi · M. Macrì · M. Mecella
Department of Computer, Control and Management Engineering Antonio Ruberti – DIAG, Sapienza University of Rome, Rome, Italy
e-mail: bianchini@diag.uniroma1.it; deluzi@diag.uniroma1.it; macri@diag.uniroma1.it; mecella@diag.uniroma1.it

A. M. Braccini
Department of Economics Engineering Society and Business Organisation (DEIM), University of Tuscia, Viterbo, Italy
e-mail: abraccini@unitus.it

R. A. Ruggiero
Department of Modern Languages and Literatures, History, Philosophy and Law Studies – DISTU, University of Tuscia, Viterbo, Italy
e-mail: rosa.ruggiero@unitus.it

A. Tursunbayeva et al. (eds.), *Technology-Driven Transformation*, Lecture Notes in Information Systems and Organisation 79,
https://doi.org/10.1007/978-3-032-01396-5_14

1 Introduction

The proliferation of chatbots represents a recent and notable advancement in the development of artificial intelligence (AI) [1]. Chatbots are generative AI applications that produce coherent and contextually appropriate text based on user inputs. Unlike other text-based technologies, chatbots utilise cognitive frameworks, enhancing their ability to provide valuable responses to user queries, simulating the experience of conversing with an intelligent human [2]. As such, chatbots are also valuable tools for various language-processing tasks. Both researchers and practitioners have shown significant interest in chatbots. Numerous studies have investigated chatbots to understand the intentions behind their use [2, 3]. However, we identify some limitations in the current research that present opportunities for further exploration, also expanding the analytical perspectives currently adopted in the literature.

First, many studies treat chatbots as agents, analysing how different targeted groups—such as employees, customers, citizens, or stakeholders in public and private organisations—perceive chatbots in terms of their anthropomorphic qualities, human-like intelligence [2, 4, 5], or as alternatives to human agency [4]. This research stream examines the implications of potential human substitution with chatbots in specific tasks or administrative processes. Still, it does not focus on the interaction of humans with knowledge management technology. Secondly, while these studies primarily focus on user perceptions, they often neglect the contextual factors surrounding chatbot use [2] and fail to consider aspects such as task characteristics and group dynamics that might impact the behavioural intention to use. Ultimately, most of the analyses focus on examining the impact of individual variables on the intention to use chatbots.

Considering these limitations, this paper aims to contribute to the literature by adopting a different perspective. We consider chatbots as text manipulation technologies that people work with. We focus on factors affecting the users' perception of chatbot functionalities and their attitude to using them. We also explore the task characteristics concerning the intention to use. Finally, we aim to examine equal combinations of these factors that explain the usage behaviour of targeted users to contribute to a more nuanced understanding of knowledge workers' behavioural intention to use chatbots. In this paper we aim at answering the following research question: *what are the causal factors influencing knowledge workers' adoption and use of AI chatbots?*

To achieve this, we have adopted a methodology of analysis called fuzzy set Qualitative Comparative Analysis (fsQCA) [5]. fsQCA allows us to explore how different combinations of conditions contribute to an outcome, identifying necessary and sufficient conditions, making it ideal for exploring multifaceted phenomena where traditional methods may fall short. We focus on knowledge workers, engaging with the ongoing discourse on the engagement of knowledge workers with AI [6], considering them individuals who handle complex tasks that require problem-solving, creativity, and critical thinking. These workers continuously interact with vast amounts of knowledge [7], and benefit from instruments that would support them in their knowledge-related practices. Specifically, this paper examines a particular category of knowledge workers within the Italian legal domain as part of the Giustizia Agile project.[1] This initiative, promoted by the Italian Ministry of Justice, seeks to enhance the efficiency and performance of judicial offices by implementing new services, organisational support for computerisation, technological innovation, and change management operations.

The paper develops as follows. Section 2 contains related literature pertinent to the type of artefacts analysed (AI chatbots) and domain of interest (legal domain). Section 3 describes the theoretical framing of our research, indicating factors and outcomes used in our analysis. Section 4 provides the needed methodological considerations, followed by the illustrations of empirical results (Sect. 5) and their discussion (Sect. 6). Section 7 concludes the paper with limitations and implications for research.

2 Related Works

Our work combines the use of AI chatbots within the legal domain. The AI chatbots serve as the artefacts under evaluation. Consequently, in the subsequent sub-section, we will briefly describe the characteristics of this type of technology and its paths of evolution. The context, however, pertains to the legal domain. We will define the legal domain as a context and explore the nature of this knowledge-intensive field in the subsequent sub-section.

2.1 AI and Chatbot

Chatbots have become increasingly widespread, evolving significantly since their inception. Initially, chatbots were rule-based with limited capabilities [8]. Today, advanced machine-learning algorithms [9] enhanced their ability to understand and generate natural language, enabling more sophisticated conversational interactions [10]. Machine learning allowed chatbots to learn from data and improve their responses over time [11]. From the early chatbots like Eliza [12], modern AI virtual assistants have evolved into advanced tools capable of simulating conversations through text or voice, finding applications in communication, automation, and customer support. The development of transformers [13] has significantly enhanced the performance of Large Language Models (LLMs), thereby boosting the capabilities of chatbots. ChatGPT, developed by OpenAI, stands out for its remarkable

---

[1] Italian Ministry of Justice PON project "Per una Giustizia giusta: Innovazione ed. efficienza negli uffici giudiziari - Giustizia Agile".

performance, and it is the chatbot we used in our empirical setting. ChatGPT is built on the GPT (Generative Pre-trained Transformer) architecture, with GPT-3 revolutionising LLMs and inspiring further projects [14]. The latest GPT-4 model has demonstrated substantial improvements over its predecessor. The achievements of GPT models and ChatGPT were unimaginable a few years ago. However, each new version of GPT brings both excitement and concern.

2.2 AI and Justice

Artificial intelligence (AI) is transforming various sectors, and the legal landscape is no exception. While AI promises advancements in efficiency, accuracy, and accessibility, its integration into the legal domain raises several concerns [15, 16]. Recognising these concerns, the European Union (EU) took a proactive step by adopting the Artificial Intelligence Act (AI Act) [2] in March 2024. This legislation aims to regulate the development and use of AI systems, prioritising fairness, transparency, and accountability. Scholars have also extensively examined the impact of AI on the justice system, exploring its potential benefits and challenges [17]. Some studies highlight AI's potential to enhance judicial decision-making by providing judges with objective data and insights, reducing bias, improving consistency, and increasing efficiency [18, 19]. However, others caution against the possibility of AI perpetuating biases embedded in the training data, leading to discriminatory outcomes [20]. Our study aligns with these calls for a deeper understanding of AI's potential use by knowledge workers within the legal domain. By employing fsQCA, we aim to identify the conditions under which AI chatbots are more or less likely to be adopted by legal professionals.

3 Theoretical Framing

The impact of chatbots on human agency is a topic of intense debate [21], especially concerning the potential changes induced in work and labour [22, 23]. Despite its recent emergence, quantitative and qualitative analyses on how chatbots impact workers still need to be made available. Some researchers have utilised the UTAUT [24] and TAM [25] to analyse its adoption in educational contexts, while others have explored its early social acceptance [26]. Studies that investigated determinants of the intention to use chatbots used quantitative variance-based methods and qualitative ones, including fsQCA [27]. Existing studies either focus on the learning dimension or the impact on workers' skills [28]. Building over existing literature, in this paper, we focus on knowledge workers in the legal domain and their interaction

[2] https://artificialintelligenceact.eu/

with chatbots in knowledge-intensive tasks, exploring their behavioural intention to use AI chatbots in their tasks. We started our exploration adopting generally validated items on technology users' acceptance from the IS literature [29]. However, we aim to deviate from these types of studies by considering new factors already described by the literature as relevant for understanding IT, but not explicitly associated with AI chatbot usage by knowledge workers.

Specifically, we set the Behavioural Intention (BI) as an outcome, whereas we consider the new characteristics that may influence the adoption of AI chatbots as described below as the causal conditions.

Considering that AI chatbots are a novelty in the landscape of digital technologies but have diffused very rapidly, we include the factor of Attitude Towards Innovation (AU) to assess how individuals feel about embracing new technologies. It has been noted that people's attitudes towards AI can shape their willingness to use such technologies [30].

Since a notable problem of AI chatbots is hallucination [31, 32], and hallucination in a knowledge worker perspective means the production of fake or non-reliable contents, we include two factors: critical thinking and perceived risk. Critical thinking-guided interaction with chatbots has been already discussed in relation to higher education [33]. We define Critical Thinking (CRI) as the ability to critically understand, evaluate, and interpret information, an essential skill for knowledge workers [34]. Perceived Risk (PRI) refers to the potential problems and uncertainties of adopting new technologies. This can encompass privacy and security concerns, which can influence how people approach AI chatbots [35].

To include instead the content of the knowledge task, we include further factors to explore the influence of team working dynamics, level of interaction and intensity of use. With Team Working (TWO) we aim to explore the impact of AI on collaborative practices. AI tools, including chatbots, may enhance teamwork [36] by providing support and fostering a sense of community. Level of Interaction (LI) refers instead to the degree of interaction of one individual with others during activities and is measured based on different levels (e.g., sequential, aggregational, group, and individual) [37]. Lastly, Intensity of Use (IU) examines the nature of individuals' activities with AI chatbots. It considers the complexity and variety of these activities, such as whether they are routine, research-oriented, or creative, and how these factors might influence the adoption and usage of AI chatbots.

Table 1 summarises the investigated factors with their description. The column *Type* specifies whether the factors are causal conditions (C) or outcomes (O).

4 Research Design

In this paper, we apply a fuzzy-set qualitative comparative analysis (fsQCA), which Ragin introduced in 1987 [38]. This technique helps us identify equifinal combinations of explanatory factors, referred to as causal conditions, that influence the outcome of interest. Using fsQCA is suitable for studying how causal factors combine

Table 1 Description of investigated factors

Causal factors	Type	Description
AU	*C*	Openness to new ideas and changes
CRI	*C*	Understanding, evaluating, interpreting information
TWO	*C*	Collaborating effectively with others
PRI	*C*	Concerns about technology adoption
LI	*C*	Interaction degree during activities
IU	*C*	Activity complexity and variety
BI	*O*	Willingness to perform a specific behaviour

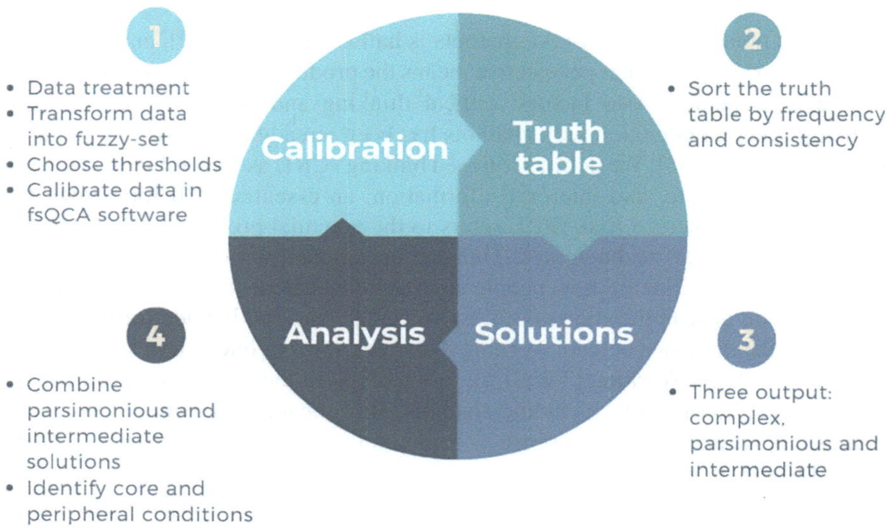

Fig. 1 Steps in a fsQCA analysis from Pappas et al. [38]

to produce outcomes. Furthermore, fsQCA is one of the most effective methods for rigorously analysing the results of interest in low to medium-sized samples. We investigate these patterns by examining the presence and combinations of each factor in relation to the outcome, utilising set theory and Boolean algebra. This approach enables us to assess whether a factor is present or absent and the degree to which it is present. We use the fsQCA 3.0 software to conduct this analysis, following a systematic procedure depicted in Fig. 1 and described in the following sub-sections.

4.1 Data Collection and Questionnaire

This study encompassed 39 participants (22 men and 17 women aged 19–50) in the targeted group. These participants are all knowledge workers in the Italian judiciary system, engaged in knowledge-intensive, problem-solving, and creative activities. Besides their familiarity with their tasks, all participants shared a common trait: a basic understanding and use of AI chatbots, particularly ChatGPT, without requiring advanced technical computer skills. We recruited them at seminars designed to teach AI chatbot usage and effective prompt engineering techniques in the legal domain. After explaining the study's goals and guaranteeing data privacy, the participants voluntarily provided information anonymously. To collect data during seminars on AI, we used an online survey, structured in four sections with the following contents:

- *Section 1*: brief overview of the Chatbot AI under investigation, highlighting its functionalities and capabilities with examples of various tasks and prompts;
- *Section 2*: demographic data from participants, including gender, age, email, and working domain, including two qualifying questions to determine participants' familiarity with AI chatbots and their usage frequency;
- *Section 3*: description of the main activities respondents would perform with AI chatbots categorised into five groups (translation, information search, text analysis, text summarisation, and code generation) representing the intensity of use (IU); characteristics of the activities performed using AI chatbots; level of interaction (LI) with peers with the activities performed (individual, sequential, aggregation, and group);
- *Section 4*: 48 questions on a five-point Likert scale (1 = Strongly disagree, 5 = Strongly agree), randomised for each participant.

We resorted on existing literature to use questions to measure constructs, and we proposed new questions for the constructs we are introducing in the analysis. Since the survey included several questions to measure the different constructs, we proceeded with the calibration of the causal factors prior the execution of the analysis.

4.2 Calibration

In the fsQCA methodology, factors must be calibrated by converting raw measurements into a 0–1 scale reflecting set membership. This involves calculating a mean value for each construct from the interview data, which serves as input for fsQCA. We adopted the direct calibration method, as recommended by [39], identifying three breakpoints to define membership levels (fully in, intermediate, and fully out). Full membership is set at the highest mean value, and full non-membership at the lowest. The crossover points mark the transition from membership to non-membership.

We constructed the fuzzy sets using the mean. Specifically, if the mean value is less than or equal to the threshold for non-membership (value 2), the membership is 0.05. When the mean value is greater than or equal to the threshold for full membership (value 5), the membership is 0.95. For mean values between these thresholds, the calculation scales the value linearly between the thresholds of 2 (completely outside the set) and 5 (completely within the set), mapping the intermediate values proportionally between 0 and 1.

4.3 True Table Construction and Minimisation

During the analysis, the fsQCA software generates a truth table that includes all possible combinations of causal conditions. Since the truth table contains the complete combinatory space of factors and outcomes, several rows will have few or no observations. To avoid noise in the fsQCA results, the truth table must be minimised before generating solutions. The minimisation happens by applying a cutoff to frequency and consistency scores [40]. Given our sample size, even if extant literature [41] suggests a cutoff of 1, we used 2 instead for two reasons: (1) it would allow use to retain 80% of cases as suggested by the literature [41]; (2) it reduces the complexity of the solution without losing additional insights. Once removing configurations with low frequency, the truth table should be sorted by raw consistency. To consider a subset of relationships as relevant, we use a consistency threshold of 0.75.

As explained by [42], after the minimisation, the analysis returns three solutions: a complex solution (containing all possible combinations of conditions); a parsimonious solution (based on simplifying assumptions, retaining the most critical conditions, and suitable for the identification of core and peripheral conditions); and an intermediate solution (derived from counterfactual analysis on the complex and parsimonious solution, including only theoretically plausible counterfactuals [43].

5 Empirical Evidence

Our analysis yielded four configurations of the causal factors (see Table 2). In our results, the complex and intermediate solutions coincide.

The parsimonious solution has been included because it contains the essential conditions for the outcome. The intermediate and parsimonious solutions are necessary to identify core and peripheral conditions, since they encompass both core and peripheral conditions. A straightforward method to identify the core conditions is to examine the parsimonious solution, which excludes peripheral conditions [44].

The configurations shown in Table 2 indicate both factors presence and absence, as well as their role of core or periphery. Below the results for each column are reported: Consistency (the degree to which cases with a specific configuration exhibit the expected outcome), Raw Coverage (the proportion of the outcome

Table 2 fsQCA results[a]

Frequency Cutoff: **2**				
Consistency cutoff: **0.752941**				
Configuration[b]	1	2	3	4
Attitude towards innovation (AU)	●		●	●
Critical thinking (CRI)	⊗	●	●	•
Team working (TWO)		●	●	⊗
Perceived risk (PRI)	⊗	⊗	⊗	⊗
Level of interaction (LI)	⊗	⊗		⊗
Intensity of use (IU)	⊗	⊗	⊗	•
Consistency	0.837368	0.901038	0.954345	0.975279
Raw coverage	0.495746	0.583072	0.580385	0.150470
Unique coverage	0.108374	0.050604	0.047917	0.015226
Overall solution consistency	0.803851			
Overall solution coverage	0.804572			

[a]Black circles (●) indicate the presence of a condition, while crossed-out circles (⊗) indicate its absence. Large circles indicate *core conditions*, small ones, *peripheral conditions*. Blank spaces indicate "*don't care*"

[b]In our configuration all absent conditions are *peripheral conditions*

explained by a particular configuration), and Unique Coverage (the proportion of the outcome explained exclusively by that configuration). The only threshold set for effective validation of the results is on the value of Overall solution consistency, which ideally should exceed 0.75, as suggested by [39]. Regarding the Overall solution coverage value, it is normal to obtain a high value (>0.80), especially for small datasets (<50), as in our case. In our situation, the overall solution consistency is 0.803851, indicating a strong fit between the configurations and the observed outcomes, while the overall solution coverage is 0.804572, meaning that the combined configurations explain approximately 80.5% of the cases. This high coverage and consistency indicate that the identified configurations are robust and reliably explain the presence of the outcome.

6 Discussion

The analysis reveals four configurations with consistency scores ranging from 0.837 to 0.975. Each configuration describes a behavioural user profile of a knowledge worker willing to use AI chatbots in her knowledge-intense tasks. The four profiles contain similarities and differences in causal explanations of the intention to use. The intersection among configurations reveals also the role of a few core factors in explaining usage behaviour towards AI chatbots by knowledge workers in the legal domain. These elements will be discussed in the following sub-sections.

6.1 Profiles of Knowledge Workers Using AI Chatbots

In the first configuration, the presence of AU is combined with the absence of CRI, PRI, LI, and IU. This configuration describes a user profile with a positive attitude towards innovation (i.e., one who would jump on innovations before others) who uses AI chatbots without a critical approach, without perceiving their risks, without interacting with other peers, and without a high intensity of use.

In the second configuration, the presence of CRI and TWO is combined with the absence of PRI, LI, and IU. This configuration describes a user profile that approaches AI chatbot usage critically in a team working context, but without perceiving its risks, interacting with peers, and without a high intensity of use. In this configuration, the significance of the team working factor lets us deduce that the knowledge worker works in a team and not individually as in the previous configuration). Since the level of interaction factor is absent in the causal explanation, we also deduce that the level of team interaction is shallow, or the knowledge worker is part of a team with a common objective but reached with a set of individual and minimal interdependent tasks.

In the third configuration, the presence of AU combines with CRI and TWO and with the absence of PRI and IU. This configuration describes a user profile positively influenced by innovations, who approaches chatbots critically in a teamworking setting but does not perceive the risks connected to them and shows a low usage intensity.

Finally, in the fourth configuration, AU combines with CRI and IU in the absence of TWO, PRI, and LI. This configuration is the only one that includes all factors in the analysis to explain BI. It is worth noticing that this configuration is also the only one that requires the presence of usage intensity for explaining the causal outcome, indicating that this user profile is one in which the engagement with AI chatbots with various and complex tasks. However, it also has the lowest unique coverage score. The configuration describes a user profile with a positive attitude towards innovation who approaches AI chatbot usage critically and uses them frequently at the same time without working in a team, perceiving their risks, and having a low level of interaction.

A cross-read of all the configurations, with the help of the parsimonious solution, allows us to indicate three factors that primarily influence the behavioural intention of knowledge workers in the legal domain to use AI chatbots: attitude towards innovation (AU) on one side and the combination of critical thinking (CRI) and teamwork (TW) on the other.

The presence of the Attitude Towards Innovation factor in three out of the four combinations identified is in line with the role that the literature assigns to early adopters and individuals who are strongly motivated to use digital technologies [26, 30].

Critical thinking has just been explored in relation to the intention to use AI chatbots because these pieces of technology can several times produce inconsistent output [31, 33]. In our analysis, critical thinking appears in all configurations; in one case, it is absent, and in the other three cases, it is present. Out of the other factors combined in the causal explanation, we find it interesting to discuss teamwork since it shows differences across the configurations. In two configurations out of four, teamwork and critical thinking are both present. In the third one, critical thinking is present while teamwork is absent. These configurations indicate a behavioural profile of a person who can critically evaluate, understand, and interpret the experience with a chatbot, either working in a team or alone. In the fourth configuration, critical thinking needs to be present.

Further considerations can be formulated concerning the outcomes that appear in the causal configuration but are negated, indicating that they are not relevant for explaining the behavioural intention to use AI chatbots: perceived risks, level of interaction, and intensity of use. Concerning the last two, the level of interaction is either absent or not significant for explaining the outcome, meaning that the context of the task does not play a role in explaining the behavioural intention. Intensity of use is instead absent in three out of four configurations, while present only in one. Finally, we would like to highlight that perceived risk (PRI) is absent in all configurations. This means that a lack of perception of risks intrinsic to the use of AI chatbots is associated with a willingness by knowledge workers in the legal domain to use AI chatbots.

6.2 *Factors Influencing Knowledge Workers' Adoption of AI Chatbots*

We started this paper to explore factors influencing knowledge workers' behavioural intention to use AI chatbots. In answering our research question, we identify that attitude towards innovation, critical thinking, teamwork, and intensity of use explain the behavioural intention to use, while perceived risk and level of interaction are not associated with use. Out of these factors, only attitude towards innovation is always present, confirming evidence in the literature indicating that users willing to adopt innovation can play a role in adopting AI chatbots among knowledge workers [30].

The other factors are instead ambivalent, as they appear in the solution either present or absent (critical thinking, team working, and intensity of use). Perceived risk is instead always absent, while intensity is mostly absent and present in only one configuration with a low coverage (as a periphery condition).

6.3 *Implications*

The results of our analysis allow us to draw implications regarding the factors influencing the behavioural intention to adopt or use AI chatbots.

One first implication concerns the empirical context of our analysis. Our results are valid for the legal domain because our targeted users originate from that domain. Further research could test the configurations identified outside this domain, to confute or confirm the identified configurations.

Second, the presence of critical thinking and teamworking factors as core conditions for the configurations identified extends the relevance of these factors, already considered by the literature in relation to AI interactions [33–35] but not explicitly explored for the usage of AI chatbots by knowledge workers in the legal domain. Furthermore, considering that these factors are not included in established theoretical models for exploring behavioural intention and attitude towards the use of digital technologies, such as TAM or UTAUT, our results stimulate future research examining the role of these new factors to extend these theoretical models.

A third implication—valid both for research and practice—concerns the perceived risk of using AI chatbots, which is always negated in our configurations. The interpretation of this result says that knowledge workers willing to adopt AI chatbots do not perceive risks in using them. Such a result calls for further research to explore the perceived risks of AI chatbots. We particularly suggest revisiting how the factor is defined since the measurement scale of perceived risk points more specifically at cybersecurity risks [29]. Such a way of measuring risks cannot be fully adequate for exploring risks of AI chatbots, first of all, because this definition of risk does not fully include the challenges implied by hallucination, and second because these systems are used over the cloud, and this usage model might not contribute to the perception of cyber risk. Moreover, the evolving nature of AI technologies suggests that new forms of risk may emerge over time, warranting continuous reassessment of risk perceptions and their implications. On the practice side, this result seems to suggest that usage happens without the perception of risks, and this calls for adequate training and sufficient comprehension of potential risks inherited by knowledge workers in their work duties prior to using AI chatbots.

Finally, still on the practical implication side, our results highlight that while openness to innovation and critical thinking are essential drivers, they are most effective when not accompanied by frequent technology usage or high interaction levels. Organizations should invest in targeted educational programs that not only address potential risks but also highlight the benefits of AI chatbot adoption, ensuring that workers are fully equipped to engage with these tools confidently.

In summary, adopting AI chatbots in the legal domain is significantly influenced by a positive attitude towards innovation and critical thinking, particularly when perceived risks and intensive usage are minimal. Considering that AI chatbots are a recent innovation, and experience and integration inside work systems are only at the beginning, these results call for future research to explore if increased usage intensity will impact perceived risk and intention to use.

7 Limitations and Conclusions

In this work, we studied the behavioural attitudes of 39 knowledge workers in the Italian legal domain concerning the use of AI chatbots in their tasks. Adopting an fsQCA-based methodology, we identified four user profiles and three core factors that explain knowledge workers' attitudes towards AI chatbots. This initial study provides preliminary results that contribute to the literature and could be further expanded by future research, exploring larger samples, or adopting different—qualitative and quantitative—analyses to strengthen the evidence presented.

This work is limited to exploring the adoption of AI chatbots within a specific sector (the legal domain), involving specific users from a cohort selected from the project Giustizia Agile. Future studies may benefit from comparative analyses across different sectors to gain more comprehensive insights. Future research should build over our findings with more diverse samples and explore sector-specific differences to build a more robust understanding of the factors influencing AI adoption.

References

1. Dwivedi, Y. K., Kshetri, N., Hughes, L., Slade, E. L., Jeyaraj, A., Kar, A. K., Baabdullah, A. M., Koohang, A., Raghavan, V., Ahuja, M., Albanna, H., Albashrawi, M. A., Al-Busaidi, A. S., Balakrishnan, J., Barlette, Y., Basu, S., Bose, I., Brooks, L., Buhalis, D., Carter, L., Chowdhury, S., Crick, T., Cunningham, S. W., Davies, G. H., Davison, R. M., Dé, R., Dennehy, D., Duan, Y., Dubey, R., Dwivedi, R., Edwards, J. S., Flavián, C., Gauld, R., Grover, V., Hu, M.-C., Janssen, M., Jones, P., Junglas, I., Khorana, S., Kraus, S., Larsen, K. R., Latreille, P., Laumer, S., Malik, F. T., Mardani, A., Mariani, M., Mithas, S., Mogaji, E., Nord, J. H., O'Connor, S., Okumus, F., Pagani, M., Pandey, N., Papagiannidis, S., Pappas, I. O., Pathak, N., Pries-Heje, J., Raman, R., Rana, N. P., Rehm, S.-V., Ribeiro-Navarrete, S., Richter, A., Rowe, F., Sarker, S., Stahl, B. C., Tiwari, M. K., van der Aalst, W., Venkatesh, V., Viglia, G., Wade, M., Walton, P., Wirtz, J., & Wright, R. (2023). Opinion paper: "So what if ChatGPT wrote it?" Multidisciplinary perspectives on opportunities, challenges and implications of generative conversational AI for research, practice and policy. *International Journal of Information Management, 71*, 102642. https://doi.org/10.1016/j.ijinfomgt.2023.102642
2. Balakrishnan, J., Abed, S. S., & Jones, P. (2022). The role of meta-UTAUT factors, perceived anthropomorphism, perceived intelligence, and social self-efficacy in chatbot-based services? *Technological Forecasting and Social Change, 180*, 121692. https://doi.org/10.1016/J.TECHFORE.2022.121692
3. Meyer-Waarden, L., Pavone, G., Poocharoentou, T., Prayatsup, P., Ratinaud, M., Tison, A., & Torné, S. (2020). How service quality influences customer acceptance and usage of Chatbots? *SMR - Journal of Service Management Research., 4*, 35–51. https://doi.org/10.15358/2511-8676-2020-1-35
4. Baird, A., & Maruping, L. M. (2021). The next generation of research on IS use: A theoretical framework of delegation to and from agentic IS artefacts. *MIS Quarterly, 45*, 342. https://doi.org/10.25300/MISQ/2021/15882
5. Ragin, C. C. (2000). *Fuzzy-set social science*. University of Chicago Press.
6. Sowa, K., Przegalinska, A., & Ciechanowski, L. (2021). Cobots in knowledge work. *Journal of Business Research, 125*, 135–142. https://doi.org/10.1016/j.jbusres.2020.11.038

7. Surawski, B. (2019). Who is a "knowledge worker"—Clarifying the meaning of the term through comparison with synonymous and associated terms. *Management, 23*, 105–133. https://doi.org/10.2478/manment-2019-0007
8. Abdul-Kader, S. A., & Woods, J. C. (2015). Survey on chatbot design techniques in speech conversation systems. *International Journal of Advanced Computer Science and Applications, 6*. https://doi.org/10.14569/IJACSA.2015.060712
9. Sinha, S., Basak, S., Dey, Y., & Mondal, A. (2020). An educational chatbot for answering queries. *Advances in Intelligent Systems and Computing, 937*, 55–60. https://doi.org/10.1007/978-981-13-7403-6_7
10. Chowdhary, K. R. (2020). Natural language processing. *Fundamentals of Artificial Intelligence, 603–649*. https://doi.org/10.1007/978-81-322-3972-7_19
11. Nuruzzaman, M., & Hussain, O. K. (2018). A survey on chatbot implementation in customer service industry through deep neural networks. In *2018 IEEE 15th international conference on e-business engineering (ICEBE)* (pp. 54–61). IEEE. https://doi.org/10.1109/ICEBE.2018.00019
12. Weizenbaum, J. (1966). ELIZA—A computer program for the study of natural language communication between man and machine | enhanced reader. *ACM, 9*, 36–45.
13. Vaswani, A., Brain, G., Shazeer, N., Parmar, N., Uszkoreit, J., Jones, L., Gomez, A.N., Kaiser, Ł., & Polosukhin, I. (2017). Attention is all you need.
14. Kalyan, K. S. (2024). A survey of GPT-3 family large language models including ChatGPT and GPT-4. *Natural Language Processing Journal, 6*, 100048. https://doi.org/10.1016/j.nlp.2023.100048
15. Dias, J., Santos, P.A., Cordeiro, N., Antunes, A., Martins, B., Baptista, J., & Gonçalves, C. (2022). State of the art in artificial intelligence applied to the legal domain.
16. Walters, R., & Novak, M. (2021). Artificial intelligence and law. In *Cyber security, artificial intelligence, data protection & the law* (pp. 39–69). Springer. https://doi.org/10.1007/978-981-16-1665-5_3
17. Akpuokwe, C. U., Adeniyi, A. O., Bakare, S. S., Eneh, N. E., Akpuokwe, C. U., Adeniyi, A. O., & Bakare, S. S. (2024). Legal challenges of artificial intelligence and robotics: A comprehensive review. *Computer Science & IT Research Journal., 5*, 544–561. https://doi.org/10.51594/csitrj.v5i3.860
18. Cortez, E. K., & Maslej, N. (2023). Adjudication of artificial intelligence and automated decision-making cases in Europe and the USA. *European Journal of Risk Regulation., 14*, 457–475. https://doi.org/10.1017/ERR.2023.61
19. Bianchini, F., Calamo, M., De Luzi, F., Macri, M. M., & Mecella, M. (2024). *Enhancing complex linguistic tasks resolution through fine-tuning LLMs, RAG and knowledge graphs (short paper)* (pp. 147–155). Springer. https://doi.org/10.1007/978-3-031-61003-5_13
20. Dietmar, H., & Two kinds of discrimination in AI-based penal decision-making. (2021). *ACM SIGKDD Explorations Newsletter, 23*, 4–13. https://doi.org/10.1145/3468507.3468510
21. Giordano, V., Spada, I., Chiarello, F., & Fantoni, G. (2024). The impact of ChatGPT on human skills: A quantitative study on twitter data. *Technological Forecasting and Social Change, 203*, 123389. https://doi.org/10.1016/j.techfore.2024.123389
22. Fui-Hoon Nah, F., Zheng, R., Cai, J., Siau, K., & Chen, L. (2023). Generative AI and ChatGPT: Applications, challenges, and AI-human collaboration. *Journal of Information Technology Case and Application Research, 25*, 277–304. https://doi.org/10.1080/15228053.2023.2233814
23. Ritala, P., Ruokonen, M., & Ramaul, L. (2024). Transforming boundaries: How does ChatGPT change knowledge work? *Journal of Business Strategy, 45*, 214–220. https://doi.org/10.1108/JBS-05-2023-0094
24. Budhathoki, T., Zirar, A., Njoya, E. T., & Timsina, A. (2024). ChatGPT adoption and anxiety: A cross-country analysis utilising the unified theory of acceptance and use of technology (UTAUT). *Studies in Higher Education, 49*, 831–846. https://doi.org/10.1080/03075079.2024.2333937

25. Awal, M. R., & Haque, M. E. (2024). Revisiting university students' intention to accept AI-powered chatbot with an integration between TAM and SCT: A south Asian perspective. *Journal of Applied Research in Higher Education, 17*, 594. https://doi.org/10.1108/JARHE-11-2023-0514
26. Chatterjee, S., Rana, N. P., Khorana, S., Mikalef, P., & Sharma, A. (2023). Assessing organizational users' intentions and behavior to AI integrated CRM systems: A meta-UTAUT approach. *Information Systems Frontiers, 25*, 1299–1313. https://doi.org/10.1007/s10796-021-10181-1
27. Foroughi, B., Senali, M. G., Iranmanesh, M., Khanfar, A., Ghobakhloo, M., Annamalai, N., & Naghmeh-Abbaspour, B. (2023). Determinants of intention to use ChatGPT for educational purposes: Findings from PLS-SEM and fsQCA. *International Journal of Human Computer Interaction*. https://doi.org/10.1080/10447318.2023.2226495
28. Ekuma, K. (2023). *Rethinking upskilling and reskilling in the age of AI and automation: A fsQCA approach*. https://doi.org/10.20944/PREPRINTS202309.0055.V1
29. Venkatesh, V., Morris, M. G., Davis, G. B., & Davis, F. D. (2003). User acceptance of information technology: Toward a unified view. *MIS Quarterly, 27*, 425–478. https://doi.org/10.2307/30036540
30. Young, A. T., Amara, D., Bhattacharya, A., & Wei, M. L. (2021). Patient and general public attitudes towards clinical artificial intelligence: A mixed methods systematic review. *Lancet Digital Health, 3*, e599–e611. https://doi.org/10.1016/S2589-7500(21)00132-1
31. Xu, Z., Jain, S., & Kankanhalli, M. (2024). Hallucination is inevitable: An innate limitation of large language models.
32. Yellowlees, P. M., & Cook, J. N. (2006). Education about hallucinations using an Internet virtual reality system, a qualitative survey. *Academic Psychiatry, 30*, 534–539.
33. Vargas-Murillo, A. R., de la Asuncion Pari-Bedoya, I. N. M., & de Jesús Guevara-Soto, F. (2023). Challenges and opportunities of AI-assisted learning: A systematic literature review on the impact of ChatGPT usage in higher education. *International Journal of Learning, Teaching and Educational Research, 22*, 122–135. https://doi.org/10.26803/IJLTER.22.7.7
34. Braccini, A. M., & Federici, T. (2013). A measurement model for investigating digital natives and their organisational behaviour. In *Proceedings of the 2013 international conference on information systems (ICIS 2013), Milano*.
35. Lee, J. H., & Song, C. H. (2013). Effects of trust and perceived risk on user acceptance of a new technology service. *Social Behavior and Personality, 41*, 587–597. https://doi.org/10.2224/SBP.2013.41.4.587
36. Skov, S. S., Andersen, J. R., Lauridsen, S., Bab, M., Bundsbæk, M., & Nielsen, M. B. D. (2022). Designing a conversational agent to promote teamwork and collaborative practices using design thinking: An explorative study on user experiences. *Frontiers in Psychology, 13*, 903715. https://doi.org/10.3389/FPSYG.2022.903715/BIBTEX
37. Thompson, J. D., & Bates, F. L. (1957). Technology, organization, and administration. *Administrative Science Quarterly, 2*, 325–343.
38. Ragin, C. (1987). *The comparative method: Moving beyond qualitative and quantitative strategies*. University of California Press.
39. Pappas, I. O., & Woodside, A. G. (2021). Fuzzy-set qualitative comparative analysis (fsQCA): Guidelines for research practice in information systems and marketing. *International Journal of Information Management, 58*, 102310. https://doi.org/10.1016/J.IJINFOMGT.2021.102310
40. Ragin, C. C. (2008). *Redesigning social inquiry: Fuzzy sets and beyond*. The University of Chicago Press.
41. Capatina, A., Micu, A., Micu, A. E., Bouzaabia, R., & Bouzaabia, O. (2018). Country-based comparison of accommodation brands in social media: An fsQCA approach. *Journal of Business Research, 89*, 235–242. https://doi.org/10.1016/J.JBUSRES.2017.11.017
42. Rihoux, B., & Ragin, C.C. (2009). Configurational comparative methods: Qualitative comparative analysis (QCA) and related techniques.

43. Liu, Y., Mezei, J., Kostakos, V., & Li, H. (2017). Applying configurational analysis to IS behavioural research: A methodological alternative for modelling combinatorial complexities. *Information Systems Journal., 27*, 59–89. https://doi.org/10.1111/ISJ.12094
44. Fiss, P. C. (2011). Building better causal theories: A fuzzy set approach to typologies in organization research. *Academy of Management Journal., 54*, 393–420. https://doi.org/10.5465/AMJ.2011.60263120

A Systematic Literature Review on Emerging Technology Adoption Across Time

Rebecca Trivelli and Stefano Za

Abstract This study presents a systematic literature review on the adoption of emerging technologies at the organizational level. Following Okoli's framework we analyzed 48 articles published in journals belonging to AJG ranking. The review identifies key adoption factors and examines how these, along with the organizational, technological, environmental and individual dimensions, are distributed across the pre-adoption, adoption, and post-adoption phases, following Damanpour and Schneider's work (2006). While existing literature has extensively explored the pre- and post-adoption stages, the adoption phase remains relatively underexplored. Moreover, although the post-adoption phase has received some attention, few studies investigate how emerging technologies become routinized and fully integrated into organizational practices. This review contributes a structured overview of the adoption process over time and offers both theoretical and practical insights to support the adoption process, while also providing directions for future research.

Keywords Emerging technologies · Pre-adoption · Adoption · Post-adoption · Systematic literature review

1 Introduction

In recent years, the academic community has shown a growing interest in emerging technologies [1]. Organizations are incentivize to explore the potential benefits of emerging technologies to respond to increased competitive pressure [2, 3]. Emerging technologies are progressively being integrated into organizational processes and

R. Trivelli (✉) · S. Za
University "G.d'Annunzio"of Chieti-Pescara, Pescara, Italy
e-mail: rebecca.trivelli@unich.it; stefano.za@unich.it

A. Tursunbayeva et al. (eds.), *Technology-Driven Transformation*, Lecture Notes in Information Systems and Organisation 79,
https://doi.org/10.1007/978-3-032-01396-5_15

practices [4–9], prompting a reevaluation of established theoretical frameworks in the literature [9]. This change requires a new organizational theory that recognizes their key role in shaping organizational processes and practices, as well as working models [9–11]. Emerging technologies represent radical or disruptive innovations, typically associated with the initial phase of the technological life cycle [12]. They are characterized by attributes, including radical novelty, rapid development, coherence, significant impact, uncertainty, and ambiguity [13]. Since the widespread adoption of emerging technologies in organizations, a thorough understanding of their main characteristics is necessary to support strategic decisions on their adoption [14]. In response to the technological landscape evolution, researchers have developed various models and theories addressing technological adoption, but only two frameworks are related to the organizational dimension [15]: the Diffusion of Innovation Theory (DOI) [16], and the Technology-Organization-Environment framework (TOE) [17], which appears also to be used for investigating the adoption of emerging technologies, in the absence a tailored model on emerging technologies [15].

Despite the significant academic attention on emerging technologies, empirical evidence related to their adoption remains limited [1].

A preliminary investigation into the adoption of emerging technology reveals that existing literature tends to focus on specific contexts and specific emerging technologies. Moreover, the temporal dimensions of adoption, encompassing the pre-adoption, adoption, and post-adoption phases, appear to be underexplored in these studies [1, 18].

To address the gaps, we conduct a systematic literature review to gain insight into existing research on the adoption of emerging technologies. This review examines emerging technologies across a broad spectrum, with a specific focus on digital technologies.

Accordingly, our research question is: *What are the factors that characterize the three phases of adopting an emerging technology?*

The paper is then structured as follows. The next section provides a theoretical background concerning the main characteristics of emerging technologies, the different models of adoption, and the delineation of adoption phases. The methodology section follows, in which we describe the research protocol adopted. Afterwards, the findings and discussion sections. The conclusion section closes this contribution.

2 Theoretical Background

This section outlines the main characteristics of emerging technologies and provides an overview of the most widely used models for organizational adoption, the DOI [16] and TOE frameworks [17]. Moreover, we introduce the conceptual foundation that frames the subsequent analysis, considering the boundaries that define each phase of the adoption process. This theoretical foundation, based on the phase's delineation proposed by Damanpour and Schneider (2006), also guides the discussion, in which we integrate our findings with their work.

2.1 Emerging Technologies Characteristics

Various interpretations have been identified in the literature concerning emerging technologies, but there is no a unique definition (Table 1, Appendix, https://urly.it/319w6q) [13]. To address definitional challenges, a recent work provided by Rotolo, Hicks, and Martin [13], based on the various definitions reviewed in the literature, identify the main qualitative characteristics of emerging technologies as: radical novelty, rapid growth, coherence, prominent socio-economic impact, and uncertainty. Furthermore, the authors define emerging technologies as:

> a radically novel and relatively fast growing technology characterised by a certain degree of coherence persisting over time and with the potential to exert a considerable impact on the socio-economic domain(s) which is observed in terms of the composition of actors, institutions and patterns of interactions among those, along with the associated knowledge production processes. Its most prominent impact, however, lies in the future, and so the emergence phase is still somewhat uncertain and ambiguous [13].

Since the adoption of emerging technologies generates organizational challenges, yet their implementation is pivotal for generating business value [19], a thorough understanding of their main characteristics is necessary in order to support strategic decisions on their adoption [14].

2.2 Adoption Models

Compared to established technologies, emerging technologies introduce distinctive and significant challenges for organizations [19]. As a result, deciding which technologies to invest in has emerged as a key strategic focus for decision-makers [19], especially as they become increasingly embedded in various organizational domains [20].

The evolution of the technological landscape has driven the development of models and theories related to technological adoption. This adoption can be examined from either the end-user perspective or the organization level [15]. While literature presents various models addressing individual technology adoption, such as the Technology Acceptance Model (TAM) [21] and the Unified Theory of Acceptance and Use of Technology (UTAUT) [22], only two models specifically address organizational level technology adoption [15]. The first model, known as the "Diffusion of Innovation" (DOI), was developed by Rogers [16]. The second model, created by Tornatzky and Fleischer [17], is called the "TOE" framework, which stands for "technology, organization, and environment."

In the DOI model, Rogers [16] outlines the different timelines at which organizations adopt innovations, influenced by their different organizational attributes. The Author classifies the adopters as pioneers, early adopters, early majority, late majority, and laggards [23]. Additionally, Rogers [16] identifies various factors that influence the adoption of innovation, including individual characteristics such as leaders' attitudes towards change, and structural characteristics of organizations, including complexity, size, and organizational slack. Additionally, the model considers system openness as an external factor that may influence an organization's adoption process [16].

On the other hand, Tornatzky and Fleischer's TOE model [17] outlines three key contexts that can influence innovation within organizations: technological, organizational, and environmental. The technological context encompasses factors such as technology complexity, compatibility and relative advantage. At the same time, the organizational context includes aspects such as organizational size and top management support [24]. Lastly, the environmental context comprises elements such as competitors, regulation, external relations, and the market [17].

Both models appear to be used to investigate the adoption of emerging technologies, although they are applied in different contexts and to different types of emerging technologies [25, 26].

2.3 Delineation of Adoption Phases

To address the temporal dimension of the adoption process of emerging technologies, we draw inspiration from the works of Damanpour and Schneider (2006), who delineate the boundaries of each phase in the innovation adoption process.

Their work is based on the investigate quantitatively how various antecedents influence each phase, considering three main dimensions: organizational (i.e., size, economic health, unions, complexity, and external communication), environmental (i.e., urbanization, population growth, community wealth, and unemployment rate) and managerial (i.e., age, education, tenure in management, tenure in position). To develop this analysis, they define each phase of innovation adoption, including initiation, adoption, and implementation, based on previous existing studies, such as Rogers (1995) [16]. These phases are grouped under the broad categories of pre-adoption, adoption, and post-adoption [27, 28].

Specifically, the pre-adoption phase (initiation phase) involves activities such as recognizing existing needs, gathering information, searching for potential solutions, evaluating options, and proposing adequate emerging technologies for the organization [27].

The adoption phase involves evaluating proposed ideas from technical, financial, and strategic perspectives, subsequently allocating resources to the chosen technology [27, 28].

The post-adoption phase (implementation phase), focuses on how the utilization of technology within the organization gradually evolves until it becomes completely incorporated into the organization's regular activities [16, 27].

Table 1 Damanpour and Schneider's result

Antecedents	Phases	Effects
Community wealth	All three phases	Positive
Population growth	All three phases	Positive
Urbanization	All three phases	No effects
Employment rate	All three phases	No effects
Organizational size	All three phases	Positive
Organizational complexity	Initiation phase	Positive
Economic health	Adoption phase	Positive
Trade unions	Adoption phase	Negative
External communication	All three phases	Positive
Tenure in management	All three phases	Positive
Tenure in position	Adoption phase	Positive
Attitude toward innovation	All three phases	Positive
Age	All three phases	No effects
Gender	All three phases	No effects
Education	All three phases	No effects

In addition, based on their results, the Authors affirm that, being multiphase, the adoption process of innovation is also multidimensional, as it is influenced by factors across environmental, organizational, managerial, and technological dimensions [27, 28] (Table 1).

This approach, which differentiates the three distinct phases of adoption, appears limited in relation to emerging technologies. This clarification could be relevant for a complete understanding of their adoption process [29]. This overview enables a deeper understanding of organizational dynamics and helps managers to handle the challenges related to the adoption.

We provide a table that presents the factors that emerged from Damanpour and Schneider's (2006) results and their related relevance across the pre-adoption, adoption and post-adoption. This literature provides a delineation of the phases in our work, and in the discussion section, we integrate and compare this literature with our findings.

3 Methodology

To analyze the existing literature on the adoption of emerging technologies, a systematic literature review is performed. This method was chosen for its rigorous methodological approach, transparent review process, comprehensive scope, and reproducibility [30, 31], which allows a correct and unbiased identification [32, 33]. We followed Okoli's [30] proposed guidelines for IS research to ensure and provide a systematic literature review, conducting four phases (Fig. 1). To carry out our analysis we selected Scopus as a database since it is considered the largest citation and abstract database that is capable of covering a wide range of topics [32, 34]. The final sample of papers analyzed, following the outlined phases, comprises 48 articles (Table 3, Appendix, https://urly.it/319w6q).

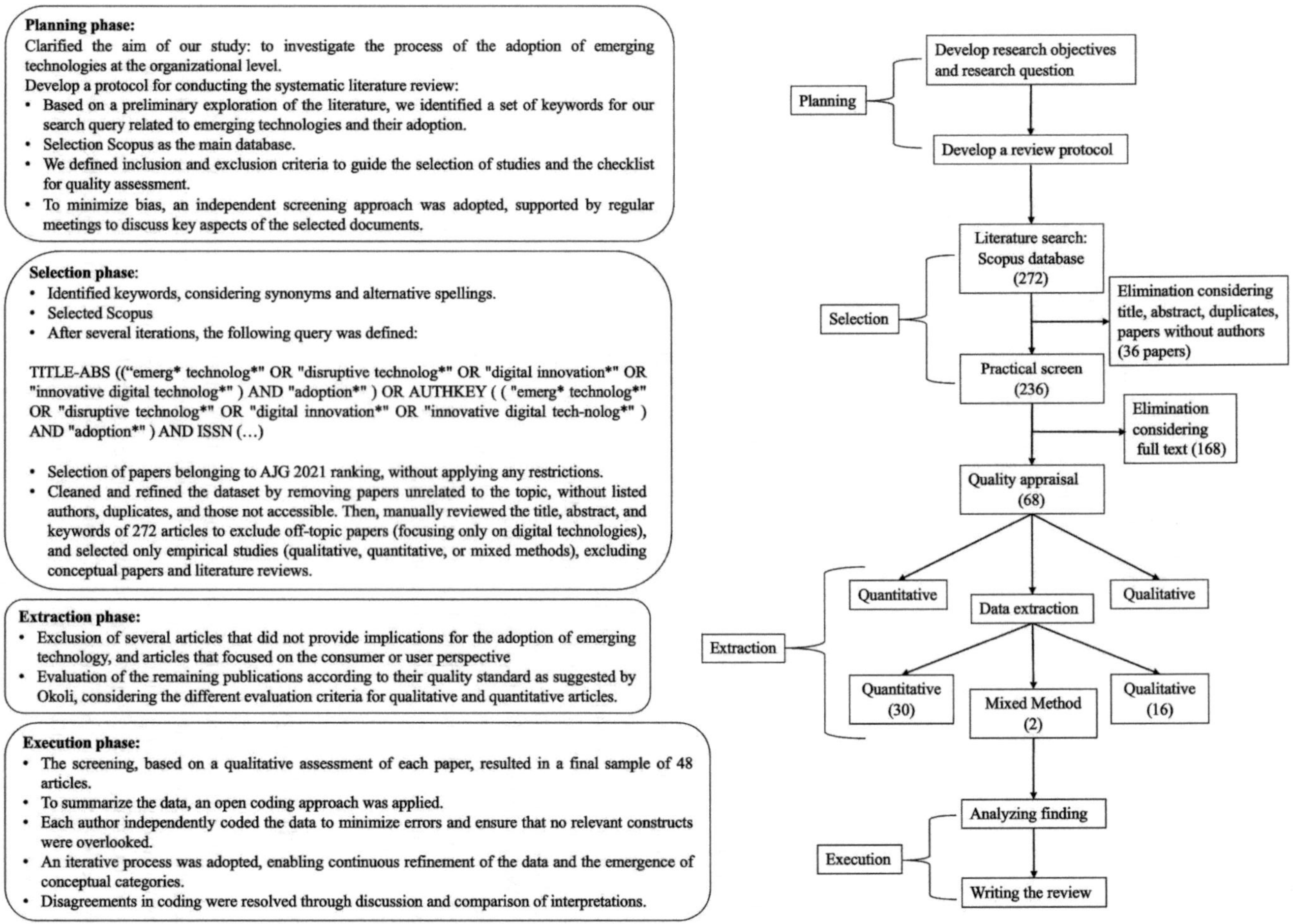

Fig. 1 Okoli’s research protocol adapted

In our analysis, we performed data coding [35] by employing an open coding approach [36–38]. The initial phase of coding aimed to identify the main factors characterizing the emerging technology adoption. These factors were categorized into four dimensions: organizational, technological, environmental, and individual. In the final phase of coding, these dimensions were aggregated with a specific phase of the adoption, such as pre-adoption, adoption and post-adoption. To reduce errors in data collection and ensure that no relevant constructs were omitted, each author independently coded the data [39] and applying an iterative approach [40] throughout the process (Table 4, Appendix, https://urly.it/319w6q).

4 Findings

Our findings reveal that several factors characterize the adoption of emerging technologies within organizations. To offer a clearer and more comprehensive analysis, we have categorized these factors into four key dimensions: environmental, technological, individual, and organizational.

Additionally, the temporal aspect has been considered, with these dimensions being distinguished across the respective phases of pre-adoption, adoption, and post-adoption (Fig. 2). In this regard, while the original phases delineated by Damanpour and Schneider (2006) associate the trial activities within the implementation phases (post-adoption), our findings suggest that pilot tests could be reconsidered as part of the adoption phase. This is the phase in which the alignment of technology within an organization is evaluated.

In the following section, we describe our findings in detail.

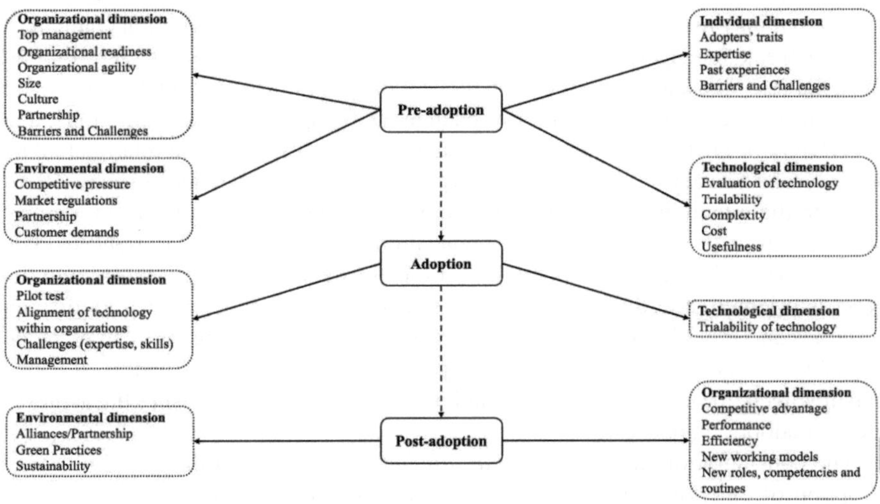

Fig. 2 Pre-adoption, adoption and post-adoption factors and dimensions

4.1 Pre-Adoption Phase

The technological dimension demonstrates that the adoption of emerging technologies by organizations is influenced by the need to maintain competitiveness and the constant evolution of technology [41]. Key factors relevant to the technological dimension include the level of awareness about the usefulness of the technology, its compatibility with the existing organizational infrastructure, its usability and trialability [41]. For example, awareness of the utility of technology can alleviate concerns about its complexity, while compatibility with existing infrastructure can improve usability and reduce risk perceived by employees [41]. Moreover, the perceived benefit of technology increases the attractiveness of adoption [42]. On the other hand, high costs can have a negative impact on adoption, leading to financial stress or uncertainty within the organization [25, 42–45].

In pre-adoption, the *organizational dimension* is characterized by the initial recognition of the need to adopt new technologies [46]. This process is supported by top management [24], through their ability to motivate employees to adopt the technology [25, 43]. Moreover, top management fosters an adequate organizational culture aimed at change that facilitates the adoption process [25, 43]. Another critical factor during the pre-adoption phase is organizational readiness, where organizations assess their internal IT capabilities, resources and expertise, along with the potential benefits of acquiring an emerging technology [42, 45, 47]. In this regard, top management allocates resources effectively, integrates efforts between departments, and reconfigures internal competencies [48–50]. Finally, our findings highlight that organizational size also plays a role: larger companies tend to have greater opportunities than SMEs to invest in technology, employee training, and scientific and market research [51].

In the pre-adoption phase, organizations often face a range of barriers and challenges that may hinder the adoption of emerging technologies. Common challenges include weak managerial support, ineffective communication strategies, limited financial resources, and underdeveloped technological infrastructure. Other critical issues involve employee resistance to change, skill gaps, technical limitations, and uncertainty or mistrust regarding the technology itself, especially in relation to data security and privacy [43, 52, 53]. To overcome these barriers and respond effectively to the intention of adopting emerging technology, organizations can identify their actions as process-related and organizational. The literature has identified key response variables that guide potential actions for managing adoption [46]. On the process-oriented side these include task selections, setting objectives, modifying activities and tool identification. At the organizational level, decisions can be made regarding the organization's culture, the project's scope, the roles and team members involved, the choice of partners, and managing timelines to ensure the achievement of adoption goals [46].

The consideration of *environmental dimension* is crucial in the initial phase of adoption of emerging technologies, as it encompasses the ecosystem in which a organizations operates and can influence the organizational decision-making process [25, 43]. Among external factors identified are market regulations [46], governmental and regulatory pressures, competitive market dynamics, and evolving customer needs [25, 43]. Institutional forces receive particular attention, as they may influence with regulatory, mimetic and coercive pressures, which often lead to isomorphism among organizations (for example, with blockchain) [54]. In this context, perceived barriers [55] such as the lack of a regulatory framework emerge as an impediment to organizations' greater adoption [52, 56, 57]. Moreover, specific social and economic contexts, such as a low cost of labor and prevalent corruption, appear to be factors that discourage the adoption of emerging technologies [26].

Another factor within the environmental dimension is the proximity of companies and the establishment of "clustered firms", which encourage the adoption of emerging technologies through the acquisition of external knowledge and information [58–61].

Considering the *individual dimension*, there are individual factors that can influence the adoption process. This dimension includes adopters' traits such as innovation or risk propensity, previous experience with other emerging technologies, and technical skills [62]. However, individuals who lack familiarity with the technology may encounter difficulties in understanding or accepting it [62]. In this regard, employees' opportunity to experiment with technology increases their confidence, perceived risks and consequent resistance [25].

4.2 Adoption Phase

The adoption phase appears to be characterized by pilot tests, considering organizational and technological dimension. Considering the *organizational dimension*, findings highlight that the organization carries out "use cases" to allow assessment whether the technology and the organization are aligned. If successful, this pilot test will be adopted on a large scale. Instead, if misalignments are found, the process of technological implementation will be interrupted [63]. While the organization evaluates its alignment with technology, challenges may arise, such as those related to the resources, skills, and expertise required. The task of management will be to address these challenges by effectively coordinating resources and expertise, adapting and developing organizational practices suitable for successfully implementing technology within the organization [64].

From the perspective of *technological dimension*, a crucial factor in evaluating the alignment of technology with the organization is the nature of its trialability. This facilitates and enables an iterative adaptation process during the pilot phase, allowing the business case to evolve based on feedback in order to achieve large-scale adoption [63].

4.3 Post-Adoption Phase

Within the *organisational dimension*, the adoption of emerging technologies can lead to significant organizational benefits [65]. For example, these technologies can enhance operational efficiency by reducing complexity and improving processes [65]. In addition, they also contribute to creating safer working environments and reducing workloads, which in turn can enhance employee satisfaction [66]. Furthermore, emerging technologies support higher production efficiency, improved product quality, and lower operating costs [66]. Emerging technologies such as blockchain, for example, simultaneously foster transparency and consumer trust while allowing organizations to optimize product development and marketing strategies through detailed consumer data analysis [51]. The adoption of other emerging technologies, such as artificial intelligence, reconfigures organizational routines [67–69]. This reconfiguration generates the potential for new working models [70], fostering the development of new skills and creating new roles within organizations by reshaping traditional boundaries through technological integration [67–69]. In this regard, it becomes crucial to provide employees with training programs aimed at improving their specific understanding of the role and developing competencies necessary to engage with new technologies [70, 71].

During this phase, key roles are played by top management, and leadership support influences the emerging technology implementation [66] and the achievement of organizational performance [48].

In the post-adoption phase, when considering the *environmental dimension*, partnerships emerge as key factors that can influence the adoption [51]. In addition, the adoption of certain technologies such as AI enables more sustainable production, reduces waste and encourages recycling, thereby positively impacting the external environment [72]. The adoption of Industry 4.0 technologies, such as the Internet of Things (IoT), big data and cloud computing, promotes the creation of digital ecosystems that combine economic growth with environmental sustainability, through the implementation of green practices and a greater commitment to social responsibility [66]. Externally, these technologies help to increase transparency and the availability of information, thus strengthening stakeholder confidence and the efficiency of the services offered [66].

In conclusion, the adoption of emerging technologies is characterized by several factors that correspond to various dimensions, including technological, organizational, individual, and environmental.

The pre-adoption phase involves assessing internal capabilities, external pressures, and identifying potential barriers and challenges. This phase requires strong leadership and the support of management to initiate and guide the organisational change associated with the adoption of emerging technologies.

The analysis of the 48 articles included in this systematic review reveals a significant gap in the literature regarding the adoption phase of emerging technologies. While one study examines pilot tests related to adoption, this phase remains underexplored. This limitation aligns with the studies of Chipizda and Polyviou, Venters, and Pouloudi [1, 18], which point to the lack of focus on the adoption phase.

In contrast, the post-adoption phase is more frequently addressed in literature, with a focus on performance improvement but also in terms of sustainability.

5 Discussion

This study investigates the emerging technology adoption through Damanpour and Schneider's work (2006), which organizes the adoption of innovation into pre-adoption, adoption and post-adoption phases. In our work, we extend Damanpour and Schneider's (2006) delineation of adoption phases to emerging technologies. The analysis reveals that each adoption phase is characterized by specific factors distributed across four dimensions: organizational, environmental, individual, and technological.

The pre-adoption phase corresponds to the initiation phase, which encompasses recognizing existing needs, gathering information, searching for potential solutions, assessing different options, and proposing suitable technology for organization [27]. Our analysis shows that the need to adopt emerging technologies is driven by both organizational necessity and the pursuit of competitive advantages, influenced by technological evolution [41]. This aligns with the initiation phase described in the literature, in which the needs are recognized, and technology solutions are explored. However, our findings provide a more detailed understanding by considering multiple factors characterizing this phase (i.e., leadership, trialability, top management, adopters' traits, regulation) and their corresponding dimensions.

While Damanpour and Schneider's (2006) work identified organizational, managerial and environmental antecedents [27], they do not consider the technological dimensions that emerge in our findings. The technological dimension is relevant given the continuous evolution of technologies. Within this dimension, perceived characteristics of technology, such as complexity, usability, and trialability, are evaluated as factors that can either incentivize the adoption or create challenges and barriers [41].

Within the organizational dimension, several factors influence the adoption process. These encompass top management and leadership support, size, and organizational readiness, which involves assessing infrastructure, skills and competencies. Conversely, challenges such as a lack of infrastructure, funding, and resistance to change may hinder the adoption process [25, 42, 43, 45, 47]. The importance of organizational size as a facilitating factor is a point of convergence with Damanpour and Schneider's findings [27].

The environmental dimension encompasses factors that can either foster or constrain the adoption process, including institutional pressure, regulations, stakeholders' perspectives, and market competitiveness. While Damanpour and Schneider (2006) address the environmental dimensions they focus on specific factors such as urbanization, population growth [27]. Conversely, our analysis highlights institutional and regulatory factors as relevant environmental influences on organizations' adoption [52, 56, 57].

The individual dimension in our findings emphasizes adopters' traits such as openness to innovation, aversion to risk, and past experiences, all of which can influence the adoption journey [62]. Openness to innovation is a factor shared with Damanpour and Schneider's work (2006), where it is emphasizes in the managerial dimension [27].

The adoption phase is characterized by organizational and technological dimension. According to Damapour and Schneider (2006), this phase involves evaluating proposed ideas from technical, financial, and strategic perspectives, subsequently followed by the decision of adoption and the allocation of resources to the chosen technology [27, 28]. Our findings reveal that, during this phase, organizations seek to align technology with the organization by developing a pilot test. This phase is characterized not only by possible challenges that may arise, but also by continuous learning and adaptation to ensure the success of the pilot test and enabling wide-scale adoption. In some cases, organizations may decide to discontinue the adoption process if significant misalignments between the technology and organizational context are identified, thus avoiding implementations that would not yield the expected outcomes [63, 64]. Although a study focuses on pilot tests, it remains evident that there is a lack of studies concerning "how" effectively an emerging technology is adopted. In this regard, while Damanpour and Schneider (2006) associate the trial activities in the implementation phase [27], our findings indicate that pilot testing and experimentation occur before the implementation phase. In our view, the pilots serve as a concrete evaluation of the alignment of the technology within organization, including its technical, financial and strategic aspects. While Damanpour and Schneider (2006) do not consider the pilot test in this phase, they describe the adoption phase as involving the evaluation of innovation along these aspects [27].

Additionally, the difference between Damanpour and Schneider's work (2006) lies in their consideration of specific organizational factors, such as economic health, which has a positive effect, and union presence, which has a negative effect [27]. Conversely, our findings highlight the organizational dimension, in terms of aligning technology within the organization, while also emphasizing the technology dimension [64].

In the post-adoption phase (implementation phase), the focus is on how the use of technology within the organization gradually evolves until it becomes fully integrated into the organization's regular activities [16, 27]. Our study confirms that previous literature has primarily focused on the organizational dimension, examining the impact of adopting emerging technologies in terms of new working models, routines, skills, tasks, and business models [67–69]. However, the explanation of how the redefinition of work processes, roles, and organizational structures effectively occurs within organizations remains limited. Despite this gap, the studies analyzed highlight how the adoption of emerging technologies contributes to increased performance and enhanced efficiency, leading to an overall perceived improvement [65].

Beyond the organizational dimension, the environmental dimension is addressed in the post-adoption phase. The adoption of emerging technologies contributes not only to improved performance but also to sustainability and the development of partnerships [66, 73]. Similarly to performance, these factors are not explicitly addressed by Damanpour and Schneider's (2006) definition of the post-adoption [27]. Our findings, therefore, integrate and extend their proposed definition of the post-adoption phase, incorporating both factors (performance and sustainability) [66].

Overall, the findings in the pre-adoption phase align with Damanpour and Schneider's initiation phase (2006). However, we propose repositioning the pilot test in the adoption phase rather than the implementation phase. This result could represent blurred boundaries between these phases, which may depend on factors such organizational context, technology adopted, size, or management decision (Fig. 3). Finally, the post-adoption phase is partially aligned with Damanpour and Schneider's work (2006), which includes the routinization of technology, but also additional insights concerning performance and sustainability factors, not addressed in their work.

In conclusion, our work not only highlights the specific factors and associated dimensions involved in each phase, differently from Damanpour and Schneider's work (2006), which considers only specific factors, but also offers an integrative perspective that refines and complements their delineations of the phases. By addressing piloting tests, performance and sustainability outcomes, our findings contribute to providing an understanding of how emerging technologies are adopted, considering the temporal aspect, and extending their work specifically outlined for innovations to emerging technologies.

Based on our findings, we develop some future research questions respectively for the three temporal dimensions (Table 2).

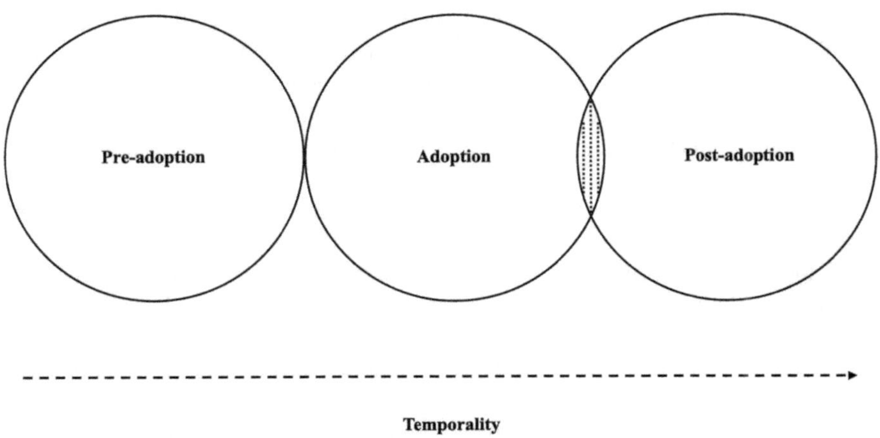

Fig. 3 Blurred boundaries of pre-adoption and adoption phases

Table 2 Ideas for future research

Pre-adoption	• How do ethical concern influence organizations decision in the pre-adoption phase of emerging technologies? • How does the characteristic of emerging technologies influence their adoption? How do managers and leaders effectively respond to these influences? • Which personality traits of decision-makers facilitate the adoption of emerging technologies in the pre-adoption phase? • What contractual power exist between the organizations and the emerging technology providers during the pre-adoption phase?
Adoption phase	• What practices lead to effective adoption of emerging technology? • What are the main challenges and barriers during the adoption phase?
Post adoption	• What organizational workarounds emerge during the implementation phase, and what are the causes? • What factors contribute to the failure of the adoption process? A case study of a failed adoption. • To what extent are processes, structures, and routines redefined during the post-adoption phase?

6 Conclusion

This systematic literature review presents the key findings of existing research conducted to investigate the process of adopting emerging technologies. The first theoretical contribution highlights the current state of the art in adopting emerging technologies, considering the temporal aspect of the process, drawing on the work of Damanpour and Schneider (2006). It highlights the limited empirical investigation into the adoption phase concerning "how" emerging technologies are effectively adopted. Moreover, the reviews reveal that few studies have explored "how" work processes, roles, and organizational structures are redefined in the post-adoption phase.

The third contribution is the positioning of pilot testing within the adoption phase, highlighting the blurred boundaries of the phases of the adoption process. These boundaries may depend on organizational context, size, technology, and managerial decisions. Moreover, we refine and complement the phase delineations proposed by Damanpour and Schneider (2006), who focus on a more limited set of factors.

Additionally, this study provides a starting point for further studies, offering research questions on the topic under investigation (Table 2).

At the level of practical contribution, this work aims to provide more in-depth insights into the pre-adoption, adoption and post-adoption phases. It offers managers a clear understanding of the adoption process they are required to manage and lead efficiently over time [29]. It allows for a better understanding of the possible challenges associated with the adoption of emerging technologies, while at the same time providing an overview of organizational dynamics and implications.

The limitations of this paper are firstly, the only one database, Scopus, further research could integrate other databases such as Web of Sciences and EBSCO, Second, we included in our dataset only papers published in the AJG journals, further steps could also include the proceedings of the main leading conferences, enriching the dataset, to grasp further issues connected with the adoption of emerging technologies.

References

1. Chipidza, W., Li, Y., Turetken, O., Mashatan, A., & Olfman, L. (2023). Quantum computing and IS - Harnessing the opportunities of emerging technologies. *Communications of the Association for Information Systems, 52*, 556–574. https://doi.org/10.17705/1cais.05219
2. Lasi, H., Fettke, P., Kemper, H. G., Feld, T., & Hoffmann, M. (2014). Industry 4.0. *Business and Information Systems Engineering, 6*, 239–242. https://doi.org/10.1007/s12599-014-0334-4
3. Blichfeldt, H., & Faullant, R. (2021). Performance effects of digital technology adoption and product & service innovation—A process-industry perspective. *Technovation, 105*, 102275. https://doi.org/10.1016/j.technovation.2021.102275
4. Faraj, S., Pachidi, S., & Sayegh, K. (2018). Working and organizing in the age of the learning algorithm. *Information and Organization, 28*, 62–70. https://doi.org/10.1016/j.infoandorg.2018.02.005
5. Malone, T. (2004). *The future of work*. Harvard Bussiness School Press.
6. von Krogh, G., & von Hippel, E. (2006). The promise of research on open source software. *Management Science, 52*, 975–983.
7. Kane, G. (2019). The technology fallacy: People are the real key to digital transformation. *Research-Technology Management, 62*, 44–49. https://doi.org/10.1080/08956308.2019.1661079
8. Davis, G. F., & Sinha, A. (2021). Varieties of Uberization: How technology and institutions change the organization(s) of late capitalism. *Organization Theory, 2*. https://doi.org/10.1177/2631787721995198
9. Bailey, D. E., Faraj, S., Hinds, P. J., Leonardi, P. M., & Von Krogh, G. (2022). We are all theorists of technology now: A relational perspective on emerging technology and organizing. *Organization Science*.
10. Bailey, D. E. (2022). Emerging technologies at work: Policy ideas to address negative consequences for work, workers, and society. *ILR Review, 75*, 527–551. https://doi.org/10.1177/00197939221076747
11. Vial, G. (2019). Understanding digital transformation: A review and a research agenda. *The Journal of Strategic Information Systems, 28*, 118–144. https://doi.org/10.1016/j.jsis.2019.01.003
12. Cozzens, S., Gatchair, S., Kang, J., Kim, K. S., Lee, H. J., Ordóñez, G., & Porter, A. (2010). Emerging technologies: Quantitative identification and measurement. *Technology Analysis & Strategic Management, 22*, 361–376. https://doi.org/10.1080/09537321003647396
13. Rotolo, D., Hicks, D., & Martin, B. R. (2015). What is an emerging technology? *Research Policy, 44*, 1827–1843. https://doi.org/10.1016/j.respol.2015.06.006
14. Boon, W., & Moors, E. (2008). Exploring emerging technologies using metaphors – A study of orphan drugs and pharmacogenomics. *Social Science & Medicine, 66*, 1915–1927. https://doi.org/10.1016/j.socscimed.2008.01.012
15. Oliveira, T., & Martins, M. F. (2010). Information technology adoption models at firm level: Review of literature. In *4th European conference on information management and evaluation, ECIME 2010* (pp. 312–322).
16. Rogers, E. M. (1995). Diffusion of innovations.
17. Tornatzky, L., & Fleischer, M. (1990). *The process of technology innovation*. Lexington Books.
18. Polyviou, A., Venters, W., & Pouloudi, N. (2024). Distant but close: Locational, relational and temporal proximity in cloud computing adoption. *Journal of Information Technology, 39*, 71–93. https://doi.org/10.1177/02683962231186161

19. Tiwana, A. (2014). Separating signal from noise: Evaluating emerging technologies. *MIS Quarterly*.
20. Bailey, D., Faraj, S., Hinds, P., von Krogh, G., & Leonardi, P. (2019). Special issue of organization science: Emerging technologies and organizing. *Organization Science, 30*, 642–646. https://doi.org/10.1287/orsc.2019.1299
21. Davis, F. D., Bagozzi, R. P., & Warshaw, P. R. (1989). User acceptance of computer-technology - A comparison of 2 theoretical-models. *Management Science, 35*, 982–1003.
22. Venkatesh, V., Morris, M. G., Davis, G. B., & Davis, F. D. (2003). User acceptance of information technology: Toward a unified view. *MIS Quarterly, 27*, 425–478.
23. Beatty, R. C., Shim, J. P., & Jones, M. C. (2001). Factors influencing corporate web site adoption: A time-based assessment. *Information Management, 38*, 337–354. https://doi.org/10.1016/S0378-7206(00)00064-1
24. Zhu, K., Kraemer, K. L., & Xu, S. (2006). The process of innovation assimilation by firms in different countries: A technology diffusion perspective on e-business. *Management Science, 52*, 1557. https://doi.org/10.1287/mnsc.1050.0487
25. Matsepe, N. T., & Van Der Lingen, E. (2020). *Determinants of emerging technologies adoption in the South African financial sector* (pp. 1–12).
26. Bhattacharyya, S. S., & Shaw, Y. (2021). *Emerging technologies in Indian mining industry: An exploratory empirical investigation regarding the adoption challenges*. https://doi.org/10.1108/JSTPM-03-2021-0048
27. Damanpour, F., & Schneider, M. (2006). Phases of the adoption of innovation in organizations: Effects of environment, organization and top managers. *British Journal of Management, 17*, 215–236.
28. Karahanna, E., Straub, D. W., & Chervany, N. L. (1999). Information technology adoption across time: A cross-sectional comparison of pre-adoption and post-adoption beliefs. *MIS Quarterly, S1*(23), 183–213.
29. Okoli, C. (2015). Critical realist considerations for literature reviews.
30. Fink, A. (2019). Conducting research literature reviews: From the internet to paper.
31. Kitchenham, B., Brereton, O. P., Budgen, D., Turner, M., Bailey, J., & Linkman, S. (2009). Systematic literature reviews in software engineering—A systematic literature review. *Information and software technology, 51*, 7–15. https://doi.org/10.1016/j.infsof.2008.09.009
32. Szvetits, M., & Zdun, U. (2016). Systematic literature review of the objectives, techniques, kinds, and architectures of models at runtime. *Software and Systems Modeling, 15*, 31–69. https://doi.org/10.1007/s10270-013-0394-9
33. Klein, H., & Myers, M. D. (1999). A set of principles for conducting and evaluating. *MIS Quarterly, 23*, 67–93.
34. Atkins, S., Lewin, S., Smith, H., Engel, M., Fretheim, A., & Volmink, J. (2008). Conducting a meta-ethnography of qualitative literature: Lessons learnt. *BMC Medical Research Methodology, 8*, 1–10. https://doi.org/10.1186/1471-2288-8-21
35. Walsh, D., & Downe, S. (2005). Meta-synthesis method for qualitative research: A literature review. *Journal of Advanced Nursing, 50*, 204–211. https://doi.org/10.1111/j.1365-2648.2005.03380.x
36. Hoon, C. (2013). Meta-synthesis of qualitative case studies: An approach to theory building. *Organizational Research Methods, 16*, 522–556. https://doi.org/10.1177/1094428113484969
37. Noblit, G. W., & Hare, R. D. (1998). *Meta-ethnography: Synthesizing qualitative studies*. Sage.
38. Miles, M. B., & Huberman, A. M. (1994). *Qualitative data analysis: An expanded sourcebook*. Sage.
39. Locke, K. (2001). *Grounded theory in management research*. Sage.
40. Alismaili, S. Z. (2021). Organisational-level assessment of cloud computing adoption: Evidence from the Australian SMEs. *Journal of Global Information Management (JGIM), 28*, 73–89. https://doi.org/10.4018/JGIM.2020040104
41. Zabel, C., Telkmann, V., Zabel, C., & Telkmann, V. (2020). The adoption of emerging technology-driven media innovations. A comparative study of the introduction of virtual

and augmented reality in the media and manufacturing industries manufacturing industries. *Journal of Media Business Studies, 00*, 1–32. https://doi.org/10.1080/16522354.2020.1839172
42. Almahamid, S. M., & Fataih, M. (2022). *AI: What determines 3D printing adoption in the GCC region?* (pp. 912–940). https://doi.org/10.1108/JSTPM-02-2022-0037
43. Cho, J., Cheon, Y., Jun, J. W., & Lee, S. (2021). Digital advertising policy acceptance by out-of-home advertising firms: A combination of TAM and TOE framework. *International Journal of Advertising*. https://doi.org/10.1080/02650487.2021.1888562
44. Mitra, T., & Kapoor, R. (2023). Studying key antecedents of disruptive technology adoption in the digital supply chain: An Indian perspective. *International Journal of Emerging Markets, 18*, 4669–4689. https://doi.org/10.1108/IJOEM-07-2021-1052
45. Selensky, S. (2022). *Towards a contingency theoretic perspective on technology pre-adoption in supply chain management*. https://doi.org/10.1108/IJLM-12-2021-0598
46. Pai, V., & Chandra, S. (2022). Exploring factors influencing organizational adoption of artificial intelligence (AI) in corporate social responsibility (CSR). *Initiatives, 14*, 82–115. https://doi.org/10.17705/1pais.14504
47. Chatterjee, S., Chaudhuri, R., & Vrontis, D. (2022). *Examining the impact of adoption of emerging technology and supply chain resilience on firm performance: Moderating role of absorptive capacity and leadership support*. https://doi.org/10.1109/TEM.2021.3134188
48. Eisenhardt, K. M., & Martin, J. A. (2000). Dynamic capabilities: What are they? *Strategic Management Journal*.
49. Roux, M., Chowdhury, S., Kumar, P., Vann, E., Vijay, Y., & Amelie, P. (2023). Small and medium-sized enterprises as technology innovation intermediaries in sustainable business ecosystem: Interplay between AI adoption, low carbon management and resilience. *Annals of Operations Research*. https://doi.org/10.1007/s10479-023-05760-1
50. Silvestri, R., Adamashvili, N., & Galati, A. (2023). *How blockchain technology generates a trust-based competitive advantage in the wine industry: A resource based view perspective* (Vol. 35, pp. 713–736). https://doi.org/10.1108/EBR-10-2022-0217
51. Rathore, B. (2022). *Identification and analysis of adoption barriers of disruptive technologies in the logistics industry*. https://doi.org/10.1108/IJLM-07-2021-0352
52. Steenhuis, H. J., & Pretorius, L. (2016). Consumer additive manufacturing or 3D printing adoption: An exploratory study. *Journal of Manufacturing Technology Management, 27*, 990–1012. https://doi.org/10.1108/JMTM-01-2016-0002
53. Jiaxin, K., Huiyue, L., & Rob, Y. (2023). Understanding the development of blockchain - Empowered metaverse tourism: An institutional perspective. *Information Technology & Tourism, 25*, 585–603. https://doi.org/10.1007/s40558-023-00262-z
54. El-haddadeh, R. (2020). *Digital innovation dynamics influence on organisational adoption: The case of cloud computing services* (pp. 985–999).
55. Kurpjuweit, S., Schmidt, C. G., Kl, M., & Wagner, S. M. (2021). *Blockchain in additive manufacturing and its impact on supply chains* (Vol. 42, pp. 46–70). https://doi.org/10.1111/jbl.12231
56. Chen, F., Hu, K., Lin, S., & Hsu, M. (2023). A decision framework for assessing and improving the barriers of blockchain technology adoption. *Journal of Global Information Management, 31*(7), 1–34. https://doi.org/10.4018/JGIM.330134
57. Molina-morales, F.X., Martínez-cháfer, L.: Disruptive technology adoption, particularities for the clustered firms. (2018).
58. Virmani, N., Author, C., Singh, R. K., Agarwal, V., Aktas, E., Kingdom, U., & Economy, C. (2024). *Artificial intelligence applications for responsive healthcare supply chains: A decision-making framework* (pp. 1–41).
59. Stock, G. N., Greis, N. P., & Fischer, W. A. (2001). Absorptive capacity and new product development. *The Journal of High Technology Management Research, 12*, 77–91. https://doi.org/10.1016/S1047-8310(00)00040-7
60. Uzzi, B. (1997). Social structure and competition in interfirm networks: The paradox of embeddedness. *Administrative Science Quarterly, 42*. https://doi.org/10.2307/2393808

61. Khanna, P. (2022). Will adoption of blockchain technology be challenging: Evidence from Indian banking industry. *Qualitative Research in Financial Markets, 15*, 361–384. https://doi.org/10.1108/QRFM-01-2022-0003
62. Maghazei, O., & Lewis, M. A. (2022). *Emerging technologies and the use case: A multi-year study of drone adoption* (pp. 560–591). https://doi.org/10.1002/joom.1196
63. Khanagha, S., Volberda, H., Sidhu, J., & Oshri, I. (2013). Management innovation and adoption of emerging technologies process innovation: An inter-organizational perspective. *European Management Review, 10*, 51–67. https://doi.org/10.1111/emre.12004
64. Sheel, A. (2019). Effect of blockchain technology adoption on supply chain adaptability, agility, alignment and performance. *Management Research Review, 42*, 1353–1374. https://doi.org/10.1108/MRR-12-2018-0490
65. Nurul, M., Reza, H., Jayashree, S., Agamudai, C., Angappa, M., & Mohiuddin, M. (2024). Towards sustainable sustainability: Exploring the impact of antecedents on industry 4.0 and sustainable performance of organizations—An empirical investigation. *Annals of Operations Research*. https://doi.org/10.1007/s10479-024-05826-8
66. Shen, L., Zhang, X., & Liu, H. (2022). *Digital technology adoption, digital dynamic capability, and digital transformation performance of textile industry: Moderating role of digital innovation orientation* (pp. 2038–2054). https://doi.org/10.1002/mde.3507
67. Asatiani, A., Kamarainen, T., & Penttinen, E. (2019). Unexpected problems associated with the federated IT governance structure in robotic process automation (RPA) deployment. (working paper).
68. Gardner, E. C., & Bryson, J. R. (2021). The dark side of the industrialisation of accountancy: Innovation, commoditization, colonization and competitiveness. *Industry and Innovation, 28*, 42–57. https://doi.org/10.1080/13662716.2020.1738915
69. Iaia, L., Basile, F., & Cavallo, F. (2023). The scientific approach to facilitate the human-machine interactions. The case of Carrozzeria Fratelli Basile. *Journal of Management History*. https://doi.org/10.1108/JMH-12-2022-0087
70. Pironti, M., & Iaia, L. (2022). *Innovazione e intelligenze artificiali e aumentate*. Riflessioni evolutive.
71. Dey, P. K., Chowdhury, S., Abadie, A., Vann Yaroson, E., & Sarkar, S. (2023). Artificial intelligence-driven supply chain resilience in Vietnamese manufacturing small-and medium-sized enterprises. *International Journal of Production Research, 45*, 1–40.
72. Silvestri, R., Adamashvili, N., Fiore, M., & Galati, A. (2023). How blockchain technology generates a trust-based competitive advantage in the wine industry: A resource based view perspective. *European Business Review, 35*, 713–736. https://doi.org/10.1108/EBR-10-2022-0217

Determinants of Blockchain Adoption in Accounting: A Case Study Analysis

Alessandro Scaletti, Sabrina Pisano, and Domenica Lavorato

Abstract This study explores the factors that influence the company's decision to adopt blockchain technology in accounting. To achieve this aim, the research employs the Technology-Organization-Environment framework and adopts a qualitative case study methodology, focusing on a leading provider of innovative solutions for document management and collaboration. The findings show that the blockchain solution enhances the company's overall information system by improving the reliability and transparency of accounting records, increasing transaction traceability, and reducing costs and human error. Moreover, the results highlight that technological factors play a more significant role than organizational or environmental factors in the adoption process. This study contributes to the literature on blockchain by offering empirical evidence from the perspective of a blockchain provider. It also adds to previous research by examining blockchain adoption within the aviation industry. From a practical perspective, the research provides suggestions to companies that want to adopt blockchain by revealing the antecedents of the implementation, especially regarding the supply chain.

Keywords Blockchain · Information system · TOE framework

1 Introduction

Blockchain is one of the most disruptive and promising emerging technologies, and it appears to have significant potential to impact the accounting field [1]. Blockchain adoption has become synonymous with considerable disruption to traditional business operations [2] and models embedded with centralized architectures, third-party

A. Scaletti · S. Pisano · D. Lavorato (✉)
"Parthenope" University of Naples, Naples, Italy
e-mail: alessandro.scaletti@uniparthenope.it; sabrina.pisano@uniparthenope.it; domenica.lavorato@uniparthenope.it

A. Tursunbayeva et al. (eds.), *Technology-Driven Transformation*, Lecture Notes in Information Systems and Organisation 79,
https://doi.org/10.1007/978-3-032-01396-5_16

intermediaries, and trusted verification [3, 4]. Although blockchain initially gained recognition as the technology underpinning the cryptocurrency Bitcoin, its ability to transform payment processing, invoicing, inventory tracking, contract management, and other documentations has significant accounting implications as well [5].

Due to its nature as a shared ledger, blockchain has the potential to revolutionize accounting by introducing a more efficient, transparent and secure way of managing financial records [6–8]. This technology can be used to record inventory and ownership, maintain invoices, process payments, and store contracts and documents, offering numerous benefits to the accounting field [5, 9].

Blockchain technology has the potential to significantly disrupt the accounting profession, with broad implications for professionals, practitioners, firms, and regulators [10–12]. It can fundamentally reshape how information is exchanged, how records are maintained, and how value is stored across sectors [13]. Therefore, it is essential to understand this technology better and assess its potential and limitations [14].

In recent years, scholars have increasingly focused on the potential of blockchain in accounting, which has become one of the most discussed topics in the field [10–12]. However, despite its promise, there is still limited empirical research on its actual impact [11]. In this regard, several scholars have called for more empirical research and case studies to better understand the blockchain adoption and its effects on accounting [14–16].

This paper aims at answering to previous call for research by investigating the factors influencing the company's decision to adopt blockchain in accounting. Specifically, the study applies the Technology-Organization-Environment (TOE) framework to explore the drivers of adoption [17]. This framework, widely used in prior studies on technology adoption [10], classifies influencing factors into three dimensions: Technology, Organization and Environment. The TOE framework has also been used to investigate the antecedents of blockchain adoption [18–20]. Most previous studies focused on the adoption of blockchain in the supply chain systems [19] or in the freight logistics industry [20]. To the best of our knowledge, the study conducted by Akter and colleagues [18] represents the only application of the TOE framework specifically aimed at examining blockchain implementation in the accounting domain. Through interviews with blockchain experts and accounting professionals, their research identified nine context-specific factors influencing the decision to adopt blockchain in accounting. This paper extends the study of Akter and colleagues [18] by providing further empirical evidence on the determinants of blockchain adoption in accounting, based on an in-depth interview with the CEO of a blockchain solution provider.

The findings show that the blockchain solution enhances the company's overall information system by increasing the reliability and transparency of accounting records, improving transaction traceability, and reducing costs and human errors. Furthermore, the analysis highlights that technological factors have a greater influence than organizational and environmental ones in the adoption process.

The remainder of the paper is structured as follows. Section 2 provides a review of the existing literature on blockchain and accounting and describes the TOE framework. Section 3 presents the research methodology, and Sect. 4 discusses the key findings. Finally, Sect. 5 offers concluding remarks, discussing the research's main contributions, implications, and limitations, and outlining directions for future research.

2 Literature Review

2.1 Blockchain and Accounting

Blockchain is a distributed digital ledger designed to record and share information across a peer-to-peer network [21]. In a blockchain, each transaction is represented by a data block, and each new block contains information about the previous one, which is immutable [9]. This structure ensures that each block of information is recorded and verified in real time, creating an immutable, chronological, and transparent history of transactions [22–24]. Blockchain's ability to store and encrypt various types of data in a way that cannot be deleted, destroyed, or changed, ensures the immutability, accuracy and reliability of the information [5, 21, 25, 26]. Blockchain and smart contracts can be used to securely store accounting data, ensuring that records are tamper-proof and trustworthy. Additionally, relevant information can be instantly shared with stakeholders, enhancing the transparency and verifiability of business data.

Unlike traditional databases, where information is stored in a central ledger managed by a central authority that controls user access, blockchains distribute a live copy of the ledger to each network participant. This means that every user has an identical copy of the ledger on their local system, which is updated in real time whenever a new transaction is added [5]. As a result, blockchain transforms accounting information systems and transactions, shifting from centralized database to a decentralized distributed ledger [27, 28].

Several scholars define blockchain as a new type of accounting information system that records verified transactions on a secure ledger [5, 29]. Its distributed, decentralized and immutable nature offers the potential to address limitations of traditional accounting systems by introducing triple-entry accounting and enabling real-time reporting [25, 28, 30].

Triple-entry accounting represents a significant advancement in the recording and verification of financial transactions [31, 32]. Although the concept of triple-entry accounting is not new [33, 34], blockchain technology has enabled its practical implementation. In traditional double-entry accounting, each transaction is recorded twice. Triple-entry accounting introduces a third component to this process: a cryptographic signature [33]. This third entry is stored on the blockchain, creating a decentralized and immutable ledger shared among relevant parties. A cryptographic receipt of the transaction is recorded on the blockchain, acting as a third entry that is visible and verifiable by both transaction parties and any authorized third parties. The cryptographic properties of blockchain ensure that, once recorded, a transaction cannot be altered or deleted. All parties involved can view and verify the blockchain records, increasing transparency and trust in financial information. By embedding the third accounting entry into a blockchain, a transparent, cryptographically secure, and self-verifying accounting information system is created, facilitating reliable data sharing between business entities [5]. In such a system, every transaction generates a blockchain entry in addition to the traditional double-entry records.

Transactions recorded on the blockchain are updated in real-time, allowing for immediate verification and reducing the delays typically associated with traditional accounting systems [30]. Such systems enable near real-time reporting by instantly broadcasting accounting information to interested parties, including managers, auditors, creditors, and stakeholders [5, 8, 25, 26, 35].

Several accounting studies have highlighted the benefits of adopting and implementing blockchain technology, including enhanced reliability and transparency of accounting records, improved traceability of transactions, cost reductions, real-time reporting, continuous auditing and a decrease in human error and fraud [5, 8, 22, 24, 30, 36]. Blockchain's decentralized nature eliminates the need for intermediaries to verify and record transactions, thereby reducing the costs of verification, information processing, and the risk of failure [7, 27]. The triple-entry ledger system inherent to blockchain provides independent verification of transactions, increasing trust in the system [5, 25, 37]. By automating transaction recording through smart contracts and minimizing the reliance on intermediaries, blockchain can significantly reduce the time and costs associated with traditional accounting processes. Routine tasks such as reconciliations and verifications can be automated, enabling accountants to focus on more strategic activities [8, 22, 38]. Real-time access to the ledger, combined with a consensus protocol for adding transactions and validation by network participants, enhances the transparency and trustworthiness of accounting information. The immutable nature of blockchain makes the manipulation or alteration of records virtually impossible [26, 39]. As a result, blockchain reduces economic uncertainty, agency costs, and information asymmetry by providing transparent and reliable records. It also improves data quality, increases trust, and significantly reduces the risk of human error and fraud [16].

Despite these benefits, other studies have discussed the challenges and risks associated with blockchain adoption in accounting. Key concerns include cybersecurity, particularly the privacy and security of corporate data [40–42]. Additional challenges relate to the scalability and flexibility of blockchain architectures, as well as the integration of blockchain with existing accounting information systems [16, 43].

However, despite the growing interest in blockchain within the accounting domain, the academic literature is still in its infancy and far from mature [44]. Empirical evidence on the topic is limited. Much of the current research is conceptual, focusing on the broader implications of blockchain technology and highlighting its theoretical benefits and challenges [16, 43]. Furthermore, several studies have examined blockchain adoption in the agrifood supply chain, with a limited focus on the management of documents related to certification and traceability purposes [42, 43].

Although blockchain technology holds significant potential to transform the accounting profession, empirical studies investigating its actual impact are still scarce [11]. Consequently, scholars have called for more empirical research and case studies to better understand the adoption and implications of blockchain in accounting [14–16]. Recent research [45] also highlights the need to explore blockchain's potential for data tracking and sharing, as well as the broader opportunities offered by decentralized networks for accounting and control.

2.2 *The TOE Framework*

The TOE framework was developed by Tornatzky and Fleischer [17] in 1990 and is considered a robust and comprehensive model for investigating the factors influencing technology implementation [10], primarily for two reasons. First, the TOE model enables the investigation of both internal and external factors that may affect technology adoption [46]. Second, the TOE framework examines the antecedents of technology implementation at the organizational level [18, 47], in contrast to models such as the Technology Acceptance Model [48], which focus on individual-level characteristics.

The TOE framework classifies the factors influencing technology adoption into three dimensions: Technology, Organization and Environment (see Fig. 1). The Technology dimension refers to the technology available to the company for adoption. Specifically, it considers the benefits of technology implementation in terms of

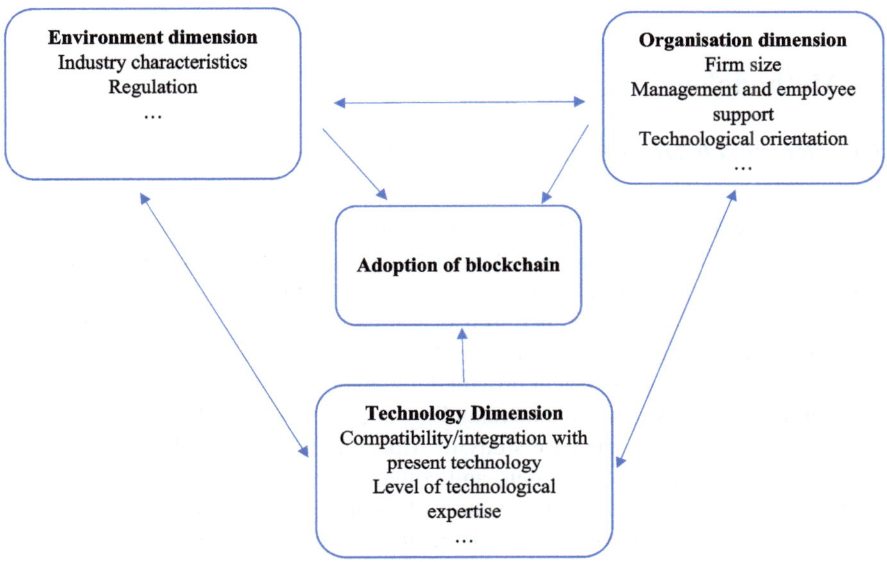

Fig. 1 The TOE framework. Source: Our adaptation from Tornatzky and Fleischer [17]

cost savings, the compatibility and integration with existing technologies, and the overall level of technological expertise within the company. The Organization dimension concerns both managerial and employee support for the implementation process, as well as organizational characteristics that indicate readiness to adopt new technologies, such as the company size and its level of technological orientation. The Environment dimension pertains to the external context in which the company operates and how it influences the organization's decision to adopt new technologies. In particular, it includes institutional pressures from competitors and regulatory bodies, and how such pressures drive the company toward implementation.

Due to its characteristics, the TOE framework has been widely used to investigate the factors affecting the implementation of various technologies, such as cloud computing [49], ERP systems [50, 51], big data [52], and artificial intelligence [53]. It has also been applied to explore the antecedents influencing a company's decision to adopt blockchain technology [18–20]. Specifically, Gokalp and colleagues [19] examined blockchain adoption in supply chain systems, while Orji and colleagues [20] focused on its implementation in the freight logistics industry. Distinct from these studies, Akter and colleagues [18] used the TOE framework to investigate blockchain adoption in the accounting domain by conducting interviews with blockchain experts and accountants. The Authors identified a range of context-specific factors acting as enablers or inhibitors in the decision to adopt blockchain in accounting. These factors were categorized into three groups: accounting-relevant factors (i.e., perceived benefits, trialability, complexity, and insufficient knowledge); general factors (i.e., perceived cost, perceived privacy risk, organization's innovativeness, top management support, and external pressure); and other factors (specifically, scalability).

3 Methodology

3.1 Research Design and Data Analysis

To achieve the research objective, this study adopted a qualitative case study methodology [54]. This methodological approach was selected because qualitative research is particularly suitable for exploring emerging or under-researched topics [55]. The case study presented herein is classified as exploratory, making it appropriate for investigating subjects that are not yet thoroughly addressed in the existing literature [54, 56]. This approach provided a holistic view of the research problem and facilitated the description, understanding, and explanation of the case context.

The study focuses on the case study of Alpha, a leading provider of innovative solutions for document management and collaboration. The company's mission is to improve the efficiency and effectiveness of creating, editing, and managing complex digital documents through state-of-the-art technologies. Alpha was selected as the case study because it has developed a blockchain-based solution for the secure creation and exchange of important documents.

A specific analysis protocol was followed, in line with the established case study methodology [54]. Initially, a comprehensive literature review was conducted, followed by a systematic collection of empirical evidence. To ensure data triangulation [54] and reduce the risk of personal bias or subjective interpretations, information was gathered from multiple sources: materials available on the company's website, YouTube videos, the organizations' LinkedIn profile, and a semi-structured interview. The sources of evidence were carefully selected and concatenated [54]. In particular, the insights gained from the analysis of information collected from the various sources were instrumental in designing the interviews, helping to focus on the most relevant aspects of the investigation.

Before conducting the interview, preliminary research was conducted to enrich the research team's understanding of Alpha's operations, the technological solutions it provides, and its key features. This research was primarily based on an in-depth analysis of the available data, including website content describing the company's solutions, YouTube videos illustrating its core business, and LinkedIn posts highlighting updates and initiatives.

The case study was developed through a semi-structured interview conducted in March 2024. The current CEO of Alpha was interviewed using a set of open-ended questions. The semi-structured interview allowed the participant to freely express personal views on the topic under investigation, enabling the researchers to gain a comprehensive understanding of the issues at hand [57]. The interview was conducted via the Microsoft Teams communication platform. Before starting the interview, the research team introduced themselves, clarified the main objective of the study, and addressed any concerns regarding the confidentiality of the information provided and the protection of company data. The interview lasted 50 min. With the interviewee's consent, the session was recorded and subsequently transcribed according to the "24-hour rule"[1] [58].

A qualitative content analysis was used to examine the interview text and to identify key concepts relevant to the research objective. This process followed a multistage approach [59, 60]. Each researcher independently reviewed the interview to ensure an unbiased analysis. The authors then collaborated to discuss and agree upon a common classification of the key concepts. Additional quality control was conducted by each author after reading the interview text. The most critical segments essential to the development of the case were synthesized and shared among the members of the research team to produce the final report.

3.2 *Case Study Description*

The company investigated is a blockchain provider. More specifically, Alpha offers two different solutions to its clients. The first consists of offering clients a smart way to create and manage digital documents starting from paper-based documents. This

[1] The interview guide is available on request.

solution involves developing a workflow management system to create standards for different organizations useful to organize their workflow, as well as an integrated system to edit the standards themselves. The second is a cloud solution for secure and reliable documents. This solution provides clients with a platform for secure long-term archiving and sharing of important documents, which are permanently and securely notarized through blockchain technology.

The company operates mainly within the supply chain of airplane manufacturing, where paper-based document management systems are still widely used today. The company was created to meet a real need in the aerospace industry, namely the handling and distribution of quality paper-based documentation to support test results and prove the origin of materials and processes.

In the aircraft industry, the handling of paper is very cost-intensive because all documents need to be printed, copied, and filed in different systems by all participants in the supply chain. In this context, it is very easy for documents to be lost or misplaced, and very difficult to trace back the origin of individual parts. In the aviation industry, it is also important to be able to prove the provenance and history of each part and to certify that each step of production has been completed according to specific standards. Therefore, it is necessary to provide a document history and to prove that the documents have not been tampered with and that their origin is correct.

Alpha began its activities by finding a way to transform the handling of paper-based documents into a digital format through blockchain technology. This kind of technology is considered the right tool to ensure not only that each document is digital and accessible, but also that the documents cannot be tampered with or changed later.

4 Findings

4.1 The Blockchain Solution

The investigated company developed a centralized and private blockchain. Therefore, the blockchain is managed by the investigated company, which can also authorize other participants to add data to the blockchain. This technology is based on proof of authority. The blockchain solution operates with any file format, which can be uploaded via a document management app. Once the documents are uploaded, the app generates an individual QR code that links back to the files in an audit-proof manner. The QR code serves as the key to the documents and can be kept or shared with others. Using the QR code, it is possible to access the documents from anywhere, at any time. After the documents have been uploaded, it is impossible to go back, modify them, and re-upload them.

Considering that the main activity of the investigated company is in the aviation industry, the documents stored in the blockchain are mainly air quality documents—for example, the results of batch tests performed on specific parts before delivery.

As reported by the CEO of Alpha, «especially in these industries, it is necessary that, for each batch of parts delivered, the production process and the materials used are both tested and certified, to prove and produce documents to verify that the parts are compliant with the standards».

The blockchain solution offers various benefits, such as security, cost savings, and sustainability. Regarding the first point, the developed technology allows clients to archive documents long-term and securely in the cloud, enabling a sustainable archiving and file management service, while still maintaining full access to the data. Once stored in the blockchain, the data cannot be altered and can only be accessed or shared using the QR code. Therefore, the data is tamper-proof and audit-proof. Moreover, the blockchain solution helps clients reduce costs, as documents can be stored and shared without ever needing to be printed. The solution also supports the achievement of sustainable development goals by eliminating the use of paper.

Another benefit is that the blockchain solution is designed to provide transparency for each transaction performed by participants in the supply chain. It is «like an open system where everybody can participate. In our system, we can also trace who did what and when. This allows for a better understanding of your processes—what happened, when it happened, and by whom—as it includes a detailed timeline».

The blockchain solution is mainly used to improve the overall information system, although it is not specifically used for accounting purposes. However, this technology could «absolutely be used for accounting purposes».

4.2 The Enablers or Inhibitors of Blockchain Adoption in Accounting

The analysis of the interview revealed several factors influencing the adoption of blockchain in accounting. According to the TOE framework [17], we structured the enablers and inhibitors of blockchain adoption into three dimensions: the technology dimension, the organization dimension, and the environment dimension.

Referring to the technology dimension, integration with existing systems was identified as a key enabler. Alpha provides a solution that is highly compatible with the client's existing systems. As highlighted by the company's CEO: «We try to touch the existing workflow within the company as little as possible. For example, we have connections to SAP systems. We work as an external storage for documents, which are then linked together in order to be proven and become part of the blockchain». This integration strategy ensures minimal disruption to the client's operations. The company begin by conducting an in-depth analysis of the client's technological environment and workflows, subsequently proposing a tailored solution that facilitates seamless integration into existing systems. As the CEO further noted: «The clients don't have to learn additional tools because our solution doesn't change the way they already do things—it just makes their lives a little bit easier and more convenient. That is very important to us».

Moreover, the company assists clients in organizing both their backlog of documents and those requiring secure archival within the blockchain infrastructure. The compatibility of the blockchain solution with existing systems is thus a key driver of adoption.

The company offers two primary implementation models. The first is a license-based access model, in which the clients are provided with login credentials to organize and manage their data directly within the company's platform. In this configuration, the system automatically generates cryptographic hashes that are recorded on the blockchain. However, this model involves a relatively high level of complexity, as clients are responsible for manually managing large volumes of documentation, an aspect that may prove burdensome for many organizations. The second model involves a customized integration, in which the blockchain solution is tailored to the client's existing technological infrastructure. In these cases, the transfer of documents to the blockchain occurs automatically, often through integration with enterprise systems such as SAP. This approach minimizes user involvement in document handling and streamlines adoption. As the CEO explained: «Often the people who work with the documents stored in our system don't really see our system on the front end, because it's happening in the background, the file transfer». The customized and automated approach mitigates system complexity, which is often cited as a key inhibitor to blockchain adoption.

The ease of use of the blockchain solution emerges as another critical factor influencing adoption. Users are not required to possess advanced technological skills, as the complexity of the system is managed in the background. As the CEO stated: «Users don't need to know about the complexity behind it. They don't need to understand or know too much about the algorithm that's working in the background». This finding is particularly relevant, given that blockchain is commonly perceived as a highly complex technology requiring significant technical expertise, an aspect that often inhibits its adoption within organizations.

Another important factor typically influencing the adoption of a new technology is its cost. In this case, the costs associated with blockchain implementation are not perceived as a barrier. The perceived benefits, such as improved document archiving, enhanced audit readiness, and reduction in document loss, outweigh the associated expenses. The solution enables clients to lower the costs related to both document handling and the potential loss of critical files. Initial implementation costs are relatively low compared to other systems or tools typically used within companies' IT infrastructures. Ongoing costs are primarily linked to licensing and adapting the technology to existing workflows and tools. As the CEO noted: «The cost of handling documents is very high because it's labor-intensive to store them securely and organize them in a retrievable way. The cost of using blockchain technology is not significant compared to these processes».

Referring to the organization dimension, top management support is important during the initial decision-making phase of blockchain adoption. Once the decision is made, the company prioritizes the technical integration of the solution into the client's existing infrastructure. As emphasized by the CEO: «It is important for us to create solutions for companies so that they don't have to dramatically change the way they work in their systems, in order to lower the barrier of change that needs to happen in the company». Therefore, unlike many technological adoptions, organizational readiness and technology orientation do not emerge as significant factors in this context. The company's strategy of ensuring compatibility with existing systems reduces the need for extensive internal restructuring or adaptation.

The size of the client organization also affects the pace and process of adoption. Smaller firms tend to implement new technological solutions more quickly, as noted by the CEO: «Usually, of course, it's quicker to work with smaller companies and they're quicker to adapt new technology solutions to help them with the problem».

Finally, regarding the environment dimension, partner support plays a pivotal role in enabling blockchain adoption. Within the aircraft supply chain, where blockchain remains an emerging technology, some partners have already implemented it. These early adopters contribute to the diffusion of the technology by sharing their experiences and promoting its benefits through informal channels. These mimetic pressures, wherein organizations adopt innovations in response to the behavior of their peers, significantly influence the diffusion of technology across the supply chain.

Unlike regulatory or coercive pressures, the adoption of blockchain technology is largely driven by mimetic forces among supply chain partners. As the CEO explained: «We're working towards a scenario where the technology is widely adopted, because the whole or the biggest benefits come when this technology is implemented end-to-end. In this way, you've got full transparency, and every part of the chain is working on this problem. But now, there isn't enough peer pressure between companies to adopt this technology. We hope there will be soon».

5 Discussion and Conclusions

The aim of this work is to investigate, through an exploratory case study, the factors influencing the adoption of blockchain technology in accounting, using the TOE framework. This study contributes to the literature on blockchain in accounting by offering a first attempt to identify the enablers and inhibitors of blockchain adoption in the field, thereby responding to the call for more empirical research on the practical implementation of this innovative technology [14–16].

Consistent with previous studies, our findings highlight that blockchain adoption offers several advantages, including enhanced reliability and transparency of accounting records, improved transaction traceability, and reductions in both costs and human errors [5, 8, 22, 24, 36].

The results of our analysis highlight how the blockchain solution improves the company's overall information system. In line with previous empirical studies on blockchain adoption in the agrifood supply chain [61, 62], the case study reveals that blockchain technology is primarily used to archive quality-related documents in compliance with regulatory standards and certifications. These documents, mainly of an extra-accounting nature, are stored in a decentralized and immutable "inventory" ledger accessible to all partners in the aircraft supply chain. In this context, the triple-entry accounting logic enables the creation of a shared inventory and certification ledger, where all transaction participants can view and verify records on the blockchain, thereby increasing transparency and trust among supply chain actors. Blockchain has significant potential to address the trust issues that typically characterize inter-organizational relationships in supply chains. Its immutable architecture makes the alteration or manipulation of documents theoretically nearly impossible [26, 39].

The increasing use of digital technologies has challenged the traditional accounting order, where qualitative information is increasingly prioritized over the quantitative, economic-financial data typically relied upon in conventional accounting information systems. Consequently, organizational decision-making is progressively based on qualitative information rather than quantitative information.

The interviewee described blockchain as "an open system where everyone can participate". This aligns with the concept of Open Book Accounting (OBA) [63, 64]. OBA is an accounting practice wherein firms within a supply chain "open their books" by sharing both financial and non-financial, qualitative and quantitative information. Historically, OBA has encountered resistance, primarily due to trust-related concerns about the sharing of accounting records. Blockchain technology addresses these concerns by ensuring data integrity and transparency, thereby enabling a more advanced form of OBA. Therefore, blockchain facilitates the overcoming of traditional trust barriers that have been well documented in the OBA literature [62].

Concerning the factors influencing the adoption of blockchain in accounting, the analysis shows that technological aspects are predominant. This finding contrasts with previous studies in the literature, which indicate that in supply chain contexts, environmental determinants are more important than technological or organizational ones [19]. In particular, integration and compatibility with existing systems have been identified as key enablers of blockchain adoption. Alpha offers its clients a solution that can be seamlessly integrated into their current systems. In contrast to many studies that portray blockchain as inherently complex [16, 40–42], our research shows that when blockchain is designed for integration, compatibility and ease of use, its complexity is significantly reduced. Therefore, complexity does not act as a barrier to the adoption of the technology. This is a significant finding, as blockchain is generally perceived as a highly complex technology requiring significant technical expertise, an element that can hinder its organizational adoption.

Another critical factor that typically influences technology adoption, according to the literature [18], is cost. However, in the case study examined, the costs associated with blockchain implementation are not perceived as a barrier. The benefits, such as improved document storage, enhanced audit readiness, and reduced risk of document loss, are perceived to outweigh the costs. The solution helps clients lower case management expenses and mitigate losses linked to missing or misfiled documentation. Therefore, the economic benefits provided by blockchain further encourage its adoption. This finding contrasts with previous research suggesting that implementation costs are a major obstacle to blockchain adoption [18].

In terms of the organizational dimension, and consistent with previous research [18, 65], top management support emerges as the most influential factor in the initial decision-making phase of blockchain adoption. In contrast to many other cases of technology adoption [49–53], organizational readiness and technological orientation do not play a significant role in this context. The company's strategy of ensuring that the blockchain solution is fully compatible with existing systems minimizes the need for extensive organizational readiness for technological change.

In terms of the environmental dimension, in line with previous studies [18, 65], our findings reveal that partner support is an important factor for blockchain adoption. Within the aviation supply chain, early adopters promote the benefits of blockchain to other partners through word of mouth and shared experiences. This dynamic creates mimetic pressure, whereby companies are influenced to adopt the technology based on the practices of their supply chain partners. This peer influence is pivotal to the widespread diffusion of blockchain technology across the supply chain.

This study has several theoretical and practical implications. From a theoretical perspective, this study enriches the literature on blockchain in accounting by analysing the case of a blockchain provider. In this sense, it extends previous theoretical research on the enablers and inhibitors of technology adoption by providing empirical evidence on the factors influencing blockchain adoption decisions [18–20]. Furthermore, the study contributes to the literature by investigating blockchain adoption within a specific industry context, i.e. the aviation sector. In addition, this research responds to the call for more empirical studies on the application of blockchain in accounting [14–16].

From a practical perspective, by providing empirical evidence and insights from a case study, this research offers guidance for managers seeking to implement blockchain solutions. Specifically, it identifies key antecedents to adoption, with a focus on the integration within supply chain processes.

Despite its contributions, the study has several limitations. First, the selected research methodology enabled an exploratory investigation, which, while appropriate for the study's objectives, limits the scope and generalizability of the findings. Although the reasons for employing a case study approach have been justified, further research involving a broader range of respondents would provide a more comprehensive understanding of the topic. Second, our analysis captures only the perspective of the technology provider. Further studies could extend this analysis to include the perspective of client organizations using the technology, in order to validate or challenge the present findings. Our study represents a preliminary attempt to identify the enablers and inhibitors of blockchain adoption in accounting and may serve as a foundation for future research on the broader implications of this emerging technology.

Disclosure of Interests The authors have no competing interests.

References

1. Wang, Y., & Kogan, A. (2018). Designing confidentiality-preserving Blockchain-based transaction processing systems. *International Journal of Accounting Information Systems, 30*, 1–18.
2. White, G. R. (2017). Future applications of blockchain in business and management: A Delphi study. *Strategic change, 26*(5), 439–451.
3. Herian, R. (2017). Blockchain and the (re) imagining of trusts jurisprudence. *Strategic Change, 26*(5), 453–460.
4. Nathan, J., & Jacobs, B. (2020). Blockchain consortium networks: Adding security and trust in financial services. *Journal of Corporate Accounting & Finance, 31*(2), 29–33.
5. Dai, J., & Vasarhelyi, M. A. (2017). Toward blockchain-based accounting and assurance. *Journal of information systems, 31*(3), 5–21.
6. Yu, T., Lin, Z., & Tang, Q. (2018). Blockchain: The introduction and its application in financial accounting. *Journal of Corporate Accounting & Finance, 29*(4), 37–47.
7. Faccia, A., & Mosteanu, N. R. (2019). Accounting and blockchain technology: From double-entry to triple-entry. *The Business & Management Review, 10*(2), 108–116.
8. Tan, B. S., & Low, K. Y. (2019). Blockchain as the database engine in the accounting system. *Australian Accounting Review, 29*(2), 312–318.
9. Kokina, J., Mancha, R., & Pachamanova, D. (2017). Blockchain: Emergent industry adoption and implications for accounting. *Journal of Emerging Technologies in Accounting, 14*(2), 91–100.
10. Jackson, D., & Allen, C. (2024). Enablers, barriers and strategies for adopting new technology in accounting. *International Journal of Accounting Information Systems, 52*, 100666.
11. Chowdhury, E. K., Khan, I. I., & Dhar, B. K. (2023). Strategy for implementing blockchain technology in accounting: Perspectives of stakeholders in a developing nation. *Business Strategy & Development, 6*(3), 477–490.
12. Maffei, M., Casciello, R., & Meucci, F. (2021). Blockchain technology: Uninvestigated issues emerging from an integrated view within accounting and auditing practices. *Journal of Organizational Change Management, 34*(2), 462–476.
13. Christidis, K., & Devetsikiotis, M. (2016). Blockchains and smart contracts for the internet of things. *IEEE Access, 4*, 2292–2303.
14. Pimentel, E., & Boulianne, E. (2020). Blockchain in accounting research and practice: Current trends and future opportunities. *Accounting Perspectives, 19*(4), 325–361.
15. Jayasuriya, D. D., & Sims, A. (2023). From the abacus to enterprise resource planning: Is blockchain the next big accounting tool? *Accounting, Auditing & Accountability Journal, 36*(1), 24–62.
16. Bonsón, E., & Bednárová, M. (2019). Blockchain and its implications for accounting and auditing. *Meditari Accountancy Research, 27*(5), 725–740.
17. Tornatzky, L. G., & Fleischer, M. (1990). *The processes of technological innovation*. Lexington Books.
18. Akter, M., Kummer, T. F., & Yigitbasioglu, O. (2024). Looking beyond the hype: The challenges of blockchain adoption in accounting. *International Journal of Accounting Information Systems, 53*, 100681.
19. Gokalp, E., Gokalp, M. O., & Coban, S. (2020). Blockchain-based supply chain management: Understanding the determinants of adoption in the context of organizations. *Information Systems Management, 39*, 100–121.
20. Orji, I. J., Kusi-Sarpong, S., Huang, S., & Vazquez-Brust, D. (2020). Evaluating the factors that influence blockchain adoption in the freight logistics industry. *Transportation Research Part E: Logistics and Transportation Review, 141*, 102025.
21. Ducas, E., & Wilner, A. (2017). The security and financial implications of blockchain technologies: Regulating emerging technologies in Canada. *International Journal, 72*(4), 538–562.
22. Iansiti, M., & Lakhani, K. R. (2017). The truth about blockchain. *Harvard Business Review, 95*(1), 118–127.

23. Lemieux, V. L. (2021). Blockchain and recordkeeping. *Computers, 10*(11), 135.
24. Tapscott, D., & Tapscott, A. (2016). *Blockchain revolution: How the technology behind bitcoin is changing money, business, and the world.* Penguin.
25. O'Leary, D. E. (2018). Open information enterprise transactions: Business intelligence and wash and spoof transactions in blockchain and social commerce. *Intelligent Systems in Accounting, Finance and Management, 25*(3), 148–158.
26. Schmitz, J., & Leoni, G. (2019). Accounting and auditing at the time of blockchain technology: A research agenda. *Australian Accounting Review, 29*(2), 331–342.
27. Walch, A.: *Deconstructing decentralization: Exploring the core claim of crypto systems*. (2019).
28. Brandon, D. (2016). The blockchain: The future of business information systems. *International Journal of the Academic Business World, 10*(2), 33–40.
29. Fullana, O., & Ruiz, J. (2021). Accounting information systems in the blockchain era. *International Journal of Intellectual Property Management, 11*(1), 63–80.
30. Han, H., Shiwakoti, R. K., Jarvis, R., Mordi, C., & Botchie, D. (2023). Accounting and auditing with blockchain technology and artificial Intelligence: A literature review. *International Journal of Accounting Information Systems, 48*, 100598.
31. Maiti, M., Kotliarov, I., & Lipatnikov, V. (2021). A future triple entry accounting framework using blockchain technology. *Blockchain: Research and Applications, 2*(4), 100037.
32. Thies, S., Kureljusic, M., Karger, E., & Krämer, T. (2023). Blockchain-based triple-entry accounting: A systematic literature review and future research agenda. *Journal of Information Systems, 37*(3).
33. Grigg, I. (2005). *Triple entry accounting* (pp. 1–10). Systemics Inc.
34. Ijiri, Y. (1986). A framework for triple-entry bookkeeping. *Accounting Review, 61*, 745–759.
35. Carlin, T. (2019). Blockchain and the journey beyond double entry. *Australian Accounting Review, 29*(2), 305–311.
36. Karajovic, M., Kim, H. M., & Laskowski, M. (2019). Thinking outside the block: Projected phases of blockchain integration in the accounting industry. *Australian Accounting Review, 29*(2), 319–330.
37. Cai, C. W. (2021). Triple-entry accounting with blockchain: How far have we come? *Accounting & Finance, 61*(1), 71–93.
38. Kwilinski, A. (2019). Implementation of blockchain technology in accounting sphere. *Academy of Accounting and Financial Studies Journal, 23*, 1–6.
39. Vardia, S., & Singh, H. (2022). Adoption of blockchain technology in accounting and auditing: Benefits and challenges. *Pacific Business Review (International), 14*(08), 95–103.
40. Fuller, S. H., & Markelevich, A. (2020). Should accountants care about blockchain? *Journal of Corporate Accounting & Finance, 31*(2), 34–46.
41. Lin, I. C., & Liao, T. C. (2017). A survey of blockchain security issues and challenges. *International Journal of Network Security, 19*(5), 653–659.
42. Sinha, S. (2020). Blockchain—Opportunities and challenges for accounting professionals. *Journal of Corporate Accounting & Finance, 31*(2), 65–67.
43. Prewett, K. W., Prescott, G. L., & Phillips, K. (2020). Blockchain adoption is inevitable—Barriers and risks remain. *Journal of Corporate Accounting & Finance, 31*(2), 21–28.
44. Kitsantas, T., & Chytis, E. (2022). Blockchain technology as an ecosystem: Trends and perspectives in accounting and management. *Journal of Theoretical and Applied Electronic Commerce Research, 17*(3), 1143–1161.
45. Lardo, A., Corsi, K., Varma, A., & Mancini, D. (2022). Exploring blockchain in the accounting domain: A bibliometric analysis. *Accounting, Auditing & Accountability Journal, 35*(9), 204–233.
46. Hossain, M., & Quaddus, M. (2011). The adoption and continued usage intention of RFID: An integrated framework. *Information Technology & People, 24*(3), 236–256.
47. Awa, H., Ojiabo, O., & Orokor, L. (2017). Integrated technology-organization-environment (T-O-E) taxonomies for technology adoption. *Journal of Enterprise Information Management, 30*(6), 893–921.

48. Davis, F. (1989). Perceived usefulness, perceived ease of use, and user acceptance of information technology. *MIS Quarterly, 13*(3), 319–340.
49. Morawiec, P., & Sołtysik-Piorunkiewicz, A. (2023). ERP system development for business agility in industry 4.0—A literature review based on the TOE framework. *Sustainability, 15*(5), 4646.
50. Walther, S., Sedera, D., Urbach, N., Eymann, T., Otto, B., & Sarker, S. (2018). Should we stay or should we go? Analyzing continuance of cloud enterprise systems. *Journal of Information Technology Theory and Application, 19*(2), 4.
51. Al-Shboul, M. D. A. (2019). Towards better understanding of determinants logistical factors in SMEs for cloud ERP adoption in developing economies. *Business Process Management Journal, 25*(5), 887–907.
52. Baig, M. I., Shuib, L., & Yadegaridehkordi, E. (2019). Big data adoption: State of the art and research challenges. *Information Processing & Management, 56*(6).
53. Nam, K., Dutt, C. S., Chathoth, P., Daghfous, A., & Khan, M. S. (2020). The adoption of artificial intelligence and robotics in the hotel industry: Prospects and challenges. *Electronic Markets, 31*, 553–574.
54. Yin, R. K. (2017). *Case study research and applications: Design and methods*. Sage.
55. Fawcett, S. E., Waller, M. A., Miller, J. W., Schwieterman, M. A., Hazen, B. T., & Overstreet, R. E. (2014). A trail guide to publishing success: Tips on writing influential conceptual, qualitative, and survey research. *Journal of Business Logistics, 35*(1), 1–16.
56. Mills, A. J., Durepos, G., & Wiebe, E. (Eds.). (2009). *Encyclopedia of case study research*. Sage.
57. Qu, S. Q., & Dumay, J. (2011). The qualitative research interview. *Qualitative Research in Accounting & Management, 8*(3), 238–264.
58. Eisenhardt, K. M. (1989). Building theories from case study research. *Academy of Management Review, 14*(4), 532–550.
59. Gioia, D. A., Corley, K. G., & Hamilton, A. L. (2013). Seeking qualitative rigor in inductive research: Notes on the Gioia methodology. *Organizational Research Methods, 16*(1), 15–31.
60. Merriam, S. B., & Tisdell, E. J. (2015). *Qualitative research: A guide to design and implementation*. Wiley.
61. Antonucci, F., Figorilli, S., Costa, C., Pallottino, F., Raso, L., & Menesatti, P. (2019). A review on blockchain applications in the agri-food sector. *Journal of the Science of Food and Agriculture, 99*(14), 6129–6138.
62. Centorrino, G., Noto, G., & Rupo, D. (2022). Management control in inter-firm relationships: Opportunities and challenges of blockchain technology adoption. *Management Control, 3*(2022), 65–88.
63. Kajüter, P., & Kulmala, H. I. (2005). Open-book accounting in networks: Potential achievements and reasons for failures. *Management Accounting Research, 16*(2), 179–204.
64. Scaletti, A., & Pisano, S. (2011). *Open-book accounting and accounting information systems in cooperative relationships* (pp. 329–336). Physica-Verlag HD.
65. Azmi, F., Abdullah, A., Bakri, M., Musa, H., & Jayakrishnan, M. (2018). The adoption of halal food supply chain towards the performance of food manufacturing in Malaysia. *Management Science Letters, 8*(7), 755–766.

State of the Art of Business Analytics for Enterprise Transformation Steering

Benedict Lösser

Abstract As Enterprise Transformations (ETs) pose significant challenges for companies, it is crucial to steer these resource-intensive endeavors rigorously. However, there is a substantial gap between ET's operational implementation and their steering committees. While existing literature suggests comprehensive information factors to support ET steering, the extent to which these factors are applied in practice and standardized through business analytics remains unclear. This manuscript aims to analyze the current state of business analytics in ET steering through a descriptive interview study. Our findings reveal that these concepts have been utilized only to a limited extent in practice, particularly for context and ET process-related factors. We further highlight and advocate for the increased adoption and implementation of specific business analytics for ET steering, addressing information gaps and enhancing decision quality. This research contributes to the discourse on ET steering by demonstrating the practical applications and benefits of business analytics in improving ET decision-making processes.

Keywords Transformation steering · Business analytics · Interview study

1 Introduction

Enterprise transformations (ETs) remain a significant challenge for organizations. Research shows that most orchestrated organizational changes fail to achieve their intended long-term benefits [1]. Despite sophisticated strategies, detailed implementation plans, and advanced project management techniques [2, 3], companies frequently fall short of meeting their ET objectives [1, 4]. Kiselev et al. [4] attribute

B. Lösser (✉)
Institute of Information Systems and Digital Business, University of St. Gallen, St. Gallen, Switzerland
e-mail: benedict.loesser@unisg.ch

A. Tursunbayeva et al. (eds.), *Technology-Driven Transformation*, Lecture Notes in Information Systems and Organisation 79,
https://doi.org/10.1007/978-3-032-01396-5_17

this shortfall primarily to inadequate governance and steering over time. ET steering refers to the act of controlling the direction in which the enterprise moves through strategic and tactical decision-making and active monitoring of the ETs progress [5]. However, steering committees—often composed of senior managers juggling multiple responsibilities—may lack a specialized training necessary for effective ET steering [6–8]. At the same time, ETs, which are frequently managed according to program logics, are extraordinary complex and unique, making decisions often irreversible and far-reaching, while also time-critical [9, 10]. This complexity necessitates a transparent, rapid, and clear flow of information to enable sound decision-making by steering committees [11–13].

To effectively support steering committees, organizations require a dedicated information logistics solution and committed transformation managers [14, 15]. Aggregated insights from the operations of the ETs are essential for preparing and making decisions, as well as for observing the impact of those decisions over time. In reality, however, the processes in steering committees are inadequately defined and information flows are often poorly controlled [16]. Furthermore, organizations lack models and frameworks for evaluating the effectiveness at the enterprise-level [17], and there is limited understanding of how organizations can gain access to relevant, often distributed, information [18, 19].

Nevertheless, developing robust business analytics for ETs—specifically, the systematic evaluation and processing of data from ongoing transformations and organizational changes—is critical for supporting decision-making. Yet, current research has not sufficiently explored such approaches, and practical knowledge remains fragmented and based on isolated solutions. Based on these considerations, we pose our research question: *How do organizations use business analytics to support their enterprise transformation steering?*

To address this research question, we conducted a qualitative interview study grounded in and informed by prior literature [20, 21]. For this, we performed ten interviews with 11 transformation managers and ET steering committee executives across various industries and companies, encompassing ten distinct cases. While the study followed an inductive approach, the coding and interpretation were guided by relevant theoretical concepts and prior research, allowing for a literature-informed, yet open-ended analysis. This process led to the identification of 16 ET steering relevant information factors, which we grouped into three overarching information areas. Based on these real-world impressions, we describe the current focus of business analytics for the purposeful use in ETs and outline a future pathway for this field. This study provides a foundation for future research, including quantitative and design-oriented studies, and offers practical insights by identifying specific information factors to enhance the quality of ET steering decisions.

2 Conceptual Background

2.1 Enterprise Transformation

ET is a significant and non-standard shift in one or more core aspects of an organization [22]. Aligned with the argumentation of Jöhnk, Ollig, Rövekamp and Oesterle [23] for digital transformation, we conceptualize ET as an umbrella term for phenomena and research areas like organizational transformation [24], IT-enabled organizational transformation [25, 26], digital transformation [27, 28], and also agile transformation [29, 30]. The relevance and commonality lies in the impact on the enterprise level, as indicated by Winter, Bender and Aier [31] and Rouse [22]. This allows for generalizable insights across different research streams. ETs are inherently strategic, complex, and resource-intensive, significantly influencing an enterprise's competitiveness, economic success, and the individual well-being of its stakeholders [32].

ETs typically involves planned changes, usually aimed at preventing disruptions or capitalizing on new business prospects [33, 34]. Increasingly, ET is seen as an ongoing process that encompasses changes in business models, organizational structures, and technologies [28, 29, 35]. At some point, however, these changes require coordination through a temporary, specialized structure [10, 36]. Organizations often use programs as structure to drive transformative changes, integrating various initiatives to achieve common strategic goals while sharing resources [37, 38]. An ET, therefore, represents a specialized type of program that focuses on integrating or developing innovative solutions, accompanied by changes in business practices, models, and value-creation pathways [28, 39].

A critical aspect of ET is the orchestration and guidance of multiple initiatives toward a common goal [40]. Sebastian, Ross, Beath, Mocker, Moloney and Fonstad [27] highlight the difficulties faced by large, established companies in managing ET, particularly in balancing strategy and operational execution. Recent solution approaches have emphasized resolving contradictions in the operational execution of ETs by introducing more adaptive governance mechanisms, such as hybrid ambidexterity [23]. However, despite these advances, many ETs continue to fall short of delivering their expected benefits [1], This is often not due to failures in the implementation of individual transformation initiatives, but rather due to difficulties in actively steering and aligning the dynamic interplay between these initiatives [2–4].

2.2 Enterprise Transformation Steering

ET steering focuses on ensuring organizations achieve their intended outcomes from concerted efforts. Following the notion of Proper [5] steering means to direct the organization along a desired course, which includes monitoring the scope, progress, dependencies, and benefits of all related initiatives over time [40]. It requires organizations to continuously review and adjust their strategies in response to internal and external changes [4, 40]. Accordingly, ET steering is mainly concerned with strategic decisions of great significance that are difficult to reverse and have high impact consequences on the organization in the long term [4, 9]. Thus, steering involves dynamic decisions *to do the right things*—in contrast to *doing the things right*, which is expressed more in operationalized project and program management [4].

Typically, steering decisions are made by a committee rather than an individual to mitigate potential biases and bring diverse functional perspectives to the table [9]. The steering committee is usually appointed by the sponsor, i.e., the managing board, as a supervising support and decision-making body. It represents the sponsor and acts as an interface between the sponsor and other stakeholders involved in the ET [6]. Thus, it is usually the highest decision-making body in the ET [37]. Comprised mostly of senior managers, the committee is tasked with resolving disputes, monitoring external factors, and adjusting the ET's direction when necessary, including terminating initiatives or reorganizing teams as needed [4].

Steering decisions in ET are made under conditions of uncertainty and are based on their expected impact on the ET and the organization's overall performance [41]. These decisions are often irreversible, highly interdependent, made under fast-changing assumptions, and affect many stakeholders at the same time [4, 9]. Due to these complexities, modeling and simulation are challenging, making it difficult to predict the utility of a decision in advance. Access to timely and relevant information as foundation is therefore crucial for effective decision-making [42].

2.3 Business Analytics for Enterprise Transformation Steering

Effective ET steering relies heavily on the availability of relevant, timely information to guide decision-making [43]. The basic paradigm states that by acquiring and analyzing data from various sources, organizations can make precise decisions that enhance their business value [44]. This aligns with the concept of information logistics, which addresses the need for enterprise-wide decision support by balancing the dynamic demand for information (such as that from a steering committee) with the supply of data available within the organization's various information systems [14].

Despite the importance of data-driven decision-making, steering committees often rely on immediate, anecdotal information provided by ET managers who prepare supporting materials for meetings. This ad hoc approach typically leaves committees without comprehensive insights into the scope, relevance, and potential consequences of their decisions [42].

To overcome this limitation, organizations must gather, analyze, and synthesize diverse information from across the enterprise to guide ET efforts effectively [42]. This is where business analytics becomes crucial. Business analytics refers to a spectrum of analytical methods used to interpret data systematically, generating insights that support decision-making, track progress, and evaluate the outcomes of ET initiatives [17, 45]. Definitions of business analytics range from narrow views emphasizing automated statistical techniques [46] to broader understandings that include both manual and automated processes for data collection and analysis [47]. In this article, we adopt the broader, evolutionary perspective, viewing business analytics as a continuum that spans from structured, manual data collection to fully automated data processing and evaluation.

Research shows that high-performing organizations are often those that leverage business analytics effectively [48]; however, the mechanisms by which these analytics create value—especially in specific decision-making contexts like for ET steering—remain largely unclear [49]. This is a significant gap, given that comprehensive business analytics solutions can be extremely resource-intensive and costly to implement [50].

To tailor business analytics to the specific needs of ETs, it is essential to identify which types of information should be captured and analyzed. Doing so ensures that data collection and analysis remain focused, relevant, and manageable—avoiding unnecessary overhead for the organization. Labusch, Aier and Winter [42], for instance, propose a comprehensive reference model for information-based ET support, which includes 11 key information factors: strategy, goals, business structure, project portfolio, design options, methods, social factors, performance, stakeholders, risks, and IT structure [42]. Moreover, Kiselev, Winter and Rohner [4] emphasize the significance of contextual factors, such as terrain, dynamics, complexity, commitment, and ability to act, which, while often beyond the direct control of ET or project managers, play a critical role in ET's success. Together, these two perspectives reflect the dual necessity of understanding both the internal configuration of the transformation and its external and situational context. Accordingly, both sets of factors should be considered essential for effective ET steering. Yet, despite their conceptual value, there is currently no systematic understanding of how these information needs are addressed through business analytics or how they inform ET steering decision-making in practice.

3 Research Design

3.1 Data Collection

We conducted an in-depth interview study to gain a profound understanding of business analytics for ET steering in its natural context [51]. We identified 11 interview partners from 9 different companies and had 10 interviews, each with a focus on a specific ET. The selection of companies and interviewees was guided by their relevance to the study's objectives. The companies were chosen based on their established involvement in ET operations across various industries, ensuring a diverse perspective. Each interviewee was carefully selected for their dual role within their organization: all participants were directly involved in the strategic steering of the

ETs through active participation in steering committee meetings while also being deeply engaged in the operational aspects of ET implementation. This dual involvement provided them with a comprehensive perspective on both the strategic and operational dimensions of ETs, making them uniquely qualified to provide the desired insights. Accordingly, the interviewees are considered subject matter experts from various organizational contexts (i.e., industries and sizes of established companies) which allowed us to accommodate the diversity of different ETs in diverse setting. We limited the interviews to one (or in one case, two) employee per ET to avoid overlap in perspectives and potential biases that might arise from internal company dynamics. By selecting a single representative, we ensured that each interview focused on a distinct ET with minimal redundancy while capturing the diverse approaches and challenges across different approaches through the multitude of interviews in different industries. This approach facilitated a broader understanding of ET steering while maintaining the depth of insights from experienced individuals. We closed the data collection after 10 interviews as no new subjects were added and the aspects mentioned were increasingly repetitive. The case number, the job title of the interviewees, the respective industry and number of the organization's employees are described in Table 1.

We followed a semi-structured interview format [21, 51] consisting of three parts: First, we created a shared understanding of business analytics for ET. Second, we asked the interviewees to openly elaborate on their ET steering and how it gets supported through business analytics. Third, we asked on the specific measures and techniques used to support their ET steering [52]. To gather detailed data and reflect the inductive nature of our study, we primarily asked open-ended questions and encouraged interviewees to share their thoughts, personal experiences, and specific

Table 1 Interview partners

Case	Job title interviewee	Industry of company interviewee is working	Number of employees
1	Head of Enterprise Architecture Management	Retail	>40,000
2	Head of Strategy Execution & Business Owner Data Driven Company Strategy	Insurance	>7500
3	Lead Project Management Office Operations	Insurance	>4000
4	Lead Lean Portfolio Operations & Enabling	Insurance	>2500
5	Head of Agile Program Management Office	Insurance	>59,000
6	Head of IT Sales	Manufacturing	>11,000
7	Lead Transformation Reporting	Financial Services	>3000
8	Business Owner Online	Telecommunications	>19,000
9	Head of IT Transformation	Manufacturing	>12,500
10	Head of Automation Platform Development	Manufacturing	>12,500

examples [21, 51]. The interviews lasted each about 60 min. If possible, the interviews were recorded and transcribed in agreement with the interviewees, as recommended by Sarker, Xiao and Beaulieu [53]. If we couldn't record them due to restrictions of the interview partner, we took extensive notes that we could analyze afterwards.

3.2 Data Analysis

For data analysis, we started with transcribing all interviews before using Atlas.ti for qualitative coding. Our coding approach was informed by the information areas of the reference model for information-based support of ET by Labusch, Aier and Winter [42] enhanced through the context information factors for steering as identified by Kiselev, Winter and Rohner [4]. These served as our analytical lens helping to structure and guide the identification and interpretation of relevant information themes. This allowed us to trace the presence and treatment of specific information factors across the interviews, such as their perceived relevance, the degree of consensus around their use in business analytics, and how they may shift in response to contextual changes. Based on the combined conceptual foundation of our analytical lens, we focused on three main areas: "ET factors", "organizational factors" and "contextual factors". We deliberately excluded individual-level aspects such as the cognitive or behavioral characteristics of decision-makers, which were outside the scope of this study. To systematically assess how organizations engage with these information areas in practice, we categorized responses into four analytical dimensions: *not considered*, *acknowledged as determinant*, *evaluated manually*, and *evaluated automatically*.

4 Findings

Our interview study resulted in an assessment of the 16 information factors for business analytics for ET steering from ten distinct ETs. Table 2 provides an overview of the information factors and a classification of the current status quo of the ETs into four different categories: not considered, given as determinant, evaluated manually and evaluated automatically. *Not considered* means that this information factor is not yet addressed in the organizational practice of the organization and therefore no structured information (in a tool or similar) is available to influence ET steering decisions. This does not mean that there is generally no information or that decisions cannot be made based on specific expert knowledge. *Given as determinant* means that the information is collected and is also implicitly or explicitly known—but is treated as a fixed determinant and is therefore not systematically tracked or systematically adjusted over time. *Evaluated manually* means that the collection of information and data is regularly adjusted over the course of the ET,

Table 2 Status quo of business analytics for ET steering

Information factor	Application of business analytics			
	Not considered	Given as determinant	Evaluated manually	Evaluated automatically
Enterprise transformation factors				
Goals	0%	70%	30%	0%
Design options	90%	0%	10%	0%
Methods	70%	30%	0%	0%
Risks	0%	10%	90%	0%
Performance	20%	0%	70%	10%
Social factors	80%	0%	20%	0%
Stakeholders	30%	50%	20%	0%
Organizational factors				
Strategy	0%	80%	20%	0%
Business structure	0%	80%	10%	10%
IT structure	0%	80%	0%	20%
Project portfolio	0%	0%	80%	20%
Context factors				
Terrain	100%	0%	0%	0%
Dynamics	100%	0%	0%	0%
Complexity	100%	0%	0%	0%
Commitment	80%	0%	20%	0%
Ability to act	100%	0%	0%	0%

albeit mostly manually. This means that data is not tracked automatically, but is obtained, for example, through manual queries to project managers. *Evaluated automatically* means that a large proportion of data is collected and processed automatically in order to support management decisions. However, this does not explicitly exclude manual assessments of analyses for specific steering decisions.

Overall, the dimensions derived from the literature were largely reflected in practice. However, a clear pattern emerged: while some organizations have begun integrating business analytics into ET steering, fully automated approaches—often associated with advanced analytics—remain the exception rather than the norm. We also observed distinct differences across the three information areas: ET factors, organizational factors, and context factors. The application of business analytics to *ET factors* shows uneven coverage, with significant variation across cases in how these factors are addressed. In contrast, *organizational factors* are more commonly and systematically supported by data collection and analysis. *Context factors* remain largely unaddressed by business analytics, with only isolated efforts or ad hoc solutions targeting specific aspects.

Below, we describe each information factor organized in the overarching information areas, the extent to which it is fulfilled across the analyzed ETs and give examples from the cases, if there is an example of implementation.

4.1 Enterprise Transformation Factors

The *ET factors* describe the factors with direct impact and relation to the ET as program and thus as a processual phenomenon. Or put in other words: These factors are related to steering the process of ET. Those factors have partly been supported by the use of business analytics. Mainly *performance* and *risk* are already evaluated on an on-going systematic basis, while also *goals*, *social factors* and *stakeholders* get (initial) attention of specified business analytics for decision-support. *Design options* or *methods* are only documented or defined and used for decision-making in individual cases.

Goals refers to aims of the ET endeavor. Goals are usually clearly defined ideas that are to be achieved from a strategic or financial perspective in the course of an ET, following the organization's strategy. In all the cases discussed, the information on the targets is already being used. In the majority of cases, this is primarily as a determining element, while in fewer cases (manual) permanent recording and analysis takes place.

Design options denotes the possibilities or solution space that an organization has in place to solve the identified problems during an ET. These design options range from evaluating emerging technologies to organizing solution ideas [42]. However, this perspective has rarely been systematically assessed or integrated into organizational processes using business analytics. Only one organization has implemented a systematic, though primarily manual, classification method for architectural design options used by the steering committee.

Methods describes the methods used to manage the transformation and the projects per se. While the majority of organizations do not record this at all and do not systematically process it for steering purposes, in 30% of cases clear information on this is provided and known but is primarily viewed as deterministic and is not systematically adapted or changed over the course of the ET.

Risks means the broad field of diverse potential threats to the ET and the organization itself. These risks are already systematically recorded, sustainably tracked and prepared for the steering committee in almost all organizations. Risks are prioritized to a certain extent, i.e., a focus is placed on earnings and legislative risks. Attempts are often made to quantify earnings risks in particular. More detailed investigations and exploratory surveys, e.g., on non-financial risks, do usually not take place to date.

Performance in this case means in particular the performance of the ET itself in the organization. We can observe that in most cases performance is already sustainably tracked and considered a relevant factor. Most of these approaches are manual, but fairly automated evaluations also take place and are assessed both quantitatively and qualitatively. At the same time, it is notable that when evaluating performance, the parameter output, i.e., the specific artifact and not its contribution to results, and the costs are measured. However, some interview partners stated that they would like to focus more on outcome and speed for ET steering (e.g., the interview partner of Case 4 has emphasized that in the future, only or almost only the outcome, i.e., the creation of value through ET, will be discussed in steering committee meetings and throughout the entire organization).

Social factors refers to the identification, analysis and targeted evaluation of various parameters, such as cultural change in the organization. The results show that most organizations have not yet systematically collected data on this change aspect. However, Case 1 and Case 2 emphasize that they are already trying to make cultural change as one main social factor measurable through systematic, regular surveys and to inform steering decisions in the ET on this basis.

Stakeholders refers to the relevant groups and individuals that need to be addressed in the course of the ET. These can be both inside and outside the organization. The aim is to identify who the stakeholders are and how they change, as well as to systematically record and process how their perspectives are fulfilled or not fulfilled by the work of the ET. In most cases, stakeholders are already regarded as determinants, but intensive analyses or even automated analyses over the course of time hardly ever take place.

4.2 Organizational Factors

The *organizational factors*, i.e., the factors that relate to the changing organization as the object of change, are often already actively known and are considered relevant accordingly. Consequently, information and analyses are already used in many cases. Meanwhile, it is notable that these factors are often seen as a determining element and are not systematically adapted or changed over time.

Strategy refers to the specific overall organizational strategy or derived strategies of the specialist departments and IT. These are widely recognized as a relevant factor, especially for deriving the needs of an ET and, in particular, the underlying goals for the ET. The strategy is usually regarded as external, as a given variable, but is often heavily relied upon. However, a special, long-term use of business analytics for the continuous acquisition of strategic information is not pursued. In a single case, the tracking of strategy and general strategic decisions can be recognized through systematic, albeit manual, tracking.

Business structure refers in particular to aspects relating to the anatomy of the organization, the functional set-up, the local distribution of tasks and functions and the nature and scope of capabilities. Only in individual cases the analyses go significantly beyond the perspective of determining effects. In one case, Case 1, however, we could identify a largely automated calculation and representation of some aspects of the business structure, e.g., the development of company-relevant capabilities based on specific maturity levels.

IT structure refers to the nature of the information technology infrastructure and application landscape in particular. This is considered to be an extremely relevant aspect of support and an active component of ET steering. In most cases, companies are already able to obtain an overview of their infrastructure based on enterprise architecture management efforts. In most cases, the IT structure is usually seen as determining and adjustments are often made, but not systematically. This is different in cases such as Case 1 and Case 2, for example, where an active and valued enterprise architecture management is in place and supported by appropriate software.

Project portfolio describes the overview of the relevant projects and programs within the entire organization as well as their interdependencies and dependencies. This is fundamentally tracked in all cases and various projects are kept in view, also over the course of time. At the same time, many companies have not yet succeeded in comprehensively tracking interdependencies, although this is a declared goal. In two cases, a high degree of automation has already been achieved in the automatic detection, recording and processing of various projects and their dependencies in relation to specific key figures, e.g., team utilization and specific resource bottlenecks.

4.3 Context Factors

The *context factors* describe the context of the ET and the organization. These are not directly manageable entities, but levels that lie outside the typical boundaries of a transformation manager. However, according to Kiselev, Winter and Rohner [4], these are particularly relevant for the success of ET and should be addressed by steering committees. Overarchingly, these have not been supported by the use of business analytics and are hardly noticed at all. While the interviewees acknowledged the relevance of such parameters, there is a lack of both motivation and capabilities for the identification and active application of business analytics on the corresponding factors. The descriptions of the different information factors are fundamentally based on Kiselev, Winter and Rohner [4].

Terrain refers to the specific situation and the prior knowledge the organization has on the abstract problem and solution spaces. Although terrain has been identified as a relevant factor for the steering of ETs and has also been confirmed by practitioners, there is a lack of specific evaluations in practice. Any decisions relating to *terrain* or that are influenced by terrain are predominantly made on the basis of gut feelings or not at all. There is no systematic evaluation through business analytics in the cases.

Dynamics concerns the speed and ambiguity of the environment of the organization and the ET. While the handling of dynamics was emphasized in particular for the steering of ETs and is often discussed in the context of business agility and traditional implementation concepts, there is a lack of metrics and systematic tracking mechanisms for the application of business analytics.

Complexity involves the complexity of the ET itself and the organization as a whole. Although complexity is a relevant underlying factor for ET steering, which deals with a complex artifact per se, it has so far remained at best at the abstract-general level in architectural logic. Specific complexity metrics are not collected and used for steering purposes. Approaches to reducing complexity are mostly based on individual specialist knowledge (e.g., through enterprise architecture managers), but not on systematic findings through the application of business analytics.

Commitment means the standing and respect towards the ET and its initiatives in the organization at senior and mid-management as well as the operational level. Although commitment is recognized as an important factor for steering ETs and practitioners agree on its pivotal role, there are few practical cases for business analytics. Most decisions related to commitment are based on intuition. However, we identified initial survey-based approaches in two cases that aim to assess stakeholders' understanding of the ET and gauge their commitment, at least at the operational level.

Ability to Act focuses on the autonomy and independent progression of the ET and its underlying initiatives. While this information factor has been identified as a relevant field, it is not captured or discussed in steering committees systematically yet. The application of business analytics to this information factor has not yet gained any significance in practice.

5 Discussion

In this study, we examined the current state of business analytics use in ET steering. Specifically, we analyzed 16 information factors across three overarching information areas to assess how systematically they are tracked and applied in steering efforts across different organizations. Our findings reveal clear differences in the treatment of these factors and indicate that, overall, the systematic use of business analytics for ET decision support remains limited. These descriptive insights offer valuable implications for both research and practice, which we discuss in the following sections.

5.1 Implications for Academia

Our results can be related to existing research findings and are discussed particularly on three main aspects. Specifically, we discuss the evaluation scheme for business analytics for ET steering with the current discourse, the introduction of new overarching information areas of business analytics for ET steering, and the broad, evolutionary definition of business analytics for the use in the context of ET.

First, our study builds heavily on the existing reference model for information-based ET support by Labusch, Aier and Winter [42] and incorporates the more recent insights of Kiselev, Winter and Rohner [4] regarding context factors relevant to ET steering. The information factors used in our study, which were validated through interviews, provide a clearer, action-oriented focus on the information requirements in ETs and serve as a robust foundation for assessing the current status of business analytics for ET steering. By adapting and expanding the original ET information factors by Labusch, Aier and Winter [42], our research contributes to the renewal of this framework, which is approaching a decade in age. In this context, business analytics that addresses both explicit and implicit information needs is positioned as a critical and systematic solution to the underlying information logistics challenges faced in ET steering.

Second, we propose a novel classification of information factors into three overarching information areas: *ET* factors, *organizational* factors and *context* factors. This structure, not previously addressed in the literature, enhances conceptual clarity and links data collection to the distinct objectives of ET governance. Our findings show that while the use of business analytics remains at an early stage, concrete examples of application already exist—particularly in the organizational domain. In contrast, context factors, though consistently described as critical by experts, are largely overlooked in practice. This gap points either to a slow uptake in the field or to underlying conceptual difficulties that future research could aim to resolve. Accordingly, our study provides a descriptive foundation for subsequent explanatory, predictive, or even design-oriented research into business analytics for ETs.

Third, our study positions business analytics as a concrete, applied use case, i.e., as a means to support ET steering. This focus is motivated by the high strategic and financial relevance of ETs [1], the inherent complexity of steering such transformations [9] the need for more informed, data-driven decisions [4]. Despite this potential, our findings show that comprehensive business analytics applications, especially those involving automated data collection, integration, and evaluation, are still rare. In many organizations, business analytics in ET steering remains conceptual, with few cases demonstrating mature, scalable implementation. This highlights a significant gap between theoretical promise and actual practice and underlines the need for further research to develop practical, domain-specific analytics solutions that support complex ET efforts.

5.2 *Implications for Practice*

The practical implications are particularly focused on addressing specific information factors to meet the needs of ET steering committees. By structuring and expanding these information factors, companies can pinpoint which areas to prioritize in their ET efforts. It's essential to identify *context* factors that have previously been overlooked or inadequately captured in organizational practice, as this might enhance the quality of steering decisions (and thus enhance the success of ET endeavors). The study also recommends that organizations place greater emphasis on data-driven support for ET steering decisions in general, focusing on the implementation of specified, situated and iterative solution approaches instead of comprehensive, end-to-end systems. Incorporating a hypothesis-driven approach to data collection and analysis into a presentation format that is accessible and useful for steering committees could further support effective decision-making.

6 Conclusion and Future Research

This study offers a descriptive account of the current use of business analytics for ET steering. We can describe an extendible coverage by actual business analytics and argue for an increased expansion with a focus on information factors in the areas *ET* and *context*. In doing so, we extend the perspective of Labusch, Aier and Winter [42] with project-external aspects that should be taken into account in ET steering, following notions of Kiselev, Winter and Rohner [4]. Our findings are grounded in interviews with experienced ET managers across diverse industries and organizational settings.

As with all qualitative research, this study is subject to certain limitations. First, the interpretive nature of the research design introduces some ambiguity in how the information factors are assessed. While our ten cases span different industries and company sizes, the sample remains relatively small, and findings reflect the perspectives of a specific group of experts at a particular point in time. Thus, the generalizability of the findings is constrained.

Second, the study relies solely on self-reports from experts primarily fulfilling the role of ET managers, without incorporating the views of other key decision-makers, i.e., other members of ET steering committees. This restricts the breadth of perspectives considered. Furthermore, the broad definition of business analytics used in this study aims to accommodate diverse requirements and the challenges of implementation in specific ET contexts. However, this broad scope may obscure the focus on developing an overarching and cohesive framework.

Future research can build on our findings in several ways. For the reason of conciseness, we point out two main streams that could be affected: First, we would encourage future research to complement the qualitative findings of the study with quantitative research methodologies and validate the results of this study accordingly, e.g., through large-sample surveys. Second, we see value in design-oriented research that explores how to better support ET steering through analytics. This includes investigating effective methods for identifying and collecting relevant data and developing visualization approaches that help ET managers and steering committee members interpret key metrics. In this context, it would also be valuable to explore how existing data sources, such as enterprise systems and project management tools, can be systematically leveraged, and how the resulting data can be processed to support timely and targeted steering decisions.

Acknowledgments Generative AI (ChatGPT) was used to enhance the linguistic clarity and coherence of selected sections of the manuscript. All substantive content and interpretations remain the sole responsibility of the author.

Disclosure of Interests The author has no competing interests to declare that are relevant to the content of this article.

References

1. Mankins, M., & Litre, P. (2024). Transformations that work. *Harvard Business Review.*
2. Campanelli, A. S., Bassi, D., & Parreiras, F. S. (2017). Agile transformation success factors: A practitioner's survey. *Advanced Information Systems Engineering (Caise 2017), 10253*, 364–379.
3. Matt, C., Hess, T., & Benlian, A. (2015). Digital transformation strategies. *Business & Information Systems Engineering, 57*(5), 339–343.
4. Kiselev, C., Winter, R., & Rohner, P. (2020). Project success requires context-aware governance. *MIS Quarterly Executive, 19*(3), 199–211.
5. Proper, H. A. (2014). Enterprise architecture: Informed steering of enterprises in motion. In S. Hammoudi, J. Cordeiro, L. A. Maciaszek, & J. Filipe (Eds.), (pp. 16–34). Springer.
6. Chandler, D., & Hall, P. A. (2017). *Improving executive sponsorship of projects: A holistic approach.* Business Expert Press.
7. Hughes, D. L., Dwivedi, Y. K., Rana, N. P., & Simintiras, A. C. (2016). Information systems project failure – analysis of causal links using interpretive structural modelling. *Production Planning & Control, 27*(16), 1313–1333.
8. Kiselev, C. (2019). Digital transformation programs – control in the context of agile and traditional approaches: A multiple-case study. Mediterranean Conference on Information Systems (MCIS), Paper 28, Naples, Italy.
9. Sáenz-Royo, C., Chiclana, F., & Herrera-Viedma, E. (2023). Steering committee management. Expertise, diversity, and decision-making structures. *Information Fusion, 99.*
10. Barthel, P., & Hess, T. (2020). Towards a characterization of digitalization projects in the context of organizational transformation. *Pacific Asia Journal of the Association for Information Systems, 12*(3), 31–56.
11. Carlsson, C. (2018). Decision analytics—Key to digitalisation. *Information Sciences, 460–461*, 424–438.
12. Lechler, T. G., & Cohen, M. (2009). Exploring the role of steering committees in realizing value from project management. *Project Management Journal, 40*(1), 42–54.
13. Moser, B. R., & Grossmann, W. (2023). Digital twins of complex projects. *The Digital Twin*, 677–702.
14. Dinter, B., Lahrmann, G., & Winter, R. (2010). Information logistics as a conceptual foundation for enterprise-wide decision support. *Journal of Decision Systems, 19*(2), 175–200.
15. Labusch, N. (2017). Information requirements for enterprise transformation. In H. A. Proper, R. Winter, S. Aier, & S. de Kinderen (Eds.), *Architectural coordination of enterprise transformation* (pp. 111–121). Springer.
16. McGrath, S. K., & Whitty, S. J. (2019). Do steering committees really steer? *International Journal of Managing Projects in Business, 12*(3), 785–807.
17. Al-Okaily, A., Teoh, A. P., & Al-Okaily, M. (2023). Evaluation of data analytics-oriented business intelligence technology effectiveness: An enterprise-level analysis. *Business Process Management Journal, 29*(3), 777–800.
18. Sunyaev, A., Dehling, T., Strahringer, S., Da Xu, L., Heinig, M., Perscheid, M., Alt, R., & Rossi, M. (2023). The future of enterprise information systems. *Business & Information Systems Engineering, 65*(6), 731–751.
19. Beese, J., Aier, S., & Winter, R. (2015). On the role of complexity for guiding enterprise transformations. In D. Aveiro, R. Pergl, & M. Valenta (Eds.), *Advances in Enterprise Engineering IX* (pp. 113–127). Springer.
20. Bouchard, T. J. (1976). Field research methods: Interviewing, questionnaires, participant observation, unobtrusive measures. In M. D. Dunnette (Ed.), *Handbook of industrial and organizational psychology* (pp. 363–414). Rand-McNally College Publishing Company.
21. Schultze, U. A. M. (2011). Designing interviews to generate rich data for information systems research. *Information and Organization, 21*(1), 1–16.

22. Rouse, W. B. (2005). A theory of enterprise transformation. *Systems Engineering, 8*(4), 279–295.
23. Jöhnk, J., Ollig, P., Rövekamp, P., & Oesterle, S. (2022). Managing the complexity of digital transformation—How multiple concurrent initiatives foster hybrid ambidexterity. *Electronic Markets, 32*(2), 547–569.
24. Greenwood, R., & Hinings, C. R. (1993). Understanding strategic change: The contribution of archetypes. *Academy of Management Journal, 36*(5), 1052–1081.
25. Henderson, J. C., & Venkatraman, N. (1999). Strategic alignment: Leveraging information technology for transforming organizations. *IBM Systems Journal, 38*(2/3), 472–484.
26. Lyytinen, K., & Newman, M. (2008). Explaining information systems change: A punctuated socio-technical change model. *European Journal of Information Systems, 17*(6), 589–613.
27. Sebastian, I. M., Ross, J. W., Beath, C., Mocker, M., Moloney, K. G., & Fonstad, N. O. (2017). How big old companies navigate digital transformation. *MIS Quarterly Executive, 16*(3), 133–150.
28. Vial, G. (2019). Understanding digital transformation: A review and a research agenda. *The Journal of Strategic Information Systems, 28*(2), 118–144.
29. Carroll, N., Conboy, K., & Wang, X. (2023). From transformation to normalisation: An exploratory study of a large-scale agile transformation. *Journal of Information Technology*.
30. Horlach, B., Schirmer, I., & Drews, P. (2019). *Agile portfolio management: Design goals and principles*. Twenty-Seventh European Conference on Information Systems (ECIS2019), Stockholm.
31. Winter, R., Bender, B., & Aier, S. (2024). *Enterprise-level IS research – Need, conceptualization, exemplary knowledge contributions and future opportunities* (pp. 6402–6411). Proceedings of the 57th Hawaii International Conference on System Sciences (HICSS 2024), Honolulu, HI, USA.
32. Proper, H. A., Winter, R., Aier, S., & de Kinderen, S. (Eds.). (2017). *Architectural coordination of enterprise transformation*. Springer.
33. Carroll, N., Hassan, N. R., Junglas, I., Hess, T., & Morgan, L. (2023). Transform or be transformed: The importance of research on managing and sustaining digital transformations. *European Journal of Information Systems, 32*(3), 347–353.
34. Riaz, S., Morgan, D., & Kimberley, N. (2023). Managing organizational transformation (OT) using complex adaptive system (CAS) framework: Future lines of inquiry. *Journal of Organizational Change Management, 36*(3), 493–513.
35. Hanelt, A., Bohnsack, R., Marz, D., & Antunes Marante, C. (2021). A systematic review of the literature on digital transformation: Insights and implications for strategy and organizational change. *Journal of Management Studies, 58*(5), 1159–1197.
36. Martinsuo, M., & Hoverfält, P. (2018). Change program management: Toward a capability for managing value-oriented, integrated multi-project change in its context. *International Journal of Project Management, 36*(1), 134–146.
37. Kiselev, C., & Winter, R. (2020). *Governance of mixed agile/traditional digital transformation programs*. AMCIS 2020 Proceedings. AIS, Salt Lake City.
38. Morris, P. (2013). Reconstructing project management reprised: A knowledge perspective. *Project Management Journal, 44*(5), 6–23.
39. Henfridsson, O., & Yoo, Y. (2014). The liminality of trajectory shifts in institutional entrepreneurship. *Organization Science, 25*(3), 932–950.
40. Gimpel, H., Hosseini, S., Ruber, R. X. R., Probst, L., Röglinger, M., & Faisst, U. (2018). Structuring digital transformation: A framework of action fields and its application at ZEISS. *Journal of Information Technology Theory and Application, 19*(1), 31–54.
41. Schoemaker, P. J. H. (1982). The expected utility model: Its variants, purposes, evidence and limitations. *Journal of Economic Literature, 20*(2), 529–563.
42. Labusch, N., Aier, S., & Winter, R. (2014). A reference model for the information-based support of enterprise transformations. In M. C. Tremblay, D. VanderMeer, M. Rothenberger, A. Gupta, & V. Yoon (Eds.), (pp. 194–208). Springer International.

43. Edwards, W. (1954). The theory of decision making. *Psychological Bulletin, 51*(4), 380–417.
44. Chatterjee, S., Rana, N. P., & Dwivedi, Y. K. (2021). How does business analytics contribute to organisational performance and business value? A resource-based view. *Information Technology & People, 37*(2), 874–894.
45. Duan, Y., Cao, G., & Edwards, J. S. (2020). Understanding the impact of business analytics on innovation. *European Journal of Operational Research, 281*(3), 673–686.
46. Davenport, T. H., & Harris, J. G. (2007). Competing on analytics. *Harvard Business School.*
47. Power, D. J., Heavin, C., McDermott, J., & Daly, M. (2018). Defining business analytics: An empirical approach. *Journal of Business Analytics, 1*(1), 40–53.
48. Phillips-Wren, G., Daly, M., & Burstein, F. (2021). Reconciling business intelligence, analytics and decision support systems: More data, deeper insight. *Decision Support Systems, 146.*
49. Božič, K., & Dimovski, V. (2019). Business intelligence and analytics for value creation: The role of absorptive capacity. *International Journal of Information Management, 46*, 93–103.
50. Farshadi, R., Nazemi, E., & Abdolvand, N. (2022). A framework for ranking critical success factors of business intelligence based on enterprise architecture and maturity model. *Interdisciplinary Journal of Information, Knowledge, and Management, 17*, 543–575.
51. Myers, M. D., & Newman, M. (2007). The qualitative interview in IS research: Examining the craft. *Information and Organization, 17*(1), 2–26.
52. Sonnenberg, C., & vom Brocke, J. (2012). Evaluations in the science of the artificial – Reconsidering the build-evaluate pattern in design science research. In K. Peffers, M. Rothenberger, & B. Kuechler (Eds.), *Design science research in information systems* (Advances in theory and practice) (Vol. 34, pp. 381–397). Springer.
53. Sarker, S., Xiao, X., & Beaulieu, T. (2013). Qualitative studies in information systems: A critical review and some guiding principles. *MIS Quarterly, 37*(4), Iii–Xviii.

The Four "E" Model—Evaluating Gen AI in a More Balanced Way

Jörg H. Mayer, Kira Bender, Markus Esswein, and Reiner Quick

Abstract Today, the use of generative AI is already ubiquitous, and industry observers expect this market to grow to more than USD1.3 trillion by 2032. However, gen AI is energy-intensive, causes carbon emissions, and consumes significant amounts of water. Beyond research which often focuses on "pure" IT issues such as GPT designs, we also consider gen AI's sustainability costs. In doing so, we conduct a survey with experienced Digital Finance leaders with 5–25 years of expertise, ultimately to assess the benefits of gen AI against its sustainability costs. Driving future discussions, we focus on three findings: (1) Only two thirds of the respondents already have ESG costs in mind. (2) Carbon emissions, energy, and water consumption are the most relevant environment criteria. (3) Weighting the categories of efficiency, effectiveness, experience, and environment, the Four "E" Model can be customized to a company's individual requirements, thus, it can help to identify best gen AI use cases.

Keywords Generative artificial intelligence · Sustainability · Cross-industry survey · Expert interviews

J. H. Mayer (✉) · K. Bender · R. Quick
Darmstadt University of Technology, Darmstadt, Germany
e-mail: jmayer@bwl.tu-darmstadt.de; kira.bender@stud.tu-darmstadt.de; quick@bwl.tu-darmstadt.de

M. Esswein
Henkel KGaA, Düsseldorf, Germany
e-mail: markus.esswein@henkel.com

A. Tursunbayeva et al. (eds.), *Technology-Driven Transformation*, Lecture Notes in Information Systems and Organisation 79,
https://doi.org/10.1007/978-3-032-01396-5_18

1 Introduction

Today, people refer to *generative artificial intelligence (gen AI)* for numerous things—even planning their vacations [1]. Industry observers expect this market to grow to more than USD1.3 trillion by 2032 [2]. As a new machine learning (ML) concept to train neural networks [3], gen AI generates previously unseen information based on data given to algorithms [4]. Well-known tools are ChatGPT and Google Gemini [5]. Another application is Microsoft's Copilot which is now integrated in the Office 365 suite.

Gen AI was often limited by the volume of data it had to learn from [6]. Today, more and more *datasets* are available even for free. Combined with *advanced computing power*, gen AI generates more accurate results for diverse topics of interest and new content [7]. Last but not least, researchers developed generative pre-trained transformers (GPT) which are already trained algorithms with adoption mechanisms [8].

Currently, gen AI is becoming increasingly popular in *offices*. A study cross-industry with 1684 participating companies laid out that one-third of the surveyed companies use gen AI regularly in one or more functions [9]. Marketing and sales (14%) are at the forefront, whereas *finance* is lacking behind (4%) [9]. After years of focusing on efficiency in the preparation of financial reports, we see the forthcoming *sustainability reporting* as a new gen AI use case.

Based on the ESG framework, which covers the environmental ("E") impact like the carbon footprint, social ("S") aspects like prosperity, and governance ("G") which refers to a company's compliance and business ethics, we focus on *internal ESG performance management reports*. Beginning with voluntary initiatives like the United Nation Global Compact [10], ESG performance *management* reports are developing towards a modern steering instrument so that they should lead to a better risk management, finally a better competitive market position [11].

We expect such reports to be less standardized than traditional financial reporting. Furthermore, they should integrate non-financial data across the company and beyond [12]. Thus, gen AI should help in generating such reports. In contrast, gen AI is energy-intensive, causes carbon emissions, and consumes large amounts of water as it runs on supercomputers and cloud infrastructures [13]. So, the question arises whether the benefits of gen AI outweigh its sustainability costs. Answers in literature are still scarce.

Accordingly, we develop a *model evaluating the benefits of gen AI against its sustainability costs*. We take internal ESG performance management reports as our case example. Considering the artefacts identified by March and Smith [14]—constructs, models, methods, and instantiations—a model is a set of propositions or statements expressing relationships among constructs. We pose two research questions (RQ):

- RQ #1: What are the most relevant requirement criteria for such a model?
- RQ #2: How does it help to assess gen AI use cases?

The contribution of the paper is threefold: (1) Beyond current gen AI research which often focuses on IT issues such as GPT designs, we also consider its sustainability costs. In doing so, we depart from prior research by a cost-benefit model beyond "pure" efficiency criteria. This makes our paper *relevant and timely*. (2) Applying a rigorous method mix that combines findings from a literature review with results from a cross-industry survey and expert interviews, our findings should be *widely acceptable.* (3) For practice, our model should assist companies to assess gen AI *use cases* in a comprehensive, *easy-to-apply manner*. Furthermore, it should help to prepare their implementations beyond "pure" experience and gut feeling.

The remainder of the article is as follows: Applying a resource-based view, we contextualize our research questions by gen AI requirement criteria *(related work)*. We then conduct a cross-industry survey *(method)* and cluster the requirement criteria in four categories (*results*). Evaluating our model, we perform expert interviews (*synthesis*). Comparing our results with prior work, we close with a summary, limitations of our work, and avenues for future research (*discussion and conclusion*).

2 Related Work

Following Webster and Watson [15] as well as vom Brocke et al. [16, 17], we identified relevant articles in a four-stage process. (1) Based on the AIS senior scholars' list of premium journals [18], we focused on leading IS journals, computer science, business, management, and accounting journals,[1] complemented by proceedings from major IS conferences[2] (*outlet search*). To obtain a practitioner perspective, we considered journals such as MIS Quarterly Executive and Harvard Business Review. (2) Accessing these outlets, we used ScienceDirect, EBSCO host, Springer Link, Emerald Insight, AIS eLibrary and the Web of Science (*database search*). (3) We then searched for articles through their titles, abstracts, and keywords (*keyword search*). Classifying an article as relevant, we focused on gen AI's capability to support ESG performance reports, especially considering sustainability costs generated by gen AI.

Applying this strategy, we combined gen AI with sustainability with the Boolean operator "and." Our research yielded 137 hits. We then delved into each of the pillars separately by substantiating sustainability with environment and life cycle management, and gen AI with GPT. In doing so, we found 372 hits for the first pillar, and for the second one we identified additional 8650 sources so that we detailed

[1] In order to select relevant journals from disciplines beyond IS, we used the Scimago Journal Ranking [19]. We selected the subject area "Computer Science" as well as "Business, Management, and Accounting."

[2] Going beyond IEEE and ACM conferences [20, 21], we followed the AIS list of leading IS conferences [22]. To cover proceedings from Semantic Web research, we included the International Semantic Web Conference and the European Semantic Web Conference.

sustainability to sustainability costs which revealed 12 hits. Finally, we conducted a *backward and forward search*. With references from all publications, we ended up with 14 publications in total.

Starting in 1987 with the United Nations' Brundtland Report [23], **sustainability** is defined as meeting *"the needs of the present without compromising the ability of future generations to meet their own needs."* The ESG framework covers the treatment of resources in three areas (Sect. 1). "E" covers environmental protection and safeguarding biodiversity such as the energy, carbon emission, and water. Prosperity, human rights, health & safety, peace per se, culture, and intergenerational justice is in the focus of "S." "G," in turn, refers to the compliance and business ethics of a company. We limit our research on the *"E" aspects* of ESG performance as they are currently most popular and best measurable.

Focusing on the **sustainability costs** of gen AI, in Jan 2023, ChatGPT4 used around 4200 MWh of *energy* to complete all its requests [24]. Another example is the transformer model BERT which consumed 1507 kWh in the 79 h needed for training [25]. For the training of ChatGPT3, 1.3 GWh were needed. Looking at the *emissions*, training a transformer with a neural network can generate 284 tons of CO_2. Running a Chat GPT-like application with 11 million requests/hour would release 12,800 tons CO_2/year [26]. ChatGPT4's training emissions are estimated to be around ten times higher [27]. Furthermore, servers need *water* cooling which accumulates to 700,000 L in training the underlaying model of ChatGPT3 [28]. It is estimated that the water withdrawal of all global gen AIs could total between 4.2 and 6.6 billion cubic meters of water by 2027 [29]—4 to 6 time the annual amount of Denmark's water usage.

Today, companies plan to *adapt gen AI to their individual business context,* which leads to an increasing amount of additional energy demand and further emissions [30]. Research is covering the sustainability costs of gen AI insufficiently. We found references for creating **ESG performance management reports** to achieve more efficiency and accuracy for data analysis [31]. They help to account and steer a company's sustainability to achieve traceability [32]. Furthermore, they should bring transparency about a company's actions [33]. However, creating ESG performance management reports is about strong efforts to *manage the non-measurable targets* and collect the associated (non-financial) data [34]. Accordingly, there is a desire to support day-to-day routines [35] by gen AI. For example, gen AI could *classify input data according to regulations* [36] or *automate data-collection, verification, and analysis* with the capability of generating report drafts [37]. In future, gen AI should help to integrate non-financial data with more reliability and ease into existing systems.

Evaluating gen AI models, we found one model with a focus on legal regulations [38]. We examined two models which defined AI sustainability costs as a *multidimensional construct* [39, 40]. Thelisson et al. offers a dashboard for monitoring *the sustainability costs of AI software* [40]. The Sætra model is a cube of "E, S, G" considering capabilities, assets, activities, and three emission scopes 1, 2, and 3 [39]. However, we identified no articles weighing the sustainability costs of gen AI against its benefits.

Cross referencing findings from *measuring IS success* [41], there are *two structural IS models* [42]. On the one hand, the Technology Acceptance Model and its extensions explain user behavior with perceived usefulness and perceived ease-of-use [43]. On the other hand, the DeLone and McLean IS success model is a multidimensional approach that covers six success categories [44]. Furthermore, there are *capital investment appraisal techniques* such as Net Present Value (NPV), Internal Rate of Return, and Payback Period. Finally, *list approaches* entail a collection of assessment criteria (often quantified and weighted) that are derived from the literature or the (individual) experience of the authors [45].

Summarizing our takeaways, we examined a lack of research evaluating the benefits of gen AI against its sustainability costs. However, requirements criteria should cover both in one model. In doing so, we opt for a list approach.

3 Method

Gaining access to companies' in-depth information, which were not available from our literature research (Sect. 2), we opted for a *survey*. It allows to address questions to a larger group of participants while maintaining anonymity and, thus, more objectivity of answers than can be expected from interviews [46].

We follow a two-step approach. Within the *pilot test*, which was conducted in September 2023, we interviewed two subject-matter experts from the department of sustainability from a manufacturing company, both experienced project managers for transformation programs with 5 and 25 years of experience in such roles, and we asked two senior scholars, one from the accounting, controlling, and auditing department at Darmstadt University of Technology and another one from the controlling department at UE Business School. They tested the usability, completeness, and consistency of our questionnaire and with their feedback we optimized the wording and predefined answers to our questions. Based on their feedback we made changes such as lack of personnel as an answer option as well as the European Sustainability Reporting Standards (ESRS) as the foundation for the ESG answer.

For the *main survey*, we asked 30 members of the manager working group "Digital Finance" (Table 1) hosted by the Schmalenbach-Gesellschaft in November 2023. The members of the Finance and Controlling department are experienced

Table 1 Characteristics of survey participants

Sector	No.	%	Department	No.	%	Market cap. [bn, EUR]	No.	%
Manufacturing	22	73.33	IT	2	6.67	<2	4	13.33
Utilities	4	13.33	Controlling	17	56.67	2–9	12	40
Others	4	13.33	Finance	7	23.33	>10	14	46.67
			Sustainability	2	6.67			
			Other	2	6.67			
Total	30	100	Total	30	100	Total	30	100

leaders with 5–25 years of experience in similar roles whilst meeting regularly to discuss trends in digitalizing the finance and accounting function.

Setting up the **questionnaire**, we employed *a resource-based view for our kernel theory* as it explains a company's development by maximizing the productivity of their resources which are physical, human, financial, technological, reputational, and organizational [47]. The survey took place in an onsite meeting and took about 60 min. Focusing on the technological benefits of gen AI and its dependent variable of sustainability costs (Sect. 1), we divided the survey into two sections:

(A) Measuring the *benefits of gen AI* and rating the gen AI status in companies, we applied predefined answers and free text fields. As a basis, we opted for the **triple "e" model**. It consists of three categories which are detailed into (sub) criteria [48]: (1) *Efficiency* is directly measurable by speed, costs (OPEX/ CAPEX), and full-time equivalents. (2) Advantages that are not directly measurable are covered by *effectiveness* consisting of better insights, flexibility, accuracy, consistency, and security. (3) Enabling efficiency and effectiveness, *experience* is the final category. Depicting for each of these categories, that is efficiency, effectiveness, and experience, we predefined answers and asked participants about the value of gen AI in their companies.

(B) Capturing the *sustainability costs*, we introduced the **European Sustainability Reporting Standards** and with the findings from the pilot of our survey, we substantiated this category, *concentrating on climate change, pollution, water & marine resources, biodiversity & ecosystems, resource use, and circular economy* [49]. An example is ESRS E1 (Climate Change) that aligns with the Paris Agreement for 2030. It addresses energy and climate change mitigation like the reporting obligations of the total energy consumption in MWh from activities of the company in high climate impact sectors per net turnover [50]. Within this part of the questionnaire, the participants chose in multi-select questions the input factors for their companies and detailed them accordingly with most influential standards regarding gen AI.

Gathering feedback about our model, we follow a naturalistic synthesis within a real-world business environment and, in doing so, we opted for *expert interviews* which took about 45 min each (Sect. 5). They determine the interviewee's knowledge regarding a phenomenon as comprehensively as possible [51]. In comparison to surveys, interviews enable delving deeper into the subject matter, so that more insights were collected. We applied *semi-structured expert interviews* (structured by an interview guide), because they combine a comparable structure within a series of interviews, whilst being flexible when interviewees want to share their individual way of thinking and any hidden facets of which they are aware [52]. To avoid adverse effects of recordings on the openness of the interviewees, even about topics that may not have gone well in the projects, we decided to *protocol the interviews* instead of recording them [53, 54]. Two members of the research team (authors of the article) conducted interviews within a software (sales: USD198.3 bn , employees: 221,000) and a manufacturing company (sales: 22.4 bn EUR, employees: 50,000).

4 Results

Within our main survey (Sect. 3), 22 participants currently use gen AI in their working environment (73%), 37% already use it weekly today. However, just nine currently use gen AI for reporting and, only two (7%) use it already for *internal ESG performance reports*. In future, more than 50% intend to use it for the latter and expect benefits from this. Adoption is currently hindered by data security issues, complexity of implementation, and lack of qualified personnel.

Then, we asked the participants about the *benefits* for internal ESG performance management reports in detail. They expect to save time, gain insights (both effectiveness criteria), and enable efficiency. 88% see time savings as the number one improvement followed by better insights (76%), and enabling efficiency per se (71%).

In the next chapter of the survey, 78% of our participants look for *environment topics* when evaluating digital technologies. This is in line with our pilot study findings, i.e., the need for extending the triple "e" model with a new category. Asked which environmental criteria they deemed most important with respect to gen AI, the participants emphasized climate change (82%), followed by water & marine resources (29%, all multi-select). Based on these two ESRS standards we selected main topics from each to integrate into our model. We detailed climate change as *carbon emission* and *energy*. The latter addresses the amount of electricity (kWh) the technology needs to process input. In the water and marine resources *water usage* stands out as being a limited resource in different parts of the world. Just 9% of the participants answered "neither."

Evaluating environmental aspects for internal ESG performance management reports, 65% of the respondents consider *sustainability costs* of gen AI. We will focus on the environmental costs in our proposed evaluation model as **carbon emissions, energy demand, and water usage**. These environmental criteria complement efficiency, effectiveness, and experience of the triple "e" model (Fig. 1).

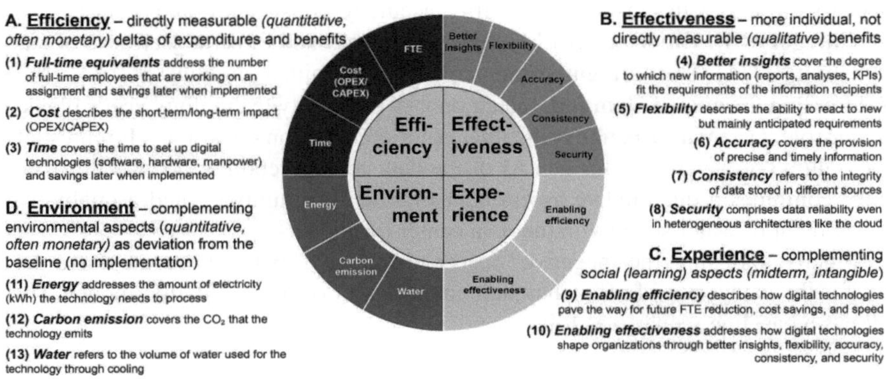

Fig. 1 Four "E" Model

Category "A. Efficiency" comprises three criteria that can be factored by a positive (economic benefits) and a negative (costs) sign and, thus, result in a delta (see Eq. 1). To enable a better understanding of the model we detail the criteria as follows: (1) **Full-time equivalents** or the impact on the size of the workforce is one benchmark for new (digital) technologies. With the adoption of such technologies, a productivity improvement can help reduce the personnel on a task. However, gen AI can also require extra FTEs for maintenance, training, or implementation as well.

(2) Addressing **cost** savings, a criterion is the ability of systems to decrease OPEX and CAPEX. On the one hand, gen AI can suggest future savings through analysis. On the other hand, it entails also costs for software licenses, new hardware, and consultancy fees if the knowledge does not exist in the company. (3) **Time** is impacted by gen AI as well. Time savings cover the reduction of redundant tasks like writing meeting notes with ChatGPT. It can also support analysis and writing recommendations. Negative impact on time can stem from inefficiencies for inexperienced users as well as time needed to train the gen AI model with the needed data.

Category "B. Effectiveness" has five criteria: (4) Benefits categorized under **better insights** capture the performance of how new information fits the requirements of the recipient. Better insight can end up in future "on top" net sales. (5) The need for **flexibility** arises from the increased demand to react to new requirements and circumstances. An example is the ability of gen AI to carry a conversation and merge information from old prompts with new criteria. (6) **Accuracy** considers precise information with gen AI being capable of detecting anomalies in large amounts of data. (7) Examining **consistency**, it is the faultlessness and unity of the data that is stored in different sources. Furthermore, gen AI provides the possibility of reducing human errors. (8) The last criterion within the effectiveness category is **security** as it is essential to enable trust in a new technology. Regarding gen AI, the model is able to control data to comply with company guidelines regarding compliance and business ethics of a company. An example is detecting threats in emails.

Category "C. Experience" has two criteria: (9) **Enabling efficiency** covers future efficiency gains such as guiding users to identify critical paths and bottlenecks based on data analyses. (10) **Enabling effectiveness** paves the way to future success through better insights, flexibility, accuracy, consistency, and security.

Category "D. Environment" has the aforementioned three new criteria of sustainability: (11) **Carbon emissions** covers the emitted amount of CO_2. (12) Addressing the **energy demand**, the amount of electricity technology needs plays a major role. (13) **Water usage** is the final criterion based on our survey. It represents the volume of water used for gen AI or the data centers' cooling. Ideally this category combines a quantitative assessment of water consumption and a qualitative assessment of water scarcity in the data center location.

Finally, to distinct the "negative" costs and "positive" benefits we integrated deltas for the categories of efficiency and environment of our evaluation model. This allows a baseline scenario as follows:

$$\begin{aligned}\textit{Use case assessment} = {} & (\alpha_1 * \textit{A. efficiency benefits} - \alpha_2 * \textit{A. efficiency costs}) \\ & + \beta * \textit{B. effectiveness benefits} + \gamma * \textit{C. experience benefits} \\ & + (\delta_1 * \textit{D. environment benefits} - \delta_2 * \textit{D. environment costs})\end{aligned} \quad (1)$$

With the help of *coefficients*, the equation depicts the ability of our model to customize the importance of the categories, that is efficiency, effectiveness, experience, and environment to a company´s individual requirements. This enables companies to balance and emphasize different categories in order to match their individual values, core beliefs, and strategies (see more details in Sect. 5).

Summarizing our findings and driving future discussions, we examined three findings from our survey: (1) Considering the use of gen AI, only two thirds of the respondents have ESG costs in mind. (2) Energy, carbon emission and water consumption are the most relevant environment criteria. (3) Weighting the four categories individually, the four "E" model can be customized to a company´s individual requirements and it can help to identify best gen AI use cases.

5 Synthesis

Discussing our Four "E" Model (Fig. 1), we opted for expert interviews and invited two experts to share their perspectives with us. The first one works as Finance Director in a software company and the second one is a Director for digitalization projects in a B2C unit of a chemical company.

Regarding the statement from the survey that the majority of participants *"currently only prioritize gen AI use cases from a cost perspective,"* the Director for digitalization projects stated that the return on investments is often the only important measure of project success. Accordingly, our Four "E" Model with its environment category departs from prior research and current practice by a first cost-benefit evaluation beyond "pure" efficiency criteria.

Furthermore, both experts noted that they *"see that many people haven't thought about the sustainability costs of gen AI."* An interesting perspective from one of the experts addressed this cost as they *"experience a different energy mix for regular or emergency use, which is most often caused by climate events."* On a different note, our expert from the software company mentioned that *"there is a shift towards upgrading data centers instead of new builds to achieve better sustainability."*

Compared to our survey results full-time equivalents reductions receive a different perspective as one of our experts confirmed that CFOs have a clear vision for the use of gen AI in combination with an FTE reduction. He added that "w*ith the possibilities of gen AI, productivity can be increased by around 10%.*" Beyond this, our other expert from the chemical industry added that she thinks "*[…] one of the overlooked benefits is that gen AI gives more room to be creative.*"

Comparing the concrete sustainability costs from Sect. 2 with the benefits highlighted in our survey, the latter currently outweigh the former. This is confirmed by both of our experts, who pointed out that it is not a question of whether to implement or not but rather when, how, and which use cases to address first.

To make this comparison more tangible in a company setting, we outlined an approach with the help of Fig. 2. Firstly, *coefficients (weights) for each category* enable finetuning of the importance of our model's categories to a company´s

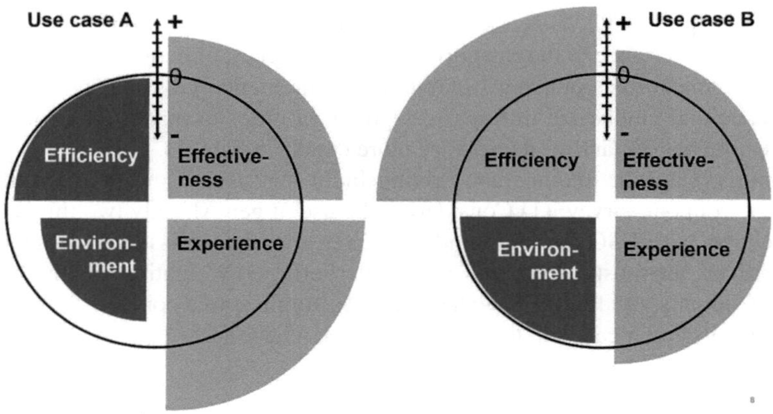

Fig. 2 Example use case comparison

individual requirements. In a visual representation, the four categories create larger quadrants the more benefits they enable, due to increased positive values of each criterion. In contrast, they shrink if more negative aspects and costs are present. For additional ease of interpretation, we have shaded negative quadrants in a darker color. (3) This approach also allows a company to "normalize" the impact of the effectiveness, experience and environment categories in comparison to the generally bigger—sometimes by orders of magnitude—efficiency category. This way, a company can put more emphasis on, e.g., accuracy of data (effectiveness) or carbon emissions (environment) that are generally hard to put a correct price tag on.

For example, *use case A* has high effectiveness benefits. However, to create those benefits the gen AI model needs more data points, computing power, and time causing the sustainability costs to increase. On the other hand, *use case B* is a simpler gen AI model (hence it is less computer intensive) that focuses on high efficiency benefits, such as writing meeting notes or aggregating media coverage of relevant topics. So, our model should help to identify best use cases and preparing their implementations more rigorously than through experience and gut feeling.

6 Discussion and Conclusion

Building on insights from a literature review and a survey among managers, we derived a model evaluating the benefits of gen AI against its sustainability costs. We evaluated our model by two expert interviews. Beyond efficiency, effectiveness, and experience, our Four "E" Model introduces the category of environment. It accounts for the sustainability costs with three criteria, that is energy, carbon emission and water.

For **research purposes**, we consider gen AI's sustainability costs in our evaluation model to become more prominent. This makes the paper *relevant and timely*. In doing so, our work combines models assessing sustainability per se like Sætra [39] and IS success models like the triple "e" model [48]. Merging both, we adopt a gen AI benefit perspective that goes beyond directly measurable efficiency criteria. As such, our research takes a step towards addressing the growing concern of environmental impact of digital technologies and gen AI in particular. In doing so, we depart from prior research by a cost-benefit model beyond "pure" efficiency criteria. Compared with practitioner articles such as Kumar and Davenport [30], the novelty of our work is that we employed a rigorous method mix by combining results from a literature review with findings from a survey complemented by expert interviews which should make our findings *widely acceptable*.

For **practice**, our research creates awareness for gen AI's sustainability costs and how to evaluate it in a balanced way. Contrary to existing models like Thelisson et al. [40], which only looks at qualitative sustainability aspects, our Four "E" Model combines quantitative and qualitative criteria for use case evaluations in a comprehensive, but always *easy-to-apply manner*. Our survey results can also give guidance for companies where they stand in comparison to our survey participants. We also translate a more balanced evaluation of gen AI mentioned by Villiers et al. [31] or Hacker et al. [38] into a model that can be applied in practice. Answering the issues that only two thirds of the respondents have ESG costs in mind, with coefficients for weighting, the Four "E" Model can help to identify best use cases in a more balanced way.

However, our research inevitably reveals certain *limitations* which open avenues for **future research**. Firstly, when more companies have gained experience with gen AI, a *broader survey* should explore more use cases and associated benefits of gen AI. Secondly, including data for different implementation options, on-premise or cloud environments, and different training approaches, will allow a more thorough evaluation of gen AI costs and benefits analysis. Thirdly, the model should be evaluated in *further use case* to gather information about its validity. Fourthly, our focus on environment should be revisited in the future as the importance of individual ESG dimensions will change over time. Finally, the model's utility should allow for the evaluation of *digital technologies* beyond gen AI as well. In conclusion, our research confirmed that gen AI will not only be a trend, but will influence all business processes, the company per se and its employees. In doing so, being tech-savvy and sustainability-minded at the same time will become a more and more important trait. In doing so, designing effective *upskilling programs* for the business department or implementing the envisioned *technical solution* will become key. Beyond others, the latter includes the development and individual training of AI as well manufacturing and maintenance of the hardware.

References

1. Roser, M. (2023). *The brief history of artificial intelligence: The world has changed fast – what might be next? Our World in Data.*
2. Bloomberg. *Generative AI to become a $1.3 trillion market by 2032, Research Finds.* Accessed April 05, 2024, from https://www.bloomberg.com/company/press/generative-ai-to-become-a-1-3-trillion-market-by-2032-research-finds/
3. Goodfellow, I. J., Pouget-Abadie, J., Mirza, M., Xu, B., Warde-Farley, D., Ozair, S., Courville, A., & Bengio, Y. Generative adversarial nets. *Neural Information Processing Systems.*
4. García-Peñalvo, F., & Vázquez-Ingelmo, A. (2023). what do we mean by GenAI? A systematic mapping of the evolution, trends, and techniques involved in generative AI. *International Journal of Interactive Multimedia and Artificial Intelligence, 8*(4), 7–16.
5. Gartner. *Generative AI: What is it, tools, models, applications and use cases.* Accessed December 11, 2023, from https://www.gartner.com/en/topics/generative-ai
6. Lazzeri, F. (2023). *Generative AI, OpenAI, and ChatGPT: What are they? - Data Science at Microsoft - Medium.* Data Science at Microsoft.
7. Nadeem, A. *The evolution of generative AI and generative machine learning.* Accessed December 1, 2023, from https://www.linkedin.com/pulse/evolution-generative-ai-machine-learning-nadeem-amin/
8. Gungor, A. (2023). *A simple guide to the history of generative AI.* Bernard Marr.
9. Chui, M., Yee, L., Hall, B., Singla, A., & Sukharevsky, A. *The state of AI in 2023: Generative AI's breakout year.* Accessed December 1, 2023, from https://www.mckinsey.com/capabilities/quantumblack/our-insights/the-state-of-ai-in-2023-generative-ais-breakout-year?cid=aisurge2023-soc%2D%2Dmar-mar%2D%2D07/23-i1a%2D%2Dbam-ip&linkId=228031498#/
10. Idowu, S. O., Capaldi, N., Zu, L., & Gupta, A. D. (Eds.). (2013). *Encyclopedia of corporate social responsibility.* Springer.
11. Whelan, T., & Douglas, E. (2021). How to talk to your CFO about sustainability. *Harvard Business Review.*
12. Christensen, H. B., Hail, L., & Leuz, C. (2021). Mandatory CSR and sustainability reporting: Economic analysis and literature review. *Review of Accounting Studies, 26*(3), 1176–1248.
13. Lanz, J. A. (2023). *AI's thirst for power may be draining water supplies.* Decrypt.
14. March, S. T., & Smith, G. F. (1995). Design and natural science research on information technology. *Decision Support Systems, 15*(4), 251–266.
15. Webster, J., & Watson, R. T. (2002). Analyzing the past to prepare for the future: Writing a literature review. *MIS Quarterly, 26*(2), xiii–xxiii.
16. vom Brocke, J., Simons, A., Niehaves, B., Riemer, K., Plattfaut, R., & Cleven, A. (2009). Reconstructing the giant: On the importance of rigour in documenting the literature search process. In S. Newell, E. A. Whitley, N. Pouloudi, J. Wareham, & L. Mathiassen (Eds.), *17th European Conference on Information Systems, Verona, Italy.*
17. vom Brocke, J., Simons, A., Riemer, K., Niehaves, B., Plattfaut, R., & Cleven, A. (2015). Standing on the shoulders of giants: Challenges and recommendations of literature search in information systems research. *Communications of the Association for Information Systems, 37*(1), 205–224.
18. AIS. *Senior Scholar's Basket of Journals.* Accessed March 02, 2025, from https://aisnet.org/page/SeniorScholarBasket/
19. SJR. *Scimago Journal & Country Rank.* Accessed April 20, 2024, from https://www.scimagojr.com/journalrank.php
20. IEEE. *Meetings, conferences, and events.* https://ieeexplore.ieee.org/Xplore/home.jsp
21. ACM. *Conferences, workshops, and symposia.* https://dl.acm.org/proceedings
22. AIS. *Conferences.* Accessed April 29, 2024, from https://aisnet.org/page/Conferences/
23. Brundtland, G. H. (1987). *Report of the World Commission on Environment and Development: Our common future.* United Nations.

24. Xue, D. (2023). *Strategies for mitigating the global energy and carbon impact of artificial intelligence*. United Nations.
25. Strubell, E., Ganesh, A., & McCallum, A. (2019). *Energy and policy considerations for deep learning in NLP*. Association for Computational Linquistics.
26. Chien, A. A., Lin, L., Nguyen, H., Rao, V., Sharma, T., & Wijayawardana, R. (2023). Reducing the carbon impact of generative AI inference (today and in 2035). In A. A. Chien, T. Eilam, G. Porter, T. Anderson, C. Josephson, & J. Park (Eds.), *HotCarbon '23: 2nd Workshop on Sustainable Computer Systems, Boston MA USA* (pp. 1–7). ACM.
27. Sundberg, N. (2023). Tackling AI's climate change problem. *MIT Sloan Management Review, 65*(2).
28. George, A., George, A., & Martin, A. (2023). The environmental impact of AI: A case study of water consumption by Chat GPT. *Partners Universal International Innovation Journal, 1*(2), 97–104.
29. Ren, S. *How much water does AI consume? The public deserves to know it*. Accessed December 1, 2023, from https://oecd.ai/en/wonk/how-much-water-does-ai-consume
30. Kumar, A., & Davenport, T. (2023). How to make generative AI greener. *Harvard Business Review*.
31. de Villiers, C., Dimes, R., & Molinari, M. (2023). How will AI text generation and processing impact sustainability reporting? Critical analysis, a conceptual framework, and avenues for future research. *Sustainability Accounting, Management and Policy Journal*.
32. Farisyi, S., Musadieq, M. A., Utami, H. N., & Damayanti, C. R. (2022). A systematic literature review: Determinants of sustainability reporting in developing countries. *Sustainability, 14*(16), 10222.
33. Benameur, K. B., Mostafa, M. M., Hassanein, A., Shariff, M. Z., & Al-Shattarat, W. (2023). Sustainability reporting scholarly research: A bibliometric review and a future research agenda. *Management Review Quarterly*.
34. Bullay, A. M. (2020). The level of sustainability reporting and its impact on firm performance. *Business and Management*.
35. de Micco, P., Rinaldi, L., Vitale, G., Cupertino, S., & Maraghini, M. P. (2021). The challenges of sustainability reporting and their management: The case of Estra. *Meditari Accountancy Research, 29*(3), 430–448.
36. Föhr, T. L., Schreyer, M., Juppe, T. A., & Marten, K.-U. (2023). Assuring sustainable futures: Auditing sustainability reports using AI foundation models. *SSRN Electronic Journal*.
37. Gu, H., Schreyer, M., Moffitt, K., & Vasarhelyi, M. A. (2023). Artificial intelligence co-piloted auditing. *SSRN Electronic Journal*.
38. Hacker, P., Engel, A., & Mauer, M. (2023). Regulating ChatGPT and other large generative AI models. In *FAccT '23: the 2023 ACM Conference on Fairness, Accountability, and Transparency, Chicago, IL* (pp. 1112–1123). Association for Computing Machinery.
39. Sætra, H. S. (2023). The AI ESG protocol: Evaluating and disclosing the environment, social, and governance implications of artificial intelligence capabilities, assets, and activities. *Sustainable Development, 31*(2), 1027–1037.
40. Thelisson, E., Mika, G., Schneiter, Q., Padh, K., and Verma, H.: Toward responsible AI use: Considerations for sustainability impact assessment (2023)
41. Grover, V., Jeong, S. R., & Segars, A. H. (1996). Information systems effectiveness: The construct space and patters of application. *Information & Management, 31*(4), 177–191.
42. Dörr, S., Walther, S., & Eymann, T. (2013). *Information systems success – a quantitative literature review and comparison* (pp. 1813–1827).
43. Davis, F. D. (1989). Perceived usefulness, perceived ease of use, and user acceptance of information technology. *MIS Quarterly, 13*(3), 319–340.
44. DeLone, W. H., & McLean, E. R. (1992). Information systems success: The quest for the dependent variable. *Information Systems Journal, 3*(1), 60–95.
45. Gurbaxani, V., & Dunkle, D. (2019). Gearing up for successful digital transformation. *MIS Quarterly Executive, 18*(3), 209–220.

46. Schmidt, W. C. (1997). World-Wide Web survey research: Benefits, potential problems, and solutions. *Behavior Research Methods, Instruments, & Computers, 29*(2), 274–279.
47. Penrose, E. T. (1959). *The theory of the growth of the firm*. Wiley.
48. Mayer, J., Ulusoy, B., Esswein, M., & Quick, R. (2021). *Receiving a triple "E" rating – Measuring IS success by balancing efficiency, effectiveness, and experience criteria*. ICIS 2021 Proceedings.
49. European Commission. (2023). *ESRS 1: General requirements*. European Commission.
50. European Commission. (2023). *ESRS E1: Climate change*. European Commission.
51. Kvale, S. (1996). *InterViews – An introduction to qualitative research interviewing* (1st ed.). SAGE.
52. Qu, S. Q., & Dumay, J. (2011). The qualitative research interview. *Qualitative Research in Accounting & Management, 8*(3), 238–264.
53. Al-Yateem, N. (2012). The effect of interview recording on quality of data obtained: A methodological reflection. *Nurse Researcher, 19*(4), 31–35.
54. McMullin, C. (2021). Transcription and qualitative methods: Implications for third sector research. *Voluntas*, 1–14.

Advances in Measuring Soft Skills in Project Management. A Technology-Mediated Approach to Capture the Enacted Behavior

Franca Cantoni, Camilla Capogreco, Marco Cerri, Emanuele Patti, and Claudio Soregaroli

Abstract The evaluation of soft skills in project management presents persistent methodological challenges due to their behavioral, relational, and context-dependent nature. This study systematically investigates (i) the dominant measurement approaches currently employed, and (ii) the diffusion of objective behavioral assessment tools capable of capturing enacted behaviors. The findings reveal a prevailing reliance on self-report measures, with limited adoption of objective behavioral assessments. To address this gap, the study proposes an innovative measurement architecture integrating technology-mediated tools—such as virtual escape rooms and e-driving simulations—and a dedicated algorithm for standardizing and interpreting behavioral data against population benchmarks. This framework offers a replicable methodology capable of generating empirically grounded, behavior-based data for theory-building and validation.

Keywords Soft skills · Project management · Behavioral assessment · Measurement methodology · Enacted behavior

1 Introduction

Traditionally, Project Management (PM) was largely synonymous with technical prowess and proficiency in the intricacies of project methodologies. The emphasis was placed squarely on the mastery of tools, processes, and techniques, often overlooking the human element [1]. However, the recognition that projects are fundamentally social endeavors, shaped by the collaboration and interaction of diverse

F. Cantoni (✉) · C. Capogreco · M. Cerri · E. Patti · C. Soregaroli
Università Cattolica del Sacro Cuore, Piacenza, Italy
e-mail: franca.cantoni@unicatt.it; camilla.capogreco@unicatt.it; marco.cerri1@unicatt.it; emauele.patti01@icatt.it; caludio.soregaroli@unicattt.it

A. Tursunbayeva et al. (eds.), *Technology-Driven Transformation*, Lecture Notes in Information Systems and Organisation 79,
https://doi.org/10.1007/978-3-032-01396-5_19

individuals [2] in ever-changing organizational landscapes [3, 4] has given way to a more holistic understanding that integrates technical competence with a rich tapestry of soft skills [5]. In contrast to hard skills, which benefit from well-established quantification protocols and standardized assessment instruments, the evaluation of soft skills—especially within project management—entails significant methodological complexity due to their behavioral, relational, and context-dependent nature [6, 7].

A key challenge stems from the inherently intangible and multidimensional nature of soft skills. Unlike hard skills, which are defined by discrete tasks, standardized procedures, and codified knowledge, soft skills emerge through complex behavioral patterns and socio-emotional interactions [8]. As a result, efforts to quantify soft skills face considerable methodological challenges arising from the complex interplay between individual dispositions, interpersonal dynamics, and contextual variability. The inherently emergent and relational character of these competencies resists standardized assessment and complicates efforts to establish consistent evaluative frameworks.

In response to these limitations, this study articulates two main research objectives. Firstly, we present an overview of the principal tools used to measure soft skills, highlighting their strengths and weaknesses. Secondly, we suggest a new perspective on measurement. Through this perspective, the research not only addresses existing gaps but also enhances the legitimacy and applicability of these skills within the broader PM community.

The structure of this paper is delineated as follows. The second paragraph furnishes a comprehensive literature review encompassing the difficulties in finding appropriate measures, the principal tools used to measure soft skills and delineates the research inquiries. Subsequently, the third paragraph elucidates the methodology adopted. Following this, the fourth paragraph expounds upon the findings, which are subsequently analyzed in the fifth paragraph. The sixth paragraph provides an additional analysis offering a new perspective on measurement. Conclusions and their implications ensue, culminating in an exploration of limitations and avenues for further research.

2 Literature Review

Soft skills are critical in project management, directly shaping the success and effectiveness of project outcomes [9, 10]. While technical expertise and domain knowledge are essential, the capacity to navigate interpersonal dynamics, lead teams with empathy and emotional intelligence [11] and communicate with clarity [12] remains equally critical. In the complex landscape of project management [13], soft skills function as a critical integrative force, enabling the alignment of diverse stakeholders through enhanced collaboration, conflict resolution, and consensus-building processes [14].

However, unlike technical skills—which can typically be evaluated through standardized academic results and certification processes—the assessment of soft skills remains inherently complex. Their evaluation often necessitates multi-source approaches, including peer and supervisor feedback [15], self-assessment instruments [16], psychometric evaluations [17], and structured interviews [18]. Furthermore, the multiplicity of assessment parameters introduces additional challenges such as inconsistencies across evaluation frameworks, measurement inaccuracies [19], incomplete coverage of the relevant skill set [20], and redundancy across overlapping criteria [21].

Such complexities underscore the need for developing more robust, reliable, and comprehensive methods for evaluating these essential competencies. As far as the tools for assessing soft skills, it appears that survey questionnaires and behavioral observation have emerged as predominant tools. Survey questionnaires offer structured and quantifiable insights into an individual's self-reported skills [22], while behavioral observations emerge as another frequently utilized approach, as indicated by the research conducted by [23, 24]. These tools involve domain experts providing feedback on questionnaire structure, assessing aspects such as representativeness, language clarity, wordin appropriateness, and item relevance [25]. Furthermore, semi-structured interviews with human resource experts, executives, and managers owe their effectiveness in capturing nuanced behavioral patterns and contextual factors [26]. Some authors suggest e-interviews, interview situation of the "look-alike" type, of the challenges linked to an approach that considers the actual work. This digital approach appears to be flexible (requiring minimal time and leaving no traces of the activity) and enables managerial staff to engage in an experience of analyzing their own activities. To conclude, the literature pertaining to the assessment of enacted behavior for the purpose of objectifying the enhancement of soft skills remains nascent and confined to a handful of pioneering studies. Our research efforts benefit from incorporating more objective methods to complement self-report measures, thereby providing a more comprehensive and reliable assessment of individuals' soft skill competencies. For these reasons, the first phase of the study commenced with the systematic selection of keywords encompassing various soft skills terminology.

Consequently, the research questions emerged as follows:

RQ1. *What are the prevailing tools employed in the measurement of soft skills?*
RQ2. *How widespread is the use of objective behavioral assessment tools capable of capturing enacted behaviors?*

3 Methodology

The intentional selection of Scopus as the primary database, coupled with the inclusion of document types such as articles and early access materials, was a methodological decision aimed at facilitating a thorough and exhaustive review process.

Scopus is recognized for its extensive collection of peer-reviewed journals across diverse disciplines, making it an ideal choice for capturing a broad spectrum of relevant studies. Additionally, Scopus offers advanced search capabilities and access to the most recent publications, which are crucial for maintaining the currency and rigor of the review process in a rapidly evolving field like project management.

To further enhance the comprehensiveness of the review, inclusion criteria were strategically formulated to concentrate on specific Scopus categories pertinent to the fields of management, education, business, and engineering. By doing so, the interdisciplinary nature of the research endeavor was accentuated, allowing for a holistic examination of relevant literature spanning multiple domains. Moreover, the establishment of language criteria, with a preference for English-language publications, was intended to promote inclusivity within the global academic community.

To answer RQ1 we will apply the following string and applied the same criteria as above specified:

(("soft skill" OR "transversal skill*" OR "personal skill*" OR "interpersonal skill*") AND ("measures" OR "measurement" OR "tools") AND ("evaluation" OR "objective evaluation") AND ("observation" OR "feedback" OR "self-assessment" OR "psychometric assessments" OR "interviews")).*

To ensure that the results align with our research objectives, we conducted an abstract review of all the selected papers. For the second objective of the study (RQ2), we performed a full-text analysis of the papers deemed relevant, with particular emphasis on investigating the extent to which objective behavioral assessment tools capable of capturing enacted behaviors are employed.

4 Findings

As far as RQ1 is concerned, the initial database search, conducted by inserting the specific search string detailed in the methodology section, yielded a total of 98 papers. However, following a careful screening process based on abstract analysis and the predefined inclusion criteria, only 14 papers were ultimately deemed directly relevant to the research question. As far as RQ2, the full-text analysis of the 14 selected papers allowed for a more in-depth investigation into the nature of the assessment tools employed. Particular attention was paid to identifying whether the studies adopted objective behavioral assessment tools specifically designed to capture enacted soft skills behaviors. The analysis revealed that the majority of the literature continues to rely predominantly on self-report measures, such as questionnaires and perception-based evaluations. Only a limited number of contributions employed methodologies that could be classified as objective behavioral assessments, including structured observations, behavioral simulations, or third-party evaluations based on observed performance. This finding highlights the still limited diffusion of objective approaches within the current body of research, underscoring a significant methodological gap and the need for further advancements in the development and application of robust behavioral assessment tools for soft skills evaluation.

5 Analysis

The analysis revealed that the self-assessment tools typically consist of structured questionnaires, Likert-scale inventories, and self-perception surveys, which, while widely used due to their ease of administration and scalability, are nonetheless subject to several well-documented limitations, such as social desirability bias, self-report inaccuracies, and restricted contextual sensitivity. Firstly, self-reported measures may be subject to biases and inaccuracies, as individuals may consciously or unconsciously inflate or downplay their abilities based on social desirability or perceived expectations. Additionally, individuals may lack self-awareness or may not accurately recognize their own strengths and weaknesses in certain areas of soft skills. Moreover, selfreported measures often fail to capture actual behavior in real-world contexts. Individuals may report their intentions or beliefs about their behavior rather than their actual actions, leading to discrepancies between stated and observed behaviors. This disparity undermines the validity and reliability of assessments based solely on selfreport data. On the other side, third-party observation of behaviors, while offering a more objective perspective, also presents limitations. External observers may bring their own biases or misinterpretations to the assessment process. Additionally, the presence of an observer can influence an individual's behavior, leading to potential discrepancies between their observed actions and their natural inclinations. Observers may inadvertently favor individuals who exhibit behaviors similar to their own or who conform to their expectations of what constitutes effective soft skills. Both self-reported and observed assessments suffer from inconsistency and subjectivity. Furthermore, these assessment approaches often lack comprehensive feedback and objective measures. Self-reported assessments may provide limited insight into areas for improvement, while observations may lack specificity or actionable feedback for individuals to develop their soft skills effectively.

A further analysis of the literature aimed at investigating the use of objective behavior assessment tools, namely tools capable of capturing "enacted behavior", yields scant results. Only Strukova et al. (2022) [26] refer to data-driven assessments, focusing on the generation of a dataset to objectively evaluate soft skills, employing tools that allow content sharing and assumption, the utilization of video games, online learning, and the use of social networks. Ramalingan et al. (2021) [27] present a pioneering hybrid model designed to delineate and assess soft skills. The model employs an intelligent controller to extract and categorize the skill profile of graduates, leveraging data derived from conventional assessment techniques such as self-evaluation and interviews. With a focus on motivation and engagement as pivotal factors, the researchers utilize an established game-based assessment approach to evaluate soft skills. Subsequently, the model generates a comprehensive graduate profile by integrating the outcomes obtained from the game-based assessment.

6 A New Perspective on Measurement

To date, the evaluation of soft skills has predominantly relied on self-assessment and thirdparty observation tools, both of which present notable limitations. Additionally, the set of soft skills and the development of associated measurement instruments have consistently encountered substantial challenges due to their inherent subjectivity. To overcome these limitations, a measurement perspective grounded in observable behaviors is advocated. The tests we propose encompass e-driving simulations, logical e-games, virtual escape rooms, and traditional games.

6.1 The New "Architectural Framework"

The new "architectural framework" comprises three distinct elements: PCAs, skills, and measures. The distinctive feature and underlying motivation for constructing the new framework lie in the absence of a unidirectional relationship between measures and PCA; in fact, a single measure can span multiple PCAs. This approach allowed each measure to be associated with multiple PCAs.

6.2 The Algorithm

An algorithm is created to ensure robustness and reliability in capturing various dimensions of soft skills manifested. The algorithm's functionality encompasses the capture of diverse behaviors, enabling the assimilation of information and measurements from a variety of tools utilized. Specifically, for tools capturing the 'learning continuum,' the algorithm is equipped to register behavioral actions in accordance with the proposed measures-skillset framework using numerical parameters. It further normalizes behavioral changes to detect any improvements and mitigate potential biases in evaluation resulting from preferences or aversions towards the characteristics of the tool used. Additionally, for all other tools employed, the algorithm adeptly captures behavioral actions through numerical parameters. An example is here provided for tools virtual escape rooms and edriving simulations. The virtual escape rooms tool provides measures of "escape time" (ET) and "escape hints" (EH), which are, respectively, the overall seconds a person takes to exit from the room and the number of hints a person asks to perform this activity. These measures are different according to the individual who is performing the test. They become relevant only if an individual is compared against the population's performances. Comparing an individual's performance over its population, rather than considering the absolute values (e.g. seconds), also provides a standardized and easy-to-interpret measure that goes beyond the specific tool in use.

At the time this article is written, we are in the process of collecting data from the escape room tool. The number of data does not allow yet to have a good knowledge of the distribution of performances across the population. Therefore, we considered the average and standard deviation of the measures in our sample and assumed they follow a normal distribution. Consider the example of ET as a random variable with mean and standard deviation. Its normal distribution will be:

$$f(ET) = \frac{1}{\sigma\sqrt{2\pi}} e^{-\frac{1}{2}\left(\frac{ET-\mu_{ET}}{\sigma_{ET}}\right)^2} \tag{1}$$

From our sample $\mu_{ET} = 10'24''$ and $\sigma_{ET} = 3'20''$. We used the function "NORM.INV" in MS Excel to return a random value of ET_i originating from the inverse of the normal cumulative distribution for the specified mean and standard deviation. For simulation purposes we generated random values of T_i with $i = 1, \ldots, 1000$. Considering the above data generation process, for an individual i it is now possible to report its performances in percentiles terms. For example, with $ET_i = 10'30''$ the corresponding percentile would be 0.485 as reported in Fig. 1.

For the e-driving simulations we followed an approach which is similar to the virtual escape room. However, measures from this tool have a fundamental difference: they monitor how an individual i is changing her/his performances across different rounds of the simulations. For example, the measure $\Delta DTi = DTi0 - DTi1$ consists in the difference of average driving times between the initial three laps $DTi0$ and the final three laps $DTi1$ performed by an individual. The expected value of ΔDTi is likely different according to the initial abilities of the performant. In fact, we expect that an individual that is lacking initial abilities could improve her/his DTi with values that could be much higher in absolute terms as compared to an individual who is already very performant at the start of the test. In other words, we expect the difference in performances being conditional to the initial performance level ($\Delta DTi | DTi0$). Considering the limited number of available data at this stage, similarly to the virtual escape time, we provide a simulation from a hypothetical data generation process. We consider DT_i^0 being normally distributed with mean $\mu_{DT}0$ and standard deviation $\sigma_{DT}0$. From our sample $\mu_{DT}0 = 2'28''$ and $\sigma_{DT}0$.Unsing the function "NORM.INV" in MS Excel we generated random values of T_i^0 with $i = 1, \ldots, 1000$. Then, we hypothesized that, for every individual i, the corresponding DT_i^1 is driven by the following process: $DT_i^1 = 0.85 * DT_i^0 + \epsilon_i$, where ϵ_i is a random value that is generated using the function "NORM.INV" in MS Excel considering the standard deviation as a reference mean point. Once T_i^0 and DT_i^1 are simulated the resulting ΔDT_i can be computed. Of course, the resulting value is strictly dependent by the data generation process in equation that could largely differ from the observed behavior that can only be ascertained with a larger number of collected driving tests. However, we believe this simulation exercise is useful to show how the

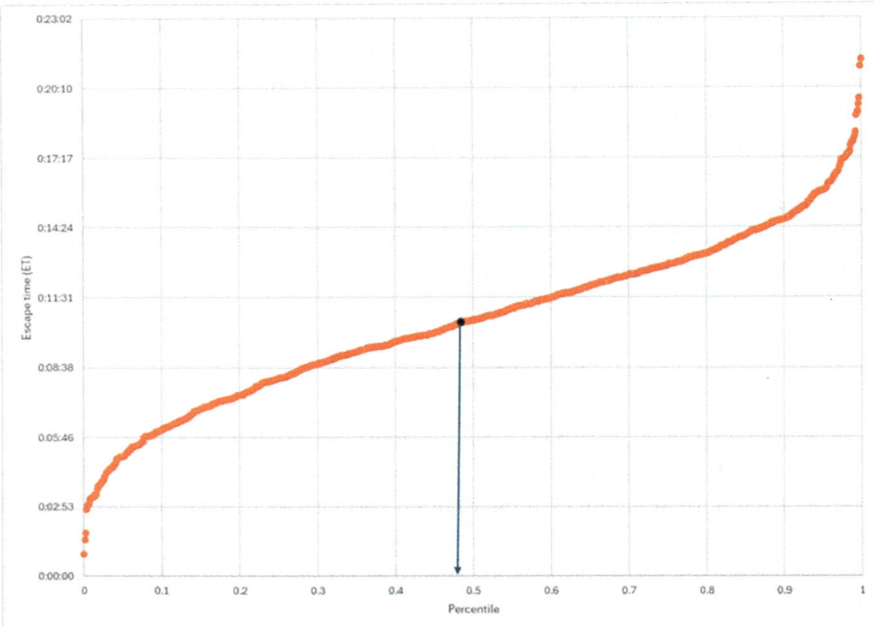

Fig. 1 Cumulative percentage of Escape Time and percentile rank for an individual performing ET = 10′30″

final metric will appear and its interpretation. Figure 2 shows the results of the simulation exercise for two individuals *i* and *j* having initial performances time of DT_i^0 = 2′46″ and DT_j^0 = 2′24″.

The two initial performances identified two different subsamples that were extracted as follows: $Subsample_i \in (DT_i^0 = 2'46'' \pm 5\%)$; $Subsample_j \in (DT_j^0 = 2'24'' \pm 5\%)$.

Figure 2 shows how an individual having a $\Delta DT_i = 0'22''$ can belong to the percentile 0.275 if her/his starting time is 2′46″ or to the percentile 0.874 if her/his starting time is 2′24″. So, the same absolute value of the measured dynamic driving skills can lead to very different interpretations when considering cumulative percentage across different subsamples originating from initial driving performances.

6.3 *The Reporting System*

In facilitating the monitoring endeavors, researchers employed pre-structured Excel spreadsheets as a versatile tool for systematic data collection and analysis. The structured format of Excel spreadsheets provided a standardized framework for recording observations and tracking behavioral nuances over time, thereby facilitating rigorous examination and interpretation of behavioral dynamics. This approach

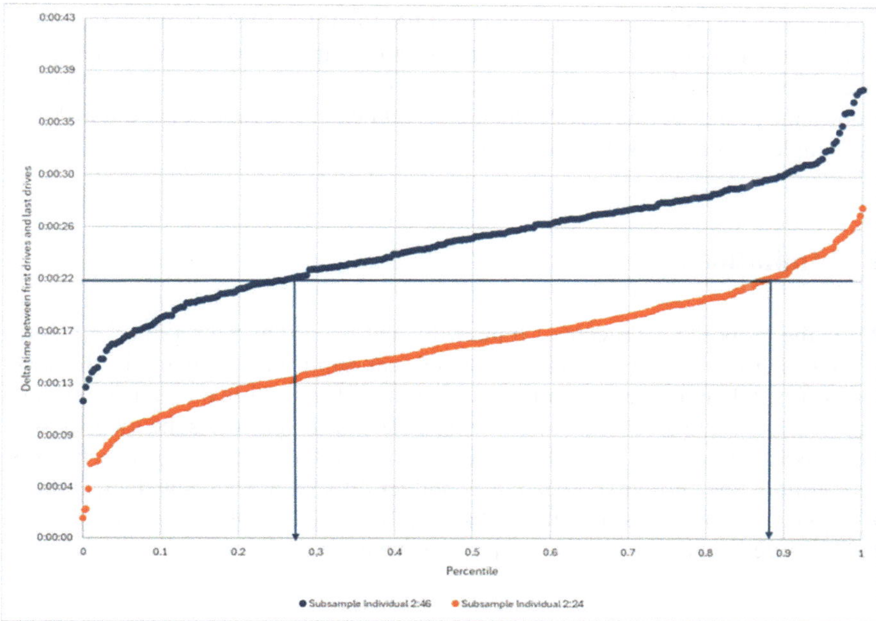

Fig. 2 Cumulative percentage of dynamic driving skills and percentile rank according to two subsamples obtained from initial performances of two individuals (2′46″, 2′24″)

not only facilitated the systematic documentation of enacted behaviors but also enabled researchers to discern patterns, trends, and fluctuations in soft skill activation across diverse contexts and scenarios.

7 Conclusion and Implications

The findings of this study underscore the persistent methodological limitations in the current assessment of soft skills within PM. Despite the growing recognition of their critical importance, soft skills remain predominantly evaluated through self-report instruments that are inherently vulnerable to bias. The scarce adoption of objective behavioral assessment tools capable of capturing enacted behaviors signals a significant methodological gap that limits both research advancement and practical application. The proposed measurement architecture represents a substantial step toward addressing this deficiency. By integrating technology-mediated simulations and algorithmic normalization processes, this framework allows for the systematic capture, standardization, and interpretation of behavioral data, enhancing both reliability and cross-context comparability. Beyond overcoming the weaknesses of self-assessment, this approach opens new avenues for dynamic, longitudinal, and context-sensitive evaluation of soft skills development.

The implications of this work are threefold. First, for research, it offers a replicable methodology capable of generating empirically grounded, behavior-based data for theory-building and validation. Second, for education and training, it enables the design of more authentic assessment environments, better aligned with the complexity of real-world project settings.

8 Limitations

While the proposed architectural framework and algorithm offer a novel approach to capturing enacted behaviors, their empirical application remains in the early stages of validation. The preliminary data collected from virtual escape rooms and e-driving simulations rely on limited sample sizes, which restricts the robustness of the statistical modeling, particularly in establishing reliable population benchmarks. Furthermore, the current approach does not yet fully integrate contextual, cultural, or organizational factors that may substantially influence soft skills manifestation and measurement across diverse project management environments.

9 Further Avenues for Research

Future research should aim to validate this framework across larger and more diverse populations, incorporate additional behavioral dimensions, and further investigate the dynamic interplay between context, individual dispositions, and skill enactment.

References

1. Al-Sa'di, A., Yamjal, P., Ahmad, E., Panjabi, R., Allott McPhee, C. A. M., & Guler, O. (2023). Assessing educators' soft skills: Developing a self-assessment instrument. *Administrative Sciences*, 1–21. https://doi.org/10.3390/admsci13090208
2. Strohmeier, S. (1992). Development of interpersonal skills for senior project managers. *International Journal of Project Management, 10*(1), 45–48. https://doi.org/10.1016/0263-7863(92)90073-I
3. Alvarenga, J. C., et al. (2020). The project manager core competencies to project success. *International Journal of Managing Projects in Business, 13*(2), 277–292. https://doi.org/10.1108/IJMPB-12-2018-0274
4. Brunet, M. (2022). On the relevance of theory and practice in project studies. *International Journal of Project Management, 40*(1), 22–24. https://doi.org/10.1016/j.ijproman.2021.11.006
5. Azim, S., Gale, A., Lawlor-Wright, T., Kirkham, R., Khan, A., & Alam, M. (2010). The importance of soft skills in complex projects. *International Journal of Managing Projects in Business, 3*(3), 387–401. https://doi.org/10.1108/17538371011056048
6. Kendall, P. C. (1984). Behavioral assessment and methodology. *Annual Review of Behavior Therapy: Theory & Practice*. https://doi.org/10.1017/S0141347300008600

7. Laker, D. R., & Powell, J. L. (2011). The differences between hard and soft skills and their relative impact on training transfer. *Human Resource Development Quarterly, 22*(1), 111–122. https://doi.org/10.1002/hrdq.20063
8. Thornhill-Miller, B., et al. (2023). Creativity, critical thinking, communication, and collaboration: Assessment, certification, and promotion of 21st century skills for the future of work and education. *Journal of Intelligence, 11*(3), 1–32.
9. Cimatti, B. (2016). Definition, development, assessment of soft skills and their role for the quality of organizations and enterprises. *International Journal for Quality Research, 10*(1), 97.
10. De Lima, L. F., & Silva, S. Q. (2020). Emotional intelligence and success of project management: the mediating effect of interpersonal skills. *International Journal of Project Organisation and Management, 2*(1), 54–73.
11. Locatelli, G., et al. (2023). Manifesto for project management research. *European Management Review, 20*(1), 3–17.
12. Marin-Zapata, S. I., Román-Calderón, J. P., Robledo-Ardila, C., & Jaramillo-Serna, M. A. (2022). Soft skills, do we know what we are talking about? *Review of Managerial Science, 16*(4), 969–1000.
13. Pant, I., & Baroudi, B. (2008). Project management education: The human skills imperative. *International Journal of Project Management, 26*(2), 124–128.
14. Sunindijo, R. Y. (2015). Project manager skills for improving project performance. *International Journal of Business Performance Management, 16*(1), 67–83.
15. Escolà-Gascón, A., & Gallifa, J. (2022). How to measure soft skills in the educational context: psychometric properties of the SKILLS-in-ONE questionnaire. *Studies in Educational Evaluation, 74*, 1–14.
16. Geithner, S., & Menzel, D. (2016). Effectiveness of learning through experience and reflection in a project management simulation. *Sage Journals, 47*(2), 228–256.
17. Heckman, J. J., & Kautz, T. (2012). Hard evidence on soft skills. *Labour Economics, 19*(4), 451–464.
18. Jang, D., Elfenbein, H. A., & Porath, C. (2023). Who succeeds in a leadership course? Achievement is predicted by ability-tested but not self-reported emotional intelligence. *Social Sciences & Humanities Open, 8*, 1–11.
19. Lin, H. Y., & You, J. (2021). Teamwork-performance prediction by using soft skills and technological savvy skills. *Journal of University Teaching and Learning Practice, 18*(8), 1–24.
20. Magano, J., Silva, C., Figueiredo, C., Vitória, A., Nogueira, T., & Pimenta Dinis, M. A. (2020). Generation Z: Fitting project management soft skills competencies—A mixed-method approach. *Education in Science, 10*(7), 187.
21. Sambell, R., et al. (2023). Opportunities to identify and develop people skills: What university students need early in their degree journey. *Journal of Teaching and Learning for Graduate Employability, 12*(2), 348–365.
22. Seinfeld, S., Prattico, F. G., De Giorgi, C., & Lamberti, F. (2024). Virtual reality body swapping to improve self-assessment in job interview training. *IEEE Transactions on Learning Technologies, 17*, 992–1006.
23. Slattery, D. K., & Sumner, M. R. (2011). Leadership characteristics of rising stars in construction project management. *International Journal of Construction Education and Research, 7*(3), 159–174.
24. Stevenson, D. H., & Starkweather, J. A. (2010). PM critical competency index: IT execs prefer soft skills. *International Journal of Project Management, 28*(7), 663–671.
25. Cantoni, F., Capogreco, C., Cerri, M., & Patti, E. (2024). *Refining the assessment of soft skills in project management*. Vita e Pensiero.
26. Strukova, S., Ruipérez-Valiente, J. A., & Mármol, F. G. (2021). Data-driven performance prediction in a geometry game environment. In *Proceedings of the Conference on Information Technology for Social Good* (pp. 283–288).
27. Ramalingam, H., Usmani, R. S. A., Hashem, I. A. T., & Pillai, T. R. (2021). A hybrid model to profile and evaluate soft skills of computing graduates for employment. *International Journal of Advanced Computer Science and Applications, 12*(7).

Empowering SMEs: The Role of Generative AI in Knowledge Retention

Haiat Perozzo, Aurelio Ravarini, Mauro Junior Dia Perozzo, Cesare Roncari, and Emanuele Strada

Abstract This study offers a comprehensive understanding of Generative AI's role in knowledge management and knowledge retention within SMEs, proposing a robust framework that integrates social and technical factors to promote continuous learning and innovation. Despite substantial research on the general impact of AI on knowledge management, there is a notable scarcity of literature focusing specifically on Generative AI and its role in enhancing knowledge retention in SMEs. This gap is critical, given SMEs' unique challenges, such as limited resources and high employee turnover rates. The research question guiding this study is: "To what extent does Generative AI impact knowledge retention in SMEs?".

The article employs a socio-technical systems framework to analyze the variables influencing knowledge sharing, emphasizing the interplay between individual motivation, organizational support and culture, and technological capability. This approach is complemented by the concept of human-centric digital technology, which focuses on enhancing human capabilities and experiences through technology. Generative AI enhances knowledge management practices by automating processes, analyzing large datasets, and generating new content, thus improving the efficiency and quality of knowledge sharing. It also reduces the administrative burden on employees, fosters a collaborative culture, and provides personalized feedback, thereby increasing individual motivation for knowledge sharing. Furthermore, Generative AI can address the inherent challenges SMEs face in knowledge retention by making critical knowledge easily accessible, reducing the learning curve for new employees, and maintaining operational efficiency. However, it is crucial to manage employees' perceptions of Generative AI to avoid resistance or sabotage due to fears of redundancy.

Keywords SMEs · Knowledge retention · Generative AI

H. Perozzo (✉) · A. Ravarini · M. J. D. Perozzo · C. Roncari · E. Strada
LIUC – Cattaneo University, Castellanza, Italy
e-mail: hperozzo@liuc.it; aravarini@liuc.it; ma16.perozzo@stud.liuc.it; ce21.roncari@stud.liuc.it; estrada@liuc.it

A. Tursunbayeva et al. (eds.), *Technology-Driven Transformation*, Lecture Notes in Information Systems and Organisation 79,
https://doi.org/10.1007/978-3-032-01396-5_20

1 Introduction

Knowledge Management (KM) is a strategic process for contemporary organizations. The effective acquisition, organization, sharing, and optimal use of internal knowledge to boost innovation and competitiveness [1–4] transforms individual and collective knowledge into substantial organizational value, making information accessible to all workers, especially new joiners [5]. KM involves both tacit knowledge, which is personal and experiential, and explicit knowledge, which is systematic and easily transferable [6, 7]. The integration of these two types of knowledge poses significant challenges and necessitates advanced methodologies and a commitment to continuous development [3, 7].

Far before the advent of ChatGPT, the introduction of Artificial Intelligence (AI) technologies into KM practices has significantly enhanced the ability to manage knowledge within organizations. AI improves the acquisition, organization, and sharing of knowledge by automating processes and analyzing large data sets to identify patterns and trends [8–10]. More recently, Generative AI (GenAI) tools such as chatbots and virtual assistants has been leading to facilitate real-time information sharing and learning from previous interactions to enhance their functionality [10, 11].

One of the areas of Knowledge Management (KM) that appears particularly suitable for the application of AI technologies is knowledge retention (KR). Retaining the knowledge developed within an organization involves, on one hand, the accumulation of data related to the activities performed and the experiences gained by employees, and on the other hand, their processing (for example, cataloging and synthesis) to make them transferable to other employees. AI technologies in fact can be exploited to support KR by ensuring that critical information is not lost when employees leave, making it accessible to new employees and maintaining operational efficiency [12, 13].

Nonetheless, these advancements are only in principle available for any organization. Small and medium enterprises (SMEs) despite facing the same challenges—if not even worse—of large companies. SMEs face unique challenges in KR due to limited resources and higher employee turnover rates compared to larger organizations. This context highlights the importance of exploring how GenAI can address these challenges. GenAI offers sophisticated tools for knowledge identification and sharing, enhancing the efficiency and quality of KM processes [14, 15].

Despite the significant advancements and interest in the integration of AI and KM, there is a notable gap in the literature concerning the specific application of AI in knowledge retention within SMEs. Existing research has extensively covered the general benefits of AI in KM [8, 9, 11], but there is a scarcity of studies that delve into the unique challenges and opportunities faced by SMEs in this domain [15]. Moreover, while some studies have touched upon the theoretical aspects of AI in KM [3], there is a lack of empirical research that examines the practical implementation and outcomes of AI-driven knowledge retention strategies in SMEs [12].

To address this gap, this article focuses on how GenAI can be leveraged to enhance knowledge retention in SMEs. By providing empirical evidence and practical insights, this study aims to contribute to the existing body of knowledge and offers valuable guidance for SMEs seeking to improve their KM practices through AI technologies.

To analyze the variables influencing KS, this article employs a framework based on the socio-technical systems (STS) perspective, which highlights the interaction and interdependence between social and technical factors in an organization [16]. This perspective is further enriched by the concept of human-centric digital technology, which focuses on enhancing human capabilities and experiences through technology [17]. The framework consists of three main variables: degree of individual motivation for KS that represents the level of internal motivation individuals have to share knowledge [18, 19], degree of organizational support and culture that is the level of organizational support and culture that promotes KS [19–21], and degree of technology-enabling capability, namely the level of technological infrastructure available to facilitate KS [14, 22, 23].

2 Theoretical Background

2.1 The Role of Artificial Intelligence in Knowledge Management

KM is a fundamental pillar in the development and innovation strategies of contemporary organizations [4]. This discipline focuses on acquisition, organization, sharing, and optimal use of internal knowledge to enhance organizations' innovation capabilities and market competitiveness [4, 22]. In summary, KM is configured as an integrated business strategy that facilitates the transformation of individual and collective knowledge into substantial added value for the organization [1]. Through the implementation of effective KM practices, organizations can maximize their innovative potential and improve their competitive position in a dynamic global economy [1, 24]. Knowledge within a business context is one of the main resources that allows companies to stay competitive in the market in which they operate [5]. KM makes information generally accessible to everyone, especially new entrants [5]. Therefore, it is essential that every company recognizes knowledge as a true resource [5]. KM thus allows the transformation of individual knowledge into organizational knowledge, i.e., the process of creating value for the company through intangible assets [3]. KM is also based on knowledge mapping, essential for effectively managing the three main categories of intellectual capital: human capital, structural capital, and customer capital. KM aims to integrate tacit knowledge, which is personal, non-formalized, and often linked to individuals' direct experience, with explicit knowledge, which is systematic and easily transferable [6, 7].

This integration represents one of KM's greatest challenges, requiring advanced methodologies and a continuous commitment to research and development [7, 25].

KM presents significant challenges such as obstruction to knowledge transfer (KT) and knowledge hiding (KH) by employees within companies [1]. Additionally, KM is fundamental within companies not only because it is a source of competitive advantage but also because it enriches the information and knowledge available for decision-making, especially for manufacturing companies. This increases the quality of decisions made by corporate managers [26, 27]. The evolution of KM in modern organizations is also deeply influenced by the integration of new technologies such as email, databases, data warehouses, collective assistance systems, search engines, internet and intranet networks, and advanced information systems based on expert knowledge [24]. However, Artificial Intelligence (AI) is certainly the technology that has recently had the greatest impact on introducing new methodologies for KM [9, 13].

AI significantly impacts KM in several ways. Firstly, it improves the acquisition and organization of knowledge by automating processes that previously required significant human intervention. AI algorithms can analyze large volumes of data, identify patterns and trends, and suggest data-driven decisions. This not only increases efficiency but also reduces the risk of human error [10, 11]. Moreover, AI facilitates KS. AI-based tools such as chatbots and virtual assistants can respond to real-time queries, providing users with the necessary information when needed. These tools can also learn from previous interactions, continuously improving their ability to answer complex questions and provide relevant suggestions [10, 28].

AI also supports KR, ensuring that critical information is not lost when employees leave the company. AI systems can store and organize knowledge so that it is easily accessible to new employees, reducing the learning curve and maintaining operational efficiency [13, 29]. The implementation of AI in KM also requires modifications infrastructural and training. It is necessary to adequately prepare data, develop knowledge graphs, and promote AI literacy among employees to maximize the benefits of AI technologies in KM. These changes ensure that the technological infrastructure is suitable for AI adoption and that workers can effectively interact with the new systems [30].

KR focuses on the challenges posed by the departure of experienced workers after long periods of service. Unlike traditional KM methodologies, KR addresses the immediate need to capture and transfer critical know-how from experts within a short timeframe, transforming it into a lasting organizational asset [31]. This subdiscipline emphasizes people over content, considering the emotional dynamics associated with employees transitioning to a new life phase. The goal is to preserve critical knowledge while respecting and valuing the experiences and emotional states of departing employees [31, 32].

The Socio-Technical Systems (STS) theory emphasizes the interplay between social and technical factors in organizational settings [16, 33]. In the context of Knowledge Management (KM), the STS perspective is particularly relevant as it highlights the need for a balanced integration of technology and human elements to optimize organizational outcomes. When implementing AI-driven solutions, such as GenAI, within SMEs, it is crucial to consider how these technologies interact with existing social structures, organizational culture, and employee behavior.

For instance, while AI tools can significantly enhance the efficiency of knowledge processes, their success largely depends on the extent to which they are accepted and effectively utilized by employees. Organizational support, proper training, and a culture that encourages knowledge sharing are essential for overcoming resistance and maximizing the benefits of AI technologies [16]. Without considering the social aspects, even the most advanced technological systems may fail to achieve their intended outcomes, leading to suboptimal knowledge retention and potential knowledge loss.

Traditional KM approaches have primarily relied on manual processes, such as documentation, mentoring, and face-to-face knowledge transfer, to capture and disseminate knowledge [2, 3]. These methods, while effective in certain contexts, often suffer from limitations, such as the potential for knowledge loss due to employee turnover and the time-intensive nature of manual knowledge documentation.

AI-driven KM, particularly with the advent of GenAI, offers a transformative approach by automating many of these processes, enabling real-time knowledge sharing, and uncovering tacit knowledge that may otherwise remain unexpressed [11, 13]. For example, AI can analyze large datasets to identify patterns and insights that are not immediately apparent through traditional methods, thereby enhancing decision-making and innovation.

However, it is important to recognize that AI-driven approaches also present challenges. These include the need for substantial initial investment in technology infrastructure, potential resistance from employees who may feel threatened by automation, and the requirement for continuous updates to keep pace with technological advancements [17]. Thus, while AI offers significant advantages in terms of efficiency and scalability, organizations must carefully manage the transition from traditional to AI-driven KM to ensure a smooth integration that complements rather than disrupts existing practices.

2.2 The Role of Artificial Intelligence in Knowledge Retention

KR encompasses all activities aimed at protecting knowledge within an organization, including its acquisition, preservation, and retrieval. KR is a division of KM where organizations leverage their collective intelligence to achieve goals by managing their cultural, social, and technological environments [5]. Successful knowledge-based organizations recognize the importance of growing, attracting, and retaining talent, or mapping their knowledge to make it available [5, 34]. KS refers to the exchange of information, skills, or experiences among individuals, groups, or organizations [35]. KS is crucial for learning and innovation, particularly in business contexts where continuous knowledge transfer and creation are essential for success and competitiveness [35]. Unlike Knowledge Exchange (KE) and

Knowledge Transfer (KT), KS is an interactive and bidirectional process where knowledge is actively constructed and reconstructed among participants [36]. Davenport and Prusak (1998) [2] emphasize the dual process of KS: externalization by the knowledge holder and internalization by the recipient. However, barriers such as temporal, spatial, and cultural factors can complicate this process [37]. The theory of organizational knowledge creation provides a valuable framework for understanding the intricate nature of human knowledge within organizations. Central to this theory are two key concepts: tacit knowledge and explicit knowledge [25]. The distinction between tacit and explicit knowledge highlights the complexity of their interaction within organizations. Research shows that tacit and explicit knowledge often overlap and integrate rather than being distinctly compartmentalized [22, 25]. Organizations that recognize the value of tacit knowledge and develop effective strategies for its identification, capture, and sharing can gain a significant competitive advantage [13]. This can include mentoring, shadowing, and storytelling practices to transmit tacit knowledge among team members and generations of employees [13]. However, these processes are often hindered by organizational silos and the complexity of human nature, which sometimes leads individuals to withhold information [13].

AI can play a crucial role in overcoming challenges associated with KS and KR. AI offers advanced tools to facilitate the sharing of tacit knowledge and make it accessible to all organization members [13]. By analyzing data, AI can identify hidden patterns and trends in employee interactions, revealing tacit knowledge that would otherwise remain unexpressed. For example, intelligent KM systems can monitor employee activities and interactions to identify specific skills or areas of expertise, facilitating connections between colleagues with similar interests or complementary skills [13, 28]. Once tacit knowledge is identified, AI can significantly contribute to its transformation into explicit knowledge. Using advanced algorithms, AI can structure and formalize this knowledge into understandable and accessible formats for all team members [13]. For instance, AI can translate an expert's experiences into a step-by-step tutorial for use by new employees or colleagues facing similar challenges [13]. Moreover, AI can overcome temporal, spatial, and functional barriers that often limit effective knowledge dissemination within the organization [13]. Through recommendation algorithms and advanced search engines, AI can identify and promote relevant content to users based on their interests, skills, and roles [13]. Enhanced corporate communication platforms with AI-based features can facilitate collaboration and knowledge exchange among employees, providing interactive channels for discussion and feedback [13].

2.3 The Impact of Artificial Intelligence on Knowledge Retention in SMEs

Small and medium-sized enterprises (SMEs) represent a crucial component of the global economy, characterized by their adaptability and agility. However, these enterprises often face significant limitations in terms of resources and access to capital, which can threaten their competitiveness. In this context, KM, and particularly KR, becomes essential to ensure the operational continuity and long-term success of SMEs [38].

KR is critical for capturing, sharing, applying, and creating knowledge, especially when key employees leave the company or when new entrants need to be quickly integrated [39]. SMEs, unlike large companies, often cannot afford a high turnover that allows for direct knowledge transfer between individuals [40]. Additionally, SMEs are often less able to retain talent due to the greater attractiveness of large companies in terms of salaries and brand [40].

AI can play a crucial role in enhancing KR in SMEs. As mentioned in the previous chapter, AI provides sophisticated tools that facilitate the identification and sharing of tacit knowledge, making it accessible to all members of the organization [13]. Through advanced data analysis, AI can uncover patterns and trends in employee interactions, bringing to light knowledge that would otherwise remain hidden [9, 38]. AI-based KM systems can monitor employee activities and interactions to identify specific skills or areas of expertise, facilitating connections between colleagues with complementary skills [38].

Furthermore, AI helps to transform tacit knowledge into explicit knowledge. By using advanced algorithms, AI can structure and formalize this knowledge into understandable and accessible formats for all team members. For example, AI can convert an expert's experiences into detailed tutorials, ready to be used by newcomers or colleagues facing similar challenges [13, 28]. AI is also capable of overcoming temporal and spatial barriers that often hinder effective knowledge dissemination within the organization. Through recommendation algorithms and advanced search engines, AI can identify and promote relevant content to users based on their interests and skills, facilitating personalized access to knowledge [38]. AI-enhanced corporate communication platforms can also facilitate collaboration and knowledge exchange among employees, creating interactive channels for discussions and feedback [30].

A particular emerging technology within the AI domain is GenAI, which offers even more advanced functionalities for KM. GenAI not only analyzes and interprets existing data but is also capable of generating new content such as text, images, and music based on patterns learned from training data [23]. This allows for the creation of high-quality content for knowledge bases, significantly reducing the time and effort required for manual content creation [14]. GenAI can also personalize generated content based on user data, improving customer satisfaction and engagement through tailored responses and product recommendations [41]. Additionally, GenAI facilitates the discovery of new knowledge by identifying patterns and relationships in large datasets, supporting more informed decisions, and improving the effectiveness of customer service teams [26, 28].

Despite the significant potential of GenAI in KR, the specific literature on the application of these technologies in SMEs is still limited. This makes the topic particularly interesting to explore, as SMEs, with their specific challenges and limitations, represent an ideal context to investigate how emerging technologies can improve KM and competitiveness [28, 38].

3 Research Gap and Research Question

While there is substantial literature on the general impact of Artificial Intelligence (AI) on KM, there is a notable scarcity of research specifically focusing on the impact of GenAI on KR. GenAI, a subset of AI that generates new content based on existing data, has shown promise in various applications such as content creation, data analysis, and decision support. However, its specific role in enhancing KR within organizations remains underexplored.

This gap becomes even more pronounced when considering small and medium-sized enterprises (SMEs). SMEs often face unique challenges related to KR due to limited resources and a higher turnover rate compared to larger organizations. Despite these challenges, there is a dearth of research examining how GenAI can address these issues within the SME context. Most existing studies on AI and KM focus on larger enterprises or provide a general overview without delving into the specificities of SMEs. Therefore, understanding the nuances of how GenAI can support KR in SMEs is critical for leveraging this technology to its full potential.

Given the identified research gaps, a pertinent research question emerges: "To what extent does Generative AI impact knowledge retention in SMEs?".

This question aims to explore the depth and breadth of GenAI's influence on KR processes within SMEs. It seeks to uncover how GenAI tools and techniques can be utilized to capture, store, and transfer critical knowledge within these organizations.

4 Proposed Theoretical Framework for SMEs

Knowledge retention (KR) is crucial for ensuring operational continuity and long-term success in small and medium-sized enterprises (SMEs). The ability to retain, share, and apply knowledge within an organization represents a significant competitive advantage, especially in environments characterized by limited resources and high volatility. Previous chapters have explored how Artificial Intelligence (AI) can enhance KR practices by facilitating the identification and sharing of tacit knowledge, transforming it into explicit knowledge, and overcoming temporal and spatial barriers. Generative AI (GenAI) has been introduced as an emerging technology that offers further advancements, allowing for the generation of new content and personalized responses, thereby enhancing knowledge sharing (KS) capabilities.

The proposed framework aims to analyze the variables influencing KS, providing a three-dimensional representation that considers individual motivation, organizational support, and technological capability. This framework aligns with the socio-technical systems (STS) model, which emphasizes the interplay between social and technical factors, and the concept of human-centric digital technology, which focuses on enhancing human capabilities and experiences through technology. The axes of the model are defined as follows: Degree of Individual Motivation for KS, Degree of Organizational Support and Culture, and Degree of Technology-Enabling Capability.

4.1 Degree of Individual Motivation for KS

This axis represents the level of internal motivation individuals have to share knowledge. In SMEs, where resources are often limited, leveraging the intrinsic motivation of employees is essential. This motivation can be influenced by intrinsic factors such as the desire to help others and personal satisfaction, as well as extrinsic factors such as organizational recognition and rewards. According to the STS model, the social component, including individual attitudes and motivations, plays a critical role in the effectiveness of organizational processes. Human-centric digital technology can enhance individual motivation by providing intuitive and engaging platforms for knowledge sharing. Studies indicate that individual motivation is crucial for the success of KS practices, as highly motivated individuals are more likely to share their knowledge, thereby contributing to the accumulation and dissemination of know-how within the organization [19].

4.2 Degree of Organizational Support and Culture

This axis measures the level of organizational support and culture that promotes KS. In SMEs, fostering a supportive organizational environment is critical. This environment is characterized by a culture that values collaboration, managerial support, and organizational structures that incentivize KS. The STS model underscores the importance of a supportive organizational culture as part of the social system, which is essential for effective KS. Moreover, human-centric digital technology can help cultivate a collaborative culture by providing tools that facilitate communication and cooperation. Literature shows that management that encourages KS can significantly enhance these practices. Organizational culture and structures that promote KS are essential for creating an environment where KS can thrive, which is particularly important for SMEs to maintain competitiveness and adapt to market changes [19, 21].

4.3 Degree of Technology-Enabling Capability

This axis represents the level of technological infrastructure available to facilitate KS. This includes tools such as enterprise social media platforms, intranets, and collaboration solutions, as well as emerging technologies like GenAI, which allow for the creation of new and personalized content based on existing data. For SMEs, which often face resource constraints, leveraging advanced information and communication technologies is crucial. The STS model highlights the technical system's role in supporting social interactions and workflows, while human-centric digital technology focuses on making these tools user-friendly and effective in enhancing human performance. These technologies play a vital role in enabling KS by facilitating knowledge dissemination and enhancing the discovery of new knowledge through the identification of patterns and relationships in large datasets, thus supporting more informed decision-making [14, 23].

In conclusion, the integration of individual motivation, organizational support, and technological capability is essential for effective knowledge sharing and retention in SMEs. Each of these variables plays a critical role in overcoming the unique challenges faced by SMEs, ensuring they can harness their collective knowledge to sustain and enhance their competitive edge. The socio-technical systems model and the concept of human-centric digital technology provide a comprehensive framework for understanding and enhancing these variables within organizational contexts, represented in Fig. 1.

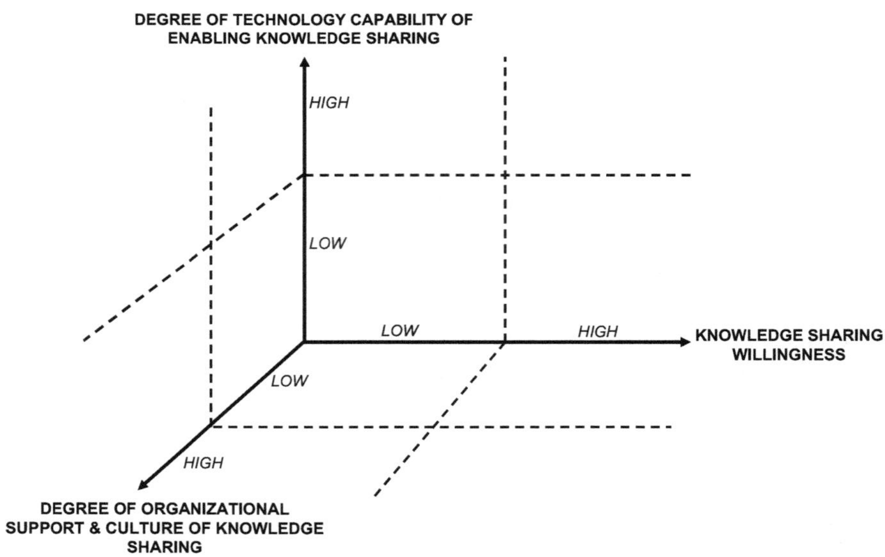

Fig. 1 Proposed theoretical framework

5 The Role of GenAI in the Proposed Theoretical Framework for SMEs

This integrated framework provides a comprehensive representation of the key variables influencing knowledge sharing (KS) in SMEs, using a scale from "low" to "high" to evaluate how the combination of these factors can promote or hinder KS.

Individual intrinsic and extrinsic motivation is essential for the success of KS practices. Motivated and competent individuals are more likely to share knowledge, contributing to the accumulation of know-how within the organization. A supportive organizational environment is crucial for promoting these practices. An organizational culture that values collaboration and managerial support can significantly enhance KS practices [19]. In SMEs, organizational support and culture are often found in the "low" quadrants due to limited financial resources and organizational culture, resulting in few incentives for employees to share knowledge. However, GenAI has the potential to shift this variable from "low" to "high," making knowledge more accessible and encouraging sharing. This shift depends on individual characteristics and the perception of incentives offered for using technology.

Information and communication technologies are fundamental in enabling KS. Adequate technological tools, such as enterprise social media platforms, intranets, and collaboration solutions, facilitate KS. Additionally, GenAI represents a significant innovation that can further enhance KS by allowing the creation of new and personalized content based on existing data, improving the discovery of new knowledge, and supporting more informed decision-making [14, 23]. The technological capability of the framework is significantly improved with the introduction of GenAI, which can analyze large amounts of data and generate new content based on this data, enhancing the efficiency and quality of KS. GenAI tools can create detailed documents, reports, and tutorials, making knowledge more easily accessible and usable. This ability to generate personalized and relevant content reduces the time needed to produce informative materials and improves the relevance and accuracy of shared information, supporting more informed and precise decision-making [14].

Compared to other technologies, the intrinsic nature of GenAI inherently promotes KS, as any input provided to GenAI is effectively shared. This shifts the focus away from quadrants of the framework where technological capability is "low" and emphasizes the other two axes, which represent the social aspect of the sociotechnical model. Moreover, GenAI strengthens organizational support and culture for KS. By automating various KM processes, GenAI reduces the administrative burden on employees, allowing them to focus on more creative and collaborative activities. This helps create a work environment that promotes continuous collaboration and innovation. Additionally, GenAI can identify knowledge gaps and suggest targeted training programs, improving organizational support and ensuring that employees have the necessary resources to effectively share and utilize knowledge. Furthermore, recent studies indicate that a robust organizational support system and a collaborative culture are essential for effective KS.

GenAI can increase individual motivation for KS, making the process more rewarding and engaging. When employees see their contributions valued and recognized through automatically generated content, their intrinsic motivation increases. Additionally, GenAI offers real-time feedback and personalized recommendations, making the KS process more interactive and engaging, further increasing user engagement [23]. However, there is a potential downside. If employees perceive that GenAI is being used to extract their knowledge, rendering them potentially redundant, they may intentionally sabotage the system by providing incorrect inputs (prompting) to confuse and undermine the model. It is therefore crucial to provide appropriate incentives and ensure that all employees understand that they can benefit from this technology, thereby avoiding resistance or sabotaging behaviors [14].

6 Conclusions and Further Research

In conclusion, this article has explored the transformative potential of GenAI on knowledge management (KM) and knowledge retention (KR) within small and medium-sized enterprises (SMEs). The introduction of GenAI into KM practices offers numerous advantages, including enhanced efficiency, improved quality of knowledge sharing (KS), and better knowledge retention capabilities. GenAI's ability to analyze large datasets and generate new, relevant content significantly reduces the time and effort required for manual content creation, thereby supporting more informed decision-making and operational efficiency.

GenAI also plays a crucial role in fostering a collaborative culture within organizations by automating routine tasks and allowing employees to focus on more strategic, value-adding activities. This shift not only improves individual motivation for KS but also enhances the overall organizational support and culture for KM practices. However, the implementation of GenAI must be managed carefully to address potential resistance from employees and to ensure that the technology is perceived as a tool for empowerment rather than replacement.

To further enrich the analysis, two sets of semi-structured interviews were conducted, targeting both employees and managers within SMEs. These interviews were designed to explore the impact of GenAI on knowledge sharing and retention from both perspectives. Although the topics covered in both interview structures were similar, the distinction between the two was crucial in obtaining a comprehensive understanding of the organizational dynamics.

Individual Sphere: Both employees and managers were asked about their roles, daily tasks, and interactions with colleagues. For employees, questions focused on their attitudes toward knowledge sharing and concerns about becoming less indispensable. For managers, the questions were tailored to understand how they perceive and promote knowledge sharing among their teams.

Organizational Sphere: This section examined the organizational culture and the incentives for knowledge sharing. Employees were queried about the support they receive, while managers were asked about the strategies and leadership practices, they employ to foster a collaborative environment.

Technological Sphere: The interviews explored the use of digital tools for knowledge sharing, with a particular focus on GenAI. Employees provided insights into their practical experiences, while managers discussed the integration of these technologies within the broader organizational strategy.

The interview frameworks consisted of 16 questions each, and the insights gathered from these interviews played a crucial role in shaping the findings of this study. The dual perspectives obtained from both employees and managers provided a nuanced understanding of the socio-technical dynamics at play in SMEs and highlighted how GenAI can either support or hinder knowledge retention depending on the organizational context.

Despite the promising capabilities of GenAI, there is still a notable gap in the literature specifically addressing its impact on KR in SMEs. Future research should focus on empirical studies to validate the theoretical findings presented in this article and to explore the practical implications of GenAI in diverse SME contexts. Such studies could provide deeper insights into how GenAI can be effectively integrated into KM frameworks, addressing the unique challenges faced by SMEs and maximizing the benefits of this advanced technology. By addressing these research gaps, through an empirical research, future work can contribute to a more comprehensive understanding of the role of GenAI in KM and KR, ultimately supporting the development of more resilient and innovative SMEs.

References

1. Abubakar, A. M., Elrehail, H., Alatailat, M. A., & Elçi, A. (2019). Knowledge management decision-making style and organizational performance. *Journal of Innovation & Knowledge, 4*(2), 104–114.
2. Davenport, T. H., & Prusak, L. (1998). *Working knowledge: How organizations manage what they know*. Harvard Business Press.
3. Nonaka, I. (1994). A dynamic theory of organizational knowledge creation. *Organization Science, 5*(1), 14–37.
4. Wasko, M. M., & Faraj, S. (2005). Why should I share? Examining social capital and knowledge contribution in electronic networks of practice. *MIS Quarterly, 29*(1), 35–57.
5. Bessick, J., & Naicker, V. (2013). The evolution of knowledge management in organizations. *Journal of Information and Knowledge Management Systems, 43*(3), 392–411.
6. Polanyi, M. (1966). *The tacit dimension*. University of Chicago Press.
7. Wang, S., & Noe, R. A. (2010). Knowledge sharing: A review and directions for future research. *Human Resource Management Review, 20*(2), 115–131.
8. Chui, M., Manyika, J., & Miremadi, M. (2018). *AI adoption advances, but foundational barriers remain*. McKinsey Global Institute.
9. Davenport, T. H., & Ronanki, R. (2018). Artificial intelligence for the real world. *Harvard Business Review, 96*(1), 108–116.
10. Taherdoost, H., & Madanchian, M. (2023). Artificial intelligence and knowledge management: Impacts, benefits, and implementation. *Computers, 12*(4), 72.

11. Huang, M.-H., & Rust, R. T. (2018). Artificial intelligence in service. *Journal of Service Research, 21*(2), 155–172.
12. Bousquet, F., & Bouchard, M. (2019). Knowledge retention practices in SMEs. *Small Business Economics Journal.*
13. Jarrahi, M. H. (2023). AI and the transformation of knowledge work. *Journal of Information Technology, 38*(1), 45–60.
14. IBM. (2023). *Scale knowledge management use cases with generative AI.* IBM Blog.
15. Sousa, M. J., & Rocha, A. (2019). Skills for disruptive digital business. *Journal of Business Research, 94*, 257–263.
16. Mumford, E. (2000). A socio-technical approach to systems design. *Requirements Engineering Journal, 5*(2), 125–133.
17. Kane, G. C., et al. (2015). Strategy, not technology, drives digital transformation. *MIT Sloan Management Review.*
18. Lin, H. F. (2007). Effects of extrinsic and intrinsic motivation on employee knowledge sharing intentions. *Journal of Information Science, 33*(2), 135–149.
19. Razmerita, L., Kirchner, K., & Nielsen, P. (2016). What factors influence knowledge sharing in organizations? A social dilemma perspective of social media communication. *Journal of Knowledge Management, 20*(6), 1225–1246.
20. De Long, D. W., & Fahey, L. (2000). Diagnosing cultural barriers to knowledge management. *Academy of Management Executive, 14*(4), 113–127.
21. Sustainability. (2020). Factors affecting knowledge sharing in virtual teams. *Sustainability, 12*(17), 7068–7084.
22. Alavi, M., & Leidner, D. E. (2001). Review: Knowledge management and knowledge management systems: Conceptual foundations and research issues. *MIS Quarterly*, 107–136.
23. Shelf.io. (2023). *Generative AI in knowledge management and contact centers.* Shelf.io.
24. Grant, R. M. (1996). Toward a knowledge-based theory of the firm. *Strategic Management Journal, 17*(S2), 109–122.
25. Nonaka, I., Toyama, R., & Konno, N. (2015). SECI, Ba, and leadership: A unified model of dynamic knowledge creation. *Long Range Planning, 33*(1), 5–34.
26. Liu, S., et al. (2012). Web sites of the Fortune 500 companies: Facing customers through home pages. *Information & Management, 31*(6), 335–345.
27. Martins, E. C., & Meyer, H. W. J. (2012). Organizational and behavioral factors that influence knowledge retention. *Journal of Knowledge Management, 16*(5), 787–810.
28. Dwivedi, Y. K., et al. (2021). Artificial Intelligence (AI): Multidisciplinary perspectives on emerging challenges, opportunities, and agenda for research, practice and policy. *International Journal of Information Management, 57.*
29. Kowalczyk, M., & Buxmann, P. (2015). Big data and information processing in organizational decision-making. *Business & Information Systems Engineering, 57*(4), 267–278.
30. RealKM. (2023). *How artificial intelligence can support knowledge management in organizations.* RealKM.
31. Levy, M. (2011). Knowledge retention: Minimizing organizational business loss. *Journal of Knowledge Management, 15*(4), 582–600.
32. Durst, S., & Wilhelm, S. (2012). Knowledge management and succession planning in SMEs. *Journal of Knowledge Management, 16*(4), 637–649.
33. Trist, E. L. (1981). The evolution of socio-technical systems. *University of Toronto Quality of Working Life Series, 2.*
34. Barney, J. (1991). Firm resources and sustained competitive advantage. *Journal of Management, 17*(1), 99–120.
35. Zeng, M. (2017). Knowledge sharing in open innovation: An empirical study of the role of boundary spanners in cross-boundary knowledge sharing. *Journal of Knowledge Management, 21*(6), 1386–1407.
36. Connelly, C. E., & Kelloway, E. K. (2000). Predictors of employees' perceptions of knowledge sharing cultures. *Leadership & Organization Development Journal, 24*(5), 294–301.

37. Hendriks, P. (1999). Why share knowledge? The influence of ICT on the motivation for knowledge sharing. *Knowledge and Process Management, 6*(2), 91–100.
38. OECD. (2021). *Artificial Intelligence: Changing landscape for SMEs*. OECD iLibrary.
39. Doan, A., Ramakrishnan, R., & Halevy, A. Y. (2011). Crowdsourcing systems on the world-wide web. *Communications of the ACM, 54*(4), 86–96.
40. Schilling, M. A., & Izzo, F. (2022). *Strategic management of technological innovation*. McGraw-Hill Education.
41. SearchUnify. (2023). *Generative AI and knowledge management FAQs*. SearchUnify.

Digital Skills and Maturity in the Public Sector: A Review of EU Guidelines

Luiza Gaysina, Aizhan Tursunbayeva, Alessia Berni, and Andrea Tomo

Abstract The development and application of digital technology have a strong impact on the way the public sector operates today and require public servants to develop and strengthen their skills. This study provides a scoping review examining grey literature around digitalization practices and digital skills in the public sector in EU member countries and proposes a framework for analyzing twenty-first-century digital skills in the public sector as per different stages of digitalization maturity. To uncover relevant "grey" literature, an established methodology was used including a search on Google.com using keywords identified from existing literature on digitalization HRM practices in the public sector. Out of 630 sources, seven relevant documents related to the relevant guidelines were included in the analysis. Then, two additional documents were added, making a total of nine documents. These were analyzed qualitatively with the help of an integrated framework of twenty-first-century digital skills, organizational dimensions, and digitalization maturity stages. This review contributes to the body of knowledge on digital transformation in the public sector by proposing a framework that can serve as a guide for understanding what digital competencies are essential and applicable at different phases of the digital transformation process. It demonstrates the importance of comprehensive policy guidelines that are linked with digital skills development. This

L. Gaysina · A. Berni
Parthenope University of Naples, Naples, Italy
e-mail: alessia.berni@uniparthenope.it

A. Tursunbayeva
Department of Business and Economics, University of Naples "Parthenope", Naples, Italy
e-mail: a.tursunbayeva@uniparthenope.it

A. Tomo (✉)
University of Naples Federico II, Naples, Italy
e-mail: andrea.tomo@unina.it

A. Tursunbayeva et al. (eds.), *Technology-Driven Transformation*, Lecture Notes in Information Systems and Organisation 79,
https://doi.org/10.1007/978-3-032-01396-5_21

study also suggests future research directions, emphasizing the need for continuous adaptation and advancement of digital skills in public sector training and development programs.

Keywords HRM · Technology · Digital skills · Maturity · Public sector

1 Introduction

Digital transformation refers to the integration of digital technologies into all areas of an organization, fundamentally changing the way it operates and delivering value to customers [1]. As governments around the world go through digital transformation to improve efficiency and service delivery, the need for new practices and digital skills among public sector employees has become more apparent. The European Union (EU) has recognised the importance of digital transformation in the public sector and has taken steps to support its member countries in their efforts to adapt to the digital age, allocating 127 billion Euro towards digital reforms and investments for the 25 national Recovery and Resilience Plans [2].

Digital change plays a critical role in the public sector since state institutions are responsible for providing essential services to citizens and businesses and technology can help to improve those services. At the same time, public sector organizations shape the digital landscape as they have the authority to create and enforce policies that direct the use of technologies [3]. According to a report by the European Commission [2], the public sector continues to be one of the largest sources of employment in the EU providing jobs for over 55 million people.

However, research indicates that the adoption of digital technologies in the public sector has been slower compared to the private sector, due to various challenges including legacy systems, organizational resistance to change, bureaucracy, and a lack of digital skills among employees [4]. To address the latter, the EU launched various initiatives including Digital Skills and Jobs platform and Digital Skills and Jobs Coalition with the mission "Digital skills for all" [5]. However, what is still not clear today is whether or how the need for digital skills is considered by EU organizations as crucial for organizational digital transformations, as well as whether or how these should vary depending on organizational digital maturity (RQ). Thus, this was set as the research aim for this explorative study. To achieve it we draw on an integrated framework built on the twenty-first-century digital skills and organizational dimensions and digitalization maturity levels frameworks. We then apply this framework to grey literature guidelines on digital transformation and Human Resource Management (HRM) in the public sector in EU member countries. The term "grey literature" refers to materials and research produced by organizations outside of the academic literature, and includes government reports and guidelines, policy documents, and working papers [6]. By focusing on grey literature, this research study aims to uncover valuable insights that may not be captured or discussed in academic literature and to explore how policies are formulating digital skills requirements and their application among public sector employees and how these skills align with different phases of digitalization.

2 Literature Review

2.1 Integrated Framework

The fast development of digital technologies and their application has a strong impact on public sector operations [7, 8]. Sidek and Ali [9] discuss that digital transformation and knowledge management are critical for the public sector to improve the efficiency, quality, and accessibility of services. At the same time, Edelmann et al. [10] drawing on the example of the Government Department of Economy, Tourism and Technology in Austria, point out that despite the benefits that digital tools can offer, there are barriers that inhibit their adoption and use within the public sector such as lack of organizational culture that supports innovation and legal frameworks that are not adapted for the new technology. Furthermore, public sector digital transformation entails a change in digital competencies requirements and also affects organizational dimensions, and the extent of this impact varies based on the digitalization maturity level of the organization. The interplay between digital skills, organizational dimensions, and stages of digital maturity can be presented in an integrated framework (Fig. 1).

2.2 Public Sector Digital Transformation

Digital Skills Since governments today increasingly rely on digital technologies to deliver services and engage with citizens, public sector workers need to have relevant skills to effectively use those new tools. Danielsen [11] exploring drivers, benefits, and challenges of digital transformation in Norwegian public organizations, shows that comprehensive policy approaches and digital competencies are critical for a successful digital transformation. In the same vein, Bhat and Rainayee [12] investigate the mediating role of person-job fit in the relationship between training and performance among civil servants, revealing the importance of aligning digital skills training with job requirements. Stofkova et al. [13] further highlight that digital skills are a critical factor in human resources development, and essential for public sector employees to effectively navigate the digital environment. However, it is critical that the development of digital skills is encouraged within the organization that seeks to adopt new technology. In this respect, top management support for innovation has been listed as one of the key factors for the success of e-government projects, while a lack of such support contributes to their failure [14].

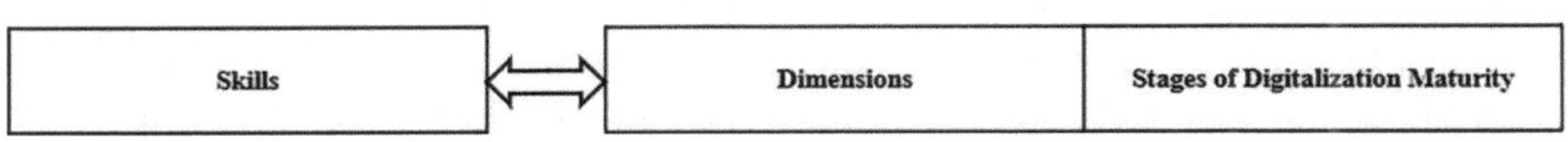

Fig. 1 Integrated framework

The literature on digital skills encompasses a wide range of competencies including digital literacy, problem-solving skills, collaboration, and communication skills [15]. Some researchers suggest the need for tailored training programs considering the specific context and needs of public sector organizations [16]. Others focus on identifying general guidelines that organizations can implement [17]. Van Laar et al. [1] based on the systematic literature review propose a framework including 12 digital skills that are essential for employees in the twenty-first century. For the purpose of this study, this framework was chosen since it is based on a thorough analysis of an extensive body of literature (75 articles) dedicated to the subject of digital capabilities. The scholars divide digital skills into core and contextual [1]. The core skills refer to abilities that are essential for carrying out duties across a wide spectrum of occupations. They include information management, critical thinking, technical skills, collaboration, communication, creativity, and problem-solving. Contextual skills are abilities that enable individuals to effectively apply and leverage their core skills. They encompass ethical awareness, flexibility, lifelong learning, cultural awareness, and self-direction. All the 12 skills are essential for public sector employees to effectively use and manage digital technologies, and to adapt to the changing demands of the digital age.

Core Digital Skills Information management refers to the skill of using digital tools such as ICT to effectively search for, choose, and organize information to make well-informed decisions about the most appropriate sources of information for a specific task [18]. It includes exploring, seeking, and accessing information to achieve a set objective [19]. Another important digital capability is critical thinking. In the context of digital skills, it refers to the ability to utilize digital tools to make informed judgments and decisions about acquired information and communication, employing reflective reasoning and adequate evidence to support the claims [1]. A critical thinking process encompasses different components such as clarification, assessment, novelty (developing new ideas for discussion), justification (providing evidence to support conclusions), linking ideas, and importance (identifying important issues) [20]. As well as critical thinking, technical skills are essential for employees to utilize innovative tools effectively [21]. Technical skills include the ability to navigate online, understand the characteristics of digital tools, and access necessary resources by using these tools [22]. Technology provides opportunities to create wide networks and meet virtually with people based in different locations. The ability to collaborate is a critical digital skill and has such components as interactive communication and participation in discussions on important work matters [23]. Closely linked to collaboration, communication, in the context of digitalization, refers to the skill of using technology to transmit information to others, clearly conveying the meaning [24]. Creativity has also been argued to be one of the key digital competencies for public sector employees [25]. Creativity, in relation to technology use, means the ability to utilize digital tools to create new or previously unknown ideas, or to approach familiar ideas in a novel manner, and to transform these ideas into a product, service, or process that is acknowledged as innovative within a specific domain [1]. Linked to creativity, problem solving can be viewed as a skill to engage in cognitive processing to understand and solve problem situations where the solution is not clear [26].

Contextual Digital Skills It is fundamental for public sector employees to have ethical awareness especially since they often work with sensitive data. Ethical awareness is the skill to behave in a socially responsible manner while using digital tools and its key components are understanding its potential risks and evaluating its impact within the given social, economic, and cultural context [27]. Since technology is developing rapidly, employees need to be able to adapt to the new tools and systems that public sector organizations adopt. The ability to adapt one's thinking and behaviour to the changing environment is defined as flexibility [28]. Strongly linked to being adaptable, lifelong learning means enabling individuals to learn, unlearn, and relearn as new technologies replace old tasks and introduce new ones [29]. Cultural awareness is another critical skill included in the twenty-first-century digital skills dimensions. It involves being conscious of and respectful towards cultural differences while communicating with people from different cultural backgrounds using digital tools [30]. Finally, public sector employees need to strengthen such a capability as self-direction. Holt and Brockett [31] use four factors to evaluate self-directed learning related to the use of digital tools: control (the ability and willingness to direct one's learning), initiative, motivation, and self-efficacy (confidence in one's own capabilities to achieve desired goals).

Recent research observed that digital capabilities are related to organizational dimensions which in turn are linked with different stages of organizational maturity [32].

Organizational Dimensions Guerrero et al. [32] identify five organizational dimensions: Customer Centricity, Strategy & Leadership, Products & Services, Process & Organization, and Technology. Each dimension represents a critical aspect of an organization that seeks to navigate the move from traditional ways of working to digital operations. Customer Centricity measures an organization's capability to use digital technologies for collaborative engagement with customers and other stakeholders within the business ecosystem. Strategy & Leadership assesses a company's ability to create and implement a plan that aligns technology with its business strategy across all organizational levels. Products & Services evaluates an organization's capacity to develop offerings through collaborative efforts within a network of partners, incorporating technology during the creation process. Process & Organization measures a company's ability to adopt technological, managerial, and agile practices to enhance its ecosystem. This dimension refers to such aspects as the organization's approach to managing knowledge, its ability to encourage collaboration, and its capacity for agility and flexibility in response to changing conditions. Finally, Technology evaluates an organization's capacity to identify emerging and potentially impactful technologies that could improve its operations and support strategic objectives. These dimensions are closely linked to stages of digitalization maturity that organizations progress through during the digital transformation process.

Stages of Digitalization Maturity Guerrero et al. [33] relate the organizational dimensions to different stages of digital maturity namely Infancy, Developing, Transforming, Optimized, and Digital Maturity. Infancy refers to the stage where there is no alignment between technology and organizational objectives, the focus is on cost reduction and technology is viewed as an extra expenditure. During the Developing stage, the organization begins to recognise the importance of technology despite most operations remain the same. There is still a lack of alignment between digital tools and strategic objectives and employees' involvement is limited. Transforming stage refers to the phase when the management leaders are open to adopting advanced technologies and make an effort to incorporate them in business planning. During the Optimized phase technology is fully integrated into the organization's strategy and used to improve communication and collaboration, encouraging new relationships with stakeholders. Digital Maturity stage is characterised by the presence of an effective digital strategy that is well-communicated throughout the organization.

3 Methods

To examine "grey" literature, we followed the methodology described by Jobin, Ienca, and Vayena [34] in "The global landscape of AI ethics guidelines" published in Nature Machine Intelligence journal. In line with best practices for "grey" literature retrieval, a search was conducted on Google.com using keywords identified from existing literature on digitalization in the public sector and new ways of working. The search was carried out while in incognito mode, with personal accounts signed out and all cookies and browsing history cleared, to ensure that the search results were not influenced by personal preferences or previous searches.

The keywords for the search were identified through the analysis of pre-existing literature reviews dedicated to three topics: public sector [35], digital technology [36], and work and HRM [37–39].

As a result, the following keywords were used to examine "grey" literature:

The keywords used were "municipal*", "public administrat", "public organi$ation*", "public management", "government*", "public service", "local government*", "e-govern*", "egovern*", "governance", "public sphere", "public sector", "digital technology", "digital platform", "industry 4.0", "internet of things", "digital transformation", "digitalization", "cyber-physical system", "big data", "virtual reality", "cloud computing", "cybersecurity", "hrm", "Human Resource", "people", "workforce", "employee", "Human Capital", "manpower", "staff", "personnel", "talent".

We examined every link in the top 30 search results for content concerning policies, guidelines, and principles related to HRM and new forms of working in the public sector in EU countries. This generic search process led to the discovery of only two unique sources after removing repeats. Then we examined the next 200 links and this search resulted in 1 additional relevant source, giving the total of 3 relevant sources.

For a more focused search, additional keywords such as "EU" and "European Union" were introduced at this stage. Out of the top 30 links, only 1 was relevant. We then reviewed the next 200 search results uncovering 1 relevant source. This search resulted in two documents.

To maximise the probability of the intended outcome, another specific keyword, "guidelin*" was used in addition to the previous search set. Then, we again reviewed Google search results up to the 30th link and found 4 relevant documents. The examination of the following 200 search results did not yield suitable sources.

As a result, by removing repeats we arrived at the total number of seven relevant documents. Then, two documents were added manually, resulting in the final number of nine sources related to the relevant guidelines for EU member states (see Appendix).

These were analyzed for key themes and issues with the help of both inductive and deductive coding [40], to elicit interpretations that matched the digital skills categories of van Laar et al. [1] and the organizational dimensions and digitalization maturity stages of Guerrero et al. [33]. Although both coding frameworks (on digital skills and digital maturity) structured the data, the inductive coding approach ensured that no important additional emerging theme was missed or neglected. For example, we observed the emergence of new skills requirements such as entrepreneurial thinking and commercial acumen.

4 Findings

4.1 Overview

For the purpose of this study, nine documents related to guidelines for digitalization practices and digital skills in the public sector in EU member countries were analysed. The documents were published between 2015 and 2024, of which three were presented in 2020. The issuers of these documents include EU institutions such as the European Commission and the Council of the EU, international organizations like UNESCO, consulting firms such as Deloitte and McKinsey, and national government agencies from Denmark and Italy. The geographical focus of these documents ranges from specific EU member countries (Denmark and Italy) to a broader scope covering multiple EU countries. The organizational types that these documents target primarily involve national governments, EU institutions, and public sector organizations. The processes discussed in the documents mainly relate to public service provision, communication, and collaboration within the public sector. In terms of technology, the documents cover a wide range including AI, chatbots, ICT, digital identity systems, and various e-government tools such as eID, eSignature, and eProcurement.

4.2 Digital Skills

The data analysis shows that the most frequently mentioned skills are technical, collaboration, and problem solving. The analysis indicates that technologies enable different public organizations to work together to achieve common objectives as illustrated by one of the quotes from Denmark, "What is ground-breaking is that these municipalities are working collaboratively" [41]. Technical skills are included in all the analysed documents. One of the sources states, "A tech-savvy workforce is integral to any organization's digital transformation strategy" [42].

Documents indicate the importance of creativity—the ability to use digital tools to create new or previously unknown ideas, or to approach familiar ideas in a novel manner, for example, a "more and faster experimentation with emerging ICT within the public administrations" [43]. As technological change brings new challenges, the role of technology should be critically evaluated, and "taking a holistic and long-term view of challenges and opportunities" it brings is critical [44].

Five out of the nine documents highlight ethical awareness as a necessary skill in the context of public sector digital transformation [44–48]. This reflects a growing concern for ethical considerations in the use of digital technologies, particularly AI. As stated in one of the documents, it is important to "critically query digital information and the impact of digital activity and reach; query corresponding ethical decisions" [47].

Cultural awareness in the analysed documents referred to the EU cultural diversity and generational differences [42, 46]. The European Declaration on Digital Rights and Principles for the Digital Decade [46] highlights "supporting effective access to digital content reflecting the cultural and linguistic diversity in the EU" as one of the key priorities. The adoption of new technologies requires flexibility and the willingness to learn, therefore self-direction and lifelong learning are also identified as essential digital skills for public sector employees. Interestingly, self-direction has been indicated in only one out of the nine analysed sources where it is referred to as "to be able to work independently on your own initiative as part of a project or an organization" [47].

A common new theme that has emerged is the importance of digital leadership as a necessary skill to be developed at all levels of seniority. The Tallinn Declaration on eGovernment [43] states, "We will in our countries: take steps to increase the digital leadership skills among top civil and public servants and digital skills more widely within the public administration at all levels, as a necessary precondition to any successful digital transformation of public administrations". Digital leadership refers to the ability to embrace and support change, as well as contribute to the creation of an environment where digital transformation can be carried out successfully [44].

The European Declaration on Digital Rights and Principles [46] points out sustainability awareness as a critical skill for digital change. This signals the importance of considering how new technologies influence the environment.

The entrepreneurial spirit is included in the list of main digital skills [42], suggesting that there is a strong need for a proactive approach to technology adaptation in the public sector which is often characterized as risk-averse.

4.3 *Organizational Dimensions and Maturity Stages*

The data analysis reveals that each organizational dimension requires multiple digital skills to be developed among public service employees. Interestingly, the findings suggest that a great number of skills are needed starting right from the early stages of organizational digitalization maturity—Infancy, Developing, and Transforming that are linked to the dimension of Customer Centricity.

Strategy & Leadership, related to the later stages of digitalization maturity, appears to be the dimension that requires the highest number of skills (12) and it is at the forefront of driving digital change. The findings indicate that the Products & Services dimension which is also linked with the Digital Maturity stage can be viewed as a starting point where the need for such critical capability as "creativity" emerges.

Unlike other dimensions, Process & Organization and Technology require lifelong learning skill, indicating that most technologically advanced public sector organizations need to make continuous learning a priority.

4.4 *Integrated Findings*

The data analysis revealed that the relationships between digital skills and organizational dimensions and digitalization maturity stages are complex, as each skill may be associated with several or even all organizational dimensions. Based on the findings, a new conceptual framework has been developed (Fig. 2) with the emerged core digital skill marked with a * sign.

The proposed framework illustrates that most digital skills are relevant across several organizational dimensions and digital maturity stages and there is a bidirectional relationship between them. Some skills, such as communication, technical competencies, and ethical awareness appear to be particularly important since they are linked to all five organizational dimensions and consequently to all stages of digitalization maturity. Interestingly, the added digital leadership skill is also linked to all organizational dimensions.

Furthermore, the developed framework demonstrates a progression of skill requirements as public sector organizations go through the digitalization maturity stages. Skills such as information management and technical competencies are relevant from the earliest "Infancy" stage, while more advanced skills like creativity and self-direction become more important in later stages.

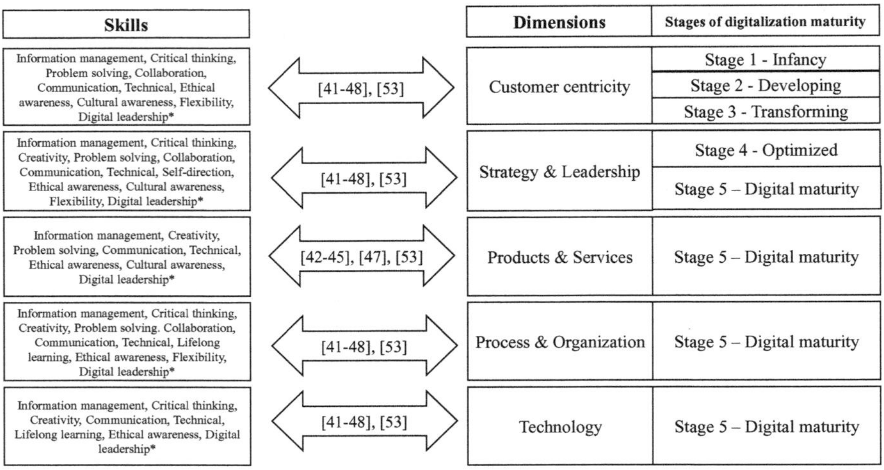

Fig. 2 Developed conceptual framework

Overall, the framework indicates that there is a need for a comprehensive approach to digital transformation since different skills are linked to various aspects of public sector operations at the same time.

5 Discussion and Conclusion

This study aimed to propose a framework mapping the digital skills requirements presented in the guidelines across different public sector contexts within EU member countries to different organizational dimensions and stages of digital maturity. By analyzing the guidelines through the lens of the core twenty-first-century digital skills framework and digitalization maturity stage model, this study contributes to the body of knowledge on digital transformation in the public sector.

The findings from this scoping review of "grey" literature confirm the need for public sector employees to develop digital skills highlighted in the academic research studies [7, 9, 13]. The analysis reveals a strong emphasis on technical skills, collaboration, and problem solving. Similar to the findings of Mergel and colleagues [3], the review of the guidelines across different public sector contexts within EU member countries shows that collaboration is a critical skill since it relates to both—internal cooperation between public servants working within the same organization and external collaboration related to involving citizens and other external stakeholders in the service development.

The conducted review revealed a critical digital skill, which was not included in van Laar et al.'s [1] framework—digital leadership. The academic literature often discusses digital leadership in relation to top management and their role in technology-driven transformation in the public sector [14]. Despite some of the analyzed documents [42, 44] demonstrate a similar approach, others [43, 48] view digital leadership as a critical skill required to be developed at different seniority levels. This expanded view of digital leadership suggests a shift in thinking about the role of each employee in the technology-driven transformation process. It indicates that successful digital change in the public sector requires not only top-down direction but also bottom-up and cross-team leadership competencies.

Another new skill that has been identified through the analysis is sustainability awareness. This competence is mentioned in only one [46] out of the nice documents reviewed and therefore was not added to the list of core skills. Along with sustainability awareness, entrepreneurial spirit [42] is mentioned in one of the sources. The presence of these competencies indicates the emergence of new skill requirements and the dynamic nature of the digital transformation demands. Sustainability awareness is particularly relevant today since digital infrastructures impact the environment and such factors as energy consumption and carbon footprint. In practice, public sector decision-makers can incorporate sustainability criteria when choosing what technology to implement.

Overall, the developed framework illustrates that most digital skills are relevant across several organizational dimensions, which suggests that a holistic approach to digital transformation in the public sector is needed. This conclusion resonates with the view of Danielsen [11] who examined the drivers, benefits, and challenges of digital transformation in Norwegian public organizations, and suggested that comprehensive policy approaches and digital competencies are critical for a successful digital transformation.

In order to apply the proposed framework to practice, public sector leaders can first identify the digitalization maturity stage of the organization and, based on the frameworks' skills categories, identify what competencies are essential to be developed. These steps can be followed by the assessment of the current employees' skill sets and identifying the gaps. Based on the results, appropriate training programs can be designed and implemented. It is suggested that in addition to technical skills, such competencies as ethical awareness, collaboration, and problem solving are introduced at early stages of training. It is proposed that tailored training programs are developed considering the specific context and needs of public sector organizations [16].

The implications of this study are considerable for both research and practice. From a research perspective, this study emphasizes the value of grey literature in understanding the complex landscape of digital transformation in the public sector. From a practical perspective, this study provides policymakers and public sector organizations with insights into the application of the proposed framework and promoting digital skills development among employees.

6 Limitations and Future Research Directions

One of the limitations of this study is its reliance on "grey" literature sources. The use of such sources poses several challenges including the lack of a peer-review process, potential bias since organizations that produce such documents can have their interests, lack of methodological transparency, and limited theoretical foundation [49]. However, analyzing grey literature can provide valuable insights into practical applications, especially in rapidly evolving areas such as advanced technology use where traditional academic publications may not capture the full spectrum of knowledge. Paez [6] discussing the benefits of searching for and using grey literature in research, highlights that manuscript submission processes are lengthy and sometimes lead to a "file-drawer" effect when researchers' valuable findings remain unpublished. Despite the challenges that the use of non-academic literature presents, it continues to provide valuable contributions to research across various disciplines including public health genomics [50], psychology [51], and human resource management [52].

In addition, since digital transformation challenges and contexts can vary significantly across different countries, the findings may not be easily generalizable to all public sector organizations located within the EU area. Each country has its own characteristics such as economic conditions, technological infrastructure, and governmental policies. However, the digital skills discussed in this research study are relevant to all public sector organizations that undergo digital change.

For the purpose of this study, a scoping review of grey literature sources was conducted. This approach allowed the researchers to synthesize and analyze existing practical knowledge and guidelines. However, empirical data collection will be carried out in the follow-up stages to validate and enrich the findings that emerged from the scoping review.

Future research could involve longitudinal studies examining public sector organizations as they progress through different stages of digitalization maturity. Such studies could provide insights into how digital skill requirements evolve over time and how public administrations in different countries adapt their training and development programs accordingly.

Another important area for future research is the assessment of the effectiveness of current digital skills training programs in public sector organizations. Such studies could involve evaluating the impact of these programs on organizational efficiency, employee performance, and quality of service delivery. The research could reveal best practices in digital skills development and inform the approach to designing and implementing more effective employee learning initiatives.

In addition, conducting comparative case studies across different EU countries could shed light on how local governmental policies and cultural factors impact the development and implementation of digital training programs in public sector organizations. Such comparative analysis could result in the identification of transferable best practices and policy recommendations within the EU.

Finally, future research should also consider the impact of advanced technologies such as artificial intelligence, machine learning, and the Internet of Things, on the digital skills requirements in the public sector. As these technologies continue to develop, it is critical to understand the evolution of digital skills and future organizational needs and adapt training programs accordingly.

Acknowledgments This study is part of a larger research project "Towards an agile public sector: reinventing the public administration by designing human-centred and sustainable organizational models, HRM practices and work(places)" funded by the Italian Ministry of University and Research within the PRIN PNRR 2022 program—CUP I53D23016460001—Finanziamento dell'Unione Europea—Next Generation EU–missione 4, componente 2, investimento 1.1. importo rendicontato V238.732".

Disclosure of Interests The authors have no competing interests to declare that are relevant to the content of this article.

Appendix: Characteristics of the Included Studies

#	Title, year	Issuer	Country of focus	Organization type/ Department	Process	Technology type	Skills discussed	Organizational dimensions	Digital maturity stages
1	Accessing Danish digital public services with Muni, 2023	Eurocities	Denmark	Virtual contact center	Communication	Chatbot	Technical, communication, problem solving, collaboration, flexibility, critical thinking	Customer Centricity, Strategy & Leadership, Process & Organization, Technology	Infancy, Developing, Transforming, Optimized, Digital Maturity
2	Tallinn Declaration on eGovernment, 2017	The Council of the EU	EU member states	The EU institutions	Public service provision	ICT, eID, eSignature, eDelivery, eProcurement and eInvoicing	Digital leadership, information mangement, technical, communication, collaboration	Customer Centricity, Strategy & Leadership, Products & Services, Process & Organization, Technology	Infancy, Developing, Transforming, Optimized, Digital Maturity
3	The journey to government's digital transformation, 2015	Deloitte Insights	70 countries including EU member states	National governments	Public service provision	ICT, Big Data and other digital tools	Digital leadership, problem solving, collaboration, flexibility, technical, business acumen, entrepreneurial spirit, creativity, lifelong learning, cultural awareness, information management	Customer Centricity, Strategy & Leadership, Products & Services, Process & Organization, Technology	Infancy, Developing, Transforming, Optimized, Digital Maturity

#	Title, year	Issuer	Country of focus	Organization type/ Department	Process	Technology type	Skills discussed	Organizational dimensions	Digital maturity stages
4	About the Agency for Digital Government, 2022	The Agency for Digital Government	Denmark	Ministry of Digital Government and Gender Equality	Public sector collaboration	ICT and other digital tools	Collaboration, problem solving, technical, information management, digital leadership, lifelong learning, ethical awareness	Customer Centricity, Strategy & Leadership, Process & Organization, Technology	Infancy, Developing, Transforming, Optimized, Digital Maturity
5	European Declaration on Digital Rights and Principles, 2022	European Commission	EU member states	The EU institutions (public and private)	Public service provision	AI	Lifelong learning, cultural awareness, critical thinking, flexibility, ethical awareness, information management, problem solving, sustainability awareness	Customer Centricity, Strategy & Leadership, Process & Organization, Technology	Infancy, Developing, Transforming, Optimized, Digital Maturity
6	Artificial intelligence and digital transformation: competencies for civil servants, 2022	UNESCO; Broadband Commission for Sustainable Development. Working Group on AI Capacity Building; International Telecommunication Union	All countries including EU member states	National governments and public sector institutions	Public service strategy, data management and service provision	AI	Critical thinking, technical, creativity, problem solving, ethical awareness, information management, collaboration, digital leadership	Customer Centricity, Strategy & Leadership, Products & Services, Process & Organization, Technology	Infancy, Developing, Transforming, Optimized, Digital Maturity

(continued)

(continued)

#	Title, year	Issuer	Country of focus	Organization type/ Department	Process	Technology type	Skills discussed	Organizational dimensions	Digital maturity stages
7	The future is now: Closing the skills gap in Europe's public sector, 2020	McKinsey & Company	EU member states and the UK	Public sector institutions	Public service provision	AI	Technical, communication, ethical awareness, collaboration, lifelong learning, problem solving, creativity, self-direction, flexibility, grit	Customer Centricity, Strategy & Leadership, Products & Services, Process & Organization, Technology	Infancy, Developing, Transforming, Optimized, Digital Maturity
8	Piano Triennale per l'Informatica nella Pubblica Amministrazione, 2023	AGID [53]	Italy	National government of Italy	Public service provision	ICT and Digital Identity Systems	Problem solving, communication, technical, information management, problem solving, critical thinking	Customer Centricity, Strategy & Leadership, Products & Services, Process & Organization, Technology	Infancy, Developing, Transforming, Optimized, Digital Maturity
9	Strategia Italiana per l'Intelligenza Artificiale 2024–2026, 2024	Digital Transformation Department; AGID	Italy	National government of Italy	Public service provision	AI	Problem solving, collaboration, technical, critical thinking, ethical awareness, information management, lifelong learning	Customer Centricity, Strategy & Leadership, Products & Services, Process & Organization, Technology	Infancy, Developing, Transforming, Optimized, Digital Maturity

References

1. Van Laar, E., van Deursen, A. J. A. M., van Dijk, J. A. G. M., & de Haan, J. (2017). The relation between 21st-century skills and digital skills: A systematic literature review. *Computers in Human Behavior, 72*, 577–588. https://doi.org/10.1016/j.chb.2017.03.010
2. European Commission. (2019). *Best environmental management practice for the public administration sector*. Accessed April 08, 2024, from https://greenbestpractice.jrc.ec.europa.eu/sites/default/files/2019-12/Best_environmental_management_practice_report_public_administration_02.pdf
3. Mergel, I., Edelmann, N., & Haug, N. (2019). Defining digital transformation: Results from expert interviews. *Government Information Quarterly, 36*(4).
4. Mergel, I. (2016). Agile innovation management in government. *Government Information Quarterly, 33*(3), 516–523.
5. European Commission. (2018). *Digital skills and jobs coalition*. Accessed April 05, 2024, from https://digital-strategy.ec.europa.eu/en/policies/digital-skills-coalition
6. Paez, A. (2017). Grey literature: An important resource in systematic reviews. *Journal of Evidence-Based Medicine, 10*(3), 153–240.
7. De Gier, J. (2018). IT governance of Dutch municipalities and digital information management. *New Review of Information Networking, 23*(1–2), 36–46. https://doi.org/10.1080/13614576.2018.1537798
8. Pautz, H. (2023). Policy making and artificial intelligence in Scotland. *Contemporary Social Science, 18*(5), 618–636. https://doi.org/10.1080/21582041.2023.2293822
9. Sidek, N., & Ali, N. A. B. (2019). Analysing the critical quality factors in IOT-based service implementation: A systematic evaluation. *International Journal of Engineering and Advanced Technology, 9*(1), 2276–2281. https://doi.org/10.35940/ijeat.A2631.109119
10. Edelmann, N., Steiner, K., & Misuraca, G. (2023). The view from the inside: A case study on the perceptions of digital transformation phases in public administrations. *Digital Government: Research and Practice, 4*(2), 1–18. https://doi.org/10.1145/3589507
11. Danielsen, F. (2021). Benefits and challenges of digitalization: An expert study on Norwegian public organizations. In *The 22nd Annual International Conference on Digital Government Research* (pp. 317–326). ACM. https://doi.org/10.1145/3463677.3463703
12. Bhat, Z., & Rainayee, A. (2019). Examining the mediating role of person–job fit in the relationship between training and performance: A civil servant perspective. *Global Business Review, 20*, 529–548. https://doi.org/10.1177/0972150918825395
13. Stofkova, J., Poliakova, A., Stofkova, K., Malega, P., Krejnus, M., Binasova, V., & Daneshjo, N. (2022). Digital skills as a significant factor of human resources development. *Sustainability, 14*, 1–18. https://doi.org/10.3390/su142013117
14. Elkadi, H. (2013). Success and failure factors for e-government projects: A case from Egypt. *Egyptian Informatics Journal, 14*(2), 165–173. https://doi.org/10.1016/j.eij.2013.06.002
15. Voogt, J., & Roblin, N. P. (2012). A comparative analysis of international frameworks for 21st century competences: Implications for national curriculum policies. *Journal of Curriculum Studies, 44*(3), 299–321. https://doi.org/10.1080/00220272.2012.668938
16. Barry, M., Gomez, R., Kaufman, B., Wilkinson, A., & Zhang, T. (2020). Is it 'you' or 'your workplace'? Predictors of job-related training in the Anglo-American world. *International Journal of Training and Development, 24*(3), 173–203. https://doi.org/10.1111/ijtd.12192
17. Barak, M. (2016). Science teacher education in the twenty-first century: A pedagogical framework for technology-integrated social constructivism. *Research in Science Education*, 1–21. https://doi.org/10.1007/s11165-015-9501-y
18. Snow, E., & Katz, I. R. (2009). Using cognitive interviews to validate an interpretive argument for the ETS iSkills™ assessment. *Communications in Information Literacy, 3*(2), 99–127.
19. Ahmad, M., Badusah, J., Mansor, A. Z., Karim, A. A., Khalid, F., Daud, M. Y., Din, R., & Zulkefle, D. F. (2016). The application of 21st century ICT literacy model among teacher trainees. *Turkish Online Journal of Educational Technology, 15*(3), 151–161.

20. Lee, H., Parsons, D., Kwon, G., Kim, J., Petrova, K., Jeong, E., & Ryu, H. (2016). Cooperation begins: Encouraging critical thinking skills through cooperative reciprocity using a mobile learning game. *Computers & Education, 97*, 97–115. https://doi.org/10.1016/j.compedu.2016.03.006
21. De Vries, H., Tummers, L., & Bekkers, V. (2018). The diffusion and adoption of public sector innovations: A meta-synthesis of the literature. *Perspectives on Public Management and Governance, 1*(3), 159–176. https://doi.org/10.1093/ppmgov/gvy001
22. Van Deursen, A. J. A. M., & Van Dijk, J. A. G. M. (2010). Measuring internet skills. *International Journal of Human-Computer Interaction, 26*(10), 891–916. https://doi.org/10.1080/10447318.2010.496338
23. Helsper, E. J., & Eynon, R. (2013). Distinct skill pathways to digital engagement. *European Journal of Communication, 28*(6), 696–713. https://doi.org/10.1177/0267323113499113
24. Siddiq, F., Scherer, R., & Tondeur, J. (2016). Teachers' emphasis on developing students' digital information and communication skills (TEDDICS): A new construct in 21st century education. *Computers & Education, 92–93*, 1–14. https://doi.org/10.1016/j.compedu.2015.10.006
25. Mengual-Andrés, S., Roig-Vila, R., & Mira, J. B. (2016). Delphi study for the design and validation of a questionnaire about digital competences in higher education. *International Journal of Educational Technology in Higher Education, 13*(1), 12. https://doi.org/10.1186/s41239-016-0009-y
26. Scherer, R., & Gustafsson, J. E. (2015). The relations among openness, perseverance, and performance in creative problem solving: A substantive-methodological approach. *Thinking Skills and Creativity, 18*, 4–17. https://doi.org/10.1016/j.tsc.2015.04.004
27. Janssen, J., Stoyanov, S., Ferrari, A., Punie, Y., Pannekeet, K., & Sloep, P. (2013). Experts' views on digital competence: Commonalities and differences. *Computers & Education, 68*, 473–481. https://doi.org/10.1016/j.compedu.2013.06.008
28. Anderman, E. M., Sinatra, G. M., & Gray, D. L. (2012). The challenges of teaching and learning about science in the twenty-first century: Exploring the abilities and constraints of adolescent learners. *Studies in Science Education, 48*(1), 89–117. https://doi.org/10.1080/03057267.2012.655038
29. Chai, C. S., Deng, F., Tsai, P.-S., Koh, J. H. L., & Tsai, C.-C. (2015). Assessing multidimensional students' perceptions of twenty-first-century learning practices. *Asia Pacific Education Review, 16*(3), 389–398. https://doi.org/10.1007/s12564-015-9379-4
30. Yang, J., Huiju, Y., Chen, S.-J., & Huang, R. (2014). Strategies for smooth and effective cross-cultural online collaborative learning. *Educational Technology & Society, 17*(3), 208–221.
31. Holt, L., & Brockett, R. G. (2012). Self-direction and factors influencing technology use: Examining the relationships for the 21st century workplace. *Computers in Human Behavior, 28*(6), 2075–2082. https://doi.org/10.1016/j.chb.2012.06.011
32. Guerrero, R., Michalke, S., & Siemon, D. (2022). *Towards the design of a digital business ecosystem maturity model for personal service firms: A pre-evaluation strategy* (pp. 1–15). Proceedings of the Pacific Asia Conference on Information Systems (PACIS), Taipei, Taiwan & Sydney, Australia.
33. Guerrero, R., Lattemann, C., & Gebbing, P. (2023). Helping personal service firms to cope with digital transformation: Evaluation of digitalization maturity model. *Pacific Asia Journal of the Association for Information Systems, 15*(2), 1–32. https://doi.org/10.17705/1pais.15201
34. Jobin, A., Ienca, M., & Vayena, E. (2019). The global landscape of AI ethics guidelines. *Nature Machine Intelligence, 1*(9), 389–399. https://doi.org/10.1038/s42256-019-0088-2
35. Cinar, E., Trott, P., & Simms, C. (2019). A systematic review of barriers to public sector innovation process. *Public Management Review, 21*(2), 264–290. https://doi.org/10.1080/14719037.2018.1473477
36. Ancillai, C., Sabatini, A., Gatti, M., & Perna, A. (2023). Digital technology and business model innovation: A systematic literature review and future research agenda. *Technological Forecasting and Social Change, 188*, 1–43. https://doi.org/10.1016/j.techfore.2022.122307

37. Bannya, A. R., Bainbridge, H. T. J., & Chan-Serafin, S. (2023). HR practices and work relationships: A 20 year review of relational HRM research. *Human Resource Management, 62*(4), 391–412. https://doi.org/10.1002/hrm.22151
38. Tursunbayeva, A., Di Lauro, S., & Pagliari, C. (2018). People analytics—A scoping review of conceptual boundaries and value propositions. *International Journal of Information Management, 43*, 224–247. https://doi.org/10.1016/j.ijinfomgt.2018.08.002
39. Tursunbayeva, A., Pagliari, C., Di Lauro, S., & Antonelli, G. (2022). The ethics of people analytics: Risks, opportunities and recommendations. *Personnel Review, 51*(3), 900–921. https://doi.org/10.1108/PR-12-2019-0680
40. Miles, M. B., & Huberman, A. M. (1994). *Qualitative data analysis: An expanded sourcebook*. Sage Publications.
41. Eurocities. (2023). *Accessing Danish digital public services with Muni*. Accessed June 05, 2024, from https://eurocities.eu/latest/accessing-danish-digital-public-services-with-muni/
42. Deloitte Insights. (2015). *The journey to government's digital transformation*. Accessed June 05, 2024, from https://www2.deloitte.com/content/dam/insights/us/articles/digital-transformation-in-government/DUP_1081_Journey-to-govt-digital-future_MASTER.pdf
43. The Council of the EU. (2017). *Tallinn Declaration on eGovernment*. Accessed June 05, 2024, from https://digital-strategy.ec.europa.eu/en/news/ministerial-declaration-egovernment-tallinn-declaration
44. UNESCO Broadband Commission for Sustainable Development. Working Group on AI Capacity Building; International Telecommunication Union. (2022). *Artificial intelligence and digital transformation: Competencies for civil servants*. Accessed June 05, 2024, from https://unesdoc.unesco.org/ark:/48223/pf0000383325
45. Digital Transformation Department and AGID. (2024). *Strategia Italiana per l'Intelligenza Artificiale 2024-2026*. Accessed July 08, 2024, from https://www.agid.gov.it/sites/agid/files/2024-07/Strategia_italiana_per_l_Intelligenza_artificiale_2024-2026.pdf
46. European Commission. (2022). *European declaration on digital rights and principles*. Accessed June 05, 2024, from https://digital-strategy.ec.europa.eu/en/library/european-declaration-digital-rights-and-principles
47. McKinsey & Company. (2020). *The future is now: Closing the skills gap in Europe's public sector*. Accessed June 05, 2024, from https://www.mckinsey.com/industries/public-sector/our-insights/the-future-is-now-closing-the-skills-gap-in-europes-public-sector
48. The Agency for Digital Government. (2022). *About the agency for digital government*. Accessed June 05, 2024, from https://en.digst.dk/about-us/#:~:text=The%20Agency%20is%20in%20charge,Digital%20Government%20and%20Gender%20Equality
49. Adams, R. J., Smart, P., & Huff, A. S. (2017). Shades of grey: Guidelines for working with the grey literature in systematic reviews for management and organizational studies. *International Journal of Management Reviews, 19*(4), 432–454. https://doi.org/10.1111/ijmr.12102
50. Avard, D., Jean, M. S., Grégoire, G., & Page, M. (2010). Public involvement in health genomics: The reality behind the policies. *International Journal of Consumer Studies, 34*(5), 508–524. https://doi.org/10.1111/j.1470-6431.2010.00914.x
51. Bellefontaine, S. P., & Lee, C. M. (2014). Between black and white: Examining grey literature in meta-analyses of psychological research. *Journal of Child and Family Studies, 23*(8), 1378–1388. https://doi.org/10.1007/s10826-013-9795-1
52. Deadrick, D. L., & Gibson, P. A. (2007). An examination of the research-practice gap in HR: Comparing topics of interest to HR academics and HR professionals. *Human Resource Management Review, 17*(2), 131–139. https://doi.org/10.1016/j.hrmr.2007.03.001
53. AGID. (2023). *Piano Triennale per l'Informatica nella Pubblica Amministrazione*. Accessed June 05, 2024, from https://www.agid.gov.it/sites/default/files/repository_files/26_07_rapporto_spesa_ict_2022.pdf

What If the Essential Were Invisible to Decision-Making? Designing an Interactive Eye-Tracking Study on the Voluntary Contribution Mechanism

Edgardo Bucciarelli, Aurora Ascatigno, Alfredo Colantonio, and Alessia Regnicoli

Abstract In experimental settings, process-tracking techniques are increasingly used to study human decision-making and its impact on decisions and outcomes. This work focuses on the use of eye-tracking to predict eye movements during decision-making and their impact on economic outcomes. Despite its widespread use in other fields, eye-tracking has not been widely adopted in experimental economics. The paper discusses various eye-tracking techniques and devices, especially their applications in economics. It also proposes a novel experimental design using the public goods game as a framework, incorporating eye-tracking to assess participants' understanding of the instructions and key elements required to make economic decisions. These elements include the amount to be contributed to the common fund, the size of the fund, and the resulting payoff. The study involves a treatment group and a control group, both answering pretest-posttest questions before and after the experiment. Eye-tracking features will be used during the experiment for the treatment group, but not for the control group. The work aims to identify links between comprehension of the instructions and responses by analysing eye movements during the reading phase. The patterns of their gaze shed light on the strategic considerations and cognitive processes underlying their choices. Although the study has limitations, it reflects on the use of eye-tracking in experimental economics and highlights the need for future research.

E. Bucciarelli
University of Chieti-Pescara, Pescara, Italy
e-mail: edgardo.bucciarelli@unich.it

A. Ascatigno (✉) · A. Regnicoli
School of Advanced Studies, University of Chieti-Pescara, Chieti, Italy
e-mail: aurora.ascatigno@unich.it; alessia.regnicoli@phd.unich.it

A. Colantonio
International Telematic University Uninettuno, Roma, Italy
e-mail: a.colantonio@students.uninettunouniversity.net

A. Tursunbayeva et al. (eds.), *Technology-Driven Transformation*, Lecture Notes in Information Systems and Organisation 79,
https://doi.org/10.1007/978-3-032-01396-5_22

Keywords Gaze movements · Experimental economics · Experimental design research

1 Introduction

The study of human decision-making and its potential impact on various aspects of research and society has significantly evolved, with a growing dependence on sophisticated process-tracking techniques. This reliance is closely intertwined with cutting-edge technological advancements, particularly the utilisation of eye-tracking technology. This non-invasive technology captures eye movements, revealing where and how long individuals fixate their gaze, potentially reflecting cognitive aspects involved in decision-making [1]. From a general point of view, while eye-tracking is a well-established tool in psychology and other social sciences, its application in economics, particularly in experimental economics, remains limited [2]. Advancements in technology, particularly the development of affordable and user-friendly systems (e.g., webcams, open-source software), have facilitated the use of eye-tracking in online economic studies, promoting research with higher participant diversity and faster data collection [3]. Among other things, this paves the way for a deeper understanding of how experimental subjects allocate their attention and manage emotions when they make economic decisions. In this spirit, according to [4], economics has become an experimental science in recent decades, where experiments are used to test theories, search for facts, provide policy advice; to teach/learn economics and to discover new behavioural patterns (for more details, see, among others, [5–7]). Traditionally, these experiments are conducted in laboratories, in classrooms or in the field (e.g., [8–12]). However, the rise of the internet has led to a surge in online experiments, which can be conducted with a wider range of participants and offer greater flexibility [13]. The validity of experimental data from online experiments is a topic of ongoing debate, but some studies suggest that the results are comparable to those obtained from traditional laboratory experiments [14]. However, conducting online experiments makes it more possible to use eye-tracking techniques, especially those that fall into the category of remote and mobile eye-tracking technology [15–17]. Thus, there is reason to believe that further applications of eye-tracking techniques may represent an evaluable potential for additional research into human decision-making and behaviour. Indeed, as argued by [18], the adoption of eye-tracking techniques allows us to enter a fascinating avenue of research that opens the door to a more in-depth analysis of human eye movements, from which human gaze can be inferred as a decision-making signal. This, in turn, can enhance our understanding of visual concentration, gaze behaviour, and the cognitive processes underlying economic decisions. Among other things, using this technique, researchers can gain valuable information to further understand a human's visual concentration, gaze behaviour and eye movements. In this way, it is possible to capture and analyse those aspects of human action that occur in all situations where people have to make decisions and learn, and that are embedded in human cognition whenever a situation of interaction between the visual system and the brain arises [19]. In order to obtain information about these aspects, researchers employ specific machine learning and deep learning techniques with the intention of estimating human gaze data. This is achieved by observing the subject's gaze position on the device's display. For further information on this point, see, among others [20–22]. Although machine learning and deep learning techniques are of fundamental importance in the estimation of human gaze data, their discussion is beyond the scope of this work. This topic may be addressed in future work.

When browsing through the literature on eye-tracking, we can see a wide range of applications in different research fields, as well as the existence of different eye-tracking technologies and devices used for this purpose. In this regard, while we recognise the wide use of eye-tracking in research areas such as healthcare [23–28], Human-Computer Interaction (HCI) [29–36], education and e-learning [37–42], car assistant [43–45], choice modelling, psychology and marketing studies [1, 19, 46–50] there is little use of it in the arena of experimental economics [51–54]. As we will see in detail, the limited application of eye-tracking in experimental economics is relatively uncommon for several reasons. Historically, economics has been a theoretical discipline focused on mathematical and conceptual models, making the incorporation of eye-tracking a recent phenomenon that has yet to gain widespread adoption. Integrating eye-tracking data with traditional economic models is complex, requiring interdisciplinary skills in economics, psychology, cognitive science, and advanced data analysis. Despite recent technological advances that have made eye-tracking more accessible and less expensive, the initial costs of purchasing high-precision devices and training personnel remain significant, deterring researchers with limited financial resources. Additionally, collecting eye-tracking data raises ethical and privacy concerns, necessitating stringent protection of participants' sensitive data and compliance with regulations, which complicates data management. Furthermore, there is considerable variation in the accuracy and reliability of eye-tracking techniques, especially in uncontrolled environments, posing challenges for experiments needing high precision. External factors such as lighting conditions, head movements, and the use of glasses or contact lenses can also introduce variability into the collected data. Addressing these issues through a comprehensive discussion of techniques and devices, and encouraging interdisciplinary collaboration, is essential for the broader adoption of eye-tracking in experimental economics.

Building on the above, our motivation is twofold. First, although it is possible to find works in literature that discuss the existence of the different eye-tracking techniques with their fields of application (e.g., [22]), these works, to the best of our knowledge, do not deal with remote eye-tracking and mobile eye-tracking also shedding lights on experimental economics applications. Secondly, it can be argued that within the existing literature, there is a limited number of published scientific articles that have conducted experiments in the field of experimental economics on the public goods game by adopting eye-tracking techniques (e.g., [55, 56]). In view of the potential of this technology to investigate human gaze and aspects of human decision-making and behaviour, it is conceivable that it could be applied relatively more widely during the conduction of a public goods experiment. In fact, according to [57], the public goods game is an experimental paradigm used in economics to study cooperation and decision-making in situations with a social dilemma. Simply put, the public goods game studies how people contribute to a common fund (public good) when the benefits of that fund are enjoyed by all, regardless of how much they have contributed [58]. This is the basis of a social dilemma in which there is a tension between individual self-interest and collective benefit [59–61]. In the game, "*Cooperation for public good provision often presents a social dilemma—contributing is individually costly but brings benefits for the group. This means that there are incentives to free-ride on others' contributions, but the public good is not provided if everybody free-rides*" (Otten et al., [62], p. 1). Although from a theoretical point of view, subjects should defect by not contributing to the common fund, experimental evidence shows instead that subjects tend to cooperate with each other and contribute to the collective welfare [63–67]. In essence, the stylisation of public goods game scenarios in which actors make contributing decisions allows us to examine the dynamics that often influence our lives and affect us both from a local and a global perspective [68, 69]. Nevertheless, regardless of the level of examination, it is essential to consider the pivotal role played by human interaction in the provision of public goods. In this context, we believe that further attention should be directed towards the way individuals make accurate economic choices within the context of public goods games. Therefore, we have reason to believe that further contributions anticipating the use of eye-tracking techniques in this direction are needed.

In this work, we aim to address these gaps by providing a detailed discussion of the commonly used eye-tracking technologies and devices, especially in experimental economics. We will also propose a novel experimental design incorporating eye-tracking in public goods games, potentially offering new insights into visual attention and decision-making in economic experiments. We propose a novel experimental design in which subjects are divided into treatment and control groups and participate in a lab-in-the-field experiment. This experiment involves playing a public goods game that includes an eye-tracking phase, which is conducted using the oTree platform [70]. As far as we know, this platform does not yet include this particular feature. This approach permits the testing of hypotheses that are challenging to investigate through alternative methodologies. These include the impact of visual attention on the accuracy of decision-making and the potential cognitive load experienced by participants during economic experiences. In this spirit, as outlined by [71], eye-tracking provides a real-time record of a subject's gaze, indicating the location and duration of their attention during interaction with teaching materials. This includes the text of the experimental instructions (e.g., see [71–73]) and the essential information needed to make an economic decision in the public goods game experiment. This approach will permit the verification of consistency between the gaze of the experimental subjects and their responses to control questions on the comprehension of the instructions, as well as between the gaze of the experimental subjects and the essential elements for making an economic decision in the public goods game, such as the amount to be contributed to the common fund, the size of the common fund and the payoff obtained. In particular, it will be possible to conduct comparative analyses between the two groups. In this context, we present a comprehensive representation of the experimental design, including all its phases, depicted through the Business Process Model and Notation (BPMN).

In addition to this introductory section, this work is organised as follows: Section 2 illustrates some eye-tracking techniques, together with the related devices often used in this field. In doing so, we refer to some of the main fields of application, paying particular attention to experimental economics. Section 3 provides the novel experimental design. To conclude, Sect. 4 discusses the main topics covered in this work and refers to further studies in this direction.

2 Eye-Tracking Devices and Applications: An Overview

This section follows the approach of [22] in discussing the various eye-tracking techniques commonly used to conduct studies in different disciplines, including experimental economics. First, the techniques are presented in order of complexity and cost, with an explanation of the economic factors limiting their widespread adoption. As each technique is defined, references are provided for further investigation. Second, we review some scientific articles in economics that use experimental approaches to study human behaviour and have utilised eye-tracking techniques.

2.1 Eye-Tracking Techniques and Devices

This part of the study examines eye-tracking techniques, and the main devices used in current literature, structured by their complexity, invasiveness, and cost. It begins with an overview of techniques that are more complex, invasive, and costly, then moves on to those that are simpler, less invasive, and cheaper. By doing so, it highlights the trade-offs involved in choosing one technique over another, such as the balance between accuracy and the invasiveness of wearing specific devices.

2.1.1 Scleral Search Coil Technique

The Scleral Search Coil Technique, as discussed by [74], is one of the most accurate methods for testing vertical saccades. Introduced in 1963 by [75], this technique uses a contact lens with mirrors connected to a metal coil that responds to magnetic fields. Despite its high accuracy, resolution, and 3D data representation, the Scleral Search Coil Technique is invasive, complex to implement, and requires expensive equipment, making it less attractive for broader use. Moreover, its susceptibility to breakage, short wear time, and incompatibility with sensitive or excessively blinking eyes further limit its adoption. Concerns about intraocular pressure and the invasiveness of the technique are significant barriers to its use in routine experimental settings [22]. This technique has since been incorporated into eye-tracking technology. By monitoring reflected infrared wavelengths, eye trackers can accurately track eye movements. Further discussion on this point can be found in [22, 76].

2.1.2 Infrared Oculography (IOG)

Infrared Oculography (IOG) is a non-invasive technique that uses infrared (IR) light and the reflective properties of the eye to track movements [22, 77]. An IR camera captures reflected IR light from the cornea and pupil, and a processing unit calculates the gaze direction. While IOG is safer and more comfortable for users, and relatively cheaper than scleral search coils, it can have lower accuracy, especially for small or rapid eye movements. Its sensitivity to ambient light and head movements further affects its accuracy. Despite these limitations, its portability and ease of setup make it suitable for various settings outside controlled laboratory environments.

2.1.3 Electro-Oculography (EOG)

Electro-Oculography (EOG) measures the corneo-retinal standing potential, resulting from different ion concentrations in the cornea and retina [78]. Electrodes are attached to the skin around the eyes to detect eye movements. While EOG is useful for studying retinal activity and small eye movements like nystagmus, it primarily measures horizontal movements, and vertical movements are less accurately captured. EOG's susceptibility to electrical noise from muscle activity or blinking also poses challenges [79]. Despite its clinical importance, its limitations in capturing vertical eye movements and sensitivity to noise reduce its attractiveness for widespread experimental use [80].

As noted by [81], EOG has some limitations: It primarily measures horizontal eye movements and vertical movements are not accurately captured due to electrode placement. EOG can also be sensitive to electrical noise from other sources, such as muscle activity or blinking.

2.1.4 Video Oculography (VOG)

Video Oculography (VOG), also known as video-based eye tracking, uses cameras to record eye movements and track specific features such as the pupil and corneal reflections [82]. For a discussion on the technical operation of the VOG, see, among others [83]. It is worth mentioning that [84] proposed a custom VOG device (an eye-tracker) to improve the quality and functionality of video frame capture. In general, VOG systems can be either single-camera or multiple-camera setups, with the latter providing higher accuracy [85]. While VOG offers a non-invasive and relatively precise method for tracking eye movements, it faces limitations in human-computer interaction (HCI) setups due to variations in head position. Despite improvements such as stereo cameras or wide-angle cameras, VOG remains costly, and its complexity can be a deterrent for extensive use in economic experiments [22].

2.1.5 Head-Mounted Eye-Tracking (HMET)

Head-Mounted Eye Tracking (HMET) integrates eye-tracking technology into head-mounted devices (HMDs), allowing researchers to track eye movements while the user wears the device [86]. HMET is particularly useful for studying human behaviour in dynamic environments, such as Virtual Reality (VR) and Augmented Reality (AR) applications [87–89]. However, the high cost and physical nature of HMET devices, which require subjects to be physically present, limit their use in larger-scale studies. Devices such as the Tobii Pro Glasses 3 [90–93] and Pupil Labs Headset, while advanced, remain expensive and cumbersome for extensive adoption in economic research [90–94]. Often, devices such as the Pupil Labs Headset are used in various fields of study such as education [95], image segmentation [96], art and culture [97]. For more information on other devices and their fields of application, see [98–124].

Broadly speaking, these head-mounted eye-tracking devices demonstrate the diversity and innovation within the field, addressing different research needs and industry requirements. Whether it is understanding consumer behaviour, improving user interfaces or advancing scientific knowledge of human vision and cognition, these devices play a crucial role in gaining insight into how we perceive and interact with the world around us. However, these devices fall under the broader umbrella of head-mounted eye tracking, which, while relatively precise and accurate, is characterised by both its considerable cost and its physical nature, requiring only the physical presence of the subjects participating in an experimental task.

2.1.6 Remote Eye-Tracking

Based on the above, to overcome some of the physical limitations typically encountered when attempting to study human gaze with a head-mounted eye tracker, different methods can be employed, such as remote eye tracking. Remote eye tracking monitors eye movements from a distance using cameras or infrared sensors, eliminating the need for physical contact [17, 125–129]. This method captures gaze data, pupil size, and gaze direction, and is calibrated to map gaze coordinates to screen positions [130]. From a general perspective, remote eye-tracking methods include those based on video, which use cameras to record eye movements, those based on infrared, which use infrared light and sensors for greater accuracy, and those integrated into mobile devices such as smartphones or tablets. In general, there are two main applications for remote eye tracking and the technology used may differ. Some interesting studies of the technologies and applications of remote eye-tracking can be found in [131–141]. At this point, it can be argued that remote eye tracking provides valuable insights into human behaviour and cognition, making it a powerful tool in various fields. Despite its non-invasive nature and applications in various research fields, remote eye tracking faces challenges in achieving high accuracy and dealing with head movements and lighting conditions [85, 131]. These factors, along with privacy concerns, can limit its adoption in broader economic experiments.

2.1.7 Mobile Eye-Tracking

Mobile eye tracking uses portable and lightweight devices, often wearable, to monitor eye movements in naturalistic environments. These systems consist of miniature cameras and infrared sensors mounted on eyewear frames or headbands, enabling real-time analysis of eye movements. Although this type of eye tracking is well known and used in several studies, an alternative approach to mobile eye tracking uses the built-in cameras of mobile devices (smartphones, tablets) to capture user interaction with the screen. More details on mobile eye tracking systems can be found in [20–22, 142–144]. This emerging technology has attracted considerable attention in recent years due to its potential applications in many disciplines, including psychology, human-computer interaction (HCI), market research and automotive safety. While mobile eye tracking offers flexibility and extensive applications in several research fields, the development of unobtrusive and comfortable devices remains a challenge. High costs and the need for on-board processing units further restrict their widespread use in economic research.

In essence, the utilisation of eye-tracking technologies provides researchers with invaluable insights into the decision-making of humans. Nevertheless, there are a number of obstacles to their comprehensive integration within the field of experimental economics. These obstacles include the high costs involved, the technical complexity of the equipment, the necessity for specialised expertise, and concerns regarding the protection of personal data. Techniques such as the Scleral Search Coil and HMET require a considerable financial investment and are invasive, which can cause participants' discomfort. The issue of invasiveness is of considerable importance regarding the utilisation of the various techniques. It is evident that techniques such as the Scleral Search Coil are invasive and may be perceived as uncomfortable by participants, which ultimately limits their practical application. Non-invasive techniques, including IOG and VOG, offer a more convenient alternative but may be less accurate due to external factors. Furthermore, concerns pertaining to privacy are also raised, particularly in the context of remote eye-tracking. It is incumbent upon researchers to consider accuracy, cost-effectiveness and participant comfort when selecting the appropriate eye-tracking technology for their studies.

2.2 Application of Eye-Tracking in Experimental Economics

Given the widespread use of eye-tracking in psychology, education and medicine, we discuss below its potential in economics experiments. While other disciplines have embraced this technology, its use in economics, especially in experimental economics, remains limited [2]. In fact, primarily, when we browse through literature on the use of eye tracking in economics, we see the presence of studies conducted in the arena of marketing. A noteworthy example is the work of [145], who investigated the efficacy of Internet advertising utilising eye-tracking technology. The study demonstrated that click-through rates are an inadequate metric for evaluating the efficacy of banner advertisements, as users frequently evade direct gaze at such advertisements. Consequently, the researchers concluded that traditional memory-based measures, such as brand awareness and advertising recall, are more reliable indicators of advertising effectiveness. This emphasises the significance of contemplating the pre-attentive processing of advertisements and proposes that a considerable proportion of this processing occurs without conscious awareness. [146] highlighted the distinction between the eye and a camera, asserting that the visual system does not generate a static image akin to a photograph. In contrast, the eyes are in a state of constant movement, gathering information from a dynamic external environment. The image that is perceived is a stable mental construct that is created by the brain. This insight is of great consequence for the interpretation of eye-tracking data, particularly in the context of economic decision-making, where the visual stimuli are in constant motion and the perceived image is a cognitive construct. [147] employed eye-tracking technology to assess the efficacy of advertising on Travel 2.0 websites. The study demonstrated the value of eye-tracking in providing insights into user interactions with online advertisements, illustrating the impact of different ad placements and designs on user engagement and memory. The findings lend support to the use of eye-tracking in the comprehension of consumer behaviour and the optimisation of strategies, with suggestions of potential applications in experimental economics to study the influence of visual attention on economic decisions.

As discussed in [2], when designing an economics experiment that employs eye-tracking technology, it is of paramount importance to develop a strong theoretical framework, to define research questions with precision, to select a suitable participant pool with care, and to design the experimental setup in a reasoned manner. Operational decisions also require careful consideration, including the choice of eye-tracking system, depending on the requirements of the study. In addition, hardware and software choices also play a crucial role in the design of this type of experiment, as they can influence subjects' perceptions and the experimental setting. In general, eye trackers are powerful tools for capturing a rich set of data that provide insights into human decision-making. This data includes a range of metrics that go beyond simply where a person is looking on the screen. These include fixation time, fixation transitions, scan paths, pupil dilation and saccades. For a detailed explanation of these metrics and the related parameters used to estimate human gaze, see, among others, [148]. More broadly, the use of eye-tracking techniques has the potential to challenge traditional economic models based on perfect rationality. As noted by [18], studies have begun to explore how eye movements can reveal the existence of signals that suggest bounded rationality and heuristics in human decision-making. Research by scholars such as [52, 149–151] provides further insights into this exciting area. By delving into the rich data generated by eye-tracking, economists can gain a deeper understanding of the cognitive processes underlying human behaviour. This newfound understanding can lead to the development of more nuanced economic models that better reflect real-world behaviour, ultimately paving the way for more effective economic policies and interventions. For instance, it is possible to merge the principles of psychophysics with economics by applying eye-tracking techniques to game theory. In this sense, [54] provides a comprehensive discussion of the response times and attention human displayed during economic experiments, captured by technical tools including eye-tracking. As introduced earlier, traditional economics models often assume perfect rationality in decision-making. However, recent research in behavioural game theory challenges these assumptions and explores how people behave in strategic situations [152]. Eye-tracking technology provides a valuable tool for investigating these discrepancies between theory and practice. In this regard, [153] used eye-tracking to investigate the cognitive abilities and strategic behaviour of subjects in one-shot games. Their analysis revealed a strong correlation between gaze patterns and strategic decisions. It is also important to consider the potential influence of being monitored by eye-tracking equipment on the behaviour of subjects. In this regard, [56] addressed this concern by investigating whether eye-tracking itself is capable of altering economic decision-making in eight standard economic games. Their results suggest that eye-tracking did not significantly alter outcomes. In addition, [15] experimentally investigated the concept of strategic gaze. They found that people generally interpret non-strategic gaze (gaze that is not intended as a signal) correctly, with variations in understanding arising from the specific gaze patterns. However, the study also showed that people strategically adjust their gaze during live interaction. When interests align, their gaze becomes more interpretable, while conflicting interests lead to more ambiguous eye movements. Further recent research has explored the potential of eye-tracking to analyse economic behaviour, decision-making and accessibility in interactive systems. For example, eye-tracking has been employed by [154] to investigate human economic behaviour in relation to financial risk, [155] to examine cost attention in discrete choices, [156] to utilise gaze data to predict behaviour in economic games, and [157] to evaluate accessible and usable interactive systems. Moreover, [158] presented an analysis of the advancements and prospective avenues for discrete choice experiments with eye-tracking, whereas [159] investigated the economic theories of choice under risk with the aid of eye-tracking. The utilisation of eye-tracking technology in experimental economics enables the testing of specific hypotheses. The first hypothesis concerns the relationship between visual attention and decision-making. Eye-tracking can reveal how participants distribute their attention during economic choices, thereby highlighting the importance of different types of information. A second hypothesis concerns the processing of information and the use of heuristics. By analysing gaze patterns, it is possible to ascertain whether participants employ cognitive shortcuts in their decision-making. A third hypothesis concerns cognitive load and complexity. Eye-tracking can be used to measure cognitive load through metrics such as fixation duration and pupil dilation, thereby allowing an assessment of the impact of task complexity on decisions. A fourth hypothesis pertains to the nexus between emotional responses and economic behaviour. By integrating eye-tracking with biometric measures, it is possible to examine emotional responses during economic decision-making processes. In addition, eye-tracking can be employed to examine learning and adaptation mechanisms by monitoring alterations in gaze patterns over time. These hypotheses illustrate the potential of eye-tracking to provide insights that are not typically accessible through other methodologies, thereby offering novel opportunities to test theories and hypotheses pertaining to economic decision-making.

3 Experimental Design

As argued in [2], if the researcher decides to design an economic experiment using eye-tracking, it is necessary to establish a strong theoretical foundation, define clear research questions, select an appropriate participant pool, and design the experimental setting itself. Following this recommendation, the theoretical foundation of our study is based on the principles of visual attention and its impact on comprehension and decision-making in economic settings. Eye-tracking technology allows us to measure where participants look, for how long, and the sequence of their gaze, providing insight into their cognitive processes during the experiment [2]. The experimental design here proposed aims to answer to the research questions that are centered around understanding how eye-tracking can enhance the comprehension of experimental instructions and whether it influences participants' behaviour in economic games. Specifically, by adopting this experimental design it will be possible to investigate if participants who are aware that their gaze is being tracked exhibit different patterns of attention and comprehension compared to those who are not tracked.

To achieve this, we propose a novel experimental design that can be employed in the field of experimental economics to investigate subjects' comprehension of experimental instructions using eye-tracking techniques. As detailed below, one group of subjects will participate in the experiment using the oTree platform [70] with the eye-tracking functionalities integrated via the WebGazer library extension [160], while the other group will participate in the experiment without experiencing the eye-tracking functionalities. To explore potential differences in instructional comprehension between the two groups, a pretest and posttest were administered prior to and following participation in the repeated linear public goods game. The approach taken was in accordance with that outlined by [71]. After randomly recruiting subjects (university students who have never participated in similar experiments, for a discussion on this point, see, among others [161]), since this is a lab-in-the-field experiment [162], subjects have to physically go to the place where the experiment will be conducted. All subjects must be equipped with a mobile device with a front-facing camera/webcam (e.g. smartphone, tablet, laptop). Once their presence is confirmed and the experimental registry is completed, the subjects are positioned in a way that avoids communication and information exchange. The informed consent was read aloud, and the experimenter provided the unique link to access the oTree platform [70]. At this point, the experimenter randomly assigns the experimental subject pool into two groups: Treatment (eye-tracking) and control (no eye-tracking). Specifically, the subjects randomly assigned to the treatment group will have to perform the facial recognition and calibration phase using the front-facing camera/webcam to enable the correct functioning of the WebGazer library [160], under the guidance of the experimenter, immediately after opening the previously provided link. Both phases will be performed according to the methods described in [160]. The experimenter then allows the subjects assigned to the control group to open the link. However, they do not have to perform the facial recognition and calibration phases, since these are not required for the control group. In this regard, it is worth mentioning that the first web page that opens for each subject, regardless of the group to which they belong, displays a prior knowledge test consisting of 12 questions with binary objective answers (1=yes, 0=no) about the repeated linear public goods game, designed according to the approach of [71]. The questions are as follows: *is this an economics experiment?; does a social dilemma emerge?; do I participate alone?; do I participate in a group?; will I make economic decisions?; do I engage in strategic behaviour?; will I obtain a payoff?; will my payoff depend on the choices of others?; do opportunistic behaviours emerge?; do cooperative behaviours emerge?; do I interact with the same people?; can I communicate with others?* To provide answers, subjects are given a time frame of 15 min. In Fig. 1, this part of the pretest is called "Pretest 1". Once these binary answers have been given, the instructions for the experiment are displayed by clicking on the "continue" button. The instructions are first read aloud by the experimenter and then in silence. Each subject, regardless of group, has 10 min to read the instructions in silence. It should be noted that in the treatment group, the oTree software [70] provides an extension with the WebGazer library [160], which allows to capture eye positions and infer human gaze. This extension is not made available to the control group. Then, after clicking the "continue" button on the web page, all subjects are asked to answer four subjective questions that indicate their level of understanding of the experimental instructions. For each question, each subject is asked to give an answer expressed on a Likert scale from 1 to 5 (1=strongly disagree, 2=disagree, 3=indifferent, 4=agree, 5=strongly agree) by ticking the appropriate box. The questions are as follows: *I have understood the content of the instructions; I have learnt something new by reading the instructions; I am able to carry out the experimental task by myself; Now the specific questions about the experiment seem clearer to me.* The experimenter allows 10 min for the answers to the above questions. In Fig. 1, this part of the pretest is called "Pretest 2".

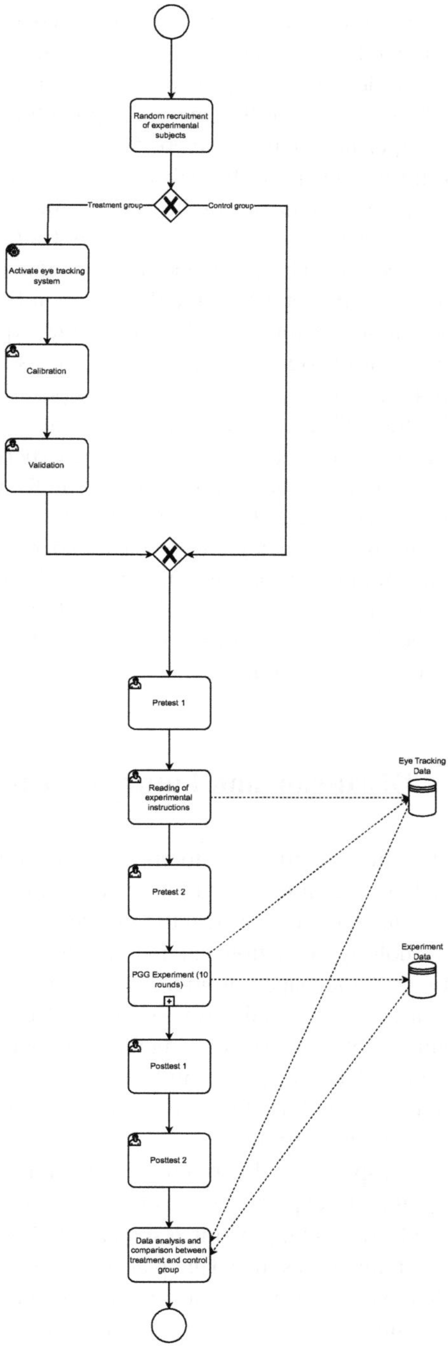

Fig. 1 A BPMN representation of experimental design

Once the answers have been provided and sent to the experimenter, the web page that enables the experimental task to be completed will appear. In detail, subjects will participate in a repeated linear public goods game for ten rounds in fixed groups of four subjects, following the approach of [163]. Also during the performance of the experimental task, the position of the face and eyes is monitored in the treatment group by means of the oTree software extension [70] with the WebGazer library [160] whereas this is not the case for the control group. Specifically, eye-tracking is employed to assess the accuracy and attention paid to the essential information required to make an economic decision in the public goods game, such as the amount to be contributed to the common fund, the amount of the common fund and the payoff obtained. At the end of the experimental task, the posttest is administered, consisting of the same questions as in the pretest, under the same conditions [164]. In Fig. 1, the parts that compose the posttest are called "Posttest 1" and "Posttest 2" respectively. At the end of the experiment, each experimental subject will be paid in cash. To do this, the experimenter will adopt the principles of the Induced Value Theory [165], providing for the payment of a fixed fee (show-up fee) and a variable fee dependent on the decisions made by each subject in the repeated linear public goods game. In each experimental phase, the experimenter will guarantee anonymity between the parties through the use of unique ID codes and by using anonymous closed white envelopes for the cash payment. Building on the above, Fig. 1 represents, by means of the BPMN, the entire configuration of the experimental design.

4 Discussion and Future Research

This study contributes to the ongoing debate regarding the integration of eye-tracking technologies within experimental economics, a field in which such technologies remain significantly underutilised relative to their widespread adoption in psychology, education, and marketing. Following the identification of this disciplinary gap, the paper provides a critical overview of eye-tracking techniques and devices as employed in diverse research domains. This review highlights the significant potential of eye-tracking technology in expanding behavioural research in economics. However, it simultaneously acknowledges the technical, financial and ethical limitations that have, to date, hindered its implementation in economic experimental settings.

In response to this observed shortfall, a novel experimental design is proposed that aims to explore the feasibility and analytical potential of integrating browser-based eye-tracking within a standard Public Goods Game (PGG). The experimental design integrates the oTree platform [70] with the WebGazer library [160] to facilitate the acquisition of visual attention data across the entire experimental sequence, encompassing both the instruction delivery and the economic decision phases. Despite the study being in the conceptual and design stages, the framework delineates a comparative analysis between subjects. Participants in the treatment group would be exposed to eye-tracking, while those in the control group would not. In order to test the hypothesis that gaze behaviour influences comprehension of instructions and decision-making, researchers would be advised to complement the current setup with pre-test and post-test questionnaires.

Despite the absence of experimental implementation, the experimental design hypothesises that metrics such as gaze trajectories, fixation durations, and screen transitions would facilitate a comprehensive analysis of participant attention allocation, information prioritisation, and interaction with the game's core variables. These variables include contribution levels, group payoffs, and social dynamics. Accordingly, the present framework constitutes the basis for future studies that are directed towards the identification of the cognitive and attentional mechanisms that underpin cooperative behaviour.

A series of anticipated limitations merit critical reflection. It is evident that browser-based tools, such as WebGazer [160], whilst being highly scalable and cost-effective, are subject to limitations in terms of precision and calibration stability. It is noteworthy that variations in device quality, browser performance, lighting conditions, and participant positioning are likely to introduce noise into the gaze data. Furthermore, the employment of a lab-in-the-field approach, whilst enhancing ecological validity in comparison with conventional laboratory environments [166, 167], may result in increased exposure to uncontrolled environmental variables, thereby complicating the interpretation of experimental results. Furthermore, comprehension would be evaluated through the utilisation of Likert-scale self-reports, a method that has been extensively adopted in behavioural studies. However, it is important to acknowledge that this approach may not always yield profound cognitive understanding or subtle misinterpretations [168–170]. The utilisation of a student cohort as a subject pool, a common practice in experimental economics, gives rise to concerns regarding external validity, particularly with regard to the generalisability across more extensive or less digitally proficient demographics.

Notwithstanding the aforementioned limitations, the proposed experimental design constitutes a novel methodological contribution. The incorporation of eye-tracking technology into the PGG framework facilitates the exploration of novel research avenues, particularly concerning the cognitive processes underpinning strategic decision-making in economic contexts. The opportunity to monitor real-time attentional shifts enables the examination of latent processes through which individuals engage with rules, social information and payoff structures, thus moving beyond traditional behavioural outputs. The analysis of visual attention data may assist in identifying how participants mentally frame the task, interpret the incentives at stake, and assess their own and others' actions. This approach is closely aligned with the theoretical literature on bounded rationality, cognitive constraints, and limited information processing, offering a refined lens through which to view cooperative behaviour.

Moreover, the heterogeneity in gaze patterns that would be observed across individuals, should such a study be conducted, could provide a basis for identifying distinct cognitive profiles. This in turn could have implications for experimental design, participant segmentation and targeted behavioural interventions. The utilisation of eye-tracking technology holds considerable promise in supporting the classification of individuals based not solely on their observable choices but also in relation to their attentional strategies, levels of cognitive engagement, and responsiveness to complexity. A comprehension of such a multifaceted nature in the realm of decision-making holds the potential to enhance the interpretation of outcomes in cooperative dilemmas and to facilitate the development of experimental tools that are more adaptive and personalised.

Beyond the experimental context, this proposal invites reflection on the broader relevance of human-centred behavioural data in environments characterised by informational complexity and strategic uncertainty. As a greater proportion of decision-making occurs within digital infrastructures and organisational systems, it is becoming ever more crucial to understand how individuals interact with interfaces and process information. The utilisation of real-time behavioural data, encompassing eye-tracking metrics, holds potential in informing the design of decision-making environments that are characterised by enhanced transparency, responsiveness, and alignment with users' cognitive capacities and strategic objectives. This standpoint is congruent with the broader interdisciplinary discourse surrounding the conceptualisation of information systems and decision architectures that are designed to facilitate informed, inclusive, and context-sensitive decision-making processes.

Future experimental studies may investigate the interaction between gaze-based indicators of attention and other sources of behavioural or physiological data, such as digital trace behaviour, heart rate variability, or galvanic skin response. The objective of these studies is to develop more integrated models of economic decision-making. Furthermore, the experimental design could be adapted to alternative experimental paradigms, including ultimatum games, trust games, and repeated social dilemmas. This would offer comparative insights into how attentional patterns vary across different strategic settings [171–178]. The integration of behavioural data into intelligent decision-support systems, particularly within policy, organisational and educational contexts, represents a promising trajectory. As such systems become more prevalent, it may prove essential to understand users' attentional profiles in order to ensure that decision-making environments are both effective and equitable.

To summarise, the present study makes a conceptual and methodological contribution to the study of cooperative behaviour by outlining a design that integrates experimental economics with eye-tracking technologies. Although the proposed experimental design has yet to be subjected to experimental testing, it presents a novel methodological approach for examining the intersection of cognition, attention, and strategic interaction. The study calls for sustained interdisciplinary collaboration that further bridges experimental economics, behavioural science, and information system design, with the objective of enhancing our comprehension of cooperation in complex, dynamic, and information-rich environments.

Disclosure of Interests The authors have no competing interests to declare that are relevant to the content of this article.

References

1. Wedel, M., & Pieters, R. (2008). Eye tracking for visual marketing. *Foundations and Trends® in Marketing, 1*(4), 231–320.
2. Lahey, J. N., & Oxley, D. (2016). The power of eye tracking in economics experiments. *American Economic Review, 106*(5), 309–313.
3. Semmelmann, K., & Weigelt, S. (2018). Online webcam-based eye tracking in cognitive science: A first look. *Behavior Research Methods, 50*(1), 451–465.
4. Friedman, D., & Sunder, S. (1994). *Experimental methods: A primer for economists.* Cambridge University Press.
5. Croson, R. (2003). Why and how to experiment: Methodologies from experimental economics. *University of Illinois Law Review*, 921–946.
6. Shogren, J. F. (2005). Experimental methods and valuation. In K.-G. Maeler & J. Vincent (Eds.), *Handbook of environmental economics valuing environmental changes* (Vol. 2, pp. 969–1027). North-Holland.
7. Viceisza, A. C. (2016). Creating a lab in the field: Economics experiments for policymaking. *Journal of Economic Surveys, 30*(5), 835–854.
8. Chamberlin, E. H. (1948). An experimental imperfect market. *Journal of Political Economy, 56*(2), 95–108.
9. Smith, V. L. (1962). An experimental study of competitive market behavior. *Journal Of Political Economy, 70*(2), 111–137.
10. Holt, C. A., & Laury, S. K. (1997). Classroom games: Voluntary provision of a public good. *Journal of Economic Perspectives, 11*(4), 209–215.
11. Harrison, G. W., & List, J. A. (2004). Field experiments. *Journal of Economic literature, 42*(4), 1009–1055.
12. Charness, G., Gneezy, U., & Kuhn, M. A. (2013). Experimental methods: Extra-laboratory experiments-extending the reach of experimental economics. *Journal of Economic Behavior & Organization, 91*(1), 93–100.
13. Arechar, A. A., Gächter, S., & Molleman, L. (2018). Conducting interactive experiments online. *Experimental Economics, 21*(1), 99–131.
14. Buso, I. M., Di Cagno, D., Ferrari, L., Larocca, V., Lorè, L., Marazzi, F., Panaccione, L., & Spadoni, L. (2021). Lab-like findings from online experiments. *Journal of the Economic Science Association, 7*(2), 184–193.
15. Hausfeld, J., von Hesler, K., & Goldlücke, S. (2021). Strategic gaze: An interactive eye-tracking study. *Experimental Economics, 24*(1), 177–205.
16. Yang, X., & Krajbich, I. (2021). Webcam-based online eye-tracking for behavioral research. *Judgment and Decision Making, 16*(6), 1485–1505.
17. Wisiecka, K., Krejtz, K., Krejtz, I., Sromek, D., Cellary, A., Lewandowska, B., & Duchowski, A. (2022). Comparison of webcam and remote eye tracking. In *2022 Symposium on Eye Tracking Research and Applications* (pp. 1–7).
18. Sickmann, J., & Le, H. B. N. (2016). Eye-Tracking in behavioural economics and finance-a literature review. *Discussion Papers in Behavioural Sciences and Economics, 2016*(1).
19. Bergstrom, J. R., & Schall, A. (2014). *Eye tracking in user experience design.* Elsevier.
20. Li, B., Fu, H., Wen, D., & Lo, W. L. (2018). Etracker: A mobile gaze-tracking system with near-eye display based on a combined gaze-tracking algorithm. *Sensors, 18*(5), 1–18.
21. Kanade, P., David, F., & Kanade, S. (2021). Convolutional neural networks (CNN) based eye-gaze tracking system using machine learning algorithm. *European Journal of Electrical Engineering and Computer Science, 5*(2), 36–40.
22. Klaib, A. F., Alsrehin, N. O., Melhem, W. Y., Bashtawi, H. O., & Magableh, A. A. (2021). Eye tracking algorithms, techniques, tools, and applications with an emphasis on machine learning and Internet of Things technologies. *Expert Systems with Applications, 166*(1), 1–24.
23. Yarbus, A. L. (1967). *Eye movements and vision.* Springer.

24. Lipps, M., & Pelz, J. B. (2004). Yarbus revisited: Task-dependent oculomotor behavior. *Journal of Vision, 4*(8), 115–115.
25. Greene, M. R., Liu, T., & Wolfe, J. M. (2012). Reconsidering Yarbus: A failure to predict observers' task from eye movement patterns. *Vision Research, 62*(1), 1–8.
26. Harezlak, K., & Kasprowski, P. (2018). Application of eye tracking in medicine: A survey, research issues and challenges. *Computerized Medical Imaging and Graphics, 65*(1), 176–190.
27. Zammarchi, G., & Conversano, C. (2021). Application of eye tracking technology in medicine: A bibliometric analysis. *Vision, 5*(56), 1–14.
28. Tahri Sqalli, M., Aslonov, B., Gafurov, M., Mukhammadiev, N., & Sqalli Houssaini, Y. (2023). Eye tracking technology in medical practice: A perspective on its diverse applications. *Frontiers in Medical Technology, 5*(1253001), 1–6.
29. Jacob, R. J. K., & Karn, K. S. (2003). Eye tracking in human-computer interaction and usability research: Ready to deliver the promises. In *The mind's eye* (pp. 573–605). Elsevier.
30. Vom Brocke, J., Thurnher, B., & Winkler, D. (2008). The impact of user experience on human computer interaction-results from a usability study. In *Pacific Asia Conference on Information Systems (PACIS) 2008* (Vol. 235, pp. 1–11).
31. Thongmool, G., & Phankokkruad, M. (2014). Analysis of interaction user interface patterns and usability study in computer assisted instruction for Tablet PC. In *2014 IEEE International Conference on Control System, Computing and Engineering (ICCSCE 2014)* (pp. 472–477).
32. Sambrekar, U., & Ramdasi, D. (2015). Human computer interaction for disabled using eye motion tracking. In *2015 International Conference on Information Processing (ICIP)* (pp. 745–750).
33. Soltani, S., & Mahnam, A. (2016). A practical efficient human computer interface based on saccadic eye movements for people with disabilities. *Computers in Biology and Medicine, 70*(1), 163–173.
34. Zhang, X., Liu, X., Yuan, S. M., & Lin, S. F. (2017). Eye tracking based control system for natural human-computer interaction. *Computational Intelligence and Neuroscience, 2017*(1), 1–9.
35. Ramírez, A. R. G., Da Silva, J. F., Savall, A. C. R., Catecati, T., & Ferreira, M. G. G. (2018). User's emotions and usability study of a brain-computer interface applied to people with cerebral palsy. *Technologies, 6*(28), 1–13.
36. Ebert, A., Gershon, N. D., & van der Veer, G. C. (2012). Human-computer interaction: Introduction and overview. *KI-Künstliche Intelligenz, 26*(1), 121–126.
37. Hyrskykari, A., Majaranta, P., Aaltonen, A., & Räihä, K. J. (2000). Design issues of iDict: A gaze-assisted translation aid. In *Proceedings of the 2000 Symposium on Eye Tracking Research & Applications* (pp. 9–14).
38. Pivec, M., Trummer, C., & Pripfl, J. (2006). Eye-tracking adaptable e-learning and content authoring support. *Informatica, 30*(1), 83–86.
39. Wang, H., Chignell, M., & Ishizuka, M. (2006). Empathic tutoring software agents using real-time eye tracking. In *Proceedings of the 2006 Symposium on Eye Tracking Research & Applications* (pp. 73–78).
40. Calvi, C., Porta, M., & Sacchi, D. (2008). e5Learning, an e-learning environment based on eye tracking. In *2008 Eighth IEEE International Conference on Advanced Learning Technologies* (pp. 376–380).
41. Porta, M., Ricotti, S., & Perez, C. J. (2012). Emotional e-learning through eye tracking. In *Proceedings of the 2012 IEEE Global Engineering Education Conference (EDUCON)* (pp. 1–6).
42. Khan, A. R., Khosravi, S., Hussain, S., Ghannam, R., Zoha, A., & Imran, M. A. (2022). Execute: Exploring eye tracking to support e-learning. In *2022 IEEE Global Engineering Education Conference (EDUCON)* (pp. 670–676).
43. Peng, J., Shao, Y., et al. (2018). Intelligent method for identifying driving risk based on V2V multisource big data. *Complexity, 2018*(1), 1–9.

44. Moniri, M. M., Feld, M., & Müller, C. (2012). Personalized in-vehicle information systems: Building an application infrastructure for smart cars in smart spaces. In *2012 Eighth International Conference on Intelligent Environments* (pp. 379–382).
45. Yi, D., Su, J., Hu, L., Liu, C., Quddus, M., Dianati, M., & Chen, W. H. (2019). Implicit personalization in driving assistance: State-of-the-art and open issues. *IEEE Transactions on Intelligent Vehicles, 5*(3), 397–413.
46. Hummel, D., & Maedche, A. (2019). How effective is nudging? A quantitative review on the effect sizes and limits of empirical nudging studies. *Journal of Behavioral and Experimental Economics, 80*(1), 47–58.
47. Yaremych, H. E., & Persky, S. (2019). Tracing physical behavior in virtual reality: A narrative review of applications to social psychology. *Journal of Experimental Social Psychology, 85*(103845), 1–8.
48. Dudinskaya, E. C., Naspetti, S., & Zanoli, R. (2020). Using eye-tracking as an aid to design on-screen choice experiments. *Journal of Choice Modelling, 36*(100232), 1–8.
49. Yegoryan, N., Guhl, D., & Klapper, D. (2020). Inferring attribute non-attendance using eye tracking in choice-based conjoint analysis. *Journal of Business Research, 111*(1), 290–304.
50. Zaki, T., & Islam, M. N. (2021). Neurological and physiological measures to evaluate the usability and user-experience (UX) of information systems: A systematic literature review. *Computer Science Review, 40*(100375), 1–19.
51. Knoepfle, D. T., Wang, J. T. Y., & Camerer, C. F. (2009). Studying learning in games using eye-tracking. *Journal of the European Economic Association, 7*(2–3), 388–398.
52. Wang, J. T. Y., Spezio, M., & Camerer, C. F. (2010). Pinocchio's pupil: Using eyetracking and pupil dilation to understand truth telling and deception in sender-receiver games. *American Economic Review, 100*(3), 984–1007.
53. Reutskaja, E., Nagel, R., Camerer, C. F., & Rangel, A. (2011). Search dynamics in consumer choice under time pressure: An eye-tracking study. *American Economic Review, 101*(2), 900–926.
54. Coricelli, G., Polonio, L., & Vostroknutov, A. (2020). The process of choice in games. In C. M. Capra, R. Croson, M. L. Rigdon, & T. S. Rosenblat (Eds.), *Handbook of experimental game theory* (pp. 69–94). Edward Elgar.
55. Bartke, S., Bosworth, S. J., Snower, D. J., & Chierchia, G. (2019). Motives and comprehension in a public goods game with induced emotions. *Theory and Decision, 86*(1), 205–238.
56. Kee, J., Knuth, M., Lahey, J. N., & Palma, M. A. (2021). Does eye-tracking have an effect on economic behavior? *PLoS One, 16*(8), e0254867.
57. Murnighan, J. K., & Wang, L. (2016). The social world as an experimental game. *Organizational Behavior and Human Decision Processes, 136*(1), 80–94.
58. Ledyard, J. O. (2020 [1995]). Public goods: A survey of experimental research. In J. H. Kagel & A. E. Roth (Eds.), *The handbook of experimental economics* (pp. 111–194). Princeton University Press.
59. Komorita, S. S., & Parks, C. D. (1995). Interpersonal relations: Mixed-motive interaction. *Annual Review of Psychology, 46*(1), 183–207.
60. Kollock, P. (1998). Social dilemmas: The anatomy of cooperation. *Annual Review of Sociology, 24*(1), 183–214.
61. De Cremer, D., & Van Vugt, M. (1999). Social identification effects in social dilemmas: A transformation of motives. *European Journal of Social Psychology, 29*(7), 871–893.
62. Otten, K., Buskens, V., Przepiorka, W., Cherki, B., & Israel, S. (2024). Cooperation, punishment, and group change in multilevel public goods experiments. *European Economic Review, 16*(104682), 1–17.
63. Andreoni, J., & Miller, J. H. (1991). Can evolutionary dynamics explain free-riding in experiments? *Economics Letters, 36*(1), 9–15.
64. Andreoni, J., & Petrie, R. (2004). Public goods experiments without confidentiality: A glimpse into fund-raising. *Journal of Public Economics, 88*(7–8), 1605–1623.

65. Walker, J. M., & Halloran, M. A. (2004). Rewards and sanctions and the provision of public goods in one-shot settings. *Experimental Economics, 7*(1), 235–247.
66. Ferraro, P. J., & Vossler, C. A. (2010). The source and significance of confusion in public goods experiments. *The BE Journal of Economic Analysis & Policy, 10*(1), 1–79.
67. Janssen, M. A., Lindahl, T., & Murphy, J. J. (2015). Advancing the understanding of behavior in social-ecological systems: Results from lab and field experiments. *Ecology and Society, 20*(4), 1–6.
68. Blackwell, C., & McKee, M. (2003). Only for my own neighborhood?: Preferences and voluntary provision of local and global public goods. *Journal of Economic Behavior & Organization, 52*(1), 115–131.
69. Ozono, H., Kamijo, Y., & Shimizu, K. (2020). The role of peer reward and punishment for public goods problems in a localized society. *Scientific reports, 10*(8211), 1–8.
70. Chen, D. L., Schonger, M., & Wickens, C. (2016). oTree—An open-source platform for laboratory, online, and field experiments. *Journal of Behavioral and Experimental Finance, 9*(1), 88–97.
71. Jian, Y. C. (2018). Reading instructions influence cognitive processes of illustrated text reading not subject perception: An eye-tracking study. *Frontiers in Psychology, 9*(387831), 1–12.
72. Luo, Z. (2021). Using eye-tracking technology to identify learning styles: Behaviour patterns and identification accuracy. *Education and Information Technologies, 26*(4), 4457–4485.
73. Riege, A., Gourdon-Kanhukamwe, A., & Vallée-Tourangeau, G. (2021). Covert eye-tracking: An innovative method to investigate compliance with instructions. *Psychological Research, 85*(8), 3084–3093.
74. Ziffer, A. J., Rosenbaum, A. L., Demer, J. L., & Yee, R. D. (1992). Congenital double elevator palsy: Vertical saccadic velocity utilizing the scleral search coil technique. *Journal of Pediatric Ophthalmology & Strabismus, 29*(3), 142–149.
75. Robinson, D. A. (1963). A method of measuring eye movement using a scleral search coil in a magnetic field. *IEEE Transactions on Bio-Medical Electronics, 10*(4), 137–145.
76. Eibenberger, K., Eibenberger, B., & Rucci, M. (2016). Design, simulation and evaluation of uniform magnetic field systems for head-free eye movement recordings with scleral search coils. In *2016 38th Annual International Conference of the IEEE Engineering in Medicine and Biology Society (EMBC)* (pp. 247–250).
77. Hammoud, R. I., & Mulligan, J. B. (2008). Introduction to eye monitoring. In *Passive Eye Monitoring: Algorithms, Applications and Experiments* (pp. 1–19).
78. Noor, N. M. M., & Mustafa, M. A. M. (2016). Eye movement activity that affected the eye signals using electrooculography (EOG) technique. In *2016 6th IEEE International Conference on Control System, Computing and Engineering (ICCSCE)* (pp. 91–95).
79. Reilly, R. B., & Lee, T. C. (2010). Electrograms (ECG, EEG, EMG, EOG). *Technology and Health Care, 18*(6), 443–458.
80. Käthner, I., Kübler, A., & Halder, S. (2015). Comparison of eye tracking, electrooculography and an auditory brain-computer interface for binary communication: A case study with a participant in the locked-in state. *Journal of Neuroengineering and Rehabilitation, 12*(1), 1–11.
81. Ryu, J., Lee, M., & Kim, D.-H. (2019). EOG-based eye tracking protocol using baseline drift removal algorithm for long-term eye movement detection. *Expert Systems with Applications, 131*(1), 275–287.
82. Larrazabal, A. J., Cena, C. E. G., & Martínez, C. E. (2019). Video-oculography eye tracking towards clinical applications: A review. *Computers in Biology and Medicine, 108*(1), 57–66.
83. Kaufmann, B. C., Knobel, S. E. J., Nef, T., Mür, R. M., Cazzoli, D., & Nyffeler, T. (2020). Visual exploration area in neglect: A new analysis method for video-oculography data based on foveal vision. *Frontiers in Neuroscience, 13*(504146), 1–14.
84. Abdulin, E., Friedman, L., & Komogortsev, O. (2019). *Custom video-oculography device and its application to fourth Purkinje image detection during saccades*. arXiv preprint arXiv:1904.07361.

85. Majaranta, P., & Bulling, A. (2014). Eye tracking and eye-based human-computer interaction. In *Advances in physiological computing* (pp. 39–65). Springer.
86. Franchak, J. M. (2017). Head-mounted eye tracking. In *The Cambridge Encyclopedia of Child Development* (pp. 113–116).
87. Narcizo, F. B., Dos Santos, F. E. D., & Hansen, D. W. (2021). High-accuracy gaze estimation for interpolation-based eye-tracking methods. *Vision, 5*(41), 1–27.
88. Franchak, J. M., & Yu, C. (2022). Beyond screen time: Using head-mounted eye tracking to study natural behavior. *Advances in Child Development and Behavior, 62*(1), 61–91.
89. Kapp, S., Barz, M., Mukhametov, S., Sonntag, D., & Kuhn, J. (2021). ARETT: Augmented reality eye tracking toolkit for head mounted displays. *Sensors, 21*(2234), 1–18.
90. Tobii. *Tobii Pro Glasses 3*. Accessed December 05, 2023, from https://www.tobii.com/products/eye-trackers/wearables/tobii-pro-glasses-3.
91. Dilbeck, M. D., Gentry, T. N., Economides, J. R., & Horton, J. C. (2023). Quotidian profile of vergence angle in ambulatory subjects monitored with wearable eye tracking glasses. *Translational Vision Science & Technology, 12*(2), 17–17.
92. Onkhar, V., Dodou, D., & De Winter, J. C. F. (2023). Evaluating the Tobii Pro Glasses 2 and 3 in static and dynamic conditions. *Behavior Research Methods*, 1–18.
93. Nasrabadi, H. R., & Alonso, J. M. (2022). *Modular streaming pipeline of eye/head tracking data using Tobii Pro Glasses 3*. bioRxiv, 2022–09.
94. Pupil Labs. *Pupil Labs core hardware documentation*. Accessed December 05, 2023, from https://docs.pupil-labs.com/core/hardware
95. Kohútek, M., Turčáni, M., & Magdin, M. (2019). Improving student reading comprehension of learning materials using the analysis of Eye-Tracking data. In *2019 17th International Conference on Emerging eLearning Technologies and Applications (ICETA)* (pp. 411–418).
96. Nguyen, N., & Sigg, S. (2017). Demo of PassFrame: Generating image-based passwords from egocentric videos. In: *2017 IEEE International Conference on Pervasive Computing and Communications Workshops (PerCom Workshops)* (pp. 76–78).
97. Reitstätter, L., Galter, K., & Bakondi, F. (2022). Looking to read: How visitors use exhibit labels in the art museum. *Visitor Studies, 25*(2), 127–150.
98. EyeTech Digital Systems. Accessed December 05, 2023, from https://eyetechds.com
99. Thompson, B., Villeneuve, M. Y., Casanova, C., & Hess, R. F. (2012). Abnormal cortical processing of pattern motion in amblyopia: Evidence from fMRI. *NeuroImage, 60*(2), 1307–1315.
100. Jin, D., Kim, M., Rhiu, I., & Yun, M. (2017). Usability study on the use of eye mouse based on all the functions of conventional mouse. *Journal of Cognitive Science, 18*(2), 153–173.
101. Boonipat, T., Brazile, T. L., Darwish, O. A., Montana, P., Fleming, K. K., & Stotland, M. A. (2019). Measuring visual attention to faces with cleft deformity. *Journal of Plastic, Reconstructive & Aesthetic Surgery, 72*(6), 982–989.
102. Smart Eye Pro. Accessed December 05, 2023, from https://www.smarteye.se/smart-eye-pro
103. Dong, L., Chen, Y., Gale, A., & Phillips, P. (2016). Eye tracking method compatible with dual-screen mammography workstation. *Procedia Computer Science, 90*(1), 206–211.
104. Wang, R. J., & Yi, A. D. (2022). Visual physiological characteristics recognition method of road traffic safety driving behavior. *Advances in Transportation Studies, 2*, 139–148.
105. SMI Eye Tracking Glasses. Accessed December 05, 2023, from https://imotions.com/products/hardware/smi-eye-tracking-glasses
106. Gao, X.-Y., Zhang, Y.-F., Zheng, W.-L., & Lu, B.-L. (2015). Evaluating driving fatigue detection algorithms using eye tracking glasses. In *2015 7th International IEEE/EMBS Conference on Neural Engineering (NER)* (pp. 767–770).
107. Tien, T., Pucher, P. H., Sodergren, M. H., Sriskandarajah, K., Yang, G.-Z., & Darzi, A. (2015). Differences in gaze behaviour of expert and junior surgeons performing open inguinal hernia repair. *Surgical Endoscopy, 29*(1), 405–413.

108. Battah, M., McKendrick, M., Kean, D. E., & Obregon, M. (2016). Eye-tracking as a measure of trainee progress in laparoscopic training. *European Journal of Obstetrics and Gynecology and Reproductive Biology, 206*(1), e13–e14.
109. Valek, R., Wendel-Garcia, P. D., Schuepbach, R. A., Buehler, P. K., & Hofmaenner, D. A. (2023). Eye-tracking to observe compliance with hand hygiene in the intensive care unit: A randomized feasibility study. *Journal of Hospital Infection, 131*(1), 148–155.
110. Chen, Y., Ou, J., & Whittinghill, D. M. (2015). Cognitive load in real-time strategy gaming: Human opponent versus AI opponent. *The Computer Games Journal, 4*(1), 19–30.
111. Bolden, D., Barmby, P., Raine, S., & Gardner, M. (2015). How young children view mathematical representations: A study using eye-tracking technology. *Educational Research, 57*(1), 59–79.
112. Eye Tracker BEAM. Accessed December 05, 2023, from https://beam.eyeware.tech/it/
113. Hossain, T., Islam, M. F., Delamare, W., Chowdhury, F., & Hasan, K. (2021). Exploring social acceptability and users' preferences of head-and eye-based interaction with mobile devices. In *Proceedings of the 20th International Conference on Mobile and Ubiquitous Multimedia* (pp. 12–23).
114. Zhu, R., Shi, L., Song, Y., & Cai, Z. (2023). Integrating gaze and mouse via joint cross-attention fusion net for students' activity recognition in E-learning. *Proceedings of the ACM on Interactive, Mobile, Wearable and Ubiquitous Technologies, 7*(3), 1–35.
115. EyeSeeCam. Accessed December 05, 2023, from https://eyeseetec.de/eyeseecam-sci/
116. Schneider, E., Villgrattner, T., Vockeroth, J., Bartl, K., Kohlbecher, S., Bardins, S., Ulbrich, H., & Brandt, T. (2009). Eyeseecam: An eye movement--driven head camera for the examination of natural visual exploration. *Annals of the New York Academy of Sciences, 1164*(1), 461–467.
117. Yang, Q., Wang, T., Su, N., Xiao, S., & Kapoula, Z. (2013). Specific saccade deficits in patients with Alzheimer's disease at mild to moderate stage and in patients with amnestic mild cognitive impairment. *Age, 35*(1), 1287–1298.
118. Klostermann, A., Kredel, R., & Hossner, E.-J. (2014). On the interaction of attentional focus and gaze: The quiet eye inhibits focus-related performance decrements. *Journal of Sport and Exercise Psychology, 36*(4), 392–400.
119. Daniel, F., & Kapoula, Z. (2019). Induced vergence-accommodation conflict reduces cognitive performance in the Stroop test. *Scientific Reports, 9*(1247), 1–13.
120. Gazepoint GP3 HD. Accessed December 05, 2024, from https://www.gazept.com/product/gp3hd/?v=cd32106bcb6d/
121. Murphy, T. I., Abel, L. A., Armitage, J. A., & Douglass, A. G. (2024). Effects of tracker location on the accuracy and precision of the Gazepoint GP3 HD for spectacle wearers. *Behavior Research Methods, 56*(1), 43–52.
122. Sibley, C., Foroughi, C., Brown, N., & Coyne, J. T. (2018). Low cost eye tracking: Ready for individual differences research? In *Proceedings of the Human Factors and Ergonomics Society Annual Meeting* (Vol. 62, no. 1, pp. 741–745). SAGE.
123. Crosser, A., Snideman, M., & Vazquez Klisans, D. (2019). Determining Static Mount Accuracy with a Mid-Range Eye Tracker. In *Proceedings of the Human Factors and Ergonomics Society Annual Meeting* (Vol. 63, no. 1, pp. 2249–2253). SAGE.
124. Xu, J., Pan, S., Sun, P. Z. H., Park, S. H., & Guo, K. (2022). Human-factors-in-driving-loop: Driver identification and verification via a deep learning approach using psychological behavioral data. *IEEE Transactions on Intelligent Transportation Systems, 24*(3), 3383–3394.
125. Bohme, M., Meyer, A., Martinetz, T., & Barth, E. (2006). Remote eye tracking: State of the art and directions for future development. In *Proceedings of the 2006 Conference on Communication by Gaze Interaction (COGAIN)* (pp. 12–17).
126. Palinko, O., Kun, A. L., Shyrokov, A., & Heeman, P. (2010). Estimating cognitive load using remote eye tracking in a driving simulator. In *Proceedings of the 2010 Symposium on Eye-Tracking Research & Applications* (pp. 141–144).

127. Pel, J. J. M., Manders, J. C. W., & Van der Steen, J. (2010). Assessment of visual orienting behaviour in young children using remote eye tracking: Methodology and reliability. *Journal of Neuroscience Methods, 189*(2), 252–256.
128. Frazier, T. W., Klingemier, E. W., Beukemann, M., Speer, L., Markowitz, L., Parikh, S., Wexberg, S., Giuliano, K., Schulte, E., Delahunty, C., Ahuja, V., Eng, V., Manos, M. J., Hardan, A. Y., Youngstrom, E. A., & Strauss, M. S. (2016). Development of an objective autism risk index using remote eye tracking. *Journal of the American Academy of Child & Adolescent Psychiatry, 55*(4), 301–309.
129. Vrabič, N., Juroš, B., & Tekavčič Pompe, M. (2021). Automated visual acuity evaluation based on preferential looking technique and controlled with remote eye tracking. *Ophthalmic Research, 64*(3), 389–397.
130. Bisogni, C., Nappi, M., Tortora, G., & Del Bimbo, A. (2024). Gaze analysis: A survey on its applications. *Image and Vision Computing, 144*(104961), 1–25.
131. Narcizo, F. B., de Queiroz, J. E. R., & Gomes, H. M. (2013). Remote eye tracking systems: Technologies and applications. In *2013 26th Conference on Graphics, Patterns and Images Tutorials* (pp. 15–22).
132. Klingner, J., Kumar, R., & Hanrahan, P. (2008). Measuring the task-evoked pupillary response with a remote eye tracker. In *Proceedings of the 2008 Symposium on Eye Tracking Research & Applications* (pp. 69–72).
133. Mele, M. L., & Federici, S. (2012). Gaze and eye-tracking solutions for psychological research. *Cognitive Processing, 13*(1), 261–265.
134. Iannizzotto, G., Nucita, A., Fabio, R. A., Caprì, T., & Lo Bello, L. (2020). Remote eye-tracking for cognitive telerehabilitation and interactive school tasks in times of COVID-19. *Information, 11*(6), 296.
135. Punde, P. A., Jadhav, M. E., & Manza, R. R. (2017). A study of eye tracking technology and its applications. In *2017 1st International Conference on Intelligent Systems and Information Management (ICISIM)* (pp. 86–90).
136. Thibeault, M., Jesteen, M., & Beitman, A. (2019). Improved accuracy test method for mobile eye tracking in usability scenarios. In *Proceedings of the Human Factors and Ergonomics Society Annual Meeting* (Vol. 63, no. 1, pp. 2226–2230). SAGE.
137. Atkins, M. S., Tien, G., Khan, R. S. A., Meneghetti, A., & Zheng, B. (2013). What do surgeons see: Capturing and synchronizing eye gaze for surgery applications. *Surgical Innovation, 20*(3), 241–248.
138. Chatelain, P., Sharma, H., Drukker, L., Papageorghiou, A. T., & Noble, J. A. (2018). Evaluation of gaze tracking calibration for longitudinal biomedical imaging studies. *IEEE Transactions on Cybernetics, 50*(1), 153–163.
139. Kim, S.-Y., Moon, B.-Y., Cho, H. G., & Yu, D.-S. (2022). Comparison of image-based quantification methods in evaluating fixation stability using a remote eye tracker in abnormal phoria. *Journal of International Medical Research, 50*(5), 03000605221098183.
140. Mardanbegi, D., & Hansen, D. W. (2011). Mobile gaze-based screen interaction in 3D environments. In *Proceedings of the 1st Conference on Novel Gaze-Controlled Applications* (pp. 1–4).
141. Purits, N., & Söderback, I. (2013). Eye tracking. In M. D. Gellman & J. R. Turner (Eds.), *Encyclopedia of behavioral medicine* (pp. 746–753). Springer New York.
142. Duchowski, A. T., Cournia, N., & Murphy, H. (2004). Gaze-contingent displays: A review. *Cyberpsychology & Behavior, 7*(6), 621–634.
143. Zhang, Y., Bulling, A., & Gellersen, H. (2011). Discrimination of gaze directions using low-level eye image features. In *Proceedings of the 1st international workshop on pervasive eye tracking & mobile eye-based interaction* (pp. 9–14).
144. Meißner, M., Pfeiffer, J., Pfeiffer, T., & Oppewal, H. (2019). Combining virtual reality and mobile eye tracking to provide a naturalistic experimental environment for shopper research. *Journal of Business Research, 100*(1), 445–458.

145. Drèze, X., & Hussherr, F. X. (2004). Internet advertising: Is anybody watching? *Journal of Interactive Marketing, 17*(4), 8–23.
146. Josephson, S. (2004). Eye tracking methodology and the Internet. In K. L. Smith, S. Moriarty, K. Kenney, & G. Barbatsis (Eds.), *Handbook of visual communication* (1st ed., pp. 85–102). Routledge.
147. Muñoz-Leiva, F., Hernández-Méndez, J., & Gómez-Carmona, D. (2019). Measuring advertising effectiveness in Travel 2.0 websites through eye-tracking technology. *Physiology & Behavior, 200*, 83–95.
148. Ryan, M., Krucien, N., & Hermens, F. (2018). The eyes have it: Using eye tracking to inform information processing strategies in multi-attributes choices. *Health Economics, 27*(4), 709–721.
149. Hristova, E., & Grinberg, M. (2005). Information acquisition in the iterated prisoner's dilemma game: An eye-tracking study. In *Proceedings of the 27th Annual Conference of the Cognitive Science Society* (pp. 983–988).
150. Arieli, A., Ben-Ami, Y., & Rubinstein, A. (2011). Tracking decision makers under uncertainty. *American Economic Journal: Microeconomics, 3*(4), 68–76.
151. Polonio, L., Di Guida, S., & Coricelli, G. (2015). Strategic sophistication and attention in games: An eye-tracking study. *Games and Economic Behavior, 94*(1), 80–96.
152. Camerer, C. F. (2011). *Behavioral game theory: Experiments in strategic interaction*. Princeton University Press.
153. Devetag, G., Di Guida, S., & Polonio, L. (2016). An eye-tracking study of feature-based choice in one-shot games. *Experimental Economics, 19*(1), 177–201.
154. Toma, F. M., Cepoi, C. O., Kubinschi, M. N., & Miyakoshi, M. (2023). Gazing through the bubble: An experimental investigation into financial risk-taking using eye-tracking. *Financial Innovation, 9*(1), 28.
155. Genie, M. G., Ryan, M., & Krucien, N. (2023). Keeping an eye on cost: What can eye tracking tell us about attention to cost information in discrete choice experiments? *Health Economics, 32*(5), 1101–1119.
156. Byrne, S. A., Reynolds, A. P. F., Biliotti, C., Bargagli-Stoffi, F. J., Polonio, L., & Riccaboni, M. (2023). Predicting choice behaviour in economic games using gaze data encoded as scanpath images. *Scientific Reports, 13*(1), 4722.
157. Molina, A. I., Arroyo, Y., Lacave, C., Redondo, M. A., Bravo, C., & Ortega, M. (2024). Eye tracking-based evaluation of accessible and usable interactive systems: Tool set of guidelines and methodological issues. *Universal Access in the Information Society*, 1–24. https://doi.org/10.1007/s10209-023-01083-x
158. Bansal, P., Kim, E. J., & Ozdemir, S. (2024). Discrete choice experiments with eye-tracking: How far we have come and ways forward. *Journal of Choice Modelling, 51*(100478), 1–26.
159. Harrison, G. W., & Swarthout, J. T. (2019). Eye-tracking and economic theories of choice under risk. *Journal of the Economic Science Association, 5*(1), 26–37.
160. Papoutsaki, A., Sangkloy, P., Laskey, J., Daskalova, N., Huang, J., & Hays, J. (2016). WebGazer: Scalable webcam eye tracking using user interactions. In *Proceedings of the Twenty-Fifth International Joint Conference on Artificial Intelligence (IJCAI)* (pp. 3839–3845).
161. Conte, A., Levati, M. V., & Montinari, N. (2019). Experience in public goods experiments. *Theory and Decision, 86*(1), 65–93.
162. Gneezy, U., & Imas, A. (2017). Lab in the field: Measuring preferences in the wild. In *Handbook of economic field experiments* (Vol. 1, pp. 439–464). North-Holland.
163. Chakraborti, R., Maloney, M., Roberts, G., & Shogren, J. F. (2018). Social capital and the voluntary provision of public goods. *Journal of Behavioral and Experimental Economics, 77*(1), 196–208.
164. Cook, T. D., & Campbell, D. T. (1979). *Quasi-experimentation: Design and analysis for field settings*. Houghton Mifflin.
165. Smith, V. L. (1976). Experimental economics: Induced value theory. *The American Economic Review, 66*(2), 274–279.

166. Grossman, G., & Baldassarri, D. (2012). The impact of elections on cooperation: Evidence from a lab-in-the-field experiment in Uganda. *American Journal of Political Science, 56*(4), 964–985.
167. Haghani, M. (2023). The notion of validity in experimental crowd dynamics. *International Journal of Disaster Risk Reduction, 93*(103750), 1–21.
168. Croasmun, J. T., & Ostrom, L. (2011). Using likert-type scales in the social sciences. *Journal of Adult Education, 40*(1), 19–22.
169. Smerecnik, C. M., Mesters, I., Candel, M. J., De Vries, H., & De Vries, N. K. (2012). Risk perception and information processing: The development and validation of a questionnaire to assess self-reported information processing. *Risk Analysis: An International Journal, 32*(1), 54–66.
170. Jones-Jang, S. M., Heo, Y. J., McKeever, R., Kim, J. H., Moscowitz, L., & Moscowitz, D. (2020). Good news! Communication findings may be underestimated: Comparing effect sizes with self-reported and logged smartphone use data. *Journal of Computer-Mediated Communication, 25*(5), 346–363.
171. Eskin, G. J., & Baron, P. H. (1977). Effects of price and advertising in test-market experiments. *Journal of Marketing Research, 14*(4), 499–508.
172. Güth, W., Schmittberger, R., & Schwarze, B. (1982). An experimental analysis of ultimatum bargaining. *Journal of Economic Behavior & Organization, 3*(4), 367–388.
173. Forsythe, R., Horowitz, J. L., Savin, N. E., & Sefton, M. (1994). Fairness in simple bargaining experiments. *Games and Economic behavior, 6*(3), 347–369.
174. Roth, A. E. (1995). Bargaining experiments. In J. Kagel & A. E. Roth (Eds.), *Handbook of experimental economics* (pp. 253–348). Princeton University Press.
175. Falk, A., & Fehr, E. (2003). Why labour market experiments? *Labour Economics, 10*(4), 399–406.
176. Wang, Z., Jusup, M., Wang, R. W., Shi, L., Iwasa, Y., Moreno, Y., & Kurths, J. (2017). Onymity promotes cooperation in social dilemma experiments. *Science Advances, 3*(e1601444), 1–7.
177. Li, X., Jusup, M., Wang, Z., Li, H., Shi, L., Podobnik, B., Stanley, E., Havlin, S., & Boccaletti, S. (2018). Punishment diminishes the benefits of network reciprocity in social dilemma experiments. *Proceedings of the National Academy of Sciences, 115*(1), 30–35.
178. Ip, E., Leibbrandt, A., & Vecci, J. (2020). How do gender quotas affect workplace relationships? Complementary evidence from a representative survey and labor market experiments. *Management Science, 66*(2), 805–822.

MIX
Papier aus verantwortungsvollen Quellen
Paper from responsible sources
FSC® C105338

If you have any concerns about our products,
you can contact us on
ProductSafety@springernature.com

In case Publisher is established outside the EU,
the EU authorized representative is:
Springer Nature Customer Service Center GmbH
Europaplatz 3, 69115 Heidelberg, Germany

Printed by Libri Plureos GmbH
in Hamburg, Germany